LEGAL SECRETARY'S STANDARD DESK BOOK

Carole A. Bruno

PRENTICE-HALL, INC.
Englewood Cliffs, New Jersey

Prentice-Hall International, Inc., *London*
Prentice-Hall of Australia Pty. Limited, *Sydney*
Editora Prentice-Hall do Brasil, Ltda., *Rio de Janeiro*
Prentice-Hall Canada Inc., *Toronto*
Prentice-Hall of India Private Limited, *New Delhi*
Prentice-Hall of Japan, Inc., *Tokyo*
Prentice-Hall of Southeast Asia Pte. Ltd., *Singapore*
Whitehall Books Limited, *Wellington, New Zealand*

To my wonderful Mother,
whose limitless love and encouragement made this book possible;

To my Father,
who has his own special way of loving me;

To my (step) Dad,
whose love and laughter lightened my load.

Library of Congress Cataloging-in-Publication-Data

Bruno, Carole A.
Legal secretary's standard desk book.

Bibliography: p.
Includes index.
1. Legal secretaries—United States—Handbooks, manuals, etc. I. Title.
KF319.B77 1986 651'.934 86-9492

ISBN 0-13-529397-9

Printed in the United States of America

ABOUT THE AUTHOR

Carole A. Bruno knows about working with lawyers and in law offices. During the past twenty-three years, she has been a legal secretary, paralegal, law office manager, law office management consultant, national legal newsletter editor, legal personnel agency entrepreneur, paralegal educator, seminar leader, and is currently a law firm marketing administrator.

In 1969 Carole became active in the local legal secretaries' association in Los Angeles. In 1973 she attended the University of West Los Angeles School of Law Paralegal Program. After moving to Atlanta she became president of the Georgia Association of Legal Assistants in 1976.

After writing her first book, *Paralegal's Litigation Handbook,* in 1979, Carole Bruno founded Legal Support Services, Inc., a national legal personnel agency. She later founded the National Institute for Continuing Paralegal Education. Carole frequently conducts seminars at colleges, universities, and for paralegal, legal secretarial, and bar associations. Attorneys, paralegals, and legal secretaries attend her intensive workshops.

Carole Bruno became editor of *Attorney's Computer Report,* a national newsletter, and then joined the Management Advisory Services Department of Holland Shipes Vann, P.C., as a senior law office management consultant in their Atlanta office. At present, Ms. Bruno is director of client relations of the ninety-attorney firm of Arnall Golden & Gregory, which has offices in Washington, D.C. and Macon and Savannah, Georgia.

Carole has written numerous articles for such publications as *The American Lawyer Management Service, Legal Assistant Today, Practicing Attorney's Letter, The Pennsylvania Lawyer, The Oklahoma Bar Association Journal,* the Georgia State Bar Association's *Bread'n'Butter,* and *Boston Association of Legal Administrators Newsletter.*

ABOUT THE CONTRIBUTING AUTHOR

Paula Turner is Manager of the Management Advisory Services Department of Holland Shipes Vann, P.C., in Atlanta, Georgia.

Mrs. Turner, C.P.A., received her B.A. degree (magna cum laude) from Oglethorpe University in Atlanta, Georgia. Her expertise as a Law Office Management Consultant includes over fifteen years' experience in administration, law office automation, evaluating and implementing timekeeping and billing systems, accounting system design and development, procedure development and documentation, and personnel administration.

Articles by Mrs. Turner have appeared in *Legal Economics, American Lawyer Management Service, Practicing Attorney's Newsletter,* and the *Boston Association of Legal Administrator's Newsletter.*

FOREWORD

Recent years have brought fast and ever-increasing changes in the role of legal secretaries. They have been expected to master not only the traditional skills of legal secretarial work—prioritizing and scheduling tasks, effective client communications and relations, and accurate and efficient production of documents—but many new tasks as well.

As sophisticated word processing machines began entering the marketplace fifteen years ago, legal secretaries began losing control of much of their traditional work. Document production was shifted to expensive word processing centers and trained operators. The result was an increasing erosion of the secretary-attorney relationship and the introduction of an additional group to work with to get documents out. As word processing machines have dropped in cost, it has been possible for many law firms to move this sophisticated equipment back to the secretarial desk—now secretaries are expected both to be expert word processing operators and to cope with the complexities of a wide range of computer-based word processing systems. These systems range from large centralized mainframe- or minicomputer-based systems to stand-alone word processors or personal computers.

Additionally, today's technology has made it possible to return the control over the timekeeping and billing functions, which were also moved to the computer centers, to the secretaries. This resulted in secretaries losing control and knowledge of the financial side of the client's work. Now, secretaries are asked to enter the time logged by the attorneys and paralegals on their computer terminals. They are asked to draft bills using computerized records and programs. In a significant way, secretaries have become computer users.

Many secretaries have long had paralegal skills and have assisted attorneys in research and document drafting. With the advent of outside computerized legal databases, secretaries are now being called upon to learn these systems. The ever-increasing use of computerized internal work-product databases is making it necessary for secretaries to learn computerized research techniques in order to better fulfill the requests for help from attorneys and paralegals.

Indeed, the high cost of providing legal services and the increasing demand by clients to reduce legal fees has put tremendous pressures on attorneys and secretaries to improve productivity. These pressures are not expected to let up in the years ahead.

More and more secretaries are being called upon to support two or more attorneys and paralegals in an attempt to lower overhead. This has become possible, largely, due to the use of sophisticated computer-based word processing, which makes the secretary's job more efficient.

In the future, secretaries will be called upon to master more and more computer equipment and programs in an effort to remain competitive. For many, this prospect is frightening; for others it is a welcome challenge. Those secretaries who take the opportunity to learn and grow will surely have more rewarding careers, both financially and emotionally.

This handbook will aid the secretary in facing the challenge ahead.

L. Donald Holland
Law Office Management Consultant
Holland Shipes Vann, P.C., CPA's
Atlanta, Georgia

WHAT THIS BOOK WILL DO FOR YOU

This handbook is a comprehensive "what-to-do" and "how-to-do-it" manual for legal secretaries. Whether you are employed in a private law firm, corporation, government agency, or legal services office, this book will make your job easier. For easy reference it is organized into twenty-one chapters, each of which details various practical methods, working tools, programs, systems, and techniques used by experienced legal secretaries throughout the country.

Included in this timely book is the latest information on the use and benefits of computers and word processors in the law office. It gives step-by-step instructions on how to select a computer or word processor, including a hands-on demo you can use to try it out. It is a "nuts and bolts" approach, showing you in simple, concise language what to do and how to get the fullest benefit from your computer or word processor.

The chapters on accounting, bookkeeping, payroll, billing, and timekeeping are written in simple-to-understand terms, unlike most texts on these subjects. You do not need any particular background or education to understand the concepts. You will especially appreciate the information on computerized billing, which will help you get bills out faster and easier.

This will be your daily guide to quick, practical, and necessary information and ideas to put to immediate use. Keep it on your desk to help you perform your job in a more efficient and productive manner. Not only will it keep you more organized, it will also give you new methods and systems of handling your daily work load. Your attorneys will be impressed both with your new knowledge and, more importantly, with your increased confidence, gained from learning these new techniques.

In addition, this book will take you through your daily tasks step by step, outlining exactly how to do each task thoroughly and effectively.

The many forms, charts, and tips provide you with added benefits. Provided are guides to information you will need in the law office, such as legal abbreviations, a dictionary of legal terms, guides to forms of address and salutations, and numerous other aids.

This handbook also offers you specific information on how to be more professional; how to assume more responsibility; and tips on how to get along with the other secretaries and paralegals in the office.

ACKNOWLEDGMENTS

I give my sincere thanks to the following friends and relatives who took the time out of their busy lives to help make this book come true: my mother, who raised me to believe that I could do whatever I wanted to do; my dad, who always loves me no matter what; my handsome son, Don, who kept me laughing even during the bad times; my beautiful daughter, Jacque, who is my special Valentine; my dear and loving sister, Mary, who gave me advice even when I didn't need it; my thoughtful brother, Jimmy, who always makes me feel special; my sensitive brother, John, for being the wonderful brother and friend he is; my altruistic brother, Smiley, for always so unselfishly helping me and the world; Paula Turner, Holland Shipes Vann, P.C., my friend and colleague, who laboriously worked alongside me every step of the way, giving me the benefit of her vast array of expertise; Don Holland, Holland Shipes Vann, P.C., for understanding my quest and enabling me to pursue it; Celena Bullard, my loyal and dearest friend, who always knows the right things to say to support me; Judi Wood, whose love and support helped me keep my eyes on my vision; my special friend, Theresa Williams, whose friendship and support gave me the lift I needed when things looked rough; Brenda Wilson, who spent many hours manicuring my manuscript and preparing the artwork; Ellen Boyer, who tediously and expertly proofed and edited every page of this manuscript; Nina Diamond, my editor, whose words of encouragement bolstered my determination and kept me going; Tony Vlamis, my former editor and personal friend; Steve Stroud, my acquisitions editor, who gave me the opportunity to write this book; Dottie Withers, my former secretary, who gave me the benefit of her legal secretarial expertise; Peggy Martin, who did nothing but wanted her name in this book; Mary Ann Fry, Director of Information Services, King and Spalding, Atlanta; Connie Weissenberger and Rochelle La Rosa, two top-notch legal secretaries at Troutman, Sanders, Lockerman & Ashmore, Atlanta; Janet Litt, attorney at law, Spruell, Jones, Fagan & Kanner, Atlanta, who gave me the benefit of her legal expertise; Professor Corneill Stephens, Georgia State University School of Law, Atlanta; and to Donna Barwick and Andy Cataldo, Troutman, Sanders, Lockerman & Ashmore, who answered many of my questions.

CONTENTS

APPENDICES

¶100 The Law Office Environment: What's It Really Like?

The law office differs from other business offices because it is centered around professionals, each practicing law in his or her own way. Every day is different. This is what makes being a professional legal secretary an exciting profession. Working with professionals in an interesting, dynamic environment provides rewards that are not available in many other secretarial positions.

¶101 The Law Firm vs. The Sole Practitioner

Law firms range in size from one attorney (sole practitioner) to as many as 350 or more attorneys. There are many firms in the United States that have over 100 attorneys.

In the past, the sole practitioner was the dominant figure in the legal profession. However, this trend is rapidly changing. Attorneys are joining together, often to pool their financial resources and to meet the ever-increasing demands of clients. The sole practitioner will not disappear, but will be unable to keep up with the capital expenditures (computers, word processing equipment, etc.) necessary to equip the modern law office. For this reason, it is the law firm that dominates the legal profession today.

As a professional legal secretary, you may find yourself working for a sole practitioner. If so, your duties will be much more diversified than if you work in a large firm. You will handle administrative matters, purchasing, and probably will even do the bookkeeping. In the larger law firm, you will most likely work for more than one attorney and perhaps will be responsible for a paralegal's work. There will be an administrative staff to handle the office facilities, supplies, and bookkeeping. In the typical law firm today, with good word processing equipment, there is a ratio of two attorneys for each secretary. The private legal secretary is rare and unnecessary. For this reason, you will notice that throughout this book the term "your attorneys" is often used when referring to the men or women for whom you will do legal secretarial work.

¶102 Organization of the Typical Firm

In most law firms there is a hierarchy, a "pecking order." If you are an experienced legal secretary you have probably already learned this. If not, it is important that you understand it.

The hierarchy is usually as follows:

Partners;
Associates;
Paralegals;
Secretaries;
Other support staff.

Depending on the size of the firm, there may be other support staff members who fit into the hierarchy at various levels. An administrator may fit between partners and associates. An office manager or bookkeeper may fit between associates and all other staff.

Within each level there is also a pecking order. The partners with the most seniority or influence in the firm will be at the top and the newer junior partners at the bottom. The same is true of associates. The attorney's names usually are printed on the firm's letterhead after the partners in order of seniority. Look at the letterhead and make sure you understand each attorney's position.

How does this pecking order affect you?

Whenever you create a listing of attorneys in the firm, you should attempt to do it in this order. You will typically find that you are expected to do the work of the attorney who is higher on the list before one who is lower. The higher on the letterhead an attorney's name is, the more power and influence in the firm he or she will have. If the letterhead has columns of names, the names in the right hand column, going from top to bottom have the most power. The second column follows, with the last column representing the person with the least power.

Figure 102-1 illustrates the organization of a typical large law firm. Although many firms have these positions, not all do.

¶103 Location: Uptown, Downtown, or Suburbia

Law offices are located all around the city because clients are all around the city. A firm usually chooses a location based on the type of services it intends to provide.

Firms that have large corporations, banks, etc., as their clientele will probably be located in the financial district of large cities. Sole

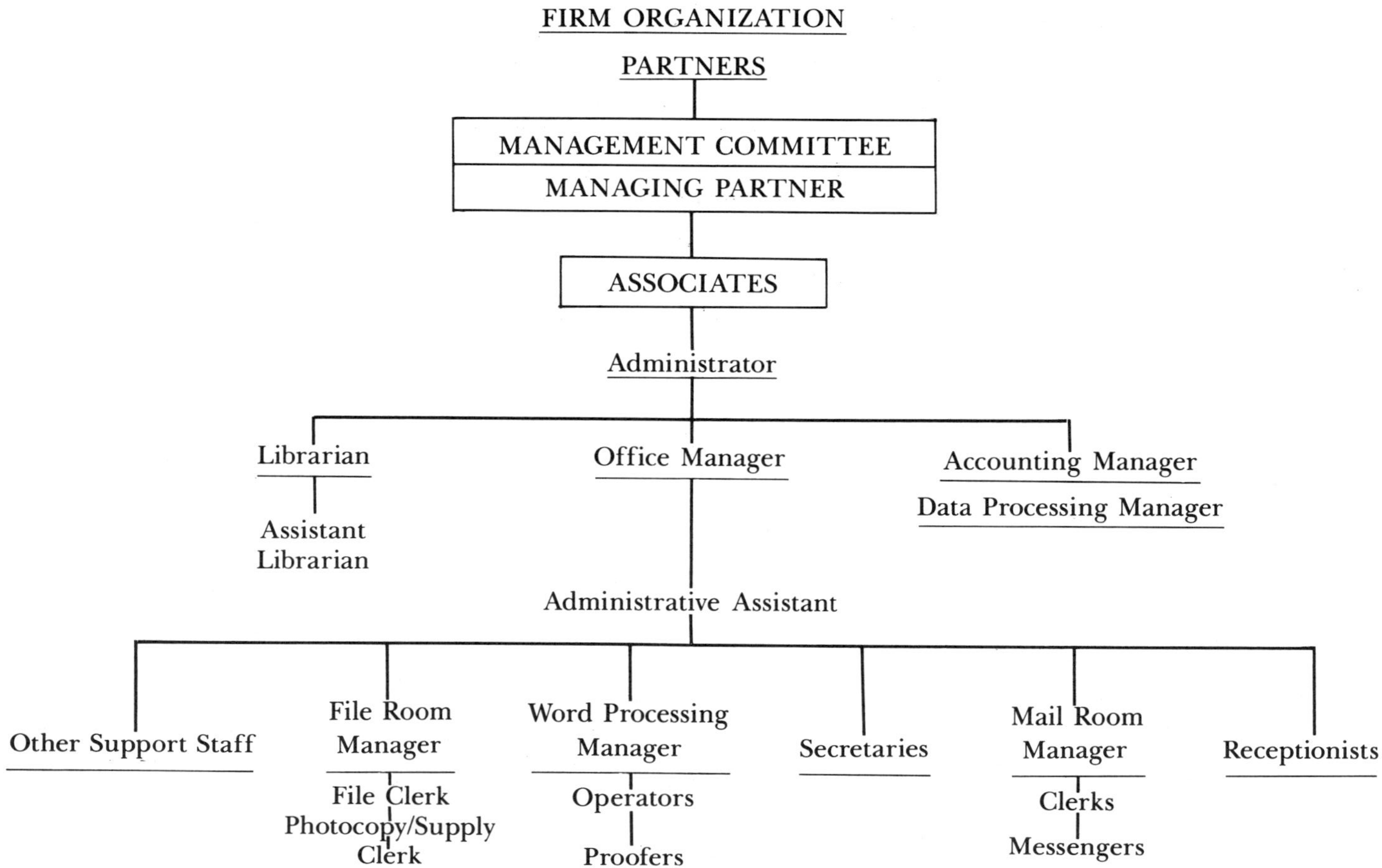

Figure 102.1 Organization Chart for a Typical Law Firm

practitioners are found all over town. If a sole practitioner does a lot of domestic relations, i.e., divorce or personal injury work, he or she may be located near a residential area. On the other hand, a tax attorney practicing alone may have an office in the financial district. Many cities have large office complexes outside of the downtown area where both small and large firms are located.

¶104 Typical Layout of the Law Office

Traditionally, law offices have been laid out in squares or rectangles. Partners' offices are usually the larger blocks with the more senior partners having corner offices, surrounded by secretarial areas which may be cubicles or small offices. Associates' offices are usually located around the outside walls of the building where the windows are found. Typically, attorneys have window offices, secretaries do not.

In most law offices, there is a secretarial cubicle or workstation just outside an attorney's office. Since most legal secretaries work for more than one attorney, you will frequently find the legal secretary outside the more senior partner's office.

Large law offices are usually arranged by departments. Attorneys and paralegals specializing in the same area of practice are grouped together. Some typical departments are:

1. Corporate and General Business
2. Real Estate
3. Banking
4. Utilities
5. Litigation
6. Tax
7. Governmental
8. Oil and Gas

There is a new trend developing in law firms due to the advent of the computer. As computer systems are added to more and more law offices, a more ergonomic design will most likely develop in the law firm (meaning one that bears in mind human comfort and ease of use).

According to *How To Manage Your Law Office* by Mary Ann Altman and Robert I. Weil, the 1960s brought a new approach to law office layout. The origination of this approach was in Germany. In Germany it is called *bürolandschaft.* However, in this country it is called "office landscaping."

Altman and Weil state that the principles of office landscaping are based on the concept that every office should have a feeling of the outdoors—privacy without isolation. Each desk in the landscaped office is screened from the other desks by means of movable partitions and plants. A technician trained in this technique of office layout is often used to control sound levels and sight patterns.

According to Altman and Weil, a combination of landscaping and traditional space use has its place in the consideration of most all organizations. The privacy that attorneys need is often obtained through private offices and walled conference rooms. At the same time, the feeling of openness is achieved in the clerical areas through landscaping. In more modern buildings with glass walls or courtyards the clerical staff receives the benefit of this contact with "nature" through the use of landscape partitions and plants.

In the larger law firms there may be a word processing center; an appropriate number of kitchens, usually one on each floor; a large law library, many with separate cubicles for the law clerks; a photocopying room; and a section for the bookkeeping and accounting department, which may be separate or combined with a computer room. The size of the accounting department in law firms is rapidly increasing in size as more and more computer equipment is added.

Another area in the large firm that takes a considerable amount of space is the file room. This room may even have a computer terminal for records management. In large firms, the file room may be located in the basement or on a centrally located floor. In smaller offices, the files may be kept outside the attorney's office in the secretarial area. Usually, even in large firms where there is a large file room there is still a file cabinet near the secretary's desk. For a further discussion of centralized and decentralized filing systems see ¶1409.

Every law firm has some type of reception area that varies in size according to the size of the firm and the nature of the firm's practice. Most reception areas are traditionally designed with a minimal amount of high-quality and conservative furniture and furnishings. Usually, there is a receptionist stationed in this area; however, in small firms a legal secretary may function as the receptionist. The best reception rooms convey a feeling of relaxation and comfort.

Another common area in most firms is the supply room. However, in smaller firms this may merely be a cabinet or the bottom drawer of a file cabinet near the secretary's desk.

¶105 How to Deal With the Office Noise Level

In the law office, noise may come from voices, telephones ringing, machines, paging systems, heating and air conditioning systems, doors opening and closing, chairs squeaking, etc. The list goes on and on.

Most law firms tackle the problem of noise by sound proofing offices with carpeting and drapes. Printers are often tucked away in heavily insulated rooms or covered with sound covers to reduce noise. People are separated by walls or movable partitions.

¶106 How to Adjust Lighting in Computer Areas

The addition of computers and word processors to the law office environment has caused most firms to carefully consider their lighting needs. Bright lights cause glare on display screens, creating eye discomfort. For this reason, overhead lighting is often decreased (taking out a few bulbs will do it) and more task lighting on the work surfaces is being used. (Video screens are usually orange on green, which is easier on the eyes.)

¶200 The Legal Secretary's Role in the Modern Law Office

¶201 How to Communicate More Effectively With Your Attorneys

Without good communication, many things can happen. For example, if your attorneys do not tell you their whereabouts, you will not be able to properly respond to clients' inquiries or inquiries from the other attorneys in the firm. Attorneys have a lot of things on their minds and are reluctant to check in as they go about their business, but you must insist that they do. Although they may seen irritated at this request, it is absolutely imperative that you ask them to tell you where they are going and the approximate time they will be back. Also, suggest to your attorneys that they call in periodically to get their messages and to see if any problems occurred in their absence that need their attention.

Other problems that may result may affect you personally. For example, if you misunderstand something one of your attorneys says to you and do not clear up the communication, it may cause you to resent him or her and perhaps your job. This resentment can grow and ultimately affect your work performance. Always keep your communications clear, saying what needs to be said, tactfully.

¶202 The Team Approach To Practicing Law

The team approach is not a new concept. In the past, the team has consisted of only the legal secretary and the lawyer. Now with the introduction of paralegals into the law office and with associates that are usually assigned to a senior partner, there are more members of the team.

Each member of the law office team has a different role. The legal secretary is the nucleus or the "core" of the team. The legal secretary "holds the fort down." The secretary, because of his or her responsibilities, usually knows exactly what is happening in the team at all times. More often, the secretary knows what each team member is doing at any given time better than any other individual member of the team.

Also, since the secretary opens the correspondence and handles the filing, she is more aware of current happenings on matters on which the team is working. In addition, the secretary knows the whereabouts of the attorneys, what meetings are going on, what depositions are being taken, and what deadlines are approaching. A former legal secretary who is now a paralegal observed that when she was a legal secretary she knew more of what was going on than she does now as a paralegal. She said, as a matter of fact, that she misses that aspect of being a legal secretary.

The following is an example of the responsibilities of the team members in a litigation department. The description would differ according to the specialization in which your team is working.

¶202.1 Responsibilities of the Litigation Team Members

Attorney

1. Sets the game plan;
2. Defines the roles of the participants;
3. Determines the strategy and tactical plans;
4. Initiates the strategy;
5. Handles problems not solvable by the paralegal or secretary;
6. Communicates with the client;
7. Initiates litigation team meetings;
8. Assigns specific tasks to members of the team; and
9. Makes decisions regarding additional support staff assistance.

Paralegal

1. Initiates and implements the Game Plan;
2. Acts as the team communicator;
3. Informs the attorney of problems or potential problems;
4. Documents the Game Plan;
5. Supervises clerical and support staff;
6. Proofreads final documents;
7. Handles minor problems;
8. Manages document control and retrieval;
9. Drafts initial documents;
10. Organizes and systematizes documents;
11. Prepares agenda for litigation team meetings; and
12. Communicates with clients as instructed by the attorney.

Secretary

1. Prepares and proofs legal documents;
2. Handles telephone communications;
3. Handles administrative problems as defined by the attorney;
4. Alerts attorney to current or potential problems;
5. Files, organizes, and controls documents;
6. Keeps abreast of court costs and fees;
7. Schedules depositions, if requested by the attorney;
8. Keeps the court calendar and the attorney's personal calendar of appointments;
9. Takes notes during litigation team meetings;
10. Acts as an assistant to the attorney in regard to clerical duties;
11. Records information; and
12. Acts as the anchorperson or team coordinator.

¶202.2 Conduct of the Litigation Team Meetings

The team should work together and meet regularly to discuss the team assignments and strategies. The following are suggestions for an effective team meeting.

1. Regularity;
2. Brevity;
3. Agenda;
4. Organization and preparation;
5. Team members' reports re:
   a. Status of case;
   b. Problems evolved;
   c. Possible solutions to problems;
   d. Revision of the game plan;
   e. Time schedules and commitments (priorities);
   f. Further task assignments and definitions of responsibilities;
   g. Subsequent meeting schedule.

¶202.3 Methods of Communication for Members of the Litigation Team

The methods of communication for members of the litigation team include:

1. Interoffice memoranda;
2. Office forms and checklists;

3. Status charts;
4. Personal communications;
5. Telephone communication;

¶203 The Legal Secretary's Role in the Team

Recorder of Information The legal secretary is the recorder of information in the team. The secretary has the task of not only recording the information, but also gathering the information from the other members of the team. The secretary should also act as a liaison among the other team members.

Coordinator of the Team The legal secretary of the team is the coordinator of all of the activities of the other team members. The secretary makes certain that all the members of the team are advised of team meetings, pleadings due, depositions to be handled, papers to be filed, calls to be made, follow-up items to be handled, and anything else that must be done by any of the members of the team.

Document Controller The legal secretary is the chief document controller, and is responsible for making sure all documents are filed in their proper places and are distributed to the appropriate members of the team. The secretary is responsible for organizing the documents in the file, making certain that any documents removed from the file are returned to the file in the proper order.

Document Locator The legal secretary is responsible for locating any documents needed by other members of the team upon their request. If a document is lost, it is the secretary's responsibility to attempt to locate the document or to obtain a duplicate from the originator. If the attorney or paralegal is on the telephone and needs a document instantly, the secretary is responsible for retrieving the document as fast as possible and returning it to the attorney or paralegal. After the attorney or paralegal has finished with the document, the secretary is responsible for returning it to its proper place in the file.

Appointment Scheduler The legal secretary is responsible for setting all appointments for the attorney unless he prefers to do so himself. The secretary is also responsible for handling any airline, hotel or car rental reservations for the attorney or paralegal and making certain that they receive itineraries of their trips.

The legal secretary is also responsible for indexing the pleading files, and preparing any subfiles that may be necessary for any particular matter. The secretary is responsible for opening a new file and preparing the new client (new business) report. The secretary is also responsible for making certain that there is a copy of every piece of correspondence that goes out of the office in the chronological or reading file.

Document Preparer The legal secretary is the chief document preparer although part-time or temporary clerical help may occasionally be available. The secretary is the person who types a document and is responsible for making the proper number of copies and distributing the document to the appropriate parties. The secretary is also responsible for making certain that a copy of each document goes into the proper file or subfile.

The legal secretary is also responsible for making certain that all follow-up dates or "tickler" dates are recorded in the proper tickler or reminder system. In most litigation departments the secretary is responsible for recording the due dates on pleadings, such as interrogatories, requests for admissions, etc. and making certain that they are entered into the system and followed up.

¶204 How To Get Along in a Law Office

It is to your benefit to become acquainted with as many people in the firm as you can. Since there will be many instances when you may need the help of other employees, it is helpful if you can establish a good rapport from the beginning. Making a friend of the messenger, for example, could come in handy when you need to get a document delivered in a hurry.

Although at times it may be difficult, most experienced legal secretaries find that it is best not to become too close to other employees in the office. Since this is somewhat impossible and you are likely to nurture a close relationship with one of the other secretaries, it is important that you continue your friendship outside the firm and not use firm time to discuss personal matters.

¶205 The Legal Secretary's Relationship with the Paralegal

Paralegals first began working in law firms in the early 1970s. At first, most legal secretaries reacted with resentment to the paralegals' entry into the law firm. Many legal secretaries felt threatened by paralegals. Some secretaries felt that they had been doing what the paralegal was hired to do, and did not understand why the firm needed a paralegal to do that work. A lot of this underlying resentment was caused by the paralegals themselves, many of whom came into firms with an uppity attitude, acting as if they were better than the legal secretaries.

As time went on and legal secretaries began to see that the paralegals were doing much different work than they were, and that the paralegals were actually relieving them of some of the heavy responsibilities that they normally carried, feelings began to ease between the legal secretary and the paralegal. Also, secretaries viewed the paralegal position as an opportunity for them to advance. In many law firms, legal secretaries are promoted to paralegals. In the past, legal secretaries had no upward mobility. However, now with the paralegal position, legal secretaries can see some advancement opportunities.

Today, there are good relationships between the legal secretaries and paralegals in most law firms. Paralegals have learned to respect the legal secretaries and their important positions. Many paralegals have realized that their secretary is really their best ally in getting their job done correctly.

As a legal secretary, you should also try to establish a good relationship with the paralegals. Since you must work together, it is important that you get along well in order to get your work done correctly. There is really little difference in status, and as many of you know, some legal secretaries command a higher salary than a lot of paralegals.

¶206 Getting Along with Court Personnel

If you are a legal secretary in the litigation department of your firm, you will find that you will have almost daily contact with the various persons who work for the city, county and state court systems. Because of this, it is important that you try to develop a friendly rapport with court personnel. Since court personnel are dealing with the public on a daily basis, and are sometimes under a lot of pressure, your consideration in making requests will make them your ally instead of your foe. Find out their names when you first talk to them on the telephone and make a notation on your Rolodex so that the next time that you talk with them, you will be able to identify them and they will be complimented by your remembering their names.

¶207 Dress for a Professional Image

When you become employed in a new law office, look around you and observe how the other secretaries are dressed. Check the office manual to see if there is an established policy for dress; most likely, this will not be noted in the law office manual. You can determine such things as whether it is acceptable to wear pants, whether the secretaries tend to wear suits, dresses, skirts, blouses or sweaters by observing those around you. In some small cities when you work in a small law office, the dress tends to be more casual. However, in metropolitan areas, especially in large firms, the dress tends to be more contemporary, up-to-date, and "corporate."

The classic style is the best style to maintain, because not only will you always look professional, but you will be able to wear the same wardrobe the next year and may change it by simply updating the accessories.

Choose professional-looking outfits, to suit your personality. Experiment with colors and you will add variety to your wardrobe. You might consider taking one of the color classes that assist you in determining which colors best complement your natural coloring. Many department stores or beauty salons offer this service, referred to as "getting your colors done." They will provide you with sample swatches of material in your colors. Take these with you when you go shopping. Select only those colors which flatter you.

If you dress properly, you will be more relaxed and comfortable with yourself, and it will be easier for you to make a more confident impression.

¶208 Pointers from an Attorney

Here are nine pointers that were suggested by Scott MacArthur, who is with MacArthur & Jennings, P.C., a professional corporation with two lawyers and five nonlawyers in Monmouth, Oregon.*

1. Display humanity to clients. We are in business to help people. Many of the people who come to our office on business are troubled and uneasy. Never lose the human touch. And never forget that if it weren't for those people, we would be out of business.

2. Don't discuss business outside the office. Never talk outside of the office about what happens here. As a lawyer, I have a privilege. No one can lawfully make me tell what I have learned from a client in confidence. As an employee of this office you have a like privilege. Violation of a client confidence is a most grievous error and grounds for instant dismissal.

*Reprinted with permission from Scott MacArthur, MacArthur & Jennings, P.C., Monmouth, OR.

3. Be assured we are concerned, regardless of appearances. Although we may laugh and joke among outselves about our clients and some of their more bizarre problems, and though we may seem at times not terribly somber about a client's problem, we are concerned. We deal with so much human misery that we have to talk about it among ourselves (and occasionally in an irreverent tone) in order to release our own tension.

4. Be attentive to economics in the office. The practice of law is a profession, but it is also a business. If you see a chance to save a dollar, let me know. We'll both benefit if you are right.

5. Be a professional in your personal appearance. Our clients pay us $60–$70–$80 an hour to help them with their problems. They expect to pay a professional fee and they expect to deal with professionals. Therefore:

- No gum chewing.
- No smoking where the public can see you. (This may be chauvinistic, but we have a lot of chauvinistic clients, and it's their money and we'll do it their way.)
- Dress like a professional. No jeans, curlers, or sandals.

6. Be a professional in your work habits. We deal in paper. What goes on in this office on paper is the hallmark of our business. Therefore:

- No misspelled words.
- No sloppy erasures.
- Make your paperwork look neat and professional.

7. Monitor the grammar of the work product. You are my right arm. I look to you to cover my tracks and to keep me from looking bad. Therefore:

- Double-check my spelling.
- Keep an eye on my grammar.
- Make sure that what I write and dictate makes sense. Do not type it; read for meaning, and tell me if I don't make sense.

8. Establish priorities and keep the work moving. Remember that our clients want action—and now. Today's work should get out today. If you have more work stacked up than you can handle today, establish priorities and check with me as to what should be done first.

9. Be communicative and cooperative. Stand up for your rights. If you don't like the way I handle things, tell me about it. We should be able to work together efficiently and cooperatively. But we can't unless we both communicate. I'll listen, I promise.

Every result has a given cause. Your every act is a result of a given cause—your motive.

Following are six techniques for motivating yourself:

1. Look at things you should do and things you want to do and eliminate things you shouldn't and don't want to do.
2. Get into action by using the self-starter "do it now" technique.
3. Start off with a small task or a small part of the project to get the momentum going. For example, if you're writing a report, just tell yourself that you are going to write one page. You will find that after you do the one page, you'll want to do more.
4. Break the project down into small tasks. Keep a chart of the tasks and check off each task as you do it. This will give you a feeling of accomplishment and will motivate you to do the next item on your list.
5. Reward yourself as you accomplish each task.
6. Give yourself credit for tasks that you have accomplished. Too frequently, we fail to give ourselves credit for what we have done, and tend to focus on what we haven't done. If you get into the habit of doing this, you will feel so good about yourself that you will want to do more.

¶209 The Secretary's Role as the Quasi-Office Manager

Irrespective of the team, the secretary has several other functions to perform as the nucleus of the office. The secretary acts as a quasi-office manager when there is no office manager or legal administrator. As quasi-office manager, you may have to do a variety of tasks.

¶209.1 Purchasing Agent

One of these tasks is purchasing office supplies and inexpensive equipment. In addition, once the supplies arrive, you have to organize them, check the invoice charges, and keep an inventory of them to make certain there is always an adequate supply. It is important for you to shop around and compare prices to get the best buy in office supplies for your attorney without sacrificing quality.

When buying small office equipment, check on maintenance contracts and references from present users before you make your decision to purchase.

¶209.2 Public Relations

As a quasi-office manager, you may frequently have to deal with salespeople who come into the office. It is important that you try to handle as many of these salespeople as possible in order to save the attorneys' time. The attorneys do not have time to be bothered with salespeople and their demonstrations.

¶209.3 Personnel Manager

One of the duties that you may have to do as a quasi-office manager is to hire support staff for the office. By doing this you can save your attorneys personnel agency fees in addition to their time in interviewing.

If you place an ad in the local paper, you can screen the calls prior to any interviews and thus save your time as well. In screening the calls, you can ask some of the basic questions and request the applicant to send a resume. When you receive a resume, you can review it and eliminate those candidates who do not have the qualifications that you desire. (See Figure 209.3-1.)

TELEPHONE INTERVIEW SHEET DATE: ______

CALL BACK ______________ AD—FULTON DAILY RPTR.
ATL JOUR/CONST.
L/S—F/T—P/T
SPEC. JOB APPLIED FOR:

NAME:

ADDRESS:

TELEPHONE NO.:

EDUCATION DEGREE: B.A.
B.S.

TRAINING-EDUCATION

PERMANENT OR TEMPORARY WORK DESIRED

LOCATION PREFERRED

SALARY DESIRED

PRESENT SALARY

Figure 209.3-1. Telephone Interview Sheet.

SKILLS: SHORTHAND ______ wpm TYPING ______ wpm

RESUME WILL SEND ☐ WILL PREPARE ☐ CAN'T PREPARE ☐

EXPERIENCE ______

REFERENCES ______

NOTES: ______

AVAIL IMMED. 2 WKS OR ______

EVALUATION: EXCELLENT GOOD FAIR POOR ______

INTERVIEW APPT: DATE: ______ TIME: ______
PLACE: ______

Figure 209.3-1 (continued)

If possible, try to do the personnel interviews yourself. This will save the attorneys a lot of time. After you have narrowed the selection down to one or two people, then let the attorneys interview them and make the final decision. Of course, they will be interested in your input. In talking with the applicant about the office, be as honest as possible as to what the duties are and the procedures in the office.

Prior to your attorneys interviewing the applicant, check the references for them. (See Figure 209.3-2.)

Once the applicant has been hired, it will most likely be up to you to train him or her. If you have any procedures in writing, it will aid in the training process. If your firm has developed an in-house legal

TELEPHONE REFERENCE REPORT

DATE ________

Candidate: ______________________________

Reference (name): ______________________________

Company Name (if any) ______________ Phone No: ____________

Address: ______________________ City & State ____________

Instructions to counselor:

Introduce yourself by name, title and company then state: Mr./Ms. (give name of candidate) has applied for a position as (give title) and has given your name as reference. Could you answer a few questions? (if not get a definite time to call back)

If reference is a former (or present) employer, ask only questions labeled (F) with all other references.

1.(F) What were the dates of his/her employment with your company? From: ______________ To: ____________
2.(F) What position did he/she hold? Starting ____________ When leaving: ______________________
3.(F) What was his/her salary rate? $ ______ per ______ hr ______ __________ mo __________ yr __________ .
4.(F) How long had he/she earned that rate? ____________
5.(F) How do you rate the quality of his/her work? ____________ Superior __________ Average __________ Inferior __________
6. How would you rate his/her attendance record? ____________ For absenteeism ________ Superior ________ Average ________ Inferior ________ . For lateness, ________ Superior ________ Average ________ Inferior ________ .
7. How long have you known him/her? ______________
8. Does he/she get along well with other people? Yes____ No ____

Figure 209.3-2. Telephone Reference Report.

9. Did he/she have any personal problems that interfered with his/her work? Yes__________ No __________
10. Does he/she have any domestic problems that might affect his/her work? Yes__________ No __________
11. Any financial problems? ________ Yes ________ No ________
12. Any drinking, drug, or gambling problems? Yes_____ No _____
____
____
____
13. Why did he/she leave your company? __________
____
____
14. Would you rehire him/her? Yes ______ No ______ if no, please explain __________
____
15. How would you rate his/her dress? ________ Very professional ________ Nonprofessional ________ Average ________ Inferior
16. How would you rate his/her organizational skills?
________ Excellent ________ Average ________ Inferior
17. How would you rate her basic work skills such as efficiency, productivity?
________ Excellent ________ Average ________ Inferior
18. Would you say he/she exercised initiative and responsibility?
__________ Yes __________ No
19. When he/she ran out of work did he/she seek additional work?
__________ Yes __________ No
20. Is there any other information you can give?
____
____
____
____

Figure 209.3-2. (continued)

secretarial training program, that would be very helpful. If you work for a large firm and they haven't developed such a program, you might suggest that they do so and offer to take on the responsibility.

¶209.4 Repair And Maintenance Coordinator

Frequently, you will need to contact repairpersons to repair office equipment. To do this efficiently, keep a file of all repair and maintenance contracts. Also, keep the repair office telephone numbers on the Rolodex with the contract numbers, date of purchase, and model numbers. Have this information ready when you call for repairs.

Be sure to be friendly and courteous to the customer service personnel, and you will get much better service.

Always get copies of the repair invoice before the repairperson leaves. Check the invoice carefully. Do not sign the invoice without your attorney's permission.

¶300 How to Improve the Secretary's Relationship with the Attorneys

¶301 How Your Attorney Is Admitted to the State and Local Bar Association

The requirements for admission to the bar vary from state to state, which basically include the following: academic training, legal training, good moral character, and belief in and loyalty to the form of the United States government.

Applicants for admission to the bar must take a state examination after graduation from law school. In some states, graduates have been admitted without examination. However, admission in one state does not allow attorneys to automatically be admitted to practice in another state. They must comply with rules that each state has for admission. In some states, attorneys from another state may be admitted without examination after they have practiced a specified time, provided the applicants meet that state's requirements.

To be able to practice in the federal courts, attorneys must have practiced three years in the highest court in their state or territory. They must be sponsored by an attorney who is a member of the bar. The requirements for admission to the Federal Courts of Appeal and District Courts vary with the circuit and the district.

In some instances, attorneys may obtain special permission to argue a particular case before court in which they are not licensed to practice.

Requirements to admission to the local bar association are usually not strict, but merely require that the attorney be admitted to the state bar.

The honorary degree of LL.D. (Doctor of Law) is sometimes conferred upon certain persons. Law schools traditionally confer a bachelor's degree, generally the LL.B. (Bachelor of Laws) after three years of study. However, recently because of the length of study required, some schools now confer a JD (Doctor of Jurisprudence, Jurum Doctor) or its equivalent.

¶301.1 Specialization

General practitioners in law are not as common as they have been in the past. Most general practitioners are sole practitioners. For several years, the trend has been toward specialization. This is more common in large cities than in small places. There are several specialties, including: corporate and business law, real estate law, trusts and estates and probate, bankruptcy, taxation, administrative law, criminal law, domestic relations, utility law, entertainment law, banking, transportation, and some others.

It is believed that the trend toward specialization is due to the fact that specialization allows attorneys to become more expert in their field. When clients come to a large firm, for example, they may work with several different attorneys, depending upon the nature of the matters they wish the firm to handle. The legal profession is analogous to the medical profession in that regard.

¶302 Assisting Your Attorneys in Building Their Practice

Your attorneys will also always be on the lookout for new clients and will always be actively or indirectly pursuing new clients. Many firms now have direct marketing strategies to attract new clients. Some firms have brochures that they distribute to the public and many firms are now using classified advertising, although the more traditional firms are still restraining from that type of advertising. Many law firms hire marketing consultants to help them build their practice.

In the typical law firm attorneys will, in most instances, receive origination credits for new clients they bring to the firm. This statistical information regarding the dollar value of fees from new business is often used to determine compensation levels according to whatever agreement the partners have among themselves. Your attorney may be called the originating attorney if he or she brings in a new client. However, another attorney may be called the billing attorney because he or she may be the one in charge of making certain that all the bills are coordinated and executed properly. There may also be an attorney deemed the working attorney who will usually be the attorney that is actually doing the work on the file.

In many of the computer management reports that are now generated within a modern law firm, you will see these different designations of attorneys. In any event, it is helpful for you to be conscious of the fact that your attorneys are actively promoting the firm's practice. Whatever you could do to further that goal or to support your attorneys in maintaining the good will that attracts and keeps clients will be appreciated by your attorneys.

¶303 Gaining Knowledge of Your Attorneys' Fee Schedules and Retainer Agreements

The method in which your attorneys bill their time varies. As you will soon learn, your attorneys will keep regular time records. The most common method of charging for legal services is by using an hourly rate. This is the reason for the time records. The following lists other methods of fee arrangements that your attorneys may use.

¶303.1 Retainer

The attorney and client may agree on a specified fee for the legal services provided. Usually this will be documented in a retainer agreement. In most instances, the client will advance an agreed amount of money to be credited towards the total fee. As this retainer is used up, depending upon the agreement between the client and the attorney, the client will advance additional monies. Various different billing arrangements may be made. The attorney may bill the client on a monthly basis at an agreed upon hourly fee. Associates or paralegals working on the matter may be billed at a specified rate. In most instances the attorney will give the final decision as to the amount of the bill. In some instances, the attorney will reduce the bill if the time seems to be exorbitant for the amount of work or result produced.

The retainer may be an annual retainer, where the attorneys are retained on an annual basis. This is the case for many large corporations. A statement of services rendered will be delivered to the corporation at specified time periods, i.e., monthly, quarterly, semiannually, annually, or otherwise.

¶303.2 Contingency Fee

Attorneys will often agree to take on a particular case for a contingency fee, especially in personal injury, or malpractice cases. This means that the attorney will take a certain percentage of the total dollar amount recovered as agreed to by the client. A common percentage for personal injury cases is one-third or 33⅓ percent of the total amount of money recovered. Usually a contingency fee agreement will be executed by the client.

If there is no amount of money awarded in the case, it is usually agreed that there will be no fee paid to the attorney. This type of fee arrangement works well for personal injury clients, because usually they will not have the money to pay the attorney's fees except out of the damages they might recover.

¶303.3 Collection Charges

There is a standard charge for collection cases, based on the percentage of the amount collected from debtors, with an additional fee if a law suit is necessary.

¶303.4 Forwarding Fee or Associated Counsel Fee

Occasionally, a case is referred to a lawyer by an out-of-town firm. A percentage of the fee earned is sometimes sent to the referring or forwarding attorney; however, the American Bar Association does not approve of the forwarding fee.

¶304 Understanding Your Attorneys' Relationships With the Clients

Your attorneys have a special fiduciary relationship with their clients. In other words, your attorneys' duty is to represent the clients' best interests to the best of their abilities. Attorneys are not allowed to discuss their clients' business with outsiders and keep all client matters strictly confidential. Your attorneys have a *privileged* communication with their clients. That is, your attorneys cannot be compelled to testify concerning any communications with their clients. Also, the attorneys' work product is protected from scrutiny by the court.

Although your attorneys will freely discuss client matters with you or other members of the firm, it is understood that these communications are to be held in confidence. You should be careful not to ask the attorneys any questions concerning another client while they are with a client. It is also important that you do not freely discuss clients' business when there are outsiders visiting the firm.

You will notice that your attorneys' utmost priorities are geared towards their clients. Therefore, all the attorneys' actions will center around pleasing the client and getting the work accomplished by the most efficient and accurate method. Anything you can do to support your attorney in furthering clients' interests and getting the work accomplished efficiently will please them.

¶305 Keeping Abreast Of Your Attorneys' Outside Activities

It is important for your attorneys to keep abreast of what is happening in the community. In addition to being active in the bar associations, most likely they will take an active part in civic affairs—school, church, charities, and any other movement that improves the communities in which they live and work.

As a legal secretary, it is important that you keep abreast of what is happening in the community as well. You will find that you will become well acquainted with your attorneys' activities, and the people with whom they spend their time in outside activities. Try to keep as interested as you can in the activities in which your attorneys are involved. If you spot something in the newspaper or in a magazine that you think will be of interest to them, by all means, show it to them. Your attorneys will appreciate this and will admire your conscientiousness and appreciate your interest in their practice. You will find personal satisfaction as well from participating in these outside activities.

¶400 Improving the Legal Secretary's Relationship with Clients

¶401 How to Gain Clients' Confidence and Respect

The legal secretary has the initial contact with the client. Therefore, it is very important that he or she immediately establish rapport with the client. This initial contact is usually through the telephone. The secretary should make certain that her telephone communications are clear, precise, and friendly.

In all relationships and communication that you have with clients and in all work that you do on behalf of clients, you should always maintain the highest ethical standards of your profession. Exhibit a professional manner at all times in each and every communication with clients, whether by telephone or in person, and you will gain their confidence and respect.

Clients must have confidence in you and know that you are dependable, trustworthy, and loyal. Remember that they are entrusting you with their personal legal problems. Attorneys are bound to the attorney—client privilege that requires them to keep clients' matters confidential. You should develop that same bond of trust between yourself and the clients. You can do this by always preserving and respecting clients' confidences.

¶402 How to Gain Clients' Cooperation

In order to do an efficient and timely job, it is essential that you have the cooperation of the clients. With the clients' cooperation you will accomplish your tasks more efficiently, your job will go more smoothly, and you will have less difficulty in obtaining necessary information and documents.

The following pointers should assist you in obtaining the cooperation of clients.

1. Be friendly, courteous, and polite at all times. Your attitude toward clients should always be positive. Your personal feelings should never affect your relationship with clients. Always call the clients by their surname, e.g., Mr. Bowen or Mrs. Bowen, unless they request you to do otherwise.

2. *Practice the art of conversation.* In your communications with the clients, remember to spend a little time with them conversing about subjects other than business to establish a friendly rapport with them. In other words, begin your conversations with common pleasantries to break the ice.

Do not try to impress clients with big words and stuffy conversation. The clients will be more impressed if you are at ease and conduct yourself in a businesslike manner. Many times clients will look to you to interpret in layman's language what the attorneys have told them. The clients will be relieved when you explain seemingly complicated legal points in simplified terms.

3. *Exude confidence.* Acting and being confident will give clients the impression that you know what you are doing. If clients feel comfortable with you and are confident in your abilities, they will be more apt to cooperate with you and relate confidences to you. This close relationship with clients is essential for you to perform your job thoroughly, expeditiously, and efficiently. If the clients feel free to reveal their personal business to you, then they will spend less time with the attorneys, and you will succeed in saving the client legal fees, and in saving your attorneys valuable time.

4. *Maintain a good attitude.* If you maintain a positive and cooperative attitude toward clients, you will most likely engender the same response from them. By offering assistance to the clients in every way you can, they will recognize your desire to be helpful and will realize your value to them; as a result, they will be more cooperative with you.

¶403 Four Simple Ways to Keep Clients Happy

In addition to the numerous suggestions given throughout the other chapters in this book, here are four guaranteed ways to keep clients happy.

1. *Keep the clients informed.* Since the attorneys have an exorbitant amount of matters to which they must attend as part of their professional and ethical responsibilities, you should act as their confidant. Clients do not realize that attorneys handle numerous cases and they naturally tend to believe and act as if their cases were the only ones the attorneys are handling. Therefore, you should endeavor to make the clients feel that their cases are very important and that you and your

attorneys want to do everything you can to let them know what is happening on their cases.

2. *Follow up on every reasonable client request.* Frequently, clients will contact your office to ask seemingly simple questions or to make what may seem to be foolish requests. Always attempt to answer every question that the clients may have regardless of how simple they may seem and attempt to fulfill every reasonable request that the clients may have within the parameters of your job. If you are unable to answer any of the clients' questions or fulfill any of the clients' requests, consult with your attorney or another attorney in the office to ascertain how you may assist the clients. If you find that you cannot help the clients, inform them that you will consult with your attorney or other proper authority on the clients' matters and that either you or the attorney will get back in touch with them as soon as possible.

3. *Acknowledge receipt of correspondence, documents, or other information sent to you by clients.* It is a good business practice to acknowledge by letter, if possible, or by telephone the receipt of any correspondence, important documents, pleadings, or other information that clients have sent to your office. As may be expected, most clients tend to worry about important things that they send through the mails. A simple telephone call or short letter will ease their minds tremendously.

4. *Make clients feel that they are important.* Clients feel that they are very important and that the legal matters they brought to your attorney's office are extremely important, or they would not have bothered to do so. Therefore, you should make every effort to treat clients as if they are one of the most important clients and as if their case is one of your attorney's most important cases.

¶404 How to Handle the Emotional Client

In a few areas of law, such as domestic relations and probate, you may have occasion to deal with an emotional client. Most likely, it will be in a domestic relation action. In most instances, it will be an upset wife; however, you may well have a husband who needs some reassurance and guidance.

In your role as a legal secretary, you can act as a temporary comfort to an emotionally upset client. Usually, clients just need someone who will listen to their problems and are not really looking for any advice or sympathy.

The trauma of a divorce is very hard for some people to handle, especially those who have been married many years. Also, there are numerous problems that arise when children are involved in the divorce. In this situation, the best thing you can do for the client is be a good listener. Simply tell the client that you are sure everything will work out. Do not try to solve the client's problems or give specific direction, as it may be construed as legal advice. Merely try to be a comfort to the client and assist in any way that you can by giving general information. If the attorney is unavailable, assure the client that your attorney will call as soon as he or she can. Tell them to relax and not to worry.

If you work in a large office and the attorneys for whom you work are not available and the client seems unreasonably upset, you might want to call in one of the other partners and have them talk with the client. Use your best judgment. A well-known divorce lawyer once said that domestic relations work is 99 percent psychological and 1 percent legal. As you work with domestic relations clients, you will realize that this is usually the case and in most instances the lawyer either acts as a mediator or a pseudopsychologist.

¶405 Dos and Don'ts for Building Your Telephone Image

- *Do* use tact if you must screen the calls so that you accomplish this without offending the caller. If you recognize the caller's name or the firm he or she works with, when he or she offers it, and if you can tactfully handle the call yourself, do so without giving any legal advice. This will save your attorneys time and effort if it is only an informational request.
- *Do* create an image of the firm by being totally professional.
- *Do* keep a pen and message pad near the telephone at all times.
- *Do* try to answer the telephone at the end of the first ring.
- *Do* complete any conversations in your office before you pick up the receiver to answer the call.
- *Do* speak directly into the instrument, keeping your mouth about an inch away, and do not begin to speak until the mouthpiece is in this position. If not, your caller may only hear the last half of the firm's name.
- *Do* put a smile into your voice whenever you speak on the telephone. Callers like to hear a clear, alert, pleasant, well-modulated, cordial, and cheerful voice.
- *Do* identify your firm and yourself, if that is the office preference.
- *Don't* say "Mr. Jones' desk."
- *Don't* add "speaking" if you give your name.

- *Don't* call a woman "Madam," since many women today object to it.
- *Don't* say "May I tell him (or her) who's calling, please?" or "May I say who's calling?" because that gives an indication that the person the caller is trying to reach is there; such a situation may be embarrassing if the one being called chose not to take the call at that particular moment.
- *Do* obtain the reason for the call so that you will be able to give your attorneys the information when you transfer the call to them. You might ask "May I say what this is regarding?"
- *Do* tell the caller what you are going to do before transferring calls. Also, give the caller the proper number for returning the call in case you are disconnected during the transfer. Know exactly how to transfer calls and put calls on hold.
- *Do* get back to the caller before thirty seconds have elapsed if you leave the phone to obtain authorized information. To the caller, thirty seconds will seem interminable.
- *Do* take a telephone number and ask the caller if you may return the call, if it looks as though your task will take longer or ask if he or she prefers to hold.
- *Do* get back on the line to let the caller know that you have not forgotten him or her if you must leave him or her on hold for longer than a half minute.
- *Don't* say, "I will have him or her call you." When you take a message, the proper phrase is something like "May I take a message for him?" or "I will ask her to call you," or "I will give her the message the moment she comes in."
- *Do* write down the complete message; don't attempt to remember it.
- *Do* use proper telephone message forms, preferably in duplicate.
- *Do* fill out all the essential information on the message form: date, time of day, name and number of caller, message, your name or initials of person taking the message, and whether the call is to be returned.
- *Do* retain your message pads for at least one year. Accurate recording of telephone calls is important for insuring that calls are returned, for billing the client, and for recording information that might be used in law suits.
- If a caller has dialed you by mistake, *do* answer courteously and ask who he is trying to reach. If it is a wrong number you can say, "You have reached the wrong number, I believe."
- If the caller asks for someone who is already using another line, *do* say, "May I help you or would you care to speak to another attorney?"

- *Don't* ever say, "She hasn't come back from lunch yet," or "He's playing golf today," or "I don't know where he went," or "She isn't in" without elaboration.
- *Do* give correct information; however, it is important that you do not state facts that could lead to a misunderstanding and that you do not divulge information you are not authorized to give.
- *Do* be discreet.
- *Do* be helpful but not too revealing.
- *Do* learn to be courteously noncommital.
- *Do* end a call with "Goodbye," but be sure to let the caller hang up first.
- After the caller has hung up, *do* replace the receiver gently.
- If the caller persists in talking, *do* say, "I'm sorry but I have a call on the other line," or "I would like to talk longer, but I'm due at a meeting now," or "Excuse me, but Mr. Bowen has just buzzed me to take dictation."

¶405.1 Difficult Situations that You May Get Into on the Telephone

The Difficult or Angry Client Frequently, an irritated client will call while your attorney is out of the office. They will try to pressure you to get an immediate response to their call even though you have told them the attorney is out of the office. In this situation, be firm and pleasant and tell the client that the attorney is not in but that you will transfer the message that the client called just as soon as the attorney returns...and then be sure to do so.

Clients Placing Toll Calls Clients frequently ask permission to use a telephone. When these are toll calls, the thoughtful client immediately suggests payment, but many clients simply do not think about it. Ask permission to place the call for the client, then record time and charges. Keep a record of these calls and bill the client for them, unless special circumstances make it more diplomatic for the law firm to charge the call to overhead.

Legal Advice Some callers will attempt to obtain legal advice free from you without talking to the attorney. Inform the client that you cannot give legal advice and that you will have the attorney call him or her.

Fee Information Some callers will attempt to try to find out the fee schedule over the telephone. Inform the caller that fees depend upon the services the attorney renders and that the attorney is the only one that can discuss fees. Suggest that the client make an appointment with the attorney.

Calls from Reporters If you get a call from a reporter with respect to a case that your attorney is handling, tell the reporter that you will have your attorney return the call when he or she comes back into the office.

¶406 Rules for Keeping Confidential Information Confidential

1. *Do not* discuss client matters with anyone outside the firm's office.
2. *Do not* deliver papers or documents to anyone without approval of the responsible attorney.
3. *Do not* answer telephone inquiries about clients' affairs. All such calls should be referred to the clients' attorney.
4. *Do not* leave materials you are typing face up if you leave your desk or anyone is standing around your desk. Turn them face down, cover them, or file them away.
5. *Do not* leave stock certificates and similar valuable papers visible and unsecured. Lock them in a desk drawer or fireproof cabinet at the end of the day.
6. *Do not* throw away discarded papers—drafts should be shredded or destroyed before being placed in the waste basket.

¶407 The Duties and Responsibilities of the Receptionist*

The following is the receptionist's manual, prepared by the firm of Kierr and Gainsburgh, of New Orleans, Louisiana. This manual will prove useful to all law office personnel. The style in which it is written may inspire a departure from the stilted office manual style found in many offices.

THE RECEPTIONIST AND THE OFFICE LAWYERS

In dealing with the lawyers in our office, the receptionist should insist that they cooperate with her in all respects.

*Reprinted with permission from *Law Office Economics & Management Manual Vol. 1* (¶14.0, 1979–1984), published by Callaghan & Co., 3201 Old Glenview Rd., Wilmette, IL 60091. (Section IV eliminated from reprint.)

They should be reminded (and, if necessary, reprimanded) about telling the receptionist when they are leaving their private offices.

They should be reminded to advise the receptionist when they leave the office entirely; she should find out where they are going, how long they plan to be away and how they may be reached in an emergency.

The lawyers should also be reminded by the receptionist to advise the secretary of their expected callers and "who they are."

When the lawyers leave messages with the receptionist, she should take down the messages in shorthand (or otherwise verbatim) and transcribe them on the typewriter so that, if she is relieved, her relief will have the message available and legible.

Great care must be taken by the receptionist to see that the lawyers receive their mail and all messages *promptly.*

This can be accomplished by the receptionist buzzing the lawyer's secretary and asking her to pick up these items, if the lawyer does not call for them himself at the receptionist's desk.

Finally, the receptionist should endeavor to protect her lawyers from embarrassment which might arise out of phone messages and appointments.

For instance, if someone calls up, mad as can be because the lawyer hasn't returned a call yet, the receptionist can help by saying:

> "He's been on the phone almost constantly, sir. Just as soon as he's free I'll remind him again."

Likewise, if the receptionist feels that a visitor has been waiting a long time, she might say to the party in the waiting room:

> "He's still tied up on the phone, sir, but I don't think it will be very much longer."

Also, the receptionist might engage such a visitor in some "light" conversation, just to help pass the time.

MISCELLANEOUS

(1) The receptionist must remember that everything written or said within or to the office pertaining to any client's business is strictly privileged, confidential and not to be discussed outside of the office with *anyone.*

No information about any client or case, including the names of clients, is to be given to anyone by the receptionist. If information is requested, the receptionist should ask one of the lawyers (preferably the one handling the case) to take the call.

(2) The receptionist should not be out of earshot of *her* telephone *and* the front office door except when relieved by the alternative receptionist.
(3) The receptionist should not engage in personal telephone conversations, especially when there are business visitors in the waiting room area.
(4) The receptionist should not read magazines or books at her desk. If she has extra time, she should ask for other work, or she should put books away onto the shelves from the library table or she should otherwise busy herself with office "chores" which she can do without being very far away from her desk.
(5) In discussing matters with clients, the receptionist should avoid making any comments to the clients which might be in the nature of "advice."
(6) The receptionist should attempt to avoid extreme coiffures and heavy make-up. Tailored street clothes should receive preference over more sophisticated attire. Skirts and blouses are deemed to be most desirable for office purposes.
(7) The receptionist should feel free to constructively criticize all of the matters mentioned herein; her comments and suggestions about these routines and procedures are invited and will be given grateful consideration. It is requested, however, that no changes be made in the various procedures outlined herein without the approval of the office attorneys.

¶500 What the Professional Legal Secretary Can Do to Organize the Law Office

¶501 Bloom Where You're Planted

If you are like most of us, you probably have had dreams of the "perfect" job or the job you don't have. You have probably spent Sunday glancing at the want ads looking for that job out there somewhere that will solve all your frustrations and make you happy once and for all. Do you want to change this pattern forever? It's actually easy to do once you decide to do it. Here's how.

Make up your mind now that you are going to start living your life as if it is exactly what you want. Begin with your job.

How? Start out by simply making your surroundings at work more attractive. Whether you have a cubicle, a nice desk, or a small office, look around you and ask yourself how can you make your work area nicer. A flower, a plant, some nice pictures, or simply cleaning off and organizing your desk? It's always nice to add a plant that puts you in touch with nature. Somehow, it makes you feel better.

Go through your work area and clean it up. File those old files. Come in on the weekend if you must to do this. It will pay off in the long run because you'll feel more in control of your life; and when you feel more in control of your life, you will be happier.

Develop the attitude that this is the perfect place for you to be the person you are and to make a contribution to the world. Also, accept the idea that it is the perfect setting to expand your life and increase your income.

Start by making a list of things you will do—little agreements with yourself.

Write a list of your agreements like the following.

1. Every day I will constantly think of good things about people. I will accept them just as they are and not try to change them. I will appreciate how different they are from me. I will not judge them or look for things in them to criticize.
2. I will smile at everyone I meet today and find something good to say to them.

3. I will speak only with good purpose. Every word that I utter to the outer will be positive, because I know that thoughts are things. What I think about will be a message to my subconscious whose job is to say "yes" to my thoughts.
4. I will live in the present moment only and not daydream about next week, next year, or whenever. I will consciously concentrate on "right now."
5. I will be on time to work every day, preferably ten minutes early.
6. I will do my best at all times. I will strive for perfection. I will not let any document or letter out of the office that may cause a client's image of our firm to be marred. I will redo the document or letter rather than send it out sloppy. I will proofread each document or letter twice or have someone else proofread it along with me.
7. I will be courteous and polite to all the people with whom I work. I will be considerate and appreciative of other people.
8. I will endeavor to manage my time more efficiently. If necessary, I will take a course in time management or read a book on time management. (Recommendation: *How to Get Control of Your Time and Your Life,* Alan Lakein, Signet Books, 1973.)

¶502 How to Help Your Attorneys Manage Their Desks

If your attorneys are like most, they are always trying to get more organized. Here's how you can help.

¶502.1 Help Your Attorneys Be Efficient and Provide Quality Service By Having a Clean Desk

Although your attorneys may not believe it, clients will not think they are unqualified simply because their desks are clean or organized. If clients see just a few files on the desk, they could think that the other files have already been serviced. It could also illustrate a new type of organization—one that brings a file to your attorneys' desks only when there is actual work to be done. The file is kept out of sight in the file cabinet until the expected correspondence or documents are received by them.

The real secret to keeping a desk organized is to find a permanent place for everything and to make sure that both you and your attorneys know what goes where and when. Of course, you all may have to break certain habits that you have had in the past, many of which were probably begun before you even became a legal secretary or they started practicing law.

Use labels and trays and perhaps even tape labels initially on specific places on their desks until you all get used to where everything belongs. If your attorneys do not want to use labels, you can use desk organizers or neatly marked trays. Or they may have specific places set aside in their credenzas so that it can be closed if a client comes in unexpectedly.

Some examples of labels you might want to use are:

1. Personal correspondence;
2. Personal receipts;
3. Firm business;
4. Expenses and miscellaneous receipts;
5. Bills to review;
6. Miscellaneous notes;
7. Correspondence from clients;
8. Interoffice memos;
9. Legal memos and briefs;
10. Discovery;
11. Seminar information;
12. Things to do;
13. Telephone messages to return;
14. Magazines, newspapers, newsletters to read;
15. New laws to review;
16. Research projects.

After you get all that organized, then you should proceed to designate certain trays for each of the following categories.

1. A tray where notes, correspondence, documents, etc., are placed by your attorneys indicating to you that they want the file in connection with that matter. Name this tray *Bring Me.*
2. A tray for interoffice items to be discussed with other attorneys in the office. Label this *Interoffice.*
3. A tray for items to be delegated or assigned to other attorneys, paralegals and other support staff. Label this *Assignments.*
4. Files needing dictation, that is all prior study and research having been completed prior to putting them in the tray. Label this *Dictation.*
5. Matters deserving review, research, and study. Label this *To Prepare.*
6. *Today's Appointments,* which should be labeled as such.

7. Telephone messages to be returned or files on which telephone calls should be placed, or files awaiting return phone calls. Label this *Phone*.
8. Your attorneys should develop the habit of placing all telephone messages, scraps of papers, correspondence, files or any other reminder of something that must be accomplished that day in *Things That Must Be Done Today,* so that by day's end, very little will be forgotten. However, they should be cautious not to overload this tray to the point of becoming overwhelmed. They must be careful to only place items that must be done that day.

Everything will now be out of sight. The important thing is that you and your attorneys know what goes where and when.

¶502.2 Checklist of Things You Can Do to Help Your Attorneys Manage Their Desks

- Scrutinize your attorneys' desks carefully. Notice where they put things. Take stock of what is on their desks.
- Go through the things on the top of their desks and credenzas and separate everything into various categories such as:

  1. Today's correspondence including only important mail from clients, other attorneys or business people;
  2. "Junk" mail,
  3. Notes and miscellaneous;
  4. Seminar brochures;
  5. Advertisements, etc.

- Help your attorneys make notes of important matters, even if they are in the middle of a conference. The notes must be placed in the appropriate tray. Otherwise, they will be forgotten. Remind your attorneys to go through the tray about an hour before they leave the office. Provide assistance by doing those tasks that you can handle.
- Don't forget to organize yourself by saving your communications with the attorneys for a time when they can be handled at one time, rather than interrupting them off and on during the day. When you think of something that you want to ask, if it doesn't have to be answered right away, make a note of it on a list that you keep handy on your desk. Reserve a specific time each day to spend with your attorneys to ask these questions and handle

matters that have come up during the day. Perhaps, around 4:00 or 4:30 P.M. when you take the day's correspondence in to them for signature would be a good time. This is the time also to review the next day's matters and to have your attorneys go through their trays of *Things That Must Be Done Today.* Be sure that you also have a location on your desk for these items to be discussed and your questions.
- Find time in your day to periodically go in and clean up and organize their desks.

Remember. A cluttered desk is a sign that things are not going well. Take action and clean up—your and your attorneys' desks.

At first you and your attorneys will have to work closely together to develop these new and helpful habits. If they are not interested in spending the time to get organized, just accept that and do as much as possible on your own to help them.

¶503 Keeping Up With the Latest Equipment: Handling Vendors

Needless to say, the legal secretary has many roles, one of which may be to supervise the ordering and maintaining of office equipment. Since the secretary usually reviews the attorneys' mail, you can keep an eye out for catalogues that will be helpful in ordering and keeping up with the latest equipment.

If you also function as the receptionist, you will have the often irritating problem of handling salespersons who come into the office without appointments soliciting business. Since your attorneys' time is valuable, you should attempt to discourage salespersons who want to talk to the attorneys. Simply tell them that the attorneys are busy or with a client and cannot be interrupted. Make sure to obtain a brochure or sales catalogue and a business card from the salesperson to keep in your files. You do not have to be rude to get the salesperson out of the office; however, you do have to be firm and should keep your discussion with them to a minimum. Your time is also valuable.

One of the ways in which you can keep up with the latest equipment is to talk to other legal secretaries in your city. This is the easiest way to find out what other firms are doing and how successful they are. It also doesn't hurt for you to review state and national bar journals, such as the *American Bar Association Journal, Legal Economics, The Legal Administrator,* or *The ABA Journal.*

¶503.1 Checklist For Ordering Supplies For A Small Office

You may add or delete from this list as necessary. This list is excellent for starting a new office.

General Office Supplies

Phone message pads
Phone message holders
Petty cash box
Typewriter ribbon
Typewriter cleaner
Correcting tape
Liquid Paper (white, yellow for drafts, white for copies, pen, pencil, and special blends)
Typewriter eraser pencils (smooth pink rubber and white rough sandpaper point)
Pencils
Pencil cups
Felt-tip pens
Erasers (ink and pencil)
Three ring binders (black)
Paper punches (2 and 3 hole)
Index tabs (clear and plain)
Dictating tapes (cassettes)
Rolodexes
Paper clip holders
Pens (red, black, and felt-tip)
Adding machine tape and ribbon
Paper clips (large and small)
Yellow and pink self-stick note pads (various sizes)
Note pads (memo)
Scotch tape and tape dispensers
Postage scale
Stamps
Mail packaging tape
Acco fasteners
Rubber bands (various sizes)
Rulers
Binder clips (various sizes)
Pressboard binders (legal and letter size; used for litigation files and real estate binders)
Manila file folders (one-third cut)
Redwald folders (also referred to as gussets or buckets)

Yellow highlighters
Letter trays (legal and letter)
Bookends
Calendars (desk, pocket, and wall)
Ink pads (black and red)
Rubber stamps (as needed)
Pendaflex folders and holders
Pendaflex tabs (plastic labels)
Business card holders
Staple removers
Staples
Index dividers (legal and letter for binders)
File dividers (A–Z)
Memo pad holders
Steno books
Storage (file) boxes
Message rack for receptionist
Letter openers
Avery file labels
Index cards (white and colored)
File room visible index holders
Card files (3 × 5 and 4 × 6)
Ledger books and paper

Computer Supplies

Disks
Ribbons
Daisy wheels
Disk holder
Paper (tractor feed)
Computer paper file binders

Cleaning and Kitchen Supplies

Paper towels
Napkins
Paper plates
Plastic spoons, forks, and knives
Styrofoam cups
Plastic glasses
Glasses
Coffee cups
Sugar

Low-calorie sweetener
Coffee cream
Dish soap
Scouring pad
Rags
Window cleaner
Plastic wrap
Aluminum foil
Cleanser
Furniture polish and cloth
Aspirin
Bandages

Paper Supplies

Plain, high-quality letter-size bond (25 percent rag), 8½ × 11
Yellow, 8½ × 11
Yellow, 8½ × 13–14
White legal bond, 8½ × 13–14
Carbon paper
Envelopes (letter—plain and engraved, billing)
Note: To save money, have your firm print the firm's name and address on a low-quality envelope and use this for unimportant mailing.

Small Furniture Items

Coat rack
Umbrella holder
Wastebaskets
Heaters
Fans
Coat hooks for doors

Miscellaneous

Hammer
Screwdriver (regular, Phillips head)
Nails
Picture hangers
Pliers

¶504 You Can Assist in the Office Move

It is very common for the typical law office, especially the small to medium-sized firms, to move quite frequently. In large firms there are a lot of interoffice moves, i.e., attorneys moving their offices due either to new attorneys being hired or to their promotion to partner, or the firms' expansion to another floor.

If a move is not handled properly, it can be a very traumatic experience. To avoid this, you can assist your attorneys with the move by planning, coordinating, and supervising the move. It is imperative that the move does not stop the normal flow of work. In other words, "business as usual" should be the motto.

To avoid wasting the attorneys' time, the firm will probably move on a weekend or holiday. This will allow personnel to get organized prior to the resumption of business on Monday after the move. Be prepared to work during the move.

Suggest to your attorneys that they hire more than two or three moving vans for shuttle runs between the old location and the new one. This way you can have one van unloading at the new location and one loading at the old site. Since loading requires much more time than unloading, arrange for loading crews at the old site and an unloading crew at the new site.

Coordinate advanced delivery of packing cartons and stick-on labels for each container, piece of furniture, office equipment and other items with the moving company. Make certain that the labels are marked to identify not only the operating area or attorney's office to which each container and separate item is to be delivered, but also the identification of the floor to which it is to be delivered. For example, a box labeled "5/CAM" indicates the box belongs in C. A. Martin's office on the fifth floor. Likewise a desk labeled "4/LIB" indicates the desk should be delivered to the library on the fourth floor.

Suggest that all attorneys and administrative staff pack their own offices with personal items and office supplies and small equipment. They would probably prefer to do this themselves.

In larger areas such as the kitchen, copy and supply rooms, teams of employees supervised by the office manager or firm administrator can be organized to label the items.

The library move should be supervised by an attorney or a paralegal. If you are in a small office, you will most likely be the person most familiar with the library and can oversee this portion of the move.

Where practical, have the commercial movers crate, pack, and mark as many of the items as possible.

The bulky and more sensitive electronic office equipment, such as computers, electronic typewriters, photocopiers, or other such items that require more attention should be moved by the company from which the equipment was purchased or by the commercial movers. Make certain that you call them in advance of the move to arrange for them to transport the equipment prior to the next day of business.

Most commercial movers will insist on noninterference during the move since they have strict liability requirements. Make certain that only one or two persons be designated as the contact person on the scene to eliminate confusion. For example, you may have one firm representative be on each floor in the old building and under your supervision or the supervision of the office manager or administrator who can observe the removal and unloading.

¶504.1 Checklist for Coordinating an Office Move

You can help your attorneys make their move run move smoothly. Plan ahead. Make a "to do" list of the items that you must take care of before you move and the things you must do during and after the move. Use the following checklist to help make your own.

1. Select a reputable, experienced moving company with quality vans and equipment at least three to four months in advance. Trying to cut corners with an inexpensive mover may turn out to be a big mistake. Go with well-known movers who are reliable, trustworthy and guarantee their moves so that if anything is broken by them, they will replace it or give your attorneys cash to replace it.
2. Obtain an estimate of the moving time from the moving company.
3. Make a list of the major items to be moved.
4. Estimate the number of boxes that will be necessary for the move.
5. Determine the moving date or dates. The best time to move is a weekend. Ask everyone to pack their own offices.
6. Order boxes ahead of time and order more than you think you will need—for some reason there are never enough boxes.
7. Inspect your new offices carefully. Take measurements and plot out the area indicating where the windows are and their sizes.
8. Weed out your attorneys' files before the move. If your firm has more than three attorneys, circulate a memo stating that all files over a certain age will be destroyed unless the attorney to whom the case had been assigned says "Don't destroy it."
9. Make a list of the major items to be moved.
10. Consult the supplier of copiers, telephone, files, computers, and so on, well ahead of time so if they are to move these items, they can work it into their schedule.

11. Keep the commercial movers continuously involved with the detailed planning of the move right up to the moving date.
12. Ask the commercial mover to recommend the packing boxes and materials and the best method for marking items, and for other details that may have an impact on the efficiency of the move.
13. Arrange for the telephone systems to be operable at the new location on moving day. In some instances you may want to get the telephone turned on at the new location prior to the actual move since there will be a couple of days of overlapping when the attorneys may be either at the old office or the new office.
14. Prepare a floor plan for office equipment, furniture, photocopying, bookkeeping, postage machines, computers, word processors, and photocopying counters.
15. Make arrangement to ensure that there will be someone to answer the phone at the new location during the move if the move takes place during working hours.
16. Arrange for the clearing and preparing of the reception and conference rooms.
17. Make certain that an adequate security system with door locks and electrical devices is in operable condition prior to the move.
18. Obtain the necessary keys for the firm personnel.
19. Assemble a group of people, depending upon the size of your firm, to assist in the move by either marking the boxes and supervising the move of the individual offices and library, kitchen, and so on.
20. You will make some mistakes; don't worry! Try to keep them to a minimum by planning, and don't cry when they come to light later.

¶505 Selecting Furniture for the Law Office

There comes a time for most secretaries to assist in selecting additional furniture or new furniture for the law office. This is not as easy a task as it would seem to be. There are numerous factors involved in choosing law office furniture. Following are several ways that you can approach the task of purchasing new furniture.

1. Consult major furniture dealers in the area to collect catalogues and obtain bids.

2. Select used furniture, which involves quite a bit of time and effort.
3. Check local ads in the business section of the newspaper to obtain good buys on used furniture.
4. Decide to save time and just go to a single furniture dealer, negotiating the best price for your selections.

When dealing with several vendors and obtaining bids, you can get very frustrated if you do not keep accurate records of what the bids are from each vendor and a description or catalogue of the furniture itself. A chart is helpful in keeping a record of the bids. (See Figure 505-1.)

NO.	ITEM	NO. ITEMS REQUIRED	VENDOR/ADDRESS/TELEPHONE	RETAIL PRICE	DISCOUNT PERCENT	NEGOTIATED PRICE	DELIVERY DATE

Figure 505-1. Vendor Bids Chart.

Most importantly, make sure you *do not sacrifice quality for price.* Frequently, what looks like a bargain may end up costing more in the long run. For example, if you get a laminated desk rather than wood over a short period of time it might start buckling. You would then just have to turn around and buy another desk. Thus, you really would not have saved at all. However, this is usually not a problem, since most law firms are careful to select solid, good-quality furniture. They know it is important to have quality furniture to impress clients. Many law firms are lavishly decorated. However, there is a current trend toward a more conservative look. In other words, you will not see as many expensive accessories in most reception areas of quality law firms.

¶505.1 Saving Space With Movable Partitions

In the past, many law firms have used permanent wall systems and when they needed to expand or decided to remodel, they found it difficult and expensive to reconfigure the office. Therefore, to meet such needs, easily changeable wall systems—known as "panel systems" —are increasingly popular with law office designers. The panel system consists of partitions, hung on posts that can be combined in various ways to form a number of law office layouts. They are usually less than ceiling height and create cubicles rather than completely enclosed offices, although full floor-to-ceiling panels are available. They range in width from one to six feet. With these panels, it is easier to separate one workstation from another or expand without a major reconstruction problem.

¶506 Finding Space for the Computer

Formerly, allocating space for the computer was not a major consideration in planning an office move or expanding present office space. However, with the current popularity of computers, the problem is twofold: first, how to find the space for all the new hardware, cables, and peripheral computer equipment, and second, how to ensure the comfort of the operators.

The simple fact is that computers take up more workspace. When you replace an electric typewriter with a word processor, the new machine may use up to 50 percent more work-surface area. The typewriter had its keyboard and printer, so to speak, both in one housing; the word processor may have a separate screen, keyboard, and printer, all of which need their own desk space. If you add a few peripherals, such as a modem (for telecommunications), the desk space formerly allotted to that operator becomes grossly insufficient.

Furthermore, the electrical needs of such a system have to be considered. Since each electrical device requires power, a single fully equipped computer terminal may demand six or more electrical outlets. In addition, specific arrangements must be made for air conditioning for some computers, although this is not always required as it used to be with the larger computers.

There are very few existing offices that have space for all that equipment, but even fewer that are equipped to handle the power supply. If your attorneys are introducing a microcomputer to your office, you can probably accommodate it. But what if they are installing ten or twenty word processing terminals?

Your attorneys, like most people, often do not think of space and power considerations when purchasing a computer or word processor. When new equipment arrives, or when they have to expand their systems to accommodate new devices, they really encounter difficulties. Computers depend on a steady, clean power source to function properly, and an overloaded electrical line can cause the computer to lose parts of documents or data. Thus, the computer which at first seemed to be a solution, can become a problem in itself.

¶506.1 Comfort and the Computer

Since so much more can be accomplished at a computer terminal, it means that word processing operators and legal secretaries spend more time at their workstations. This has caused a number of health complaints, including: headaches; blurred vision and other eye discomfort; muscle, joint and tendon pain; and irritability, anxiety, and depression.

In the past, a standard swivel chair for use by a secretary at a standard desk was sufficient. It was hard to adjust, but there was seldom a need to. Once adjusted, the chair stayed in position. However, an easily adjusted chair is essential at the modern computer terminal. For one thing, not all the devices an operator is likely to be working with are likely to be at the same height. Additionally, all those extra hours spent in the same seat will create all kinds of discomfort if the chair cannot be adjusted periodically to let the operator sit in a new position or at a new angle. This seems to relieve the common cause of backaches.

Moreover, some chiropractors and orthopedists have suggested that word processing operators who share terminals with other operators may suffer from chronic backaches, neckaches, and other aches and pains if they are stuck in a position that was suited only to the first operator.

Another problem is acoustics. Some computer equipment, notably printers, can be excessively noisy. This can be irritating and distracting. Moreover, when a lot of this equipment is jammed into a relatively small space, it can generate an uncomfortable amount of heat.

With all this noise, glare, heat, and body discomfort, it is not surprising that there are so many complaints from word processing operators and legal secretaries. Recently, there have been more workers' compensation cases resulting from using computers. Fortunately, office furniture designers have developed some revolutionary ways to deal with these problems. One need only attend a computer show, glance through a computer catalogue, or contact a furniture dealer's association to discover that there are numerous products that will assist in alleviating many of these problems.

¶507 For Your Attorneys: Ten-Point Questionnaire of Design Factors to Consider in Designing the Law Office

If your attorneys are moving into a new office in which they will have a say regarding space planning, give them, or the law firm's administrator, this design questionnaire.

1. Secretarial assignments:
   a. Are secretaries to be assigned on a one-to-one basis?
   b. Will secretaries work together as a team, sharing the workload?
   c. Will a secretarial pool be formed to serve the younger associates or as a training facility for new legal secretaries?
   d. Who will do the secretarial work for summer clerks?
   e. Do secretaries act as a buffer between attorneys and internal interruptions?
   f. Will overflow or substitute "floating" secretaries be needed to keep things moving during vacations or illnesses?
   g. Will secretaries input time for their attorneys? Do they need to be near enough to be aware of their movements?
2. Equipment considerations:
   a. Is the firm increasing its use of word processing equipment? Will each secretary have a workstation? Where will cabling have to be done?
   b. Where will printers be located? Will a printer room be necessary? Will they need to be close to secretaries or will printed documents be delivered?
   c. Will secretaries need typewriters? Can they share typewriters if they each have word processing equipment? Where will the typewriters be located?
   d. Will remote dictation equipment be installed to carry legal dictation directly to the secretarial workstation? Should conduit be installed during construction?
   e. What sound control will be required?
   f. Will satellite copying equipment prove advantageous?
   g. Should a central duplicating facility with an operator be provided?
   h. Does the firm wish to purchase its own telephone equipment?
   i. How much telephone equipment space is required and

how far from the receptionist's desk can the main equipment be located?

j. Should the firm use a message center?
k. Should a paging system be installed to make it easier to locate attorneys?
l. Does the firm need controls for multi-floor operations, such as a check-in system, which automatically reports the fact that attorneys are leaving and tells them whether they have messages upon their return?
m. Are there electrical current fluctuations in the building which will interfere with the proper functioning of the equipment?
n. Will special sound controlling walls, ceiling, and floor be needed?
o. Does the dust level of a computer area have to be controlled?
p. Where will computer printouts be stored? Computer supplies?

3. Filing system:

a. Is it time for the firm to consider centralizing its files?
b. How much centralization will take place, and what additional filing facilities will be required throughout the office?
c. Will separate filing rooms or areas be needed for special departments or for office accounting records?
d. Should a vault or other fireproof facility be built in for storage of client papers and valuable documents?
e. How many file clerks will the firm have by the time its lease is up?
f. What kind of filing equipment will best serve the future needs of the firm?
g. Will the loaded weight of the file equipment fall within the acceptable floor load requirements of the building or is additional bracing needed?
h. What other duties—e.g., conflict checks, forms filing—will the file personnel perform? What equipment will this require?
i. Can access to the file room be controlled by means of a "dutch door"?
j. What volume of closed files must be kept on the premises?

k. How many files can go to a warehouse facility or be microfilmed?
l. Where will microfilm equipment be placed when and if it is acquired?
m. Has file room planning considered a five- to ten-year expansion factor?
n. Where will file room supplies be stored?

4. Duplicating:
a. Is a change needed in the type of copying or duplicating equipment?
b. Is special ventilation needed?
c. Will any special electrical wiring be required?
d. Are there electrical current fluctuations in the building that will interfere with the proper functioning of the equipment?
e. How close or far away from the secretaries should the copying equipment be?
f. How much room will collating equipment require?
g. Will special sound controlling walls, ceiling, and floor be needed?
h. How large should the storage cabinets for supplies be?

5. Mail room:
a. Will messengers (internal or external) be required at the new location?
b. Will larger postage meters and other mail equipment be needed in the next few years?
c. Should individual pigeonholes for attorneys' mail be built into the mail room or some other location?
d. Is the office postage scale sufficiently accurate or is a new one required?
e. How will bulk items, such as parcel post shipments of books, be received? Will it be possible to deliver packages to the mail room directly from a freight elevator without carrying them through the halls?
f. Are receptacles for mail and deliveries needed at various locations in the office and should they be built in?
g. Can the freight elevator be monitored at all times to prevent intruders from entering?

6. Private offices:
a. Is it possible to standardize attorneys' offices to one, two, or three sizes?

b. Will they be large enough to accommodate small meetings or will they be strictly work locations?
c. Will furnishings be paid for by the firm, through a budget allocation to the attorneys, or by the attorneys themselves?
d. How much latitude in furnishing will be allowed?
e. How large should the largest office be?
f. Will attorneys be grouped in accordance to specialties with associates and partners in each specialty near each other?
g. Where will the office administrator be located—near the managing partners, near the entrance, near the secretaries, near the accounting department?
h. Should the administrator have an office large enough to accommodate a secretarial applicant?
i. Would attorneys benefit from work rooms that can be used to ready cases for trial or to house large litigation case files?

7. Conference rooms:
a. What is the minimum and maximum size required for conference facilities and how many conference rooms are desired?
b. Can one large conference room be made divisible into two smaller ones?
c. Will an extra exhaust ventilation be required?
d. Would rheostat lighting controls be beneficial?
e. Will the conference room be well insulated from surrounding noise?
f. Should facilities for a court reporter be provided in a deposition room?

8. Reception rooms:
a. Can the reception room be placed conveniently near the elevators and yet out of the traffic flow of the office?
b. Will the receptionist's desk either be clear of all client work or well shielded from the eyes of visitors?
c. How many persons must be seated in the reception room on a normal day? An exceptional day?
d. Has a back-up receptionist been located nearby so that the reception room can be constantly attended?
e. Has sufficient closet space been provided?
f. Will employees put their coats in the reception room closet or are other facilities available?

g. Is a "local call only" phone available for visitors? Should the phone be located in a small private room?
h. Does the receptionist have a need for a security bell to summon assistance?
i. Is a boot and umbrella storage unit desirable?

9. Library:
a. Will the library be a separate facility or will it be combined with the conference room?
b. Will the library be visible to clients or will it be a working library?
c. Have adequate carpeting and sound-absorbing ceiling been included to reduce noise?
d. Will all internal library aisles be wide enough when the furniture is placed in the room?
e. Has library planning included a factor for five to ten years of expansion?
f. If a librarian is to be used, has an office been included in the planning? Will it quiet typewriter and telephone noise? Will the librarian need a computer terminal and printer?
g. Will computerized legal research be done in the library? Is space for computer equipment provided for? Is the printer soundproofed?
h. Will one central library be provided or should there be smaller specialized libraries for departments?
i. Is there storage space for infrequently used volumes in the library or elsewhere?
j. Will any books be purchased in microfilm form and, if so, where will the reader be placed?
k. Can space be saved with double-stacked shelves or movable library shelving?
l. Will the working facility be a table or a series of library carrels?
m. Have special adjustments for the extra lighting needed in the library been taken care of?
n. Should a copying machine and/or dictation booths be incorporated in the library design to assist attorneys in their research?

10. Other major considerations:
a. Does the firm plan to extend its use of paralegal assistants? What planning has been done to provide space for them?

b. Will paralegals be located near the secretarial work force or near the attorneys?
c. Where will their secretarial help be located?
d. Is sufficient parking available for staff and clients?
e. Does the building provide good maintenance?
f. Is the building known as a quality one or "just another office building"?
g. Is elevator service adequate to the floor to be occupied?
h. Are rest rooms kept clean?
i. Will special rest room facilities be built within the office suite?
j. Does the firm desire to have lunchroom facilities available to the staff and attorneys?
k. Would it be useful to have a shower and dressing room in the offices?
l. Has a reasonable, accurate firm growth factor been included in the layout and lease planning?

¶600 How to Prepare Picture Perfect Correspondence

One of your primary duties as a legal secretary is the preparation of accurate and professionally prepared correspondence. Properly prepared letters present a professional image for your attorneys. The letters an attorney writes are often the only thing clients see (other than the bill) as a representation of the work being done. Therefore, it is important that there are no erasures or words corrected with liquid paper or correction tape. It is essential that you present the best prepared letter you can as a representation of the work your attorneys do.

¶601 Keys to Better Letter Design

Generally, there are four letter styles:

1. full-block;
2. modified block;
3. modified semi-block;
4. official.

The first three styles are more commonly used in law offices. The official style is seldom used but is sometimes used for personal informal letters.

Full Block (See Figure 601-1.) The full-block style is sometimes preferred by the attorneys. It has no indentations and the left margin is flush. The date and complimentary close (e.g., Very truly yours) are aligned with the paragraphs that begin at the left margin. Open punctuation is generally used.

Modified Block (See Figure 601-2.) The modified block style is used more often for legal correspondence. The date is in the upper right hand corner, the address is flush left, and the salutation or greeting is also flush left along with the "regarding" clause. The complimentary close is approximately five spaces to the right of the center of the page, and the typed signature is aligned with the

LEGAL SUPPORT SERVICES, INC.
3216 Post Woods Drive, Suite G
Atlanta, Georgia, 30339
(404) 952-8468

August 3, 1985

Debbie Kay Designs
2059 Lake Park Drive, Suite P
Smyrna, GA 30080

Attention: Ms. Debbie Keller

Re: Design No. 890

Dear Ms. Keller:

This office represents John Yellowjay who has informed us that he placed an order with your company over ninety days ago, a copy of which is enclosed. He sent you a letter dated April 1, 1985, and enclosed a check in the amount of $9,800. He has received no response from you or anyone in the company. The check has cleared the bank.

This letter is to inform you that unless we receive a response from you within ten (10) days, we will have no choice but to file suit against you and your company.

We shall expect your response or the items that Mr. Yellowjay ordered from your company by August 13, 1985.

Yours very truly,

Colleen Ferrington

CF:cab

Enclosures

bc: John Yellowjay

Figure 601-1. Full-Block Letter (mixed punctuation).

LEGAL SUPPORT SERVICES, INC.
3216 Post Woods Drive, Suite G
Atlanta, Georgia, 30339
(404) 952-8468

August 3, 1985

PERSONAL AND CONFIDENTIAL

Ms. Sylvia Jones
9 Outer Road
Norwalk, CT 67846

Re: Jones v. Pugh

Dear Ms. Jones:

We have received your request for information about the above-referenced matter, along with your check no. 687 in the amount of $6.50.

We are returning your check no. 687 because it is the incorrect amount. We need a check from you in the amount of $8.25 for the copies of the will you requested.

Please send a check for $8.25, and we will send the copies you requested. We are sorry for this inconvenience and appreciate your cooperation.

Very truly yours,

Jacque Caryl Mills

JCM:cab

Enclosures (1)

cc: Christine Johnson Bowen
Newton County Courthouse

Figure 601-2. Modified Block Letter (mixed punctuation).

complimentary close line. The title of the person signing the letter may be placed directly under the signature line and aligned with the complimentary close. However, in law firms the title is seldom used since the signatories are normally attorneys. You can put "Esquire" or "Esq." if your attorneys prefer that you do.

Modified Semi-block (See Figure 601-3.) The modified semi-block style is the most popular with attorneys. The paragraphs are indented. Some offices indent five spaces and others indent twelve. The regarding clause is also indented the same number of spaces as the paragraph. If there is a second line carried over in the address, it is indented three spaces. For example:

Mr. Joseph Marino
Holland Shipes Bennett
   Thrasher
5995 Barfield Road, Suite 100
Atlanta, GA 30328

The signature line is aligned with the complimentary close. The data is typed flush with the right-hand margin.

Official (See Figure 601-4.) The official style is generally used by attorneys for informal personal letters written on their personalized letterhead. The significant difference from their regular letter styles is that the inside address is placed at the bottom of the letter below the signature line flush left, instead of at the beginning of the letter. Very seldom do you see the official style; it is becoming outmoded.

¶602 Keeping a Looseleaf Form Book

Many law offices have a book, usually a looseleaf binder, that contains copies of letters that the attorneys use frequently. These are called form letters, which are usually boilerplate or standard letters for routine correspondence. If you have a collection of these letters, you can handle a lot of your attorneys' correspondence for them and save them from having to dictate many letters. All you usually have to do is change the names and addresses and perhaps the dates mentioned in the letter.

One common boilerplate is the *transmittal letter.* The transmittal letter is used to mail an enclosure to another party or to the court for taking care of routine matters. If you don't have a book of form letters, you can make one by getting in the habit of keeping an extra copy of

LSS

LEGAL SUPPORT SERVICES, INC.
3216 Post Woods Drive, Suite G
Atlanta, Georgia, 30339
(404) 952-8468

March 2, 1985

CONFIDENTIAL

Ms. Joanne Bolthan
10227 Alcovy Road
Covington, GA 30209

Re: Newton County Probate Court Case No. 238

Dear Ms. Bolthan:

The above-entitled case will be heard on June 10, 1985, in Courtroom B-2. Please bring all documents relating to this case at this time.

If you have any questions regarding this matter, please don't hesitate to contact us.

Thank you for your cooperation in this matter.

Very truly yours,

Patricia Graves
Clerk of the Court

PG:jcm

cc: Ann Mather
Skip Johnson
Judi Wood
Carole Love
Bob Love

Figure 601-3. Modified Semi-Block Letter (mixed punctuation).

LEGAL SUPPORT SERVICES, INC.
3216 Post Woods Drive, Suite G
Atlanta, Georgia, 30339
(404) 952-8468

JUDI SMITH JOHNSON & ASSOCIATES
2211 West Paces Ferry Road
Atlanta, GA 30305

Office of the City Attorney

February 14, 1984

Dear Ms. Williams:

I regret that I was unable to come to your reception. However, please be assured that you will get my vote in your campaign for city councilwoman. I intend to support you in every way that I can.

Enclosed is my check for $500 for your campaign. I hope that I will be able to come to your reception on March 27, 1985.

Warmest personal regards.

Sincerely yours,

Ms. Theresa Williams
1284 Brannon Wood Road
Clarkston, Georgia 30021

Figure 601-4. Official Letter Style (mixed punctuation).

each letter that is frequently used. Punch three holes in the letter and put it in your form book after indexing it.

For example: Letter to the court clerk transmitting a pleading and a check (See Figure 602-1.)

LEGAL SUPPORT SERVICES, INC.
3216 Post Woods Drive, Suite G
Atlanta, Georgia, 30339
(404) 952-8468

John I. Bruno
Attorney at Law
P.O. Box 471
Conyers, Georgia 30207
(404) 922-8489

August 26, 1985

Ms. Fran Awtry
Clerk of the Court
DeKalb County
188 East Pontem Street
Kelly, West Virginia

Re: Marlene Arnold v. Mark Citrin
DeKalb County Superior Court File No. 898

Dear Ms. Awtry:

Enclosed are an original and two copies of Plaintiff's Requests For Admissions of Matters and Genuineness of Documents to Defendant in the above-entitled case, together with check no. 899 in the amount of $14.00.

Please file the original and stamp-file two copies and return to this office in the enclosed stamped self-addressed envelope.

Thank you for your assistance in this matter.

Very truly yours,

William Chappini

WC:jcm

Enclosures (3)

Figure 602-1. Transmittal Letter.

¶603 Preparing Opinion Letters

Attorneys commonly write letters that give a legal opinion on a certain point of law or particular transaction. These letters are signed by a partner in the firm with the firm name just below it, since they represent advice from the firm and not just the individual attorney who wrote the letter. For example, the signature line will be like this:

(Two spaces) Very truly yours,
BARWICK & BARWICK

(Four spaces) ______________________
Nancy Barwick
For the Firm

¶604 Making The Letter Picture Perfect

A letter should literally be perfect enough to be enclosed in a picture frame. To have a picture-perfect letter, you should plan ahead before starting to type the letter. If you have a word processor, this will be easy. With word processing you can send the same letter to different persons with the merge capability. This allows you to insert different names and addresses in the same letter. It is almost automatic.

¶605 Checklist for Designing and Preparing an Attractive Letter

1. Figure out the approximate length of the letter by making a rough draft and counting the number of lines in the letter. If you don't have time to make a rough draft, learn to gauge the letter's length by the length of the dictation tape.
2. For a short, one-page letter, set the left margin about 17 to 20 spaces from the left-hand edge of the paper. Set the right margin approximately 22 to 27 spaces from the right-hand edge of the paper. This allows five spaces for the typewriter bell to go off so that you can end the line.
3. For a medium length letter set the left margin about 12 to 17 spaces from the right edge of the paper, and the right margin 12 to 17 spaces from the left-hand edge of the paper, allowing five spaces for the bell signal.

4. For a very long letter, set the margins about 12 spaces from the left-hand edge of the paper, and 17 spaces from the right-hand edge of the paper.
5. Before you put your paper in the typewriter, put a light pencil mark on the right-hand side of the paper about 1½ inches from the bottom. This will give you a visual warning when you have reached the end of the paper. With each page marked, you can end the pages at the same place on the paper. If you have a word processor, you can use formatting techniques.
6. The margins in the second-page sheets should match those of the first sheet. Never leave just one line of a paragraph on the last line of the letter. Always type at least two lines of the paragraph before going to the second page.
7. You should single-space your letters and double-space between paragraphs.

¶606 You Can Punctuate Properly

The most popular pattern that is commonly used by most attorneys nationwide is mixed punctuation. Closed punctuation is rarely used in law offices. Attorneys now consider this style outdated.

¶606.1 Mixed Punctuation (See Figure 606.1-1)

1. There is no punctuation in the date line, except for the comma after the day of the month.
2. The address is not punctuated, except if an abbreviation such as J.D. or M.D. appears at the end of the line.
3. The salutation is ended with a colon.
4. A comma appears after the complimentary close, e.g., Sincerely,.
5. There is no punctuation at the end of the signature lines.
6. Mixed punctuation can be used with any of the letter styles.

¶606.2 Open Punctuation (See Figure 606.2-1.)

1. There is no punctuation in the date line, except for the comma at the end of the day of the year and before the year.
2. There is no punctuation used at the end of the address line, unless an abbreviation, e.g., Jr., ends the line in which case the period ends the line.
3. There is no punctuation in the salutation, e.g., Dear.

LEGAL SUPPORT SERVICES, INC.
3216 Post Woods Drive, Suite G
Atlanta, Georgia, 30339
(404) 952-8468

JACOBSON, SMITH & FERRINGTON
4128 Bolton R
Stamford, CT 67821

September 5, 1985

Your Ref: 1–34

CERTIFIED MAIL

Logic Creations, Inc.
8883 Snowden Avenue
Los Angeles, California 92300

Attention: Mr. S. Symington

Re: Smithson V. Symington
Los Angeles County Civil File No. 12313

Dear Mr. Symington:

Thank you for your letter of September 1, 1985. We appreciate your offer to settle this suit. Of course, I need to discuss your offer with my client.

Your offer to settle must be considered in light of your original agreement with Mr. Smithson. According to our records, the construction was to begin on April 1, 1984, but did not in fact begin until May 31. There is a loss of one month under the original contract, and the value of that lost month can be precisely determined.

Therefore, it is urgent that we get together to discuss this further amicabally. I will be in touch with you next week.

Very truly yours,

Arnold Arrington

AA:jcm

bc: John Smithson

Figure 606.1-1. Mixed Punctuation.

LSS

LEGAL SUPPORT SERVICES, INC.
3216 Post Woods Drive, Suite G
Atlanta, Georgia, 30339
(404) 952-8468

October 12, 1985

Mr. M.A. Madison
101 South Terrace
Norwalk, CT 67846

Dear Mr. Madison:

I am sorry that I could not attend the shareholders meeting last week. However, I do need a copy of the minutes. Would you please send me a copy of the minutes.

I will be attending the next meeting. I would like to add the subject of the sale of the Minkke's stock to the agenda. I understand that the meeting is going to be held on November 3, 1985. If this is incorrect, please call me.

I appreciate your assistance in this matter.

Yours very truly

David A. Samson

DSJ:jcm

Figure 606.2-1. Open Punctuation.

4. There is no punctuation in the complimentary close, e.g., Yours very truly,.
5. There is no punctuation after the signature line, e.g., John I. Bruno.
6. Open punctuation is used with the modified block letter (Figure 601-2) or the full block letter (Figure 601-1).

¶607 Becoming Familiar With the Different Parts of a Letter

There are several parts to a letter which are listed below in the order in which they appear in the letter.

¶607.1 The Date Line

1. Always date the letter the day it is dictated, not the day it is typed, unless your attorney tells you otherwise. If you date the letter the day it is typed, be sure and change references to time made in the dictation, such as today or yesterday.
2. Type the date on one line.
3. Do not use *d, nd, rd, st,* or *th* after the day of the month.
4. Do not abbreviate or use figures for the month.
5. Do not spell out the day of the month or the year, except in very formal letters.

   For example:

   March 2, 1985, not March 2nd, 1985, or March second, Nineteen hundred and eighty-five.
6. The date line can appear on the right side of the letter or centered in middle, whichever your attorneys prefer.

¶607.2 The Reference Line

The reference line in most business letters is immediately below the date line. Attorneys commonly don't use the reference line unless they are writing to an insurance company and must reference a particular file or policy.

For example:

November 10, 1984
Reference: File No. 2356-A

June 16, 1984
Ref.: Your file no. 55838-1

¶607.3 The Subject Line

The subject line in legal correspondence is sometimes referred to as the "regarding" clause. Most attorneys use the subject line, especially when it involves a particular lawsuit, probate matter, real estate transaction.

For example:

Re: *Jones vs. Williams*
County Superior Court No. 3438-84

In re: San Diego County Probate No. 3829-85

In most law offices, the subject line is underlined. The court, case name, and case number are usually included for the convenience of the person receiving the letter.

The subject line usually follows the salutation. It is preferable to match the indented paragraphs in the letter.

¶607.4 Mailing Notations

When a letter is to be hand delivered, special delivery, or by certified mail, note the method of delivery in capital letters two spaces above the address.

Example No. 1:

BY HAND

THOMPSON, GARNER, TODD & REINJOHN
Attorneys at Law
4311 Barfield Road, Suite 6000
Atlanta, GA 30349

Example No. 2:

HAND DELIVERY

Ms. Janice Evans
3978 Jacobson Drive
Simi Valley, CA 92888

Example No. 3:

SPECIAL DELIVERY

Mr. Richard Goede
Jones, Bird & Spalding
390 Equitable Building
Norwalk, CT 06854

¶607.5 Personal And Confidential Notations

If a letter is to be sent to the addressee and opened only by the addressee, you should indicate PERSONAL on the letter. If a letter is to be sent to the addressee and opened either by the addressee or another person authorized by the addressee to open the letter, you should indicate CONFIDENTIAL on the letter. Type these notations two spaces above the address or just under the mailing notation.

For example:

June 6, 1984

SPECIAL DELIVERY
CONFIDENTIAL

Always put these notations on the envelope two spaces above the address.

¶607.6 The Address

The address is placed about 12 lines below the date line. For a longer letter, it may be 8, but never more than 12 lines. The address line is always single spaced.

¶607.7 Title

The title such as *Mr., Ms., Mrs., Miss, Dr.,* or *The Honorable* is typed before the addressee's full name, even if a business or professional title such as Treasurer follows the surname (last name). Never use a courtesy title with Esquire or when an abbreviation for a degree follows the name. For example, never say *Mr. James L. Bowen, Esquire.* The trend now is not to use *Esquire* after an attorney's name.

Refer to previous correspondence, if there is any, to determine how to address the letter. Use the title indicated on the previous letter. If the title is unknown, either ask your attorney or another secretary in the office, or consult your file and rolodex. If you are unable to find the correct title, you may call the party's secretary or receptionist and ask the correct title. Never guess. Always ask someone or check previous correspondence. (See also ¶608.1.)

¶607.8 Attention Line

The attention line should be typed two spaces after the last line of the address and before the regarding clause.

If the company name uses Co. instead of Company, write the name the way the company uses it in their correspondence. Some common words that are spelled differently are: *Inc., Incorporated, Co., Company,* and *&*. Some law firms and CPA firms now omit commas from their name, so you should review their letterhead for proper presentation.

Example No. 1:

Ledbetter Mills Frank Pittman

Example No. 2:

Ledbetter, Mills, Frank & Pittman

It is always safe to address a woman with *Ms.*, especially if you are unsure of her marital status.

¶607.9 The Salutation

The salutation, e.g., *Gentlemen/Ladies:* is typed two spaces beneath the last line of the inside address or two spaces below the attention line. It is the "Dear to" salutation. If you are going to enclose the letter in a window envelope such as a bill, you may add additional lines of space after the inside address.

The first letter of the salutation is always capitalized, as well as the first letters of the title of the addressee and last name.

With mixed punctuation, a colon (:) follows the salutation. With open punctuation, there is no punctuation after the salutation.

The most commonly used salutations are:

Gentlemen:
Dear Mr. (or Ms., Mrs., Miss, Dr.,
Professor) Keller

More formal salutations include:

My dear Justice Janus;
Your Excellency;
Reverend and Father.

The salutation *Dear Sir* is rarely used by attorneys. The salutation *Gentlemen* is used less frequently due to the women's rights movement and the Equal Rights Amendment. The most commonly used phrase is *Gentlemen/Ladies:* or *Ladies/Gentlemen.*

The use of *Madam* or *Mrs.* may be offensive to a single woman. You may use the salutation *Ladies* to address a group of single women.

Use the following salutation for a married couple.

Dear Mr. and Mrs. Street;
Dear Dr. and Mrs. James W. Bruno,

Refer to Special Forms and Addresses and Salutations in Appendix E for more specific salutations.

¶607.10 The Body of the Letter

Type the body of the letter on the text two spaces below the salutation line, indenting either five or twelve spaces, whichever your attorneys prefer.

Single-space the text of the letter and double-space between paragraphs. Very short letters may be double-spaced.

Some attorneys prefer that you use quotation marks for long quotations or legal descriptions, e.g., real estate land descriptions. They may be indented five or ten spaces from the left margin and the right margin. Other attorneys prefer to omit the quotation marks; it is considered appropriate to do so. If you are using a word processor, it may have the capability to automatically indent. The quotations should be single-spaced. If your attorney requires you to use quotation marks, put the quotation marks only before the first line of the quotation and on each subsequent paragraph; only one quotation mark is used at the end of the last quotation. In other words, only the last paragraph ends with a quotation mark.

Example:

"Section 742. *Exemption from taxation.* Except as otherwise provided by law, all stocks, bonds, Treasury notes, and other obligations of the United States, shall be exempt from taxation by or under State or municipal or local authority."

If you have to list several items, you may number the items and indent five spaces from the end of the left margin or, if your attorneys prefer, you may indent another five spaces.

Example:

The following items should be purchased from Advanced Office Products:

(5 spaces)

1. Legal paper
2. Pens
3. Message note pads

or

The following items should be returned to Advanced Office Products:

(10 spaces)

1. Legal paper
2. Pens
3. Message note pads

¶607.11 Continuation Pages

Again, never leave one line of text ending a paragraph at the bottom of a page. Always leave at least two lines of text before continuing on to the next page.

Example: Full block letter—(continued on second page)

Page 2
Pat Patterson, Esq.
August 16, 1985

(4 lines)

will meet with you on August 31, 1986, at the Colony Square Hotel. If this meets with your approval, please let my secretary know as soon as possible.

Very truly yours,

James L. Bowen, Jr.

JLB:lg

The format for the full block letter is typed flush left.

Example: Modified block, modified semi-block and official styles—(continued on second page)

Page 2
Pat Patterson, Esq.
August 16, 1985

(4 lines)

are planning to attend the conference at Colony Square Hotel on August 31, 1986.

Very truly yours,

James L. Bowen

JLB:lg

¶607.12 Complimentary Close

Full Block The complimentary close is used in most correspondence by attorneys. The complimentary close is typed two lines below the last line in the text. The complimentary close is always aligned with the right-hand margin in a full block letter.

Modified Semi-block The complimentary close may be placed directly under the date line (e.g., about five spaces to the right of the center of the text) or flush with the right-hand margin. For example, if the center is 65 spaces on a pica typewriter, then the complimentary close would be about 70 spaces. Some secretaries prefer to type it in the center of the page. Be sure to allow enough space on the right to avoid running beyond the right margin.

Capitalize the first word of the complimentary close. Do not punctuate the complimentary close if open punctuation is used. Insert a comma after the complimentary close if mixed punctuation is used.

Attorneys use a variety of complimentary closes. It is a matter of preference as to which one they choose. You might look at previous letters written by your attorneys and use a similar complimentary close. Some of these are:

Respectfully yours This is usually used in extremely formal matters or to a judge or the court to show respect.

Very truly yours This is a safe complimentary close to use in a letter to most any person regardless of their position.

Sincerely yours This is a friendly and informal complimentary close usually used in legal and other correspondence.

Cordially yours This complimentary close is more friendly and informal. Use this when your attorneys are on a first name basis with the addressees.

¶607.13 Signature Block

The first line of the signature block indicates the sender of the letter. The next line may be *Attorney at Law* or other title, e.g., *General Counsel.* The sender's name is usually typed at least four lines below the complimentary close.

For example:

Very truly yours,

John P. Potter
Attorney at Law

If your attorneys prefer, you may type the firm name two spaces below the complimentary close and then type the sender's name four spaces below the firm name.

For example:

Very truly yours,

LEE & GORDON

Raymond L. Lee
Attorney at Law

There are many variations of the previous two examples. The best thing to do is to ask your attorneys what style they prefer or to check the correspondence files to determine the most used style.

¶607.14 Secretary's Initials

There are several ways that your attorneys may choose for indicating your initials. In most instances, they will leave it up to you. Again, check the style used in previous correspondence and use that unless told otherwise. Some examples are:

PFT/CB
PFT:CB
PFT:CAB
PFT:cab
pft:cab

If a letter is dictated by an associate and signed by a partner, you may want to type the associate's initials and the partner's initials followed by your initials. For example:

PFT:DRJ:cb

¶607.15 Enclosure Line

If an enclosure is to be included with the letter, it is always indicated either one or two lines below the signature line. Type it directly below the initials flush against the left-hand margin. It may be abbreviated, e.g., *Encl., Enc., Encls.,* or *Encs., Enclosures.* Some offices also indicate the number of enclosures or name the enclosures.

Example No. 1:

Very truly yours,

Deborah I. Goodman

DIG:cb
Enclosures

Example No. 2:

Very truly yours,

Deborah I. Goodman

DIG:cb
Encs.

Example No. 3:

Very truly yours,

Deborah I. Goodman

DIG:cb
Encl.

Example No. 4:

Cordially yours,

Deborah Goodman

DIG:cb

Enclosures: 1. Copy of Warranty Deed
2. John Tyler's Will

Many attorneys will usually indicate in the letter what enclosures accompany the letter. If not, always check with your attorney to see if there are any enclosures to be included in the letter. Also, it may be helpful to you to note the items enclosed on a copy of the letter if it is not indicated in the letter.

¶607.16 Copy Notation

If a copy is to be sent to another party and your attorney wants you to indicate on the letter to whom the copy or copies are to be sent, you do as follows:

Example No. 1

Sincerely yours,

Robert O. Schuller

ROS:dw
Enclosures (3)

cc: Donald F. Mills

Example No. 2:

Respectfully yours,

Robert O. Schuller

ROS:dw
Encls. (3)

cc: LDH
CAB
DRJ

In some instances your attorney may want to indicate the address or addresses of the parties receiving copies. If so, type the address directly below the recipient's name as:

Example No. 3:

Yours very truly,

Dennis I. Bull

DIB:dw
Enc.

cc: Celena I. Bullard
120 Pineland Street
Smyrna, Georgia 30080

Also, your attorney may want to indicate the items to be enclosed to each of the parties, such as:

Example No. 4:

Cordially yours,

Sharon W. McElvany

SWM:lg

cc: Darlene Johnson (lease)
Michael McChesney (note and lease)

¶607.17 Postscript

A few attorneys will add a postscript at the end of a letter as an afterthought. It is typed like this:

Kindest regards,

Marlene Arnold

MA:dw

P.S.: Thank you for the flowers.

There is a period and a colon after the S in postscript.

¶608 Knowing the Proper Forms of Address

It is important to properly address people and show respect for their titles. Always precede a name by a title, unless initials indicating degrees or Esquire follow the name. A general discussion of special titles, designations and abbreviations follows. For more specific forms of addressing persons in official or honorary positions, see Special Forms of Addresses, and Salutations, Appendix E.

Mr., Jr., Sr. The use of a business title or position or of Sr. or Jr. after a name does not take the place of a title.

Example:

Mr. John J. Bowen, Jr.
Mr. Fred Kelly, President

¶608.1 When Should You Use the Title of Esquire?

Esquire The abbreviation Esq. for Esquire is being used less and less in law offices. If it is used, it is also used after a woman attorney's name. Esquire or Esq. never precedes a name and is never used with any other title, not even Mr. In business correspondence Esquire or Esq. is used only to address high-ranking professionals who have no other title, but in the law office the practice is different. Many law offices always address an attorney as Esquire. You should check with your attorneys for instructions.

Clerks of courts and justices of the peace are properly addressed as Esquire. Do not use Esquire in a salutation. If a courtesy title such as Dr., Hon., Miss, Mr., Mrs., or Ms. is used before the addressee's name, Esq. is omitted. The plural of Esq. is Esqs. and is used with the surnames of multiple addressees.

If in doubt, it is always safe to write Attorney-at-Law after the lawyer's surname.

Esquire is never used after a firm name composed of two or more surnames.

Examples:

RIGHT—

Kent and Totton, Attorneys at Law

or

Ronald A. Millkey, Esq.
Norman E. Maller, Esq.
Millkey & Maller, Esqs.

or

Messrs. Milkey and Maller
Attorneys at law

You would address the attorneys as follows:

Gentlemen
Dear Mr. Millkey and Mr. Maller
Dear Messrs. Millkey and Maller

WRONG—

Millkey and Maller, Esquires

¶609 Preparing Envelopes

Always type the name and address, together with any mailing notation, on the envelope the same way it appears in the letter. You can use the abbreviation for the state if your attorneys prefer. Single space the address. Put any mailing notation or personal or confidential notation two spaces above the address in all capitals. It may also be underlined.

The sender's full name and address, including the firm's name, should always appear on the envelope. If your attorneys do not have preprinted stationery, you will have to type their names, the firm's name, and address in the upper left-hand corner of the envelope. Write the name of a foreign country in upper case on the envelope. Always use intitial caps for the name and address.

¶610 Letter Writing Hints

You may frequently be asked to write a letter for your attorneys. This section will give you some techniques to assist you in writing simple and direct letters.

When writing a letter, pretend as though you were talking with the person. Do not use big or stilted words. Use plain English properly written. The most favorable technique is to use as little as possible to get your message across to the addressee.

One technique that you can use after you write the letter is to go back and rewrite the letter, crossing out all unnecessary words and phrases. Writing is rewriting. Don't be concerned if you have to rewrite the letter several times before it is to your satisfaction. No one will ever know. Use draft paper until the letter is perfect. Even though there is no such thing as "perfect," if you have done the best you can do, then that is usually sufficient. If you are doubtful, have one of the other, more experienced secretaries read your draft.

Sometimes we get so involved in the technique that we lose sight of the purpose of the letter. The purpose is to inform, advise, or get a message across to the other party.

¶611 Suggestions for Writing a Better Letter

1. Never use trite phrases.
2. Avoid unnecessary words or phrases.
3. Do not use superfluous words to impress the reader.
4. Do not use two words with similar meanings for emphasis.
5. Avoid favorite words or expressions.
6. Try not to use the same word twice in a letter, except for necessary words.
7. Do not use big words.
8. Use short sentences.
9. Make a separate paragraph when a new subject is introduced.
10. Write and rewrite your letter.
11. Proofread the letter yourself, or ask someone else to do it.

¶612 Trite Expressions to Avoid in Legal Correspondence—and What to Say Instead

1. acknowledge receipt of—we received
2. advise—say or tell
3. approximate (or the next)—give exact date
4. as a matter of fact—don't use
5. as per; per—use only with per annum and per diem
6. as per your request—pursuant to your request
7. as stated above—omit
8. assuring you of our interest—we are interested
9. at all times—always
10. at this time—present or now
11. at your convenience; at an early date—be specific
12. at your earliest convenience—as soon as possible
13. avail yourself of the opportunity—take avantage of
14. await the pleasure of a reply—look forward to hearing from you
15. beg to state, beg to advise, beg to acknowledge, beg to suggest, beg to remain—say or tell

16. complying with your wishes—as you requested
17. contents carefully noted—received
18. contents duly noted—we received
19. deem it a privilege—we are privileged to
20. duly—don't use
21. enclosed herewith please find—enclosed is
22. enclosed please find—enclosed is
23. esteemed—don't use
24. favor—don't use
25. favor us with your reply—please respond
26. for your information I might explain—omit
27. handing you—enclose
28. have before me—in answer to your response: or reply
29. hereto—to this letter
30. herewith—don't use
31. hoping to be favored—don't use
32. hoping to hear from you in due course—look forward to your reply
33. in accordance with your wishes—pursuant to your request
34. in answer to (or response; or reply)—I received your letter of
35. in compliance with your request—as you requested
36. in connection therewith—regarding
37. In re—regarding or concerning; use only in reference line
38. in reference to the above—regarding
39. in reply to yours of recent date—we received your letter, etc.
40. in this connection please note—regarding
41. it has come to my attention that—I note that
42. it will be our endeavor—don't use
43. kindly be advised—don't use
44. kindly inform us of your wishes—please let us know
45. kindly send check by return mail—please send your check by return mail
46. let me call your attention—please note
47. may I say—don't use
48. may I take the liberty—don't use
49. may we call your attention—please note that
50. merit your kind attention—please attend to
51. owing to the fact that—because
52. permit me to state—say or tell
53. please advise accordingly—please respond

54. please be assured—I assure you that
55. please favor us with your check—please send your check
56. please find enclosed—enclosed is
57. pursuant to yours of recent date—pursuant to your letter of, request, etc.
58. recent date—give exact date
59. referring to yours of the 10th—refer to exact date
60. regret exceedingly to advise—I wish to inform you that
61. same date—omit or give exact date
62. state—say or tell
63. take pleasure—are pleased; are happy
64. thanking your for your interest—thank you for your interest
65. thanking you in advance—thank you for your assitance in this matter
66. the favor of a reply—please reply
67. the pleasure of your patronage—thank you for your interest
68. the privilege of serving you—happy to assist you
69. the writer wishes to state—say or tell
70. this is to advise you—don't use
71. this is to inform you—don't use
72. under separate cover—separately
73. valued—don't use
74. we are pleased to advise—don't use
75. we note from our records—according to our records
76. we shall endeavor to merit—we will
77. we take pleasure in announcing—we wish to announce
78. wish to advise you—don't use
79. wish to call to your attention—please note
80. wish to inform you—omit (just say it)
81. wish to say; wish to state; would say—don't use
82. wish to take this opportunity to say—don't use
83. with kindest regards—warmest regards
84. with your kind permission—with your approval
85. your Mr. Bloome—your associate or just Mr. Bloome
86. your communication of recent date—your letter (memo, note, etc.) of June 26, 1985
87. your reply by return mail—appreciate your quick response
88. your valued patronage—appreciate your business
89. yours of recent date to hand—your letter (memo, note, etc.) of June 28, 1985

¶613 Extra Words and Phrases to Omit in Your Correspondence

1. She arrived at *the hour of* nine.
2. There is truth to *both of* her reasons.
3. In *the state of* New York.
4. The table is made *out* of oak.
5. The brief came *at a time* when we were ready.
6. Property appreciated *in value* with time.
7. During *the year of* 1986.
8. The book cost *the sum* of $90.
9. At the banquet *held* in Boston.
10. We will send your letterhead *at a* later *date.*
11. In about two months *time.*
12. The idea *first* arose when she called.
13. A *certain* book entitled Legal Research.
14. His *true and invariable* policy is known.
15. Someone *or other* is at the bank.
16. I am *now engaged in* writing a brief.
17. Within *close* proximity of your land.
18. During *the course of* her stay with us.
19. *Perhaps* it may be better to call her.
20. She entered by *means of* the gate.
21. The land sells for *a price of* $18,000 an acre.

¶700 Legal Documents Are Easy to Prepare

Attorneys prepare a variety of documents which are not filed in the courts. A good example is a legal agreement or contract. Learning how to recognize and prepare these documents is important. This chapter will define and describe some of these legal documents, and give you hints how to prepare them.

¶701 The Difference between Legal Documents and Pleadings

A *legal document* is a written instrument that may evidence a legal duty or agreement. For example, if Steve and Joan Durdin agree to renovate Bob and Sue Leigh's house for a certain sum, the Durdins and the Leighs may put that agreement in writing in the form of a legal contract, also called a legal agreement. The words *contract* and *agreement* are often used interchangeably, even though there is a technical legal difference in their meanings.

Legal documents include pleadings. Again, there is a technical difference between pleadings and other legal documents which are filed in court. A *pleading* is any of the formal legal papers filed with the court that states the facts each party will try to prove to uphold his or her claim or his or her defense. Court pleadings include: complaints, answers, replies, counterclaims, and crossclaims. Other court papers may include notices, interrogatories, requests for admissions, motions, briefs, etc. (See ¶1800.) A pleading consists of formal written allegations or statements of the parties who file it with the court to maintain the suit, or to defeat it, for the judgment of the court. A copy of the pleading or court paper must be served on the attorney(s) for the other party(s) under most court rules.

Other legal documents are usually designed for the use of the parties who sign them and they constitute evidence of an agreement between the parties or an act performed by one or both of the parties. If the terms of the agreement are not met by one or all of the parties to the agreement, a suit may be filed in the courts by the other parties. Usually the offended parties will ask the court for money damages or they may, under certain circumstances, ask the court to make the other parties comply with the terms of the agreement. A copy of the legal document on which a lawsuit is based is attached to a pleading as an exhibit and is incorporated in the pleading by reference.

¶702 An Introduction to the Most Common Legal Documents

Here is a brief description of the more commonly used legal documents, excluding pleadings and other court papers. The sample documents are not representative of all documents of that nature, but are presented for illustration only.

1. Agreement or Contract is a written understanding or agreement between two or more parties (See Figures 702-1(a) and (b).)

SAMPLE LEGAL DOCUMENTS

STATE OF GEORGIA
COUNTY OF FULTON

SALES CONTRACT

The undersigned Seller agrees to sell and the undersigned Purchaser agrees to purchase all that tract or parcel of land which is more particularly described as follows:

[legal description]

together with all easements and rights appurtenant thereto, all of Seller's right, title and interest in and to all public and private ways adjoining the same, and all buildings, equipment, fixtures and other improvements located thereon, all of which are hereinafter referred to as the "Property."

The purchase price shall be:______________________________ ______________________________ ($) Dollars.

The purchase price shall be paid in accordance with the provisions set forth in Exhibit "A" attached hereto and incorporated herein by reference.

Seller represents and warrants to Purchaser that Seller has good and marketable fee simple title to the Property and shall convey the property to Purchaser by general warranty deed, free and clear of any liens, security interests, easements or other encumbrances.

Figure 702-1(a). Sample Sales Contract

Purchaser shall have until five (5) days prior to the Closing Date in which to examine title to the Property and in which to furnish Seller a written statement of objections affecting the marketability of such title. Seller shall have until the Closing Date to satisfy all valid objections on or prior to the Closing Date, then Purchaser may either (i) waive the objections and elect to close, or (ii) satisfy the objections, after deducting from the purchase price the cost of satisfying objections which can be satisfied by the payment of money, or (iii) extend the Closing Date for a period of not more than sixty (60) days until such objections are satisfied by giving written notice of such extension to Seller, in which case the Closing Date shall be extended to the date specified by Purchaser, or (iv) terminate this agreement by giving written notice of such termination to Seller, in which case Purchaser's earnest money shall be refunded promptly, all rights and obligations of the parties shall expire and this agreement shall become null and void. In the event of an extension of the Closing Date under subparagraph (iii) above and the subsequent failure or refusal of Seller to satisfy the objections, then Purchaser may elect between the options set forth in subparagraph (i) and (ii) above, or Purchaser may elect to exercise such rights or remedies as may be provided for or allowed by law or in equity.

The sale shall be consummated at a place designated by Purchaser, at a time and on a date which is mutually designated by Purchaser, at a time and on a date which is mutually agreeable to the parties but in no event later than ________________, (the "Closing Date"), unless the Closing Date is extended as provided for elsewhere in this agreement. All ad valorem taxes shall be prorated between the Purchaser and Seller as of the Closing Date. Seller shall pay the Georgia realty transfer tax. All other charges, fees and expenses of the closing shall be paid by the party incurring the same.

Between the date hereof and until the transaction is consummated on the Closing Date, the risks of ownership and loss of the Property and the correlative rights against insurance carriers and third parties shall belong to Seller. In the event of damage to or destruction of the Property by fire or other casualty prior to the Closing Date, Purchaser may elect either to receive the insurance proceeds payable as a result of the event and consummate the transaction, or to terminate this agreement by giving written notice of such termination to Seller, in which case Purchaser's earnest money shall be refunded promptly, all rights and obligations of the parties shall expire and this agreement shall become null and void.

In the event of the taking of all or any part of the Property by eminent domain proceedings or the commencement of any such proceedings prior

Figure 702-1(a). (continued)

to the Closing Date, Purchaser shall have the right, at his option, to terminate this agreement by giving written notice thereof to Seller on or before the Closing Date. If Purchaser does not so terminate this agreement, the purchase price for the Property shall be reduced by the total of any awards or other proceeds received by Seller at or prior to the closing with respect to any such taking, and at the closing Seller shall assign to Purchaser all rights of Seller in and to any awards or other proceeds payable by reason of any such taking.

Between the date hereof and until the transaction is consummated on the Closing Date, the Purchaser and Purchaser's agents and employees, shall have the right to enter the Property for the purpose of inspecting the same, and making soil tests, engineering studies and surveys; provided, however, that such activities shall not materially damage the Property.

This agreement may be assigned by Purchaser without the consent of Seller, and any such assignment shall relieve Purchaser of Purchaser's obligations. This agreement shall be binding upon and enforceable against the parties and their respective heirs, their representatives, successors and assigns.

Purchaser has deposited with ______________________________
______________________________ the sum of $______________________
as an earnest money deposit. At the time the sale is consummated, the said deposit shall be applied as part payment of the cash portion of the purchase price. IF the sale is not consummated in accordance with the terms and conditions of this agreement due to circumstances or conditions which are no fault of Purchaser, then said deposit shall be returned to Purchaser upon request, and Purchaser may, at Purchaser's option, pursue any remedies available to Purchaser at law or in equity, including an action for specific performance of this agreement. If the sale is not consummated in accordance with the terms and conditions of this agreement due to a default by Purchaser, then the earnest money shall be forfeited to Seller and shall be retained by Seller as full liquidated damages for Purchaser's default.

This agreement supersedes all prior discussions and agreements between the Seller and Purchaser with respect to the purchase of the Property and other matters contained herein, and this agreement contains the sole and entire understanding between the parties hereto with respect to the transactions contemplated herein. This agreement shall not be modified or amended except by an instrument in writing signed by or on behalf of the parties hereto.

Figure 702-1(b). Sample Agreement.

This agreement shall be governed by and construed and enforced in accordance with the laws of the State of Georgia. This agreement may be executed in several counterparts, each of which shall be deemed an original, and all such counterparts together shall constitute one and the same instrument.

Purchaser agrees to allow Seller to retain possession of premises until 6:00 P.M. on ______________________, rent free.

Seller warrants that all appliances remaining with the dwelling and the heating and air conditioning systems will be in normal operating condition at time of closing. Purchaser shall have the privilege and responsibility of making inspections of said equipment and systems prior to closing of sale.

Seller shall provide at time of closing this transaction a clearance letter from a pest control operator certified in Wood Destroying Organisms certifying apparent freedom from termites and other wood-destroying organisms and from structural damage caused thereby and carrying a guarantee that the property will be treated free for a period of one (1) year from the date of issuance, said letter to be issued under Chapter 620-7.02(9) of the Rules of the Georgia Structural Pest Control Commission. Said inspection will be acceptable only if made no longer than thirty (30) days prior to the date of acceptance of this contract.

The provisions set forth in Exhibit "A" attached hereto are incorporated herein by reference. In the event of any conflict between the printed portion of this agreement and such provisions, then the provisions of Exhibit "A" shall control.

IN WITNESS WHEREOF, the parties have executed and sealed this Agreement this the ______ day of ____________________, 19____

______________________	______________________
UNOFFICIAL WITNESS	PURCHASER
	______________________
	PURCHASER
	______________________
	SELLER
	______________________
	SELLER

Figure 702-1(b). (continued)

2. *Will* is a written legal instrument expressing the wishes of a deceased person as to the distribution of his or her property and to possibly appoint a guardian for his or her children, if any. (See Figure 2002-1, ¶2000.)

3. *Codicil* is a supplement or amendment to a will which may change, delete, or add certain provisions.

4. *Lease* is a contract between an owner and a tenant for the use and possession of real property. (See Figure 702-2.)

______________________, 19 ____

THIS LEASE, made this day of , 19 , by and

between , first party, (hereinafter called "Landlord");

and , second party, (hereinafter called "Tenant");

and YOUR FIRM NAME , third party, (hereinafter called "Agent");

WITNESSETH:

Premises 1. The Landlord, for and in consideration of the rents, covenants, agreements, and stipulations hereinafter mentioned, reserved, and contained, to be paid, kept and performed by the Tenant, has leased and rented, and by these presents does lease and rent, unto the said Tenant, and said Tenant hereby agrees to lease and take upon the terms and conditions which hereinafter appear, the following described property (hereinafter called premises), to wit:

and being known as______________________________

No easement for light or air is included in the premises.

Term 2. To have and to hold the same for a term of beginning on the day of , 19 and ending on the day of 19 , at midnight, unless sooner terminated as hereinafter provided.

Rental 3. Tenant agrees to pay Landlord, by payments to Agent of Landlord, who negotiated this lease, at office of Agent in Atlanta, Georgia, promptly on the first day of each month in advance, during the term of this lease, a monthly rental of

Figure 702-2. Sample Lease.

5. *Deed* is a document signed by the owner of real property evidencing transfer of ownership of that particular piece of property. A deed may be a warranty deed, a special warranty deed or a quitclaim deed, depending upon what guarantees as to title the grantor (owner) is willing to make. When told to type a deed, be sure to ask your attorney which type of deed is desired, if not told in your instructions. (See Figure 702-3.)

6. *Mortgage, Deed to Secure Debt, or Deed of Trust* is a document showing ownership of a particular piece of real property subject to payment of a loan on the property. (See Figure 702-4.)

Form 10–8

GEORGIA STATE OFFICE
TITLE BUILDING
ATLANTA, GEORGIA 30303

Lawyers Title Insurance Corporation

ATLANTA BRANCH OFFICE

WARRANTY DEED

STATE OF COUNTY OF

THIS INDENTURE, Made the day of , in the year one thousand nine hundred , between

of the County of , and State of Georgia, as party or parties of the first part, hereinafter called Grantor, and

as party or parties of the second part, hereinafter called Grantee (the words "Grantor" and "Grantee" to include their respective heirs, successors and assigns where the context requires or permits).

WITNESSETH that: Grantor, for and in consideration of the sum of ( ) DOLLARS in hand paid at and before the sealing and delivery of these presents, the receipt whereof is hereby acknowledged, has granted, bargained, sold, aliened, conveyed and confirmed, and by these presents does grant, bargain, sell, alien, convey and confirm unto the said Grantee,

Figure 702-3. Sample Deed.

7. *Promissory Note* is an agreement to pay a loan or other sum to the party named in the note (payee). The debtor signs the note. The debtor is the maker of the note (payor). (See Figure 702-5.)

8. *Bill of Sale* is evidence that the party named in the bill of sale got title (evidence of ownership) from the person who signs the bill of sale. (See Figure 702-6.)

9. *Corporate Documents* are documents such as articles of incorporation, amendments to articles of incorporation, minutes, by-laws, etc. (See Figure 1903-2, ¶1900.)

10. *Power of Attorney* is a written document by which one party gives another party named in the document the right to execute any legal documents on the first party's behalf or to act on the other party's behalf in any other specified way. A power of attorney may be *general* or *special*, depending on its terms. A *general* power of attorney gives unlimited power to the party whereas a *special* power of attorney may permit the other party to only consummate a specific act. (See Figure 702-7.)

DEED TO SECURE DEBT

STATE OF

COUNTY OF

THIS INDENTURE, Made the day of , in the year

A. D., one thousand nine hundred , between

of the County of , and State of

as party, or parties, of the first part, hereinafter called Grantor, and

of the County of , and State of

as party, or parties, of the second part, hereinafter called Grantee,

WITNESSETH, That Grantor, for and in consideration of the sum of

($) DOLLARS, to Grantor in hand paid by Grantee at and before the sealing and delivery of these presents, the receipt whereof is hereby acknowledged, has granted, bargained, sold, aliened, conveyed and confirmed, and by these presents does grant, bargain, sell, alien, convey and confirm unto said Grantee, all that tract or parcel of land lying and being in

Figure 702-4. Sample Mortgage.

$ ATLANTA, GEORGIA , 19

FOR VALUE RECEIVED, the maker or makers hereof, jointly and severally, promise to pay to the order of the principal sum of

($) DOLLARS,

with interest (payable monthly) at the rate of (%) per centum per annum on said principal sum, or on so much thereof as may from time to time remain unpaid; said principal and interest being payable in monthly instalments of ($) DOLLARS each, on the day of each and every month, commencing on the day of , 19 , and continuing to and including , 19 ; each instalment, when paid, to be applied first to the payment of interest accrued on unpaid principal, and the residue thereof to be credited on the principal, and the balance of principal and interest shall be payable on the day of , 19 ; both principal and interest payable in lawful money of the United States of America, at the office of: in Atlanta, Georgia, or at such other place as the holder of this note may designate, in writing.

Figure 702-5. Sample Promissory Note.

BILL OF SALE

KNOW ALL MEN BY THESE PRESENTS, that ("Owner"), in consideration of Ten And No/100 Dollars ($10.00) and other good and valuable considerations to it paid by ("Purchaser"), the receipt and sufficiency of which are hereby acknowledged, does hereby sell, assign, transfer, set over and convey to Purchaser, its successors and assignees, all right, title and interest of Owner in and to all fixtures, chattels and articles of personal property owned by the Owner on the date hereof placed upon or attached to or used in connection with the operation of the real property more particularly described on Exhibit "A" attached hereto and by this reference made a part hereof (the "Property"), including, but not limited to, all furniture, fixtures, kitchen equipment and utensils, office supplies and equipment, washers, dryers, linens, air conditioners, television sets, maintenance room small tools and equipment, meeting room chairs, tables and equipment.

TO HAVE AND TO HOLD the said personal property above described unto Purchaser, its successors and assignees, forever.

The items conveyed hereby are sold "as is" and without any warranties, express or implied, concerning condition or fitness for intended purpose.

IN WITNESS WHEREOF. Owner has caused this Bill of Sale to be executed, this ______ day of ______.

"OWNERS"

Figure 702-6. Sample Bill of Sale.

POWER OF ATTORNEY

STATE OF GEORGIA
COUNTY OF DEKALB

KNOW ALL MEN BY THESE PRESENTS: That, the undersigned, ____,an individual residing at ____, does hereby constitute and appoint ____________________ as the true and lawful Attorney-in-Fact for the undersigned and in her name, place and stead to manage and transact all and every part of the business of the undersigned.

Without in any way limiting the generality of the foregoing, shall have the following specific powers to be exercised in the name of and on behalf of the undersigned:

Figure 702-7. Sample Power of Attorney.

1. To sell, mortgage, encumber, convey, lease, pledge or otherwise dispose of, any property, real or personal, which the undersigned may have an interest, located in the State of Georgia, for cash or upon such terms as may deem advisable, and to execute appropriate deeds, promissory notes, deeds to secure debt or other instruments for said purposes.

2. To deposit or withdraw in the name of the undersigned and for her account with any bank, trust company or other financial institution any funds resulting from exercising her powers as herein granted or all moneys payable or belonging to the undersigned which are from or for her and to sign her name and endorse same for deposit or collection on all bills of exchange, drafts, checks, bonds, notes, stocks or other instruments for money payable or belonging to the undersigned.

3. To collect, sue for, settle, adjust or compromise any claim for money arising by contract or tort, to execute releases, cancellations or satisfactions.

4. To do any other thing or perform any other act, not limited to the foregoing, which the undersigned might do in person, it being intended that this shall be a general power of attorney.

The undersigned does hereby ratify and confirm on behalf of herself, her heirs and assigns, all such acts which shall lawfully do or cause to be done by virtue hereof. All persons shall be entitled to rely upon the within Power of Attorney without further confirmation or validation hereof by the undersigned.

The within Power of Attorney is irrevocable and shall remain effective until the same is revoked by written instrument.

IN WITNESS WHEREOF, the undersigned has caused this Power of Attorney to be executed under seal, this ____ day of ____.

____(SEAL)

Signed, sealed and delivered in the presence of:

____

Witness

____

Notary Public

Figure 702-7. (continued)

¶703 Who Are the Parties to a Legal Document?

The parties to a legal document or those who execute it include persons who obtain or lose a right, or undertake a duty, as set forth in the written document signed by them. In some legal documents a third party may be named as a beneficiary of the document, as in a will.

A party or third party beneficiary may be a partnership, an individual, a corporation, a professional corporation, a trust, an estate, an association, or any other recognized legal entity. Most legal documents are signed by at least two parties, but there are some that need be signed by only one party. For example, powers of attorney and assignments. An assignment is a document whereby one party turns over his or her rights in or to a particular piece of property or other legal right to another person. Other examples—a lessee may assign a lease; a party may assign certain rights under a purchase contract; an author may assign his rights to royalties from a book or a person may assign his or her rights to a patent or a copyright.

In a modern contract, a party's name or a designated term is used for each party to the agreement, depending on the transaction. For example, parties to a book contract may be referred to as *author* and *publisher.* Another example is the designation of parties to a purchase agreement as *seller* and *buyer.* Sometimes the last names of the parties are used as designations throughout the contract. For example, Theresa Williams is designated *Williams* and Creative Options, Inc. is designated *Company* or *Corporation.*

¶704 Typing Legal Documents Made Easy

The legal secretary is responsible for preparing a vast array of legal documents. Many of these involve filling in blanks on a printed form. Although the attorneys are responsible for the content of all documents, their preparation and their final form are the responsibility of the secretary.

As a legal secretary you may sometimes find a new document that you have never seen, especially if you are inexperienced. When you encounter a new legal document, don't panic or be confused. Just look at the document to see how it is formatted. Find a similar document if you can from one of the other legal secretaries in your office to use as a sample form from which to prepare the new document. Or ask one of the other attorneys if they have a similar form.

¶704.1 Heading, Introductory Clause, and Provisions

The first part of a legal document is the title or type of agreement designated as a heading. Next, there is the introductory clause which names the parties involved in the legal document. After that, the word WITNESSETH: is usually typed although many attorneys consider that style archaic. After the introductory clause, the various provisions or clauses of the agreement follow in logical sequence. At the bottom of the agreement, the words *It is agreed:* may appear, or *Therefore,* etc., may be used.

¶704.2 Testimonium Clause

The last clause of the legal document is the testimonium clause which indicates who will sign the document. If a corporation or a partnership is a party to the legal document, this clause will state what officer of the corporation will sign the document and what his or her title is. In the case of a partnership or limited partnership, the testimonium will indicate what partner(s) will sign the agreement.

¶704.3 Signature Lines

The legal document will have signature lines to indicate the persons who will be signing the document and their titles, if any. In some instances, identifying words may be used and words such as Buyer or Seller may follow. Your attorneys will tell you who is to sign the document and what their titles are.

¶704.4 Corporate Seal

In the case of a corporation, a corporate seal may appear below the signature lines. A corporate seal is the official seal of a corporation imprinted or impressed by a metal seal on the document. The seal is engraved on a metal plate and impressed on paper by an officer of the corporation, usually the corporate secretary. It attests that the corporation approves the document. Usually the testimonium clause will indicate whether a corporate seal is to be affixed to the document. Most corporate documents require a corporate seal to be affixed in the indicated place on the document. In many instances your attorney may be the secretary of the corporation and keep the corporate seal along with the corporate documents (in a binder) for the client. Below the place for the corporate seal is a place for the corporate secretary to sign. For example:

...its corporate seal to be affixed hereto, and attested by its secretary, and signed by its president, this 30th day of August, 1985.

If a corporation is a party to a legal document, the document is signed in the name of the corporation, typed in all capital letters, with the corporate officer indicated below the signature line. An example follows:

(Corporate Seal) JOHN SIMPSON & ASSOCIATES

By: ______________________
John Wood, President

ATTEST:

____
Secretary

Four lines are usually left after the corporate name and the signature lines are typed five spaces to the right of the center of the paper. Leave at least two lines of the legal agreement on the page on which the signature lines will be typed. *Never put the signature lines on the page alone,* because someone could fraudulently attach the signature lines separately to another agreement.

¶704.5 Attestation Clause

When witnesses sign a document after the parties sign the agreement, they are attesting to the signature(s) of the party(s). Sometimes a clause precedes the signatures which is referred to as the "attestation clause." If the document is witnessed, an attestation clause will precede the witnesses' signature. For example:

IN WITNESS WHEREOF, we, the Buyer and the Seller, have hereunto set our hands and seals to the foregoing agreement, consisting of twelve (12) pages, on this 25th day of August, 1985.

Signed, sealed, and delivered
by the Buyer in the presence of:

____

____

¶705 What You Need To Know About Acknowledgments

A good legal secretary must know the difference between an acknowledgment and an affidavit. An *acknowledgment* is a declaration by a signer of a legal document to a notary public or officer of the court that he or she is in fact the person who signed or executed the legal document. An *affidavit* is a statement by a person that is believed to be that person's true statement. Many times affidavits are prepared in an attempt to establish facts.

The notary public or officer signs the document at the place indicated in the document. The acknowledgment clause is sometimes inaccurately referred to as a subscribed to and sworn to clause or a notary clause. One who acknowledges the signing of a legal document does not swear to its truth. That person merely acknowledges that the named person signed the document. The words *subscribed* and *sworn* are to properly appear after the signature lines on an affidavit.

¶705.1 If A Document Is Notarized, Is It Legal?

Many people think that if a document is notarized, it means it correctly reflects what it says in the document or that it is legitimate; however, when a notary signs a document, he or she is merely attesting to the fact that he or she witnessed the signature of the person indicated on the document.

There are laws in each state governing acknowledgments. When a document is introduced into court, it frequently contains an acknowledgment by a notary. Many states have adopted the Uniform Acknowledgment Act. In these states the clause is uniform and the form is similar. Otherwise, it varies from state to state. The law of the state where the document is recorded governs the form rather than the laws of the state where the document is executed.

¶705.2 What Documents Should Be Acknowledged?

Documents that must be recorded, such as leases, liens, deeds or mortgage notes, should be acknowledged. Your attorneys will tell you what type of acknowledgment they prefer or will refer you to a similar form of legal document containing the acknowledgment they want to use. For example:

STATE OF GEORGIA)
) SS:
COUNTY OF COBB)

On this 16th day of June 1985, before me, PEGGY MEDLIN, notary public of said county and state, duly commissioned and sworn, personally appeared PAUL PHILLIPS, known to me to be the person whose name is subscribed to the within instrument, and acknowledged that he executed the same.

IN WITNESS WHEREOF, I have hereunto set my hand and affixed my official seal the day and year in this certificate first above written.

____

Notary Public

¶705.3 What Are the Two Kinds of Acknowledgments?

The two kinds of acknowledgments are individual and corporate. The acknowledgment on a document executed by a corporation must state the name of the corporation, the corporate office held by the person or persons executing the document, and a statement that the person or persons have been authorized by the corporation to sign the acknowledgment on behalf of the corporation. For example:

STATE OF CALIFORNIA)
) SS:
COUNTY OF SAN DIEGO)

On this 14th day of February, 1985, before me, a notary public of the State of California, personally appeared SYLVIA JONES, President of Whodonit Corporation, known to me to be the person who executed the within Instrument in behalf of said corporation and acknowledged to me that SYLVIA JONES executed the same for purposes therein stated.

____

Notary Public

¶705.4 What is Venue?

An acknowledgment always states the venue or specific state and county where the document is signed. In some states the commonwealth is recited instead of the state. In Louisiana, the parish instead of the county is noted. Type the state, then the county followed by the parenthesis followed by *ss:*, the abbreviation for *scilicet*. The abbreviation may be in capital or small letters. Scilicet also means *to wit.* A colon should follow.

¶705.5 What Date Do You Put on the Acknowledgment?

The date on which the acknowledgment is made is entered in the acknowledgment clause. When you type an acknowledgment, leave blank spaces for day of the month and the year, at least sixteen spaces. Thus, if the party comes in on a different day and month than what you expected, you do not have to retype the acknowledgment. The person making the acknowledgment should never execute the acknowledgment before the document it is acknowledging is signed.

¶705.6 How to Indicate the Party or Agent Making the Acknowledgment

The name of the person making the acknowledgment always appears in the acknowledgment. It should be typed in all capitals. If the person making the acknowledgment is making it in a particular capacity as attorney in fact or as a secretary or other officer of a corporation, then the title of the signer is designated in the acknowledgment clause.

¶705.7 Where Should You Indicate the Officer or Notary Taking the Acknowledgment?

The title of the officer or notary who signs the acknowledgment should appear below the signature line, approximately four spaces below. In some states the person's name is also typed as well as signed. If you do not know who is going to make the acknowledgment, leave a long line for the average name, approximately 32 spaces.

¶705.8 Where Do You Put the Expiration of the Notarial Commission?

In some states, it is required that a notary show the date of the expiration of the commission. The words *My commission expires* should be typed two spaces below the signature. Most notaries have a rubber stamp or a metal seal which shows this information. However, you can type this below the line. For example:

____
Notary Public
My commission expires:

In most states the notary seal must appear beside the notary's signature. In some states, a justice of the peace may make an acknowledgment or swear in a witness. In some counties justices of the peace no longer exist. Check your local laws.

¶706 More About Notary Publics

A notary public is a commissioned officer of the state who has the power to administer oaths and affirmations and take acknowledgments, depositions, verifications, and affidavits. The oath is documented in the form of a *jurat.* The jurat is a certification at the end of the affidavit that indicates when, before whom, and where the affidavit was notarized. For example:

Sworn and subscribed to before
me this ________day of September, 1985.

____
Notary Public

On the other hand, to notarize a document means to attach an acknowledgment that the signature on the document is authentic. No oath is necessary for an acknowledgment.

If you, as a notary do not know the person who is going to execute a document or if the person is not a client, you should ask for proper identification. Only notarize documents that have been signed in person. Do not take acknowledgments over the telephone or notarize a document that someone has brought to you already signed.

¶706.1 What is an Authentication?

An authentication is a statement by the clerk of the court that the notary or officer is authorized in the particular county to take acknowledgments and that the signature on the acknowledgment is theirs. Sometimes, your attorney may have you obtain an authentication from the county in which the notary is registered. This is rarely done, except when required by some states or when the document is introduced as evidence in a court of a different state.

¶706.2 How to Become a Notary Public

If your attorney wants you to become a notary, call the clerk's office in the county in which you wish to become a notary and request the forms to apply for a notarial commission. It will be very convenient for you to be a notary to take acknowledgments for your attorneys' clients. When you obtain your notarial certificate and take your oath, usually the clerk will give you a pamphlet with the local notarial statutes. Be sure to review them carefully. Any errors, omission, or misconduct in your duties as a notary public may cause you criminal and civil penalties. In some states you will be required to take a test. You will usually be given a booklet of notarial laws in that county or state to study prior to the test. The tests are not difficult.

After your commission is received, you will need to order a notary seal and stamp. You must also register your commission with the clerk of the court (or other designated official) in your county, so the officer can authenticate your certificate of acknowledgment on papers that are to be recorded in another state.

In some states, justices of the peace are notaries. The justice of the peace has no judicial functions, except that he or she may perform marriages. In other states, the justice of the peace is still a judicial officer. However, the functions of a notary are statutory.

¶706.3 Rules for Notarizing Legal Documents

1. Be sure that the corporate seal is impressed or stamped on the document, if required.
2. Make sure all the blanks are filled in.
3. Make sure that you have included the date of the expiration of your commission, if required in your state.
4. Make sure your notarial seal is impressed or stamped on the document.
5. Be sure that your stamp makes a legible imprint. A black stamp photocopies better than other colors.
6. Be sure to attach your certificate of authentication if you are sending the documents to other states or if it is required or requested.
7. Be sure to keep a record of the document that you notarize. Most stationery or office supply stores have notarial record books.
8. Be sure that the proper date is put on the acknowledgment.
9. If you don't know the party, ask for identification.

¶707 How to Record Legal Documents

Legal documents are usually recorded in a public office so that the record will be available to anyone who is interested. The purpose of recording legal documents is to protect the interests of all persons by giving constructive notice to all of its existence. For example, if Ann Mather wants to purchase some property from Sue Freeman, she may learn from the public record that Ross Stearns holds a mortgage on the property. Ms. Mather purchases the property, but she makes legal arrangements that will protect not only her own interests but those of Ross Stearns as well. If Mr. Stearns owns a second trust deed, for example, Ms. Mather may want to pay off that note to clear the title.

¶707.1. What is the Difference between Recording and Filing Legal Documents?

Recording a document is delivering the original document to a public officer designated by law to copy and record the copy of the document. The document may be copied for the record by typewriting in a record book, photocopying or copying on microfilm.

Filing is delivering the original of a pleading or other court paper to the office of the Clerk of the Court in which the particular lawsuit is pending to be filed in the official court file.

A recorded or filed legal document becomes a part of the official public record in the jurisdiction or in the court where it was entered. The public record then furnishes evidence of the existence and contents of the legal document. The time and date of receipt is stamped on the document when it is recorded by the clerk. After the document is recorded, it is again stamped by the clerk to show the official book and page number where it is recorded. The original legal document is returned to the person who delivered it for recording, usually the attorney.

When a pleading of other court paper is filed, the original is placed in the court case file and kept in the custody of the court official, usually the Clerk of the Court. The clerk enters the date and time of receipt of the document on the court docket, stamps it with the date of filing, and keeps it in his or her office in the court case file. The document is available to the parties of a lawsuit or to the public for inspection, except in rare instances when the court orders case records sealed. A court paper or pleading is filed whereas other legal documents or instruments are tax-stamped and recorded. Recorded documents are photocopied to be inserted permanently in the court record books and then returned to the proper party.

Legal documents that are recorded or filed can be easily located if you know the official record and page number of the recorded instrument or the court case number where the court papers were filed. Where records are kept on microfilm or microfiche, it is absolutely necessary that all documents submitted for recording be clearly readable. However, the court's employees will appreciate legible documents in any case.

Your attorneys will usually tell you in what county to record the document. It depends on the circumstances surrounding the document. Don't ever assume where it is to be filed without first checking with your attorney.

The fees for recording documents vary from county to county so always check before you send a document to be recorded by mail.

After an out-of-town court official records and stamps the document, he or she will usually return it to your office. If possible, enclose a stamped self-addressed envelope for the official to use. Send the original document by registered mail, return receipt requested. Keep the transmittal letter and copy of the document in a follow-up file until you receive the original back from the court official. Your attorneys will instruct you what to do with documents after they have been recorded and returned.

¶708 How Legal Documents Are Signed

The execution of a legal document is the actual signing of the document by the parties to the document who declare by the signing that they agree to the terms and provisions of the preceding document. The document may or may not have a notary clause or witnesses, depending upon the nature of the document. If you are unsure who will be signing a document, ask your attorneys before the client arrives. If an officer of a corporation is going to sign a document, the corporate seal may be necessary. If you are not a notary public and the document is required to be notarized, arrange for a notary to be present. In most law offices, there are several secretaries who are notaries.

¶800 Keys to Increasing Your Office Efficiency and Productivity

¶801 You Can Get Organized Once and For All

One of your most difficult challenges in being an efficient legal secretary is to get organized. For example, one basic tool of organization is to have an efficient calendar and appointment-keeping system. This may be a looseleaf calendar or a bound calendar. There are several personal time management calendar systems on the market, but what is important is that you like it and that it suits your needs. Also, you may take a looseleaf calendar system and add your own sections with individual divider tabs for items that do not come with the systems.

You may also combine your personal calendar system with your business calendar system so that you do not have two calendars to keep up with. Whatever system you choose, be sure that it has a place for things to do, notes and memos, and a month-at-a-glance calendar. The Day-Timer™, Inc., P.O. Box 6168, Allentown, PA 18001, makes an excellent calendar system that comes in pocket, junior, and senior sizes. It not only has those features, but also has a calendar to record your services performed daily in six minute divisions in the event you are required to keep time records.

¶802 How to Organize Your Time and Set Priorities

You can get that raise, increase your output, and increase your attorneys' profits by proper time management. You can be more efficient, more organized and more on top of things if you learn to plan and control your time. One of the most concrete ways to prove to your attorneys that you are worth more money is to be more efficient so that they increase their productivity, their profits, and their billable hours. You can do that by managing your time and producing more work in less time. An increase in your attorneys' billable hours means more money to your firm and eventually to you. Your attorneys' billable hours are reflected in two very important ways:

1. time reports;
2. current accounts receivable.

Moreover, your effectiveness parallels that of your attorneys'. If you make them look good, then they will reward you when review time comes.

¶803 Steps to Setting Priorities

Step 1. List all of the tasks you have to do for the next day, the next week, the next month, and any long term projects.

Step 2. Go through the list and use the ABC Priority System: Write a capital letter A to the left of those items on the list that have a high value; a B for those with medium value; and a C for those with low value. Be aware that as you do this, that you will be, to some extent, guessing. Based on your current knowledge, rate these tasks. As you compare the items on the list, you will be able to make priority choices.

Step 3. Now go through the list and take all of the A items and rate each one within this category with a 1 for high priority, a 2 for the next priority, and a 3 for the low priority. Remember this pertains to the A items only.

Step 4. After you finish with the A items, go to the B items and then the C items.

Step 5. Now you can rearrange the items in priority order or just leave them where they are on the list.

Step 6. As you handle each item on the list, use the following designations:

X = task completed;
D = task dismissed;
T = task transferred to another day.

Step 7. Use a sample form such as the one in Figure 803-1 and insert the date the item is due and the date the item is completed. If the item is transferred, put the date transferred.

Step 8. Put a reference abbreviation for each item if there is one. For example, you might insert FD for file documents.

Items marked A should be those that are the most important at the time. Of course, you can always rearrange your priorities as circumstances and situations change. Many times just a call from a client will cause your attorney to change his or her focus on what he or she is currently doing and shift to the client's current problem or crisis. Most law firms are crisis-oriented to meet the client's needs. A law office may

TO DO

PRIORITY (A,B,C)	XDT	CLIENT	ITEM	DATE DUE	DATE COMPLETED

Figure 803-1. To Do list.

be analogous to a hospital in that your attorneys many times must react to situations and often cannot plan exactly how their day will go. You get the most out of your time doing the A's first, and saving the B's and C's for later. One expert who teaches time management recommends that you forget C's altogether.

Learning to control your time will increase your value to your attorneys. If you are organized, then they will feel organized. Learn how to make time work for you. Time is your tool, your key to increased productivity and efficiency, your key to your career advancement and a better future.

Develop time consciousness. You must become fully aware of how you are utilizing your time. Analyze your methods of doing routine tasks. Becoming aware is the first step to changing your work habits and improving your skills. One good way to do this is to keep a clock nearby and for a period of one week keep a diary of your activities at work, including coffee breaks, lunch activities, social interactions, etc.

It will not take you much more than a few minutes to enter everything you do in this diary. Note the time you begin the activity and the time you finish. The small amount of time you take to make this time record diary will pay off in making you aware of your time losses.

Review and study your time record diary at the end of the week. Then subject your office habits and activities to rigorous examination with these questions:

Self-Analysis of Work Habits

- Are there any tasks that I can combine?
- Do I have the proper equipment to do these tasks (transcribing equipment, good writing pens, reference materials such as a dictionary, word division and spelling book, thesaurus, etc.)?
- Can any of these tasks be delegated or done better by someone else? (See ¶ 808)
- Is there an easier way to do this task?
- Do I use the telephone as often as I can to save time?
- Do I arrive at work on time?
- Does my lunch time extend to one hour or one hour and a half?
- Do I chit-chat in the halls or the rest room?
- Do I spend time at my desk snacking?
- Do I plan my day?
- Do I work on one item at a time, keeping only documents relating to that item on my desk at one time?
- Do I control my telephone time by being businesslike but pleasant?
- Do I spend time looking at what everybody else is doing and not concentrating on what I am doing?
- Do I spend time gossiping or taking unnecessary personal telephone calls at work?
- Do I miss deadlines or cause myself to lose control of time?

- Can any of my tasks be eliminated entirely?
- Do I stew over things rather than discuss them with the person who is affecting my reactions.
- Do I make notations of things I must do when I think of them or when someone calls or asks me to do something?
- When I am given a task, do I get all the information I need at the time that I am given the task?

Think About It

You will be amazed at the amount of time you spend in chatting, reading junk mail, or in doing tasks that could easily be delegated to others. You may find that you waste time waiting to see someone to ask a question. Would a quick telephone call do just as well? The telephone can be either an asset to saving time or a hindrance to efficient time management. This self-analysis should give you insight into your nonproductive and time-wasting habits by making you more aware of how you are wasting time and perhaps by starting you to action.

Evaluate Your Tasks

Another good way to utilize this time consciousness study to your advantage is to keep a pad on your desk during the same week. Use this pad to jot down ways in which you could save more time. As you begin each task evaluate it. Say to yourself: "How can I do this faster, better, and more efficiently? What shortcuts can I take?" Then write your ideas down. You'll be surprised to see how your list will grow.

¶804 Unnecessary Time Wasters

Self

1. Lack of daily tasks to do.
2. Failure to plan.
3. Failure to anticipate.
4. Inability to organize work.
5. Cluttered desk/work area.
6. Lost or misplaced files and documents.
7. Disorganized files or inappropriate filing system.
8. Filing everything including junk mail.
9. Waiting at copy machine and chit-chatting.
10. Failure to delegate.
11. Reading unimportant material.
12. Can't say no.
13. Correcting other people's mistakes.

14. "Trying to be nice" and doing everything for everybody else and cleaning up everyone else's mess.
15. "Trying to be perfect" to a point of ridiculousness.
16. Being careless and klutzy.
17. Lack of self-discipline.
18. Lack of self-control: temper/impatience/haste.
19. Procrastination.
20. Not listening and taking notes.
21. Not following instructions.
22. Daydreaming.
23. Inability to stick with one task until completed.
24. Poor memory.
25. Not paying attention to important details.
26. Misunderstanding instructions.
27. Not correcting your own mistakes.
28. Poor typing and shorthand skills.
29. Not learning how to use machines properly.
30. Being late.
31. Being absent.
32. Quitting early.
33. Long coffee breaks/lunch hours.
34. Eating at desk/drinking coffee constantly.
35. Not getting enough sleep.
36. Not taking care of your health.
37. Constantly going to the restroom.
38. Doing nonwork related activities.
39. Receiving and making personal phone calls.
40. Chit-chatting with coworkers.

Attorney-Related

1. Not informed of where attorneys are.
2. Not informed of attorneys objectives, plans, or changes in firm policy.
3. Lack of planning by attorneys.
4. Lack of teamwork.
5. Lack of or unclear instructions.
6. Miscommunication.
7. Unorganized attorneys.
8. Poor decision making by attorneys.
9. Inability of attorneys to make decisions.
10. Attorneys' poor handwriting.
11. Attorneys' lack of clear speech or poor dictation habits.

12. Waiting for attorney.
13. Personal errands for attorneys.
14. Socializing with clients waiting to see your attorneys.
15. Unnecessary written correspondence and memos.
16. Duplication of effort.
17. Making attorneys' telephone calls.

Firm-Related

1. Lack of office policy manual.
2. Duplication of effort.
3. Unnecessary interruptions by coworkers.
4. Outdated and unrepaired equipment.
5. Lack of instructions/manuals for office equipment.
6. Poor instruction by firm regarding equipment.
7. Skimpiness by firm to save money.
8. Lack of communication between departments/law office manager-administrator/management or executive committee.
9. Equipment problems (downtime for repairs); lack of service contracts for equipment.
10. Unsatisfactory performance by coworkers.
11. Unnecessary interruptions by coworkers.
12. Lack of consistency by management.
13. Lack of direction or goals by firm.
14. Heavy turnover.
15. Poor support services, i.e., mail, couriers, etc.
16. Inefficient and inadequate photocopying equipment.
17. Lack of standard accounting procedures.
18. Lack of firm support for peak workload periods.
19. Poor management by office manager-administrator.
20. Inattention to firm common areas, i.e., rest room, reception area, supply room.

Miscellaneous

1. "On hold" on telephone calls.
2. Drop-in visitors.

¶805 How to Control Common Time Wasters

1. Poor skills or lack of necessary skills. If you lack the necessary skills to do parts of your job, you will spend excessive time in doing those tasks. For example, Patti's job includes completing the quarterly tax returns. Although Patti has had no training in accounting or taxes, she has learned how to do this portion of her job. However, when her attorney asks her to do other types of computations she's not familiar with, she has to ask one of her coworkers to help her. This wastes not only her time but also that of her coworkers. Obviously, the solution to this problem would be for Patti to take some courses in accounting so that she can do her job without wasting time.

Poor skills cause a similar problem. Secretaries who are poor typists or have poor shorthand skills spend a lot of time correcting their mistakes, trying to read their notes, or redoing work. Perhaps they oversold themselves to get the job or have not used their skills enough to improve them but now find that they need better skills. Every secretary knows that if you don't use your shorthand, you will lose it. A refresher course in typing or shorthand will help in both these areas. Perhaps some practice on your own will be all that is needed. The important thing is to recognize your weak areas and do something about it rather than muddling through your work. ¶500 contains information you can use to plan a self-improvement program dealing with your skills, abilities, and knowledge. There are also numerous self-improvement books and other self-teaching books on the market that can help you. Look in the business, reference, or self-help sections of the bookstore. There is a book written for most anything you might want to learn.

2. *Telephone calls.* There are several ways that you can become more efficient using the telephone. The following are tips to save you time on the telephone and improve your telephone effectiveness:

- Before you make a call, organize your thoughts or questions. If you are going to give information out, write that down too. If you have to, write the questions or information out in detail before you call to help you be more precise and assertive during your call. This will prevent your having to make a second call because you forgot something. Taking notes during your call will also help you realize that you have completed the purpose of your call, and it is time to end it. Also, if you have to document the conversation later in a letter or a memorandum, it will be much easier with the notes right before you. While you are obtaining the information from the other person, take notes on their responses and other things that you are supposed to do or to follow up on.
- If you think you may need to refer to a report, letter, file, memo, etc., during your conversation, have this information in front of you when you place the call. This will eliminate your having to ask the other person to hold while you get the information and will shorten the time you spend on that telephone call.

- Make calls at the right time of day. Will the person you are calling be at lunch? You may start work at 8:30 A.M. but maybe the person you are calling doesn't. Wait until 9:30 A.M. or so before you make calls. If you are calling long distance, don't forget about the time zones. Save yourself time by calling when you will have the best chance of reaching the party. It's best not to make calls Monday morning. Most people are trying to organize their day and get back into their work after the weekend. Late Friday afternoon is also a bad time to call since people are trying to complete their day and prepare for the weekend.
- Make sure you have the right telephone number and that you dial carefully. If you are on a discount telephone service, make sure you dial all the numbers necessary to get into the system properly. If you are calling a large business or a government office, check to see if there is a direct number rather than going through the main switchboard.
- Try to call a specific person or department to eliminate having to have your call transferred (sometimes more than once).
- Keep your conversations as short as possible. Don't begin with, "Hello, Mr. Pennington. This is Nancy Edwards. Welcome back. Did you have a nice vacation?" You may know Mr. Pennington well enough to ask him about his vacation, but he'll appreciate your leaving out the nonbusiness chatter. It will save time for both of you. You will also prevent a long-winded party from going on and on about their vacation or whatever.
- Telephone etiquette states that the caller is the first one to hang up. If you're the caller, you should draw the conversation to a close when you have completed the purpose of your call. A simple "Thank you for your help, Mr. Pennington" (if he helped you in some way) or "That completes the information I have to give you, Mr. Pennington. Before we hang up, do you have any questions?" will usually signal your conversation has ended pleasantly.
- Occasionally, you will receive a long-winded call from someone who just doesn't know how to end a conversation or likes to talk about personal matters. When you are finished with your business, be assertive and tactfully end the call. Some possible ways to do this are:

  "Thank you for calling, Ms. Williams. I'll take care of this matter right away and send you a copy of Mr. Bowen's letter. Goodbye."

  "I appreciate your calling, Ms. Williams. We always like to know if the deposition is completed. Thank you for letting me know. Goodbye."

"Ms. Williams, I'm sorry to interrupt, but my attorney just motioned me into his office to take dictation. I'm going to have to hang up. Thank you so much for calling. Goodbye."

"Someone else is calling me on the other line."

"I have someone here to see Mr. Bowen. Goodbye."

- If someone calls and asks you "Are you busy?" or "Do you have a minute?" or "Can you talk now?" reply with, "Yes, Paula, I can talk for a few minutes." This puts a time limit on the conversation and provides you with an excuse to end the conversation if necessary.
- If you have someone else or a receptionist to answer your calls, let him or her do so.
- Stay away from personal calls at the office. For one thing, it distracts you from your work and may upset or disturb you if you get in an emotional conversation. Further, it tends to cause other secretaries or attorneys to frown on your having a personal conversation on firm time. Moreover, you will most likely just wind up feeling uncomfortable and guilty. It just isn't worth it. Try to tell your friends and your family not to call you unless it is absolutely necessary, or if it is an emergency. If you have to call someone while you are at work, do it during your lunch hour or after work. If possible, you might consider going to a pay phone to make your call. Most of us don't want other people in the office to know our business anyway. This is definitely a time waster, so beware!

3. *Procrastination.* For some reason we all tend to procrastinate. The one thing about procrastination is that the longer you put a task off, the harder it is to do it. Unfortunately, the unwanted task won't disappear; it just will grow out of proportion in your mind. Take what is called a "symbolic gesture."

A symbolic gesture is a successful accomplishment or a step taken toward your goal that helps build momentum toward successful accomplishment of a number of different tasks. By deliberately devising a symbolic gesture, you can create momentum.

How do you create and use a symbolic gesture?

- Choose a particular result or end goal you desire.
- Pick a small step toward that goal that you can accomplish *easily* that can be seen as a step toward that result or goal.
- Consciously direct your mind to take this symbolic success as a

strong suggestion of the full accomplishment of the complete result you choose.

For example, a secretary felt overwhelmed by the amount of disorganized clutter in her attorney's office and realized she wanted more order in the office to help her do her job more efficiently. To support this choice, she cleaned out and reorganized the In box on her attorney's desk. She took pride in this accomplishment, making herself feel better, giving her mind a clear, strong suggestion, building momentum, and creating an orderly office for her attorney. She found, to her surprise, that she no longer felt overwhelmed. In fact she was eager to take further steps. As she did so, her energy and ability to take the right steps at the right time continued to build. Soon she had completed the job of reorganization with the order she had chosen to create.

Symbolic gestures of this type enhance momentum while making use of what you are doing anyway. These gestures are an easy way to create movitation when all else fails.

4. Correcting others' mistakes. Judi gives you a letter with poor corrections. You retype it instead of having her do it. If you continue to do this, Judi will continue to give you letters with poor corrections. Have Judi correct her own work.

5. Perfectionism. Many of us grow up hearing:

"If something is worth doing, then it's worth doing well."

"Remember what you represent."

"Take pride in whatever you do."

"Do your very best always, no matter what!"

Thus, we decide that:

"If I'm judged by what I do, then I have to do everything perfectly."

"If I want to be proud of what I do, then I have to do it perfectly."

"Whatever I do, I do perfectly."

"I must always do my very best no matter what it takes or what I have to do."

So you become a perfectionist and set unreasonably high standards for yourself. For example, everything you type has to be perfect—there are no corrections and material is placed "just so" on the paper. If it isn't, you do it over. Is there anything wrong with that attitude?

Think about all the typing tasks that you do each day. Does every one have to be perfect? For example, if your attorney told you to do a draft on the word processor, does your format for this draft have to be absolutely perfect? If you feel uncomfortable with this, type "draft" on it so your attorney will remember that it is only a draft. Unless your attorneys insist on perfect drafts, don't try to make them perfect. In fact you might point out to your attorneys that it is stored on the word processor and can easily be changed for the final copy. Since your attorneys are going to make changes to their documents anyway, it is simply a waste of time for you to labor over draft documents.

If you do not have a word processor, computer, or a memory typewriter, then "cut and paste." For example, take the paragraph or paragraphs that you want to move to another part of the document and cut them out. After moving them to the place where you want them to be, cut off the old paragraph and tape in the new paragraph between it. This is a method that has been used by attorneys, legal secretaries, paralegals, and law clerks for years, but with the advent of the computer, this technique is often not necessary.

Be wary of running off too many drafts on the computer just to give your attorneys clean copies. Try to have them make all changes on the first draft before you make corrections on the computer and run off the final draft.

Strive for excellence in your work but beware of perfectionism, as it can be frustrating and a waste of time. Know when to quit. This holds true for whatever tasks you have to do. For example, if you have been assigned a research project and asked to prepare a memorandum, know when to stop. You can keep doing research forever or writing and rewriting forever. While it's good to be thorough, it can be counterproductive.

6. *Don't know how to say NO.* You work for a senior partner and an associate comes up to you and says that his secretary is really swamped and he has to get this pleading in the mail right away. What do you do? It depends on what your workload is. If your attorney has you busy on a project that must get out, then you have to gracefully refuse the associate's request. A good way to do that is to say:

> "Corneill, I know you need help, but I have to finish this pleading for Mr. Cohen and I have to do it right away. If I finish and still have some time and you still do not have the pleading typed, perhaps, I can do it. I'll check back with you."

Now, if you have time to type the pleading, be aware that Corneill will probably be back the next time he needs a letter, memorandum, pleading, etc., typed. If you're not careful, Corneill will take your humanitarian desire to help for granted. Perhaps you should qualify your response with:

> "Certainly, Corneill, I have time to type your pleading this time. But understand that I'm usually too busy with Mr. Cohen's work to

take on extra work, so don't assume I can type a document whenever you need it."

Or, you may respond:

"Corneill, have you checked with the receptionist to see if she has time to type your pleading? She is always glad to help out and she needs the experience."

There are many secretaries, especially in large firms, who will ask you to help them with their work. Sally may ask you to type some transmittal letters for her because she has so much to do she can't possibly get them finished by this afternoon. Should you help Sally? You know Sally is probably exaggerating about the amount of work she has to do. Also, you notice she had time to take a long lunch hour and spend ten minutes talking to one of the other secretaries about her boyfriend. Although you have had to help Sally before in similar situations, you decide to say no this time to let Sally know she won't always be able to count on you to help her do her work, today, or in the future.

"Sally, I'm sorry, but I just don't have time to help you. I am overloaded with work from Mr. Cohen that has to get out today."

Then there are the office birthdays or gift collections someone has to make—for Celena who's getting married, for Sheryl who's leaving the firm, for Anne who's having a birthday. Once you play the good egg and take up the collection (including shopping for the gift and card, wrapping the gift, and seeing that everyone signs the card), you've not only used your working time but also your personal time. The next time your office wants to give someone a present, all eyes turn toward you to take charge. When you're asked in more than one instance to collect money (or anything else), say,

"I'm sorry, but I just don't have time to do that. But thanks for asking me."

Or,

"Gee, I would like to help out, but Mr. Cohen is counting on me to get this memorandum drafted to go down to word processing; therefore, I won't be able to help you. I'll be glad to make a contribution, however."

7. *Duplication of effort.* Did one of your attorneys ever ask you to do something, such as "Check with word processing to see if my complaint is finished" and when you go down to word processing, which is on another floor, you find out that he or she already called them. Not

only do you feel like a fool but you've wasted a lot of time. Obviously, your attorney was worried about the document but didn't value your time too much. Perhaps in the future you could ask him or her if they have already called the word processing department.

8. Lack of communication between other attorneys and other departments of the firm. Unfortunately, the various departments in some large firms are sometimes located on other floors or in an area far away from each other. This causes attorneys to forget that they're all part of a team; instead they operate in their own "world." As a matter of fact, many attorneys in the same department operate in their own world almost unconsciously. They tend to operate on their own "island." This may be their nature or they may have been trained to be so independent. Either way it causes communication problems.

As a secretary you can alleviate a lot of havoc that goes with the problem. When you do a project that involves more than your department, for example, the accounting department, be sure to check with each department to make sure there are no conflicts. Be careful how you handle this, though, as you don't want to create ill will between departments. Cooperate in any way that you can not only with other departments, but also within your department.

9. Unclear or incomplete instructions. If you start an assignment with no instructions or incomplete instructions, most likely you will have to do the assignment over, because it wasn't done to someone else's satisfaction. At the time you are given an assignment, be sure to ask all of the questions you can think of. It is much easier to ask the questions while the person is concentrating on giving you correct instructions then to go back to your desk unsure, only to have to run back in your attorney's office with questions. Don't worry about taking their time. They want you to understand so the project can be done right the first time.

Many attorneys think you are a mind reader and should know exactly what they want. If the assignment is similar to previous assignments, these attorneys might be justified in thinking this. If the assignment involves unfamiliar material, procedures, or subjects, however, you don't always know when you lack complete instructions or information.

Don't be afraid of appearing stupid. When given instructions that are unclear, ask questions right then. Say, "Ms. Turner, let me make sure I understand what you mean." Not asking questions is being stupid and a waste of time because you end up redoing an assignment you did incorrectly. If you don't understand, *say so.* Make sure you are completely clear on the assignment before going back to your desk.

10. Unnecessary written correspondence. If your attorneys dictate letters, when you think a telephone call would serve the same purpose, then question the need for this written corespondence. Anything that you can eliminate will save time for you and your attorneys. Perhaps, they can send short handwritten memos or their business cards with a note. Maybe they can just write a note on the letter, photocopy it, and return it. They have to make this decision, because they may want a letter to go out for the purpose of documenting a conversation, for example.

If you do a particular letter repetitively, check with your attorneys to see if you can put it on the word processor or make a form out of it, especially letters to the court or government offices which don't have to be originally typed.

11. Not informed of attorneys' objectives, departmental plans or changes in firm policy. Ask your attorneys to please keep you informed about any changes in firm policy that will enable you to give them better assistance. This will save your having to redo work because you were uninformed.

12. Not informed of attorneys' whereabouts. Many attorneys have a habit of leaving their offices in a hurry and forgetting to tell their secretaries where they are going and when they will be back. As a result, you may spend unnecessary time trying to locate them when an important telephone call comes in or someone comes to see them.

When your attorneys start to leave their offices, ask them where you can locate them, if necessary, and when they expect to return. Let them know that in order for you to be efficient, they have to let you know where they are going and when they will be back. You might have to exercise your assertiveness here. But as soon as your attorneys realize that their best interests are in your mind, they will try harder to keep you informed.

¶806 Put a Stop to Interruptions Once and For All

Besides learning how to spend your time, you also need to know how to control the interruptions that limit your productivity. Anything that stops you from doing what you are doing at a particular time is an interruption. For example, if you're typing a pleading and the telephone rings, the telephone is an interruption. If you're posting a check in the ledger and someone comes into your office and speaks to you, that person is an interruption. If you're filing and start thinking about whether you want to go to the movie tonight, you're the interruption. If you're meeting with the office manager and your attorney buzzes you, your attorney is an interruption. If the secretary across the hall starts talking to the courier loudly and disturbs your concentration, they're the interruption.

Most interruptions tend to get you off track and make you lose your concentration. The flow of your work is halted temporarily, and it may be hard to refocus on what you are doing.

You're working on a complaint that has to be filed today. First, you pull out the standard complaint forms and start the process of creating a new document on your word processor. As you are getting your format set up on the word processor, someone comes by your desk to hand you some mail that was delivered to them by mistake. You stop to listen. Now you've lost your train of thought, so you go back to the beginning to start over.

Just as you get moving again, the bookkeeper comes to you to check about the travel and expense report you turned in the other day for one of your attorneys. After the bookkeeper leaves, you return to your word processor and try to find the place in the complaint where you left off. Now where were you? Once again you have to reorient yourself to typing the complaint.

You should begin to become aware of how interruptions cause you to waste time. Perhaps, if you have an office to yourself, you can close your door to discourage interruptions. Most secretaries do not have an office that can be closed, however. Therefore, you need some practical tools to help you limit the number of interruptions you have daily and increase your productivity and efficiency. The following list will help you limit and control the interruptions that you commonly face each day. Some of these suggestions may not fit your work situation; some may help you. You may have your own ideas of what to do.

¶807 Practical Ways to Control Interruptions

Telephone Calls

1. If you make a call and the person is not in, try to find out when they will be back in the office so that you can call back. Don't leave messages for people to return your call because these calls will not be in your control and will interrupt you throughout the day. However, if you have a difficult time trying to reach someone then it would be best to leave a message rather than waste time trying to keep calling.

2. If someone calls your attorney and he or she is not available, encourage them to leave a message for your attorney to return the call. This will allow your attorneys to make all their calls themselves at one time and limit people who might keep calling back.

Coworkers Interruptions

3. Suggest to your attorneys that they circulate a memo around the office requesting everyone to put everything in writing. Many businesses have the philosophy: "Don't say it, write it."

4. Try to train coworkers and people you supervise to consolidate their requests for information or assistance. Suggest that they make a list of the questions or information they need before coming to you. Tell them that you will do the same. For example, say you have given Sylvia a research memorandum to proofread, and she keeps hopping up and down to show you the errors. Very tactfully, say to her:

> "Sylvia, to save your time and mine, why don't you wait until you have read the whole memorandum, and then let's discuss it."

5. When you ask someone to get information to you or to follow up on some item, end your request with:

> "Beth, after you find the name of the book regarding legal research, would you just write me a note and put it in my In basket (or, just put the information in my In basket). If I have any questions, I'll let you know. Thanks."

6. Always be very thorough in giving instructions to your coworkers or people you supervise when you ask them to do something for you. At the end of the instructions, always ask:

> "Do you understand what I want? Do you have any questions to ask me?"

If the task is a new procedure, put it in writing for future use as well. Be sure your instructions are clear and easy to understand. If you are writing a new procedure, you might ask one of your coworkers to read the new procedure and see if they think it is clear enough to be correctly understood.

7. If you can, try and set certain times of the day for instructions and questions, a time when you are not to be interrupted. Let everyone know what time this is and at what time they can come to you with questions or requests for information.

8. Always get your work done prior to the time it is due to save people having to come and interrupt you to get the information they requested earlier. For example, if your attorneys' time slips or computer time entry sheets are due every day, make sure that they are turned in before the end of the day or the following morning when the bookkeeping or accounting department wants them. If you forget to do this, you can be sure that you will be interrupted at an inconvenient time, plus

you will have to apologize and be embarrassed for not being efficient in getting the time slips or time sheets in on time.

9. If you can delegate the handling of certain routine requests to a subordinate, such as the receptionist or clerk, do so. For example, if you see that the receptionist is not very busy, ask her or him if he or she would mind collecting the telephone charge slips and postage charge slips for you. Most likely, he or she will be delighted to do something because he or she is bored just sitting around trying to look busy. Of course, if your receptionist is too busy, don't ask because he or she may volunteer to do it but may not really have the time to do a good job.

10. If one of your coworkers comes to you more than two times with the same question, talk with him or her about what is happening. Suggest that he or she write down your answers for future references or to take sufficient notes. Explain to him or her tactfully that you have already explained that twice and you would appreciate it if he or she would write it down this time because you are busy and must get this document out that you are working on.

11. If one of your coworkers is always coming to you to borrow supplies, because he or she does not want to go to the supply room to get the supplies tactfully suggest that you are about out of these items and would he or she mind going to the supply room to get them.

12. Some coworkers may become pesty about asking your opinion or asking you to help them make a decision. You should say that:

> "It really is important for you to make this decision because you know better than anyone else what is best for you and for the situation."

13. If one of your coworkers is constantly coming by your office to gab, you are going to have to be firm and discourage him or her from doing this any longer. You might say:

> "Donna, I really would like to hear about it (whatever it is she is wanting to chat about), but Mr. Reinhart really gets upset with me when I talk and don't concentrate on my work. Could we talk about it during lunch (or whenever is convenient for you)."
>
> Most likely, by lunchtime she will have forgotten about it.

Family, Friends, and Visitors

14. Ask your family and your friends to call you at home. If they call you at work, just simply say:

> "Can I call you back after work? I'm really busy."
>
> If you have children who are small and want to let you know that they are home from school and are okay, you might ask your attorneys if

they mind if they just call to check in with you and tell them that you will keep the call short. Tell them that this is the only call they will make unless it is an emergency, and be sure to thank them.

15. Don't give your work number to organizations that publish rosters or lists. Ask them not to publish your work telephone number and indicate that you are not to be called at work.

16. If all else fails and you can't get coworkers to stop interrupting you, just continue working and don't look up from your work; eventually, they will get the message. Don't look up and give the interruptors any sign that they are welcome. If you look up and smile, they will feel welcome. You will be inviting conversation. If they are interrupting you about business, then by all means, look up and give them your full attention, but keep it short.

17. If you are located in a traffic area and you can tell when someone goes by, don't look up and smile because that will give them the idea that they are invited to stop and talk.

Drop-In Visitors

18. If you are in the main reception area, from time to time it is assured that you will have salespersons drop in unannounced and without an appointment. They may want to see your attorney or to talk to you for some reason not related to your work. For example, frequently temporary employment agencies send personnel to call on law offices. They usually do not make an appointment. You might handle this by saying:

> "Thank you for stopping by, Ms. Wood, but right now we do not need any temporary help. If you will leave your card or a brochure, we will contact you if we need some help. Thank you for coming by."

Then put your head down and continue working. Be polite but be firm.

Distractions

19. The first place to eliminate distractions is in your immediate work area. Look at your desk. Is it cluttered with cute knick-knacks? One or two useful knick-knacks, like a paper weight or memo clip, might be helpful, but little statues and other memorabilia are unnecessary. Sure, you are proud of your little boy's kindergarten drawing, but ask whether a smart businessperson would have that on their desk. Save those priceless treasures to display at home.

Also, several times during the day, take a long hard look at your desk. Is it cluttered with more than one project? If so, get rid of everything but what you're working on. Files belong in the file drawer. Have a box or folder for your things to do, an in and out box and a pending box—nothing else. All you really need on your desk is your telephone, calculator, address file and message pad, your In-Out baskets, your pending box and a "To Do" box or folder, your pencil holder and what you're working on. Everything else should be put away. This may be hard to do at first, but once you get in the habit of keeping your desk organized and uncluttered, you'll see how easy it is.

Self-imposed Distractions

20. There are many things that may distract you that are within your self-control. For example, if you are bored with what you are doing and find it difficult to concentrate, you might take a look at how you can make this task more interesting. Throw yourself into the project and get interested in it. No matter what you do, you can somehow make it interesting by making a challenge out of it. The challenge can be to do it within a certain time or to do a certain number of items per hour, per day. For example, if you have the project of reorganizing the whole file drawer and all you are doing is making new file folder labels and punching down the documents in the file, you can set little goals for yourself. You might set a goal to have the first drawer done in one day, the second drawer done in five or six hours, and third and fourth drawer to be done by the end of the third day. Now you've given yourself some motivation. And remember motivation doesn't come by waiting for the motivation to do a task but rather *by doing*.

21. Are you tired? Being sleepy is a primary distraction and will affect not only your mood and your productivity but also your response time and thinking abilities. Try to discipline yourself to save your late night adventures for the weekend. See that you get enough rest at night so that you can make it through the day easily and be efficient as well. You'll be glad you did. All it takes is one late night to remember how hard it is the next day.

22. Are you thirsty? Try keeping a glass of water at your desk where it can't spill instead of making numerous trips to the water fountain or the kitchen.

23. Are you bored and restless? Perhaps taking a short walk or doing an errand will break the routine. Or, if you can, take a break and do nothing but relax. Try to get out during lunchtime even if you don't eat out. If you brown-bag it, eat your lunch, then go window shopping (but leave your checkbook back at the office). If there is a park nearby and it is safe, bring an interesting book and sit there and read. Or just look at the leaves or the flowers in bloom to relax your mind. Don't get in a rut! Break the routine.

Turn-about is fair play. Remember that others don't like unnecessary interruptions any more than you do. Respect their right to work without interruptions.

Be patient with yourself. It takes time to break bad habits. Don't be discouraged if at first you don't succeed. Just keep trying and eventually you'll break through the barriers. Experts say it takes twenty-one days to break a habit. Keep track of the days of your calendar.

Stop and think why you are being interrupted. If you are being interrupted for a legitimate purpose, recognize that it's okay. But if you're being interrupted for a nonbusiness purpose, then recognize that and act accordingly as was suggested here or in any other way that you feel comfortable doing.

¶808 Easy-To-Use Techniques for Delegating Tasks

It's an accepted practice for attorneys to delegate tasks, but what about legal secretaries? Can they delegate? Yes, but in a different way and to a limited number of people. If you are like most legal secretaries, you are afraid to delegate and insist on handling everything yourself. Why do you do this? There are several possible reasons.

1. You're not used to having someone available to help you. You're used to doing everything yourself and find it hard to ask someone else to help you. You're somewhat afraid and intimidated to ask someone to help you. It seems easier to do it yourself. But ask yourself, Do I have to do everything? Do all these tasks require my skill, my knowledge, and my experience? Can someone else do some tasks just as well as I can?
2. You don't want to take the time to show someone else how to do a task at the time the task has to be done, or you feel it's going to take just as long to explain it as doing it yourself. By the time you explain it, you could have done it, you think. Rather than rationalize and continue to do the task, stop and realize that if you show Cindy how to do this task now, then the next time she will be able to do it. You'll save time in the future, reducing your time burdens and pressures.
3. You feel that you can do the work better than anyone else. After all, haven't you been doing it for years. While this may be true, many tasks can be done in a number of ways. The end product or end result is what counts. As long as the end result is satisfactory, what difference does it make how it's done, except that it be done as efficiently as possible. Someone else may not be able to do the work as well as you can, but the satisfactory job you turn in on time may be more valuable to your attorney than the perfect one you finish late. After all,

legal work is based on a lot of short-notice deadlines that have to be met. Just constantly keep in mind the goal you have to meet. Let go and let others help you. Most likely, they will be more than happy to help you. Let them also have the satisfaction of helping you; this is important to their self-esteem too.

4. You feel threatened and insecure in your position. What if Cindy does do it better than you? Would this mean that she might take your job? So you think that if no one else knows how to do your job, your attorney will be less likely to replace you. You will become indispensible and thus be forever secure. Nonsense. What happens if you're ill or on vacation? Do your attorneys just wait for you to return? Do you expect someone to fill in for you and do your work just the way you would do it? Is that fair? Do you want your attorneys to be so frustrated that they cannot function when you're out? The best thing you can do for your attorneys and for yourself is to let others learn your job. Then, if some personal emergency comes up, you won't have to worry about the work getting done and feel guilty about being gone.

5. You don't want to be responsible for others and their mistakes. When you delegate, you do accept the responsibility for others' work, but don't let that keep you from delegating. Just as you do, other people make mistakes and your attorneys are going to understand that if you have Cindy help you, you're not entirely at fault if she goofs up. So relax. Getting tasks done through others is only one part of delegating work. The other part is helping others develop skills and trusting them to be as efficient as you would be. People usually live up to our expectations of them. So give other people the benefit of the doubt and let go.

6. You don't want to delegate because you want all the credit. If you think this way, you operate on the principle that there is only so much credit to go around, and if someone else gets credit, that's less for you. This isn't true. There is plenty of room for everyone to succeed. Give up pettiness and enjoy working with others. The team effort is very rewarding.

7. Trying to be a superwoman keeps you on a treadmill. You soon become overwhelmed with all you have to do. You are so worried about the whole project that you can't see that things are done a step at a time, minute by minute, hour by hour and day by day. You become frustrated and feel overworked. Eventually, you'll become resentful and unhappy and even go so far as to look at the weekend's classified section and dream about a new job that will be different (you think).

You need to stop and look around you. Ask yourself the following questions:

1. Is the receptionist busy?
2. Is the receptionist eager to learn?
3. Is she bored?
4. Are the other secretaries busy?
5. Who can help you?
6. Can the courier do some errands for you?
7. Is one of the secretaries going to the same bank that you must go to?
8. Is there anything you can delegate by telephone? For example, can you ask the teller at the bank to send a statement by courier rather than you running to the bank on your lunch hour and wasting half an hour?
9. Do you know the abilities of each of your coworkers?
10. Do any of them have skills or experience that would qualify them to do any of your tasks? For example, can the assistant in the library locate a statute for you and copy it to take to your attorney.
11. Could any of them be easily trained to do some of your tasks?
12. What are their outstanding skills? Their weak areas? For example, Sharon is an excellent typist but is weak in grammar and punctuation; Marge has good command of grammar and punctuation but is weak in composing letters; John has accounting skills but is weak in typing.
13. Can the other secretaries take turns delivering documents or getting supplies?
14. Can the mailroom clerk pick up your mail?
15. Can you get a high school student to help you a couple of hours each day and delegate routine tasks to him or her?

Once you know who is available and what talents they have, you can review all your job functions and decide which ones you must do and which ones others can do for you. It's a matter of matching the person with the task. Be careful, though, that you do not place undue workloads on your delegatees or shirk your responsibilities.

If you're considering whether to delegate a task, stop and ask yourself, "Is it necessary that I do this task? If so, why?" If you can honestly say that no one else has the ability to do that particular job, then you should not delegate it. But don't kid yourself. Remember, you must learn to let go and let others help you.

¶808.1 Step-by-Step Procedures for Delegating Work

Step 1. Analyze the task thoroughly and write down every piece of information you would need to do the task.

Step 2. Write out the various steps for doing the task.

Step 3. Organize that information in a logical, orderly fashion.

Step 4. Break the task down into small segments if the task is complicated. For example, say Shelley is going to help you prepare some papers for filing with the court. This involves copying the documents, preparing the court backs (usually referred to as "blue backs" although they may be any color depending on the court), and assembling the exhibits. Shelley has never prepared court papers before. If you were to explain the whole project to her at once, she probably wouldn't remember everything you told her to do and would have to keep coming back to you for new instructions. For Shelley, this is an involved task that you should break down into smaller segments.

Step 5. Demonstrate as you explain. Depending on the task, you may need to demonstrate the process to use. For example, you might prepare a sample court back for Shelley to refer to; then have her type one court back and assemble the court papers to fasten the court back. Then show Shelley how to prepare the civil filing memo.

Step 6. Give the person time to absorb the information. For example, if the copying Shelley has to do is lengthy, have her do all the copying before explaining how she should do the court backs. Then explain how to do the court backs. Let her do a few, then explain to her how to fill out the civil filing memo.

Step 7. Ask the person to repeat instructions to ensure that they understood you and that you gave complete instructions. Give the person time to ask questions. Make sure the person understands. People frequently say they understand when they do not.

Step 8. Provide written instructions if a task is involved or if the person will perform the task infrequently. This will save your having to reinstruct delegatees the next time they have to do the task. Hand them a tablet to take notes and give them time to do it. If you have an office procedures manual, let the delegatee read the procedure, then explain and allow them to reiterate what they understand the task to be. If this task is done frequently and you do not have it in written form, it would be a good idea to do so for future reference and for training of new employees. Also, it will help if you are out and someone has to take over for you.

Step 9. Refrain from checking on the progress of the delegatees; however, encourage delegatees to check back with you whenever they have questions about procedure or are unsure what to do next. Give them leeway to do so by reminding them that it is okay to check back with you and to ask you questions.

Step 10. Let the delegatees correct their own mistakes. Just telling them they made a mistake doesn't teach them how to do a task correctly.

Step 11. Explain how a portion of a task the delegatee is doing fits in with the whole picture. Such explanation can give them a perspective of the whole task and the end product desired; therefore, they may be able to realize if they are proceeding in the wrong direction.

Step 12. Ask delegatees to keep you informed by reporting back to you from time to time. For example, you might say, "Shelley, let me know if you have any problems getting the court backs from the supply room." Also, if this is a long project, ask them to let you know how they are coming along so that you can decide whether they will need help.

Step 13. Give delegatees deadlines for completing the work or for reporting back to you. For example, "Shelley, I will need these papers filed before four o'clock, so let me know how you are doing about two o'clock."

Step 14. Most of all, give the delegatees feedback. If they are on the right track, let them know. If they are doing a good job, let them know.

Delegation does not mean assigning a task to someone else and then forgetting about it. You may think that because you passed the task on that you can just forget it. You may have confidence in your delegatees to do their jobs, but you still must keep control of the tasks you delegate and follow through to their completion. You can do this by having a method of checking to assure that the work is accurate and complete. Just remember that although you are getting work done through someone else, you are still responsible for the end results.

¶809 Train Your Attorneys to Dictate Properly

If your attorneys are like most attorneys, they usually dictate in a rather haphazard way with little planning and organizing. You can train them to maximize their dictating time which in turn will help you maximize your time. How do you do this? By asking them to do the following items when they are preparing to dictate and when they are actually dictating. You'll have to be tactful in suggesting these techniques. You must also realize that they may or may not accept any of your suggestions, but even if you only get them to accept one, it will be worth your effort.

¶809.1 Suggestions For Better Dictation

1. Have a definite time set aside every day for dictation. If you are at your best and your thoughts are clearer in the morning, then this is a good time to dictate.

2. Have all of the files and documents you need prior to beginning your dictation. If you have to make any telephone calls regarding matters on which you are dictating, make those calls before you start.
3. Allow ample time for your secretary to transcribe your dictation before the mail closes.
4. Make every effort to prevent unnecessary interruptions during the dictation period. Close your door, if necessary. Have your secretary hold your calls.
5. Concentrate on your dictation so that you do not waste your time and that of your secretary.
6. Indicate clearly whether material dictated is memorandum, letter, report, or other type of communication.
7. Indicate how many copies you need before the material is typed.
8. Indicate which letters are to be rushed.
9. Mark the date, item dictated, and your initials on each tape or on a note attached to the tape, especially if your secretary works for someone else in addition to you.
10. Ask for a rough draft when you anticipate changes.
11. Spell unusual words and proper names and clearly enunciate figures.
12. Regulate your dictation speed to your secretary's writing speed if he or she is taking shorthand.
13. Give your secretary an opportunity to ask questions on points which are not clear to her.
14. Make yourself responsible for grammar and sentence structure since you know more of what you are trying to say.
15. Compliment your secretary when he or she gets out a nice looking letter or report.
16. Take the blame yourself for errors that are your fault.
17. Indicate minor corrections in such a way that the material does not need to be retyped.
18. Make corrections in longhand on informal communications.
19. If possible, correct any rough drafts with a red pen or pencil so that your secretary can spot your changes easily.
20. If an error can be corrected without retyping, make your notation of change lightly in the margin or on a note attached to the paper.
21. Avoid keeping your secretary after office hours to do work that can be done just as well the next day.
22. If you have items to be enclosed with the document you are

dictating, let your secretary know ahead of time so that she can prepare the appropriate copies.

23. If your secretary prefers that you dictate punctuation, then do so. However, ask your secretary because she may prefer to use her own judgment on punctuation if that is one of her skills. Some secretaries are insulted when attorneys dictate commas and periods. However, some prefer that you do. Always check. Or if you explicitly want certain items punctuated in a certain way, say so.
24. Be reasonable in your expectations of the amount of work that can be done. What looks like it will take a short time may be an unrealistic assessment on your part. Talk to your secretary to get an idea of a reasonable time that you can expect your dictation to be finished.

¶810 Clear-Cut Ways to Save Your Attorneys' Time with Clients

Much of attorneys valuable time is wasted unnecessarily in meetings and other contacts with the client as a result of lack of organization and preparation. Scrutinize the office procedures, methods, and systems that cause this to happen in your attorneys' office.

The following techniques are some of the many ways that you can save your attorneys' time with clients, which will not only save the client money, inconvenience and aggravation, but will also make a good impression on the client.

1. With your attorneys' approval, communicate with the client yourself as much as possible by telephone or by letter to handle all the client's matters not requiring the expertise of the attorneys.
2. Before your attorneys meet with clients, check all the clients' files to make certain that they are current and in order. This will prevent your attorney from having to leave his meeting with the client to locate the missing documents.
3. Whenever possible and with your attorneys' approval, meet with clients to give them documents or to have them sign documents, or other routine matters that would be time consuming for your attorneys.
4. Gather all documents and collect all information your attorneys will need prior to meeting with clients to save your attorneys from interrupting their meetings with the clients

and having to make telephone calls or inquiries to other persons to obtain necessary information and documents.

5. Prepare checklists and forms for your attorneys' use when interviewing and meeting with clients.
6. Prepare any necessary verifications or acknowledgments in advance of your attorneys' meetings with clients. This will enable your attorneys simply to ask the clients to fill in the remaining information and will save an enormous amount of time. Whenever possible and with your attorneys' approval, prepare any papers in advance that you can to save the time that your attorneys will have to meet with the client.
7. Make any copies that your attorneys will need to give to clients prior to their meetings so that they don't have to interrupt their meetings to ask you to copy documents.
8. Have all necessary papers, pencils, pens, paper clips, legal pads, notary seals, and other items that your attorneys and their client might need in the conference room or in your attorneys' offices prior to the clients' visit.

¶811 Time-Saving Techniques

Take advantage of these fifteen time-management techniques to systematize and organize your time. These techniques will help your attorneys increase their billable hours. The end result will be the hastening of your career advancement.

1. Schedule your work. It is important to schedule your time yourself. Develop a habit of scheduling your work on a daily, weekly, monthly, and long-term basis as much as possible, recognizing that priorities may change as the need arises. Make scheduling your work and setting your priorities a routine function so that it will become habit and will allow you to judge the length of your work activities and to balance your time. Keep your daily schedule on your desk in front of you so that you can refer to it and check off items as they are accomplished. Realize that you will constantly be rescheduling your work and your priorities.

2. Plan ahead to avoid crises. You must pay close attention to your attorneys' deadlines and priorities to avoid crisis situations. Try to anticipate any deadlines or crises which may occur in the future. Crises are often caused by lack of communication, failure to plan your work, failure to follow through on delegated work, and failure to make contingency plans. Think about your attorneys' due dates, appointments, meetings, depositions, court appearances, etc., prepare for them and plan ahead. Keep on your toes constantly and remind your attorneys of their work priorities. Check with them often to see if they are keeping on track. Some attorneys will not allow you to "bug" them in this manner, and others will want you to. You'll have to assess your own situation and act accordingly. Use a tickler system to remind your attorneys of important dates and deadlines. (See ¶1400.) There are enough unanticipated crises in practicing law without creating more.

For example, you know that your attorneys have a board meeting to go to on behalf of one of their corporate clients, and you have to prepare the minutes of the last meeting and other relevant documents. You should allow yourself ample lead time in which to accomplish this task. Schedule a portion of these minutes to be prepared each day. Then a few days before they must attend the meeting, you will not have to put all your other work aside to accomplish this task on schedule. This would cause you unnecessary stress, and you could not do an efficient job. It is certainly much safer to overestimate the amount of time it will take you to accomplish a task than to underestimate it. Then, if you complete it before the estimated time, you will have time for the emergencies you cannot anticipate.

When you have a crisis situation, analyze it to avoid its repetition in the future. Then you will save time for the really unavoidable crises. If you plan ahead to avoid these situations, your work will go smoother, you will be happier, and your attorneys will be impressed with your efficiency.

3. Make deadlines. If you are one of those people who usually work better under pressure, give yourself a deadline if you do not have one given to you. It will provide the pressure you need to pursue your assignment until it is completed. This technique is excellent if you are not a self-motivator.

Announce your deadline to the person who has given you the assignment. Knowing that that person is depending on you to accomplish the job by a certain time will help you to work better. Ask for an approximate time frame of when he or she wants the job done; use this time to set a realistic deadline, giving yourself ample time for unanticipated events that may occur. Qualify your deadline by saying that it is your "expected" or "anticipated" deadline. If you find that you are not going to make your deadline, give your attorneys an idea of your progress and your new anticipated completion time.

Most important of all, respect your deadlines. Do not get into the habit of stretching them or they will lose their effectiveness. You will get a given task done more quickly by making less time available for it. Remember Parkinson's Law: *Work expands to fill the time available for its completion.* Avoid "spinning your wheels" needlessly while you are trying to do the task perfectly.

4. Learn to communicate. Good time management requires concentration on one thing at a time. When you are being spoken to or are engaged in a conversation, concentrate on the content of the conversation. Observe the speaker's facial expressions and body language. Taking notes will force you to concentrate. Even though at the time you are listening to a work assignment you think you will have no problems remembering it, take notes anyway. You will be surprised how quickly you may forget the details.

5. Gather all the information you need in advance. Before you can do a competent job on any project, it is imperative that you get all the facts or information you need in advance. If your attorneys call you into their offices to ask you to do a project, always take your pad with you. Take thorough notes on everything, even though they may seem irrelevant. Ask questions on any portion of the project that is not entirely clear to you even if the question may seem simple or dumb. Your attorneys will be impressed with your interest in clearly understanding the project. Also, make sure you clearly understand the project's priority. Getting this information in the beginning will save you from wasting time later. Although there will be times when this is impossible, make sure you obtain the necessary information as soon as you can.

Make sure you understand what your attorneys want you to do and what they expect the outcome or end product to be. They may be unavailable when you begin working on projects, and if you don't understand it, you will be stuck and unable to reach them for help. This will result in wasted time on your part and theirs too since you gave them the impression that you understood the projects and really didn't. Ask. Ask. Ask.

6. Tackle the most important tasks first. The most important items in a given group normally constitute a relatively small portion of the total items in the group. This means that these tasks are only a small percentage of your total tasks.

For example, if you have a long list of projects which overwhelms and perhaps discourages you, instead of being frustrated and bogged down with the list, choose two or three of the most important items on the list. At the end of the day, don't feel guilty about those items you did not get done. The most important tasks will be taken care of, and you should feel so good about it that you will be able to do the other tasks with ease. Keep this in mind when assigning priorities.

7. Aim for excellence but don't spin your wheels. All of us want to do the best job we can, to strive for accuracy, excellence and even perfection in our work. However, you must be realistic in your endeavor to do this. You should always do the best job you can, but at the same time you should avoid spinning your wheels by going to the extreme in always expecting total perfection of yourself. You are going to make occasional mistakes. Learn from them. Guard against wasting needless time. Give your best; then relax and don't worry about it. Interestingly enough, you will find that relaxing and being at ease with yourself will enable you to be freer and more productive.

8. Learn to delegate. Your first reaction to the word "delegate" is probably "to whom?" To the receptionist, office clerk or office courier? Yes. And delegate to someone you never thought of—another secretary. One of the most basic principles taught to management trainees is delegation. Although most legal secretaries are not in management positions, they do hold positions of heavy responsibility. Anyone with a great deal of responsibility can use assistance. Delegation is one way of obtaining this assistance.

Let's take the receptionist, for example. The work of most receptionists is light, especially those whose sole duty is to answer the telephone in a small- or medium-sized firm. Most conscientious receptionists would much rather be busy than try to look busy or sit around looking bored. If you have developed a good working relationship with the receptionist, and other clerical staff, then the chances are they will be glad to help you.

Try to give the receptionist or office clerk meaningful jobs that will allow them to utilize their creative or intellectual abilities and secretarial skills. If they don't have any secretarial skills then maybe they can learn from you. Don't just give them menial tasks. Give them a chance to learn to do something interesting. Perhaps, they want to advance to a legal secretarial position and with your help they can. Give them room to learn new skills. If the work you give them is a challenge, their egos may be nourished. *Warning—Don't overdelegate.* Always be sure you show your appreciation to the person who assists you. Let others see the chance to assist you as an opportunity for them to learn more about being a legal secretary.

Other more simplified and clerical jobs can be delegated to the file clerk or the office courier or mailroom clerk who is not tied down to a busy telephone. Perhaps, the clerk can make routine calls for you, verify addresses, type address labels or make Rolodex cards for you. The office courier can run errands such as going to the post office, delivering rush packages, or letters, or purchasing special supplies.

9. Don't procrastinate—do it! You may have, over the years, developed the unfortunate habit of procrastination. You do not need to have anyone tell you that it is a bad habit. You know it! But what can you do about it? How can you change this wasteful habit?

You must change your thinking to change the habit of procrastination. Instead of thinking: "This unpleasant task must be done, but I will do it tomorrow when I am more in the mood," think: "Although I know this is an unpleasant task, it will probably take less time to do it than to think about doing it, so I'll do it now; then I can do the things I enjoy." Often, if you will just pick one of the most unpleasant things you must do on your To Do list and make yourself do it the first thing in the morning, you will obtain a feeling of achievement. This will motivate you and make you want to finish your other work.

10. Increase your knowledge, skills and techniques. Working in the practical aspects of the law, you must constantly keep up with court rule changes, new court procedures, pleadings, forms of legal documents, and changes in civil procedure, among others. Keeping abreast of these changes is another way to better utilize and manage your time.

Increasing and broadening your knowledge and refining your secretarial skills, techniques and procedures in your day-to-day work will undoubtedly increase your output. As you become more knowledgeable and experienced in your area of expertise, it will take you less time to do your job. For example, time will be saved in some instances because you will no longer have to stop to look up a legal procedure or court rule. In addition, your increased knowledge and new skills will enable you to develop systems, procedures, and habits that will save you time.

Be alert to national and local legal secretarial continuing education seminars and classes. Many local and state legal secretarial associations conduct seminars on a regular basis. Also, business colleges, colleges, private associations, and businesses frequently advertise and hold valuable and worthwhile seminars. Attend as many of these seminars as you can. Check with your firm or your attorneys to see if they will cover the cost of the seminars. In many cases the cost of the seminars is tax deductible.

11. Improve your note-taking. One of the most valuable skills that you can develop in your job as a legal secretary is the ability to take good notes. It is not necessary for you to have the ability to take notes in shorthand since shorthand is not a required skill of most legal secretaries today. In fact, using shorthand in taking notes is oftentimes inefficient, because there is not always time to transcribe them, and your attorney may want you to do the task right away. Take brief, concise and readable notes so that you understand what it is you are supposed to do.

Find the note-taking method that will be the most comfortable and the easiest for you. Develop your own system of abbreviations or use the list given in the Appendix to save time. Take complete notes on everything, as previously mentioned. Again, you cannot always trust your memory, and it is easy to forget something when you are under pressure. You will definitely increase your efficiency by taking concise notes.

12. Monitor your social interactions. Often we do not realize how much time is wasted in small talk or gossip. While it is helpful to develop good interpersonal relations with office personnel, it is important to keep in mind the priorities of your work and not to let social amenities get out of hand. Successful people find that it is better not to become too personally involved in work relationships. Save your social activities for after work when you can enjoy them more.

13. Be observant and learn from others. One of the best ways to obtain new ideas is to observe and model other people and to learn from them. We all learn from each other. Observing efficient people may help you determine the secrets of their efficiency. Many times you can model the things you like in other persons and use their techniques for their success in their jobs.

Talking with other legal secretaries, paralegals, attorneys, and other law office personnel may give you good ideas on how to do things better, more efficiently, or even faster. Ask them questions. This is another good reason for attending legal secretarial association meetings and continuing education seminars. You can use this opportunity to exchange ideas with other legal secretaries and perhaps learn new methods, techniques or procedures. Or you can learn about new books, magazines and seminars that are available. If you have a particular problem or if you reach a stumbling block in your work, having a network of legal secretarial and paralegal friends is a good way to get new solutions to your work problems. Discuss it with another legal secretary, even one in another firm. This is a good way to find a possible solution or to discover valuable ideas that you may use.

14. Exercise self-discipline. It is a human trait to have difficulty getting started in a task, and sometimes it is even more difficult to finish it. To overcome this natural inertia, you will have to use extra push and energy.

By exercising self-discipline in your working habits, you can accomplish your goals more efficiently and expeditiously. One proven way to do this is to reward yourself when you exercise self-discipline and accomplish your goals. Buy yourself a new book or a plant for your office. Take a long walk at lunch and enjoy the fruits of your accomplishments in your mind.

15. Take regular work breaks. It is important to take frequent small periods of time during the day to relax. A coffee or a soda break serves this purpose well. However, sometimes you may find an occasional change of pace from periods of concentration in talking with clients or in conversations with office personnel. You should alternate short tasks with longer, more difficult tasks to break the monotony.

Plan your work schedule to suit your best work pattern. Some people work better with periods of continuous concentrated work, while others work in spurts of short, intensive work. Some people are morning people and can accomplish the more difficult tasks or projects early in the day, while others tend to get revved up in the late afternoon. Find the way you work best and learn to judge your fatigue level. For example, if you are a morning person, then schedule tasks that require more concentration for that time.

If you have heavy telephone duties, make it a point to get away from the telephone for short periods of time. Perhaps the main receptionist or switchboard operator can relieve you while you take a break.

It is is also a good idea to get out away from the office at lunch. Although there will be days when this is impossible, try to get out of the office as many days as you can. Window shopping or just enjoying the sunshine can lift your spirits and recharge your batteries for the rest of the day. If you always stay in and work during your lunch hour, it will soon be expected and when you do want to get away, your attorney will wonder why. It is really better for both of you to leave your desk and your office for at least an hour.

¶812 Simple Ways To Be More Organized

The purpose of this section is to help you discover your personal organizational habits and give you ideas on how you can improve them. Here are nine simple ways to be more organized:

1. Plan, organize, and schedule your work;
2. Organize and combine routine tasks;
3. Organize your desk and office to eliminate clutter;
4. Utilize office aids and equipment;
5. Make and use forms and checklists;
6. Handle paperwork and correspondence expeditiously;
7. Make an information notebook;
8. Develop a pleading form file; and
9. Keep a file index.

1. Plan, organize and schedule your work. One of the best ways of planning your work is to make lists of things to be done, often referred to as "To Do" lists. Another thing you must do is to learn to set priorities. Make lists on a long-term, monthly, weekly, and daily basis in the following manner. Of course, much of your work cannot be organized this way, but try to organize as much of your routine and anticipated work in this manner. (See ¶803.)

Long-Term:

Make a list of long-term projects and goals. If you currently do not have any outstanding projects or assignments, then set some long-term goals, which may include personal work-related and management goals. Examples of good long-term goals are:

- Organizing and indexing form files;
- Reorganizing filing system;
- Developing systems and procedures to expedite work;
- Improving dictation or shorthand skills; and
- Programming new forms on the word processor.

It is best to set a time limit and/or priority for these goals. Separate each long-term goal or project into smaller portions. Then allocate a part of your time each month for a separate portion of the project. Set mini-deadlines for each segment. Add the initial portion of the project or goal to your first month's list. Then after you complete the first part, add the next to the following month and so on. Review this long-term list periodically to revise your projects or goals, realign your priorities, or add new ones.

Monthly:

At the beginning of each month, make a list of work projects that are due for that month or that you want to accomplish for that month. Sometimes this list will be short since you may not always know in advance what projects you will have that month. Use this list to make notations of your attorneys' scheduled trials, hearings, depositions, meetings, document productions, and other prescheduled functions. Noting these on a monthly list will help you remember your time commitment for that month and assist you in planning your work accordingly. Add new items as they are scheduled.

Weekly:

At the beginning of each week, make a list of the work projects you must complete for that week, indicating the day they must be completed. Then number each according to its priority or the order in which each project is to be completed (see ¶803).

Daily:

Each afternoon before you leave for the day, make a list of the things you must do the next day. Write down only those tasks that have to be done tomorrow, numbering them by priority. Estimate how much time you think each assignment will take. If you anticipate an assignment will take longer than a day, and it is not due immediately, enter it on your list, allocating a portion of time for it each succeeding day. The next morning after you open your attorneys' mail, review the list and add any additional items that need to be done promptly. Check your calendar and your attorneys' calendars to make sure that you have included all their projects as well as your projects that you must work on that day. Refer to your long-term monthly and weekly lists when reviewing your daily lists.

Time-Available Basis:
Make another list of miscellaneous tasks that can be done at any time or on a time-available basis. These will usually be low-priority tasks that you might do when your attorneys are out of the office. Give these items a priority on the basis of their importance. Be sure to include even the most minute tasks. Add new items as they arise. Delete completed items as they are accomplished.

2. *Organize and combine routine tasks.* Many of you may have to do a lot of routine tasks and errands such as obtaining or ordering your own supplies or delivering or picking up your work from the word processing room, mail room, or copy room, and so on.

To save time, you should be alert for ways in which you can combine routine tasks. For example, coordinate your interoffice errands. If you work in an office which occupies several floors, anticipate your visits to different floors. Keep a tray or a place on your desk for accumulating notes which concern interoffice errands. Make each trip productive by delivering or picking up as many items as you can at the same time. Of course, if you have an interoffice delivery system, you will not have this problem, but many times you may want to handle certain things yourself.

Note the supplies you need so that when you go to the supply room, you obtain all the items you need in one trip. Making a list will prevent you from forgetting something and having to make another trip. If you know another secretary that you can take turns with in doing these tasks, by all means share the responsibility.

Some law offices do not have the convenience of an attorney service company which handles the filing of court documents and other routine errands. Thus, a secretary may be assigned these tasks. Be sure you get all the information you need for filing a court document or handling an errand. A handy Courthouse Filing Request Form and an Errand Request Form (Figures 811-1 and 811-2, respectively) follow.

Courthouse Filing Request

Client Name: ______________________ **Client No.:** __________

Responsible Attorney(s): ________________ **Date:** __________

Case Title: ______________________________________

v.

____

Document To Be Filed: ______________________________

Date To Be Filed: ____________________ **Court:** __________

Return Conformed Copy to: __________________________
(name of attorney, paralegal, or secretary)

Other Instructions: ______________________________
____
____
____
____

Signed: ________________
(name of person making request)

Conformed Copy Returned With This Request to: __________

Date of Filing: __________ **Time of Filing:** __________ (.m.)

Remarks: ______________________________________
____
____
____

Signed: ________________
(name of person handling request)

Figure 811.1 Courthouse Filing Request.

ERRAND RUN REQUEST

DATE: ______ REQUESTED BY ______ TIME Rush ______
2:00 Run ____
4:00 Run ____
Other ____

ERRAND IS (check category): DRIVING ____ WALKING ____

ERRAND IS (check category): PICK UP ____ DELIVER ____
BOTH ____

MATERIAL IS (check one): ATTACHED ____ SEE ATTORNEY ____
SEE SECRETARY ____

DESTINATION OF ERRAND: SPECIAL INSTRUCTIONS:

______________________ ______________________

______________________ ______________________

______________________ ______________________

______________________ ______________________

CHARGE TO: CLIENT NUMBER: ______ FIRM EXPENSE: ______

CLIENT NAME: ______________________

WORK COMPLETED: DATE ____________ BY ____________

COMMENTS ______________________

____________ CHARGES: ____________

Figure 811.2 Errand Run Request Form.

They will help you to get your attorneys to give you all the necessary information to file documents properly and take care of errands. They avoid inefficient oral directions or illegible handwritten notes and also serve as written reminders to you. Also use these forms to give the courier proper information.

3. Organize your desk and office to eliminate clutter. Your desk is your primary working area. It should be kept organized at all times. Keep your desk clear and free of clutter. Clutter distracts and can create tension and frustration, as well as a feeling of being disorganized and "snowed under." You may find that if you remove personal articles from your desk, such as knick-knacks, family photos, souvenirs, and other trinkets, you will have more working space and less visual distraction. Keep only the materials and files with which you are currently working on your desk. Keep your pens and pencils in a container in your desk. Use In and Out trays to prevent accumulation of paper. Keeping your desk clear will give the impression of neatness and efficiency, will help you think more clearly, concentrate more easily, and will help you feel more organized. A desk scattered with too much paperwork will not impress others and make them think you are very busy, but rather it will make you look disorganized and disheveled.

Look around your work area and ask yourself if there is anything that is there that you can do without. Do not have files in your area unless they are in the filing cabinet, or unless you are currently working on them. Return those files with which you are not currently working to the file room. Do not let other office personnel store their files in your work area. Ask them if you can store them in the filing room or elsewhere. Too many files scattered about your work area will tend to give clients and others the impression of being disorganized. Keep your work area orderly at all times.

4. Utilize office aids and equipment. There are many office aids that will help you be more organized and do your job more efficiently. Calendars, diary appointment and address books, business card files and Rolodex™ systems are invaluable for recording information and having it accessible. Make good use of a tickler system (see ¶1500).

Make use of office equipment such as transcribers, tape recorders, calculators, adding machines, and personal computers or word processors whenever you can. For example, personal computers can be invaluable in maintaining your attorneys' time and billing records. (See ¶1100.) Another example, calculators can be invaluable in computing interest on a promissory note or figuring damages in a personal injury action.

When using dictation transcribers, it is important that you ask your attorneys to use efficient dictation techniques or they may waste a lot of your valuable time (see ¶809).

5. Make and use forms and checklists. Review the various forms, checklists, charts, and graphs in this book and use those that are helpful to you. Look for other forms and checklists that will systematize and organize your work. Create your own forms and checklists that will be pertinent to your work. If you find that you often gather the same information on certain files, make a form that will help you record that information systematically. Standardize your work in every way possible. Creating your own forms and checklists can be both fun and practical.

6. Handle paperwork and correspondence expeditiously. Review your attorneys' mail quickly and separate it for them. Discard anything that they have told you that you have permission to get rid of. Many attorneys instruct their secretaries to throw away all junk mail; others want to keep everything.

Divide the mail into separate stacks, such as:

1. Correspondence from clients and other attorneys
2. Pleadings and court documents
3. Interoffice memoranda
4. Seminar brochures
5. Junk mail, advertisements, etc.
6. Personal
7. Files and invoices regarding client disbursements

You might want to put these in separate folders for your attorneys if they prefer this method. If not, just stack these materials in the order of their importance, with the junk mail being on the bottom of the stack, and put them on the middle of their desks or wherever they instruct you to put it.

7. *Make an information notebook and use other reference materials.* There are many details that you must know in handling legal documents and papers that you frequently refer to, such as information regarding local court rules, filing fees, number of copies required of certain documents, service of process information, names of judges, calendar clerks, and attorneys.

You will find it extremely helpful to compile a notebook containing this necessary information and any other information that you need frequently. A letter-sized or small three-ring binder is good for this purpose. It will soon become your office bible. You might ask the other experienced legal secretaries in your office if they have already compiled any of this information and if you could copy it. Index the separate categories of information. For example, your notebook might contain the following information:

- Frequently applied local, federal and state Supreme Court rules;
- Marshal/sheriff or attorney service of process information;
- Notes regarding pleadings, such as number of copies and pleading "court backs" required;
- Garnishment and attachment procedure information;
- Notes regarding frequently used codes of civil procedure;
- Letter-size maps of counties in your state (you may be able to obtain this from the public information department of your state capitol);
- Relevant information regarding your Secretary of State's corporation department and telephone numbers for checking registered agents for service of process; and

- Notes regarding obtaining police and automobile accident reports, driver's license information, death certificates and other vital statistics. Keep the telephone numbers and addresses.

Inasmuch as court rules, filing fees, civil procedures, etc., change from time to time, be sure to keep your notebook current. Many states have printed official directories of state and county offices available. Check with your Secretary of State's office. Many city and county government offices also have various printed materials which may be helpful. Additionally, you can copy the following helpful telephone numbers and addresses out of the telephone book to put in your notebook:

- City, county, state and federal government agencies, including courts and names of judges;
- Local attorneys;
- Local physicians and hospitals (for personal injury matters);
- Area codes and local dialing prefixes; and
- Long distance calling information.

Your dictionary is another reference book from which you can copy handy information to include in your notebook. However, as you know, this book is copyrighted and should only be copied for your personal use. Most good dictionaries have the following helpful information:

- Proofreader's marks
- General guides to marks of punctuation
- Abbreviations and symbols
- Names of colleges and universities
- Names of large cities
- Names of foreign countries

Of course, you may find other helpful information to include in your notebook, such as English writing and usage tips, rules of hyphenation, and lists of spelling of cities and states, along with zip code information. As time goes on, you will accumulate more and more valuable information.

Other reference materials which you may find useful to keep in your office are: a law dictionary, thesaurus, and medical dictionary; Latin terms and phrases; an accounting reference book; miscellaneous handbooks and law books in various areas of law such as research, civil procedure, real estate, torts, evidence, bankruptcy, creditors' rights and remedies, criminal law, administrative agencies, domestic relations, tax, business law, corporations, trust, wills and estates. These handbooks and law books may now be used only by your attorneys, but if you have them handy and have an opportunity to have a more advanced project, you can refer to them. If you are striving to become a paralegal, the more information and reference sources you can accumulate, the more opportunity you will have to learn.

8. Develop form files. A good legal secretary knows the inherent value of a court paper (sometimes referred to as a pleading) form file. This file may contain sample forms of pleadings and other documents which are to be filed with the court in a legal action. They will include complaints and answers, and may also include interrogatories and other discovery documents, as well as motions and notices. It is almost a necessity that you develop and accumulate a pleading form file not only for your attorneys but also, for your reference purposes in preparing those documents.

Every time you type a new pleading or court paper that you expect to use again, although it may need changes, you should make a copy of it and insert it into your form file. You may want to have separate indexed file folders for each type of court paper such as pleadings, interrogatories, requests for admissions, motions, etc., in which to insert these samples loosely (see ¶700). Perhaps, you may prefer to bind the sample forms together and index them. If your office utilizes word processors, you can record the sample court papers or other pleadings for future use. It is best to number and index the sample forms to make them easily accessible.

Of course, if your attorneys do not do any litigation and are corporate or real estate attorneys, then your form files will be entirely different, but they will be organized under the same principle and the techniques discussed here will apply. Your form files for such attorneys may contain sample articles of incorporation, meeting notices, by-laws, minutes, resolutions, mortgages, deeds, promissory notes or others.

You should also make a form file for letters that you prepare repetitively, such as transmittal letters to court clerks and recorders, routine collection letters, medical authorizations, letters requesting corporation, medical, and policy report information, or any other type of routine letter that you frequently prepare.

Regardless of what type of law your attorneys practice, you should learn to organize and keep form files whether they be corporate, real estate, bankruptcy, labor law, or any other type of law.

9. Keep a file index. In addition to your New Client Memorandum (or New File Memorandum), it is very helpful to keep either a card index, Rolodex,™ or a separate list of all the client files on which you work. These may be on your word processor or in a more elaborate electronic data system in large offices as well. On these records, indicate the client name, matter, file number, adverse party, responsible attorney, court file number and other relevant information. This index should include all open files on which your attorneys work. Cross-index this information by adverse party, or by related or similar names. For example, if your client, Harold Jameson, has a civil action pending against ABC Corporation doing business as (d/b/a) "Ready Concrete," you would cross-index the file under "Ready Concrete" and "ABC Corporation." If your client's name is Lynda Pittman, formerly known as (f/k/a) "Lynda Stadille," you would cross-index her former name, "Lynda Stadille." (See ¶1400 for further discussion of file setup procedure.)

¶900 Accounting and Bookkeeping Made Simple

by Carole A. Bruno and Paula F. Turner

Chances are you may never have to be concerned with accounting for your firm's financial transactions. However, if you are a legal secretary in a small firm or work for a sole practitioner, you may very well be involved in the day-to-day recordkeeping. That is all accounting is—keeping records. Records must be kept of money coming into the firm and money going out.

¶901 Fundamental Accounting Principles

There is one fundamental accounting principle that you should know: *For every debit there must be a credit.* Debits and credits are not really hard to understand.

Accountants use a concept of the "account." An account is a group of similar transactions, i.e., a checking account is made up of deposits and checks for one individual firm. A client's account consists of bills sent and payments made for that client. An expense account is a summary of all checks written to pay that type of expense, i.e., salaries. "Secretarial Salary Expense" is the sum of all payroll checks written for secretaries' salaries for a certain period.

The transactions of a law firm cause increases and decreases in the accounts of the firm. A separate account is used to record all transactions of a similar nature.

An account is sometimes explained by the use of a "T-account" (see Figure 901-1).

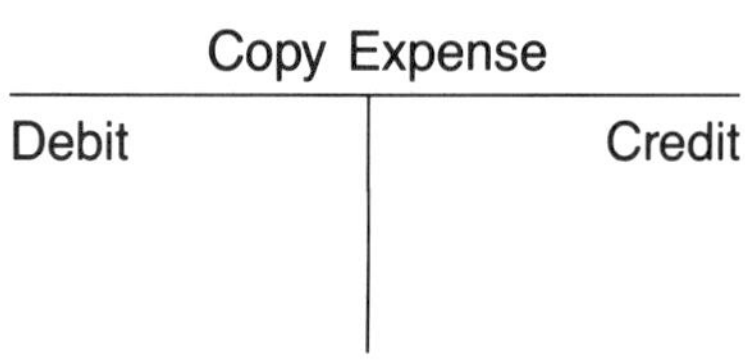

Figure 901-1. T-account.

Notice that it is shaped like a "T." The T separates the left side from the right and provides a place to write the name of the account, Copy Expense, at the top. A debit is an entry to the left side of a T-account, a credit is an entry to the right side.

Example: If you write a check to pay for the rent on the copy machine in your office for $300, a debit would be made to the left side of the Copy Expense Account. Remembering the rule *for every debit there must be a credit* you would have to make a credit to some other account. Most transactions include either a debit or credit to the checking account, since they involve either receiving or spending cash using a check. Therefore, since you spent $300 with a check, you would "credit" cash for $300. Now picture two T-accounts like this (see Figure 901-2).

Figure 901-2. Two T-accounts.

The difference between the debits and credits in an account will give you the account's balance. This balance represents the dollar amount of what the firm has spent, owns, or owes at the time the balance is figured.

You will not actually see T-accounts in your firm's bookkeeping system, although some recordkeeping books are similar to T-accounts. T-accounts are only used to explain the concept of debits and credits.

¶901.1 What Kind of Accounts Does a Law Firm Use?

A law firm uses several different kinds of accounts in recording its transactions. The accounts look the same. Only the name identifies the type of account it is.

1. *Asset accounts* are used to record transactions that reflect increases or decreases in the assets of the firm. Assets are what the firm owns: cash, equipment, furniture, etc. The normal balance in an asset account is a debit.

2. *Liability accounts* are used to record transactions that reflect increases or decreases in the liabilities of the firm. Liabilities are what the firm owes: notes payable, payroll taxes, and other debts. The normal balance in a liability account is a credit.

3. *Capital accounts* are used to record transactions which reflect increases or decreases in the partners' capital invested in the firm. Capital is the amount of money or other equity the partners have contributed to the firm. Capital is used to buy such things as office furniture and equipment and to pay the expenses of operation if there are not sufficient legal fees collected to cover them. The normal balance in a partner's capital account is a credit.

Some law firms are professional corporations rather than partnerships. The partners in a professional corporation are technically shareholders, but are often referred to as partners. Professional corporations have common stock, paid in capital and retained earnings accounts instead of partner capital accounts. The normal balance in these accounts is also a credit.

4. *Revenue accounts* are used to record transactions which reflect increases or decreases in revenues, sometimes called income. Most revenues in a law firm come from legal fees collected from clients. The normal balance in a revenue account is a credit.

5. *Expense accounts* are used to record transactions which reflect increases or decreases in the expenses of the firm. Expenses are the goods and services which the firm consumes when it operates. The normal balance in an expense account is a debit.

Every time you receive money from a client or other source, you will debit the account that represents the bank in which the money was deposited. Remember, you must then credit some account, usually "Legal Fees Received."

Every time you or one of your attorneys write a check, you should debit some account, usually an expense account. The corresponding credit will be to the checking account.

There are also other types of transactions to be handled. It is impossible to explain accounting procedures in depth in a few short pages. However, most firms use bookkeeping systems that are easy to learn, even if you don't understand fully how it works.

¶902 What Are Books Anyway?

In general, law firm accounting records consist of documents such as invoices, bank statements, cancelled checks, deposit slips, insurance policies, etc. These documents provide detailed information and evidence of the firm's financial transactions.

Most law firms have several books, called *journals* or *ledgers,* where the details of these financial transactions are recorded. These books contain a record of the transactions in chronological order and show, among other things, which accounts should be debited or credited. The firm's books may be kept manually, writing each transaction in by hand, or they may be kept by typing in the details of the transactions on a computer. In many firms, the books are a combination, some manual, some computerized. Many small firms use "one-write" systems that record transactions on the client ledger card and journal pages at the same time a check is written (see Figure 902-1).

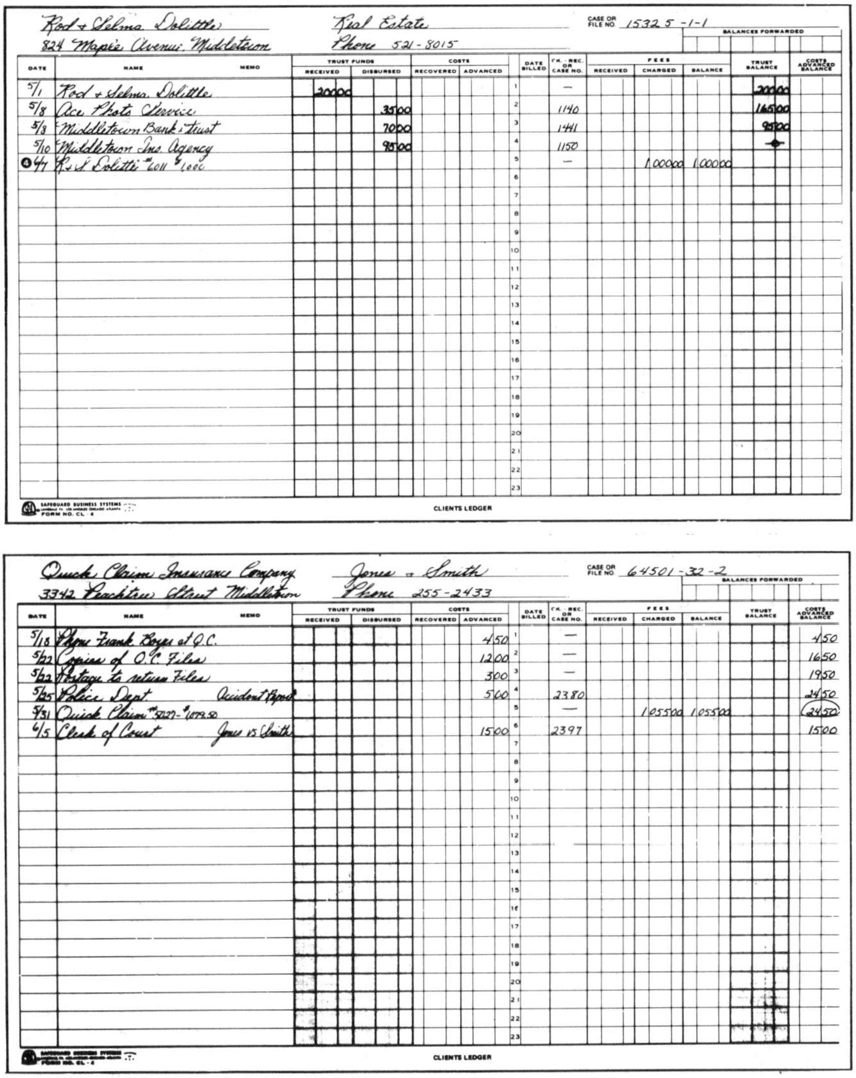

Rod + Selma Dolittle — 824 Maple Avenue, Middletown — Real Estate — Phone 521-8015 — CASE OR FILE NO. 1532 5-1-1

DATE	NAME	MEMO	TRUST FUNDS RECEIVED	TRUST FUNDS DISBURSED	COSTS RECOVERED	COSTS ADVANCED		DATE BILLED	CK.-REC. OR CASE NO.	FEES RECEIVED	FEES CHARGED	FEES BALANCE	TRUST BALANCE	COSTS ADVANCED BALANCE
5/1	Rod + Selma Dolittle		200 00				1		—				200 00	
5/8	Ace Photo Service			35 00			2		1140				165 00	
5/8	Middletown Bank + Trust			70 00			3		1141				95 00	
5/10	Middletown Ins. Agency			95 00			4		1150				-0-	
6/7	R + S Dolittle #6011 $1000						5		—		1,000 00	1,000 00		

CLIENTS LEDGER — SAFEGUARD BUSINESS SYSTEMS — FORM NO. CL-4

Quick Claim Insurance Company — 3342 Peachtree Street Middletown — Jones v Smith — Phone 255-2433 — CASE OR FILE NO. 64501-32-2

DATE	NAME	MEMO	TRUST FUNDS RECEIVED	TRUST FUNDS DISBURSED	COSTS RECOVERED	COSTS ADVANCED		DATE BILLED	CK.-REC. OR CASE NO.	FEES RECEIVED	FEES CHARGED	FEES BALANCE	TRUST BALANCE	COSTS ADVANCED BALANCE
5/18	Phone Frank Boyer at Q.C.					4 50	1		—					4 50
5/22	Copies of Q.C. Files					12 00	2		—					16 50
5/22	Postage to return Files					3 00	3		—					19 50
5/25	Police Dept.	Accident Report				5 00	4		2380					24 50
5/31	Quick Claim #5027-$1079.50						5		—		1,055 00	1,055 00		(24 50)
6/5	Clerk of Court	Jones vs Smith				15 00	6		2397					15 00

CLIENTS LEDGER — SAFEGUARD BUSINESS SYSTEMS — FORM NO. CL-4

Figure 902-1. Client Ledger Card. Forms courtesy of Safeguard Business Systems, Inc., Fort Washington, PA.

The books of a law firm, whether manual or computerized, usually consist of the following journals or ledgers:

1. Cash receipts journal: Every time a check is received from a client to pay for legal services or to reimburse the firm for costs advanced, the date and amount of the check should be recorded in the cash receipts journal along with the client's name and matter description. The firm occasionally receives money from nonclients, which should also be recorded in this journal. The normal entry will be to debit Cash—Checking Account and to credit Legal Fees Received (see Figures 902-2 and 902-3).

2. Cash disbursements journal: Every time a check is written on one of the firm's checking accounts, it should be recorded in the cash disbursements journal. The normal entry will be to debit the account that best describes the transaction and to credit Cash—Checking Account (see Figures 902-4 and 902-5).

A separate cash disbursements journal is usually kept for trust account checks since money held in trust for clients should be kept in a separate bank account (see Figure 902-6).

3. Payroll journal: Payroll checks are often written from a separate account and recorded in a payroll journal that is designed to easily record the salary and payroll taxes withheld from an employee's check. Sometimes, the payroll journal is part of the cash disbursements journal. If a separate payroll journal is used, only payroll checks should be recorded in it.

4. Fees charged journal: When a bill is sent to a client, it is sometimes recorded on a fees charged journal. The amount of fees and disbursements are usually separately recorded. Sometimes the fees charged journal is combined with the cash receipts journal (see Figure 902-3).

5. General journal: Any transaction that does not logically belong in one of the above journals is usually recorded in a general journal. These transactions arise because either money was not received, or a check was not written. Examples of general journal transactions are the recording of interest earned on a savings account, depreciation entries or correction of errors.

6. General ledger: The general ledger is a summarization of all of the entries made in the other journals used by the firm. The details of transactions are kept in the general ledger through a process called *posting*. The total of activity in each account is transferred to the general ledger. A separate page is maintained for each account on the chart of accounts if a manual system is used. Many computerized general ledger systems maintain the detail of transactions in the general ledger (see Figures 902-5 and 902-6).

CASH RECEIVED AND FEES CHARGED SYSTEM WITH CLIENT LEDGER

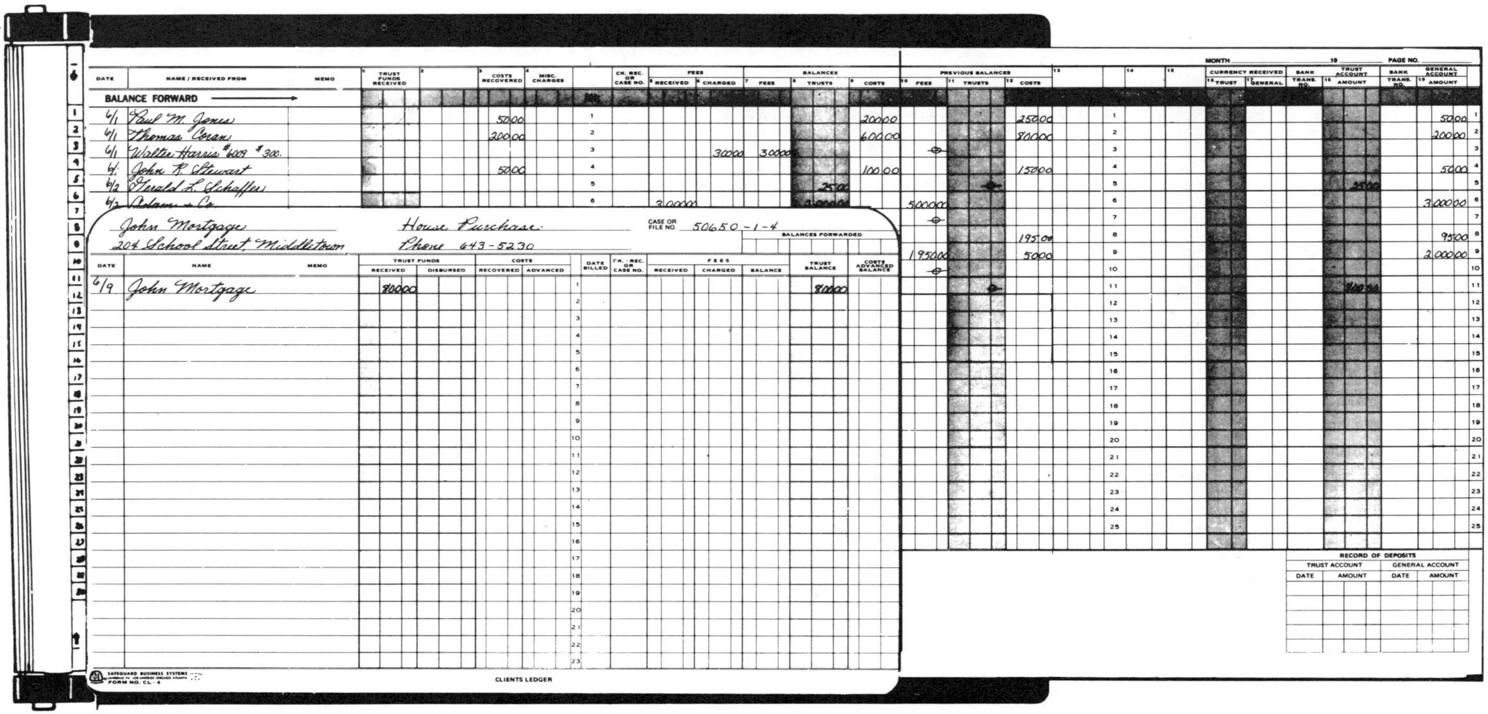

Figure 902-2. Fees Charged Journal. Forms courtesy of Safeguard Business Systems, Inc., Fort Washington, PA.

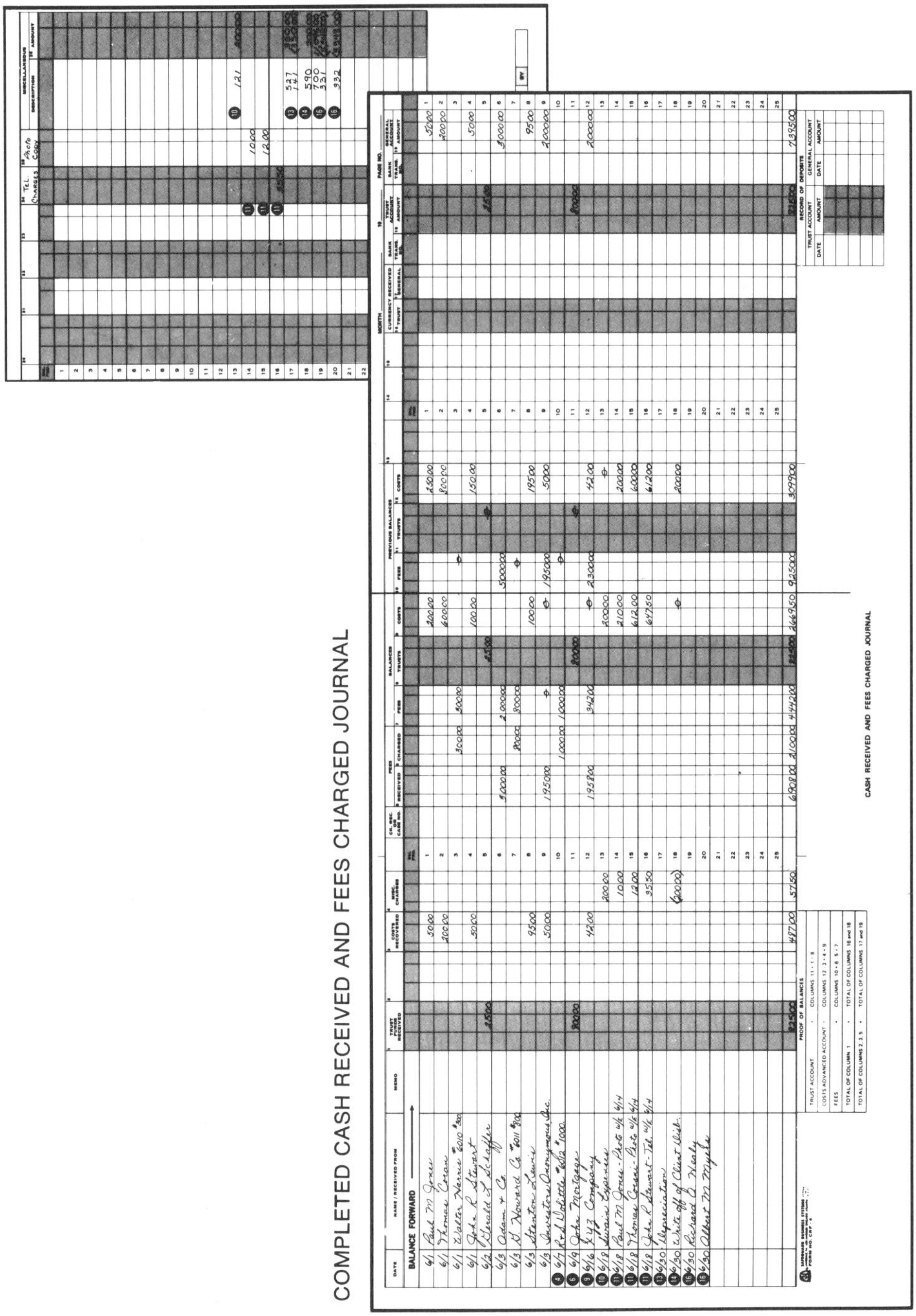

Figure 902-3. Completed Cash Received and Fees Charged Journal. Forms courtesy of Safeguard Business Systems, Inc., Fort Washington, PA.

CASH DISBURSEMENT SYSTEM WITH CLIENT LEDGER—GENERAL ACCOUNT

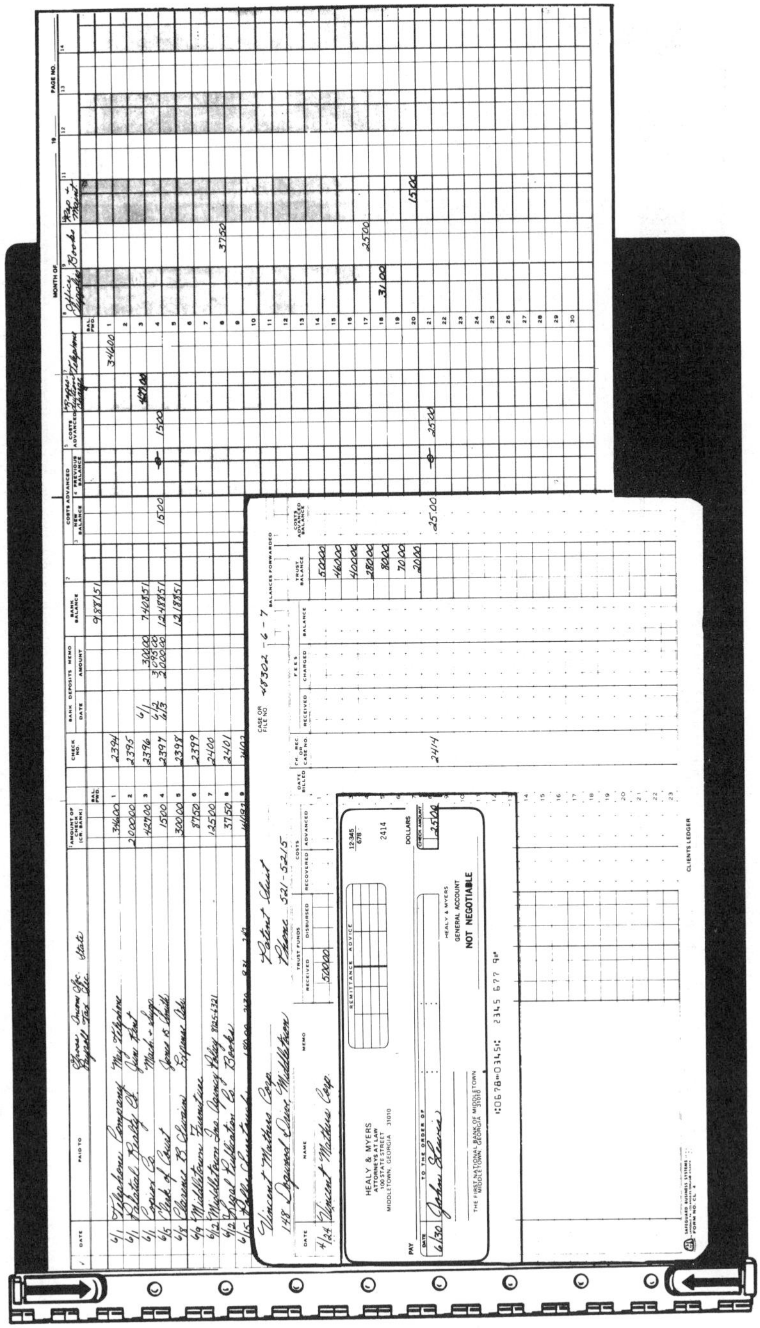

Figure 902-4. Cash Disbursements Journal. Forms courtesy of Safeguard Business Systems, Inc., Fort Washington, PA.

COMPLETED DISBURSEMENTS JOURNAL—GENERAL ACCOUNT

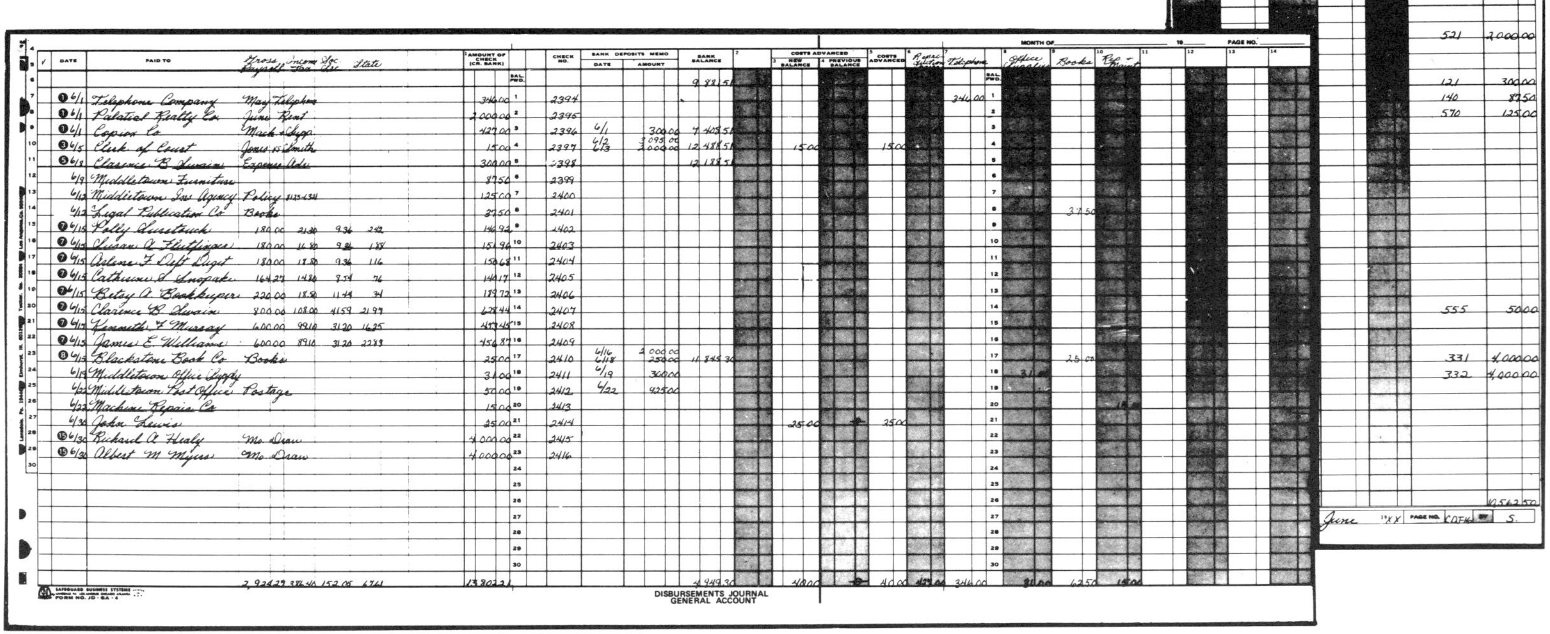

Line	Date	Paid To	Gross Payroll / Memo	Income Tax	Soc. Sec.	State	Amount of Check (Cr. Bank)	Bal. Fwd.	Check No.	Bank Deposits Memo Date	Amount	Bank Balance
												9,881.51
①	6/1	Telephone Company	May Telephone				346.00	1	2394			
①	6/1	Palatial Realty Co	June Rent				2,000.00	2	2395			
①	6/1	Copier Co	Mach + Supp.				427.00	3	2396	6/1	300.00	7,408.51
③	6/5	Clerk of Court	Jones vs Smith				15.00	4	2397	6/2 6/3	3,095.00 2,000.00	12,488.51
⑤	6/8	Clarence B Swain	Expense Adv.				300.00	5	2398			12,188.51
	6/9	Middletown Furniture					87.50	6	2399			
	6/12	Middletown Ins Agency	Policy #125-634				125.00	7	2400			
	6/12	Legal Publication Co	Books				37.50	8	2401			
⑦	6/15	Polly Lusetouch	180.00	21.30	9.36	2.42	146.92	9	2402			
⑦	6/15	Susan A Flutfingers	180.00	16.80	9.36	1.88	151.96	10	2403			
⑦	6/15	Arlene F Deft Digit	180.00	18.80	9.36	1.16	150.68	11	2404			
⑦	6/15	Catherine S Snoopake	164.27	14.80	8.54	.76	140.17	12	2405			
⑦	6/15	Betsy A Bookkeeper	220.00	18.50	11.44	.34	189.72	13	2406			
⑦	6/15	Clarence B Swain	800.00	108.00	41.59	21.97	628.44	14	2407			
⑦	6/15	Kenneth F Murray	600.00	99.10	31.20	16.25	453.45	15	2408			
⑦	6/15	James E. Williams	600.00	89.10	31.20	22.83	456.87	16	2409			
⑧	6/15	Blackstone Book Co	Books				25.00	17	2410	6/16 6/18	2,000.00 250.00	11,845.30
	6/18	Middletown Office Supply					31.00	18	2411	6/19	300.00	
	6/22	Middletown Post Office	Postage				50.00	19	2412	6/22	425.00	
	6/22	Machine Repair Co					15.00	20	2413			
	6/30	John Lewis					25.00	21	2414			
⑮	6/30	Richard A Healy	Mo. Draw				4,000.00	22	2415			
⑮	6/30	Albert M Myers	Mo. Draw				4,000.00	23	2416			
			2,924.29	386.40	152.05	67.61	13,802.21					4,949.30

Line	Costs Advanced New Balance	Costs Advanced	Repair & Upkeep	Telephone	Office Supplies	Books	Rep. + Maint.	Misc. Description	Misc. Amount
1				346.00				521	2,000.00
3								121	300.00
3								140	87.50
4	15.00	15.00						570	125.00
8						37.50			
14								555	50.00
17						25.00		331	4,000.00
18					31.00			332	4,000.00
20							15.00		
21	25.00	25.00							
Totals	40.00	40.00	471.00	346.00	31.00	62.50	15.00		10,562.50

June 19XX Page No. 5

DISBURSEMENTS JOURNAL GENERAL ACCOUNT

SAFEGUARD BUSINESS SYSTEMS FORM NO. JD-GA-4

Figure 902-5. Completed Disbursements Journal. Forms courtesy of Safeguard Business Systems, Inc., Fort Washington, PA.

COMPLETED DISBURSEMENT JOURNAL—TRUST ACCOUNT

DATE	PAID TO	MEMO	AMOUNT OF CHECK (CR. BANK)	BANK DEPOSIT MEMO DATE	BANK DEPOSIT MEMO AMOUNT		CHECK NO.	BANK BALANCE		TRUST BALANCE	PREVIOUS TRUST BALANCE	DEBIT TRUST ACCT.	
						BAL. FWD.		6 103 20					
6/27	Clerk of Court	Filing Fee	15 00			1	1214		Alan Adams	485 00	500 00		1
6/27	Lawyers Service Co.	Serve Papers	12 00			2	1215		Chas. Solo	588 00	600 00		2
6/27	Middletown News	Third Notice	10 00	6/27	900 00	3	1216	6 966 20	Ronald Clark	65 00	75 00		3
6/28	Middletown Realty	Down Payment	100 00			4	1217		Gerald Schaffer	400 00	500 00		4
6/28	Crest Photo Service	Car Photo's	30 00			5	1218		John Stewart	30 00	60 00		5
6/28	Mr. + Mrs. Paul Jones	Property Damage	150 00			6	1219		Ronald Peters	700 00	850 00		6
6/28	ABC Brokers	Brokers Fee	200 00			7	1220		John Adams	⊖	200 00		7
6/28	Middletown Clinic	Physical Exam	25 00			8	1221	6 461 20	Adam Wise	75 00	100 00		8
6/29	Middletown Police Dept.	Accident Report	3 00	6/29	1 405 00	9	1222	7 863 20	Lee West	27 00	30 00		9
6/30	John Eye	Witness Fee	15 00			10	1223		John Smith	1 165 00	1 180 00		10
6/30	Healy + Myers	Client Dist. + Fee	875 00			11	1224		Adam Smith	⊖	875 00		11
6/30	Martin Beason	Settlement	600 00			12	1225		Martin Beason	1 200 00	1 800 00		12
6/30	Paul Aurt	Witness Fee + Cost	50 00			13	1226		Adam Wise	550 00	600 00		13
6/30	Clerk of Court	Filing Fee	15 00			14	1227		Vincent Mathers Corp.	5 00	20 00		14
6/30	Home Developers	Downpayment	800 00	6/30	150 00	15	1228	5 658 20	John Mortgage	200 00	1 000 00		15
								5 658 20					

SAFEGUARD BUSINESS SYSTEMS — FORM NO. JD · TA · 4

DISBURSEMENTS JOURNAL TRUST ACCOUNT

MONTH OF June 197X PAGE NO. 2 BY [illegible]

Figure 902-6. Trust Account Journal. Forms courtesy of Safeguard Business Systems, Inc., Fort Washington, PA.

The balances in the general ledger are computed, either by hand or electronically, by adding the current month's debits and credits to the previous month's balance to arrive at a new year-to-date balance. These balances are then used to prepare financial statements (see Figure 902-7).

¶903 A Typical Law Firm Chart of Accounts

A Chart of Accounts is simply a listing of all the names of the accounts used by the firm in its bookkeeping system. To keep from having to write out the name of an account every time a transaction is recorded in it, most firms assign numbers to the accounts. If the firm is using a computer to keep track of its transactions a numbering system is always necessary.

Figure 903-1 shows a typical law firm Chart of Accounts. It is patterned after a Chart of Accounts prepared by the American Bar Association. If you are setting up the books for a new firm, or need to improve the bookkeeping system in your firm, you should consider using this Chart of Accounts. The accounts are grouped in a way which will provide meaningful information to the attorneys in the firm who are responsible for managing the firm's business, rather than alphabetically. Also, it is easier to compare your firm's operations to other firms who use a similar Chart of Accounts. Many economic surveys are done by state bar associations and accounting firms with the results reported in the same format as this Chart of Accounts.

ASSETS

100–000 *Cash*

- 100–001 Bank account #1
- 100–002 Bank account #2
- 100–003 Bank account #3
- 100–025 Savings account
- 100–075 Petty cash

110–000 *Client trust funds*

- 110–001 Client trust funds

120–000 *Short-term investments*

- 120–001 Marketable securities

Figure 903-1. Chart of Accounts.

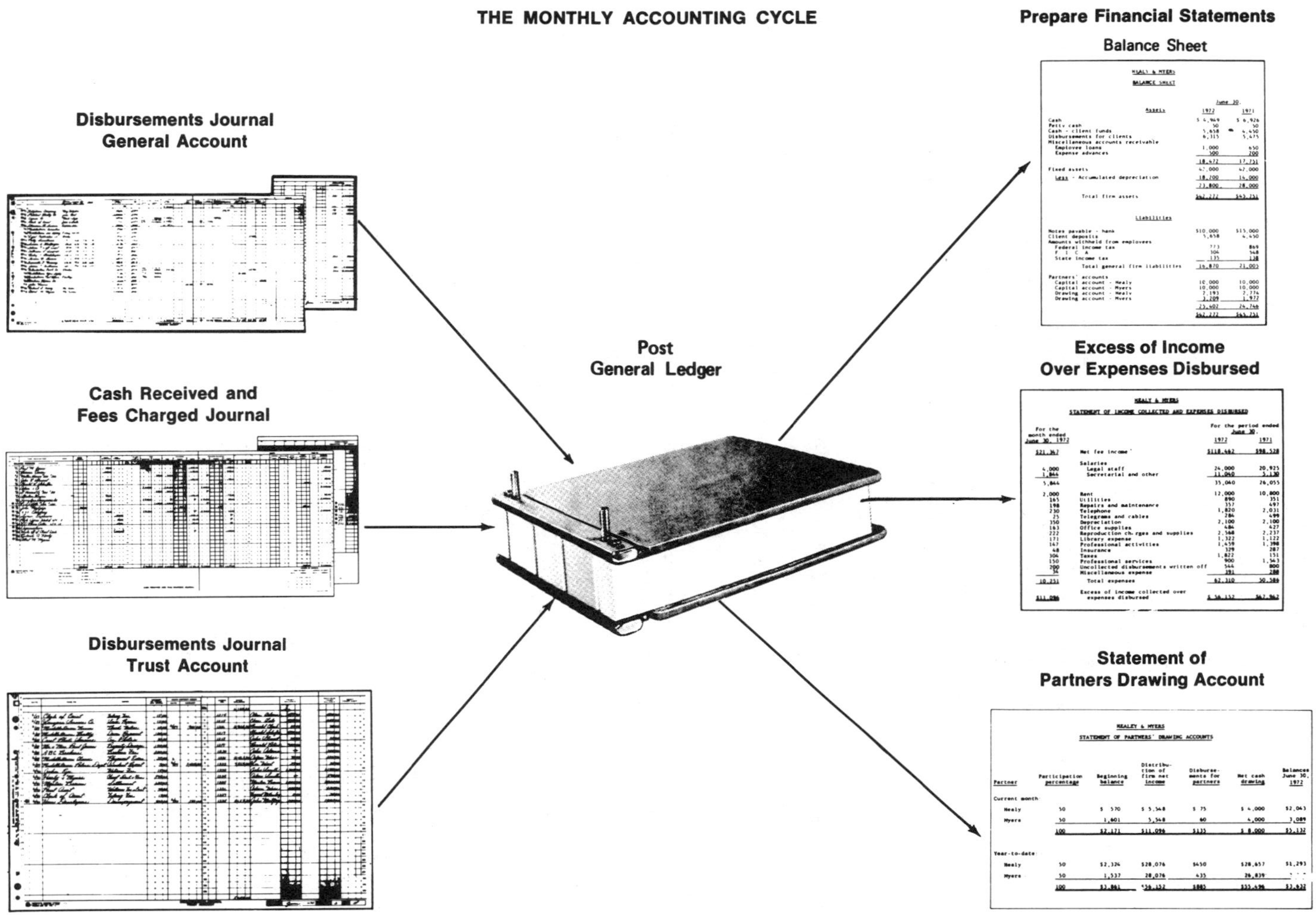

Figure 902-7. Monthly Accounting Cycle. Forms courtesy of Safeguard Business Systems, Inc., Fort Washington, PA.

130–000 *Costs advanced*

130–001 Costs advanced—Billed
130–002 Costs advanced—Unbilled

140–000 *Other accounts receivable*

140–001 Employee advances—Partner A
140–002 Employee advances—Partner B
140–003 Employee advances—Associate A
140–004 Employee advances—Associate B
140–100 Deposits (refundable)
140–101 Employee notes and loans receivable
140–102 Miscellaneous receivables

150–000 *Fixed assets*

150–001 Furniture and fixtures
150–002 Office equipment
150–003 Leasehold improvements

160–000 *Reserve for depreciation*

160–001 Reserve for depreciation—furniture and fixtures
160–002 Reserve for amortization—office equipment
160–003 Reserve for amortization—leasehold improvements

170–00 *Other assets*

LIABILITIES AND PARTNERS' CAPITAL

300–000 *Notes payable—current*

300–001 Bank loans—current
300–002 Other loans payable—current

310–000 *Accounts payable and other liabilities*

310–001 Accrued expenses—billable to clients
310–002 Group insurance deductions
310–003 Other payroll deductions

320–000 *Payroll tax liability*

320–001 Federal income tax withheld
320–002 State income tax withheld
320–003 Employee FICA tax withheld

Figure 903-1. (continued)

	320–004	Employer FICA tax accrued
	320–005	Federal unemployment tax accrued
	320–006	State unemployment tax accrued
330–000	*Liability for client funds*	
	330–001	Liability for client trust funds
340–00	*Client deposits and other credit balances*	
	340–001	Retainers and deposits
350–000	*Notes payable—long term*	
	350–001	Bank loans—long term
	350–002	Other loans payable—long term
400–00	*Partners' capital*	
	400–001	Partner A
	400–002	Partner B
	400–003	Partner C
	400–004	Partner D
410–00	*Partners' drawings*	
	410–001	Partner A
	410–002	Partner B
	410–003	Partner C
	410–004	Partner D

INCOME STATEMENT

Account		
500–00	*Fees from legal services*	
	500–001	Fees—General practice
	500–002	Fees—Litigation
	500–003	Fees—Real Estate
	500–004	Fees—Trust and Estate
	500–005	Fees—Contingency
	500–006	Fees—Other
510–000	*Miscellaneous revenue*	
	510–001	Directors' fees
	510–002	Interest income
	510–003	Miscellaneous revenue

Figure 903-1. (continued)

600–00 *Compensation—legal staff*

600–001 Salaries—associates
600–002 Salaries—legal assistants
600-003 Bonuses and profit sharing accounts

610–00 *Compensation—secretarial/word processing staff*

610–001 Salaries—secretarial
610–002 Salaries—word processing staff
610–003 Salaries—other
600–004 Bonuses—secretarial/word processing staff
610–005 Overtime—secretarial/word processing staff
610–006 Overtime billed to clients (credit)

620–000 *Compensation—administrative staff*

620–001 Salaries—administrative staff
620–002 Bonuses—administrative staff
620–003 Overtime—administrative staff

630–000 *Payroll taxes/other employee costs*

630–001 FICA taxes
630–002 Unemployment taxes
630–003 Disability insurance expense
630–004 Medical insurance expense
630–005 Group life insurance expense
630–006 Profit sharing plan contributions
630–007 Workers' compensation insurance expense

640–00 *Miscellaneous employee costs*

640–001 Temporary office services
640–002 Parking
640–003 Other miscellaneous employee costs

650–000 *Occupancy expenses*

650–001 Rent expense
650–002 Utilities
650–003 Amortization of leasehold improvements
650–004 Maintenance and repairs to premises
650–005 Janitorial and trash service
650–006 Miscellaneous occupancy expense

Figure 903-1. (continued)

660–000 *Stationery, printing and supplies*

- 660–001 Stationery
- 660–002 Printing
- 660–003 Office supplies

670–000 *Furniture and equipment/depreciation*

- 670–001 Furniture rental
- 670–002 Typewriter rental
- 670–003 Word processing equipment rental
- 670–004 Computer equipment rental
- 670–010 Depreciation—furniture
- 670–011 Depreciation—equipment

680–000 *Reproduction expense*

- 680–001 Copier lease costs
- 680–002 Copier supplies
- 680–003 Outside reproduction services
- 680–004 Reproduction costs billed to clients (credit)

690–000 *Other office operating expense*

- 690–001 Small equipment purchases
- 690–002 Repairs and maintenance
- 690–003 Automotive expenses
- 690–004 Taxi
- 690–005 Coffee service expenses
- 690–006 Office meal allowances

700–00 *Professional activities*

- 700–001 Travel costs—professional activities
- 700–002 Luncheon and dinners—professional activities
- 700–003 Other professional activities

710–00 *Association dues and expenses*

- 710–001 Bar associations
- 710–002 Professional associations
- 710–003 Other dues and expenses

720–000 *Firm meetings*

- 720–001 Meetings, luncheons/dinners

Figure 903-1. (continued)

730–000 *Practice development*

- 730–001 Luncheons and dinners
- 730–002 Staff entertainment

740–000 *Continuing legal education*

- 740–001 Continuing legal education

750–000 *Recruiting costs*

- 750–001 Recruiting costs

760–000 *Insurance*

- 760–001 Professional liability
- 760–002 Personal liability and property damage
- 760–003 Other

770–000 *Communications*

- 770–001 Telephone and teletype
- 770–002 Postage
- 770–003 Communication costs billed to clients (credit)

780–000 *Reference materials*

- 780–001 Books
- 780–002 Subscriptions

790–000 *Taxes other than payroll*

- 790–001 Personal property taxes
- 790–002 Real estate taxes
- 790–003 Business taxes
- 790–004 Other taxes

800–00 *Professional services*

- 800–001 Accounting services
- 800–002 Consulting services

810–000 *Client disbursements written off*

- 810–999 Client disbursements written off

820–000 *Interest expense*

- 820–001 Interest expense

830–000 *Miscellaneous*

Figure 903-1. (continued)

¶904 Learning How to Handle Money and Petty Cash

Most law firms have very few cash transactions. That is, most transactions are handled by check. Clients usually mail checks to pay their bills and most firm expenses are paid by check.

¶904.1 What to Do When Clients Pay Cash

Occasionally a client will pay in cash. If you receive cash from one of your attorneys or a client, handle it carefully. The client *should* be given a receipt, signed by either you or the attorney collecting the money. If your firm receives cash payments often from clients, perhaps preprinted and prenumbered receipts could be used. If cash payments are unusual, you may simply type up a receipt for the client similar to the one in Figure 904.1-1. The important thing is that the client receives something in exchange for his payment to prove that he paid the money to the firm.

The cash should be deposited in the bank as soon as possible. If your firm has a bookkeeping department, take the cash immediately to the bookkeeper and ask for it to be deposited. If you make the deposits, do so as quickly as possible.

RECEIPT

Date ______________________________

RECEIVED FROM ______________________________

$ ______________________, (__AND __/100 DOLLARS)____

FOR ______________________________.

____

Figure 904.1-1. Cash Receipt.

¶904.2 How to Handle Petty Cash

Most law firms have a petty cash account, a small amount of cash to pay things for which a check is not appropriate. Items like postage due, parking tolls for messengers or attorneys, copies at the local library or lunches for attorneys and clients are often paid out of petty cash.

If you have been given the responsibility for keeping the firm's petty cash fund, it is important that you understand how it works. A petty cash fund is usually a fixed amount, either $50, $75 or $100. Let's assume your firm's petty cash fund is $75. Every time you give someone money from the fund, they should fill out a petty cash voucher like the one in Figure 904.2-1. You should also ask them to bring you a receipt for the money spent which you should staple to the petty cash voucher.

No. ____________ Amount $____________

PETTY CASH VOUCHER

____________ 19____

For ____________

Charge to ____________

____

____________ ____________

Approved by Received by

Figure 904-2.1. Petty Cash Voucher.

At any given time, the total of the petty cash vouchers and the cash remaining in the fund should total $75, the amount of the petty cash fund. When the cash in the fund is low you should total all of the vouchers and request a check for that amount. Provide the bookkeeper with a description of each of the uses of the cash so that the proper expense accounts are charged. When you receive the check, or cash if the check is cashed for you, you should again have $75 consisting of cash and vouchers.

¶905 How to Accept Checks from Clients—Regular and Trust Funds

Most law firms keep at least two bank accounts, one for general purposes of the firm, and the other for money they hold in trust for clients. Cash receipts should be deposited daily as soon after they are received as is practical.

Preprinted deposit slips should be prepared in duplicate in order to compare to the receipt from the bank after the deposit has been made. The information recorded on the deposit slip should include the name of the payor (client) and the amount of the check.

¶905.1 Regular Funds

When a payment is received from a client for billed services, give the check to the person in your firm who is responsible for making deposits to the bank account. If you have a copy of the client's bill in a billing file, first mark the bill with the date and amount of payment. Do not hold the check—it should be deposited on the same day it is received.

¶905.2 Trust Funds

You will occasionally receive checks from clients for other purposes than paying their account. The most common reason for this is the payment of trust funds. Attorneys often hold money for clients for many purposes until some event takes place. A common use of trust funds is for real estate closings. The purchaser usually pays an amount to the seller's attorney to indicate a willingness to buy. The money is then applied toward the purchase price of the property when it is legally finalized (closed).

Trust funds should not be commingled with the firm's funds. The money belongs to the client, not the firm. A separate bank account should be maintained and detailed records kept of the amounts belonging to each client. If the money is deposited in an interest-bearing savings or checking account, a separate account should be opened for each client. The interest earned on the money in the account belongs to the client, not to the firm. If several clients' money is put in the same interest-bearing account, it is confusing when trying to decide how much of the interest belongs to which client, so don't do it.

¶906 How to Take Care of Disbursements for Clients

It is normal practice in law firms to pay certain costs for clients. These costs are then included on the clients' bills, labeled costs advanced, disbursements, or client costs. A firm may have to spend large amounts of cash on behalf of their clients making it very important to keep good records so the money can be recovered from the clients.

There are two types of client disbursements, cash and non-cash disbursements. A cash disbursement is one which requires the writing of a firm check or payment in cash using the firm's cash; e.g., court filing fees, travel expenses. A non-cash disbursement is a charge to the client for some use of the firm's facilities or services other than the attorneys' time, e.g. copy charges, long distance phone calls. Typical cash and noncash disbursements are listed in Appendix G.

Your firm will probably require you to fill out a check request form (Figure 906-1) when you need to pay filing fees, legal advertising, or other costs for your attorneys' clients. Fill in the correct client and matter name and number if your firm uses a client numbering system. This is the only way the bookkeeping department will know to whom to charge the cost.

Most firms charge clients for making photocopies at the rate of 15¢ to 25¢ per copy. Either you will be required to write down the number of copies you make for a client or the copier will be equipped with a copy control device that requires you to input the client and matter number before it will work. This is the best method of keeping track of copies. The machine counts them for you and in some firms updates the client's account when you are through. Your responsibility, unless you are also the bookkeeper, is to record the correct information when you make the copies (see Figure 906-2).

Long distance calls are usually charged to clients, also. Unless your firm has invested in sophisticated telephone equipment, including a call controller which works very much like the copy controllers mentioned above, manual records will have to be kept of the telephone calls. Some attorneys write the phone number on their time slips. Others keep a log of telephone calls. The most common method is to fill out individual slips (Figure 906-3) which can be sorted and compared to the telephone bill when it comes.

Many of the new long distance services, like Sprint and MCI, allow you to punch in your employee number or even a client number when you make a call. The telephone bill is then sorted by these numbers when you receive it. This simplifies the accounting for telephone calls considerably. Your job is to make sure you enter the correct information when you place the call.

¶907 Writing Checks: Some Dos and Don'ts

Check preparation in your law firm depends on its size. In the small firm, one of the secretaries might keep the checkbook. In the large firm, the bookkeeper or accounts payable clerk will write all checks, either by hand or with the use of the computer. In some firms the secretary is able to call up a check form on the screen of his or her word processor, fill it out and have it print out in the bookkeeping depart-

DISBURSEMENT REQUEST ☐ REGULAR FILE NO. ______

DATE ______ AMOUNT ______ ☐ TRUST ☐ PETTY CASH

CLIENT ______

MATTER ______

PAY TO ______

PURPOSE OF PAYMENT ______

☐ DELIVER TO ______

☐ MAIL TO ______

______

DATE REQUIRED ______ CHECK NO. ______ REQUESTED BY ______

Figure 906-1. Check Request Form.

CLIENT/MATTER: ____________________

DATE: ____________________

POSTAGE: ____________________

COPIES: ____________________

COURIER: ____________________

FILING FEES: ____________________

BUSINESS MEALS & TRAVEL: ____________________

PARKING & MILEAGE: ____________________

Figure 906-2. Miscellaneous Expense Slip.

LONG DISTANCE TELEPHONE CALL

CLIENT: ____________________

MATTER: ____________________

DATE: ____________________

TO: ____________________

PLACE: ____________________

TELEPHONE NO.: ____________________

MADE BY: ____________________

Figure 906-3. Long Distance Telephone Call Slip.

ment where it is approved and signed. A messenger will then deliver the completed check to the secretary within just a few minutes. However it is done in your firm, there are some general rules to follow.

1. *Do* fill out some type of check request form (Figure 906-1) stating the purpose of the check, the amount, date, and the client and matter, if it is to be charged to the client. Fill out the form completely.

2. *Do* have an attorney approve the check request by initializing the check request form.
3. *Don't* wait until the last minute to request a check. Give the bookkeeping department staff time to adjust their schedules to accommodate your request.
4. *Don't* ask for or allow blank, signed checks to be given to attorneys or other personnel.
5. *Don't* write a check unless the proper, approved check request form accompanies it.
6. *Don't* interrupt the attorney who signs checks more often than necessary. Save up all the checks for the day, if possible, and get them signed all at once.
7. *Do* record the check as soon as it is written.
8. *Don't* hold onto a check which you had prepared, but did not use.
9. *Do* void checks by destroying (tearing off) the signatures on it. Don't forget to mark the check voided in the checkbook and cash disbursements journal.
10. *Do* write the client's name and ID number on a check for a cost advance.

¶908 You Can Reconcile the Bank Account—It's Easy!

At the end of every month, the bank will send a statement of each of the firm's checking accounts. This statement is just like the one you receive for your personal checking account. The only difference is that there are usually more cancelled checks in it.

Each checking account should be reconciled every month. This is the only way to find errors made by the bank, or in the checkbook or bookkeeping records. Here are step-by-step instructions for preparing a bank reconciliation, using the form shown in Figure 908-1.

Step-by-step procedure for reconciling the bank account:

1. Gather this month's bank statement, check stubs or check register, deposit slips or cash receipts journal and the prior month's bank reconciliation.
2. Put the canceled checks in numerical order. If the bank lists the checks in numerical order on the bank statement, this step may be skipped.
3. Put the date of the reconciliation and your initials at the top of the form. The reconciliation date is the date of the bank statement.
4. Enter previous month's bank account balance in the area labeled (A).

BANK RECONCILIATION

Reconciliation Date ____________

Prepared By ____________

Bank ____________ Acct. # ____________

General Ledger Account ____________

BALANCE $ (A)

add debits

$

(B)

Total Dr. TOTAL (B)

Total $ (A&B)

less credits:

$

(C)

Total Credit Total (C)

BANK BALANCE-Per General Ledger $(A&B − C)

BALANCE PER BANK STATEMENT

As of ____________ 19____ $ (D)

Add Deposits in Transit:

$

(E)

Total in Transit Total (E)

Total $ (D&E)

Less Checks Outstanding:

(See List) $

(G)

$

Total TOTAL (G)

BANK BALANCE - Per Statement Reconciliation $ (D&E − G)

OUTSTANDING CHECKS

Number	Amount	Number	Amount
(F)			

Figure 908-1. Bank Reconciliation Form.

BANK RECONCILIATION

Reconciliation Date ____________

Bank ____________ Acct. # ____________ Prepared By ____________

General Ledger Account ____________

BALANCE $ ________

add debits

$ ________

____

____

____

____

____

Total Debits

Total $ ________

less credits:

$ ________

____

____

____

____

Total Credits ________

BANK BALANCE-Per General Ledger ________

BALANCE PER BANK STATEMENT

As of ________ 19____ $ ________

Add Deposits in Transit:

$ ________

____

____

____

Total in Transit

Total ________ $ ________

Less Checks Outstanding:

(See List) ________ $ ________

____

____

________ $ ________

Total ________

BANK BALANCE - Per Statement Reconciliation $ ________

OUTSTANDING CHECKS

Number	Amount	Number	Amount

Figure 908-1. (continued)

BANK RECONCILIATION

Reconciliation Date ______

Bank ______ Acct. # ______ Prepared By ______

General Ledger Account ______

BALANCE		$ 2808.50
add debits		
	$	
CASH RECEIPTS	5500 00	
RET'D CHECK DEPOSIT	125 00	
Total Debits		5625.00
Total		$ 8433.50
less credits:		
CHECKS 251-372	$ 6134 96	
BANK CHG	2 50	
RET'D ITEM	137 00	
BANK INS. DRAFT	250 00	
Total Credits		6524.46
BANK BALANCE-Per General Ledger		$ 1909.04
BALANCE PER BANK STATEMENT As of 1/31 1978		$ 2350.60
Add Deposits in Transit:		
1/28	$ 200 00	
1/31	565 00	
Total in Transit		765.00
Total		$ 3115.60
Less Checks Outstanding:		
(See List)	$ 1206 56	
	$	
Total		1206.56
BANK BALANCE - Per Statement Reconciliation		$ 1909.04

OUTSTANDING CHECKS

Number	Amount	Number	Amount
153	6 56	(date	12/15/77)
263	100 00	current	month
298	1000 00	out	standing
370	100 00		
	1206 56		

Figure 908-1. (continued)

5. Enter the total of the current month's deposits in the area labeled (B).
6. Add up all the checks written in the current month. Enter the check number range, i.e., 495–567, and the total amount of the checks in the area labeled (C).
7. Enter any bank service charges, returned items, or miscellaneous charges appearing on the bank statement in the area labeled (C).
8. Add the total of area (B) to area (A) and subtract area (C). This should give you the bank balance per your checkbook (and general ledger if you keep one).
9. Enter the bank balance per bank statement in the area marked (D).
10. Enter in the area labeled (E) any deposits included in area (B) which do not appear on the current month's bank statement. These are called deposits in transit.
11. Review the past month's bank reconciliation and mark off all checks which are listed on the bank statement as being paid by the bank. Enter the other checks, check number and amount, in the area labeled (F).
12. Go through the current month's check stubs and determine which checks were paid by the bank and which are still outstanding and enter them, check number and amount, in the area labeled (F).
13. Total the amounts listed in area (F) and enter this total in area (G).
14. Add area (E) to the balance per bank statement—area (D). Subtract area (G) and the resulting total should agree with the balance per checkbook calculated in step 8.

¶909 Preparing the Monthly Financial Statements

At the end of each month, the bookkeeper should prepare certain statements that show the financial picture of the firm and how well it did during the previous month for the partners. These statements are used by the partners to manage the firm, to control costs and maximize profits.

Financial statements in a law firm are usually extremely confidential. If you are involved in the preparation of such statements, be very careful not to disclose the information to other attorneys or staff members. Usually, only the partners see the financial statements. It is not uncommon for employees to be terminated because they breached

FIRM NAME
ASSETS

CURRENT ASSETS	
Cash	$XXX
Client trust funds	XXX
Short-term investments	XXX
Costs advanced	XXX
Other accounts	XXX
Total current assets	XXX
FIXED ASSETS	
Furniture and fixtures	XXX
Leasehold improvements	XXX
Office equipment	XXX
Reserve for depreciation and amortization	(XXX)
Total fixed assets	XXX
OTHER ASSETS	
Other assets	XXX
Total assets	$ XXX

LIABILITIES AND PARTNERS' CAPITAL

CURRENT LIABILITIES	
Notes payable—current	$XXX
Accounts payable and other liabilities	XXX
Payroll tax liability	XXX
Liability for client funds	XXX
Total current liabilities	XXX
LONG-TERM LIABILITIES	
Notes payable—long term	XXX
PARTNERS' CAPITAL	
Partners' capital	XXX
Partners' drawings	(XXX)
Current period earnings	XXX
Total partners' capital	XXX
Total liabilities and partners' capital	$XXX

Figure 909-1. Sample Balance Sheet.

FIRM NAME
Income Statement
For the Month Ended February, 1987

	Current Month	YDT
Income:		
Legal Fees	$XX,XXX.XX	$XX,XXX.XX
Interest	X,XXX.XX	X,XXX.XX
Directors' Fees	X,XXX.XX	X,XXX.XX
Other	X,XXX.XX	X,XXX.XX
	XX,XXX.XX	XX,XXX.XX
Expenses:		
Compensation—Associates	X,XXX.XX	X,XXX.XX
Compensation—Secretarial	X,XXX.XX	X,XXX.XX
Compensation—Administrative	X,XXX.XX	X,XXX.XX
Payroll Taxes	X,XXX.XX	X,XXX.XX
Group Insurance	XXX.XX	XXX.XX
Worker's Compensation	XXX.XX	XXX.XX
Temporary Office Help	XXX.XX	XXX.XX
Parking	XXX.XX	XXX.XX
Misc. Employee Expenses	XXX.XX	XXX.XX
Auto Expenses	X,XXX.XX	X,XXX.XX
Beverages	XXX.XX	XXX.XX
Continuing Legal Education	XXX.XX	XXX.XX
Courier	XXX.XX	XXX.XX
Equipment Rental	X,XXX.XX	X,XXX.XX
Firm Relations	X,XXX.XX	X,XXX.XX
Professional Liability Insurance	X,XXX.XX	X,XXX.XX
Interest Expense	X,XXX.XX	X,XXX.XX
Library	XXX.XX	XXX.XX
Misc. Expense	XX.XX	XX.XX
Office Supplies	XXX.XX	XXX.XX
Dues and Subscriptions	XXX.XX	XXX.XX
Rent	X,XXX.XX	X,XXX.XX
Telephone	X,XXX.XX	X,XXX.XX
	XX,XXX.XX	XX,XXX.XX
Net Income	$ XXX.XX	$ XXX,XX

Figure 909-2. Sample Income Statement.

FIRM NAME
Cash Flow Statement
For the Month Ended February, 1986

	Current Month	YDT
Beginning Cash Balance	$XX,XXX.XX	$XX,XXX.XX
Net Income (Loss)	XXX.XX	X,XXX.XX
Add:		
Depreciation and Amortization	X,XXX.XX	X,XXX.XX
Proceeds for Bank Loans	XX,XXX.XX	XX,XXX.XX
Capital Contributions	X,XXX.XX	X,XXX.XX
Client Disbursements Collected	X,XXX.XX	X,XXX.XX
Total Cash Available	$XX,XXX.XX	$XX,XXX.XX
Deduct:		
Partner Draws	XX,XXX.XX	XX,XXX.XX
Principal Payments	X,XXX.XX	X,XXX.XX
Office Equipment Purchased	XX,XXX.XX	XX,XXX.XX
Furniture/Accessories	X,XXX.XX	X,XXX.XX
Leasehold Improvements	XXX.XX	XXX.XX
Undeposited Payroll Taxes	XXX.XX	XXX.XX
Client Disbursements Paid	XXX.XX	XXX.XX
	$XX,XXX.XX	$XX,XXX.XX
Ending Cash Balance	$XX,XXX.XX	$XX,XXX.XX

Figure 909-3. Sample Cash Flow Statement.

the trust the partners had placed in them to keep this information strictly confidential.

The basic financial statements are the balance sheet, the statement of income (sometimes referred to as the profit and loss statement), and the cash flow statement. These statements are simply summaries of the information found in the general ledger at the end of each month.

The balance sheet (Figure 909-1) shows the balances of the asset, liability, and partners' capital accounts. It shows the firm's financial condition as of a certain date—what the firm owns and what it owes.

The statement of income (Figure 909-2) shows the balances of the revenue (fees) and expense accounts for the current month and year-to-date. The expenses are deducted from the revenue received from fees to arrive at net income.

The cash flow statement (Figure 909-3) shows the beginning cash balance, cash activity during the month, and the ending cash balance. It is prepared after the statement of income is completed. The statement of income is used as a basis, but is adjusted for items which do not require the use of cash, like depreciation. Also, items which were paid in cash but not included in the statement of income, like principal payments on bank loans, purchases of office furniture and equipment, are deducted. The resulting balance should agree with the balance in the bank. Client trust funds should not be included in the cash balance.

¶1000 Taking the Mystery Out of Payroll

By Carole A. Bruno and Paula F. Turner

In the sole practitioner's office or the small law firm it is often the responsibility of a legal secretary to prepare payroll checks and maintain the payroll records. Handling payroll transactions is not really difficult. Follow the guidelines found in this chapter and you will find this out for yourself.

¶1001 Circular E: Your Questions Answered

The Internal Revenue Service (IRS) publishes a guide for employers called Circular E, Employer's Tax Guide. You may find the latest Circular E with the payroll files. If not, call the nearest IRS office and request one (Figure 1001-1). This publication will provide you with the necessary tables for withholding taxes and the current tax rates, deposit rules, and payroll tax return information.

¶1002 How to Secure the Employer Identification Number

Every employer must have a nine digit identification number, which is obtained from the IRS. In order to apply for a number, a new employer should fill out IRS form number SS-4 (Figure 1002-1). When the IRS receives this form they will issue an Employer ID Number similar to this:

58-1234567

You should use this number on all federal payroll tax returns, checks in payment of federal payroll taxes and all correspondence to the IRS regarding payroll tax matters.

Identification numbers are also required from state agencies for payment of state income taxes and unemployment taxes. Each state is different so you will need to call the appropriate income tax department of your state to request the proper application form. When you call, ask if you also need to apply for a number for employer's unemployment

Circular E

Employer's Tax Guide

Publication 15
(Rev. January 1985)

Highlights of Changes in Law

This revision includes changes made by the Social Security Amendments of 1983 (Public Law 98-21) and the Tax Reform Act of 1984 (Public Law 98-369).

Income Tax

This publication contains the income tax withholding rates and tables for wages paid after December 31, 1984. The income tax withholding tables reflect the indexing for inflation of the tax rate schedules, the zero bracket amount, and the personal exemption amount, as these affect the amount of income tax withholding.

Income tax must be withheld on certain pension, annuity, and deferred income payments unless the recipient elects to have no tax withheld by filing a **Form W-4P**, Withholding Certificate for Pension or Annuity Payments. Payers and plan administrators may substitute their own forms for this purpose.

You should figure income tax witholding on periodic pension, annuity, and deferred income payments by using the tables and methods explained in this publication or in **Publication 493**, Alternative Tax Withholding Methods and Tables. Publication 493 also contains details and examples on withholding and tables for withholding income tax from qualified total distributions.

Note: Employees can file **Form W-4S**, Request for Federal Income Tax Withholding from Sick Pay, with third-party payers to have income tax withheld from payments of sick pay.

Employment Taxes

The social security tax rates increase to 7.05% each for employers and employees for wages paid in 1985.

The maximum amount of wages subject to social security taxes referred to in this publication is $39,600 for 1985.

The maximum amount of wages subject to Federal unemployment (FUTA) tax is $7,000 for 1985 and the FUTA tax rate increases to 6.2%. The credit against the FUTA tax for payments to State unemployment funds increases to a maximum of 5.4% in 1985.

Backup Withholding

Payers must generally withhold 20% of taxable interest, dividend, and certain other payments if payees fail to furnish payers with their correct taxpayer identification numbers. There are other circumstances where the payer is also required to withhold. This withholding is referred to as backup withholding. Please see **Form W-9**, Payer's Request for Taxpayer Identification Number and Certification, and the 1985 **Instructions for Form 1099 Series, 1098, 5498, and 1096** for more details.

Report backup withholding amounts on the same Form 941 you use to report social security and income tax withholding (or Form 941E for reporting income tax withholding). See section 13 for information on depositing backup withholding.

Whole Dollar Withholding and Paying

Beginning in 1985, the amounts in the wage bracket tables for income tax withholding (pages 22 through 41) and advance earned income credit payments (pages 46 through 48) are rounded to whole dollar amounts. See page 19 for details.

Internal Revenue Service
Cincinnati, OH 45999

Official Business
Penalty for Private Use, $300

Bulk Rate
Postage and Fees Paid
Internal Revenue Service
Permit No. G-48

Publication 15
(Rev. January 1985)

Postmaster: Deliver Immediately

Figure 1001-1. Circular E, Employer's Tax Guide.

Form **SS–4**
(Rev. 9–82)
Department of the Treasury
Internal Revenue Service

Application for Employer Identification Number

(For use by employers and others as explained in the instructions. Please read the instructions before completing this form.)
For Paperwork Reduction Act Notice, see page 2.

OMB No. 1545–0003 Expires 9–30–85

1 Name (True name and not trade name. If partnership, see page 4.)

2 Social security no., if sole proprietor

3 Ending month of accounting year

4 Trade name, if any, of business (if different from item 1)

5 General partner's name, if partnership; principal officer's name, if corporation; or grantor's name, if trust

6 Address of principal place of business (Number and street)

7 Mailing address, if different

8 City, State, and ZIP code

9 County of principal business location

10 Type of organization
☐ Individual ☐ Trust ☐ Partnership ☐ Other (specify)
☐ Governmental ☐ Nonprofit organization ☐ Corporation

11 Date you acquired or started this business (Mo., day, year)

12 Reason for applying
☐ Started new business ☐ Purchased going business ☐ Other (specify)

13 First date you paid or will pay wages for this business (Mo., day, year)

14 Nature of principal business activity (See instructions on page 4.)

15 Do you operate more than one place of business? ☐ Yes ☐ No

16 Peak number of employees expected in next 12 months (If none, enter "0") ▶ Nonagricultural | Agricultural | Household

17 If nature of business is manufacturing, state principal product and raw material used.

18 To whom do you sell most of your products or services?
☐ Business establishments (wholesale) ☐ General public (retail) ☐ Other (specify)

19 Have you ever applied for an identification number for this or any other business? ☐ Yes ☐ No
If "Yes," enter name and trade name. Also enter approx. date, city, and State where you applied and previous number if known. ▶

Under penalties of perjury, I declare that I have examined this application, and to the best of my knowledge and belief it is true, correct, and complete.

Signature and Title ▶ Date ▶

Telephone number (include area code)

Please leave blank ▶	Geo.	Ind.	Class	Size	Reas. for appl.	**Part I**

Figure 1002-1. IRS Form SS-4, Application for Employer Identification Number.

insurance contributions. Like the federal employer ID number, these numbers should be used on all returns, checks and correspondence with the state agencies.

¶1003 How to Secure the Employee Identification Number

Every employee which the firm pays must have a Social Security number which also serves as a tax ID number. When a new employee joins the firm, request a Social Security number. If the employee does not have such a number, he or she should fill out the Social Security Administration's form SS-5 (Figure 1003-1). This form can be obtained by calling your local Social Security office or the firm's accountants will be able to supply you with one.

The general rule should be that no employee is ever paid until the firm has a Social Security number on file for that employee. If the employee is applying for a number for the first time, when you are satisfied that the application has been properly filled out and mailed, the payroll check may be released. The important thing to keep in mind in these situations is that it is the employer's responsibility to get the appropriate ID number from the employee. You are the employer's representative in this situation, therefore, it is your responsibility.

¶1004 How to Handle Social Security Taxes (FICA)

Every employer is responsible for withholding Federal Insurance Contributions Act (FICA) taxes from the gross wages of all employees.

Wages include salary, fees, bonuses, and commissions paid to employees as compensation for services performed for the employer. In the law firm, the most common forms of wages will be salaries and bonuses. If your firm is a traditional partnership, the partners are not considered employees. The money paid to them is not considered wages. They are withdrawing (drawing) a portion of the firm's (and hence, their) profits. No taxes will be withheld from the "draws." If the firm is a professional corporation or professional association, the partners will be shareholders and will be paid a salary like all other employees. In this case, FICA taxes will be withheld from their salaries just like it is from the other employees.

The FICA tax rate is imposed on both the employer and the employee. The tax is calculated on wages up to a certain limit. The limit and the tax rate change from year to year so you will need to refer to Circular E to find out what the current rate and limit is.

DEPARTMENT OF HEALTH AND HUMAN SERVICES
SOCIAL SECURITY ADMINISTRATION

Form Approved
OMB No. 0960-0066

FORM SS-5 – APPLICATION FOR A SOCIAL SECURITY NUMBER CARD
(Original, Replacement or Correction)

MICROFILM REF. NO. (SSA USE ONLY)

Unless the requested information is provided, we may not be able to issue a Social Security Number (20 CFR 422.103(b))

INSTRUCTIONS TO APPLICANT — Before completing this form, please read the instructions on the opposite page. You can type or print, using pen with dark blue or black ink. Do not use pencil.

NAA NAB 1 — NAME TO BE SHOWN ON CARD: First | Middle | Last
FULL NAME AT BIRTH (IF OTHER THAN ABOVE): First | Middle | Last
ONA — OTHER NAME(S) USED

STT 2 — MAILING ADDRESS (Street/Apt. No., P.O. Box, Rural Route No.)
CTY STE ZIP — CITY | STATE | ZIP CODE

CSP 3 — CITIZENSHIP (Check one only)
- ☐ a. U.S. citizen
- ☐ b. Legal alien allowed to work
- ☐ c. Legal alien not allowed to work
- ☐ d. Other (See instructions on Page 2)

SEX 4 — SEX: ☐ Male ☐ Female

ETB 5 — RACE/ETHNIC DESCRIPTION (Check one only) (Voluntary)
- ☐ a Asian, Asian-American or Pacific Islander (Includes persons of Chinese, Filipino, Japanese, Korean, Samoan, etc., ancestry or descent)
- ☐ b Hispanic (Includes persons of Chicano, Cuban, Mexican or Mexican-American, Puerto Rican, South or Central American, or other Spanish ancestry or descent)
- ☐ c Negro or Black (not Hispanic)
- ☐ d North American Indian or Alaskan Native
- ☐ e White (not Hispanic)

DOB 6 — DATE OF BIRTH: MONTH | DAY | YEAR
AGE 7 — PRESENT AGE
PLB 8 — PLACE OF BIRTH: CITY | STATE OR FOREIGN COUNTRY

MNA 9 — MOTHER'S NAME AT HER BIRTH: First | Middle | Last (her maiden name)
FNA — FATHER'S NAME: First | Middle | Last

PNO 10 — a. Have you or someone on your behalf applied for a social security number before? ☐ No ☐ Don't Know ☐ Yes
If you checked "yes", complete items "b" through "e" below; otherwise go to item 11
SSN PNS PNY — b. Enter social security number | c. In what State did you apply? | What year?
NLC — d. Enter the name shown on your most recent social security card | e. If the birth date you used was different from the date shown in item 6, enter it here. MONTH | DAY | YEAR

DON 11 — TODAY'S DATE: MONTH | DAY | YEAR
12 — Telephone number where we can reach you during the day: HOME | OTHER

ASD — **WARNING: Deliberately providing false information on this application is punishable by a fine of $1,000 or one year in jail, or both.**

13 — YOUR SIGNATURE
WITNESS (Needed only if signed by mark "X")

14 — YOUR RELATIONSHIP TO PERSON IN ITEM 1: ☐ Self ☐ Other ________ (Specify)
WITNESS (Needed only if signed by mark "X")

DO NOT WRITE BELOW THIS LINE (FOR SSA USE ONLY)
DTC | SSA RECEIPT DATE ________
☐ SUPPORTING DOCUMENT-EXPEDITE CASE
☐ DUP ISSUED
SSN ASSIGNED OR VERIFIED
SSN
NPN
BIC
DOC | NTC | CAN
SIGNATURE AND TITLE OF EMPLOYEE(S) REVIEWING EVIDENCE AND/OR CONDUCTING INTERVIEW.
TYPE(S) OF EVIDENCE SUBMITTED
☐ MANDATORY IN PERSON INTERVIEW CONDUCTED
DATE
DATE
IDN | ITV | DCL

Form **SS-5** (2-81)

Figure 1003-1. Form SS-5, Application for a Social Security Number Card.

If an employee joins your firm who has worked for another employer and has already reached the maximum FICA salary level, your firm must still withhold and pay FICA taxes on that employee. Also, you cannot add the former employer's wages to the wages earned at your firm to reach the FICA limit. The limit is based on earnings from any one employer. The employee will resolve the overpayment problem by claiming a refund when he or she files a Federal Income Tax return for the year.

The employer is liable for the collection, by withholding, and payment of both the employee's and the employer's FICA taxes. The tax withheld as well as the employer's portion must be "deposited" (see ¶1006) and every employer who is liable for FICA taxes must file a quarterly return on IRS Form 941 (Figure 1008-1).

¶1005 How to Determine Income Tax Withholding

The firm, as an employer, is required to withhold income taxes from all wages paid to an employee. The amount to be withheld is computed on gross wages before any deduction for FICA taxes, insurance, etc.

¶1005.1 Federal Income Tax Withholding

Each new employee should complete a Form W-4 (Figure 1005.1-1), Employee's Withholding Allowance Certificate. The certificate should show the employee's name, exactly as it appears on the social security card, address, marital status, social security number and the number of withholding exemptions claimed. An employee may be entitled to withholding exemptions in addition to those claimed for dependents on income tax returns. Form W-4 outlines the circumstances under which additional exemptions may be claimed.

The amount to be withheld is generally determined from the wage bracket tables published by the IRS in Circular E, Employer's Tax Guide. If the employee fails to complete a Form W-4, you should withhold income taxes at the rates for a single person with no exemptions.

¶1005.2 Withholding from Bonuses, Overtime, and Back Pay

If supplemental wages, such as bonuses, overtime pay, or back pay are paid in the same payment with regular wages, you should determine the amount of tax to be withheld as if the total of the supplemental and regular wages were a single wage payment for the regular payroll period.

Form **W-4** (Rev. January 1984)

Department of the Treasury—Internal Revenue Service

Employee's Withholding Allowance Certificate

OMB No. 1545-0010

1 Type or print your full name	2 Your social security number
Home address (number and street or rural route)	3 Marital Status: ☐ Single ☐ Married ☐ Married, but withhold at higher Single rate
City or town, State, and ZIP code	**Note:** If married, but legally separated, or spouse is a nonresident alien, check the Single box.

4 Total number of allowances you are claiming (from line F of the worksheet on page 2) . . . .

5 Additional amount, if any, you want deducted from each pay . . . . $

6 I claim exemption from withholding because (see instructions and check boxes below that apply):

a ☐ Last year I did not owe any Federal income tax and had a right to a full refund of **ALL** income tax withheld, **AND**

b ☐ This year I do not expect to owe any Federal income tax and expect to have a right to a full refund of **ALL** income tax withheld. If both a and b apply, enter the year effective and "EXEMPT" here . . . ▶ Year

c If you entered "EXEMPT" on line 6b, are you a full-time student? . . . . ☐Yes ☐No

Under penalties of perjury, I certify that I am entitled to the number of withholding allowances claimed on this certificate, or if claiming exemption from withholding, that I am entitled to claim the exempt status.

Employee's signature ▶ Date ▶ , 19

7 Employer's name and address **(Employer: Complete 7, 8, and 9 only if sending to IRS)**	8 Office code	9 Employer identification number

Detach along this line. Give the top part of this form to employer; keep the lower part for your records.

Privacy Act and Paperwork Reduction Act Notice.—If you do not give your employer a certificate, you will be treated as a single person with no withholding allowances as required by law. We ask for this information to carry out the Internal Revenue laws of the United States. We may give the information to the Dept. of Justice for civil or criminal litigation and to the States and the District of Columbia for use in administering their tax laws.

Purpose.—The law requires that you complete Form W-4 so that your employer can withhold Federal income tax from your pay. Your Form W-4 remains in effect until you change it or, if you entered "EXEMPT" on line 6b above, until February 15 of next year. By correctly completing this form, you can fit the amount of tax withheld from your wages to your tax liability.

If you got a large refund last year, you may be having too much tax withheld. If so, you may want to increase the number of your allowances on line 4 by claiming any other allowances you are entitled to. The kinds of allowances, and how to figure them, are explained in detail below.

If you owed a large amount of tax last year, you may not be having enough tax withheld. If so, you can claim fewer allowances on line 4, or ask that an additional amount be withheld on line 5, or both.

If the number of withholding allowances you are entitled to claim decreases to less than you are now claiming, you must file a new W-4 with your employer within 10 days.

The instructions below explain how to fill in Form W-4. **Publication 505,** Tax Withholding and Estimated Tax, contains more information on withholding. You can get it from most IRS offices.

For more information about who qualifies as your dependent, what deductions you can take, and what tax credits you qualify for, see the Form 1040 Instructions.

You may be fined $500 if you file, with no reasonable basis, a W-4 that results in less tax being withheld than is properly allowable. In addition, criminal penalties apply for willfully supplying false or fraudulent information or failing to supply information requiring an increase in withholding.

Line-By-Line Instructions

Fill in the identifying information in Boxes 1 and 2. If you are married and want tax withheld at the regular rate for married persons, check "Married" in Box 3. If you are married and want tax withheld at the higher Single rate (because both you and your spouse work, for example), check "Married, but withhold at higher Single rate" in Box 3.

Line 4 of Form W-4

Total number of allowances.—Use the worksheet on page 2 to figure your allowances. Add the number of allowances for each category explained below. Enter the total on line 4.

If you are single and hold more than one job, you may not claim the same allowances with more than one employer at the same time. If you are married and both you and your spouse are employed, you may not both claim the same allowances with both of your employers at the same time. To have the highest amount of tax withheld, claim "0" allowances on line 4.

A. Personal allowances.—You can claim the following personal allowances:

1 for yourself, 1 if you are 65 or older, and 1 if you are blind.

If you are married and your spouse either does not work or is not claiming his or her allowances on a separate W-4, you may also claim the following allowances: 1 for your spouse, 1 if your spouse is 65 or older, and 1 if your spouse is blind.

B. Special withholding allowance.—Claim the special withholding allowance if you are single and have one job or you are married, have one job, and your spouse does not work. You may still claim this allowance so long as the total wages earned on other jobs by you or your spouse (or both) is 10% or less of the combined total wages. Use this special withholding allowance only to figure your withholding. Do not claim it when you file your return.

C. Allowances for dependents.—You may claim one allowance for each dependent you will be able to claim on your Federal income tax return.

Note: *If you are not claiming any deductions or credits, skip D and E, add lines A, B, and C, enter the total on line F and carry the total over to line 4 of W-4.*

Before you claim allowances under D and E, total your non-wage taxable income (interest, dividends, self-employment income, etc.) and subtract this amount from estimated deductions you would otherwise enter in D1. If your non-wage income is greater than the amount of estimated deductions, you cannot claim any allowances under D. Moreover, you should take one-third of the excess (non-wage income over estimated deductions) and add this to the appropriate "A" value in Table 1 if determining allowances under E.

D. Allowances for estimated deductions.—If you expect to itemize deductions, you can claim additional withholding allowances. See Schedule A (Form 1040) for deductions you can itemize.

You can also count deductible amounts you pay for (1) alimony (2) qualified retirement contributions including IRA and Keogh (H.R. 10) plans (3) moving expenses (4) employee business expenses (Part I of Form 2106) (5) the deduction for a married couple when both work (6) net losses shown on Schedules C, D, E, and F (Form 1040), the last line of Part II of Form 4797, and the net operating loss carryover (7) penalty on early withdrawal of savings and (8) charitable contributions for nonitemizers. **Note:** Check with your employer to see if any tax is being withheld on moving expenses or IRA contributions. Do not include these amounts if tax is not being withheld; otherwise, you may be underwithheld. For details, see **Publication 505.**

The deduction allowed a married couple when both work is 10% of the lesser of $30,000 or the qualified earned income of the spouse with the lower income.

Once you have determined these deductions, enter the total on line D1 of the worksheet on page 2 and figure the number of withholding allowances for them.

E. Allowances for tax credits.—If you expect to take credits like those shown on lines 41 through 48 on the 1983 Form 1040 (child care, residential energy, etc.), use the table on the top of page 2 to figure the number of additional allowances you can claim. You may estimate these credits. Include the earned income credit if you are not receiving advance payment of it, and any excess social security tax withheld. Also, if you expect to income average, include the amount of the reduction in tax because of averaging when using the table.

Form **W-4** (Rev. 1-84)

Figure 1005-1.1. Form W-4, Employee's Withholding Allowance Certificate.

Example: An employee's regular salary is $400 per week. The partner granted her a merit bonus of $250. You should find the tax to be withheld in Circular E, using the table for weekly wages in the amount of $650.

If the supplemental wages are not paid in the same payment as regular wages, you may:

1. Withhold at a flat rate of 20 percent on the gross wage; or
2. Add the supplemental wage to the last regular wage and determine the income tax to be withheld as if it were a single payment (like the example). Then you should subtract the normal tax usually withheld from the regular wage payment, and withhold the remaining tax from the supplemental wage payment.

¶1005.3 State Income Tax Withholding

Every state does not impose an income tax on its residents. If your state does, it will publish an employer's tax guide similar to the IRS' Circular E. You will need to find the appropriate state income tax agency in the phone book and call to request the necessary tax tables and forms.

When a new employee fills out the W-4 form, you should have them fill out a similar form for your state.

¶1006 How to Pay Withheld Taxes

The income tax withheld and FICA taxes (both employer and employee portions) must be deposited with an authorized, commercial bank depositary or a Federal Reserve Bank, with a Federal Tax Deposit Form 8109-B (Figure 1006-1).

Tax deposits are a means of getting funds quickly into the government treasury and should not be confused with tax returns. The amount of taxes due determines the frequency of tax deposits. The firm owes taxes as soon as wages are paid, not when the payroll period ends.

The rules for making tax deposits are found in Circular E. These rules change periodically, so be sure to review Circular E to make sure you understand the current rules.

It is good practice to write the checks for the payroll taxes due when the payroll checks are written. The federal taxes should be deposited in the bank right away (usually within three banking days), but the checks for state taxes may be held until the payroll tax return is due. By writing the checks, it is more likely that there will be enough money in the checking account when it is time to pay the payroll taxes. Many firms have gotten themselves in trouble with the IRS because

FEDERAL TAX DEPOSIT

Type of Tax **MARK ONE** | Tax Period **MARK ONE**

FISCAL YEAR MONTH →

EMPLOYER NUMBER →

BANK NAME/ DATE STAMP

Name ______________________

____

Address ______________________

____

City ______________________

State ______________ Zip __________

32

DO NOT WRITE OR STAMP BELOW THIS LINE

FOR BANK USE IN MICR ENCODING

SEPARATE ALONG THIS LINE AND SUBMIT TO DEPOSITARY WITH PAYMENT.

OMB NO. 1545-0257

IMPORTANT

Read instructions carefully before completing form.

Enter your name exactly as shown on your return or other IRS correspondence, address, and employer identification number in the space provided. If you are required to file Form 1120, 990C, or 990T, enter the month in which your fiscal year ends in the applicable boxes. Example: If your fiscal year ends in January, enter 01, if it ends in February, enter 02, etc.

Kind of Tax—Mark one kind of tax only. Make sure you darken the space that corresponds to the kind of tax you are paying.

Right 941 | Wrong 941 | Wrong 941

The following kind of tax must be paid through the Federal Tax Deposit System.

Form 941 —Withheld Income & Social Security (FICA)
Form 943 —Agricultural Withheld Income & Social Security (FICA)
Form 940 —Federal Unemployment Tax FUTA
Form 720 —Excise Tax
Form CT-1 —Railroad Retirement
Form 1120 —Corporate Income Tax
Form 990C —Exempt Cooperative Association Income Tax
Form 990T —Exempt Organization Income Tax
Form 1042 —Withholding at Source—Non-Resident Alien. Foreign Corporations, Tax Free Covenant Bonds
Form 945 —Backup Withholding

Tax Quarter—Mark only one space to indicate the tax quarter for which you are making a deposit. Note: When depositing taxes for forms 1120, 990C, or 990T be sure to mark the quarter that corresponds to your fiscal year. For example, if your fiscal year ends in June, your first quarter would be July through September.

Amount of Deposit—Enter amount of deposit in space provided.

DO enter amounts legibly, forming the characters as displayed here.

1	2	3	4	5	6	7	8	9	0

DON'T type money amounts. Don't use dollar signs, commas, decimal points, or enter leading zeros, as below.

0	0	0	$	7,	6	3	5.	0	0

How To Order Deposit Forms—Request deposit forms by calling IRS or by writing any IRS office. If you write, your request should show your name, address, employer identification number, and the month in which your fiscal year ends, if you are required to file Form 1120, 990C, or 990T. There are 15 coupons to a book for use in depositing any kind of tax for any tax year. You should receive the forms in about 3 weeks. Be sure to request forms early enough to make your deposits on time.

How to Make Deposits—Mail or deliver the completed form with a check or postal money order for the amount of deposit to a qualified depositary for federal taxes or to the Federal Tax Department of the Federal Reserve Bank or Branch (FRB) for your area. Make the check or money order payable to that depositary or FRB. Federal agencies should make deposits at FRB's only.

Deposits at Depositaries—Authorized depositaries are required to accept from a taxpayer cash, a postal money order drawn to the order of the depositary, or a check or draft drawn on and to the order of the depositary. If you want to make a tax deposit by a check drawn on another financial organization, you may do so only if the depositary is willing to accept that payment as a deposit of Federal taxes.

Deposits at FRB's—If you want to make a deposit by check at an FRB, you must make it with the FRB for your area with a check or other payment for which immediate credit is given in accordance with the check collection schedule of the receiving FRB. Checks generally considered as immediate credit items at FRB's include, but are not limited to, checks drawn on commercial banks located in the same city as the receiving FRB. Information about the FRB for your area and checks that are considered by that FRB as immediate credit items can be obtained from FRB's and commercial banks.

Timeliness of Deposit—The date they are received by an authorized depositary will determine whether deposits are made on time. All deposits made at an FRB will be dated on a collection basis. But deposits made with a payment instrument that complies with the above payment requirements will be considered timely if the FRB receives them by the due date. For deposits made at an FRB that do not comply with payment requirements, the date the funds are collected will determine timeliness of deposit regardless of when they are mailed.

When to Make Deposits—Instructions are provided in IRS publications and tax returns. You can get copies of these documents and other information about tax procedures from the IRS District Director's office.

PAPERWORK REDUCTION ACT NOTICE

We ask for this information to carry out the Internal Revenue laws of the United States. We need it to ensure that taxpayers are complying with these laws and to allow us to figure and collect the right amount of tax. You are required to give us this information.

Department of The Treasury
Internal Revenue Service

☆U.S. G.P.O. 1984-455-685 E.I. 43-0787287

Form 8109-B (10-83)

Figure 1006-1. Form 8109-B, Federal Tax Deposit.

there is not enough cash to pay the taxes because someone forgot about them and spent the cash on other items. By writing the checks, subtracting the amounts from the checkbook balance, it is as if the money is already spent, even if you have the checks tucked away safely in a drawer.

¶1007 Understanding the Payroll Tax Calendar

January 1	Determine each employee's withholding status for the new year. Request new Form W-4 to be completed by each employee.
January 31	Prepare and furnish to each employee a Form W-2, showing wages paid and taxes withheld during the prior year.
	File Federal Unemployment Tax Act (FUTA) (Form 940) for prior year.
	File Employer's Quarterly Federal Tax Return (Form 941) for the last quarter (October, November and December) of the prior year.
February 28	Prepare and furnish to recipient Annual Information Returns (Form 1099) for all nonemployee compensation and other payments of $600 or more made during the course of business during the prior year.
	Last day for filing copies A (originals) of all Forms W-2 issued for the year. Use Transmittal of Wage and Tax Statements (Form W-3). File with the Social Security Administration.
April 15	File individual income tax and self-employment tax returns for the prior calendar year.
April 30	Prepare quarterly payroll tax return (Form 941) for the quarter ended March 31.
	Deposit accrued FUTA taxes if in excess of $100.
July 31	Prepare quarterly payroll tax return (Form 941) for the quarter ended June 30.
	Deposit accrued FUTA taxes if in excess of $100.

October 31	Prepare quarterly payroll tax return (Form 941) for the quarter ended September 30.
	Deposit accrued FUTA taxes if in excess of $100.
December 1	Last day for an employee to file an amended withholding exemption certificate for current year where exemption status has changed.

¶1008 Understanding Payroll Tax Returns

Every employer who withholds federal income tax from wages or who is liable for FICA taxes must file an Employer's Quarterly Federal Tax Return, Form 941 (Figure 1008-1). Do not file more than one calendar quarter on any return. In other words, one return per quarter. The months for each payroll quarter are:

First Quarter	January, February, and March
Second Quarter	April, May, and June
Third Quarter	July, August, and September
Fourth Quarter	October, November, and December

The return is due on or before the last day of the month following the close of the quarter.

You will need the following information in order to complete the return:

1. A listing of all employees and their Social Security numbers;
2. The total amount of gross wages paid to each employee during the quarter;
3. The amount of income tax withheld from each employee's gross wages;
4. The amount of FICA taxes withheld from each employee's gross wages;
5. The amount of federal taxes due at each pay period (both withheld and employer's portion of FICA);
6. The date and amount of each deposit of payroll taxes made during the quarter;
7. The amount of any undeposited payroll taxes.

With this information, you should be able to complete the payroll tax return by answering each question, one at a time. Look at the completed return in Figure 1008-2. Notice that the amount deposited

Form **941**
(Rev. January 1985)
Department of the Treasury
Internal Revenue Service

Employer's Quarterly Federal Tax Return

▶ For Paperwork Reduction Act Notice, see page 2.

Please type or print

Type or print in this space your name, address, and employer identification number as shown on original.

Return for calendar quarter ending (Enter month and year as on original)

If you are not liable for returns in the future, write "FINAL" . . . . ▶ Date final wages paid . . . . ▶

Complete for First Quarter Only

1 a	Number of employees (except household) employed in the pay period that includes March 12th . ▶	1a	
b	If you are a subsidiary corporation AND your parent corporation files a consolidated Form 1120, enter parent corporation employer identification number (EIN) . . ▶ 1b –		
2	Total wages and tips subject to withholding, plus other compensation . . . . ▶	2	
3	Total income tax withheld from wages, tips, pensions, annuities, sick pay, gambling, etc . . . . ▶	3	
4	Adjustment of withheld income tax for preceding quarters of calendar year (see instructions) . . ▶	4	
5	Adjusted total of income tax withheld	5	
6	Taxable social security wages paid . . . . . $ ______ X 14.1% (.141) . .	6	
7 a	Taxable tips reported . . . . $ ______ X 7.05% (.0705) . .	7a	
b	Tips deemed to be wages (see instructions) . . $ ______ X 7.05% (.0705) . .	7b	
8	Total social security taxes (add lines 6, 7a, and 7b)	8	
9	Adjustment of social security taxes (see instructions) . . . . ▶	9	
10	Adjusted total of social security taxes	10	
11	Backup withholding . . . . ▶	11	
12	Adjustment of backup withholding tax for preceding quarters of calendar year	12	
13	Adjusted total of backup withholding	13	
14	Total taxes (add lines 5, 10, and 13) . . . . ▶	14	
15	Advance earned income credit (EIC) payments, if any (see instructions)	15	
16	Net taxes (subtract line 15 from line 14). **This must equal line IV below** (plus line IV of Schedule A (Form 941) if you have treated backup withholding as a separate liability.)	16	
17	Total deposits for quarter, including overpayment applied from a prior quarter, from your records . ▶	17	
18	Undeposited taxes due (subtract line 17 from line 16). Enter here and pay to IRS . . . . . . ▶	18	
19	If line 17 is more than line 16, enter overpayment here ▶ $ ______ and check if to be: ☐ Applied to next return or ☐ Refunded.		

Record of Federal Tax Liability (Complete if line 16 is $500 or more)

See the instructions under rule 4 for details before checking these boxes.

Check only if you made eighth-monthly deposits using the 95% rule ▶ ☐ Check only if you are a first time 3-banking-day depositor ▶ ☐

Date wages paid	Tax liability (*Do not show Federal tax deposits here.*)					
	First month of quarter		Second month of quarter		Third month of quarter	
1st through 3rd	A		I		Q	
4th through 7th	B		J		R	
8th through 11th	C		K		S	
12th through 15th	D		L		T	
16th through 19th	E		M		U	
20th through 22nd	F		N		V	
23rd through 25th	G		O		W	
26th through the last	H		P		X	
Total liability for month	*I*		*II*		*III*	

IV Total for quarter (add lines *I*, *II*, and *III*) . . . . ▶

Under penalties of perjury, I declare that I have examined this return, including accompanying schedules and statements, and to the best of my knowledge and belief it is true, correct, and complete.

Signature ▶ **Title** ▶ **Date** ▶

Figure 1008-1. Form 941, Employer's Quarterly Federal Tax Return.

Form **941** (Rev. January 1985) Department of the Treasury Internal Revenue Service

Employer's Quarterly Federal Tax Return

▶ For Paperwork Reduction Act Notice, see page 2.

Please type or print

Type or print in this space your name, address, and employer identification number as shown on original.

Return for calendar quarter ending (Enter month and year as on original)

If you are not liable for returns in the future, write "FINAL" . . . . ▶ Date final wages paid . . . . ▶

Complete for First Quarter Only

1 a	Number of employees (except household) employed in the pay period that includes March 12th . ▶	1a	
b	If you are a subsidiary corporation AND your parent corporation files a consolidated Form 1120, enter parent corporation employer identification number (EIN) . . ▶ 1b –		
2	Total wages and tips subject to withholding, plus other compensation . . . . ▶	2	
3	Total income tax withheld from wages, tips, pensions, annuities, sick pay, gambling, etc . . . . ▶	3	
4	Adjustment of withheld income tax for preceding quarters of calendar year (see instructions) . . ▶	4	
5	Adjusted total of income tax withheld	5	
6	Taxable social security wages paid . . . . . $ ______ X 14.1% (.141)	6	
7 a	Taxable tips reported . . . . $ ______ X 7.05% (.0705)	7a	
b	Tips deemed to be wages (see instructions) . . $ ______ X 7.05% (.0705)	7b	
8	Total social security taxes (add lines 6, 7a, and 7b)	8	
9	Adjustment of social security taxes (see instructions) . . . . ▶	9	
10	Adjusted total of social security taxes	10	
11	Backup withholding . . . . ▶	11	
12	Adjustment of backup withholding tax for preceding quarters of calendar year	12	
13	Adjusted total of backup withholding	13	
14	Total taxes (add lines 5, 10, and 13) . . . . ▶	14	
15	Advance earned income credit (EIC) payments, if any (see instructions)	15	
16	Net taxes (subtract line 15 from line 14). **This must equal line IV below** (plus line IV of Schedule A (Form 941) if you have treated backup withholding as a separate liability.)	16	
17	Total deposits for quarter, including overpayment applied from a prior quarter, from your records . ▶	17	
18	Undeposited taxes due (subtract line 17 from line 16). Enter here and pay to IRS . . . . . . ▶	18	
19	If line 17 is more than line 16, enter overpayment here ▶ $ ______ and check if to be: ☐ Applied to next return or ☐ Refunded.		

Record of Federal Tax Liability (Complete if line 16 is $500 or more)

See the instructions under rule 4 for details before checking these boxes.

Check only if you made eighth-monthly deposits using the 95% rule ▶ ☐ Check only if you are a first time 3-banking-day depositor ▶ ☐

Date wages paid	Tax liability *(Do not show Federal tax deposits here.)* First month of quarter		Second month of quarter		Third month of quarter	
1st through 3rd	A		I		Q	
4th through 7th	B		J		R	
8th through 11th	C		K		S	
12th through 15th	D		L		T	
16th through 19th	E		M		U	
20th through 22nd	F		N		V	
23rd through 25th	G		O		W	
26th through the last	H		P		X	
Total liability for month	*I*		*II*		*III*	

IV Total for quarter (add lines ***I***, ***II***, and ***III***) . . . . ▶

Under penalties of perjury, I declare that I have examined this return, including accompanying schedules and statements, and to the best of my knowledge and belief it is true, correct, and complete.

Signature ▶ **Title** ▶ **Date** ▶

Figure 1008-2. Completed Form 941, Employer's Quarterly Federal Tax Return.

and the amount of tax calculated on the return is a little bit different, by a few cents. When this happens you can adjust the amount on Line 9 labeling it Fractions Only. These differences occur when the FICA taxes are calculated and are usually due to rounding off cents.

You may need to complete a similar return for your state income tax department. Since every state is different and some do not even have income taxes, you will need to get the information from your state agency.

¶1009 What Is the Federal Unemployment Tax Act (FUTA)?

Unemployment insurance is a coordinated federal state program designed to provide economic security for a worker during temporary periods of unemployment. Although a federal tax is imposed, the Federal Act provides no direct benefits. Benefits are paid by the states through contributions of employers and the federal government. This tax is imposed on employers only and must not be collected or deducted from employee's wages.

An employer is subject to FUTA if the following is true:

1. One or more persons are employed, on at least some portion of one day, in each of twenty or more calendar weeks during the taxable year, or during the preceding taxable year or;
2. If wages of $1,500 or more are paid during any calendar quarter in the calendar year or preceding calendar year.

As soon as either test is met, the employer becomes liable for the FUTA tax for the *entire calendar year.*

The FUTA rate (3.5 percent in 1985) is outlined in Circular E and is imposed on the first $7,000 (1985) of wages paid during the calendar year to each employee. A credit is allowed against the tax for contributions paid by the employer into state unemployment funds. This credit is generally 2.7 percent of the taxable wages, regardless of the actual state rate, which usually varies according to an employer's unemployment experience. Law firms generally have very low state unemployment rates, because legal employees seldom apply for unemployment pay. It is the unskilled worker who draws a lot of unemployment, therefore it is only right that those employers who use unskilled workers foot the bill for their unemployment claims.

Deposit rules provide that the FUTA tax must be computed every quarter for the first three calendar quarters. The amount subject to deposit is determined by multiplying .008 (3.5 percent less 2.7 percent) by the part of the first $7,000 of each employee's annual wages paid during the quarter.

If the total amount computed is more than $100, a deposit must be made with an authorized commercial bank or a Federal Reserve Bank. You should fill out a Federal Tax Deposit Form 8109-B (see Figure 1006-1 in ¶1006) and deposit the FUTA tax (accompanied by form) on or before the last day of the month following the close of the quarter.

If the amount is less than $100, a deposit is not required until the next quarter when the total for that quarter plus the undeposited tax for the prior quarter exceeds $100. You do not need to make a deposit for the last quarter. You may wait and pay the remaining amount when the annual return is filed.

You will need to fill out an Annual Federal Unemployment Tax Return on Form 940 (Figure 1009-1) for the prior year on or before January 31. At that time the balance of the tax due may be paid if it is less than $100. If it is more than $100, you must deposit it in the firm's bank.

Each state will have its own rules for payment of unemployment taxes. You will have to find out what they are by calling your state income tax department or unemployment insurance agency.

¶1010 How to Use Form W-2 (Wage and Tax Statement)

At the end of each year, your firm is responsible for preparing a Form W-2 (Figure 1010-1) for each employee from whom income tax or FICA taxes were withheld during the prior year. Form W-2 shows the total wages and other compensation paid to employees and the amounts deducted for income tax and FICA taxes.

Give each employee at least two copies of their W-2 form—three if your state has an income tax—four if both your state and city have an income tax. In other words, the employee should have a copy for themselves and one to file with each income tax return required.

The Form W-2 must be given to the employee not later than January 31 of the following year. If an employee leaves the firm before the end of the year and requests a W-2, the firm is required to prepare it and furnish it to the employee not later than 30 days after the request.

The original (Copy A) of Form W-2 must go to the IRS on or before the last day of February. Use Transmittal of Income and Tax Statements, Form W-3 (Figure 1010-2) to summarize the W-2s and as a transmittal form. Keep a copy of each W-2 for the firm's records.

Form **940**
Department of the Treasury
Internal Revenue Service

Employer's Annual Federal Unemployment (FUTA) Tax Return

▶ **For Paperwork Reduction Act Notice, see page 2.**

OMB No. 1545-0028

1984

If incorrect, make any necessary change. ▶

Name (as distinguished from trade name) | Calendar Year 1984
Trade name, if any | Employer identification number
Address and ZIP code

T	
FF	
FD	
FP	
I	
T	

A Did you pay all required contributions to your state unemployment fund by the due date of Form 940? (If none required, check "No.") ☐ **Yes** ☐ **No**

If you checked the "Yes" box, enter amount of contributions paid to your state unemployment fund ▶ $

B Are you required to pay contributions to only one state? ☐ **Yes** ☐ **No**

If you checked the "Yes" box, (1) Enter the name of the state where you are required to pay contributions ▶

(2) Enter your state reporting number(s) as shown on state unemployment tax return ▶

Part I Computation of Taxable Wages and Credit Reduction (To Be Completed by All Taxpayers)

1 Total payments (including exempt payments) during the calendar year for services of employees . . . **1**

2 Exempt payments. (Explain each exemption shown, attaching additional sheet if necessary) ▶ . . . **2** Amount paid

3 Payments for services of more than $7,000. Enter only the excess over the first $7,000 paid to individual employees not including exempt amounts shown on line 2. Do not use the state wage limitation . . . **3**

4 Total exempt payments (add lines 2 and 3) . . . **4**

5 **Total taxable wages** (subtract line 4 from line 1). (If any part is exempt from state contributions, see instructions) ▶ **5**

6 Credit reduction for unrepaid advances to the states listed (by 2-letter Postal Service abbreviations). Enter the wages included on line 5 above for each state and multiply by the rate shown.

(a) CT	x .007	(f) MI	x .007	(l) VT	x .006		
(b) DC	x .011	(g) MN	x .008	(m) WV	x .007		
(c) IL	x .008	(h) NJ	x .006	**Outside the United States**			
(d) IA	x .003	(i) OH	x .007	(n) PR	x .006		
(e) LA	x .003	(j) PA	x .008	(o) VI	x .009		
		(k) TX	x .003				

7 Total credit reduction (add lines 6(a) through 6(o) and enter in Part II, line 2 or Part III, line 4) ▶ **7**

Part II Tax Due or Refund (Complete if You Checked the "Yes" Boxes in Both Items A and B Above)

1 FUTA tax. Multiply the wages in Part I, line 5, by .008 and enter here . . . **1**

2 Enter amount from Part I, line 7 . . . **2**

3 **Total FUTA tax** (add lines 1 and 2) . . . **3**

4 Less: Total FUTA tax deposited for the year, including any overpayment applied from a prior year (from your records) . **4**

5 **Balance due** (subtract line 4 from line 3—if over $100, see Part IV instructions). Pay to IRS ▶ **5**

6 **Overpayment** (subtract line 3 from line 4). Check if it is to be: ☐ Applied to next return, or ☐ Refunded ▶ **6**

Part III Tax Due or Refund (Complete if You Checked the "No" Box in Either Item A or Item B Above. Also complete Part V)

1 Gross FUTA tax. Multiply the wages in Part I, line 5, by .035 . . . **1**

2 Maximum credit. Multiply the wages in Part I, line 5, by .027 . . . **2**

3 Enter the smaller of the amount in Part V, line 11, or Part III, line 2 . . . **3**

4 Enter amount from Part I, line 7 . . . **4**

5 **Credit allowable** (subtract line 4 from line 3) (If zero or less, enter 0.) . . . **5**

6 Total FUTA tax (subtract line 5 from line 1) . . . **6**

7 Less: Total FUTA tax deposited for the year, including any overpayment applied from a prior year (from your records) . **7**

8 **Balance due** (subtract line 7 from line 6—if over $100, see Part IV instructions). Pay to IRS ▶ **8**

9 **Overpayment** (subtract line 6 from line 7). Check if it is to be: ☐ Applied to next return, or ☐ Refunded ▶ **9**

Part IV Record of Quarterly Federal Tax Liability for Unemployment Tax (Do not include State liability)

Quarter	First	Second	Third	Fourth	Total for Year
Liability for quarter					

If you will not have to file returns in the future, write "Final" here (see general instruction "Who Must File") and sign the return ▶

Under penalties of perjury, I declare that I have examined this return, including accompanying schedules and statements, and to the best of my knowledge and belief, it is true, correct, and complete, and that no part of any payment made to a state unemployment fund claimed as a credit was or is to be deducted from the payments to employees.

Signature ▶ Title (Owner, etc.) ▶ Date ▶

Form **940** (1984)

Figure 1009-1. Employer's Annual Federal Unemployment (FUTA) Tax Return.

1 Control number	OMB No. 1545-0008	
2 Employer's name, address, and ZIP code	3 Employer's identification number	4 Employer's State number
	5 Stat. employee ☐ Deceased ☐ Legal rep. ☐	942 emp. ☐ Subtotal ☐ Void ☐
	6 Allocated tips	7 Advance EIC payment
8 Employee's social security number / 9 Federal income tax withheld	10 Wages, tips, other compensation	11 Social security tax withheld
12 Employee's name, address, and ZIP code	13 Social security wages	14 Social security tips
	16	
	17 State income tax / 18 State wages, tips, etc.	19 Name of State
	20 Local income tax / 21 Local wages, tips, etc.	22 Name of locality

Form **W-2 Wage and Tax Statement 1984** Copy 1 For State, City, or Local Tax Department
Employee's and employer's copy compared ☐

Figure 1010-1. Form W-2, Wage and Tax Statement.

Each state that imposes an income tax on residents will have its own rules regarding the reporting of wages and withholdings. Most states will require you to send them a copy of Forms W-2 by the end of January or February.

¶1011 How to Write Payroll Checks

Everyone loves payday. If you are responsible for preparing payroll checks, everyone will love you—on payday. As you deliver those checks you will get smiles you may never see any other time. That is, unless you make a mistake. You will be the first to know if you have underpaid someone. You may forget to include some secretary's overtime, or an associate's raise. The writing of payroll checks should be done very carefully.

Payroll periods differ from firm to firm. There are only a few general pay periods, however.

Monthly	Once a month
Semi-monthly	Twice a month on the 15th and the last day of the month
Bi-weekly	Every two weeks
Weekly	Once a week

Here are the general guidelines for writing payroll checks.

1. Determine the employee's regular pay. This will probably be the same every pay period. You may have to calculate this only once when

Please do not staple

1 Control number	33333	OMB No. 1545-0008			
☐ Kind of Payer and Tax Statements Transmitted ▶	2 941/941E ☐ Military ☐ 943 ☐ CT-1 ☐ 942 ☐ Medicare Fed. emp. ☐		3 W-2 ☐ W-2P ☐	4	5 Number of statements attached
6 Allocated tips	7 Advance EIC payments		8		
9 Federal income tax withheld	10 Wages, tips, and other compensation		11 Social security (FICA) tax withheld		
12 Employer's State number	13 Social security (FICA) wages		14 Social security (FICA) tips		
15 Employer's identification number			16 Establishment number		
17 Employer's name			18 Gross annuity, pension, etc. (Form W-2P)		
			20 Taxable amount (Form W-2P)		
19 Employer's address and ZIP code (If available, place label over boxes 15, 17, and 19.)			21 Income tax withheld by third-party payer		

Under penalties of perjury, I declare that I have examined this return and accompanying documents, and to the best of my knowledge and belief, they are true, correct, and complete. In the case of documents without recipients' identifying numbers, I have complied with the requirements of the law in attempting to secure such numbers from the recipients.

Signature ▶ Title ▶ Date ▶

Form **W-3 Transmittal of Income and Tax Statements 1984** Department of the Treasury Internal Revenue Service

Please return this entire page to the Social Security Administration address for your State as listed below.

If your legal residence, principal place of business, office or agency is located in ▼	Use this address ▼
Alaka, Arizona, California, Colorado, Hawaii, Idaho, Iowa, Minnesota, Missouri, Montana, Nebraska, Nevada, North Dakota, Oregon, South Dakota, Utah, Washington, Wisconsin, Wyoming	Social Security Administration Salinas Data Operations Center Salinas, CA 93911
Alabama, Arkansas, Florida, Georgia, Illinois, Kansas, Louisiana, Mississippi, New Mexico, Oklahoma, South Carolina, Tennessee, Texas	Social Security Administration Albuquerque Data Operations Center Albuquerque, NM 87180
Connecticut, Delaware, District of Columbia, Indiana, Kentucky, Maine, Maryland, Massachusetts, Michigan, New Hampshire, New Jersey, New York, North Carolina, Ohio, Pennsylvania, Rhode Island, Vermont, Virginia, West Virginia	Social Security Administration Wilkes-Barre Data Operations Center Wilkes-Barre, PA 18769
If you have no legal residence or principal place of business in any State	Social Security Administration Wilkes-Barre Data Operations Center Wilkes-Barre, PA 18769

Paperwork Reduction Act Notice.—We ask for this information to carry out the Internal Revenue laws of the United States. We need it to ensure that taxpayers are complying with these laws and to allow us to figure and collect the right amount of tax. You are required to give us this information.

Figure 1010-2. Form W-3, Transmittal of Income and Tax Statements.

the employee joins the firm and periodically as the employee is given raises. If a secretary is paid an annual salary, say $20,000 and the firm's payroll period is weekly, the regular pay is $384.62 ($20,000/52).

2. Determine any bonuses, overtime, back pay, or severance pay. Determine the amount of supplemental pay for each employee. Overtime should be approved by the responsible attorney. Attorneys generally do not receive overtime pay, only secretarial and other support staff. Overtime should be calculated at one and a half times regular pay. A secretary who makes $20,000 annually and works a 40-hour week makes $9.62 ($20,000/52/40) per hour regularly. Overtime should be paid at $14.42 ($9.62 × 1.5) per overtime hour.

Merit bonuses or Christmas gifts should also be added to regular pay before withholding taxes. These types of payments are subject to income taxes and FICA withholdings just like regular pay.

Sometimes an employee is owed back pay. The most common type of back pay is when the employee is granted a raise but the person who prepares the payroll is not informed, or the raise is retroactive. The employee's check is usually adjusted in the next period.

Often when an employee is terminated, the firm will pay them several weeks' salary rather than give them notice. This is called severance pay or "salary in lieu of notice." When this happens, you will need to pay the terminated employee for the current pay period, plus the severance pay.

3. Calculate the amount of FICA tax to be withheld. Add up the regular wages and supplemental pay to arrive at the gross wages for each employee. Multiply this figure by the current FICA tax rate (7.05 percent in 1985). This will give you the amount to withhold from the employee's wages. A secretary who has a salary of $384.62 for the pay period would have $25.76 withheld from his check for FICA taxes.

For attorneys who are paid a salary, be careful not to withhold FICA taxes after they reach the limit. Check Circular E or with the firm's CPA to find out what the limit is. ($39,600 in 1985)

4. Determine the amount of federal income tax to be withheld. Use the tax tables in Circular E to find the amount of federal income tax to withhold. The amount will differ depending on the marital status and number of exemptions of each employee as reported on Form W-4. Assume our secretary will have $65.00 withheld for federal income taxes.

5. Determine the amount of state income tax to be withheld. If your state has an income tax, use the appropriate tax tables from your employer's tax guide to determine the amount of state income tax to be withheld from each employee. Assume our secretary will have $23.00 withheld for state income taxes.

6. *Determine if any miscellaneous deductions should be withheld.* There are several types of other deductions which you may need to withhold from an employee's check:

Health insurance premiums (if the firm does not pay them all);
United Way contributions;
Repayment of employee advances;
Profit sharing contributions by the employee;
Payment of expenses paid by the firm on behalf of the employee (postage, copies, long distance calls, personal office supplies, etc.)

These amounts may vary with each employee and should be explained on each employee's earnings card.

Let's assume our secretary has agreed to give $2.00 per pay period to the United Way.

7. *Determine the amount of net pay.* The net pay is the amount for which the payroll check will be written and is calculated like this:

Gross pay		$384.62
Less:	FICA taxes	– 25.76
	Federal income tax	– 65.00
	State income tax	– 23.00
	United Way	– 2.00
Net pay		$268.86

You should write a payroll check to our secretary, James Dillon, which shows the amount of gross wages, less each deduction. The amount of the check will be $268.86. This is how much James can spend. The deductions will be paid to the appropriate agency by depositing the payroll taxes in the bank, paying with a payroll tax return or a check to the United Way for all employee's contributions.

Hopefully, your firm will use a pegboard system, also known as a "one-write" system for payroll. This eliminates many posting errors because the payroll check, the earnings card and the payroll journal are all created at one time. These systems are specially designed for writing payroll checks, with boxes for each type of deduction on the check, the payroll card and the payroll journal. If your firm does not have such a system, you should recommend one. If you write regular checks, be sure to write the amount of gross pay and all deductions on the check stub for the person doing the firm's bookkeeping.

8. *Total each column or part of the payroll.* You will need a total of each item making up the payroll transactions:

Gross wages
FICA wages
FICA withheld
Federal income tax withheld
State income tax withheld
Other deductions (United Way, insurance premiums, etc.)

Gross wages are the amount of payroll expense your firm will have for the period. *FICA* wages are the total wages subject to FICA taxes. FICA wages and gross wages will be the same until some point in the year when some employees' salaries exceed the FICA limit. After that point, their wages will be excluded from FICA wages because you will not be withholding FICA taxes from their pay.

FICA wages are used to calculate the amount of the employer's portion of FICA taxes due to the IRS. You will need to multiply the employer's FICA rate times the total FICA wages to determine this amount.

FICA withheld is the amount you will need to deposit in the bank or pay to the IRS with the quarterly payroll tax return, depending upon the amount. (See Circular E for deposit rules.).

Federal income tax withheld also must be deposited in the firm's bank or paid to the IRS with the quarterly payroll tax return, depending on the amount. (See Circular E for deposit rules.)

State income tax withheld must be paid to the appropriate state agency. Each state has different rules and it will be up to you to find out what those are in your state. Call the firm's CPA or the state income tax department for details.

Other deductions should be paid to the appropriate party or recorded in the firm's books to reduce the proper account. For example, United Way deductions should be totaled and a check written to United Way for the total deducted for all employees. This check can be written once a month rather than every pay period.

Insurance premiums which are withheld should be credited to the insurance expense account in the firm's general ledger, reducing the firm's total insurance expense. The firm will probably pay the premiums in full and then will collect the employee's portion by payroll deductions. Often these premiums are for dependent coverage which the employee elects to have when the firm's policy is to not pay dependent coverage.

9. Write the checks for payroll taxes withheld. You should go ahead and write the checks for any liability for payroll taxes at the same time you prepare payroll. This has the effect of getting on the firm's books all of the payroll tax expense for the pay period and accounts for the payroll taxes due to the various governmental agencies. If you are required to deposit the payroll taxes, fill out the appropriate forms (Form 501) and see that both the employee's and the employer's portion are deposited. If the state taxes are not required to be deposited, save the checks until the return is filed according to your state's requirements.

10. Maintain confidentiality at all times. There is probably no type of business which requires as much confidentiality of payroll transactions as the law firm. Other businesses have pay scales that are published and employees are paid according to seniority or other criteria. It is no secret how much other employees make. This is not the case in the law firm. Secretaries may be paid based upon performance, seniority or anything else the attorney wishes. New employees coming into the firm are often paid a higher salary than present employees because the market requires it.

If you are preparing payroll, you have been given a position of trust. Distribute paychecks in envelopes, or put them in the hands of each employee yourself. Do not lay them down on the employee's desk if they are away from their desk. Don't leave payroll records lying on your desk. Put them away before you leave to distribute paychecks. Don't leave payroll checks in plain view on the partner's desk, who will sign them. More than one employee has been terminated because they breached this position of trust and confidentiality. If you have a problem with the amount of someone's pay, including your own, discuss it with your attorneys, not with the other secretaries.

¶1100 How to Use the Various Timekeeping Systems

By Carole A. Bruno and Paula F. Turner

Attorneys are in the business of selling time. It is an attorney's education, skills, and experience, that make his or her time worth something. Every day your attorneys work for their clients, solving legal problems. They expect clients to pay them for their efforts. How do clients know how much to pay? How do attorneys know how much to charge? This is where timekeeping comes in.

Actually, attorneys cannot charge clients solely on the basis of time spent on behalf of the client, but it is a good place to start. The attorney considers what was done for the client, the amount of time the service to the client required, the benefit the client received from the service when making a decision about how much to charge.

Attorneys usually have an hourly rate that they use in their timekeeping system. Generally, the more experience and expertise an attorney has, the higher his hourly rate. In some types of practices, however, the rates are set by the client. For example, in insurance defense work, the large insurance companies have a lot of influence on the rates attorneys can charge them for their services.

¶1101 Learning the Difference Between Standard Value vs. Matter Value

Even if clients are billed a flat rate for services, i.e., $500 for a divorce, $450 for a residential real estate closing, timekeeping is still beneficial to the firm. A timekeeping system helps the attorneys know if they are profiting from certain clients or areas of practice. It may be that the real estate closings are profitable and the divorces are not. The firm may never know that if they do not know how much time is spent on each area of law and compare the value of that time to the amount collected from clients.

The value of the time an attorney spends working for a client is determined by multiplying the time spent by the attorney's standard hourly rate. Each attorney in the firm should have a *standard hourly rate.* This is the rate used to calculate the value of the attorney's time to be compared against the amount collected for that time. Most attorneys use a standard hourly rate even though they quote higher or lower rates on certain cases or matters.

Example: Assume attorneys A and B both worked on a real estate closing for Client C. Attorney A worked two hours and Attorney B worked four hours. Attorney A's standard hourly rate is $100 while Attorney B's is $75. The value of the services rendered to Client C, based upon time spent, is $500, calculated as follows:

Attorney A	2 hrs × $100 =	$200
Attorney B	4 hrs × 75 =	300
Total time value		$500

This value is referred to as the *standard value.* If Attorney A or B had made an arrangement to do the real estate closing for client C for a flat rate of $400, the *matter value* would be $400. When the matter value is compared to the standard, the difference is called *under-* or *over-realization.* In our example, the attorneys under-realized $100, the difference between the standard value of $500 and the matter value of $400.

If certain areas of law allow the attorneys to collect their standard hourly rates most of the time, with a small amount of under-realization, then the attorneys can concentrate on building up that area of practice. The attorney may refuse to take on matters which repeatedly show a large under-realization, or may decide to increase the amount of fees quoted to clients.

Without a timekeeping system, the nonprofitable areas of practice may be shrouded by the profitable ones, with the attorneys thinking they are both profitable.

¶1102 How Time Records Are Kept

As your attorneys work during the day, they probably record the clients worked for, the amount of time spent on an activity, and a description in a diary (such as a Day-Timer or bound calendar book), on timeslips, or on a timesheet. This constant necessity to record each activity requires a lot of discipline. To gain the maximum benefit out of the timekeeping system, the attorneys should record the information as soon as the activity is completed.

With most timekeeping systems, the smallest increment of time used is tenths of hours. Some firms use quarter hours as the smallest unit of time. In those firms, a telephone call would be charged to a client at 0.25 times Attorney A's hourly rate even though the call lasted only five minutes. Sometimes you may notice that the time recorded on the timeslip or time sheet is not comparable to the time spent. This is because attorneys often make a decision about the value of the activity to the client when the time is recorded. If the attorney did an especially good job for the client in a short amount of time, he or she may go ahead and charge the client with more time than actually spent.

More and more firms are using computerized timekeeping systems because the computer takes a lot of the drudgery out of the billing process. It does not eliminate the timekeeping process, however. The attorneys' requirement to keep accurate time records is a necessity, whether a manual or computerized system is used. While computers are used more for timekeeping, it still makes sense for some firms to use manual systems. Sole proprietors or small firms or new firms lacking the necessary capital for the purchase of a computer system can use a manual system effectively. It is only when the volume of time transactions becomes so great that the manual system becomes unmanageable.

¶1102.1 Timeslips systems

Most manual timekeeping systems use *timeslips* to record the attorneys' time. The slips are small pieces of paper, preprinted with spaces for the attorney to fill in the date, client, matter (or file number), time spent and a description of the services rendered (See Figure 1102.1-1).

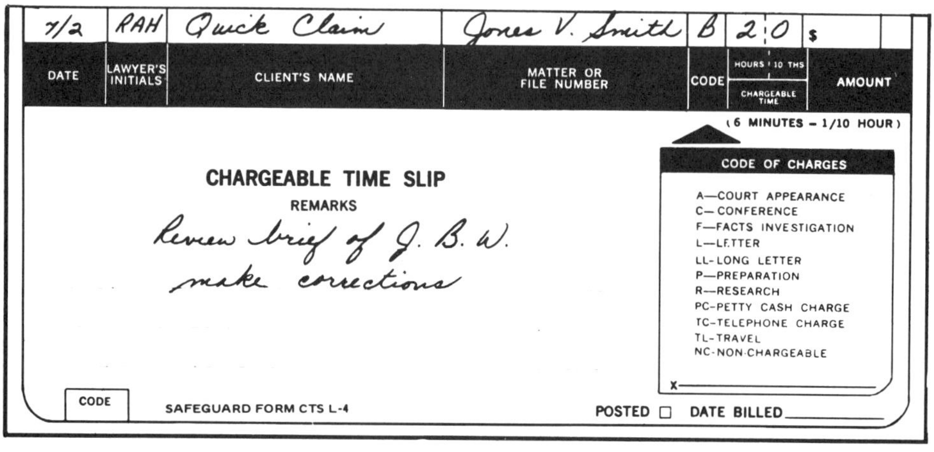

DATE	LAWYER'S INITIALS	CLIENT'S NAME	MATTER OR FILE NUMBER	CODE	HOURS : 10 THS CHARGEABLE TIME	AMOUNT
7/2	RAH	Quick Claim	Jones V. Smith	B	2 : 0	$

(6 MINUTES – 1/10 HOUR)

CHARGEABLE TIME SLIP

REMARKS

Review brief of J. B. W.
make corrections

CODE OF CHARGES
A—COURT APPEARANCE
C—CONFERENCE
F—FACTS INVESTIGATION
L—LETTER
LL-LONG LETTER
P—PREPARATION
R—RESEARCH
PC-PETTY CASH CHARGE
TC-TELEPHONE CHARGE
TL-TRAVEL
NC-NON-CHARGEABLE
X

CODE SAFEGUARD FORM CTS L-4 POSTED ☐ DATE BILLED

Figure 1102.1-1. Timeslip.

The best timeslip systems are the *pegboard systems.* The timeslips are attached on the left side and have holes that fit over the pegs on a board (Figure 1102.1-2). A single sheet, with holes on the left side that fit over

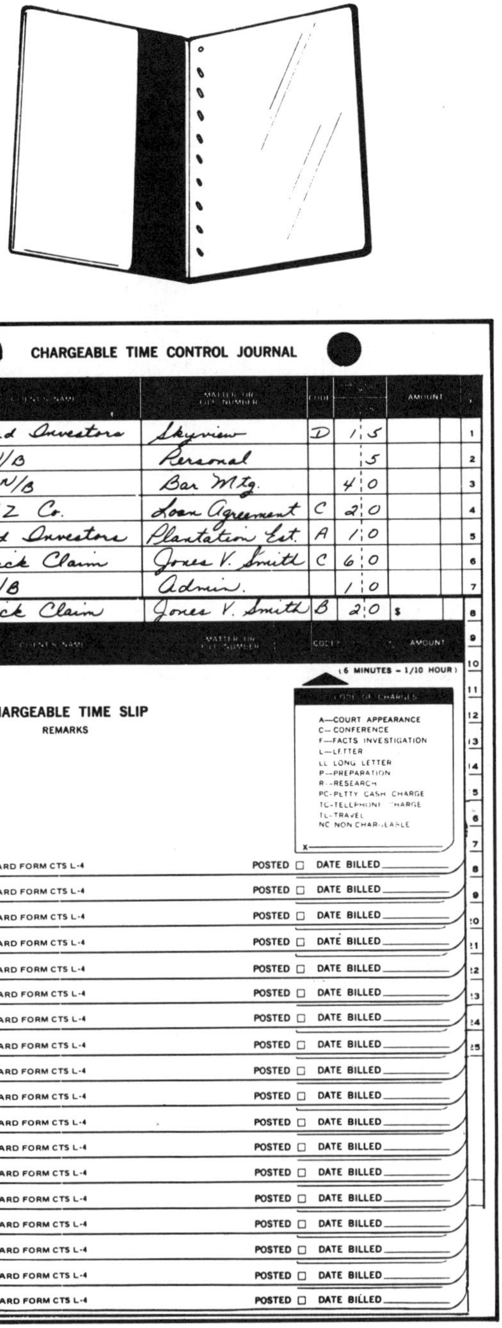

Figure 1102.1-2. Pegboard System. Forms courtesy of Safeguard Business Systems, Inc., Fort Washington, PA.

the pegs, is under the timeslips. As entries are made on the timeslip, they are duplicated on the control sheet underneath. This gives the attorney a record of the time turned in once the timeslip has been torn off and given to the secretary or bookkeeper.

Example: On Tuesday, March 5, Attorney A made a telephone call to Client B. They discussed an upcoming trial and some documents which the attorney needed to review in preparation for the trial. They made arrangements for the client to send a messenger to the law firm to deliver the documents. The telephone conversation lasted five minutes. When Attorney A finished with the telephone call, she filled out a timeslip with the following information:

Date	*Client*	*File*	*Time*	*Description*
3/5	Client B	Trial	.1	Telephone conference with Client B re required documents for upcoming trial; made arrangements to have documents delivered.

Notice that the time recorded was one-tenth of an hour, or 6 minutes, while the telephone conversation lasted only 5 minutes. In this case, tenths of hours is the smallest increment of time the attorney can use.

Similar events happen throughout the attorneys' day. The timeslips are filled out, then torn off and given to the secretary or person responsible for organizing them (Figure 1102.1-3).

The reason the small slips are used is because they can be sorted and filed by client and matter (or file) to be used at the end of the month for billing purposes. Usually, the bookkeeper or receptionist does the sorting and filing. If several attorneys are doing work for the same file, all of their time for the month should end up in the file box under the matter name.

At the end of the month, the attorney takes the slips that have been sorted and dictates a bill to the client. There are a variety of billing formats. Check with your attorneys to get a form that they prefer (Figure 1102.1-4). The time and disbursements made on behalf of the client may be first summarized on a billing memo (Figure 1102.1-5). The attorney, or the secretary, must sort out the slips by each attorney

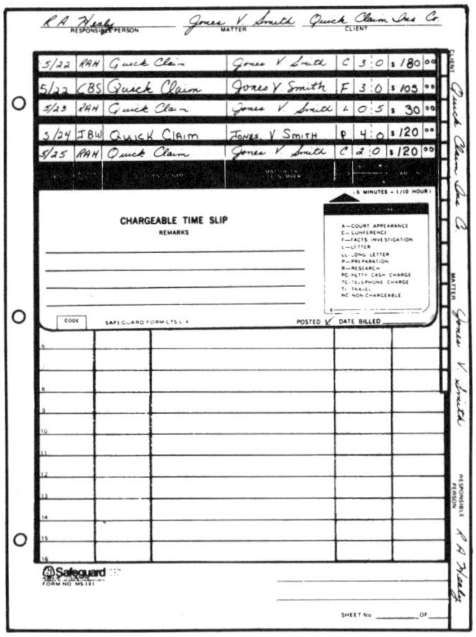

A standard, indexed file tray may be used for filing billable time tickets, as shown on page 10. The "Time Ticket Mount Sheet", illustrated, is an alternate method of maintaining these tickets. This simplified method can offer several advantages depending on policies set by the firm.

The secretary or bookkeeper collects and sorts billable time tickets, by client, each day. Tickets pertaining to a particular client are then attached to his reserved Mount Sheet, regardless of which lawyer in the firm worked on the matter. A column of check-off blocks, printed on the right hand side of each Mount Sheet, is used for indicating time tickets billed. A total fee for billable time, applicable to a specific billing period, may be taken directly from the mounted time tickets and bulk posted in the "Fees Charged" column on the "Accounting Side" of the client ledger card. Posting the "Work in Progress" side of the client ledger card may be optionally eliminated. In either case, time tickets are securely held in position and are displayed in chronological order for ease in photocopying and/or review. Mount Sheets may be stored in an up-right file tray or standard 3-ring binders.

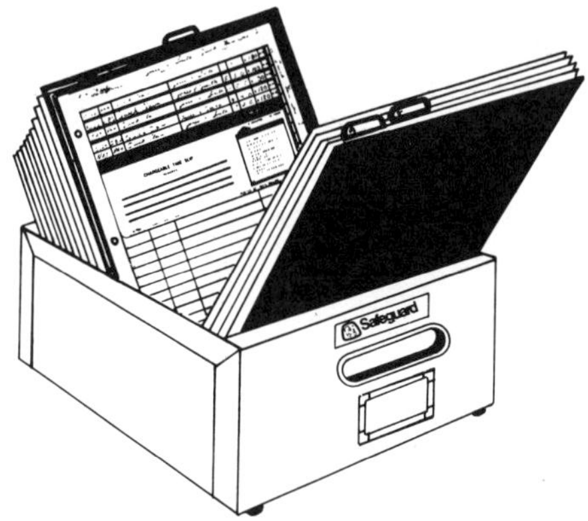

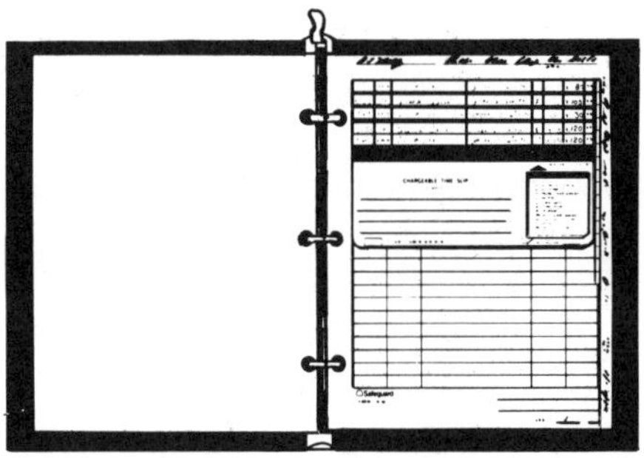

Figure 1102.1-3. Time Ticket Filing Procedures. Forms courtesy of Safeguard Business Systems, Inc., Fort Washington, PA.

worked, read them, and decide how to describe the services rendered during the month. In some firms, a paralegal or the legal secretary prepares a draft bill from the timeslips, especially if the attorneys have provided a clear description of the activity on each timeslip (Figure 1102.1-6).

If you are responsible for preparing a draft bill, you should take care to use standard phrases and formatting. Each attorney has a personal style of timekeeping and unless your firm requires a standard

October 31, 1985

Name of Client
Street Address
City, State and ZIP Code

Legal services rendered from December 1, 1984 through October 31, 1985 in connection with the following matters:

Option to purchase Jones Corporation, including telephone conferences with John Doe, meeting with Joe Smith and other related parties in Chicago regarding proposed option agreement, preparation and review of option agreement and other related office and telephone conferences regarding transaction		$2,000.00
Advice and counsel regarding year-end accounting matters including preparation and depreciation schedules and pro forma of financial statements and other various accounting matters; and various other services not detailed here		500.00
		$2,500.00
Less: Retainers through October 1985 (10 at $100.00)		1,000.00
		$1,500.00
To reimburse for the following expenses:		
Long distance telephone calls to Nashville, Tennessee, Chicago, Illinois and New York, New York	$20.00	
Xerox copies of various documents	10.00	
Postage for mailing document to Chicago	5.00	35.00
Balance Due		$1,535.00

Mark off 15.0 hrs. on client #________

Figure 1102.1-4. Three Sample Bill Computations.

August 15, 1985

Name of Client
Street Address
City, State and ZIP Code

Legal services rendered from February 1, 1985, through August 15, 1985, in connection with the eviction and prosecution of detainer warrant against John Doe; office conference on March 2, 1985, relative to tenant problems and desired eviction; drafting and filing of detainer warrant in General Sessions Court, Hamilton County, Tennessee; investigation and miscellaneous telephone conferences relative to location of defendant for service of process; drafting and filing of alien Summons; telephone conference with John Doe relative to status of eviction; appearance in Hamilton County General Sessions Court on June 8, 1985, for trial of detainer action against Joe Doe; correspondence relative to disposition of trial and bankruptcy of defendant; miscellaneous telephone conferences with John Doe and others; and all other related services	$260.00
To reimburse for fee to Lucile Hixson, Clerk, for detainer warrant	9.25
	$269.25
Less: Advance payment received on February 1, 1985	150.00
Balance Due	$119.25

Mark off 8.3 hours on client # ________

Figure 1102.1-4. (continued)

July 15, 1985

Mr. and Mrs. John Doe
1317 Paula Lane
Chattanooga, Tennessee 37404

Legal services rendered in the cases of John Doe v. Milford Price, No. 10057-J, and Mrs. Jane Doe v. Milford Price, No. 10058-J, in the Circuit Court of Hamilton County, Tennessee (1/3 of Gross Recovery)		$3,000.00
To reimburse for the following expenses:		
Jim Arledge—Investigative Service	$41.94	
Richard Smith, Court Reporter—Attendance Fee	23.65	65.59
Total		$3,065.59

COMPUTATION

Gross Recovery	$9,000.00
Deduct: Fee to Simms & Simms (1/3 of Gross Recovery)	3,000.00
Client's Portion of Recovery	$6,000.00
Deduct: Reimbursement for Expenses (See detail above)	65.59
Net Check to Client	$5,934.41

Mark off 31.3 hours on client # ________

Figure 1102.1-4. (continued)

BILLING MEMORANDUM

Bill No. 5027

Client Quick Claim — Responsible lawyer RAH

Matter Jones V. Smith — Matter number 64501-32-2

Period covered 5/18/72 to 5/31/72 — Date of bill 5/31/72

Unbilled Time and Client Disbursements

Time Charges	Last Date	Unbilled Hours	Unbilled Standard Value	Current Billing* Hours	Current Billing* Billing Value
Lawyer time					
RAH	5/25/72	9.5	$ 570		$
CBS	5/25/72	7.0	245		
JBW	5/25/72	8.0	240		
	/ /				
Total lawyer time		24.5	1055		
Steno time					
	/ /		–		
	/ /		–		
Total steno time					
Total all time charges		24.5	1055		
Less: Unapplied advances received					
Net unbilled time		24.5	$ 1055		$

Client Disbursements	Standard Value	Billing Value
Reproduction	$ 12.00	$
L. D. Telephone charges	4.50	
Travel	–	
Supplies	–	
Postage	3.00	
Accident report	5.00	
Total client disbursements	24.50	
Less: Unapplied advances received	–	
Net unbilled client disbursements	$ 24.50	$

	Hours	Standard Value	Hours	Billing Value
Total all unbilled time and client disbursements	24.5	1079.50		

After consideration of the standard value of the above time charges and

1. Skill and experience involved
2. Prevailing local practice in the field of law involved
3. Amount involved and benefits to client
4. Preclusion from other employment
5. Contingency or certainty of compensation
6. Casual or continuing client relationship

I hereby fix a reasonable fee to be billed the client at $1,079.50.

Safeguard BUSINESS SYSTEMS P.O. BOX 106 FORT WASHINGTON, PA 19034

Responsible lawyer

*Responsible lawyer should enter hours and value to be billed for each lawyer if all time is not to be billed currently. Bookkeeper will assume all time and client disbursements as billed unless otherwise indicated.

Figure 1102.1-5. Billing Memorandum. Forms courtesy of Safeguard Business Systems, Inc., Fort Washington, PA.

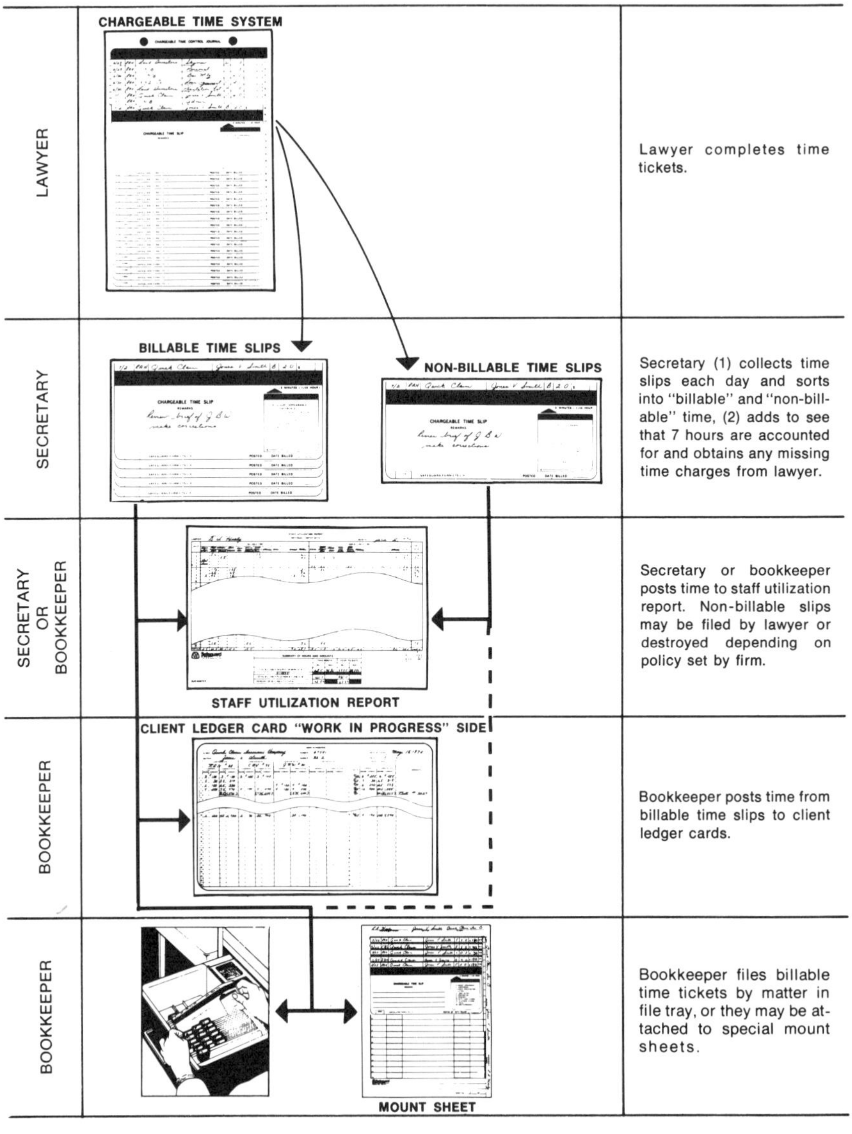

Figure 1102.1-6. Daily Timekeeping Procedures. Forms courtesy of Safeguard Business Systems, Inc., Fort Washington, PA.

style (which many do) the bill will read like it was written by many different authors unless you edit the descriptions.

Example: Attorney A and B worked on the same file for Client C. At the end of the month, you are required to prepare a draft bill from the following timeslip information.

Attorney A	Meeting with Client C to discuss problem with tenant; prepared draft of letter to tenant.
Attorney B	Met with Attorney A to discuss possible need to prepare eviction papers for Client C's tenant; Research re same.
Attorney A	Proofread and edit letter to tenant; telephone call to Client C to determine necessity of proceeding with eviction process.

Notice the different verb tenses used in these time entries. Some are present tense, others past tense. Your job is to make them all the same. Your firm or your attorneys may have a preference which to use. If not, choose one tense and use it throughout the client's bill.

Example: The completed draft bill may look like this:

Attorney A	Meeting with Client C to discuss problem with tenant; preparation of draft letter to tenant.
Attorney B	Meeting with Attorney A to discuss possible need to prepare eviction papers for Client C's tenant; Research re same.
Attorney A	Proofreading and editing of letter to tenant; telephone call to Client C to determine necessity of proceeding with eviction process.

Notice that each activity for a single attorney on the same day is separated by a semicolon. If two attorneys are involved in the same activity, i.e., attended the same meeting, the entries may be combined as follows:

Attorney A	
Attorney B	Meeting with Client C to discuss...

¶1102.2 Diary systems

Attorneys may use a diary system to record their time on a daily calendar which is divided into fractions of a day, either quarters or tenths of hours. The client, file or matter is entered on the diary as soon as an activity is completed, with some type of designation, like bracketing, of the part of the day spent working for that client (Figure 1102.2-1).

SERVICES PERFORMED TODAY

THURSDAY 1
213th Day • AUGUST, 1985

HOURS	FOR	IN REF:	DESCRIPTION OF SERVICES	TIME HRS. 1/10
8				
9				
10	Creative Options		Telephone call to JoAnn Boltham, Prepare business plan	1.0
11				
12				
1				
2				
3				
4				
5				

DAY TIMERS IN U.S.A. BOX 2368 ALLENTOWN, PA 18001 • IN CANADA 4875 KENT AVENUE, BOX 1028, NIAGARA FALLS, ONT. L2E 6X6 • IN UNITED KINGDOM 24A BARTHOLOMEW VILLAS, LONDON NW5 2LY

Figure 1102.2-1. Daily Calendar.

At the end of the day, the secretary may take the completed diary and transfer the information to a ledger sheet. At this time the amount of time is calculated into hours or fractions of hours.

The advantage (perhaps the only advantage) of the diary system is the ability for the attorney to view the entire day at a time, unlike timeslip systems. The disadvantages are the duplication of effort expended by the secretary when "posting" the time entries to the ledger card and the frequency of errors during the posting process.

¶1102.3 Paste-up systems

The paste-up systems are similar to timeslip systems. The difference is in the way the slips are sorted. The paste-up slips have an adhesive backing which is pasted (rather than posted) to the individual client's card instead of being filed in a box. At the end of the month at billing time, the card is delivered to the attorneys for billing purposes. The elimination of the posting process, as in the diary system, reduces the amount of error.

¶1102.3 Computerized systems

Computerized timekeeping systems are explained in detail in ¶1200. The computerized system is really only different after the timekeeping process is completed by the attorneys. The attorneys must still complete timeslips or a timesheet with the appropriate information.

Some firms continue to use timeslips after installing a computer, however, this is an unnecessary expense. Remember, the only reason for the timeslips was for sorting purposes. If the computer is to do the sorting, the timeslips are unnecessary. The use of many small pieces of paper also increases the chance that one will be misplaced. The preferable way to keep time is with a single timesheet for each day. Like the diary system, the use of the timesheet allows the attorneys to see the whole day at a glance. As many as eight or ten time entries may be made on a single timesheet. This requires handling only one piece of paper rather than eight or ten, a much more efficient method.

Another difference you may notice with computerized systems is the use of *work* or *activity codes* or *acronyms*. Many systems allow a code to be entered rather than writing out an extended explanation. Codes are usually defined by each firm and there are really no standards. An example of a work or activity code would be TC for telephone call. Each time an attorney needs to record a telephone call, instead of writing out telephone call the code TC may be entered into the computer. When the bill is produced by the computer the words *telephone call* will appear every place that the work code was input.

¶1103 How You Can Help Your Attorneys With Timekeeping

While most attorneys keep time records, few enjoy it. It is a "necessary evil." As mentioned before, timekeeping requires strict discipline on the part of the attorneys. Anything you can do to help make the timekeeping process easier is sure to be appreciated.

It won't take long to determine your attorneys' attitudes about timekeeping. One may turn timesheets in daily while the other procrastinates, finally agonizing over them at the end of the month, trying to remember what in the world was done during the month. Here's how other legal secretaries helped their attorneys who had difficulty keeping time.

Secretary No. 1

This secretary made an agreement with his attorney. He told him that if the attorney would dictate his time every morning (which he later transcribed onto a timesheet) as soon as he came into the office, he would get his coffee for him. The time spent going to the break room fixing the coffee, chatting with a few other attorneys or secretaries was enough time for him to dictate his daily time. It worked! Every day the secretary reminded him to do his time as soon as he came in and while the attorney did it, the secretary brought him his first cup of coffee.

Secretary No. 2

This secretary kept a time sheet at her desk for her attorney. Every time a client called she wrote it on the timesheet. If another attorney stopped by to talk about a case, she wrote it down. If she didn't know what matter or file they talked about, she asked. If her attorney had a meeting with a client, she asked what it was about. She was not being nosy, she was filling out the attorney's time sheet as the day progressed. He loved it! She was a valuable secretary to him and he rewarded her generously for it.

Secretary No. 3

This secretary was required to keep a timesheet of her own because her time was also billed to the clients. She kept her time accurately and in detail because her attorney was not a very disciplined timekeeper. Almost every month, he had a few days in which he was just too busy to keep a record of his time. She was able to help him fill out his missing timesheets using hers as a basis. If she had typed a letter, then he must have dictated a letter. If she had greeted a client, then he must have met with the client. Without her records, he would have missed much of the time entries, and would not have been able to bill the clients for the time spent.

Secretary No. 4
This secretary prepared a list of people who called or were called during the day, conferences held, letters received or sent and gave it to her attorney at the end of each day to help him with his timekeeping. He was often able to include items on his timesheet that would have otherwise been overlooked.

¶1104 A Sure-Fire Way to Make Your Attorneys More Profitable

There are only a few ways for your attorneys to become more profitable. One is to spend more hours working. If your attorneys are like most, they are already working long, hard hours. Another way is for all attorneys to account for a full working day.

Full day accounting means that a set number of hours are to be accounted for each day. If your attorneys work an average of nine hours every day, then each day's timesheet should total nine hours. At the end of each day, the total hours worked is calculated to see if the full day has been recorded. If not, the attorney must review the events of the day to determine which items have been overlooked. This will usually require the use of a timesheet (Figure 1104-1) rather than individual timeslips.

Experts in the legal industry say that law firms that require their attorneys to account for a full working day often increase their profits by as much as 20 to 30 percent. Suggest to your attorneys that they consider full day accounting. If they do and decide to proceed with it, you will be responsible for improving the firm's profits. Who knows, perhaps some of the increase will find its way to you.

¶1104.1 Keeping Track of Nonbillable Time

Some of your attorneys' time must be devoted to nonbillable activities, such as firm administration, continuing legal education, civic activities and other matters. When full day accounting is used, the nonbillable time must be recorded along with the billable time to arrive at the day's total hours.

A knowledge of how much time is devoted to these matters is helpful in planning future activities and in determining how much must be earned from billable hours in order to maintain a reasonable level of compensation. For this reason, all nonbillable time should be included in the day's time. The nonbillable time should be kept by categories so the managing partners will know how much time was spent on each activity.

HOLLAND SHIPES BENNETT THRASHER	DAILY TIME LOG					MO. DAY YR.	STAFF NO.	NAME

ADMINISTRATIVE TIME: 9999 Holland Shipes Bennett Thrasher, 11 Administrative, 21 Prof. activities, 31 Prac. Dev., 41 Vac/Hol/Ill, 51 Continuing education, 61 Staff training/recruitment, 71 Other

	CLIENT AND MATTER NAME	ACCOUNT NUMBER		TIME		ADDITIONAL NARRATIVE
		CLIENT	MATTER	HRS	1/10	
1	CLIENT NAME					
	MATTER NAME					
2	CLIENT NAME					
	MATTER NAME					
3	CLIENT NAME					
	MATTER NAME					
4	CLIENT NAME					
	MATTER NAME					
5	CLIENT NAME					
	MATTER NAME					
6	CLIENT NAME					
	MATTER NAME					
7	CLIENT NAME					
	MATTER NAME					
8	CLIENT NAME					
	MATTER NAME					
9	CLIENT NAME					
	MATTER NAME					
10	CLIENT NAME					
	MATTER NAME					
		PAGE TOTAL				

Figure 1104-1. Daily Time Log. Courtesy of Holland Shipes Bennett Thrasher, P.C., CPAs, Atlanta, GA.

Some common nonbillable time categories are:

Firm administration;
Bar activities;
Practice development;
Vacation, holiday, and illness;
Personal leave;
Religious, civic and charity;
Continuing education;
Staff training;
Unaccounted for time;
Other.

Both billable and nonbillable time may be shown on a report called the *firm utilization report* (Figure 1104.1-1). This report may be prepared at the end of each month to help the managing partners assess the productivity of the attorneys in the firm.

¶1105 Billing—The Most Important Task

Attorneys sell time. They go to law school to learn enough to make the time they spend using their acquired skills worth something to their clients. An attorney can do excellent work for a client, but if a bill for that work is never sent to the client, the attorney will never be paid. It's as simple as that.

Most firms bill clients once a month for the time attorneys and paralegals have spent doing work for the clients. The time, which has been recorded in some fashion during the month, is multiplied by the attorneys' hourly billing rates and a bill is prepared. Most firms show the detail of what the attorneys did during the period. See Figure 1102.1-4 for sample bills. Sometimes, the only thing a client will see during the month from the firm is the bill. For this reason, the bill should be neat, complete, and correct. It is a reflection of the work done by the firm.

As a rule, attorneys dislike (some even hate) billing time. Taking time to review the time spent and deciding how much to bill a client takes away from the attorney's working time. If the firm does not have a good timekeeping and billing system, manual or computerized, the process is even more agonizing. If the timekeeping system is manual, the bills are often dictated by the attorney, a time consuming task.

Anything you can do to make billing time easier for your attorneys is sure to be appreciated. First, you should determine your attorneys' attitudes toward billing. One may be eager to get the bills out, while the

HEALY & MYERS

FIRM UTILIZATION REPORT

Current Month — Month Ending June 30, 1972

Lawyer	Billable (1) Hours	Billable (2) Value	Billable (3) Per Cent	Non-Billable Hours (4) Admin	Bar Prof Dev	Prac Dev	Vac Hol Sick	Pers	Rel Civic Char	Other	(5) Total	(6) Total Hours
Current Month												
RAH	68.0	$ 4,080	42.5	18.0	11.0	7.5	35.0	6.5	6.0	8.0	92.0	160.0
AMM	98.0	4,900	60.9	23.0	10.0	5.0	-	3.0	10.0	12.0	63.0	161.0
CBS	125.0	4,375	81.2	2.0	9.0	6.0	-	4.0	8.0	-	29.0	154.0
KFM	101.0	3,535	65.6	-	7.0	6.0	14.0	-	14.0	12.0	53.0	154.0
JBW	124.0	3,720	68.9	-	10.0	6.0	-	6.0	14.0	20.0	56.0	180.0
	516.0	$20,610	63.8	43.0	47.0	30.5	49.0	19.5	52.0	52.0	293.0	809.0
Year-To-Date												
RAH	573.0	$ 34,380	62.3	94.0	45.0	62.0	70.0	19.0	35.0	22.0	347.0	920.0
AMM	635.0	31,750	68.8	81.0	56.0	45.0	35.0	10.0	25.0	36.0	288.0	923.0
CBS	729.0	25,515	71.9	40.0	63.0	42.0	35.0	9.0	56.0	41.0	286.0	1,015.0
KFM	653.0	22,855	70.2	32.0	70.0	35.0	21.0	14.0	65.0	40.0	277.0	930.0
JBW	747.0	22,410	76.4	38.0	63.0	36.0	7.0	12.0	46.0	29.0	231.0	978.0
	3,337.0	$136,910	66.8	285.0	297.0	220.0	168.0	64.0	227.0	168.0	1,429.0	4,766.0

Figure 1104.1-1. Firm Utilization Report.

other may not care. Usually, the attorney who is involved in the management of the firm is more concerned about billing than one who is not. Regardless of their attitudes, you should understand that the preparation of bills usually has priority over other work. There are exceptions, of course, but the general rule should be "bills first."

¶1106 Understanding Accounts Receivable and the Rebilling File

Once a bill has been sent to a client, an account receivable is created. The firm may now expect to receive the amount of the bill to pay the client's account. Usually, the bill should be paid within thirty days after it is received. Sometimes special arrangements are made with the client for a payment schedule other than this.

Clients have different attitudes toward paying their bills, just like attorneys have about sending them. Some clients pay promptly on the tenth or fifteenth of the month, regular as clockwork. Other clients put off paying their bill until reminded several times. Others never pay.

You have probably heard the old saying, "The squeaking wheel gets the grease." In business, this means that the person or firm that asks the most often to be paid, gets paid. This is why it is important to remind clients to pay their bills.

In some firms the bookkeeping department handles the accounts receivable and sends reminder statements to the clients, but usually it is the attorneys who are expected to do it. If your attorneys are responsible for reminding clients about past due payments you can help them. Keep a copy of all bills as you send them out in a billing file. As they are paid, pull them out of the billing file, and put them in the client's file. After the bills are sent out for the month, review the billing file for bills which remain unpaid from previous months.

Be sure to check periodically with the bookkeeping department to make sure you know which bills are unpaid. If your firm is on a computerized system your attorneys will probably receive an accounts receivable aging each month. This report will show which clients have not paid and how many days past due the bills are. Ask if you can check your billing file against this report.

Once you have determined which bills have not been paid, a simple way to remind the client to pay is to make a copy of the bill and mark it REMINDER with a rubber stamp you may order from the office supply store. Often the client loses the bill or sometimes they never receive it. The reminder bill will alert them to the fact that there is a problem.

Before you send out reminder bills you should review them with your attorneys. They may know of unusual circumstances or payment agreements of which you are unaware. When you have agreed upon the clients to be rebilled, mail the duplicate bills. Both you and your attorneys may be surprised at the results you get.

If sending a duplicate bill does not work it is usually necessary to call the client. This is usually done by the attorneys. You can help, however, by providing your attorneys with a list of past due bills, the dates and amounts due, and the clients' telephone numbers. Make it easy for them to pick up the phone. If they have all the information at their fingertips, they will have no excuse to put it off.

In some cases, the attorney may wish for you to call the client's bookkeeping department to ask why a bill has not been paid. You should do so politely, asking if there is a problem with the bill. Again, many times the bill never reaches the client due to an incorrect address or other reason. If this is the case, sending a duplicate bill to the correct address corrects the problem.

Sometimes clients find them in the position of having to hire an attorney unexpectedly. The client's budget may not include attorneys' fees. It may be difficult for them to pay and special arrangements may be worked out with the attorney. Sometimes partial payments are made over a period of months. It is important for you to keep track of these payments in the billing file, writing the date and amount on the bill as they are received. You should exercise care not to rebill clients for whom special payment arrangements have been made.

¶1200 Getting the Most Out of the Microcomputer

By Carole A. Bruno and Paula F. Turner

As a legal secretary, you probably will not be involved with the computer selection process unless your firm is small. Small firms do not invest their money in large computer systems, but more often they choose *microcomputers,* also called personal computers. You may be required, however, to learn to use a large computer, a *minicomputer,* and should understand something about them.

This chapter will teach you about computers and what they can and can't do. It will also outline the necessary steps to selecting a computer for your firm and tell you how to make it work once you have it.

Before you can determine what a computer can do for you, you need to understand what a computer does and how it works. You do not need to know all the technical terms but there is some basic terminology which you should know.

¶1201 What a Computer Can Do

The computer can perform almost any task that you can divide into a number of procedures and express in terms of a series of instructions. The seven major tasks that computers are used for in law firms are:

1. Word processing;
2. Legal accounting;
3. Calendar and docket control;
4. Conflict of interest;
5. Special legal applications;
6. Litigation support;
7. Telecommunications.

What is the advantage of doing these functions with a computer rather than by hand? All of these functions involve repetitive tasks that are very time consuming and often boring. The computer tends to eliminate the drudgery involved in doing them.

¶1201.1 Word Processing

Every law office produces both long and short documents; letters, wills, memos, trusts, contracts, briefs, court pleadings, and opinion letters. Most microcomputers bought by attorneys are to help in the preparation of these documents. Typically, the process of document preparation in a firm without a microcomputer or other word processing equipment goes something like this:

1. The attorney dictates;
2. The secretary types;
3. The attorney reviews and revises;
4. The secretary retypes;
5. The attorney proofs and revises;
6. The secretary retypes;
7. Etc.

Computerized word processing allows the secretary to store the document after it is typed and recall it for later editing. The entire document doesn't have to be retyped if the attorney writes all over it with a red pen, only the necessary parts are changed. The result? More documents may be produced, in less time, making both the secretary and the attorney more efficient.

¶1201.2 Legal Accounting

Computers which help with legal accounting provide management assistance to the attorneys. Recordkeeping and report preparation are tedious and time consuming when done manually. Legal accounting may be divided into two basic categories:

1. Timekeeping and billing;
2. Financial accounting.

¶1201.2.1 Timekeeping and Billing Keeping track of attorney and paralegal time can be streamlined with the aid of a computer. No more sorting time tickets and typing bills from them if you have the proper system. The computer does the sorting for you. The bill may even be produced from the description which was typed in with the time, no need to retype it. Even disbursements for clients may be entered into the system to be automatically added to the bill.

A computerized system makes it easier to keep track of client accounts. When a bill is produced, it is added to the client's account, a payment is subtracted. All transactions affecting the client's account are then summarized. With most systems you can get a status report at any time by typing in the client's name or client ID number. A history of the client's account will then by displayed on the screen and/or printed on your printer. Just think how this will save both you and your attorneys time when a client calls with a question about his or her account.

¶1201.2.2 Financial Accounting Financial accounting includes the recording, summarizing and reporting of all the financial transactions of the firm, i.e., cash received, checks written, payroll, etc. Manual systems that require copying information from check stubs or deposit slips are both inefficient and subject to error. Many computer systems allow you to type in the information about a transaction only once, with the computer doing all the work after that. The computer may print out the check, "post" the transaction to the general ledger and sumarize it on the appropriate financial statement. Used properly, the books will never be "out of balance."

¶1201.3 Calendar and Docket Control

The attorneys in your firm have numerous appointments, court dates and document filing deadlines of which to keep track. This is a natural application for the computer. The typical calendar control system prints out yearly, monthly, weekly, or daily calendars to remind the attorneys when to activate files or prepare for appointments.

Most malpractice insurance carriers offer discounts on premiums to attorneys or firms using a computerized calendar and docket control system. The reason for this is that missed deadlines is the singlemost reason for malpractice suits against attorneys. Computerized systems, properly used, are more dependable than manual ones.

¶1201.4 Conflict of Interest

Attorneys may not represent both sides of a lawsuit, or parties who are related in some way, business or personal, to the opposing side of a client's lawsuit. To avoid accepting cases in which a *conflict of interest* may arise (and possible malpractice suits) the firm should have a system to check the parties in a new matter against existing clients and related parties.

Many computerized systems are available to assist in conflict of interest or adverse party checking. Those names involved in matters which the firm is involved are entered into the system and new names are compared against existing names. If similar names are discovered and a possible conflict arises, a determination must be made by the attorneys whether or not a valid conflict of interest exists.

Computerized systems which allow the use of the client and matter information used in the timekeeper file are often the most efficient. This eliminates the need to re-key the information into the conflict checking system. However, many firms successfully use a database manager software to create their own systems.

¶1201.5 Special Legal Applications

An attempt has been made to computerize almost every aspect of practicing law. Some special systems which are available ate:

1. Real estate closings;
2. Trust accounting;
3. Tax planning and preparation;
4. Estate planning and administration;
5. Debt collections.

As mentioned earlier in this chapter, any process which is a set of procedures with definite instructions can usually be done more efficiently on a computer. Attorneys have many areas of practice which are ideal for computerization. Sorting, calculating, printing checks, tax returns, and summarizing information into management reports are things computers do well.

¶1201.6 Litigation Support

One of the areas of practice which can benefit most from computerization is litigation. From legal research to indexing documents, the computer, properly used, will be a blessing to the litigation attorneys, paralegals and secretaries. The use of a good computerized calendar and docket control system is a good place to start.

¶1201.6.1 Legal Research Legal research is the search of codes, regulations, administrative rulings, legislative history, and case law. The traditional method of research is for an attorney or paralegal to search indices and books for the proper information and then make photocopies for the client file.

Computerized legal research does not require ownership or availability of a single book. The key words or situations are entered and the system finds the appropriate information, and displays it on the screen. The references may be printed out for later use. There are two major legal data bases which law firms may search via telephone lines with their computers, Lexis and Westlaw. Their use is quickly cost justified when you consider the attorney or paralegal time saved. (See ¶1600.) Information America also is becoming a widely used and beneficial research tool. This system allows users to search title insurance policies, court records and calendars, and public records, including making corporate name reservations from the firm's microcomputer.

A firm may also create its own legal research system. Every time a legal research memo is created, you need only to store relevant information about it on your computer for later searching and retrieval.

¶1201.6.2 Document Indexing The litigation support file contains the documents related to the case, potential evidence. They must be catalogued and indexed in order to later locate them. Computerization doesn't make the cataloging and indexing procedures any simpler, perhaps even more time consuming, but the retrieval is considerably quicker.

¶1201.7 Telecommunications

One of the most exciting uses of computers today is *telecommunications,* the ability to transmit documents or electronic files over telephone lines via microwave or satellite. Copies of documents may be sent to clients or other law firms in a matter of seconds if both firms have the proper equipment. This reduces the dependency on the Postal Service or courier service.

Legal research is often accomplished by means of telecommunications. There are other *electronic databases* to which you can subscribe to get information on airline schedules, stock market quotations, news releases, restaurants and entertainment, even the weather.

Some of the public databases like ABA/Net, The Source, Electronic Mail Corporation of America (N.Y.), and Compuserve also have *electronic bulletin boards.* You can scan advertisements or messages, or leave a message for someone to "pick up" later. This is a good means of communicating with attorneys who travel frequently. If they have access to a computer with communications capability, they can call up the bulletin board after normal working hours to get messages.

¶1202 Checklist of Computer Applications for the Law Office

I. Word processing
    - Document creation
    - Editing
    - Spelling check
    - Printing
    - Storage

- Document reproduction
- Typesetting

II. Legal accounting
- Timekeeping
- Billing
- Accounts receivable
- Client disbursements
- Cash disbursements
- Payroll
- Cash receipts
- General ledger
- Bank account reconciliation
- Financial statement preparation
- Budgeting
- Long-range planning
- Profit distribution
- Fixed asset accounting

III. Law office administration
- Conflict of interest search
- Client files
- Calendar and docket control
- Mailing lists
- Work product retrieval
- Case tracking
- Library management
- Personnel management
- Recruiting (applicant tracking)
- Information storage and retrieval
- Client newsletters

IV. Special legal applications

Real estate
- Closing statement preparation
- Title opinions
- Loan amortization schedules
- Check preparation
- Management information

Tax
- Return preparation
- Tax planning
- Financial planning

Estates and trusts
- Will preparation

Estate planning
Estate return preparation
Document preparation
Estate administration
Trust accounting
Debt collections
Correspondence
Tickler system
Debtor accounting
Corporate formation
Patent searches
Oil and gas
Division order opinions
Mineral interest calculations
Litigation support
Document indexing
Document storage and retrieval
Financial modeling
Calculation of personal injury damages
Evaluate profitability of case
Evaluate syndications
V. Telecommunications
Legal research
LEXIS
WESTlAW
Information America—local court records
Databases
ABA/Net—The Lawyer's Network
OAG—Official Airline Guide
Compuserve, Incorporated—financial data, etc.
Dow Jones & Company, Inc.—stock quotes and SEC reports
Library of Congress
NEXIS—news wire access
Dialog—Information Services, Inc.—legal resource index
Program access (time sharing)
Time and billing
Tax return preparation
Statistical analysis
Economic models
Off premise data storage (for backup)

Message transmission
- Western Union
- Telex
- Facsimile transmission
- User-to-user communication

¶1203 What Is a Computer?

A computer is a machine which does work. It cannot think, but is dependent upon people like you to make it work. What the computer can do is built into it when it is made.

A computer does not have mechanical, moving parts like many other machines—it is electronic. Because it is electronic, it works much faster than mechanical machines. When you consider the amount of work a computer can do, it is very compact in size.

¶1203.1 What Can a Computer Do?

Most computers have the ability to do these three basic operations:

1. Move data;
2. Compare data;
3. Compute data;

That's all. Everything that happens in a computer is a combination of these three operations.

Data are the information used by computers. It is *moved* in and out of the computer. It is *compared* with other data in the computer and *computations* are made with it.

Data are moved into the computer, or input, several ways, via:

1. Keyboard;
2. Magnetic tape;
3. Another computer;
4. An electronic file;
5. Telecommunications.

Data are moved out of the computer, or output, also by several methods:

1. A screen or display;
2. A printer;
3. Another computer;
4. An electronic file;
5. Telecommunications.

The computer performs basic arithmetic operations, (addition, subtraction, multiplication, and division) on the numerical data, even square root calculations. Computers do this "number crunching" much faster than people and without error.

A computer assigns values to numbers, letters and other data it receives. Then, it can, when instructed, compare data to find similar or equal values, i.e., numbers that equal or names that match. Near matches or values which meet other criteria such as greater than or less than may also be found.

¶1203.2 Components of the Computer

A computer is a system, made of several components, like your stereo system. In fact, if you think of a computer like your stereo, it may take much of the mystery out of it.

Computer systems consist of four basic components very much like stereo systems:

Computer	Stereo
1. The central processor unit (CPU)	1. Receiver
2. Input devices	2. Turntable or tape player
3. Output devices	3. Speakers or tape recorder
4. Storage	4. Records or tapes

The central processor (CPU) is the part of the computer where the work is done. A CPU has memory that allows it to hold a certain amount of instructions and data for later processing, like writing down a list of numbers before adding them up.

¶1203.2.1 Kilobytes and Megabytes Memory is usually expressed by a unit of measure, the *kilobyte* (K or Kb). A kilobyte is 1024 bytes of information. The more memory your CPU has, the more data and instructions it can store. Most microcomputers have from 64 K to 640 K of memory. A typical typewritten, double-spaced page is about two kilobytes of memory. Larger computers have memory measured in megabytes (M or Mb). A *megabyte* equals one million bytes.

¶1203.2.2 Input and Output Devices The most common input and output device is the *workstation,* or computer *terminal,* consisting of a *keyboard* and a *display screen.* As the keys are pressed (input), characters are generated and displayed on the screen (output). The screen may be green or amber with white letters, or it may be a color *monitor* which displays bright colors.

Workstations, or terminals, are usually referred to as "dumb" or "intelligent." If a workstation is intelligent, it means that some work can be done at the workstation before being sent to the CPU for processing. Dumb terminals depend entirely upon the CPU for all work that is done. Intelligent workstations cost about two to three times as much as dumb terminals, but computer systems with intelligent workstations usually require less processing power and memory in the CPU.

There are several ways to get data into the CPU, but the most common is the keyboard. Most keyboards have a numeric ten key pad and function keys on them in addition to the regular typewriter keys. Your firm may have an *optical character reader (OCR)* which scans a typewritten page and transmits the data read to the CPU. This scanning eliminates the need to rekey data and reduces errors. You may already be familiar with an OCR at your neighborhood supermarket. Special magnetic coding on products is scanned so the cashier does not have to key in the information at the cash register. The concept is the same, except in a law office the data scanned are mostly words, not codes.

Computers are almost always configured with a *printer* to print out a record of what has been input and processed. The printout from a computer is called *hard copy.* Printers are described by the

1. Type
2. Speed
3. Means of handling paper
4. Characters printed

There are two basic types of printers, *impact* and *nonimpact.* Impact printers operate very much like the typewriters, striking an ink or carbon ribbon to form characters on the paper. Nonimpact printers rely on heat, electricity or jets of ink to form the characters. Laser printers are an example of nonimpact printers. As a rule, impact printers are noisier than nonimpact printers. See ¶1303.2 for a more indepth description of printers.

¶1203.2.3 Storage All of the data you need to use cannot be stored in the CPU's memory. Even if it could, when the computer is turned off everything in the CPU's memory is lost. All computer systems have some type of storage, usually disks for storing large amounts of data. When the power is turned off this data remains on the disk.

The amount of data that can be stored on a disk is expressed in the same kilobytes (K or Kb) or megabytes (Mb) as memory. But memory and disk storage are not the same. When the computer is turned off, the data stored on a disk is retained, like the music on your stereo records and tape.

There are two types of disks, floppy or hard. Floppy disks are made of flexible plastic and are encased in a plastic jacket. Hard disks are made of ceramic or aluminum material, encased in a housing. Hard, or fixed, disks are usually contained in the same cabinet as the central processor on microcomputers. On larger computer systems, disks may be in separate cabinets, directly attached by a cable to the CPU. Floppy disks, on the other hand, are stored outside the computers.

Hard disks are often referred to as *Winchester disks.* This name arose because the first hard disk made by IBM was the 3030, the same as the 3030 rifle made by Winchester Arms Company. The name stuck.

There are advantages to having a computer with a fixed disk. More data can be stored on a hard disk. On a microcomputer, hard disks hold 10–50 MB of data and the amounts are increasing every year. By comparison, a floppy diskette holds 360 KB to 1.2 MB of data. Diskettes are inexpensive, easy to store and transport. However, they are much more susceptible to damage and wear than hard disks.

Hard disks are fast and self-contained. They last longer and are more reliable than floppy disks. The greatest disadvantage to hard disks is the difficulty in backing up. It takes about 30 floppy disks to back up a 10-MB hard disk. Computer manufacturers are now offering magnetic tape systems for backing up microcomputers. Many of these are cartridge tapes, like a cassette tape you would play on your stereo. The tapes usually hold 10 MB of data and make backing up much quicker.

¶1204 How Does a Computer Work?

The computer system cannot do anything without instructions. The instructions are known as *software* or *programs.* The instructions, or programs are written in a language that the computer can understand. The computer language allows people to communicate with the computer system, the machine.

Computers do not think. Computer systems can do only the things they are instructed to do by means of the programs. There are different languages for different computers. They do not all speak the same language. The programs that operate on one computer will not necessarily operate on another.

The CPU "reads" the instructions in the program and performs the tasks as required. The tasks are usually performed on data that have been entered into the CPU via the keyboard.

There are several types of computer software programs:

1. Operating system software;
2. Applications software;
3. Utility software.

¶1204.1 Operating System Software

The operating system is supplied by the computer manufacturer. It works similar to a translator, helping you communicate with the applications software. Without the operating system software, your computer will not operate.

You do not really need to understand how the operating system works. There are only a few basic facts which you should know to help you understand computer systems and to choose the right computer for yourself or your firm.

There are two basic types of operating systems, standard (generic) and proprietary. A *standard operating system* is one which will function on more than one computer system.

Example: A software company by the name of Microsoft Corporation created an operating system for micro computers which they named Microsoft Disk Operating System (MS-DOS). Many micro computers use MS-DOS operating systems. IBM uses a variation of MS-DOS, called PC-DOS. Many applications software packages requiring MS-DOS or PC-DOS may be run on many different computers. These computers are usually referred to as IBM compatibles.

Other standard operating systems for micros are XENIX, UNIX, PICK, CP/M and CP/M-86. The advantage of a standard operating system is that it reduces the risk of your computer system becoming obsolete. If it becomes necessary to replace computer hardware and your system is obsolete, you can purchase a different vendor's system which runs the same operating system and transfer your applications programs and data files to the new system.

A *proprietary operating system* is one which is unique to a manufacturer's computer.

Example: Apple computers use a proprietary operating system. This means that the application software that runs on an Apple computer under its proprietary operating system cannot also run under an MS-DOS or other operating system.

Most computer manufacturers wtih proprietary operating systems try to provide compatibility with other standard operating systems by use of hardware or software converters or emulators.

Another thing to consider about operating systems is whether you need a single-user or multi-user system. The operating system determines whether one or more persons can use the same (CPU) at the same time. For example, the MS-DOS operating system is a single-user operating system. Only one person at a time can do only one thing at a time. The UNIX operating system is a multi-user system, allowing more than one person to use the same applications software at the same time. Of course, you must have the hardware that allows multiple terminals to be tied into a central processor to have a multi-user system.

Which type operating system is best? It all depends on the availability of the applications software that runs under a particular operating system. If the software you need runs under a MS-DOS operating system, then that is the best system for you.

Manufacturers are making great strides toward making their computer systems compatible with other computer systems. In the microcomputer industry, IBM is definitely the leader. This is not because their computers are so much better than the others, but because IBM is such a strong, financially sound company with excellent marketing strategies. Consumers in the market for a computer, including attorneys, are comfortable buying IBM because of their strength. The confidence that the company will still be around when the machine needs to be repaired is worth a lot.

Because of IBM's strength, many microcomputer manufacturers attempt to make their computers compatible with the IBM line of microcomputers. What this means is that the computers will operate using the MS-DOS operating system so that applications software which was written for the IBM micros will also run on their brand of computers.

¶1204.2 Applications Software

Operating systems don't really do anything for you, the user. Nothing that you can see, anyway. *Applications software* is the set of instructions, the programs, that will help you in your daily tasks. Word processing is an applications program. It is merely a set of instructions which tells the computer what to do with the words formed by you, the user, when you type them on the keyboard.

Time and billing software is an applications program. So is docket and calendar control or general ledger software. Each of these "applications" provide benefit to you.

¶1205 Understanding Peripherals

As you get involved in computers you are certain to hear the term *peripheral.* What is a peripheral? It is something which is not a part of the CPU, but is connected to it.

The only thing a CPU can do is process data. It cannot process this data, however, unless it is input in some way into the CPU. Once it is processed, in order for it to be of value to you, the user of the computer, it must be output in a form usable by people. This input and output is what peripherals do.

Peripherals are connected to the CPU by means of an *interface.* An interface is often a circuit board in the CPU that is connected to the peripheral by a cable. The data processed by the CPU is *transmitted* to and from the CPU and the peripherals via this interface and cable.

The standard peripherals you may see in the law office are the keyboard, display and printer. There are, however, many other types of peripherals that are often used.

OCR;
Modem;
Copy controller;
Telephone controller;
Graphics plotter;
Disk drives;
Magnetic tape drive for backup.

¶1206 How to Tell If You Are Ready for a Computer

Your attorneys may be talking computers. That's how it all begins. It is difficult today to not talk computers. Everyone seems to be doing it, computerizing, that is. When the talk begins, the first question which needs to be answered is "Do we really need a computer?." The investment in computerizing is significant, both in time and money. Many attorneys are not willing to invest in a project until they are convinced it is really necessary.

Here are some guidelines to help you and your attorneys decide if the time has come for your firm.

1. Is billing time almost unbearable? Is too much attorney time spent dictating bills, time which could otherwise be billable. A computerized time and billing system should allow bills to be automatically produced from the time entries which were input during the month. The attorneys review the time entries for the client, edit the narrative and decide how much to bill. This process usually takes half or less of the time required to sort timeslips and dictate bills.

2. Are you unable to control client disbursements? Do advances made on behalf of clients get lost, never being billed or collected from the client? Do the charges show up on the client's account too late, after the matter is closed, or never at all? Are photocopy and telephone charges accounted for haphazardly? A good time and billing system, with a checkwriter or accounts payable system can help. If checks for client costs are produced by the system, the client's account should be automatically updated, as soon as the check is written. Telephone and copy controllers can be directly connected to your computer system to calculate charges as they are made and post the charges to the client's account.

3. Is the level of errors produced by your time and billing system too high? When time or disbursements are charged to the wrong client are they easily transferred to the correct client, or are the timeslips often lost in the correction process? A computerized time and billing system should allow you to transfer the incorrect charge to the correct client for billing. Time cannot be lost from the system, it remains until either written off or billed.

4. Does your firm lack good financial and management information? Do the partners know which attorneys produce the most fees and which clients or areas of practice are most profitable? Do they know how old their receivables are and how much time and disbursements have built up in work-in-progress? This is the type of information that is automatically produced by computerized time and billing systems.

5. Has the quality of service to clients diminished because the staff is overloaded? Do secretaries have to type and retype documents? Is the turnaround time for documents too long? Is the firm spending considerable dollars on overtime to clerical personnel trying to keep up?

6. Is the firm experiencing cash flow problems? Are bills going out late because of the increased volume of time and disbursement entries? Is the firm unable to bill regularly because of the administrative time required to produce a bill. Are accounts receivable too high and increasing? The firm should be billing most clients on a regular monthly cycle, as soon after the end of the month as is possible. With a good time and billing system, bills can be produced easily within the first week of every month.

7. Are staff ratios too high for firms in your area and your size? Has your firm had to hire more and more bookkeeping and billing personnel? Is the attorney to secretary ratio less than 2 to 1? The money saved by not having to hire new personnel will usually pay for a computer system in two or three years. In other words, the firm will spend the same amount of money, either in staff salaries or equipment and after the firm reaches a certain size the equipment can do a better job than more people.

8. Is the firm management in agreement about the purchase of a computer system? Are one or two attorneys pushing the project or are all interested? Are the partners who will be required to make the investment in agreement and behind the project? Change is difficult for most people. The firm management can make it easier if all members of the staff are kept well informed and a positive attitude about the new system is expressed. This support can only come from the top.

9. Have several important deadlines been missed lately? Is an inordinate amount of time spent trying to make sure it doesn't happen again? Has the firm outgrown its manual docket and calendar control system? Has the firm grown to the point it needs to have a calendar control system? A computerized docket and calendar system may be in order. These systems print out reminders, daily, weekly or monthly as required.

10. Are the firm's current automated systems inadequate? Has the firm outgrown the capacity of current systems? Does the firm need more secretarial or accounting workstations? Is the equipment obsolete? Is the maintenance too high? Often new systems can be purchased with the money saved from high maintenance charges on old equipment. Vendors make the charges high because they want to sell new equipment. They will get your money, one way or another.

A final word of advice. If your firm's manual records are in a mess, the computerized version will also be a mess. This brings us to an important rule:

DON'T COMPUTERIZE A MESS

All that will have been accomplished is the ability to mess up quicker. The time and money spent on the system will have been wasted, thrown down the drain. If your firm is serious about computerization, then clean up your act before you start.

There is one more basic rule of computerization. Keeping in mind that computers do not make mistakes, people do, remember this important rule.

GARBAGE IN—GARBAGE OUT

All this means is that the information you get from your computer is only as good as the data you input. Therefore, it is important to not haphazardly enter data into the system. There should be some control over the data entered, making sure it is correct.

¶1207 Computers—Too Many Options?

The electronics industry has exploded in the past few years. The legal industry has been affected like most every other industry, if not more. Every day it seems there is a new product on the market. The trade journals are full of them. Half or more of all advertising done in legal publications is computer related.

With so many options, how does one pick a computer system? In ¶1208 the computer selection process is outlined in detail. However, before you begin, unless you have hired a legal automation consultant, you should know what your options are. You do not need to become a computer expert, but if you are involved in the selection process, you should become informed about the options available.

How does one become informed? Here is a list of ten things you and/or your attorneys can do to begin the process.

1. Attend a computer seminar sponsored by the local bar association or Association of Legal Administrators in your area.
2. Read a book like *A Commonsense Guide to Law Office Automation,* by Sara Piovia, Prentice-Hall, Inc., Englewood Cliffs, N.J. 07632. Softcover, 182 pages, $12.95 (1984).
3. Review recent copies of *Legal Economics* or *ABA Journal* for articles on computerization.
4. Find out what other firms your size in your area are doing about computerization.
5. Look in the yellow pages under computers or word processing to see which hardware vendors are located in your area.
6. Consider paying a legal automation consultant to come to your firm for a few hours to explain what options are available to firms your size.
7. Visit a local computer store to see, feel and touch a computer. Look at the different types of printers, including the new laser printers. Find out what a modem looks like. When you begin talking about the hardware items, if you have actually seen them, you are more likely to understand them.
8. Ask another firm if you can visit them to see their computer system in operation. It doesn't matter whether you are considering a similar system, they all operate basically the same. It will increase your understanding.
9. Ask some of the computer or software salespeople that are always calling to educate you. Don't let them talk you into a decision before you have really evaluated your needs, but take advantage of their willingness to spend time with you.

10. Subscribe to one of the legal computer newsletters, like *Attorneys Computer Report* (P.O. Box 80280, Atlanta, GA 30366) or *The Lawyer's PC,* R.P.W. Publishing Corp., P.O. Box 1108, Lexington, SC 29072. These newsletters are full of tips about new products and the ways computers are being used by other firms throughout the country. They typically have short articles that are easy to read.

¶1208 How to Find the Right Microcomputer

Once you have determined that your firm is committed to a computer selection project, and only then, the project is ready to begin. If you are involved in such a project you may want to offer the suggestions found in this chapter as a guide.

The computer selection project should be organized, with a beginning and an end. Each step should be scheduled, with a time limit, and a scheduled completion date. It is easy to get bogged down when there are so many options and so much to learn, but keep in mind this one important maxim:

THERE IS NO PERFECT COMPUTER SYSTEM!

The system you choose will not do everything you want. Before you purchase it, hopefully, you will understand what it will and will not do, but more likely you will not. Each day, week or month that you use it, you may discover some new capability or deficiency. Hopefully, the deficiencies will not have a major impact on the firm's operations. This will be the case if you and the other attorneys involved in the selection process proceed logically and systematically. Computer purchases should never be made on impulse, like buying a new dress or suit. The investment is too high and too much is at stake.

You may be wondering now, if there is no perfect system and any system selected will have deficiencies, why bother? In today's world, law firms are forced to automate. The competition is stronger every day and to keep the quality of service and billing rates down, automation is essential. This brings us to a second maxim:

YOU HAVE TO START SOMEWHERE!

You will not find the perfect system, but the system you select carefully should provide value to the firm for a time. It will eventually wear out, be outgrown, become too costly to maintain or become obsolete. When that happens, you replace it, like trading cars. You will, however, be much more informed the second time around. You will know what deficiencies you wish to correct and what additional capabilities you need.

¶1208.1 The Selection Process

There is a basic rule that should be followed when selecting a computer system.

FIND THE SOFTWARE THAT DOES WHAT YOU WANT AND THEN BUY THE HARDWARE THAT IT RUNS ON

This is a good rule to use. The place to start is with the software, the instructions and the ability of the computer to perform certain tasks. This does not mean that you do not consider the ability of the hardware, it just means that you do so after you consider the ability of the software. You may know of the most up-to-date, state-of-the-art computer available today, but if it does not have software that does what your firm needs, it is of no value to you.

Here are the steps to follow. It is important to not skip any of them. For example, don't start attending demonstrations until you are sure you know what you are looking for.

¶1208.2 Find Out the Computer's Capabilities

From your knowledge of what other firms are doing with computers and what they can do for you, list all of the tasks now being done manually in your firm which you think a computer can do better or quicker. Your list may look something like this:

I. TIME AND BILLING

1. Allow maximum of 15 (or 20 or 25 depending on expected number of timekeepers in your firm over the next 3–5 years) timekeepers at one time on system.
2. Allow input of time entries with unlimited number of characters in each time entry.
3. Automatically sort time and client disbursement entries.
4. Allow the following fee arrangements:
   Five hourly billing rates per timekeeper;
   Flat rate;
   Contingency billing (out of pocket costs only).
5. Produce prebill for selected clients and matters in billing attorney order for attorney review.
6. Automatically print bills in letter quality print.
7. Produce past due statements.

8. Allow for interest charges to clients on past due amounts.
9. Allow four originating attorneys per client.
10. Produce the following management reports:
    Accounts receivable;
    Work-in-progress aging;
    Billing and realization;
    Staff utilization report (hours worked, billable and nonbillable)
11. Allow input of time for new month before all billing complete for previous month.
12. Ability to bill by each matter or all matters for one client.
13. Ability to group clients for billing and reporting purposes.
14. Print a client listing with or without addresses and telephone numbers.
15. Ability to do cycle billing, i.e., half of clients on the fifteenth of the month, the other half at the end.
16. Ability for secretaries to input time from their word processing workstations.
17. Ability for secretaries to produce bills from their workstations.
18. Automatically charge client's account for copies when client and matter entered at copier.
19. Management reports by branch office and area of law.
20. Calculate and report attorney fee credits the way the firm is accustomed to.

II. GENERAL LEDGER AND CHECKWRITING
1. Print checks from information entered, i.e., client and matter, vendor name, type of disbursement, amount.
2. Update client's account and general ledger automatically from checks written.
3. Allow firm to use its own chart of accounts.
4. Produce financial statements in same format of present manual statements.

III. WORD PROCESSING
1. Type copy.
2. Allow corrections to be made quickly and easily.
3. Copy repetitive work.
4. Substitute standard paragraphs on document.
5. Keep track on typing done on the system.
6. Print duplicate copies.
7. Edit and re-edit text.

IV. CONFLICT OF INTEREST
1. Check for conflicts of interest from information entered into system.
2. Use client and matters entered in time and billing system. No need to re-enter them.

V. OTHER
1. Ability to use electronic spreadsheet for projections, tax planning, etc.
2. Keep track of all clients for which the firm has prepared wills.
3. Ability to do legal research via telecommunications.
4. Ability to send and receive documents from clients' word processing systems.

Once you have listed all the things you would like a computer to help your with, you should *prioritize* them. Keep this thought in mind as you and the attorneys working with you on the project establish priorities:

AUTOMATE THE BASICS—NOT THE FRILLS

Remember that each attorney will have different priorities. The tax attorney will want to do tax planning while the real estate attorney will want to do real estate closings. Eventually, each should have what they need, but the priorities should be to:

1. Get the bills out more efficiently.
2. Provide better management information.
3. Provide word processing capabilities (if needed).

Everything else should be examined closely to see if it is a frill or basic to the practice.

After you have your list of tasks you want to do on the computer, you should examine it to determine if any of them are unique to your firm. You should also try to establish what other requirements may be unique. You may require an eight digit client or matter number in order to avoid renumbering all client files. You may have a special way of calculating fee credits for attorneys. Some of the unique requirements will not become evident until you have seen the way some of the systems operate.

1. Document your present systems and procedures. The best way to communicate to vendors what you need a computer system to be able to do is to give it to them in writing. This also assures that every vendor will be given the same information. The preparation of such a document is also the best way of insuring that you have analyzed your needs thoroughly.

The document should begin with a statement of what you wish to accomplish with the new system. Following that should be a description of the manual systems you wish to automate. You should describe how much data needs to be processed, how often and how fast.

The documentation should include statistics about the operation of your firm which will help the vendor determine file sizes and hence, the amount of disk storage space you will need. These statistics should include the following:

	NOW	*5 YEARS FROM NOW*
Number of attorneys		
Number of paralegals		
Number of other timekeepers		
Total timekeepers		
Number of time tickets per day per timekeeper		
Average number of characters per time ticket		
Number of clients		
Number of active matters (files)		
Number of client invoices produced each month		
Number of cash receipts each month		
Number of checks written each month		
Number of client disbursement checks written each month		
Number of noncash transactions per month:		
Photocopy charges		
Long distance charges		
Messenger charges		
Legal research charges		
Other noncash charges		
Number of trust account checks written per month		
Number of general ledger account		
Number of journal entries per month		

You should also include a description of all computer or word processing equipment the firm is currently using and how it is used in this documentation. It may be possible to upgrade your present system or integrate it into the new system.

2. Decide on your hardware requirements. Now that you have decided what you want your computer system to do, you must decide what capabilities you need in hardware. By answering these few questions, you will have determined what your hardware needs are:

Do you want a stand-alone system or shared-logic system? See ¶1303.1 for an explanation of standalone and shared-logic systems.

How many workstations do you need? Do you need only one computer to do both word processing and financial applications? If you have decided you want a shared-logic system, how many terminals will you need? One for each secretary and one for the bookkeeper? Do the attorneys want workstations? The number of required terminals will to a great extent determine the size system you will need.

How many printers will you need? What kind of printers do you want? Will every secretary have a printer or will they share? How fast should they be? Can a laser printer be connected to the system? How many letter quality printers are needed? What is the fastest draft printer (for accounting reports) you can afford? Printing is a time consuming process. Don't pinch pennies on printers, they are as important as the computer itself.

How much memory will be needed on the new system? Are you planning to use the electronic spreadsheets which require a lot of main memory? How much memory does the word processing software you are considering require?

How much disk storage will you need? How many bytes will the data files use? How many pages of word processing documents need to be stored on the system? A good measure of disk storage requirements for a time and billing system is to have available one megabyte of space for every timekeeper. Therefore, an eight timekeeper firm will need eight megabytes of storage just for time and billing.If you plan to do word processing on the sample computer you will need more than a 10 MB hard disk.

Does the new computer system need to be integrated with other present systems? Does the firm already have a word processing system? Do the secretaries need to be able to tie into the computer system? Is there another computer in the firm, say for real estate closings or in one of the other departments? Do the systems need to be able to talk to one another and share files?

Does the computer system need to be able to communicate with the outside world? Do you intend to do legal research like Westlaw and Lexis on the new system? Do you need a modem? Does the firm need to send and receive documents to and from clients? Does the firm need telex ability?

3. Select vendors to consider. The best way to select vendors is to hire the services of a qualified legal automation consultant for a few hours to explain to you and your attorneys the options available today. If this is not possible, find out what other firms in your area are doing and discuss with them their likes and dislikes about their systems. Make certain that repair and support is available in your locality.

Send your written requirements to these vendors, asking them to propose the system they think your firm needs.

4. Evaluate proposals. Once you have received several proposals from vendors you will need to compare them. The best approach is a systematic one. Otherwise you may overlook an important flaw in a system or find that the systems you are comparing are not really comparable.

5. Evaluate software. There are some basic things to consider about each system. Many of the questions you should get answered can only be answered by someone who has used the system long enough to become really familiar with it. You should request at least five customer references from the software vendor, along with their telephone numbers and a name to contact. Vendors expect this and are usually prepared to provide such information. You may want to rate each system on a scale of one to ten for each consideration and use the total scores in your decision process.

Ease of installation. Software installation usually includes making backup copies of the applications programs, copying the operating system onto the backup diskette or "loading" the software onto the hard disk of your computer. In addition to the installation of the software on the computer, the start-up of the system, loading your firm's data is considered installation. You can ask the vendor to show you the installation instructions in the manual and explain the steps to you. Better yet, ask several of the customer references if the manual was easy to understand and the software easy to install. If the vendor installed the software, was it done properly?

Ease of learning. Ease of learning means how simple or difficult it is to learn to use the software. You will not be able to tell this for yourself from demonstrations, however, you can ask other users of the software how easy it was to learn to operate. Were there meaningful examples in the manual? Is it easy to find answers to your questions in the manual? Is there an online help function? How helpful is it? Did the vendor provide training? Was it adequate?

Ease of use. Ease of use means how good is the documentation and operator's manuals which come with the system. Are they adequate? Do they explain in simple, everyday language (not "computerese") how to use the system? Does the system have menus which are well organized and consistent? These are questions which you will have to ask other users of the software since you will not know how easy the software is to use until you have used it.

Performance. How fast does the system run? Software packages are written in different languages by different people who think differently. Many do the same tasks, but do them differently—some more efficiently than others—just like people. You cannot tell how fast a software package runs by looking at a demonstration. It may appear fast, but what happens when you load in all of your data? Does the system slow down while trying to process all of that data? Are there errors (bugs) in the system? Does the software do what it claims to do? If there were bugs in the system were they corrected by the vendor? How long did it take to get them corrected?

Vendor support. Does the vendor provide adequate support for the system? Are there qualified people to answer your questions? Is the support reasonable in cost?

6. *Evaluate hardware.* Evaluating microcomputer hardware is not really difficult. Most microcomputers work well. The major questions are:

- What is the hardware vendor's financial strength and commitment to the microcomputer market?
- Will the vendor still be around several years from now?
- Where can you get your computer repaired?
- Can you get a loaner to use while your computer is being repaired?
- Does the computer have enough capacity (main memory, disk storage, and speed) to process your firm's data?
- Can the system be upgraded if necessary if the firm outgrows it?
- Can more workstations or printers be added if needed? How many?
- Are there places in the back of the computer to physically plug in more devices? If not, can they be added?

Look at the cost of adding another workstation for a new secretary. Be careful to not get your firm in a dead end situation where no upgrades are available and their only choice is to scrap the system and buy a completely new one. Remember, that is a costly mistake.

7. *Prepare a cost justification.* Cost should be the last thing to be considered in the selection process. Most systems are similar in price if they have the same functionality. The decision should not be too heavily influenced by differences in cost unless the difference is dramatic. Usually, when the differences in cost are looked at on a per month basis, or a per workstation basis, they are insignificant.

How will your attorneys justify the cost of a computer system? A microcomputer for a small firm will cost the firm $10,000–$20,000 by the time the software and all peripherals are added. What will be gained? Many of the advantages of a computerized time and billing system cannot be translated into dollars, but others can. For example, if your system will help you collect information to better charge clients for copies you can make some assumptions which will convert into dollars. *Example:* Assume you will be able to collect 100 copies per day from clients that you do not now collect. If you charge each client 25¢ per copy that is $25 per day in income which you do not have now. If you multiply $25 times 250 working days in a year you will have $6,250 more than you presently have. This is one way you can pay for a computer system.

Many firms are charging their clients for computerized word processing charges. Secretaries keep time just like attorneys and paralegals and the time is billed to the client at an hourly rate of, say, $25. All secretarial time is not usually billed but if just two hours a day per secretary is collected, the dollars add up.

It is hard to put a dollar value on the amount of time attorneys will save during the billing process with a good time and billing system. If just two or three hours a month can be spent doing billable work instead of administrative work, the dollar benefits will add up quickly.

Here is a simple schedule to use to compare the costs of the systems under consideration (Figure 1208.1-1). Make sure the hardware and software includes the same capabilities in all systems before you begin comparing prices. One system may seem like a bargain, but you may find, much to your dismay, that the capabilities are greatly diminished over the other systems.

8. Check References. Usually, vendors provide a list of satisfied customers. You should insist on references from at least *five* other law firms in your area. Once you have narrowed your search down to a few possibilities, check the references. Here are some questions you should ask.

a. Was the system delivered and installed on time?
b. Did you encounter any problems during the installation period that a prospective user should be aware of?
c. What kind of training was provided by the vendor? Lecture, video tapes, audio tapes?
d. Where was the training done and by whom?
e. Was the training adequate?
f. How useful are the manuals?
g. How easy or difficult was it to learn to use the system? To operate the system?
h. What is the overall impression of the system by the secretaries in your firm? The attorneys?

TURNER, WITHERS, JACOBSON & BRUNO

HARDWARE AND SOFTWARE

DATA AND WORD PROCESSING

	COMPAQ DESKPRO					
	PROPOSED	QUANTITY	UNIT PRICE	TOTAL PRICE	MONTHLY MAINT.	TRAINING & INSTALLATION
COMPUTER:						
1. CPU and accessories	Compaq Deskpro	2	3,670	7,340	73	I*
PERIPHERALS:						
2. Disk storage	30MB Hard disk	2	1,400	2,800	28	I
	Diskettes	1	40	40	NA	I
3. Back up	10MB Tape backup	2	I	0	I	I
	Tapes	4	29	116	NA	I
4. Display terminals	Amdek color	2	495	990	10	I
5. Communications/controllers	Serial/clock card	2	I	0	I	I
6. Printer - draft	Okidata 84	1	700	700	7	I
7. Printer - letter quality	HP Laserjet	1	2,495	2,495	25	I
8. Printer - check writing	None required	--	---	---	---	---
9. Operating system software	MS DOS 2.11	2	59	118	NA	I
10. Time and billing software	Clockwork	1	1,500	1,500	NA	1,000
11. Geneal ledger software	Timberline	1	1,090	1,090	NA	800
12. Word processing	Mass 11 - PC	1	995	995	NA	500
				18,184	143	2,300
	Add sales tax		5%	909		
13. Total hardware and software				19,093	143	2,300

Figure 1208.1-1. Sample Comparison of System Costs.

i. Have any software errors (bugs) been encountered since installing the system?
j. Does the system break down frequently?
k. How did you convert your documents to the new system?
l. How responsive has the vendor been in answering questions or responding to problems related to the system?
m. Has the vendor provided technically competent personnel to assist you with problems?
n. Do you ever experience a slowing down (degradation) of the system? When does this happen?
o. Have you upgraded your original system? How was it accomplished?
p. If you had to do it over again, would you purchase the same system?

9. Select vendor. Based upon your study, make your best guess of which vendor can provide the software and computer hardware for your firm. Tell the vendor you are also considering other proposals to give your firm some leverage in the negotiating process.

10. Negotiate contract. This part of the computer selection project will most likely be handled by the attorneys involved. In the purchase of a microcomputer there is not really a lot of negotiating to be done. A clear understanding is important of the responsibility of the vendor and the warranties that accompany the software. Issues such as training and ongoing support should be clearly defined prior to the signing of a contract.

11. Schedule implementation. Now that the decision is made, it is important to plan the implementation of the system. Here are a few tips to keep in mind when doing so.

The best-planned word processing workstations offer the most features within the least amount of space. Poorly planned workstations lead to increased noise and traffic. Consider carefully the space requirements of the systems under consideration. Where will the printers be placed? If they are noisy, they may need to be down the hall, in a room away from the attorneys. If so, this may require many unnecessary trips to pick up documents.

Don't place the computer in an attorney's office or on a secretary's desk. This does not promote sharing of the equipment and maximizing its use. The only time the computer should be placed on a secretary's desk is when it was purchased for word processing for that secretary. If it is to be shared, a more centrally located station is more practical.

Most word processing terminals take up no more room than a typewriter. However, you will still need a typewriter nearby. Certain forms (like Federal Express), Rolodex cards, index cards and labels need to be prepared on a typewriter. It is usually possible for several secretaries to share a typewriter by placing it in a central location. If your work space gets too cluttered with equipment you will not be able to work effectively or efficiently.

Be sure to purchase the proper furniture for the computer. Don't try to make do with old desks and chairs. Comfort at the computer is extremely important. Many hours may be spent by you or other secretaries and improper furniture that is not adjustable will cause fatigue and possible back pain.

Consider anti-glare screens to reduce glare and eye fatigue.

Arrange for electrical wiring for the system. Most systems require a dedicated line for the CPU. If the computer is operated on a line with other machines in the office, the uneven power supply may cause damage to the electronic data files. A power surge protector may be a good investment.

Suggest a clean up of all client files before implementing a computerized time and billing system. Close as many files as possible, collect outstanding receivables, bill time and disbursements, write off old time and disbursements and uncollectible receivables. The less "garbage" you put in the system, the less cluttered it will be.

12. Enjoy! This is sometimes the most difficult part of owning a new computer system. People, generally, don't like to change and this becomes especially obvious with the advent of a new computer. Take it slow and easy. Don't try to change everything at once. Get one program up and running before tackling the next one. Do the easiest part first to help you become comfortable with the computer. Be careful, however, or you may be one of those bitten by the computer bug and have a love affair with your computer.

¶1300 Guidelines to Selecting and Using Word Processors

By Carole A. Bruno and Paula F. Turner

Purchasing word processing equipment in the large law firm, either for the first time or to replace existing equipment, is usually done by the office manager or administrator; sometimes a group of interested attorneys will head up the project. An outside consultant is often hired to assist in the selection process. As a rule, the higher the expected investment, the more attorney time and consulting fees spent. Mistakes can be very costly to the firm and must be minimized as much as possible.

It is usually a good idea to consider your firm's data processing needs along with its word processing requirements since these two functions are often done with the same equipment. Also, there is a trend today for secretaries to be involved in the time and billing process, entering time and disbursements and requesting and printing bills right from their word processing workstations. See ¶1200 for advice on selecting a computer system for your firm.

There is a lot to learn about computers and word processors before an informed decision can be made. Since attorneys' time is valuable and there is no real advantage to their becoming computer experts, this task is usually passed on to the administrator or office manager. In the small firm it is often one of the secretaries who is given responsibility for the project.

If you become aware that your firm is considering the purchase of word processing equipment, get involved. It is the best way to get what you want. Volunteer to assist in the process, even if you have to do it after normal working hours. It will be worth it in the long run. A word of caution, however. Don't take full responsibility for the final decision and don't be too disappointed if your first choice is not selected. Be as helpful as possible by supplying information, meeting with vendors and attending demos. Leave the final decision up to the attorneys whose money will be used to make the purchase.

¶1301 Determining Your Word Processing Needs

The first step in selecting a word processor is to determine your firm's requirements. An analysis should be made of present document preparation. You can survey the attorneys (authors) and other secretaries regarding the firm's present situation. What problems do they encounter? What documents do they produce? How can they benefit from better word processing equipment?

Providing secretaries with good word processing equipment usually improves the document production process; however, if the problems are due to poor secretary or attorney work habits, purchasing equipment won't solve them. It is best to try to determine what the real problems are before getting too far along in the project.

¶1301.1 Surveying the Word Processing Situation

A document survey form like the one in Figure 1301.1-1 may be filled out by the secretaries to help determine the volume and frequency of documents produced in the firm. This is a critical step since it will help the vendors determine the size of system you need. The use of this form will also provide information about the number of revisions which are required and by whom. It is true that some attorneys do it right the first time, but most attorneys almost always change a document before sending it out.

The firm's type of practice will often dictate the type of word processing equipment needed. For example, if the firm does heavy litigation, it may need the ability to sort documents. You should request that each attorney and his or her secretary furnish you with samples of the types of documents they produce. These should be reviewed with the vendors to make sure you both have a good understanding of the firm's requirements.

Don't forget to take an inventory of the firm's present equipment. It is sometimes possible to use existing equipment effectively, supplementing or upgrading it. Unless the firm is extremely unhappy with its present equipment or vendor or you are certain it is obsolete, don't make the decision to scrap it until you are sure that it is necessary. Remember, all of the documents on your present system will have to be converted to a new system.

¶1302 What Word Processing Software Can Do for You

Before you can decide what you want in a word processing system, you must first understand what the system can do. Word processors are supposed to help, not hinder, as you write or prepare documents. A word processor should make writing simpler, whether a short letter or long brief. If it doesn't, it is of no value to you.

NAME ______________________ Phone Extension __________ Department ______________________

AUTHOR ______________________ Phone Extension __________ Equipment Used ______________________

Document Name	Orig. Form	Estimated		Paper Size	Frequency		Proof	Corr. Allowed	Carbon	Copies	Font/ Type Style (2)	Turn around Time (hours)	Boiler-plate %	Reten-tion Period (Diskettes)	Comments
		No. of Pages	Revi-sions		(daily, weekly, etc.)	Vol.									
Memos															
Letters															
Pleadings															
Briefs															
Formal legal documents (list)–Leases, Will, etc.															
Preprinted forms (list)(1)															
Mass Mailings (list)															
Envelopes															
Other (list)															

(1) e.g., Tax returns, GBREB forms, Stock Certificates (2) A–Legal Courier; B–Delegate; C–Prestige Elite; D–Other

Figure 1301.1-1 Word Processing Survey Form. Reprinted by permission of Holland Shipes Bennett Thrasher, P.C., CPAs, Atlanta, GA.

Word processors are often described by the software features they have or the functions of the hardware. Vendors will try to convince you that they have more features than their competitors and vice versa. Keep in mind that the number of features is not important. What is important is whether the word processor has the features you need and if they are easy to use.

If you do not understand the concepts of hardware and software, you should turn to ¶1200 and read about computer systems before continuing.

Probably 80 percent of all word processing requires the use of five basic features:

Type;
Insert;
Delete;
Move;
Format.

If these software features are present, easy to learn and use, then the word processor will be a valuable tool. Of course most word processors *do* much more than these five things. See Figure 1302-1 for a complete checklist of word processing software features.

Word Processing Software Feature Checklist

This list is intended to familiarize novices with the types of commands commonly found on word processing software packages. Smaller, less expensive packages will contain only a subset of these features. More sophisticated packages may contain most or all of these features. Since WP commands can be grouped in different ways, including simply as *editing* and *printer/formatting* features, and since new features are being added as software technology evolves, this checklist should not be considered as definitive. We are indebted to *Mini-Micro Systems,* May 1982, for the basic outline of this listing.

TEXT INPUT/DOCUMENT CREATION

Cursor Movement
- Forward/backward one char/word/ line/sentence/paragraph
- Up/down one line
- Top/middle/bottom of screen
- Beginning/end of text
- Start of next line
- Specified page
- Next screen

Scrolling
- Vertical by line/screen
- Horizontal

Screen Formatting
- Set/release left/right margins
- Set page width/length
- Set/clear single/all tabs
- Indentation
- Underlining
- Centering

Figure 1302-1. Word Processing Software Feature Checklist.

- Reformat paragraph
- Manual/automatic page breaks
- Hyphenation
- Variable word wrap
- Split screens

BASIC EDITING

Insertion and Deletion

- Move forward/backward one char/word/line/sentence/paragraph/block
- Insert char/word/line/sentence/etc.
- Delete forward/backward one char/word/line/sentence/paragraph/block
- Delete rest of page/to end of document
- Word wrap

Block Operations

- Copy/move/merge/delete block
- Erase all block markers
- Hide/display block
- Write block to file

Search Operations

- Search forward/backward for string of characters
- Find/replace string with verification n times
- Substitute with/without query
- Global search and replace
- Repeat last operation
- Ignore a specific string occurrence when searching
- Match whole words only
- Search and replace operations using "wild cards"
- Search and delete

PRINTER/FORMATTING FEATURES

Page Layout

- Set top/bottom/left/right margins
- Set/clear tabs/multiple tabs
- Set titles
- Set/suppress headers/footers
- Set header/footer margin
- Set page length
- Set number of char/lines per inch
- Set single/double/triple vertical spacing
- Out/indent first lines/paragraphs
- Number paragraphs
- Line between paragraphs
- Page numbering/suppression
- Pagination/stop pagination
- Book-style page numbering (odd numbers on right)
- Force new page

Justification

- Right/no right justify
- Centering
- Block justify
- Hard (unsplittable) spaces/hyphens
- Automatic decimal data alignment
- Double/triple/etc. columns with right justify

Character Attributes

- Underline
- Boldface/boldface underline
- Shadowed (double strike)
- Variable intensity boldface
- Super/subscript
- Overprint
- Ribbon color shift
- Proportional spacing
- Microspace char spacing
- Continuously variable char spacing
- Explicit alternate char spacing
- Pitch-independent line lengths
- Special characters

Printer Control

- Print specified page from file
- Print from/through specified page
- Print from cursor position
- Print with values from specified disk record
- Print until specified record is read
- Read keyboard
- Print multiple copies
- Interrupt/resume printing
- Line/form feed
- Display/change print format
- Test page
- Pause and display message
- Pause for paper insertion

Figure 1302-1. (continued)

Continuous printing of multiple documents (print spooling)
Convert to all uppercase
Convert to upper/lower case
Change fonts
Typesetter
Unformatted printer

DOCUMENT UTILITIES/SPECIAL FEATURES

Document/File Operations
Display file directory
Display space used/unused
Save file
Exit file without saving
Save file and continue editing
Save from cursor to end of file
Automatic backup—one/n generation(s)
Read file/part of file
Delete file
Line/merge WP documents with non-WP documents

Programming
String/integer/dollar/system variables
Input to variables from disk
Input to variables from operator (fill in blanks)
Prompt operator from input
Output variable information to disk (simultaneous WP, data capture)
Conditional branching

OFFICE AUTOMATION/SPECIAL FEATURES

Draft and finish printer drivers
Programmer mode
Calculator utility
Business graphics (character graphics)
Mail list create/update/select/sort
Columnar math
Automatic table of contents/document index
"What you see is what you get" display (print enhancements on screen)
Security passwords by library/document
Electronic mail
Administrative support (phone index, calendar card file routines)
Spelling check/correct (English/law/medical dictionaries)
Thesaurus
Syntax check

Figure 1302-1. (continued)

The most important thing a word processor does is to help you prepare documents. Once the document has been typed, it is saved, electronically, on either a hard or floppy disk, for future use. You can print it out on paper, proofread it, and give it to your attorney for revision. When you are ready to revise it, you simply retrieve the electronic file from the disk. The document will again be displayed on the screen for you to edit. You can make as many revisions as you wish, keying in only the necessary changes. Some word processing software programs automatically mark the changes so only the changes need to be proofed. This feature is called redlining and can save you and your attorneys valuable time. Special features of word processors that you should know follow.

Search and replace	Searches throughout a document for a word or phrase and replaces it with another word or phrase.

Pagination	Automatically separates the document into pages, either in the background or as you type.
Spelling checker	Checks the spelling in a document against a dictionary which should include legal terms. Also allows you to add words or names you use often.
List processing	Allows the one-time creation of a form document that can be used over and over again, by merging a list of information into it, i.e., form letters for mass mailings or a standard will or lease.
Merge	Allows you to merge two documents or parts of another document into the document on which you are currently working.
Headers and footers	Prints information at the top or bottom of each page, e.g., the page number or document name. Automatically numbers the pages.
Footnoting	Automatically places footnotes on the proper page along with its reference. Automatically numbers and renumbers footnotes.
Math capabilities	Performs simple calculations, printing the solution in a location defined by the operator.
Sorting	Alphabetizes or sorts in numeric sequence.
Redlining	Marks text that has been edited, deleted or inserted to make proofreading easier.

Table of contents	Automatically creates a table of contents, complete with alpha characters or numbers, including Roman numerals.
Help key	Provides a help manual on the screen for the function you are trying to do. Eliminates the need to find the instructions in a larger manual.

¶1302.1 Other "Tricks" Your Word Processor Can Do

While it is true that document preparation is the major use of word processors, it is not the only use. If you choose a computer with word processing software, of course, there are numerous tasks it can perform, as described in ¶1200. Even standalone and dedicated word processors have other capabilities.

Communications

With the aid of a modem (a device used to transmit data over telephone lines from one computer to another), you can send documents or information cheaper and faster than by courier. Most word processors have the ability to connect and use a modem. You can also use your word processor as a Telex machine or you can send a document to a typesetter over the telephone lines.

One of the most popular uses of communications on word processors is to subscribe to services such as Westlaw and Lexis to do legal research (see ¶1600). You can also subscribe to newswire services, stock market operations and electronic bulletin boards to exchange and receive information.

Other features like those listed in the following, which may be available on the same computer equipment as word processing, are discussed in ¶1200:

Conflict of interest;
Calendar control;
Electronic spreadsheets;
General accounting;
Time and billing;
Trust accounting.

Data Processing Integration

Law firms are becoming more computerized. Many secretaries have word processing terminals right on their desks, rather than a few word processors in a word processing center. In many firms the word processor operates off of a larger computer which also processes the firm's time and billing and financial information.

You may be able to sit at your desk and type in your attorneys' time for the day, request a check for a client disbursement, request and print out a client's bill, right from your terminal. Your word processor, in other words, may do "double duty," both word processing and data processing.

There is a trend throughout the country to charge clients for the use of computerized word processing, either by the completed page or by the hour. Some systems even require you to enter the client and matter number relating to the document you are producing before you can leave the document. When you do this, the client's account is charged (all electronically) for the amount of the word processing charge. A few seconds later you could request to see the status of the client's account on your screen and the word processing charge would be there.

¶1303 A Concise Guide to Word Processors

There are basically two types of word processing systems being used in law offices today—standalone and shared-logic. They each have their places in certain situations. Both standalone and shared-logic have common characteristics: a display, a keyboard, and a printer.

¶1303.1 Standalone vs. Shared-Logic

Standalone Systems These word processors do just what their name implies—they stand alone as self-contained units. One person at a time uses them. A standalone system may be a word processor with a screen, or a microcomputer with its own printer. Usually, documents are stored on diskettes which hold about 100 pages. Some electronic or memory typewriters fall into the category of standalone word processors. Standalones are often used in the smaller law office with only a few secretaries, because they are usually much less expensive than shared-logic systems.

Shared-logic Systems Shared-logic systems consist of several workstations tied to a main computer. The terminals depend on the computer to operate. Shared-logic systems usually store documents on a fixed disk drive that may hold as much as 350,000 pages. A document on a shared-logic system may be used by other users on the system. This is one of the advantages to the shared-logic system, since attorneys and secretaries may use the same documents, i.e., standard wills, leases, estate planning documents, etc.

Another advantage to the shared-logic system is that secretaries may share printers. Ideally, a secretary should be able to print a document on any other printer on the system. If your firm needs more than two workstations, you should consider a shared-logic system.

¶1303.2 Pros and Cons of Shared-Logic and Standalone Word Processing*

Once a firm decides to automate or decentralize its word processing department, the question of whether to purchase a shared-logic system or invest in standalones for the individual secretaries arises.

When a firm is making an automation decision, it wants to make sure the equipment it purchases will serve the firm for many years. With the fast decline of dedicated word processors, some firms are somewhat gun-shy of investing in soon-to-be-outmoded hardware.

This article will discuss the pros and cons of both systems in an attempt, hopefully, to assist you in making an informed decision.

The main distinction of a shared logic system is that it has series of terminals that share one central processing unit (CPU), i.e., a minicomputer. These shared logic configurations are in either a cental location or distributed throughout the larger office. This differs from the independent standalone word processor which is an intelligent terminal, complete in itself with its own memory and storage capabilities. Many standalones also include a printer.

Pros and Cons of SHARED LOGIC Word Processing Systems:

PROS

1. *Ability to share documents from the firm's boilerplate files.* With a shared logic system, any attorney can utilize other attorneys' form documents that are in the system. This prevents "reinventing the wheel" and also encourages standardization of the forms that the attorneys use. In other words, the format and contents of the boilerplate documents can be perfected by the input of various attorneys in the firm.

*Reprinted with permission, L. Donald Holland and Paula F. Turner, Holland Shipes Bennett Thrasher, P.C. CPAs, Atlanta, GA.

2. *The ability to share workloads by dividing documents and having more than one secretary work on them.* Frequently, an attorney will have a peak workload crisis, with a voluminous amount of documents to prepare. With a shared logic system, the secretary can get additional help from other secretaries in the firm, since they will be able to access the same document data base. Also, when secretaries are not busy, they can assist each other more efficiently.

3. *The standardization of text editing capabilities among all secretaries and word processing operators.* The firm can develop a document preparation manual that each employee would be instructed to use. Thus, there will be overall consistency in the format of the documents prepared by the attorneys.

4. *The ability of the firm to secure its word processing documents through controlled backup.* A system manager can be appointed to monitor the backup procedures of the entire system. With a standalone system, it is more difficult to control the individual backup procedures.

5. *The inability of a secretary to "file away" her documents so that they are unavailable for use when she is ill or on vacation.* When the secretary is out, many attorneys have spent frantic days looking for documents, information and forms that only the secretary could locate. With a shared logic system, if a secretary is absent, another secretary or temporary can take her place and be able to access any of the documents that are in the system. Thus, the attorney does not suffer a crisis when his secretary is out.

6. *The standardization of training procedures for all secretaries.* With the ability to standardize the work product and document preparation process, the training of new secretaries and the continued training of the present secretaries can be standardized. When new secretaries are trained, the manual would allow the secretaries to be self-trained more easily, because the procedures, forms and formats would be in the manual. This would also be helpful when using temporary office workers.

7. *The ready ability to use background printing.* Background printing is when the operator can continue to use the word processor while the printer is printing out another document. With some standalone systems, you cannot do background printing as you can with a shared logic system.

8. *The shared logic system is usually more cost effective.* Large disk drives store information at a lower cost than storage on the smaller disks

of standalone systems. A shared logic system also provides more sophisticated capabilities.

9. *Data processing can be added easily.* If the firm has a shared logic system, it is easier to add data processing software at a later date.

10. *Ability to input time directly into the time and billing system.* With a shared logic system, if the firm has the appropriate data processing software, each secretary can input the attorneys' time directly into the system on a daily basis, preventing duplicate keying by the accounting or bookkeeping department personnel.

    The use of a shared logic system, which allows secretaries to do time and billing work at their desks, often decreases the accounting support staff. Furthermore, secretaries can more easily make time entries since they are most familiar with the attorney and his work. Personnel and client/record departments that process client matter and representation information can often be reduced because the secretary has on-line data input and inquiry capabilities to use information maintained in the firm's master file.

11. *Ability to fill out new matters and new clients directly on the system.* A shared logic system allows a secretary to enter new client matter and information into the time and billing system. Thus, new client information and matter information will be more accurate and updated more quickly.

12. *Conflict searches on a firm-wide database.* Since new clients and new matters can be directly entered into the system, it becomes easier to check conflicts almost immediately, whereas with a standalone system, the new matter memorandum and client information would have to be sent to another department to be entered later in the firm's filing and conflicts of interest system.

13. *Automated docket and calendar control for the firm as a whole.* With a shared logic system, each secretary can enter pertinent docket and calendar information into the firm's database. This gives the attorneys more control over the information for docket and calendar purposes. Another advantage is that docket and calendar information can be entered more expeditiously as opposed to being sent to another department or another person for input.

14. *The use of an automated Rolodex system for the firm.* With a shared logic system, an automated Rolodex system or mailing list could be prepared for the firm. Secretaries can produce Rolodex cards for everyone working on a file automatically. This Rolodex system

would also give any attorney access to any client's name, address and telephone number, along with the contact name. Thus, if an attorney wanted to send an announcement to all of the firm's clients, the firm Rolodex system would be available. This would be extremely helpful in the case of attorneys working on another attorney's client file.

15. *Secretaries can share printers.* With a shared logic system the more expensive high speed laser printers can be used by all secretaries on the system. Other printers for shorter documents can be placed throughout the office or tucked away in a soundproofed printer room, rather than at the secretary's desk.

CONS

1. *The entire system can go down and the secretaries cannot continue to operate.* In a shared logic system, terminals are connected to one CPU. If the CPU is nonoperational, so are the secretaries.
2. *Secretaries are usually required to share printers.* The sharing of printers is usually not a problem, unless there are too many secretaries assigned to one printer. Attorneys may have to wait while other attorneys' work product is being processed, causing the work to have to be prioritized constantly, causing possible conflicts among attorneys and secretaries.
3. *Fewer printers with more distant locations require secretaries to be away from their desks.* When the secretaries are away from their desks, their attorneys' telephones will not be answered and visitors may not be greeted. Clients may feel neglected, not to mention attorneys.

Pros and cons of STANDALONE word processing systems:

PROS

1. *Flexibility of design.* There is more flexibility in the office layout because the hardware can be moved around more easily.
2. *Secretaries do not have to leave their desks to inquire about or retrieve printed documents.* All secretaries may have a printer at their work-stations, like the new desktop lasers. Also, if a secretary handles the printer, it is easier to make frequent changes in the paper rather than go to a distant location set aside for the printer and its function.
3. *When a standalone system is down, other standalone stations are unaffected.* Other secretaries will continue to be productive. The only

documents which may be lost or inaccessible will be the ones on the nonoperational workstation.

4. *Cabling costs are greatly reduced.* The need to string cable to each secretary's workstation for a shared logic system is absent with the standalone. The workstation can usually be brought in and immediately installed.
5. *Per workstation cost may be less.* For the small firm, the per workstation cost and total system cost is usually less when standalones are used. However, in the larger firm, the shared logic system is usually the most cost effective solution.

CONS

1. *Secretaries cannot share documents efficiently.* Standard documents may be duplicated by each secretary and a significant amount of time will be lost. Also, changes to the standard form by any attorney will not be available to other attorneys, creating different versions throughout the office. In other words, standard documents will not be standard.
2. *Standalone word processing encourages unique procedures at each workstation.* Each secretary may create documents a different way, thereby causing nonuniform procedures and documents in the firm. It is more difficult to standardize using standalone workstations.
3. *Standalone word processing does not promote work sharing.* Because the secretaries are using individual workstations, they do not seem to be as willing to help each other as they are in a shared logic system where they must work together.
4. *A standalone system often requires secretaries to handle diskettes.* Diskettes are cumbersome to handle and backup of diskettes is time consuming. It is also difficult to ensure proper backup of documents.
5. *With a standalone system, more sophisticated software cannot be used.* Minicomputers can use more sophisticated software, giving the firm greater capabilities in its word and data processing systems.
6. *A standalone system tends to not promote interdependence among the various departments of the firm, making each workstation a satellite center.* When the departments are working together, the attorneys maintain a higher level of cooperation.
7. *With a standalone system, data processing cannot be added as easily.* It will be difficult to add data processing software for firm-wide time-

keeping and accounting functions unless the standalone can be tied into a central CPU at a later date.

Having considered the pros and cons of the two types of systems, the firm's decision will be based upon many factors. There is, of course, no perfect system and what is right for your firm is not necessarily right for another.

A general conclusion that can be drawn, however, is that the benefits of a shared logic system are valuable and the medium to large law firm should consider this approach. The smaller firm may want to start with standalones that can later be used as terminals on a shared logic system.

¶1303.3 Printers

In addition to the word processor itself, you will need to consider the types of printers your firm will need. There are three basic types of printers used for word processing today.

Letter Quality Printers These printers produce documents that look as if they have been typed on a good typewriter. They look professional. These printers are usually described by the speed at which they print. The speeds range from 20 characters per second to 60 characters per second.

Most letter-quality printers work by striking the paper through an ink ribbon, forming the character on the paper. This striking, or impact, can be a noisy process. For this reason, impact printers are often hidden away in a printer room or covered with a sound hood to minimize the noise. Letter-quality printers usually have sheet feeder attachments which eliminate the need for a secretary to hand feed paper or letterhead into the printer. If at all possible, dual bin sheet feeders should be used so two types of paper may be used at one time.

Draft Printers These printers are usually called dot matrix printers. They also operate by making an impact on the paper, forming the characters by an arrangement of dots. The quality of the print is usually not good enough to use for legal documents or correspondence in final form, but they are popular because they print much faster than the letter-quality printers.

Most draft printers print at speeds of from 160 characters per second to 600 lines per minute. The first drafts of a document may be printed on the draft printer in half or more of the time of a letter-quality printer. Draft printers usually have a tractor feed device and use continuous form paper, the kind with holes in each side to fit on the tractor feed.

Laser Printers These printers are becoming more and more popular, especially since many vendors are now selling desktop lasers. The small lasers cost no more than a good impact printer and should certainly be considered.

There are two distinct advantages of the laser printer over impact printers. They are quieter and they are faster. A laser printer can be placed near the secretary's desk without disturbing those working around her. The new desktop models print eight pages per minute. This is four to eight times faster than the letter-quality printers.

The quality of the print of a laser printer is usually excellent and consistent. Before you commit to purchasing a laser printer, however, be sure to try your firm's letterhead in it, since some paper types or heavily engraved paper will not work properly in them. It may be necessary for you to have both a laser for legal documents and an impact printer for correspondence.

¶1303.4 State-of-the-Art Simply Stated

The word processing industry has new vendors and new products showing up and disappearing almost daily. You may be tempted to buy a machine that is no longer made because it is a bargain. The initial cost may be low, but consider the aggravation when you can't find anyone to fix it when it breaks, or you can't find anyone who knows how to use it.

Even well-known, established vendors discontinue their products because of newer technology. The discontinued system may be more than adequate for your needs, but what typically happens, is that the maintenance costs get higher every year until it is cheaper to go out and buy another new system than to maintain the old one.

State-of-the-art, simply stated, means the most recent version of a vendor's product which is comparable to the vendor's competitors' most recent products.

¶1304 Selecting the Right Word Processor for Your Firm

When you have completed your analysis of the firm's requirements you should have a list of requirements to present to the vendors you will consider. The best way to select the vendors is by finding out what other firms have selected for word processing and what they like or dislike about it. Find out which are the most popular systems and why. This will give you a good place to start. Don't try to look at every word processor on the market. It is a waste of your time. The systems in place in other firms are there because they have something good to offer the legal environment.

Another important point to consider is which vendors are located in your area. There may be an excellent word processing system which you have read about and would like to purchase, but if there is no local service for that system, it is not a good choice.

A simple way to find out which vendors are located in your area is to review the Yellow Pages under computers or word processing sections. Find out where service personnel are based. Are they in your town, or would they have to travel from a nearby city? Obviously, the former is preferable to the latter.

You should learn something about the vendors who sell the word processing equipment in addition to learning about the features of the equipment.

¶1304.1 Hands On or Hands Off

Once you have selected several systems to consider, arrange for a "hands on" demonstration. Don't take the word of the vendor that his or her equipment can do just what you want. It may very well be able to do it, but you must determine how easy or difficult it is to do.

Ask the vendor if you can have one workstation installed in your firm for an evaluation period. Give it to the most reluctant secretary, or use it yourself. This may require getting some word processing training, but it is the best way to evaluate the equipment.

Above all, don't be swayed in your decision by factors that have nothing to do with the equipment's ability to function properly in your office, such as the vendor's personality, the amount of attention the vendor paid to your project, or "gut feel." Once the sale is made, you are stuck with what you bought. You may never see the salesperson again.

¶1305 Step-by-Step Word Processing Hands On Demo*

Here are step-by-step instructions of things to do at a demo of word processing software on a microcomputer.

1. Arrange with the salesperson to have the software loaded on the computer and a letter quality printer connected to the computer prior to your arrival. This will save you time.

*Adapted from an article "How to Buy a Word Processor" with permission by Michael P. Froman, Law Office Management Associates, Atlanta, GA, 1984.

2. Take a note pad along with you for taking notes.

3. Take along about a dozen sheets of your stationery as well as billing stationery and your firm's envelopes.

4. First, review the instruction manual. Does it make any sense? After the salesperson has installed your computer and gone on to the next sale, will you be able to read the manual?

5. Turn on the computer and start the word processing program yourself. Do you like the color, size, and format of the screen? Look at the displays, instructions and what computer people strangely call "menus." Can you read them? Are they pleasing to you?

6. Type the following test paragraph, exactly as shown:

> The quick brown fox jumped over the lazy dog. Simpson v. Howard, 576 F.2d 385 (5th Cir. 1984) [cited] {overruled} "THE QUICK BROWN FOX JUMPED OVER THE LAZY DOG?; 'U.S.C.A. §20-3567:' 1+½*4=3 and $3@5%< > 15 & don't forget that #↕/\ | ~ ¶ are also there!

Did you find that the keyboard did not have all of these characters? That is to be expected. A number of years ago, computer professionals decided that there would be 94 standard printable characters, all of which are in the test paragraph. The list did not include ½, ¼, ¶,§,™,°,®,© and ¢. If you have any other "favorites," try them out now.

WARNING: Even if your keyboard *does* have all of these characters it may not be representing these characters internally in accordance with the so-called ASCII standard, and may cause problems when communicating with other computers such as Lexis, Westlaw or Dow-Jones News/Retrieval or with any other printer other than the one that comes with the equipment. Ask the salesperson about this.

Did you like the feel of the keyboard? Is the touch good? Are the keys where you are used to them?

7. Now print this paragraph on the printer. Did you get all of your characters printed? Do you like the type style? How many other printwheels can you get? Can you get a printwheel that substitutes the nonstandard characters, like §, when you type a standard character that you rarely use, like [or ~?

8. Have the salesperson change the ribbon and the printwheel and feed sheets of plain paper and computer paper through the printer. Now try it yourself. How hard is it to do? How much do ribbons cost? How long do they last? Where can you purchase them?

9. Ask the salesperson how and when the word processing program makes a backup copy of what you are typing. Is it done automatically, or do you have to remember to save it?

10. Now edit the test paragraph. Ask the salesperson to show you how to do the following:

a. Interchange the lowercase "quick brown fox" sentence with the all caps "QUICK BROWN FOX" sentence.
b. Replace "[cited] [overruled] with "(cert. denied, 467 U.S. 478)".
c. Reformat the paragraph from a 65 character line to a 25 character line and back. Make sure to notice how the program handles hyphenation.
d. Underline the case name *Simpson v. Howard.*
e. Make the first "quick" boldface type.
f. Make the first "brown" double-strike. Are e. and f. the same?

11. Print the new paragraph. Did the printer faithfully print exactly what you wanted it to? If not, why not?

12. Ask the salesperson to show you how to print with right-justified margins. Print the paragraph again. How does it look? Did the printer do proportional spacing? Some printers justify by inserting extra spaces between words, some by inserting microspaces (1/120th inch) between characters. The former sometimes looks like you are using a cheap typewriter that mistakenly skips spaces when it is not supposed to.

13. Erase the edited paragraph and recover the backup paragraph which you previously stored. Make sure that there is a carriage return at its end. Your paragraph now has approximately 250 characters. Copy it again in the same document so that it now has 500 characters. Repeat four more times, so that you now have 8,000 characters. This is approximately the size of a three page, single-spaced document.

14. Print the document, double-spaced on your own letterhead or billhead. Remember to use the option that allows you to insert a new page of letterhead after each page has finished printing, otherwise you will be printing on the platen.

How easy was the printing? How long did it take? If you were using a 35 character per minute printer, it should have taken almost four minutes to print, plus an additional one to two minutes to feed the paper. Do you need a faster printer? Do you need a cut sheet feeder, a mechanism which automatically feeds single sheets? Do you need two printers, a faster dot matrix printer for drafts and internal documents and a slower letter-quality printer?

15. Place the cursor, the marker that tells you where you are working, at the end of the 8,000 character document. Back it, character by character, through the document. Is the response sluggish? Word

processing programs slow down as you reach the limits of memory of your computer.

16. Copy the document on itself again so that it contains 16,000 characters. Test the cursor backwards again. Keep copying the document on itself and testing the cursor movement until you find the largest document the program will take without rebelling or stalling.

17. Now edit this large document. Move a paragraph from one page to another. Insert your name and address in the middle of one paragraph. Notice if the program seems slow now.

18. Go to the beginning of the document and search for your name. Do it again, only search for your name and replace it with your mother's name.

19. Now do a global search and replace, replacing Simpson with your last name throughout the document. Notice how long it takes. How many keystrokes does it take? Can this procedure be done in the background while you continue to work on the same or another document? If so, try it.

20. Now ask the salesperson to show you some features which you have not tested. Write them down so you can later decide if they are of value to you or your firm.

21. Ask the salesperson how to print envelopes. Type your name and address with your firm name as the return address and print the envelope.

22. Review your notes. Are they good enough for you to remember what has happened? If not, go back over and retest if necessary.

23. Write down the model numbers of the equipment you used during the demo, the version of the software and the prices of all items, including options.

24. Take your information and experience back to your office for the decision-making process. Compare your notes with those from other demos and make your decision.

¶1306 Training on the Word Processor Can Be Easy

Word processing training must occur when a new system is purchased, a new secretary is hired or when temporaries are working for the firm. There are three ways to train new word processing operators:

1. Send them to the vendor's training class;
2. Have an experienced secretary train them;
3. Let them teach themselves.

Each of these methods may be desirable in certain situations.

In the case of the new secretary, it may be worth the money it costs to have the word processing vendor do the training. The investment will probably pay off in the long run. This is probably the quickest way for the new secretary to obtain maximum benefit from the equipment. This method will not keep you or the other secretaries from your work. Your time may be spent keeping the attorneys' work completed. After the new secretary finishes the training class, you and the other secretaries can provide additional support and training.

When a temporary employee is using the equipment, it is not usually necessary to provide complete training. A temporary is generally called in when there is heavy typing that does not require most of the sophisticated functions of the equipment. During these periods either you or the other secretaries can provide training as needed. A temporary is usually not hired for an assignment that requires the use of word processing equipment if not already experienced in the use of word processors, making extensive training unnecessary.

It is occasionally preferable to let a secretary train himself or herself, with the support of the other secretaries. If time is not critical, if the secretary has an aptitude for the equipment, and if good training materials are available, the secretary can train "on the go." As functions are required they can be looked up in the manual and learned. Some word processing vendors have developed both audio and video tapes for self-training which are very good. They are also very expensive but may be worth the investment if they are well done. The disadvantages to letting secretaries train themselves is that they often don't discover the full potential of the system. They learn only the basic functions and don't even know some of the others exist. Time may also be wasted trying to figure out how to do something, when a simple explanation could shortcut it considerably. An experienced secretary should be made available to answer questions and assist whenever needed.

When a new word processing system is installed, everyone must be trained. There are several methods used by vendors to provide training to the entire secretarial staff:

1. Classes in the vendor's facilities;
2. Classes in the firm's facilities (conference room, library, etc.);
3. Video tape presentations in either location;
4. Individual instruction.

Some vendors train the supervisors, or senior secretaries, only, who in turn train the other secretaries. Other vendors train all of the secretaries. The amount and type of training should be negotiated prior to signing the contract for the purchase of the word processing system.

If you are chosen to be trained and then expected to train other operators, you will have been given a great responsibility. If your trainees do poorly after their training, it will probably be because you have failed in your training efforts. If they are good secretaries, there is no reason they won't be good word processing operators unless they are inadequately trained. Training word processing operators can be done effectively and painlessly...both for the trainer and the trainee.

During the training be sure to emphasize what the secretary can do with the machine, not what the machine can do. This will show your concern for the secretary's needs, as a person. The word processor is only a tool, while the secretary is a human being, with worries, feelings and fears.

One of the greatest fears of new word processing operators is that they will somehow damage the machine. They know the equipment is expensive and that the documents they are working on are valuable. They often fear that pushing a wrong key, deleting the wrong document or some other operator error will cost them their jobs. Be sensitive to these fears and concerns. Trainees need assurance that they can't hurt the machine. Most of all don't broadcast your trainee's mistakes around the office. You may need that secretary to help you one day.

When a secretary completes the training by whatever method is selected, the following functions should have been mastered:

1. Set up the system (turn it on, off, etc.).
2. Create a document.
3. Store and file a document.
4. Perform minor editing and revising.
5. Reformat text.
6. Print a document.
7. Recall and retrieve text.

The time between learning these functions and being able to practice them should be as short as possible. If several secretaries are trained at one time, it is preferable for each one to have a terminal to practice on as the training progresses. This is one advantage of holding the training classes in the vendor's facilities, since they usually provide a terminal for each trainee.

During the training process, keep your sense of humor. Learn to laugh at your mistakes and with others when they make mistakes. Eventually, you will all learn and will master the machine, making it your slave. All it takes is a wrong attitude to feel you are a slave to the machine.

Be sure to check on your trainees periodically after the training is completed to make sure they are getting the most out of the word processor. The more sophisticated functions may be taught once the basics have been mastered. Remember, your trainees' skills on the word processor will be a reflection of your efforts to train them. Make them successful.

¶1307 General Guidelines for Backup Procedures

Backup simply means copy. Generally, word processors use either diskettes or tape for backing up. Backup copies should be kept in a safe place, preferably outside of the firm. Some secretaries take the backup diskettes home with them for safekeeping. A better place is to have a safe deposit box at the bank or a fireproof safe or cabinet.

The purpose of the off-site storage is to have backup copies in the event of a fire or other kind of disaster in your office. The disaster could be that you or another secretary deleted the document by mistake. Sometimes, power surges or a malfunction of the word processing equipment causes a document to either disappear, or become damaged. A control log should be maintained of files which are stored at the off-site location. The log should contain, at a minimum, the name of the file and date it was created or last updated.

The procedures for backing up files and rotating them to the off-site location should be documented in writing. Ask your attorneys to tell you how long documents should remain in the system before being archived (copied) to diskettes for off-site storage.

Following are some general rules for backing up your word processing system:

1. When making backup diskettes, always rotate the diskettes being used. This means you will have two or more backup copies at one time. Make your first backup copy, then the next time you back up, use a different diskette. If a power failure occurs during backup, both your original and backup will be destroyed. This is the reason for using a different diskette. When making the next backup copy, use the original diskette, safeguarding your most recent backup.
2. Make a backup of standard documents and forms after they have been finalized. Store these backup copies at an off-site location, one that is temperature and humidity controlled like a safe deposit box.
3. Make periodic backup copies of standard documents and forms and rotate them to the off-site location. Also, if standard docu-

ments are changed, new backup copies should be made and stored off-site. By rotating backup diskettes in this manner, the chances of not being able to read a backup diskette because of degradation of the magnetic encoding due to age will be reduced.

4. As a general rule, it is a good idea to make intermediate backup copies of documents which require significant time to enter and/or edit.

5. Make backup copies of documents as critical dates approach, such as court filings. Copies should be made one or two days in advance of the deadline date, and periodically as you work on them. The closer to the critical date, the more important to have the latest version backed up. Don't forget the rule about rotating diskettes when making several backups of the same document.

6. Periodically review the files which are stored on the hard disk and archive (copy) to diskettes any that are not going to be required in the near future. If you are required to keep a permanent copy of the document, you might want to consider storing the diskette off-site in order to backup the "hard copy" or paper copy that you keep in the file.

7. You don't really need to worry about making backup copies of very short documents, like one or two page letters or memos.

8. Backup copies of the operating system software and word processing software should be kept at the off-site storage location mentioned above.

Some secretaries think of backing up as an inconvenience. However, when you consider the amount of time it takes to retype, proofread and edit a long document, it makes sense. You should develop a positive attitude toward the backing up process. The first time you lose a critical document, for whatever reason, you will be glad you took the time to backup. If you didn't, it will be a lesson learned the hard way. It will happen, so be prepared.

¶1308 Understanding Document Indexing—Method or Madness?

Now that you have your word processing equipment, how do you keep track of all those documents you are creating? Your attorneys will be asking you to find a letter they wrote last month to such and such a client, or the brief from a particular matter from last year. How will you know where it is, or what you called it?

Some word processors have a document summary page that allows you to type in the name of the client or a description of the document. You and the other secretaries should devise a system for naming documents which you will all use. Then if another secretary has to try to find one of your documents, she will know your system. Even if the client's name and a document description have been entered, if no system for naming the document is used, you will have to scan all the documents on the system to find the one you are looking for.

Periodically, you should print out a listing of documents on your word processor. They may print out in chronological order or alphabetical order, depending on your system. On some systems, the list will contain only the name of the document, eight or nine letters or numbers. Other systems will print out the description you entered, the author, and the date created or last revised. When you need to find a document, you can use this list.

Here is an example of a document indexing system you can use. If this one doesn't fit your needs or your system, develop one that works for you. Make sure all the secretaries understand it. If you use these codes or similar ones you should type them up and circulate them to all secretaries.

Here's how it works. Let's assume your system allows you to enter nine digits to name a word processing document. You can break up the nine places into sections. The first three digits can contain the initials of the author of the document, your attorney. The next four digits can contain the client number or, if your firm does not use client numbers, several letters that describe the client. The last two digits can contain a code which describes the type of document, like "LT" for letter. It would look something like this.

Author	Client	Document
PFT	1045	LT

When the document is named, you would type in "PFT1045LT." If several letters are sent to one client you may use just "L" for letter and name them "L1, L2, L3, etc." Here are some other codes you may use:

LT	= letter	BR	= brief	IM	= internal memo
CT	= contract	WL	= will	LS	= lease
BL	= bill	FM	= file memo	RM	= research memo
EP	= estate plan	SP	= speech	OC	= offering circular
AR	= article	MM	= minutes	AI	= articles of incorporation
FP	= financial plan	BL	= by laws	PA	= partnership agreement

You can develop others that fit your attorneys' type of practice. The key is to develop a system and to get in the habit of using it. If you simply name a document anything that comes to mind, what seems logical to you may not be what another secretary thinks of when trying to figure out what you might have named the document she is looking for. A good system will help both you and the other secretaries become more efficient.

Circulate a list of documents on the system to your attorneys from time to time and ask them to decide which documents may be deleted. You should ask them to initial the ones they wish to delete. If you need room on your system, you may also archive (copy) documents that you will not be using in the near future. Also ask your attorneys to indicate which documents may be archived. You should not make the decision to delete any documents. That is not your decision. It should be your attorneys' decision. They may know of a reason they will be needing that document which you do not know. Before deleting any document from the system (other than short letters and memos) make sure you have your attorneys' initials beside it on the document listing.

¶1309 Decentralized vs. Centralized Word Processing

¶1309.1 How to Determine Advantages and Disadvantages of Decentralized Word Processing*

Advantages

1. Decentralization reduces costs that were necessary in a centralized strategy when the cost of hardware relative to the cost of personnel required to operate it was high. Now, since personnel costs are higher than the hardware, the idea is to get more hardware and less personnel for the same money.
2. There is increased physical control over the production of the document. Since the secretary is most familiar with the document, she can control its production more efficiently.
3. Attorneys receive more personalized and individualized secretarial support. They can get their documents typed and prepared in their own particular style rather than having to adhere to a style standardized by the word processing department.

*Reprinted with permission of L. D. Holland and Paula F. Turner, Holland Shipes Bennett Thrasher, P.C., CPAs, Atlanta, GA.

4. If a printer is accessible to the secretary, there is increased printer access as opposed to a centralized word processing center located away from the secretaries' offices, where the printers are controlled by others. Also, if a secretary handles the printer, it is easier to make frequent changes in the paper rather than to go to a distant centralized area set aside for the printer and its functions.

5. Secretaries do not have to leave their desks to inquire about or retrieve printed documents.

6. Decentralization gives the firm the ability to start out small and upgrade as needed. Therefore, start-up costs can be lower.

7. In a decentralized system, there is less paperwork necessary to get the typing done, i.e., word processing department logs and forms, and additional edits due to communication problems.

8. Decentralization returns accountability to the attorney.

9. Decentralization reduces dependence on satellite centers and support personnel.

10. Decentralization increases the value of client services.

11. Decentralization focuses the work on the secretary.

12. Decentralization increases attorney and secretary productivity. Since the secretary and attorney can see the end product quicker, they will be psychologically motivated to produce more with this immediate feedback. Increasing secretarial productivity makes it possible for the attorney to be more effective and handle more work. Increasing attorney productivity has the effect of providing greater service value to the clients.

13. Decentralization reduces support staff in relation to the number of attorneys. Giving secretaries easy-to-use, automated tools eliminates the need for hard-to-find, highly skilled personnel. In other words, because the automated tasks are easier, it is not necessary to seek as highly qualified and paid legal secretaries. Highly skilled secretaries are in short supply. Most firms' economic goals cannot be maintained if the systems installed require everyone who uses them to be superstars.

14. Decentralization gives the attorneys autonomy over their work, returns decision-making about schedules and priorities to the attorney.

15. Decentralization leaves fewer people for the attorney to deal with. The paperwork, red tape and persons with whom the attorney has to interact to get his work done are significantly lessened.

16. Decentralization lets secretaries do time and billing work at their desks, which decreases the accounting support staff now doing this work. Furthermore, secretaries can more easily make time entries since they are most familiar with the attorney and his work. Personnel in

client-record departments that process client, matter and representation information can be cut back because the secretary has on-line data input and inquiry capabilities to implement information maintained in the firm's master files.

17. Reducing the number of support staff in relation to the number of timekeepers lowers the cost of legal services. For most firms, this objective should be implemented in conjunction with systems that maintain or enhance the quality of firm's services.

Disadvantages

1. It is more difficult for secretaries to share documents if they are using standalone systems. However, if they are using a shared logic system or networking configuration, they can share documents.

2. Decentralized word processing encourages unique procedures at each workstation. In other words, each attorney may do his or her work a different way thereby causing nonuniform procedures and paperwork.

3. Decentralization sometimes requires a printer at each workstation. If there is not a printer at each workstation, secretaries may bunch up to share a printer, causing delays in getting the end product processed.

4. Decentralization does not promote work sharing. Because the secretaries are segregated at their individual workstations, they do not seem to be as motivated to help each other out as they would in a centralized word processing environment.

5. Decentralization may require secretaries to handle diskettes or be familiar with computer terminology they are not currently familiar with.

6. Decentralization creates a lack of direct word processing supervision. In a centralized word processing center the operators can usually get immediate assistance from a word processing supervisor or from each other about problems they may be having handling the hardware and/or software.

¶1309.2 Advantages of Centralized Word Processing

1. In a centralized word processing center that is shared logic or shared resource (networked), there is usually the ability to access all data from any workstation. (Although this may be done in a decentralized system as well if standalones are not used.)

2. Centralized word processing sometimes provides more sophisticated capabilities. In other words, more complex hardware such as minicomputers may be used.

3. Centralized word processing usually enables more efficient processing of large documents due to increased work capacity.

4. Most word processing centers have supervisors. It is easier to train new operators and they can usually get immediate assistance.

5. With centralized word processing, data processing can be added easily.

6. In most instances, centralized word processing optimizes the use of word processing equipment. In other words, there is less downtime because work is shared among the operators.

¶1309.3 Disadvantages of Centralized Word Processing

1. Centralized word processing causes resistance to change by staff. Attorneys are used to having private secretaries and they resist having to redirect their work to another area where they will lose control over their work product.

2. Attorneys suffer the lack of status that comes with having a private secretary.

3. When the centralized system is down, everyone is down.

4. With a centralized word processing system, personal relationships and rapport are lessened between the secretaries and attorneys. This is psychologically demotivating to both.

5. Fewer printers with more distant location requires secretaries to be away from their desks.

6. In a centralized word processing center, the operators are alienated from the rest of the firm and are generally not as psychologically motivated and thus unhappy. They do not get the personal interaction with the attorneys they are working for.

7. With a centralized word processing center, there is increased paperwork to get typing done, i.e., word processing logs and forms.

8. Entry level costs of a centralized system are higher. Centralized word processing centers demand expensive hardware and software necessary for a shared logic, shared resource or distributed system.

9. More office space is required to house a word processing staff in a centralized word processing center.

10. With centralized word processing, the attorney is placed in the role of an information distributor who is highly dependent upon support personnel.

11. Centralized word processing causes secretarial downtime because they must wait for work to be done in the center. Also, how long

attorneys are willing to wait ultimately determines the staffing of the centers. Establishing staffing levels to satisfy peakload periods causes downtime and an expensive and high support-staff-to-attorney ratio.

12. Transferring documents between the attorney, secretary and word processing center can be cumbersome and involves considerable "double-handling," such as optical scanning and revision work in cases where the secretaries do the original typing and revisions are later performed in the satellite center.

¶1400 Designing, Implementing, and Maintaining an Effective Filing System

¶1401 Becoming Familiar with the Different Kinds of Files in Law Offices

Let's talk about what types of paper or documents attorneys usually have in their offices. Attorneys have a variety of documents in their files, some of which are ruled and produced according to certain laws and court procedures. Others are maintained to help them run their business and in some cases, their lives. Some of the documents attorneys have include:

1. Personal records;
2. General business correspondence;
3. Client records;
4. Collections files;
5. Miscellaneous brochures, periodicals, bulletins, advertisements, investments materials, etc.;
6. Civic activities;
7. Seminar and speech materials;
8. General research files;
9. Legal and general information;
10. Specially designed form files;
11. Blank form files—court forms, etc.

1. Personal records are the type of records that attorneys collect in their offices; they vary according to the degree that they want their secretary to handle their personal business. Some attorneys prefer not to have their personal business brought into the office. Others want their secretaries to help them keep their lives straight. Many secretaries do such things for attorneys as:

- Handling their personal and business checking accounts.
- Paying personal bills and handling personal bookkeeping, investments and financial recordkeeping.
- Assisting them in personal errands, such as buying gifts for their friends, business associates, and in some cases, their families.

- Running personal errands, such as picking up their cleaning, going to the post office or parcel service company, purchasing personal items, making personal travel arrangements, etc.
- Handling bar association and other professional activities.

2. *General business correspondence* refers to various correspondence relating to the running of their practice that attorneys collect. Some of the items that may be included in this type of correspondence are:

- Financial and bookkeeping records (see ¶900);
- Personnel records;
- Tax records and information;
- Business and professional license information;
- Legal documents affecting the business such as partnership agreements, etc.;
- Warranties and equipment purchase and repair information;
- Other miscellaneous records and papers.

3. *Client records* are files that include all matters relating to the clients, except for commercial collections when kept separate. There are litigation files as well as general business files. However, the active files are usually separated from the closed or inactive files. These documents may be systematized according to an alphabetical or numerical filing system (see ¶1402).

4. *Collections files* are sometimes handled and organized separately from the main client files. For example, if your client is First Olympic Bank, and the bank has a number of outstanding loans that they want to collect, you would set up a separate series of files according to the various loan names and/or numbers. This would require a separate system within the client system so to access these files more easily, it is helpful to separate them. These separate files may also be indexed either alphabetically or numerically.

5. *Miscellaneous files* are, generally speaking, anything that doesn't fit in the other files; it can be filed here according to subject. For example, if your attorneys practice real estate law, you might collect real estate seminar brochures, various brochures relating to investments, articles on certain subjects related to real estate law, bulletins, newsletters, advertisements on office supplies and products, etc. You may set up these various items in a subfile by subject. Then you can file them together and label the file drawer "Miscellaneous." These files can be more flexible than some of your other files.

6. *Civic activities* files relate to your attorneys' charitable and civic activities, such as the Chamber of Commerce, a particular church, various charities, etc. You might want to keep these files separate by subject or title of the charity. You can work with the attorneys to find out

how they want them labeled. The easiest way for you and them to remember what is where will do the trick.

7. *Seminar and speech materials* can sometimes be placed in the miscellaneous file, depending on how much material you have. It is best to separate them if your attorneys are quite active in continuing education and seminars or give frequent speeches and/or seminars. Be sure to keep these files organized and control the amount of paper that goes into them. A lot of these documents can be thrown away once the speech is given. For example, any notes or rough drafts of outlines can be discarded once the outline is prepared in final.

8. *General research files* contain the research that all attorneys do to varying degrees. Litigation attorneys tend to do much more research than other practitioners. Of course, in large firms, law clerks or paralegals may do the research for your attorneys. Still, you will need to keep track of it. It is a good idea to have a duplicate of research memos relating to your attorney's practice even if the law clerk or associate actually did the research. These can best be indexed by subject. Also, you might want to prepare a card index of these memoranda. Some firms have a main research file and a card index by subject. Many more firms are now setting up these files on the computer with data base management software. You can set up a system on your word processor by just using the subject name and preparing a typewritten index. To locate the document, you could do a global search by subject.

9. *Legal and general information* files contain new laws, regulations, court rules, etc., if there is no other specific file set up for them. For example, you might keep the court rules by county or all federal trade information by subject. You might keep local city ordinances (laws) in this file in addition to appellate procedures. This can be a whole set of individual subfiles or just one general file. If it is one general file, you should make subfiles once it gets too big or complicated.

10. *Specially designed form files* may contain sample forms or legal documents such as complaints, wills, interrogatories (questions), court pleadings, real estate documents, etc. These files should not contain blank printed forms, but rather forms that can be used in the future to draft similar forms.

11. *Blank form files* should contain any blank forms or preprinted documents, such as a deed or an income tax return form. These can be organized in a very simple way. See ¶1411 for an excellent reference system.

Be sure that all these files are organized in a systematic way. From time to time take a look at how they are changing with additional files being added. At some point you might want to set these up with a numeric system (see ¶1402). Just keep them under control and weed out old documents.

¶1402 What Kind of Filing System is Best for Your Firm: Alpha or Numeric?

Filing is probably one of the most important functions of a legal secretary. Even so, it is probably the least preferred and most often put off task, until it becomes the most dreaded task as it begins to stack up on the secretary's desk. Most secretaries find that when they file a document at the time that they are finished with it, it is easier to do. It is a good solution to this often detested chore.

There are basically three types of legal filing systems: numeric, alphabetic and alpha-numeric. Obviously, whatever filing system your attorneys have, you most likely will have to live with it. If you are able to change or modify the system, you may be able to get a better system that will work well for your attorneys' practice.

¶1402.1 Numeric

A numeric system is usually used in large firms because of the large number of clients and the complexity of the files. Numeric filing is more accurate for several reasons:

1. The sorting systems are more easily developed on a computerized filing system.
2. There is less chance of misfiling.
3. With an alphabetic system, room must be left for additional inserts in each letter of the alphabet. With numeric files, new files are added to the last drawer and a minimum of space is left in the file cabinet.
4. There is more flexibility for expansion.

The numerical system has many variations. Basically, the files are arranged according to the file number with the last file opened being the most recent number. For example:

2345.678900-1

could be Gerald H. Fritz client number and the "1" could be the matter number and may stand for the first matter handled for that client, or in some systems that could be the type of matter such as personal injury or probate. There could be codes for the different areas of law. For example:

2345.678900-1 could be a general corporate file,
2345.678900-2 could be a will file,
2345.678900-3 could be a probate file.

¶1402.2 Alphabetic

The alphabetic system of filing is easy to understand since you merely look up the name of the client. It does not require that you look up the file number in a file index card or in a Rolodex system. A lot of small offices have the A–Z system. The variation to this type of system is where the file is filed under the plaintiff's name in a litigation matter. Today, this is a method which is seldom used.

¶1402.3 Alpha-numeric

The alpha-numeric system is a combination of the two systems. In many systems the alphabetical system stands for the type of matter. For example:

2345.67890-A could be a personal injury action,
2345.67890-B could be a will written for the client,
2345.67890-C could be the formation of a corporation.

Regardless of your current filing system, make an effort to learn to use it while always looking for ways to improve upon it.

¶1403 A Simple Way To Design a Foolproof Numeric System

This section will help you design a file system. If your firm already has one, you will pick up hints on how to use that system more effectively. If your firm is dissatisfied with its present system and finds it inadequate, this section will give ideas for redesigning the system.

There are many variations of numeric systems. They vary from office to office. However, the following basic system will suit most filing needs and can be the core of your system. It is very simple. The numeric system consists of four digits for the client number, two digits for the area of law designation and three digits for the different matters the client may have. For example, the entire number may be as follows:

0001.01001

The first four digits would be the client number, which in this case would be 1. The next two digits following the client number and the period would be the type of law, i.e., litigation, corporate, bankruptcy, etc. The last three digits would be the matter number, i.e., personal injury accident, a particular corporate matter such as a tax question, a particular breach of contract action, etc.

Thus, you can have up to 9999 clients; up to 99 different areas of law; and 999 different matters that your attorneys would be handling. Practically speaking, your firm should need no more than those numbers of clients, areas of law, or matters.

Now, you can go even further and use a year code and/or an attorney code number or alphabetic designation. For example:

0001.01001-85.DFM

This would be in year 1985 and the attorney's initials; in this case, the attorney is Donald F. Mills.

With this system you can vary the arrangement of the numbers. You can put 85 before the file number, like:

85-0001.010001-DFM

or

DFM-85-0001 01001

This is essentially a generic system that you can adapt to suit your firm's needs. Take this number:

4329.12001-DFM-85

That would be client number 4329, area of law 12001, and the particular matter involved in this file is the first matter your attorney (DFM) handled for this client. And, of course, the year the file was opened was 1985.

¶1404 How to Open New Files Easily

The procedures vary from firm to firm as far as the methods of opening files are concerned. Basically, it is a very simple process.

¶1404.1 Simple Steps for Opening a New File:

1. Obtain all the client information from the responsible attorney.
2. Prepare the New Matter Report (see Figures 1404.1-1 and 1404.1-2).
3. Obtain a file number and enter that number in the file index log.

NEW MATTER REPORT

In any law office, a new matter normally requires that certain things be done:

1. The client must be interviewed and the necessary information obtained regarding the case.
2. A file must be opened.
3. Time and accounting records must be set up.

These three things can be handled efficiently by using forms that are simple to complete and easy to understand. The responsibility for preparing the form and distributing the information may vary with the size of the firm; however, the standardization of the procedures used to obtain and distribute client matter information virtually eliminates any problem of assigning the clerical duties inherent in the process.

Experience has shown that the use of a New Matter Report is the easiest and most direct way of obtaining all the administrative information necessary to enter a new matter into the firm's filing and accounting system. An example of the New Matter Report is shown on the following page.

The New Matter Report is normally completed by the attorney during his initial interview with the client. It is prepared in *longhand*. There is no need to type the New Matter Report since its purpose is to serve as a checklist for the attorney and not as a formal filing or accounting record. (Some firms prefer the receptionist or lawyer's secretary to complete parts of the New Matter Report prior to the lawyer's interview with the client.) Usually, the New Matter Report is prepared with one carbon copy. The original is placed in the client's file, should it be needed for future reference, and the duplicate copy is routed to the firm's lawyers in order to keep them up to date on the new business coming into the firm. Some firms prepare a weekly listing from the New Matter Reports for circulation to the lawyers.

NOTE: The New Matter Report should not be viewed as a substitute for specialized checklists used in the legal handling of a matter. It is designed to provide a checklist for data required in the internal administrative operations of the firm only.

Each lawyer should maintain a supply of New Matter Reports in his desk for use when interviewing a new or prospective client or a present client with a new matter.

Instructions for Preparing the New Matter Report

The following instructions will aid the lawyer in completing the New Matter Report:

[A] Client Information

1. Enter client name and address.
2. Indicate whether it is a new client or a present client. (If it is a present client, the address and phone numbers required are normally already on file and can be entered by the secretary.)
3. The lawyer's secretary should obtain a client file number from the file clerk or secretary responsible for assigning numbers.
4. Enter the business phone number of the client.
5. If the client is a company, enter the name of the responsible individual at the client's office.
6. Enter the home phone number of the client if an individual.

[B] Matter Information

7. Enter the file name exactly as it should appear in the firm's records.
8. Make any notes desirable on the nature of the matter.
9. Enter amount of estimated damages or other money information involved in the case.
10. Enter area of practice code.
11. Enter the name of the opposing party or parties.
12. Enter the name of the opposing attorney.

[C] Fee Arrangements

The data called for in this block will vary depending on the fee arrangement with the client. The lawyer merely checks the line best describing the fee arrangement and enters the necessary details. All other lines may be left blank. Enter the following information on each line checked:

13. Enter the dollar amount of the fixed fee or the estimated range quoted to the client.
14. Enter the hourly rate quoted to the client or indicate that the normal hourly rate will be charged.
15. Enter the details of the contingency arrangement or refer to the fee contract signed by the client.
16. Enter the estimated fee the firm may expect from the case. This information will be helpful in analyzing the results of billing at the completion of the matter.

[D] Billing Procedure

This section provides instructions for and information needed by the bookkeeper. Only those lines that are applicable should be checked, and the following information should be entered:

17. Enter the amount of the retainer, whether it is monthly, quarterly, semi-annual, or annual; and the effective date of the retainer arrangements.
18. Enter the amount of the advance received from the client prior to undertaking the case. (Many law firms find it advantageous to require the client to advance funds to cover, at a minimum, out-of-pocket expenses.)
19. Enter instructions for the bookkeeper to bill, or remind the lawyer to bill, the fee on client disbursements as indicated.

[E] Files

This section contains instructions to the file clerk on file requirements:

20. Check whether a new file is required, or whether any documents are to be included in an existing file, or whether no file is required.
21. The secretary should check the master alphabetic index (See NEW MATTER INDEX SET) for a possible conflict of interest as soon as possible after receiving the New Matter Report, and indicate with initials and date that this check has been made.
22. If a new file is required, file cards should be prepared for proper control and cross-references. The Secretary preparing the file cards should enter her name and the date she prepared the cards.

[F] Firm Administration

This section contains information to establish responsibility for bringing in new business and for its completion. Enter the following:

23. The name or initials of the lawyer completing the New Matter Report.
24. The name of the person outside the firm who referred the client to the firm.
25. The name or initials of the lawyer responsible for *billing* the work.
26. The name or initials of the lawyer responsible for bringing in the new business.
27. The names or initials of the lawyers assigned to the case.
28. Any instructions as to each lawyer's share of the fee or other arrangements.

[G] Remarks

29. Enter any additional information or data.

Figure 1404.1-1. How to Prepare a New Matter Report. Reprinted with permission from *Law Firm Administrative and Accounting Manual*, Safeguard Business Systems, Inc., Fort Washington, PA, 1974.

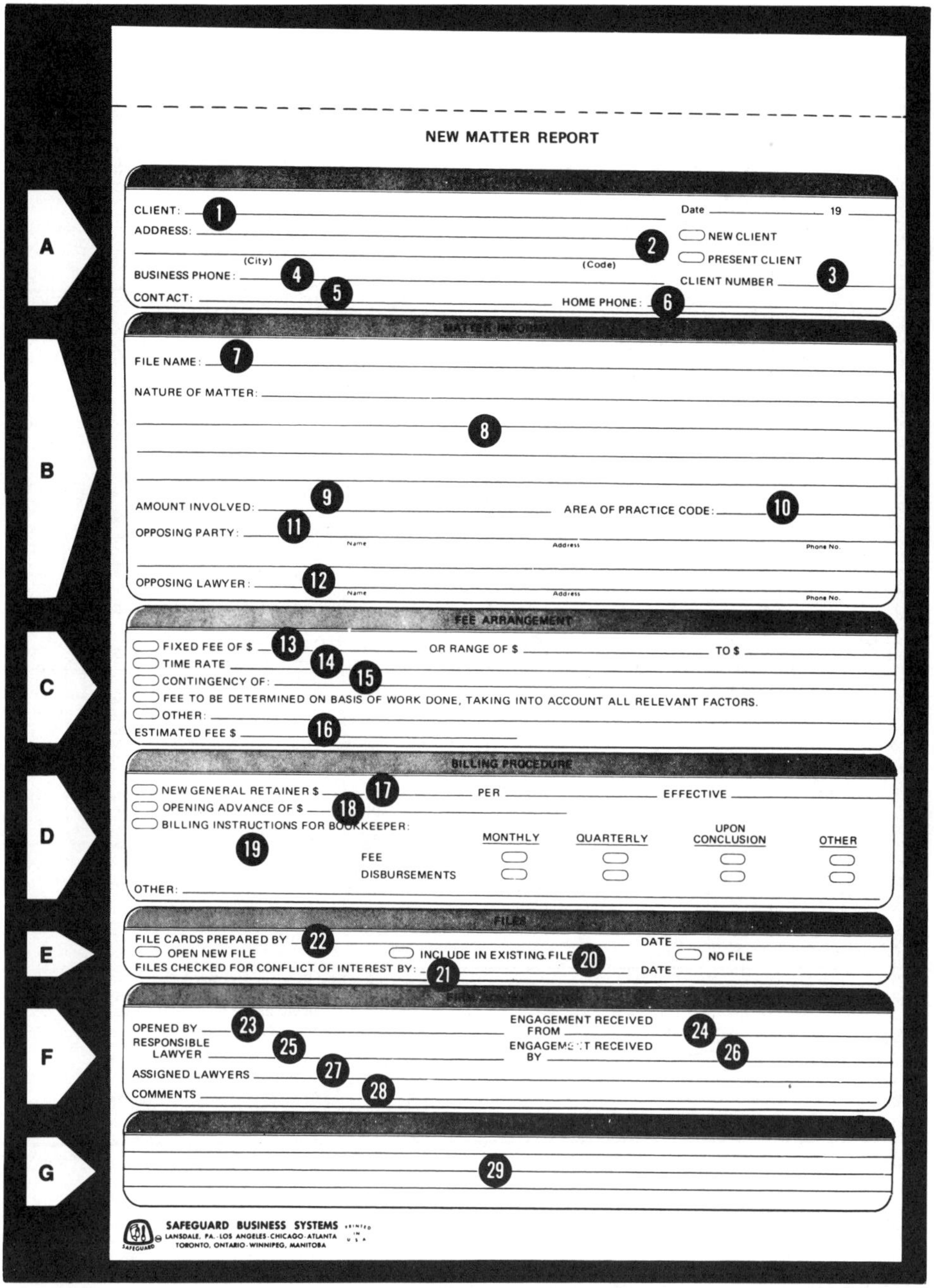

NEW MATTER REPORT

A

CLIENT: ________ Date ________ 19 ____

ADDRESS: ________

(City) (Code)

☐ NEW CLIENT

☐ PRESENT CLIENT

CLIENT NUMBER ________

BUSINESS PHONE: ________

CONTACT: ________ HOME PHONE: ________

B

FILE NAME: ________

NATURE OF MATTER: ________

AMOUNT INVOLVED: ________ AREA OF PRACTICE CODE: ________

OPPOSING PARTY: ________ Name Address Phone No.

OPPOSING LAWYER: ________ Name Address Phone No.

C

FEE ARRANGEMENT

☐ FIXED FEE OF $ ________ OR RANGE OF $ ________ TO $ ________

☐ TIME RATE ________

☐ CONTINGENCY OF: ________

☐ FEE TO BE DETERMINED ON BASIS OF WORK DONE, TAKING INTO ACCOUNT ALL RELEVANT FACTORS.

☐ OTHER: ________

ESTIMATED FEE $ ________

D

BILLING PROCEDURE

☐ NEW GENERAL RETAINER $ ________ PER ________ EFFECTIVE ________

☐ OPENING ADVANCE OF $ ________

☐ BILLING INSTRUCTIONS FOR BOOKKEEPER:

	MONTHLY	QUARTERLY	UPON CONCLUSION	OTHER
FEE	☐	☐	☐	☐
DISBURSEMENTS	☐	☐	☐	☐

OTHER: ________

E

FILES

FILE CARDS PREPARED BY ________ DATE ________

☐ OPEN NEW FILE ☐ INCLUDE IN EXISTING FILE ☐ NO FILE

FILES CHECKED FOR CONFLICT OF INTEREST BY: ________ DATE ________

F

OPENED BY ________ ENGAGEMENT RECEIVED FROM ________

RESPONSIBLE LAWYER ________ ENGAGEMENT RECEIVED BY ________

ASSIGNED LAWYERS ________

COMMENTS ________

G

SAFEGUARD BUSINESS SYSTEMS

LANSDALE, PA. · LOS ANGELES · CHICAGO · ATLANTA

TORONTO, ONTARIO · WINNIPEG, MANITOBA

Figure 1404.1-2. How to Prepare a New Matter Index Set. Reprinted with permission from *Law Firm Administrative and Accounting Manual*, Safeguard Business Systems, Inc., Fort Washington, PA, 1974.

4. Prepare the New Matter Index Set (see Figure 1404.1-3).
5. Set up the client ledger.
6. Prepare tabs for the file.
7. Prepare a file gusset (also called expandable file, redwald, or bucket).
8. Prepare subfiles, if any.

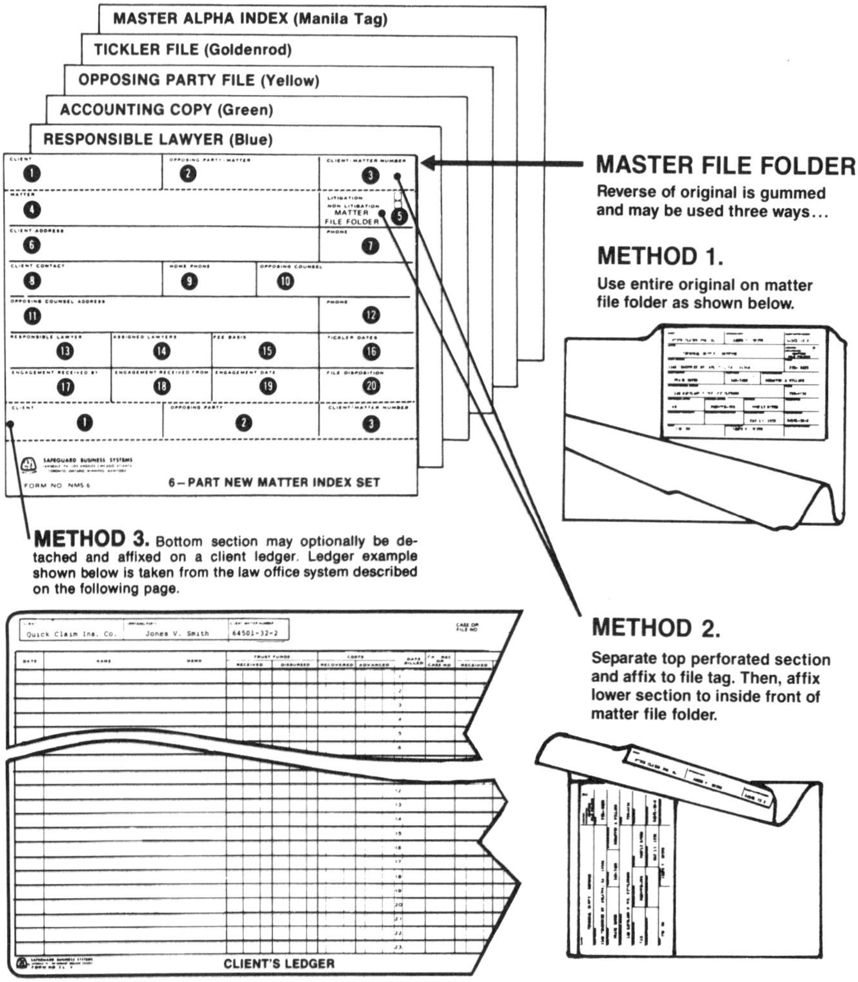

Figure 1404.1-3. New Matter Index Set. Forms courtesy of Safeguard Business Systems, Inc., Fort Washington, PA.

9. Enter the client number, telephone number and relevant information for the Rolodex.
10. Add file number to New Matter Report.

The New Matter Report is a memorandum that is circulated throughout the firm to inform the staff of the new client and new client number for their records.

¶1405 Subfiles Must Be Set Up Correctly

Most client files will need certain subfiles other than the main file. For example, in a litigation matter, you may have the following subfiles:

1. Correspondence file;
2. Pleading file;
3. Interoffice memorandum;
4. Research and legal memos files;
5. Medical reports;
6. Medical expenses, lost earnings and miscellaneous expenses;
7. Interviews and witnesses' statements;
8. Evidence;
9. Attorneys' notes;
10. Deposition and official court transcripts; and so on.

Ask your attorneys what subfiles they want; as you progress, you should be able to get a good idea of what subfiles are needed yourself.

¶1406 Time Saving Methods of Organizing the Contents of Individual Subfiles

There are various types of files in different areas of law. While it is difficult to cover every type of file here, the following covers most of the more common files you will have.

Correspondence Files Fasten the New File Memorandum on the left inside of the file. It should be in an accessible place in the file since the information contained will be used frequently. Insert the correspondence on the right inside of the file in chronological order with the most recent correspondence on top. If you prefer, separate interoffice and outgoing correspondence from incoming correspondence, putting one set of correspondence on each side.

Interoffice Memoranda This file should contain interoffice memoranda in chronological order. Some law offices do not use this type of file since they file the interoffice memos in with the correspondence.

Research and Legal Memos All legal memos and research briefs should be accumulated in this file by date, together with copies of any related cases. The legal memos should indicate the author and issues discussed. An index should be kept of the contents. The index should organize the memos by subject and should show the client file number to locate it if separate copies of memos are not kept in a memo file. This will allow the attorney to locate the memo when the subject comes up in another case.

The following lists files pertinent to litigation, worker's compensation, personal injury, or medical malpractice matters.

Pleadings File Arrange the pleadings in chronological order with the most recent pleading on the top. Separate the pleadings with numbered or lettered dividers. Prepare a transcript index with the style of the file and number. Then list the complete title of the pleading and its filing date. If the case is transferred or appealed to another court, it is best to begin a new separate file for the pleadings in the other court. Be sure to cross-reference the old and the new file. Always insert a court conformed (file-stamped) copy of the pleading in this (see Pleadings Index, Figure 1406-1). Interrogatories, requests to produce, etc., may be filed in the pleading file but copies of the answers and responses may be more appropriately filed in one of the files described in the following.

Medical Reports Arrange the medical reports in chronological order. Prepare a chart of all the reports in the file showing the name, physician or hospital that prepared the report, the date of the report, to whom copies were provided, and the date thereof. Fasten this index on the left-hand side of the folder and the reports on the right.

Medical Expenses, Lost Earnings, and Miscellaneous Expenses This file should contain receipts and invoices for medical and other miscellaneous expenses. Since most receipts and invoices are often different sizes, they may be difficult to organize. Therefore, you may want to staple the smaller items on letter- or legal-size paper before you insert them in the file. It is best not to tape these items down, since they may be used as evidence later. Arrange the documents in chronological order, fasten them on the right-hand side of the file. Prepare a chart of all the information contained in the file. Use the following Medical Expenses Record (Figure 1406-2), Lost Earnings Records (Figure 1406-3) and Miscellaneous Expenses Record (Figure 1406-4) to have the attorney or paralegal record this information. These charts will assist

Pleadings Index

In the ____State____ Court of ____Shelby____ County
State of ____Tennessee____

Joanne Bolthen)
)
)
Plaintiff(s),)
)
) **Civil Action**
)
v.)
)
) **File No. C-12889**
)
Michael Heath and Company)
)
)
)
Defendant(s).)
)

Date Complaint Filed: 1/11/85 Date Answer Filed: 2/10/85

---

1. **Complaint**
   Filed: January 11, 1985; Served: January 13, 1985
2. **Answer**
   Filed: February 10, 1985
3. **Plaintiff's First Interrogatories to Defendant**
   Filed: March 3, 1985
4. **Extension of Time (for Def. To Answer Plaintiff's Interrogatories)**
   Filed: April 3, 1985
5. **Defendant's Answers to Plaintiff's First Interrogatories to Defendant**
   Filed: April 30, 1985
6. **Defendant's First Interrogatories to Plaintiff**
   Filed: April 30, 1985
7. **Plaintiff's Answers to Defendant's First Interrogatories to Plaintiff and Plaintiff's Motion To Produce to Defendant**
   Filed: May 29, 1985

Figure 1406-1. Pleadings Index.

Medical Expense Report

Client Name & Matter: ____________ **File No.:** ____________ **Responsible Attorney(s):** ____________ **Date:** ____________
Name of Patient: ________________ **Patient's Address:** ______________________________________

Date of Treatment/ Expense	Name & Address of Doctor, Hospital, Etc.	Code*	Description of Treatment/Expense	Treatment Over/ Continuing	Total Cost	Date Paid	Type of Record**	OK

*Codes to be used in this column: D = Doctor; H = Hospital; P = Pharmacy; M = Medical Supplier; O = Other.
**E.g., receipts, paid bills, cancelled checks, etc.

Paralegal: ____________

Figure 1406-2. Medical Expenses Report.

Lost Earnings Record

Client Name & Matter: ____________________ **File No.:** __________

Responsible Attorney(s): ____________________ **Date:** __________

Date of Accident: ______________ **Time of Accident:** ____ ____ .m

Location of Accident: ____

____

Name of Injured Party: ________________________________ P/D*

Home Address of Injured Party:

________________________________ **Phone No:** __________

Employer(name & address): ________________________________

________________________________ **Phone No.:** __________

Job Title: ____________________ **Date of Employment:** ________

Supervisor (name & title): ________________________________

Salary:		**Yearly Income:**		
$ ________	per hour.	19________	$ ________	Verified ____
$ ________	per day.	19 ________	$ ________	Verified ____
$ ________	per week.	19________	$ ________	Verified ____
$ ________	per month.	19________	$ ________	Verified ____
$ ________	per year.	19________	$ ________	Verified ____

Claimed Lost Time: ____________

Dates	Length of Time Lost	Earnings Lost
From ________ To ________	Hr. ___ Da. ___ Wk. ___ Mo. ___	$ ____________
From ________ To ________	Hr. ___ Da. ___ Wk. ___ Mo. ___	$ ____________
From ________ To ________	Hr. ___ Da. ___ Wk. ___ Mo. ___	$ ____________
From ________ To ________	Hr. ___ Da. ___ Wk. ___ Mo. ___	$ ____________
From ________ To ________	Hr. ___ Da. ___ Wk. ___ Mo. ___	$ ____________
TOTALS	Hr. ___ Da. ___ Wk. ___ Mo. ___	$ ____________

* P = Plaintiff, D = Defendant (circle one).

Figure 1406-3. Lost Earnings Record.

Miscellaneous Expenses

Client Name & Matter: ______ **File No.:** ______ **Responsible Attorney(s):** ______ **Date:** ______

Expenses For (give name and address): ______

Date of Expense	Description of Expense	Expense Payable to (give name & address)	Notes	Amount	Date Paid	Type of Record*	OK

* E.g., receipts, paid bills, cancelled checks, etc.

Paralegal: ______

Figure 1406-4. Miscellaneous Expenses Record.

the attorney in assessing the total amount of damages to allege in the plaintiff's complaint or, in the case of the defendant, to assess the amount of damages the defendant may counterclaim, if any.

Interviews and Witnesses' Statements This file should contain transcripts of all interviews and statements taken relating to the case including those to be used at trial.

Evidence Insert all documents, photographs, charts, and other written evidence which may be used at trial. You may need a large file-bucket or box for these. Also insert a memo in the file as to the location of physical exhibits that may be needed at the trial.

Depositions and Official Court Transcripts This file-bucket should contain transcripts of all depositions taken in the case. An index of each deposition taken may be prepared, indicating the name of the deponent, date and place of deposition, number of volumes in each deposition and, if known, the relation of the deponent to the case, i.e., witness, relative or employer of the plaintiff or defendant, indicating which (see Deposition Index, Figure 1406-5). This file should also contain digests of depositions, indicating who prepared the digest and date thereof. Remove the fasteners in the deposition and insert the digest and index in front of the deposition under the plastic cover, noting the deponent's name, volume, i.e., Vol. I of III, and date of deposition on the first page. This makes the digest more accessible and prevents the attorney or paralegal having to shuffle through the depositions to determine the name of the deponent and the date of the deposition (see Deposition Digest, Figure 1406-6).

Legal Documents All legal documents not being used as evidence should be placed in this file, including contracts, agreements, notes, leases, bills of sale, wills, etc. Do not include any valuable documents that should be in the safe, like stock certificates, original copies of wills, bonds, etc.

Client's Papers and Materials Papers belonging to the client other than those kept in the safe should be kept in this file, but they should not be punched or fastened since they ultimately will be returned to the client. An inventory noting the type of document, date, and other identifiable information of the client's materials should be prepared and inserted in the file. Also, it would be a good idea to keep a separate copy of the index in case the other one is lost or misplaced.

Extra Copies and Drafts It is useful and in many instances necessary to retain prior drafts and extra copies of documents, plead-

Deposition Index

Client Name & Matter: R.H. Shaw v. M.L. Brown **File No.:** 455L-185

Responsible Attorney(s): K. Owenby/S. Arnold **Date:** 10/20/85

Name of Deponent	Date of Deposition	Place of Deposition	No. of Volumes	Relation to Client
Russell H. Shaw	12-5 & 6-85	110 E. Third St., N.E., Atlanta, Ga. 30309	II	Client
Cathy Shaw	12-10-85	110 E. Fifth St., N.E., Atlanta, Ga. 30309	I	Client's daughter; occupant of car and witness to accident
John White	12-11-85	110 E. Fifth St., N.E., Atlanta, Ga. 30309	I	Witness to accident
Mary Lou Brown	12-12-85	77 Peachtree St., N.E., Atlanta, Ga. 30303	I	Defendant; driver of car which struck Mr. Lewis' car
Jean Jones	12-12-85	77 Peachtree St., N.E., Atlanta, Ga. 30303	I	Occupant in Defendant's car and witness to accident
Deborah Smith, M.D., Ph.D.	12-17-85	100 Doctors Bldg., Atlanta, Ga. 30303	II	Client's doctor
Murray Louis	12-18-85	137-A Twenty-Third St., N.E., Atlanta, Ga. 30305	I	Witness to accident
Martha Ann Wagner, M.D.	12-18-85	2334 Thomas Dr., East Point, Ga. 30344	I	Defendant's doctor

Figure 1406-5. Deposition Index.

Deposition Digest

Client Name & Matter R.H. Shaw v. M.L. Brown **File No.:** 455L-185

Responsible Attorney(s): K. Owenby/S. Arnold **Date:** 12/20/85

Deposition of: Russell H. Shaw

Date(s) Taken: October 5 & 6, 1985

DESCRIPTION	**Pages**
1. General Background Information	1
2. Medical History	1-2
3. Mr. Lewis' Version of Accident	2-4
4. Description of Scene of Accident	4
5. Mr. Shaw's Injuries and Medical Treatment	4-6
6. Mr. Shaw's Present Condition	7
7. Mr. Shaw's Medical Expenses	8
8. Mr. Shaw's Present Emotional Condition	8-9
9. Ms. Cathy Shaw's Injuries and Medical Injuries	9-10
10. Ms. Shaw's Present Condition	11
11. Ms. Shaw's Medical Expenses	12
12. Ms. Shaw's Present Emotional Condition	12-13
13. Traffic Court Hearing	13-16
14. Property Damage	17-18

Figure 1406-6. Deposition Digest.

ings and briefs. These may be kept loosely in a separate file, indicating the dates of the drafts in pencil on the upper right-hand corner of the first page. That way you won't have to sort through the document to find the date and because it is in pencil, it can easily be erased if it needs to be copied.

Miscellaneous This file should contain any documents or information that does not fall under the description of the contents of the other files. This file may contain such things as photographs, diagrams of the location of the accident, tax returns, maps, newspaper clippings, and financial statements. Since most of these items are originals, they should not be punched or fastened down, but may be kept in an envelope, the top of which may be punched and fastened down in the file. Be sure not to punch it when the documents are in it, but rather before the documents are inserted.

Of course, there are numerous other files that your attorneys may want depending upon the nature of the matter.

¶1407 Follow These Basic Rules and You'll Have a Successful Filing System

Rule 1. Keep Files in a Centralized File Room. Attorneys collect paper, and as their practice grows they soon can no longer remember all the information about their clients that is in the files. The nature of practicing law is to make, use and interpret documents. Attorneys tend to collect files in their office. Therefore, when someone else is looking for a file, they have to go in all of the offices to find it.

A common scenario is when a client calls, and the attorney asks for the file. Then the attorney and the secretary go bustling around the office looking everywhere for the file. Much time is spent looking for a lost document or a file. The files should be in one centralized location where the attorney can trust that the file will be there. You should constantly be taking files out of the attorneys' offices and returning them to the file room to keep the attorneys from hoarding them in their offices. Keep constant guard on their files. It is up to you to exercise some organization and control of your attorneys' files. But remember, it is a continual process.

Rule 2. Open New Files Immediately. When a new client comes in or a new matter is going to be handled by one of your attorneys, open a file right away. Even if your attorneys say not to officially open the file or give it a number, still go ahead and put it in a manila folder and pencil in the name of the prospective client. This way the documents won't be loose on the attorney's desk, and if a file is never opened, you can merely erase the penciled-in name.

Use the New Matter Report if your office has one. If not, see Figure 1404.1-1 for sample forms that you can adopt for your office. If you want to redesign the form, it will be easy for you to add or combine the items you want on your memorandum. It is *important* to have a new file memorandum.

Usually when a new file is opened, two or three copies of the New Matter Report are prepared. One may go to the accounting department, one to the file room, and one in the file. Some offices make additional copies. Check the procedures in your office and conform to that, or improve the system, if possible.

When a new file is opened, a Rolodex card is usually made, along with a client file card.

Rule 3. File Everything Right Away. Be sure to file each document as soon as possible to keep it from getting lost. Never let papers float around the office. Grab them and make sure they get fastened down in the file as soon as possible. Go into your attorneys' offices periodically and see if there is anything that they are through with that you can file. You will have to be assertive with your attorneys because they will tend to let documents, papers, and magazines stack up. Just go into their offices when they are free, perhaps at the end of the day when the telephone stops ringing, or first thing in the morning before the busy day begins.

Rule 4. Make Subfiles. Most legal matters involve different processes or have different types of documents other than correspondence. When you see the different papers accumulated, look to see if they fall in any logical order. Try to make all the files in your office conform to a standard form of organization. For example, a personal injury action may contain sections on research, pleadings, discovery, medical reports, etc. Create a system that suits the type of file on which your attorneys work. At first, you may have to check with your attorneys to determine a system of organization. After you do, document this procedure and follow it religiously. It is a common practice to fasten the correspondence on the left side of the file, although some offices fasten the correspondence on the right and leave the new file memorandum on the left. Just conform to whatever the present system is, or if you design your own, be consistent in your internal organization of the file (see ¶1404).

Rule 5. Maintain File Security. Your attorneys should keep their files in a fireproof file cabinet that only costs a little more than a standard file cabinet. A smoke detection alarm and a sprinkler system should be installed in the offices.

In addition to these safeguards, your attorneys should store valuables in a safe, including such items as bonds, wills, stock certificates. They should not be kept in the file. A photocopy can be kept in the file or a notation can be inserted in the file to show that they are in the safe.

A word of caution—you and your attorneys should take care to make sure the documents are not left carelessly around the office where other clients, adversaries, salespersons, and maintenance people pass through the office. When someone else is in your office, you should leave the documents on your desk face down to discourage any prying eyes.

Rule 6. Purge Files Regularly. A problem soon arises in law offices more than a year or two old of what to do with old files. Often a client comes in with a problem and never comes back. Thus, a file is opened that must be closed.

Establish a regular closing system to purge old files and store them. Also, as a file grows, have your attorneys look through the files and discard documents that they don't need to keep. Drafts of old agreements may be kept for negotiation purposes or to prove the legality of an agreement and other documents should always be kept. Check with your attorneys before throwing anything away, but keep guard on the growth of documents in the file. Again, subdivide, if necessary.

Some offices have standard procedures as to the proper amount of time to keep old files. Usually, the firm stores the old files off-site. There are services that store file boxes that you can have delivered to your firm upon request. It might be a good idea to get your firm to establish a time limit on how long to store certain files. Some specialties of law require a longer storage due to tax laws and other laws, or just to be safe.

Rule 7. Use Numeric Filing System Instead of Alphabetic. It may not be your choice as to which file system to choose. If your firm has an alphabetic filing system, most likely it is a small office. However, if they do use the alphabetic system, perhaps you can convince them to change the system. You might volunteer to take on the project. Of course, if you are extremely busy, this may be hard to do. But most attorneys do travel, appear in court or attend meetings. Perhaps you can use small blocks of time while they are out of the office to handle the project. For sure you will impress the attorneys.

Rule 8. Become a File Monitor. If your firm does not have a "file monitor" to watch over the files, you become one. Basically, what this involves is having one person with some authority make sure that all files presently in use be returned to the central file room. This means periodically going through the attorneys' offices, the secretarial work areas, the library, the conference room, or anywhere else the files may be left.

The file monitor should be uncompromisingly firm and not allow the attorneys to hoard files in their offices, which they will do if they can. Perhaps one of the attorneys in your office will support you in this effort, or perhaps the office manager will assist you. In any event, this file monitor must be thorough and make the search daily. Talk to your attorneys about this. If no one is officially appointed, just get in the habit of going through the offices and asking the attorneys if they are not using the files today and if you can return them to the file room or file cabinet.

Rule 9. Use a Standard Internal Filing Format. It is important to be consistent in handling your files. Frequently other attorneys may have to go into your file and if you have a standard format for the office, they will be able to locate documents easier. If you are in a small firm, under eight to ten attorneys, try and get the other secretaries to agree on a standard internal filing format. This will allow others to obtain information out of the file more easily.

You might want to keep a running log of the documents that are in the file and place it on top of the last filed document. Also, you could keep a copy of this log in a separate book on your desk to provide you an easy reference guide. Of course, litigation transcript files that contain pleadings usually have a pleadings index (see Figure 1406-1 and ¶1800 for further reference).

Rule 10. Use Color Codes. If you are in a small firm, it might be helpful to assign a color code to either the different areas of law or to the individual attorneys. You can use either colored labels or colored dots on each file. Most office supply companies carry a variety of colored tabs, labels, dots, etc. Obviously, if you have more than ten or twelve attorneys, this wouldn't work. Color codes for attorneys will only work in small law offices. If you use a color code for the different areas of law, for example, real estate files can be yellow, estate files purple, criminal files blue, worker's compensation files red, and personal injury files green. Using color codes for different areas of law might prevent misfiling of documents in the wrong section.

¶1408 How to Select the Right Filing Equipment

Some secretaries are asked to purchase the filing system for their attorneys, or to assist in the selection. This section will give you a general idea on the different types of equipment available so that you can assist your attorneys.

Your part in the selection of filing equipment is to help the attorneys pick the proper filing equipment that will be the most efficient system for the least possible overall cost.

The best equipment for some other attorneys may not be the most suitable equipment for your attorneys. To determine the type of filing equipment for your attorneys, you should consider the following:

1. *Frequency of use:* Are these filing cabinets for active or closed files? Obviously, if they are for inactive files, you need not get an expensive filing cabinet for those files because they will not be used as often.
2. *Location:* Whether your attorneys keep their files outside of their office or in your office work area or whether they will be in a centralized location.
3. *Quantity:* The amount of filing to be placed in the cabinets.
4. *Space constraints:* Cost and availability of space, and office layout.
5. *Staff:* Who is going to do the filing? If it is you, then perhaps the files should be located in your work area. Maybe, your attorneys want them in their offices for convenience. (Few attorneys do—it spoils their image.)
6. *Budget:* Money allocated for the filing equipment.

Standard Drawer Files Until recently, the only file available to attorneys was the standard two-, three-, four-, and five-drawer file that pulls straight out the entire length of the files, commonly called vertical files. These tend to topple over if more than one file drawer is pulled out, so caution should be used not to pull out one drawer while another is out. These drawer files are 24, 26, and 28 inches deep. A standard 26-inch drawer holds up to 5,000 sheets plus file guides and manila folders (not gussets).

The width of the drawers can be either letter or legal size. The letter size is 12½ inches and the legal is 15½ inches. Of course, the most practical size is the legal size although some attorneys will have their personal and general files in letter-size folders.

Four-drawer filing cabinets are the most popular although five-drawer filing cabinets are as common. For small offices with a low volume of filing, these are the most inexpensive and the most adequate. Many times you can purchase these files in used condition that will be perfectly fine for your attorneys. If your attorneys are just starting out, a good suggestion would be for you to check the local want ads under office equipment.

To prevent the file toppling over, purchase files with telescoping slides to give support. These slides are on ball bearings. Your attorneys might want to bolt the files together or to a wall.

When just beginning to use a file cabinet, you will need a block to hold the files until the drawer is full and holds itself. Usually the file drawers have sliding blocks.

Compact Drawer Filing Cabinets These files are used to save space, however, the space they save is usually not worth the inconvenience of the files. They do not hold some oversize documents. Special file folders and dividers must also be used in the cabinets. In addition, you are now working with a standard-size legal folder, and it may be difficult to locate the proper size of files. These files are not recommended for attorneys.

Expandable File Cabinets An expandable file cabinet has a feature that allows the front drawer to open and fall foward at an angle, or the rear may fall back. Although this feature permits tighter packing of the materials in the drawer, it is not worth the small amount of space it saves.

Lateral Movable Shelf Files Now there are lateral files that are arranged so that the farthest they pull out is only the length of the actual file, i.e., 15½ inches. In other words, the files are arranged from the left side of the cabinet to the right rather than from the back of the vertical cabinet to the front. They allow access to a complete file folder from the side and top. Lateral files operate as though a regular cabinet file drawer were opened through the side of the cabinet instead of the front. With these files, it is not necessary to convert the file folders.

Lateral files are generally more expensive than vertical files. They are excellent for private or public areas. Closed-front stationary shelving is more expensive than plain open shelving. Attorneys are using these files more and more, mainly because they will hold more files than the typical vertical file and are easier to fit in small spaces.

The price of these files varies depending upon the grade and capacity. They also come in a variety of colors. Their main advantage is the minimum of aisle space they require and the complete visibility. Some manufacturers have safety features on these cabinets that prevent them from toppling over. If not, you should suggest that the cabinets be bolted to the floor.

Open Shelving Open shelving may be used in a centralized file room. Basically, they are built-in shelves or floor-to-ceiling units. You can purchase open shelving in either steel or wood to put against the wall. These files must be sturdy to hold the volume of files that will be put on them.

There are a variety of other types of shelves, but most likely if your firm needs these types of files, it is probably big enough to have an office manager or legal administrator that can choose other systems. You probably won't be involved in those purchases, and most likely you won't have time. If you do have to look at these other systems, such as side-movable, multiple-stacked shelves, electrically operated shelf files, or visible indexing systems, you can find articles in legal books and periodicals that will tell you more about them.

¶1409 Centralized Filing vs. Decentralized Filing: What Works?

The question of a centralized vs. decentralized filing system may not be within your control. An explanation of the difference between the two follows.

Centralized filing is where the main files are located at another part of the firm and not near the attorneys' offices. Some firms have a combination of centralized and decentralized systems. They may have some of their files outside their office and the rest in the main central filing room. Or, they may only send those files that are inactive to the main filing room, keeping their active files outside their offices. The most important thing to keep in mind is that the files are organized and put away properly.

If your firm has a centralized file area, you may prepare the new file memorandum, and the file room may assign the file a number and prepare the folders. Or you may prepare the whole file and assign it a number. The procedure varies from firm to firm according to the personnel the firm has in the centralized file room. However, if you do have a centralized file room, be sure you keep an index of your files and prepare the card files (see ¶1404).

In a decentralized system, attorneys have their own files in their general work area outside their offices. In this case, you will have more control over the files. You still may have to close the files and send them to another location (see ¶1410). Be sure to keep accurate records to indicate whether a file is open or closed, i.e., active or inactive.

¶1410 Quick File Closing Procedures

If you have a good active filing system, then you will be able to develop a good inactive one. When a case is closed, you should remove the file index card, and make a notation on that card that the file is closed. If you have a system whereby inactive or closed files are given separate numbers, then you will then assign the closing file a number. There are variations on this system. A quick file closing method is as follows:

1. Pull the active file card.
2. Mark it "Closed" (a rubber stamp can be used for this). You may also stamp the date on the card. Some file cards have a place for the inactive file number as well.
3. Assign an inactive file number even if your file uses an alphabetical filing system so that you are always adding to the end of a file rather than inserting files internally into the system. You may use a "C" before the closed file number.
4. Write the inactive file number in a bound closed file book.
5. Move the file card to the back of your file index box in numerical order.
6. Remove all paper clips, duplicate material, and unnecessary envelopes and materials.
7. Have the attorney review the file and remove any necessary material.
8. Mark the file "Closed."
9. Transfer to an inactive file or storage area.
10. Do not send valuable or client documents to storage. Ask the attorney what he or she wants to do with these.
11. Arrange for microfilming, if used.
12. If you are to physically store the files, arrange them in closed file number order.

¶1411 A Direct Reference Form Filing System*

The form system presented in this section allows you to locate rapidly any one of thousands of forms, *without* knowing the name of the form and *without reference to any index.* Alphabetization, and the classic inexactitudes that accompany it, can practically be rendered obsolete.

The system can be used with or without a computer. Bear in mind that a computer alone (without the system) would not necessarily reduce retrieval time, since, before a particular form could be located, it would still have to be identified and "named," in any event. Either way, because the methods presented slash retrieval time, form files can be expanded well beyond current conventional use. The system provides the requisite base for such expansion. Correspondingly, the quality of forms can be

*Reprinted with permission of Ashley S. Lipson, 1983.

greatly augmented, since the increased numbers allow for greater variation, flexibility and "tailoring."

A person wishing to locate any particular form need only know the use or purpose of the form; the system takes over from there. The forms are arranged in "logical grouping," by function, instead of by alphabetization, thereby eliminating the ambiguities that are prevalent in alphabetical systems. Related forms are located close to one another for inspection and companion use.

For example, assume that an attorney wishes to commence garnishment proceedings. A typical alphabetical filing system would cause an Affidavit for Writ of Garnishment and the Writ of Garnishment to be separated by 21 letters of the alphabet; the two forms, though always used in tandem, would be at opposite ends of the filing system. This makes no sense. Moreover, after mentally debating the whereabouts of the form, the average attorney would probably look under the letter G and not find either form. His next step would involve reference to the form file index, which would either be in alphabetical order or in some other haphazard grouping. That index would then perhaps assign numbers, which would have to be located within the filing system. However, if the attorney could not remember the exact title of the form, it might *never* be found either in the index or in the file drawer.

If, having found the printed garnishment forms, the attorney then wants to refer to a completed set of garnishment pleadings (as a sample), he would very likely encounter a different procedure entirely. Most often, he would resort to the apex of inefficiency—the random search through client files.

The system proposed herein is a topical grouping system that avoids all of the problems encountered in the example. Under the system, the Writ and the Affidavit of Garnishment would be side by side, and moreover, any related checklists, completed "sample garnishments," briefs or other relevant memos or documents would be close at hand. The proposed system thus cuts across the traditional lines of separation between standard printed forms, constructed forms, interview sheets, checklists, prototype pleadings and sample pleadings. All of these different law office aides are brought together by topic under "one roof," thereby keeping wasted research, dictation and finger walking to an absolute minimum. In essence, the system causes the forms to be grouped in accordance with the manner in which a lawyer, paralegal or secretary should think, and not by the random manner in which the title of the form happens to fall with respect to alphabetization. The system also has many other advantages that will later be considered.

Speaking of forms in general, experienced practitioners are somewhat unanimous in their opinion that a well-devised form system is one of the most important tools that a law firm can possess. Three requirements relating to the quality of a system are paramount:

First, constructed forms must be devised for efficiency, quality, accuracy, and that most neglected trait of a "nonform" appearance (i.e., the reader should not be able to tell by inspection that a preprinted form was used). Constructed forms can be of great value if properly used, or can be quite embarrassing if misused.

Second, the system must allow for addition, deletion and modification of the forms. A typical numerical system would not efficiently accommodate the second requirement. Unless a fractional or decimal system were devised, new forms would be placed at the end of the system, in numerical order, thereby destroying any topical or other arrangement upon which the system was originally predicated. Fractional and decimal systems tend to be complex and unwieldy. Our goal is simplicity, and therefore, only integers (whole numbers) are used.

Third, one must be able to locate any particular form immediately. For attorneys, nothing is quite as wasteful of temper and time as knowing that a needed form or sample pleading exists—somewhere—and being unable to locate it quickly. There is a simple test for locatability: direct someone to find the most obscure and rarely used form in the office; if the search takes the person more than 60 seconds, the system has failed with respect to this most important requirement. As previously stated, alphabetical systems are poor at best. To use an alphabetical system, one must know the exact title of the form. Moreover, even knowing the exact title might not be enough (consider locating tax form 1020).

¶1411.1 The Direct Reference System

Each form is delegated a five-digit number, with a comma between the second and third digit. Five-digit numbers, in general, seem to be easy to vocalize, and thus easy to remember. The first digit denotes one of nine major substantive practice categories, representing the types of matters handled by a particular law firm. The second digit denotes the first major subgroup within the category. The third digit denotes a subheading within the subgroup, etc.

This might sound complicated, but it really isn't. If the reader exhibits the patience to follow through the examples set forth hereunder, the simplicity and practicality of the system will become apparent.

The most important grouping consists of the nine major categories encompassed by the first digit. Selecting the categories and their numerical order can reflect the emphasis in particular areas of practice in a given law firm. The following designations seem to work well for most general practice or litigation-oriented firms, and often, even for firms which heavily emphasize or specialize in one (or fewer than nine) of the categories:

1. Litigation (black)
2. Probate (red)
3. Corporate and Business (green)
4. Real Estate (brown)
5. Tax (yellow)
6. Labor (blue)
7. Motor Vehicle (purple)
8. Administrative (orange)
9. Other

The colors denoted correspond to the color of folder labels to be used in conjunction with the several categories. These colors possess no great significance per se, though for the author, they seem to provide a good mnemonic scheme for remembering the categories they represent.

Because of the nature of litigation and the fact that it often overlaps other office matters, it is highly recommended that it be assigned the first position, even though a firm may emphasize probate work or some other matter. Whatever numerical order is selected, it must be followed consistently. Unlike any of the remaining numbers assigned for purposes of subgrouping, this first digit will correspond not only to the office form file system but will also relate to client files (later discussed).

The second digit of our five-digit numbering system will correspond to a major subgroup within the major category. We will use litigation for our initial illustration since it is the most complex category.

As with our eight other major categories, for litigation there exists a natural, *"rememberable"* hierarchy or pecking order. Litigation's hierarchy is the Federal-State Court system. The first major subgroup under the litigation category best conforms to court structure. This will assist those attorneys and/or secretaries afflicted with a propensity for filing motions in Federal District Court, on forms obtained from a State District Court. Thus, the second (of our five digits) designates one of the following:*

*Tax court forms fall within the scope of the litigation category, 15,000.

1. U.S. Supreme Court
2. U.S. Circuit Court of Appeals
3. Federal District Court
4. Federal Court of Claims
5. Tax Court
6. California Supreme Court
7. California Court of Appeals
8. California Superior Court
9. California Municipal Court
10. Other

The next subheading, represented by the third digit, designates the stage of the proceeding for the particular court; it also has a natural order (chronological in nature), which can best be represented as follows:

1. Commencement
2. Response
3. Discovery
4. Pretrial
5. Trial
6. Judgment
7. Execution
8. Appeal
9. Substantive Law

The nine subheadings are obviously best suited to the courts of original jurisdiction (Federal District Court, California Superior Court, etc.); however, for simplicity, they should be left intact and used as a subheading for each of the nine courts. The fact that there may not be any pretrials conducted in the California Supreme Court, for example, creates no major problems; it just means that there will be no forms within that particular numerical heading.

A concrete example may be useful at this juncture. Consider the prior example of the litigation attorney searching for his garnishment forms, this time without his index and without his alphabet. He might not be conversant with all nine of the major categories, but he would certainly be familiar with the subgroups pertaining to *his* particular field (i.e., litigation). Of course, he would know the court in which he intended to file the garnishment (8. California Superior Court), and it is hoped that he would know whether the garnishment was being filed at the "commencement" of the lawsuit or after judgment. Having no more facts at his fingertips than those indicated, the attorney will know that his form is circa 18,701 (see Figure 1411.1-1).

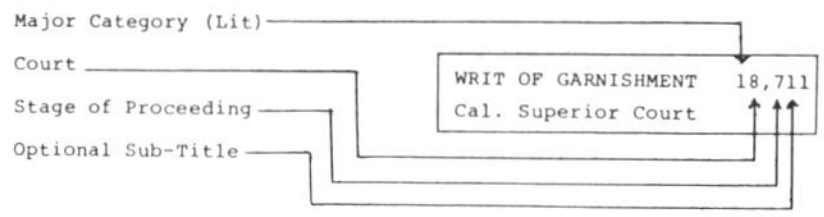

Figure 1411.1-1.

The optional subtitles (fourth digit) would pertain only to the execution phase of the proceeding. An example of such denotation could be as follows: 1. Garnishment forms, 2. Execution forms, 3. Post Judgment Debtor proceedings.

To be consistent, if the Writ of Garnishment were given the designation 18,711, then the Affidavit in Support of the Writ of Garnishment would be given the number 18,712, etc. Proceedings involving garnishments before judgment have been rendered all but obsolete due to the restrictions imposed by *Fuentes v. Shevin,* 407 U.S. 67, 92 S.Ct. 1983, 32 L.Ed2d 556. Sample garnishments or "filled in" forms pertaining to garnishments should be circa 18,715, etc.

By way of a second example, assume that you wished to commence litigation in Federal District Court. You would have a hunch that a summons might be required; and, although you might not know the exact title of the document (i.e., District Court Summons, Federal Court Summons, Summons, etc.), you would certainly know that you were dealing with a court of general federal jurisdiction (subgroup three). Thus, quickly you would be led to those forms circa 13,101. To find the documents that would accompany the filing of your suit, you would need only glance at the adjacent form file labels to see such accompanying titles as a "Marshall's Service form," a "Federal Court Face Sheet," or any other documents required in conjunction with local court rules. The fact that the forms are located close together and grouped by usage assists the attorney or paralegal in *remembering* what is necessary for the particular procedure under consideration.

It is therefore important once again to emphasize the fact that the person wishing to find the form *does not* have to know the exact form number; the person need only be "close." It takes but a few seconds to flip through folders that are "close together." The finger flipping will always be kept to a minimum. At the outset, perhaps as many as 90 percent of the forms will be eliminated totally from consideration solely by reason of the colored labels.

Some numbers may not be quite so obvious; a little thought might be required. For example, assume that you wished to locate a set of sample or form interrogatories for a products liability case. Applying the rule of subject matter jurisdiction, you know that such a case may be tried in a Federal District Court, a State Court of general jurisdiction, or a State Court of inferior jurisdiction. Which do you choose? The rule is simple: If the case arises under federal law, choose subgroup three; if it does not, then apply the rule of *Erie v. Thompkins* and look to the State Court system.

You know that the jurisdiction may overlap the State Courts, so once again apply a simple rule: Choose the court of general jurisdiction (subgroup number eight) regardless of the amount in controversy (see Figure 1411.1-2).

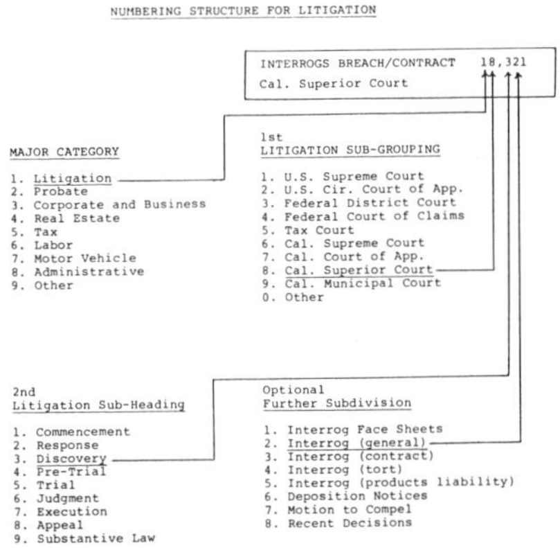

Figure 1411.1-2.

Another area where thinking might be required concerns "appeals." Forms circa 18,800 would pertain *only* to those appeal forms to be filed in the Superior Court (for example, a Motion to Stay Proceedings pending appeal to the Court of Appeals). The Claim of Appeal would be the first document filed in the California Court of Appeals, and even though a copy of the same might be served upon the Superior Court, the forms concerning the actual Claim of Appeal would be found circa 17,100.

¶1411.2 Alternative Indexing

It is not absolutely essential that *every* user learn the system; die-hard alphabetizers can peacefully coexist. Once the forms are organized in the fashion herein presented, an alphabetical index can be prepared as a back-up location device. Moreover, several different indices could be prepared, according to individual preference. One such index could contain a breakdown corresponding to the nine major categories, with alphabetical sublistings; another could consist of a simple numerical list (which of course would per se fall into the topical patterns).

The indices would only serve as back-up devices, so as to guarantee that almost everyone should be able to locate any form within the system.

It is important to emphasize that by using the number system a person could come very close to the particular form within a matter of seconds. And in this particular situation "close counts." Adjacent forms could serve as location aids and reminders with respect to other related proceedings, forms and/or sample documents.

¶1411.3 Client Files

Before developing the remaining major categories, it would be helpful at this juncture to mention the corresponding client file system. That system is quite a bit simpler than the form filing system. A six-digit number is recommended. For those firms that may open more than 99 files within any given quarter, a seven-digit system would probably be more appropriate. Once again, as with the form file system, the first digit will denote one of the nine major practice categories (litigation, probate, etc.). The next two digits will denote the year in which the file is opened, and the fourth digit will indicate the quarter of such opening.

This method of numbering will group the files by major categories. Within each category, files will be placed according to the period in which they were opened (see Figure 1411.3-1). An alphabetical cross-index would be advisable, even though recently opened files could be located very quickly.

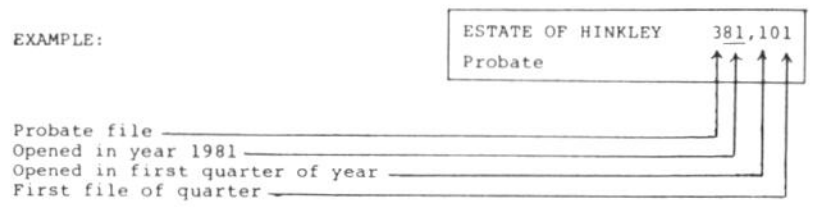

Figure 1411.3-1.

A "closed file" system is automatically constructed. As the files are pulled from the active drawer and placed into the "closed filing system," each of them would fall into its appropriate chronological order. The file clerk could simply handwrite the letter C before the first digit of the file to designate the particular file as "closed."

Closed files would be as easy to locate as active ones; the same rules apply.

¶1411.4 The Remaining Major Categories

For those "general office forms" that seem to cut across all of our traditional grouping categories, the first digit should be designated 0. These forms would include such matters as: time sheets, billing sheets, forms relating to intraoffice matters. Such a designation will cause these forms to appear first in the filing drawer, which makes sense, since they are the most commonly used forms.

Numbering systems for all the remaining major groupings will be constructed in the same manner as that for litigation. First, a hierarchy or natural order will be created that encompasses *all* of the forms for the category in question. Second, for each element of this "natural order," it will be determined whether or not a natural subgrouping hierarchy exists. Thereafter (beyond the third digit), substructuring is optional (see Appendix).

¶1411.5 Closing Note

This is perhaps your first encounter with a filing system description that exceeds a paragraph in length. Is the system worth the trouble of learning? To answer, consider the average law library; it contains volumes of indices and "systems" designed to lead you to a particular case. If you're an average practitioner, you devote far more time to preparing documents than to finding cases. How many books in your library assist you in locating forms?

¶1411.6 Appendix

Probate (Major Category 2) For our purposes, the term "probate" is much broader than the legal definition implies. The natural order of the grouping system, in effect, corresponds to a person's corporeal station. Subgroup one pertains to *inter vivos* transfers; subgroup two provides a framework for testamentary instruments. Subgroups three through seven all pertain to surrogate administration. The Estate Administration subheading could be used in conjunction with each of the latter five groups (see Figure 1411.6-1).

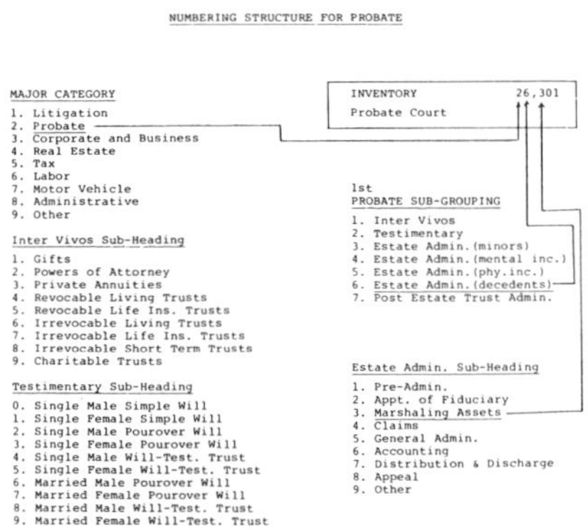

Figure 1411.6-1.

Corporate and Business (Major Category 3) By far, the greatest number of "business" forms pertain either to Corporations or to Uniform Commercial Code (U.C.C.) matters. Partnerships, joint ventures and sole proprietorships account for relatively few forms that pertain exclusively to those entities.

The subgroups titled "U.C.C.-Matters" and "Contracts" don't fit our "entity hierarchy" but are nevertheless quite necessary. Those proficient with the Code will notice that the subheadings correspond to its chapters *both* in title and in number. The "Contracts" subgroup would consist predominantly of sample agreements (e.g., buy-sell agreements, etc.). The sample structure for the category is as follows (see Figure 1411.6-2).

Real Estate (Major Category 4) Real Estate has a natural order about it. Interests which are the subject of transfers form a nice quantitative hierarchy, commencing with the "fee simple." From there, the list works its way down through limited possessory Estates (leases) to nonpossessory interests (mortgages and liens).

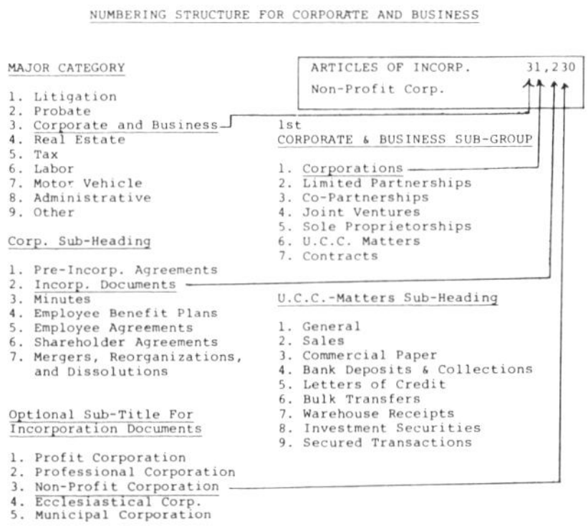

Figure 1411.6-2.

Concurrent Estates involve joint and common ownership, while Divisible Estates pertain to future interests. Any forms pertaining to either of these two groups would most likely consist of sample deeds or related prototype documents (see Figure 1411.6-3).

Tax (Major Category 5) Tax practitioners speak, think and communicate with numbers; they address one another by social security numbers. It would therefore be a sacrilege to reassign to tax forms, numbers that don't correspond to their common titles.

With litigation forms excluded from this category,* there remain

*The California Court system is being used as an example. Like most State Court systems, it possesses a court of general jurisdiction (Superior Court), two Appellate Courts, and one or more courts of inferior jurisdiction. It should also be noted (with respect to subgroup three) that Federal District Court includes Bankruptcy Court.

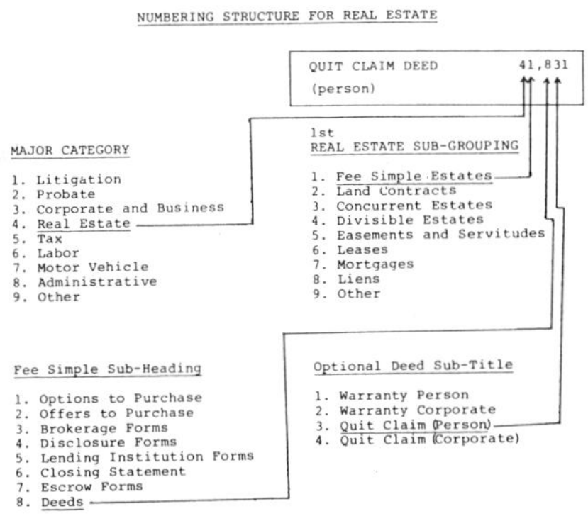

Figure 1411.6-3.

few forms that do not have "official numbers" (a prototype Notice of Taxpayer's Protest would exemplify such an exception).

The official forms, recognized as such by the Treasury Department, exceed 300 in number and are all named on the Official Treasury List of forms and returns (form 701). All such forms are numbered such that no number exceeds four digits; some have letters preceding the numbers (e.g., form SS-4) and some have letters following (e.g., form 1040-C, sometimes referred to only as "Schedule C").

For our system, we will ignore the letters, regardless of whether they precede or follow the numbers, and label the last four digits so as to correspond to the official form number. For example, tax form 941 would be assigned to label number 50,941. Likewise, form 1040 would correspond to label number 51,040. The letters constitute variations; and all such variations could be placed in one folder. This would mean that the SS-4 form and the W-4 form would both fall into form folder 50,004. This system would seem adequate for most practitioners, even though form 50,004 would contain several different schedules and forms.

State forms would also "fall into" the system by number. It should not be unduly disturbing that state and federal forms would, in some cases, be kept within the same folder. For, in many cases, state returns and forms are intentionally assigned federal numbers (with accompanying state abbreviations), indicating companion use.

In the alternative, for those practitioners who make use of many of the odd-ball forms in volume, a separate folder could be assigned for each lettered variation of a given form. For example, form 1040-C would be assigned form number 51,040C; while Schedule C would be given form number 51,040-C, etc. Further breakdowns and separations could also be required with respect to the year of the particular form. Some forms are revised from year to year (e.g., the 1040), and others are periodically abolished (e.g., Schedule 1040-TC). These variations depart significantly from our "pure five-digit number" system, and would be efficacious only for tax law specialists or C.P.A. firms.

Labor (Major Category 6) Labor is a specialized and complex matter, which unless restrained could cut across the lines of several other groups, causing much confusion. It should not be permitted to overlap Category eight, even though it most definitely concerns itself with many administrative and governmental agencies; nor should it be permitted to overlap Category one, even though many labor forms are tailored for litigation.

The labor subgrouping (infra) is tailored to particular proceedings. Subgroup five contains *only* those litigation forms that pertain directly to labor matters, so as not to be confused with the litigation forms of major Category one. Practitioners utilizing labor forms will most likely be specialists and have no problems identifying those particular forms that would fall within the scope of subgroup five; an example of such a form would be a Petition for Removal of action from State Court to Federal Court predicated upon Section 301 of the Labor Management Relations Act.

Though tenuously related, labor practitioners consider Workers' Compensation cases outside of their sphere; such matters concern a specialty onto itself. Therefore, Workers' Compensation matters will be treated within major Category eight.

Much of the labor practitioner's time, if not most of it, concerns arbititration proceedings. The most helpful forms would be sample briefs or memoranda pertaining to particular arbitration issues (see Figure 1411.6-4).

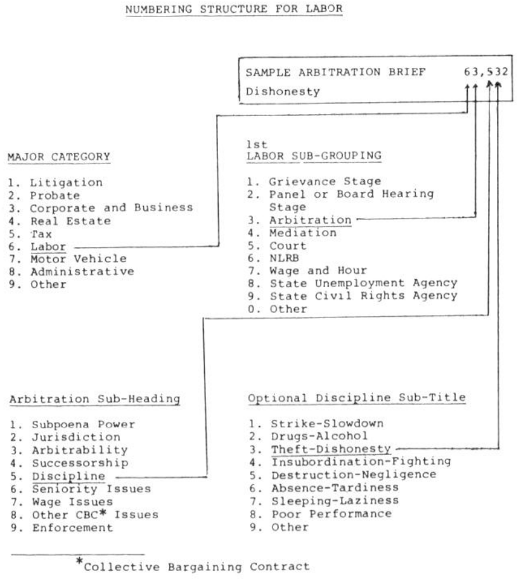

Figure 1411.6-4.

Motor Vehicle (Major Category 7) This category is too minor, and concerns too few forms to justify extensive structuring. The category would encompass applications pertaining to motor vehicle titles and other Secretary of State forms. Perhaps form Petitions for Restoration of Driving Privileges might be included. Because the forms are so few, any simple consecutive numbering would be adequate.

Administrative (Major Category 8) This particular category will be subject to some variation, depending upon a law firm's particular emphasis. As with litigation, the first five members of the subgroup have been reserved for federal agencies, with the remainder delegated to the states. The number of forms for a general practice firm that would be included within each of the members of the group would be somewhat limited, in any event (see Figure 1411.6-5).

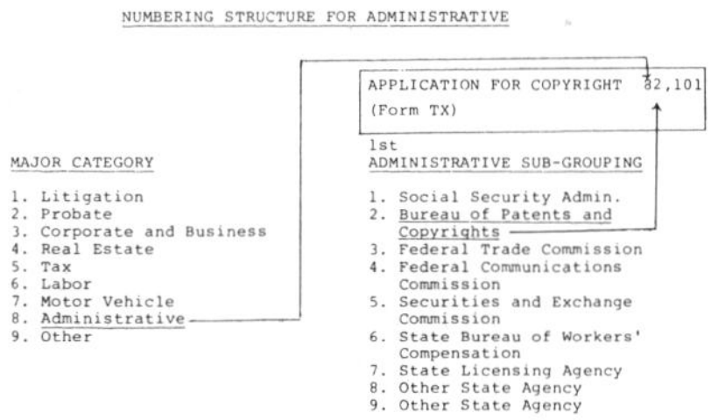

Figure 1411.6-5.

¶1412 Some Basic Indexing and Filing Rules

The following are some basic indexing and filing rules.*

I. INDIVIDUAL NAMES

1. Reverse names of individuals considering first surname, then given name and middle name or their abbreviations.

Name	**Index and File**
John J. Brown....................	*Brown* John J
William Henry Carter	*Carter* William Henry
Howard A. Jones................	*Jones* Howard A
Lawrence B. Lindquist...........	*Lindquist* Lawrence B
Harvey R. Miller	*Miller* Harvey R

*Reprinted with permission of Kardex Systems, Inc., Marketing Department, P.O. Box 171, Marietta, OH 45750.

1a. In individual names, if possible to determine given name and middle name or their abbreviations, apply Rule 1 and index and file all remaining as the surname. See also Rule 23.

Name	**Index and File**
C. D. Abd El Nour	*Abd El Nour* C D
Joseph D'Agostino...............	*D'Agostino* Joseph
Laura De La Torre	*De La Torre* Laura
H.L.G. De San Marzano	*De San Marzano* H L G
Edward J. Du-No-Van............	*Du-No-Van* Edward J
D. El Koury.....................	*El Koury* D
Edna Fitz Gerald	*Fitz Gerald* Edna
Henry C. GaNun.................	*GaNun* Henry C
Albert I. Gell Man...............	*Gell Man* Albert I
William H. La Boyteaux	*La Boyteaux* William H
Jaques Le Compte	*Le Compte* Jaques
David L'Esperance...............	*L'Esperance* David
Andrew Li Causi	*Li Causi* Andrew

1b. Hyphenated surnames are indexed usually as one complete surname. Exceptions may occur where name following hyphen is ignored, or it may be used as the given name or middle name. A cross reference is helpful.

Name	**Index and File**
R. Burton-Opitz.................	*Burton*-Opitz R (optional)
Harriet Chapman-Catt...........	*Chapman-Catt* Harriet
Charles Cholmeley-Jones	*Cholmeley-Jones* Charles
Julian K. Ex-Sprague	*Ex-Sprague* Julian K
John H. Fitz-Gerald	*Fitz-Gerald* John H
J. Forbes-Robertson..............	*Forbes-Robertson* J
John Foster-Brown...............	*Foster-Brown* John
Fernando Gomez-Rodriguez......	*Gomez-Rodriguez* Fernando
James Smith-Elliott	*Smith*-(Elliott) James (optional)

1c. In individual names, if not possible to determine the given name, the middle name or their abbreviations, index and file as written.

Name	**Index and File**
Ah Hop Akee...................	*Ah* Hop Akee
Chin Hing Sing	*Chin* Hing Sing
Einosuke Hayase	*Einosuke* Hayase
Hun-Ka-Hop-Py.................	*Hun* Ka-Hop-Py
Ng King Wong..................	*Ng* King Wong
Phra Leha Avudh	*Phra* Leha Avudh
Yee San Lung...................	*Yee* San Lung

2. Titles or degrees of individuals, whether preceding or following the name, are disregarded in indexing and filing.

Name	Index and File
Dr. John Brown	*Brown* John (Dr)
Capt. William Clarke	*Clarke* William (Capt)
Horace Cook L.L.D.	*Cook* Horace (LLD)
Mrs. A. R. Crawford	*Crawford* A R (Mrs)
Mayor John Marshall	*Marshall* John (Mayor)
Mr. Henry Miller	*Miller* Henry (Mr)
Prof. W. N. Rice	*Rice* W N (Prof)
William Walton, Treas.	*Walton* William (Treas)

3. Abbreviated designations (e.g. "Jr.," "Sr.," "2nd" etc.) appearing as part of name are usually disregarded in indexing and filing.

Name	Index and File
James G. Blaine, 2nd	*Blaine* James G (2nd)
Henry Hale, Jr.	*Hale* Henry (Jr)
Arthur Nelson, 3rd	*Nelson* Arthur (3rd)
Howard Peters, Sr.	*Peters* Howard (Sr)

4. If a title is followed by a recognized surname, with no given name, index under Surname. Disregard title. See Rule 26. Exception: Religious titles. See also Rules 4a, b and c.

Name	Index and File
Madame Allston	*Allston* (Madame)
The Misses Dennis	*Dennis* (The Misses)
Mrs. Johnson	*Johnson* (Mrs)
Monsieur Jaques	*Jaques* (Monsieur)

4a. Titles, including both foreign and religious titles, followed by one name, *not recognized* as a surname are indexed as written. A cross reference is helpful.

Name	Index and File
Brother Anselm	*Brother* Anselm
Duke of York	*Duke* (of) York
Father Joseph	*Father* Joseph
*Father Lyons	*Father* Lyons
Lord Aberdeen	*Lord* Aberdeen
Madame Lucile	*Madame* Lucile
Prince William	*Prince* William
Princess Alicia	*Princess* Alicia
Sister Mary Beatrice	*Sister* Mary Beatrice

*Exception to Rule

4b. If a nickname is followed by a recognized surname, index under surname and use nickname as given name. Cross reference if correct given name is known.

Name	Index and File
Tubby Jones	*Jones* Tubby
Baby Face Nelson................	*Nelson* Baby Face
Toughy Richards	*Richards* Toughy

4c. In case of nickname with no recognizable surname, index as written.

Name	Index and File
Boston Jimmie	*Boston* Jimmie
Little Jeff......................	*Little* Jeff
The Spider	*Spider* (The)
Tony The Rat...................	*Tony* (The) Rat

5. The legal name of a married woman is the one considered in filing, and the husband's name is cross-referenced, if known.

Name	Index and File
Mrs. Mary A. Brown.............	*Brown* Mary A (Mrs) Mrs. John A **Cross Reference** *Brown* John A (Mrs) *See Brown* Mary A (Mrs)

II. FIRMS, CORPORATIONS, INSTITUTIONS AND ORGANIZATIONS

6. Names of firms, corporations and institutions are indexed as written, word for word, except where they embody full names of individuals. See Rules 1 and 1a. Cross reference when necessary. See also Rules 6a through 24a.

Name	Index and File
A La Jeunesse Elegante	*A* La Jeunesse Elegante
Antoine de Paris	*Antoine* de Paris
Au Cour de France Store	*Au* Cour de France Store
Bay State Finishing Corp.........	*Bay* State Finishing Corp
Blue Bird Hat Shop	*Blue* Bird Hat Shop
Church of the Epiphany	*Church* (of the) Epiphany
D E K Company	*D* E K Company
El Krino Cigar Company.........	*El* Krino Cigar Company
El Oro Mining Co	*El* Oro Mining Co
Harris Forbes & Company	*Harris* Forbes (&) Company
II Giornale della Casa	*II* Giornale della Casa
II Progresso Italo	*II* Progresso Italo
Junior League of City of N.Y......	*Junior* League (of) City (of) N Y
La Banque D'Hochelaga	*La* Banque D'Hochelaga
La Belle Iron Works.............	*La* Belle Iron Works

La France Novelty Co. Inc.	*La* France Novelty Co. Inc
Lamson & Hubbard Company	*Lamson* (&) Hubbard Company
Las Dos American Restaurant	*Las* Dos American Restaurant
Lo Priore Santa	*Lo* Priore Santa
Los Angeles Evening Herald	*Los* Angeles Evening Herald
Loy Da Renovating Company	*Loy* Da Renovating Company
Maison du Roi	*Maison* du Roi
Mount Hope Garage	*Mount* Hope Garage
New Amsterdam School	*New* Amsterdam School
Non Woven Fabric Co.	*Non* Woven Fabric Co
North End Union	*North* End Union
North Munroe Avenue Garage	*North* Munroe Avenue Garage
St. George Bros. Co.	*Saint* George Bros Co
St. Mark's Church	*Saint* Mark's Church
Saint Moritz Knitting Mills	*Saint* Moritz Knitting Mills
San Juan Land & Oil Co.	*San* Juan Land (&) Oil Co
Ten Eyck Glass Company	*Ten* Eyck Glass Company
Ten Minute Taxi Company	*Ten* Minute Taxi Company
The T Shop	*T* Shop (The)
The Vogue	*Vogue* (The)
Ye Manor House Catering Co	*Ye* Manor House Catering Co

6a. Firm or corporate names which have titles abbreviated or written in full as their first word are indexed by name. Titles are disregarded. Cross reference under title if helpful. See also rule 24.

Name	**Index and File**
Count Berresford Travel Bureau	*Berresford* Travel Bureau (Count)
Madame Blanc Hats	*Blanc* Hats (Madame)
Mr. and Mrs. Foster's Place	*Foster's Place (Mr and Mrs)*
Mme. Juliette Shop	*Juliette* Shop (Mme)
Capt. Post Pickle Company	*Post* Pickle Company (Capt)
Dr. Reed's Cushion Shoes	*Reed's* Cushion Shoes (Dr)
Mistress Smith Bake Shop	*Smith* Bake Shop (Mistress)
Col. Walter Smith Military Supply Co.	*Smith* Walter Military Supply Co (Col)

7. A firm or organization name, embodying full name of individual, is indexed and filed in accordance with Rules 1 and 1a. Cross reference when necessary.

Name	**Index and File**
Robert De Haven Mfg Co.	*De Haven* Robert Mfg Co
Marshall Field & Company	*Field* Marshall (&) Company
Ben Franklin Steamship Co.	*Franklin* Ben Steamship Co
John Hancock Mutual Life Ins. Co.	*Hancock* John Mutual Life Ins. Co
Walter E. Harrison & Co.	*Harrison* Walter E (&) Co

Washington Irving High School . .	*Irving* Washington High School
H. W. Johns Manville Co.	*Johns* H W Manville Co
Henry E. Kane & Company	*Kane* Henry E (&) Company
Condé Nast Publications Inc.	*Nast* Condé Publications Inc.
Wm. P. St. Lawrence Drug Co.	*Saint Lawrence* William P. Drug Co

8. Firm names which contain the full names of two or more individuals are indexed and filed by first individual name only. Cross reference second name if desired.

Name	**Index and File**
John Brown & Edward Field	*Brown* John
C. H. Evans & Roy Carey	*Evans* C H
Harry Kellogg & Robert Moore. . .	*Kellogg* Harry

Correct Filing Arrangement

Brown James
Brown John (&) Edward Field
Brown John B
Brown John (&) Co

9. Hyphenated firm names are indexed as separate words.

Name	**Index and File**
A-1 Locker Company	*A*-One Locker Company
Ad-E-Fect Studio	*Ad*-E-Fect Studio
Anglo-American Purchasing Co. . .	*Anglo*-American Purchasing Co.
Anti-Saloon League	*Anti*-Saloon League
Au-Win Hat Company	*Au*-Win Hat Company
Bona-Fide Press	*Bona*-Fide Press
Du-Wel Steel Company	*Du*-Wel Steel Company
Ex-El-Ent Stationery House	*Ex*-El-Ent Stationery House
G-Art Embroidery Company	*G*-Art Embroidery Company
Ho-Made Cakes	*Ho*-Made Cakes
Hum-pah-ta-kah	*Hum*-pah-ta-kah
Pan-American Lines	*Pan*-American Lines
Tak-em Home	*Tak*-em Home
Tel-o-Pad Company.	*Tel*-o-Pad Company
Ti-It Machine Company	*Ti*-It Machine Company
U-Drive It Garage.	*U*-Drive It Garage
Val-King Corporation	*Val*-King Corporation
Walsh-Weiner Boiler Co.	*Walsh*-Weiner Boiler Co.

9a. Names which may be spelled either as one word or two words *may be* indexed as one word. Cross reference when necessary. See also Rules 9 and 10.

Name	**Index and File**
Auto Piano Company	*Auto Piano* Company
Co-Operative Press	*Co-Operative* Press

Inter City Mfg. Co.	*Inter City* Manufacturing Co
Inter State Drug Co.	*Inter State* Drug Co
Mid West Metal Products Co.	*Mid West* Metal Products Co
Non Pareil Hat Company	*Non Pareil* Hat Company
North East Railway Co.	*North East* Railway Co
Tri-Boro Electric Co.	*Tri-Boro* Electric Co

10. Compound geographic and location names are filed as two words or more in order given. Cross reference when necessary. Congestion may necessitate exceptions. See also Rule 9a.

Name	**Index and File**
Cedar Hill Nurseries	*Cedar* Hill Nurseries
De Kalb Lumber Co.	*De* Kalb Lumber Co
Fall River Steamship Co.	*Fall* River Steamship Co
Fort Hamilton Transportation Co.	*Fort* Hamilton Transportation Co
Los Angeles Hardware Co.	*Los* Angeles Hardware Co
Mount Vernon Holding Co.	*Mount* Vernon Holding Co
New Jersey Coal Co.	*New* Jersey Coal Co.
New London Hardware Corp.	*New* London Hardware Corp
Park Avenue Hotel Co.	*Park* Avenue Hotel Co
Port Chester Savings Bank	*Port* Chester Savings Bank
Red Oak Country Club	*Red* Oak Country Club
Ridley Park Club	*Ridley* Park Club
San Alto Cigar Co.	*San* Alto Cigar Co
San Francisco Real Estate Co.	*San* Francisco Real Estate Co
Three Rivers Lumber Co.	*Three* Rivers Lumber Co

11. Firm or corporate names beginning with such phrases as "Board of" "Bureau of" "Commission for" etc. are indexed and filed as written and cross referenced under any caption which may be helpful. See also Rule 11a and Government Rule 18.

Name	**Index and File**
Board of Missionary Preparation	*Board* (of) Missionary Preparation
Bureau of Envelope Manufacturers of America	*Bureau* (of) Envelope Manufacturers (of) America
Commission for Relief in Belgium	*Commission* (for) Relief (in) Belgium
District of Columbia Paper Manufacturing Co.	*District* (of) Columbia Paper Manufacturing Co

11a. Index and file Boards of Trade and Chambers of Commerce by location.

Name	**Index and File**
Boston Chamber of Commerce	*Boston* Chamber (of) Commerce
Board of Trade Cleveland Ohio	*Cleveland* (Ohio) Board (of) Trade
Chamber of Commerce of Newark	*Newark* Chamber (of) Commerce

11b. Names of institutions, corporations, associations, etc., which incorporate the words "City," "Town," "State," or similar words as the first word of title are indexed and filed as written. Do not reverse. See also Rule 18.

Name	**Index and File**
City of Boston Realty Trust Co...	*City* (of) Boston Realty Trust Co
City Investing Co. of Chicago ...	*City* Investing Co (of) Chicago
County of Norfolk Fire Ins. Co. .	*County* (of) Norfolk Fire Ins Co
State & City Realty Co. of Baltimore....................	*State* (&) City Realty Co (of) Baltimore
Town of Lancaster Dry Goods Co.	*Town* (of) Lancaster Dry Goods Co

12. The name of an organization which is part of a larger organized group is indexed and filed under its individual name and cross referenced under parent organization, if desired. See Rules 6, 6a and 7.

Name	**Index and File**
Azure Lodge A.F. & A.M........	*Azure* Lodge A F (&) A M
Camp Roosevelt of Boy Scouts of America.....................	*Camp* Roosevelt (of) Boy Scouts of America
John Pershing Post of World War Veterans	*Pershing* John Post (of) World War Veterans

13. Names of hospitals, schools, colleges, hotels, libraries, banks, and similar institutions are indexed and filed under distinctive titles. If title is not distinctive, location may be prefixed. This is also good practice to overcome congestion under any common names beginning with corporate titles. Cross reference if desired.

Name	**Index and File**
Peter Bent Brigham Hospital....	*Brigham* Peter Bent Hospital
Broad Street Hospital	*Broad* Street Hospital
Hospital for Joint Diseases......	*Hospital* (for) Joint Diseases
Lakeside Hospital..............	*Lakeside* Hospital
Katherine Gibbs School.........	*Gibbs* Katherine School
University of Maine	*Maine* University (of) (optional)
Spence School for Girls.........	*Spence* School (for) Girls
Bancroft Hotel.................	*Bancroft* Hotel
Hotel Gotham	*Gotham* Hotel
Francis Scott Key Hotel.........	*Key* Francis Scott Hotel
Astor Library..................	*Astor* Library
Carnegie Library, Westwood	*Carnegie* Library Westwood
Free Public Library of Newark ..	*Newark* Free Public Library (optional)
Enoch Pratt Public Library......	*Pratt* Enoch Public Library
Chase National Bank New York .	*Chase* National Bank New York *New York:* Chase National Bank (optional)

Citizens National Bank of Baltimore	*Citizens* National Bank (of) Baltimore *Baltimore:* Citizens National Bank (optional)
Commercial National Bank of Austin Texas	*Commercial* National Bank (of) Austin Texas *Austin* (Tex): Commercial National Bank (optional)
Corn Exchange Bank Trust Co. Chicago	*Corn* Exchange Bank Trust Co Chicago *Chicago:* Corn Exchange Bank Trust Co (optional)
First National Bank of Auburn Maine	*First* National Bank (of) Auburn Maine *Auburn* (ME): First National Bank (optional)
Old Colony Trust Co. Boston	*Old* Colony Trust Co Boston *Boston:* Old Colony Trust Co (optional)
Third National Bank of Cleveland	*Third* National Bank (of) Cleveland *Cleveland:* Third National Bank (optional)
Banco Di Napoli, Italy	*Italy:* Banco Di Napoli (optional)
Lazard Freres	*Lazard* Freres
Lloyds Bank Ltd	*Lloyds* Bank Limited

14. Receivers, Guardians, Trustees, etc., are indexed and filed under names of individuals or organizations for whom they act, and permanent cross reference is made for the name of receiver, guardian, etc.

Name	**Index and File**
Flora Grimm, Admx .... Estate of Lee Grimm	*Grimm* Lee Estate (of)
	Cross Reference
	Grimm Flora Admx See *Grimm* Lee Estate (of)
Anna H. Swift, Guardian .... Robert S. Campbell	*Campbell* Robert S
	Cross Reference
	Swift Anna H Gdn See *Campbell* Robert S
C. D. Thompson Receiver for.... Carnegie Foundry Co.	*Carnegie* Foundry Co

	Cross Reference
	Thompson C R Receiver See *Carnegie* Foundry Co
Arthur N. Boering Trustee ...... under Trust of Theodore H. Keller	*Keller* Theodore H Trust
	Cross Reference
	Boering Arthur N Tr See *Keller* Theodore H Trust

15. Names of firms doing business under two titles are indexed and filed under the more active or important name and a permanent cross reference is made under the other name. This would include

a. Change of name due to successorship.

Name	**Index and File**
Turnbull & Evans .... Successors to Borden & Turnbull	*Turnbull* (&) Evans
	Cross Reference
	Borden (&) Turnbull Succeeded by *Turnbull* (&) Evans

b. Proprietors' and Trade Names

Name	**Index and File**
William Farley, Prop. .... A & J Garage	*A* (&) J Garage
	Cross Reference
	Farley William (Prop) See *A* (&) J Garage
Ess Bee Garment Co. .... (Einstein & Behrman)	*Ess* Bee Garment Co
	Cross Reference
	Einstein (&) Behrman See *Ess* Bee Garment Co

c. Doing business as, sometimes written d/b or d/b/a, Trading as, Operating as, and/or, etc.

Name	**Index and File**
Max Eigeld Jensen .... d/b/a Ace Van Lines	*Ace* Van Lines
	Cross Reference
	Jensen Max Eigeld See *Ace* Van Lines

M. Ivan and L. Orval .... Tr/as Miller's	*Miller*'s
	Cross Reference
	Ivan M See *Miller's* *Orval* L See *Miller*'s
Frank Gaglioro .... Oper/as The Italian Tavern	*Italian* Tavern (The)
	Cross Reference
	Gaglioro Frank See *Italian* Tavern (The)
Healy's, Inc. and/or .... Healy's Special Tours	*Healy's,* Inc
	Cross Reference
	Healy's Special Tours See *Healy's,* Inc
J. Mandel & Sons Co. .... &/or Standard Furniture Co.	*Mandel* J (&) Sons Co
	Cross Reference
	Standard Furniture Co See *Mandel* J (&) Sons Co

III. GOVERNMENT

16. Federal departments are indexed and filed under "United States Government" and are subdivided by name of department. In small files and records this rule may be varied. For example, there are many independent agencies which may be grouped under United States Government or filed as the name reads.

Name	**Index and File**
Home Owners Loan Corp........	*United* States Government: Home Owners Loan Corp *Home* Owners Loan Corp (optional)
Social Security Board	*United* States Government: Social Security Board *Social* Security Board (optional)
United States Dept. of Agriculture	*United* States Government: Agriculture (Dept of)

Name	Index and File
United States Collector of Internal Revenue	*United* States Government: Treasury (Dept): Internal Revenue (Coll of)

17. Names of States, Cities, Counties, Towns, etc. are indexed by name of location subdivided by departments. In small files and records, this rule may be varied.

Name	**Index and File**
Town of Berwick	*Berwick* Town (of)
City of Boston	*Boston* City (of)
Borough of Manhattan	*Manhattan* Borough (of)
State of New York	*New York* State (of)
Probate Court Norfolk County	*Norfolk* County: Probate Court
Commonwealth of Pennsylvania	*Pennsylvania* Commonwealth (of)

18. Phrases such as "Bureau of," "Board of," "Commission for," "Department of," "District of" are placed after the word they modify and are disregarded in indexing and filing. See also Rule 11.

Name	**Index and File**
New York Board of Aldermen New York City	*New* York City (of): Aldermen (Bd of)
Commission for the Blind New York State	*New* York State (of): Blind (Comm for the)
Department of Education New York State	*New* York State (of): Education (Dept of)
United States Department of Justice	*United* States Government: Justice (Dept of)

19. Names of foreign governments are indexed under name of country subdivided by department or bureau.

Name	**Index and File**
Dominion of Canada Department of Agriculture	*Canada* Agriculture (Dept of)
Republic of France Department of the Seine	*France:* Seine (Dept of the)

IV. NUMERALS

20. Captions beginning with numerals of *one or two digits* are read in units and tens, and the numeral is indexed and filed as one word. Consider only lowest number in captions beginning with inclusive numbers.

Name	**Index and File**
5 Cent Souvenir Company	*Five* Cent Souvenir Company
10 East 4th Street Garage	*Ten* East Fourth Street Garage

28 West End Ave. Store	*Twenty Eight* West End Ave Store
86 Madison Ave. Realty Co.......	*Eighty Six* Madison Ave Realty Co
92-96 W. 18th St. Corp.	*Ninety Two* (96) West Eighteenth Street Corp

Captions beginning with *three or four digits* are read in hundreds and the numeral is indexed and filed as one word.

Name	**Index and File**
100 Broadway Corporation	*One Hundred* Broadway Corporation
630 Fourth Street Corp..........	*Six Hundred Thirty* Fourth Street Corp
706 Chestnut St. Company	*Seven Hundred Six* Chestnut Street Company
1000 Lexington Ave. Corp.......	*Ten Hundred* Lexington Ave Corp
1198 Park Ave. Corp.	*Eleven Hundred Ninety Eight* Park Ave Corp

Captions beginning with *five or more digits* are read in thousands or hundred thousands and the numeral is indexed and filed as one word. The word "hundred" is supplied when called for in reading the last three digits.

Name	**Index and File**
11675 Commonwealth Ave. Garage	*Eleven Thousand Six Hundred Seventy Five* Commonwealth Ave Garage
28000 University Ave. Co.	*Twenty Eight Thousand* University Ave Co
32026 Bay Shore Rd. Corp.......	*Thirty Two Thousand Twenty Six* Bay Shore Rd Corp
61005 Monadnock Ave. Corp.....	*Sixty One Thousand Five* Monadnock Ave Corp
200000 Strong Committee.......	*Two Hundred Thousand* Strong Committee

20a. Captions beginning with numerals spelled in full or abbreviated are indexed and filed as if spelled in full. Numerals of *two or more words* are indexed as one word.

Name	**Index and File**
4th Ave. Corp..................	*Fourth* Avenue Corp
96th St. Bldg. Associates.........	*Ninety Sixth* Street Bldg Associates
182nd St. Building Corp.........	*One Eighty Second* Street Building Corp
One Hundred W. 72nd St. Corp..	*One Hundred* West 72nd St. Corp
One Hundred Twenty-four E. 91st St. Inc.	*One Hundred Twenty Four* East 91st Inc
One Fifty Broadway Corp........	*One Fifty* Broadway Corp

One Eighty Second Ave. Inc......	*One Eighty* Second Ave Inc
Two Ninety Nine Park Ave.......	*Two Ninety Nine* Park Ave

V. ABBREVIATIONS

21. Abbreviations are indexed and filed as if spelled in full. See also Rule 6a.

Name	**Index and File**
Amer. Paper Bag Co.............	*American* Paper Bag Company
Ave. B Theatre.................	*Avenue* B Theatre
E. 59th St. Garage..............	*East* Fifty Ninth Street Garage
Wm. Foster, Inc.................	*Foster* William Incorporated
L. I. Railroad Co................	*Long* Island Railroad Company
La. Securities Co. New Orleans ..	*Louisiana* Securities Company New Orleans
Nat'l. Audit Company...........	*National* Audit Company
No. 11 E. 48th St. Corp..........	*Number* Eleven East Forty Eighth Street Corporation
Penna. Iron & Steel Products Co.	*Pennsylvania* Iron (&) Steel Products Company
R. R. Bldg. & Loan Assn.........	*Railroad* Building (&) Loan Association
Ry. Signal Corp.................	*Railway* Signal Corporation
R. E. Title & Trust Co...........	*Real* Estate Title (&) Trust Company
Jos. St. Clair Coal Co............	*Saint Clair* Joseph Coal Company
S. Central Park Corp............	*South* Central Park Corporation
St. Car Conductors' Union.......	*Street* Car Conductors' Union

21a. "Co," "Inc," "Bros," "Son," "Mfg," "Ltd," and "Corp" are indexed and filed as if spelled in full.

Name	**Index and File**
Childs Co.......................	*Childs* Company
Hartley Mfg. Co................	*Hartley* Manufacturing Company
Smith & Bros...................	*Smith* (&) Brothers

Correct Filing Arrangement

Henderson Lanning (&) Co	Loft George L
Henderson Ltd (Limited)	Loft Inc (Incorporated)
Henderson Locke Corp	Loft John J

21b. In foreign firm names abbreviations of Company, Brothers, etc., are indexed and filed as if spelled in full.

Name	**Index and File**
Cie Generale Transatlantique	*Compagnie* Generale Transatlantique

Duval Cie	*Duval* Compagnie (Company)
Fernandez & Cia	*Fernandez* (&) Compania (Company)
Fernandez Hnos	*Fernandez* Hermanos (Brothers)

21c. Abbreviations of fraternal, welfare and similar organizations including government agencies are indexed and filed as if spelled in full.

Name	**Index and File**
A A O N M S	*Ancient* Arabic Order of Nobles of the Mystic Shrine
A B S	*American* Benefit Society
A F & A M	*Ancient* Free & Accepted Masons
A F M	*American* Federation of Musicians
A I B	*American* Institute of Bankers
A & I O K M	*Ancient* and Illustrious Order Knights of Malta
A O F	*Ancient* Order of Foresters
A O H	*Ancient* Order of Hibernians
A O U W	*Ancient* Order of United Workmen
A R C	*American* Red Cross
B P O E	*Benevolent* & Protective Order of Elks
B S A	*Boy* Scouts of America
C F of A	*Companion* Foresters of America
D A R	*Daughters* of the American Revolution
D of L	*Daughters* of Liberty
D O H	*Degree* of Honor
D of P	*Degree* of Pocahontas (Improved Order of Redmen)
D of R	*Daughters* of Rebekah
D of V	*Daughters* of Veterans
F of A	*Foresters* of America
F & A M	*Free* and Accepted Masons (now obsolete)
F F A	*France*-Foresters of America
F O E	*Fraternal* Order of Eagles
G A R	*Grand* Army of the Republic
G I A to B L E	*Grand* International Auxiliary to Brotherhood of Locomotive Engineers
G S A	*Girl* Scouts of America
G U O of O F	*Grand* United Order of Odd Fellows
H of J	*Heroines* of Jericho
I B P O E W	*Improved* Benevolent & Protective Order of the Elks of the World
I C A	*Independent* Companions of America
I O B A	*Independent* Order of Brith Abraham
I O B B	*Independent* Order of B'nai Brith
I O D St G	*Independent* Order of Daughters of St. George
I O G T	*Independent* Order of Good Templars
I O O F	*Independent* Order of Odd Fellows (M. U. added-Manchester Unity)

I O O L. . . . . *Independent* Order of Odd Ladies
(M. U. added-Manchester Unity)
I O S St. G . . . . *Independent* Order Sons of St. George
K of P . . . . *Knights* of Pythias
K of T . . . . *Knights* of Tara
K T . . . . *Knight* Templars
L G A R . . . . *Ladies* of the Grand Army of the Republic
L O M . . . . *Loyal* Order of Moose
M A S E . . . . *Massasoit* Assn. of Stationary Engineers
M C O F . . . . *Massachusetts* Catholic Order of Foresters
M S I . . . . *Mutuo* Soccorso Italiana
M V M. . . . . *Massachusetts* Volunteer Militia
N D I . . . . *National* Daughters of Isabel
N E O P . . . . *New* England Order of Protection
O of A . . . . *Order* of the Amaranth
O D H R. . . . . *Order* der Hermann Soehner (Order of the Sons
of Herman)
O E S . . . . *Order* of the Eastern Star
O S B . . . . *Order* of the Shepherds of Bethlehem
O S C . . . . *Order* of the Scottish Clans
O U A M . . . . *Order* of the United American Men
O of V . . . . *Order* of Vasa (Vasa Ordern)
P of H . . . . *Patrons* of Husbandry
P J . . . . *Princes* of Jerusalem
R A. . . . . *Royal* Arcanum
R & S M . . . . *Royal* & Select Masters
S P R S . . . . *Sublime* Princes Royal Secret
S W V . . . . *Spanish* War Veterans
T A B . . . . *Total* Abstinence & Benevolent Society
U O P F . . . . *United* Order of Pilgrim Fathers
U S W V. . . . . *United* Spanish War Veterans
W S D B . . . . *Workmen's* Sick and Death Benefit
Y M C A. . . . . *Young* Men's Christian Assn.
Y P S C E. . . . . *Young* People's Society of Christian Endeavor
Y W C A. . . . . *Young* Women's Christian Assn.

VI. ARTICLES, PREPOSITIONS, ETC.

22. Article "The" included as part of title is disregarded in indexing and filing. If initial word, it is placed at the end.

Name	**Index and File**
The Castle Hat Company.	*Castle* Hat Company (The)
Hart The Florist.	*Hart* (The) Florist

Exceptions: In corporation names the foreign article is indexed as written. See Rules 6 and 9. Also "Ye," old form of writing "The," is indexed as written.

23. "And," "&," "of," "for," "on," "to," "by," etc., are disregarded in indexing and filing, but not omitted in writing titles.

Name	Index and File
Avon-by-the-Sea Hotel...........	*Avon* (by-the)-Sea Hotel
Committee of Seventy...........	*Committee* (of) Seventy
Croton-on-Hudson Amus. Co. ...	*Croton* (on)-Hudson Amusement Co
Davis and Lawrence Co..........	*Davis* (and) Lawrence Co
Dawson & Meade, Inc.	*Dawson* (&) Meade Inc
Home for Blind	*Home* (for) Blind
Home of Childhood.............	*Home* (of) Childhood
House of the Good Shepherd....	*House* (of the) Good Shepherd
Pusey & Jones	*Pusey* (&) Jones
Society for Ethical Culture.......	*Society* (for) Ethical Culture

Exceptions: Foreign prepositions are indexed as written. See Rules 1a, 6, 7 and 10 etc.

24. Apostrophe s ('s) indicating possessive case is not considered in indexing and filing.

Correct Filing Arrangement

Baker A R
Baker's Book Shop
Baker Charles

24a. S apostrophe (s') is considered in indexing and filing.

Correct Filing Arrangement

Girl Scouts
Girley John
Girlow William
Girls' Friendly Society
Girls' Home
Girlum Howard

VII. ADDRESSES

25. Local addresses ending with word "City" are indexed and filed as if name of city were spelled in full.

Name	Index and File
W. K. Emerson 10 Post Office Square City.....	*Emerson* W K 10 Post Office Square Boston Mass
National City Company City	*National* City Company New York N Y

25a. Addresses containing name of building as well as street and number are indexed and filed by street and number.

Name	Index and File
Standard Oil Company Equitable Building 120 Broadway N Y C..........	*Standard* Oil Company 120 Broadway New York N Y

25b. Street addresses embodying more than one number are indexed and filed by the lowest number.

Name	Index and File
Harrison & Treflow 10-12 Martin St...............	*Harrison* (&) Treflow 10 Martin St

25c. Arrangement of different addresses for the same name is alphabetic by city. If city name is duplicated, index and file next by name of state.

Correct Filing Arrangement

Western Foundry Co Birmingham Ala
Western Foundry Co Connellsville Pa
Western Foundry Co Newark N J
Western Foundry Co Newark Ohio

VIII. FILING ARRANGEMENT

26. Surname or single titles when used alone precede the same surnames having initials or given names. See Rule 4a.

Correct Filing Arrangement

Kurzman's
Kurzman .... (Madame)
Kurzman .... (Mrs)
Kurzman A
Kurzman George H

27. The following list shows correct arrangement of a group by secondary filing word or initial.

INDEX	- *and* -	FILE
Smith		A
		Albert
		B
		Benjamin
		Brothers
		C
		C A
		C Albert
		C (&) B

INDEX - *and* - FILE

Charles
Charles (&) Henry Jones
(See Rule 8)
Charles A Co
Charles Benjamin
Charles Brothers
Charles C
Charles Coal Co
Charles (&) Company
Charles Cutter
Charles F
Charles H
Charles Henry
Charles Inc
Charles Irving
Charles Ltd
Charles Robert
Charles S
Charles Samuel
Charles (&) Sons
Charles Stewart
Chester
Chester B
Clark Co
Coal Co
Company
Corner Market
Crawford H
D
Daniel
David A
David Woolen Co
David Y

¶1500 Tickler Systems Can Be Your Best Ally

Every secretary should be aware that a reliable and infallible system of reminders is essential to every law office. Failure to take legal action at the proper time could have serious consequences. Relying solely on the memory of office personnel is not only inefficient, but could also result in a malpractice action. Most malpractice insurers require that a firm have a double method of reminder or calendar systems.

In some smaller law firms, the reminder system, or *tickler system,* as it is more frequently called, may be as simple as a desk calendar. In larger firms, it may be as complex as a computerized calendar and docket control system.

The purpose of this section is to introduce you to different types of tickler systems so that you can find one that can be adapted to the particular needs of your work. A court docket system which reminds attorneys of scheduled court trials, motions, and other hearings, is discussed in ¶1506. If your firm is already using a tickler system, you may wish to review it to determine if it can be improved, or if it needs total revamping. If your firm presently does not have a reliable tickler system, it would be beneficial to convince the responsible person of the necessity of having a dependable tickler system.

¶1500.1 Tickler System Applications

There are many potential applications of a tickler system. They include:

Approaching Deadlines An approaching deadline should be announced well in advance of the actual day, for example, a three-month reminder, a one-month reminder, and so on, depending on the matter. A tickler system is designed not only to meet deadlines, but to avoid the disruptions and inefficiencies that accompany frantic, last-minute efforts.

Periodic Tasks Almost all practicing attorneys have some periodic responsibilities (either weekly, monthly, quarterly, or annually) that cannot be overlooked. A tickler system provides a reminder to do the task and then advances to the next duty period. This helps ensure that nothing is forgotten. Use a tickler card fully by not only putting the date and the task on the card, but also names and addresses, client and matter numbers, phone numbers, file numbers, docket numbers, and any useful information that will help complete the task as soon as the card appears.

End-of-Day Matters This tickler card can be used as a simple reminder of things to take home or do before leaving the office. For example, it might remind the attorney to take home a particular file because he or she has a meeting the next day with a client concerning that file.

Correspondence Every piece of correspondence, both incoming and outgoing, should be accompanied by some tickler file activity. Prompt responses to incoming mail and methodical follow-up on outgoing letters move cases and please clients.

Future Matters Use the tickler system for any day in the future even if it is one or two years away. Put it in the system and get it off your mind.

Confusion Minimizers Rather than the attorneys accumulating files on their desks of things to do, make a list of those files and the items to be done in the tickler file, and file away those files. They only serve to overwhelm and confuse the attorneys.

Client Activities Attorneys have a certain number of clients for whom they handle regular routine matters. If these matters are put in a tickler system, they are less likely to be forgotten. For example, put a tickler card in the file to remind your attorneys to prepare the annual meeting of shareholder minutes for each year in advance. This will help them remember to do this routine task. Be sure and put the reminder several days prior to the time that the task needs to be done.

Memory Improvers If your attorneys have problems remembering names, jot down the names of the people they meet. Or put their business cards in the file to appear at a certain time when they can contact them to establish rapport. Have them put certain bits of information on the cards that are useful to recall and can make a favorable impression upon a potential client.

Also, if your attorneys are trying to remember certain information, such as the amount of the exemption of gain on the sale of a personal residence, put the information on a tickler card that will appear regularly. When the facts have been memorized, put the card away.

Idea Accumulators Have your attorneys get in the habit of jotting down ideas whenever they think of them. Ideas are like slippery fish: They get away if we don't reduce them to paper. Have your attorneys carry a couple of tickler cards in their calendars or Daytimers™ just for those unpredictable times when they get an idea. Or you might put a certain task on a card and insert it in the file every few days so that they can add new ideas to it.

Seven basic tickler systems are described in the following section: the Card Tickler, the Tickler Memo, the Follow-up Files, the Statute Book, the Periodic File Review, the Diary and Court Calendar System, and the Automated Calendar System.

¶1501 The Card Tickler System

The Card Tickler is the simplest type of reminder system and has been used in many law offices for years. One of the reasons for its popularity is its practicality. Materials needed for this system are 3 × 5 index cards, numbered divider guides (numbered 1 through 31), monthly dividers and a metal filing box.

To use this system, you should arrange the numbers in chronological order and place the monthly dividers behind the last numbered day (30 or 31). When you schedule a deposition, obtain a court trial date, schedule a board of directors meeting, or need a reminder to your attorneys to complete a particular document, fill out a blank index card, noting the task, the pertinent date, the client name, file, and matter number. Then insert the card behind the appropriate monthly divider. If it is within the current month, file it under the proper numbered date tab. If it is in another month, file it behind the monthly divider in chronological order. You may want to use daily dividers for three or four months, and then after that to insert the card behind the monthly divider rather than a numbered card behind the monthly divider. You may want to expand your tickler system to cover more than one month at a time.

Be sure and give yourself additional reminders in advance of certain dates so that you may remind your attorneys to make the necessary preparations.

For the purpose of reminding the attorneys of the expiration of statutes of limitations, you may use this system by adding index dividers for subsequent years to place behind your monthly reminders. The use of special colored tabs for these very important dates is helpful.

If you are setting up a larger tickler system for several attorneys and paralegals, it is important to make sure that there is centralized control over the system to avoid confusion. Distribute a memorandum to all personnel fully explaining the system and enlisting everyone's cooperation. Have the attorneys or paralegals use the tickler request form to have particular dates calendared (see Figure 1501-1). If your firm relies on the system heavily, you might consider having preprinted tickler cards made. This system can be varied or expanded to meet the needs of your firm.

¶1502 The Tickler Memo

The Tickler Memo system is one of the most convenient and reliable reminder systems. It is also one of the least time-consuming methods.

Basically, it uses a pretyped form that lists routine services that are usually performed by your attorneys. You simply check the more common matters that need to be followed up, such as particular legal documents that need to be prepared or reminders of important dates. Moreover, this form can be expanded for use in complex matters by adding more blanks, or it can be redesigned for your firm's particular practice (see Figure 1502-1).

The Tickler Memo is then placed in an expanding legal-size file, or in numbered file folders under the approppriate reminder date. The file should be checked daily. The Tickler Memo is then removed from the tickler file and clipped to the relevant file and given to the appropriate person to take the necessary action.

¶1503 Follow-Up System

This system is merely a variation of the card tickler system in which a particular piece of correspondence or other paperwork is placed in the appropriately numbered file folder for follow-up on the noted date. It is sometimes called a "suspense" file. The file folders are handled similarly to the card tickler system in that 31 folders marked 1 through 31 are prepared, together with dividers for subsequent months. They are checked daily.

The main disadvantage to this system is the necessity for creating an extra copy for the follow-up file and the inconvenience of handling additional sheets of paper. This system may be more efficiently used as a supplement to any other reminder system. It is very useful in following up on routine correspondence, court filings, registered mail, collection letters, or interoffice correspondence to which a reply has been requested.

Tickler Request

To: ______________________________
(name of secretary or calendar clerk)

From: ______________________________
(name of attorney or paralegal)

Date: ______________________________
(current date)

Re: ______________________________
(client name) (client no.)

Date(s) To Be Calendared: ______________________________

Reminder: ______________________________

____

____

____

____

____

Date received by secretary or calendar clerk: ______________________________

Date returned to attorney/paralegal above: ______________________________

Signed: ______________________________
(secretary or calendar clerk)

Figure 1501-1. Tickler Request.

Tickler Memo

Client Name: ______________________ **Client No.:** ____________
Responsible Attorney(s): ________________ **Date:** ____________

Reminder:

________ Appointment with ______________________________
________ Meeting scheduled with __________________________
________ Deposition of ___________________________________
Place: ____
Date: ______, Time: ______, Confirmed with opposing attorney ____
________ Interview with (witness name) ____________________
________ Response to demand letter due.
________ Statute of Limitations expires ____________.
________ File Complaint.
________ Check service of Complaint.
________ Answer due (30 days).
________ File Amended Complaint.
________ Enter Default Judgment.
________ Extension of time expired.
________ File P's/D's* Interrogatories to P/D.
________ File P's/D's Answers to P's/D's Interrogatories.
________ File P's/D's Requests for Admissions.
________ File P's/D's Answers to P's/D's Requests for Admissions.
________ Pre-trial hearing set; Date: ________, Time: ________.
________ Hearing set; Date: ________, Time: ________.
________ Jury/Non-jury** trial set, Date: ________, Time: ________.
________ Judgment recorded.
________ Post-judgment proceedings ____________.
________ Bill Client.
________ Close file.
________ Follow-up.

Notes: ____
____
____
____

*** P = Plaintiff/D = Defendant (circle one).** **** Jury/Non-Jury (circle one).**

Figure 1502-1. Tickler Memo.

¶1504 The Statute Book

A Statute Book is a ten-year diary with one individual page for each month in each year. The only dates that are entered are the dates the statute of limitations expires for particular causes of action, the dates failure to complete service of process statutes run on lawsuits, and the dates a mandatory dismissal for failure to prosecute statute runs on a given lawsuit. It is not necessary for you to completely understand this, because it is the attorney's responsibility to tell you what dates to calendar. If you are ever in doubt, ask your attorney.

To avoid forgetting these important dates, your attorney should instruct you to enter them in the Statute Book immediately upon completion of the initial client interview and after the file has been prepared. When a new client leaves your attorney's office, ask your attorney if there are any dates that you need to calendar, such as dates relating to the statute of limitations. The statute of limitations is merely the time within which the attorney has to file a lawsuit. They vary for different types of matters. After you calendar a date, either make a notation in the file or make a notation on the New File Memorandum of that particular file. In any event, putting a notation that the date has been calendared in writing assures the attorney the matter has been taken care of.

¶1505 The Periodic File Review

A Periodic File Review system is a method whereby the attorneys review clients' files at a regularly scheduled time, preferably once a month but certainly not less than once every three months. The system's main purpose is threefold: to close out inactive and completed files; to extract current file information regarding future billings; and to ensure that the client is kept up to date on the status of the file. A Periodic File Review system in itself is not a complete and efficient reminder system. This system should be used in conjunction with another tickler system.

Another variation of this type of system is the practice of reviewing files on a periodic basis by calendaring all the firm's files to be reviewed routinely. However, because of the time-consuming nature of the system, this type of system is more suitable to a small law office.

¶1506 The Diary and Court Calendar

The Diary and Court Calendar system is perhaps the simplest reminder system. Caution should be taken to use it in conjunction with another reminder system and not to rely solely on this system. The diary can be an appointment book or an attorney's daily journal or calendar. Many printing firms offer variations of this type of diary or daily journal. A calendar pad that shows a "month at a glance" is preferred by some attorneys. Whatever diary or calendar you use, make sure it is kept up-to-date with new dates being calendared immediately.

The problem with using a Diary and Court Calendar system by itself is that oftentimes the diary does not have a sufficient amount of space in which to calendar numerous files. Therefore, it is best to use the diary specifically for noting court dates, depositions, hearings, meetings, and office appointments. Many small offices have a master calendar. Usually this calendar is placed on the wall within view of all attorneys. Some people find this to be unsightly and prefer not to put it in view of the clients. Moreover, this may become somewhat cumbersome to administer in larger law offices.

If your attorneys are frequently out of the office for meetings or appointments, it is helpful for them to carry a pocket appointment book which duplicates dates noted on your office diary or calendar. It is important to make sure the dates and other items are calendared in both the pocket calendar and the office calendar.

There are many variations of the calendar system. One method frequently used by larger law firms is the Memorandum Calendar system. The responsible paralegal or associate checks the local legal newspaper and extracts the trial calendar dates of the attorneys in the office. Then a memorandum is prepared noting the pretrials, trials, and motions scheduled (including date, time, court, department or division, and the presiding judge). This memorandum is distributed to all the attorneys and paralegals in the firm (see Figure 1506-1).

Once the trial calendar is distributed, a follow-up Reminder of Calendar Call is distributed to the appropriate attorneys just prior to the set date. The attorneys are requested to note the action taken at each calendar call and file the notice in the pleading or transcript file.

This system may vary from court to court depending upon the local court's method of notifying attorneys of court dates. In some states, court dates are set upon a written request from the attorneys and notification is made by mail. In other states, it is necessary to consult the local legal newspapers.

¶1507 The Automated Calendar

Surprisingly enough, if you have a good manual system and then decide to automate, you should have no problem. The main difference is that you will be inputting information into the computer that you will be

Daily Court Calendar

Court: Superior Court of Washington County **Date:** January 11, 1980

CASES			ATTORNEYS
Before Judge Smith			
Civil Non-Jury Motions Calendar			
Monday, January 14, 1980—9:30 a.m.			
6th	B-53479	Randy Richmon v. D.H. Earle & Co., Inc., et al.	D. Brown/S. Ames
Monday, January 21, 1980—9:30 a.m.			
8th	C-20748	Daniel Ross v. Kathy Lawrence & Ben Lawrence	K. Waters/G. Fisher
Before Judge Anderson			
Civil Jury Trial Calendar			
Week of January 28, 1980			
Calendar call will be at 9:30 a.m. on Monday, January 28, 1980. Any case not answered at the call of the calendar will be dismissed for want of prosecution. Requests for continuances must be made in writing by Tuesday, January 22, 1980. Judge Anderson requests that you not call his office; for calendar information call J. Howell. Any case in which service has not been perfected will be dismissed unless good cause is shown to do otherwise.			
5th	C-37925	Dorothy E. McRae, et al., v. William B. Richards	V. Johnson/S. Ames
15th	C-37987	Gilbert H. Jones v. Carroll Management Company	D. Brown/F. Lewis
Before Judge Mundy			
Civil Non-Jury & Motions Calendar			
Tuesday, January 22, 1980—11:00 a.m.			
3rd	C-21107	Baker Co., Inc., v. Martin Bros. & Co., Inc.	T. Earle
7th	C-22190	Mrs. Roy Albert Day v. Teele & Albertson Contr.	K. Waters/F. Lewis
17th	C-31101	Lee Franklin, et al., v. Broad St. Printers, Inc.	T. Earle/J. Macey

Figure 1506-1. Daily Court Calendar.

able to retrieve for each particular day. The retrieval will be easy and there will be less chance for error. Software can be obtained for this purpose. (See list of software vendors in Figure 1507-1.)

Aid Data Systems, Inc.
Post Office Box 750
Millersville, Maryland 21108
(301) 987-6822

Alpine Datasystems, Inc.
8043 S.W. Cirrus Drive
Beaverton, Oregon 97005
(800) 547-1837

Barrister Information Systems Corporation
One Technology Center
45 Oak Street
Buffalo, New York 14203
(716) 845-5010

Cognition Corporation
2160 Broadway
Boulder, Colorado 80302
(303) 440-3541

Compute-R-Systems
5165 Campus Drive
Plymouth Meeting, Pennsylvania 19462
(215) 825-7500

Custom Management Systems, Inc.
187 Office Plaza Drive
Post Office Drawer 10588
Tallahassee, Florida 32302
(904) 878-5155

Cybernetics Resource Corporation
10 Maple Street
Port Washington, New York 11050
(516) 883-7676

Data Law Company
6341 S. Troy Circle
Suite E
Englewood, Colorado 80111
(303) 790-8193

Figure 1507-1. Automated Calendar Control Programs.

Dickens Data Systems, Inc.
3050 Holcomb Bridge Road
Suite A
Norcross, Georgia 30071
(404) 448-6177 or 446-0255

Inmagic, Inc.
238 Broadway
Cambridge, Massachusetts 02139
(617) 661-8124

Law Management Systems Ltd.
420 Sun Life Place
10123-99 Street
Edmonton, Alberta T5J 3H1
Canada
(403) 423-2675

Lawtomation
TYCON Courthouse
2070 Chain Bridge Road
Suite 140
Vienna, Virginia 22180
(703) 790-8900

Legal Data Systems, Inc.
50 Franklin Street
Boston, Massachusetts 02110
(617) 426-1040

Legal Decision Systems, Inc.
145 Soo Line Building
5th & Marquette Avenue
Minneapolis, Minnesota 55402
(612) 338-2585

MCM Systems, Inc.
750 Third Avenue
New York, New York 10017
(212) 883-6520

Micro Craft, Inc.
2007 Whitesburg Drive
Huntsville, Alabama 35801
(205) 534-4190

Figure 1507-1. (continued)

Royce-Edward Systems
5101 N.W. Gateway Drive
Kansas City, Missouri 64151
(800) 821-8637

Figure 1507-1. (continued)

You will merely add new data to the system each day and the computer will sort it out and put it in the appropriate location for retrieval at a later date. You can obtain daily, weekly, monthly, semimonthly and yearly reports. The computer can print out a report for distribution to the entire firm on a daily or other basis for just one attorney. The computer will sort and retrieve the data according to your instructions.

¶1600 You Can Assist Your Attorney in the Law Library

Learning your way around the law library is a must. Its books are the tools of the trade for your attorneys. Your attorneys must interpret the way the law is applied to the facts of each client's case. They do this by researching the law and finding *precedents,* or that which was law *before,* and how it affects that which comes *after.* If your attorneys have a case involving an injury relating to a glass door in a rented apartment, they will want to look at all the past cases involving glass doors in rented or leased property and try to find a case with similar facts or facts that support the legal theory they are trying to apply. Precedent is also referred to as *stare decisis,* which is the doctrine that when a court in the same jurisdiction has once laid down a principle of law as applicable to a certain set of facts, it should adhere to that principle, and apply it to all future cases (*Black's Law Dictionary,* West Publishing Company, p. 1577).

¶1601 How Law Books Are Cited

A *citation* is reference to an authority that supports a statement of law or a quotation source.* A citation may also be a writ or summons issued by the courts, but that type of citation is not related to legal research references. When an attorney writes a brief, a memorandum of law, or an opinion letter, he or she will reference the citation following the statement of the law. To cite a law book or other legal authority there are uniform rules which are set forth in the small hand-size paper-bound pamphlet entitled *A Uniform System of Citations* published by the Harvard Law Review Association in Cambridge, Massachusetts (13th edition). It is commonly called "the Harvard citator." You should check with your state's supreme court rules to see how the forms of citations are required in the appellate courts.

**Legal Secretary's Encyclopedic Dictionary,* Mary A. De Vries, Prentice-Hall, 3rd edition, 1982.

¶1602 Easy Guide to Citations

Most of your typing of citations will be in briefs, law memoranda, and opinion letters. If your attorneys specialize in litigation, you will do a lot of typing of citations.

The important thing about typing citations is that they be done correctly and accurately. You should check and double check the citation. If at all possible, take the citation and refer to the book itself to make sure that the reference is correct.

A citation has three or more parts. Many citations fall into the following category:

24 U.S.C.A. 23

In this example, the first two numbers represent the volume number of the book or reference, the letters represent the name of the book or authority referenced, and the last two or more letters are the page number.

Citations reference the following:

1. Statutory sources:
   Constitutions;
   Statutes (or laws);
   Codes;
   Regulations.
2. Reports of cases in official and unofficial reporters.
3. Secondary sources:
   Encyclopedias;
   Books;
   Periodicals.

Citations are found in opinion letters, memoranda of law, briefs, and in the end section of supporting documents that accompany motions. In briefs, citations appear as footnotes, and in summary form *(table of authorities)* at the end.

There are so many ways of citing authorities that it is impossible to cover them all. Again, the best book available on the subject is *A Uniform System of Citations,* published by the Harvard Law Review Association; it is commonly referred to as the "Blue Book." It is important to check your own supreme court rules to determine how to cite the official state reports in appellate briefs. This chapter attempts to give you some basic guidelines to follow when typing citations.

Official and Unofficial Reports All of the opinions of the highest state courts and the United States Supreme Court, and many of the opinions of the appellate courts, are published both in official and unofficial reports. The official report is the publication under the direction of the state reporter, and is always recognized by the courts.It is the preferred cite. However, the unofficial reports are the reporters in the *National Reporter System* that are usually cited after the official report and are published much sooner than the official reports. For example:

official cite: 45 Ga. 88
unofficial cite: 89 S.E. 98

The first cite is volume number 45 of the Georgia Reports at page 88. The second cite is the 89th volume of the Southeastern Reporter at page 98 (see Appendix J, Guide to the National Reporter System).

Codified and uncodified form Codification is a process of collecting and arranging the laws of a country or state into a code, i.e., into a complete system of positive law, scientifically ordered, and promulgated by legislative authority. When laws are passed, they are then systematically arranged into the codes for the state or federal jurisdiction. Until they are codified, they are known as *slip laws.* There are two types of codes: *annotated* and *unannotated.* Annotated codes include references to cases at the end of the code section.

¶1602.1 Statutory Sources

These sources are constitutions, statutes, codes, and administrative regulations.

¶1602.1.1 United States Constitution Citations to the U.S. Constitution give article, section, and clause number, but dates are only shown for prior constitutions. For example,

U.S. Constitution, Article X, Section 9, Clause 7

or

U.S. Const. Art. X, §9, Cl. 7

¶1602.1.2 State Constitutions Citations to state constitutions contain four parts:

1. the jurisdiction or name of the constitution, usually abbreviated;
2. the article or amendment number, usually in Roman numerals preceded by the abbreviation *art.* or *amend.;*

3. the section, chapter, or clause number, if applicable, in Arabic numerals;
4. the date of the constitution in parentheses if it is no longer applicable. For example:

U.S. Const. Amend, XIV
Ga. Const. Art. III, §3, cl. 8

The punctuation is minimal; no comma is used between the name of the constitution and the article or amendment number. You may capitalize *Art.* and *Amend.* You may also use the abbreviation *Sec.* if you do not have a section symbol on your typewriter or word processor. You can type the section symbol on a typewriter without such a key by typing a capital S, backspace, turn the platen up slightly and strike another S. Or you may type the capital S, backspace, and strike a lower case s on the same line.

¶1602.1.3 Federal Statutes When a statute that is uncodified has been passed and has not been published, in the *Statutes at Large* or in the *United States Code,* it is referred to as a *slip law.* The citation appears in the following order: (1) name of statute, if known; (2) public law number; (3) chapter and section number, if applicable; (4) the congress that passed the law; (5) published source, if the slip law itself is not available; and (6) date of enactment in parentheses, if necessary. For example:

Arms Agreement, Pub. L. 84-89, 78th Cong.,
2nd Sess. (June 25, 1985).

When a statute is found in the *Statutes at Large,* the information appears in the following order: (1) name of statute if applicable; (2) chapter and section number of the statute if applicable; (3) volume number of the *Statutes at Large* in Arabic numerals; (4) the official abbreviation *Stat.;* (5) the number of the page on which the law begins, but not the word page or its abbreviation; and (6) the date of the *Statutes at Large* edition in parentheses. For example:

National Wildlife Preservation Act of 1984, c. 58, 89 Stat. 2311 58

or

National Wildlife Preservation Act, 89 Stat. 2311 (1984)

Uncodified federal statutes are cited as follows: (1) volume number of the code, in Arabic numerals; (2) name of the code abbreviated—U.S.C. (United States Code) or U.S.C.A. (United States Code Annotated); (3) section number of the code; (4) date of the codification or date of the code volume when necessary in parentheses; (5) any needed supplementary information, including identification of the codification in parentheses and other information as needed, such as the original session law number. For example:

31 U.S.C.§18
31 U.S.C.§18 (1960)
32 U.S.C.§18 (1960), as amended
(Supp. III, 1964).

The citation *U.S.C.A.* is the United States Code Annotated.

¶1602.1.4 State Statutes State statutes appear in both uncodified and codified form. Each state has its own unique way of citing its codes. For example:

In Georgia, a state statute is cited:

Ga.Code Ann. § 12-2080

whereas, in Kentucky, it is cited:

KRS 201.00(5)

Check with your attorneys to find out the method used in your state. Citations generally include: (1) name of the state compilation, in abbreviated form; (2) year of the session, usually not preceded by a comma; (3) chapter, title, or section number of the law (capitalize the abbreviation for *No.* or *Number);* (4) page number, using "page" if it immediately follows a section number; and (5) additional information, if needed, in parentheses. For example:

Minn. Acts 1969, No. 123 at 89

Citations to state code compilations usually appear in this order: (1) name of the state compilation, properly abbreviated; (2) number of the statute; (3) date of the compilation, usually in parentheses; and (4) additional information, if necessary, in parentheses. For example:

Minn. Stat., Arts. 1911 (1942)

Your attorneys might omit the name of the state in which they practice. For example:

Stat., § 239.34 instead of Maine Stat., Sec. 239.34

¶1602.1.5 Administrative Regulations The regulations of federal administrative agencies are cited to the *Code of Federal Regulations* (C.F.R.O.) to the Federal Register (Fed. Reg.) or to the exact form in which they were originally issued. For example:

22 C.F.R.	§393.9 (1985)
44 Fed. Reg.	§54999(1984)
Treas. Reg. 119,	§29.04 (1966)

The numbers preceding *C.F.R.* and *Fed. Reg.* denote the volume numbers of the reference; the last number is the page on which that statute begins in volume 44.

¶1602.2 Cases

Citations to cases include either official or unofficial reporters. A brief explanation of case citations follows.

¶1602.2.1 Title of the Case Always cite the name of the case as it appears in the running head of the report, not as it appears at the beginning of the opinion. The first word of a litigant's name is never abbreviated. A case may be entitled: *Goede v. Johnson.* The first name is the plaintiff, the second is the defendant. The case is either italicized or underlined. In cases that do not involve two opposing parties, they are cited: *In re Harris* or *In the matter of Harris.* Only surnames appear in the case title, but for business, the full name of the business appears, such as: *Morgan Computer Company v. Jones.* However, they may be abbreviated such as *Morgan Computer Co. v. Jones.* If the *United States* is a party, it is spelled out in full: *Keller v. United States.* Never substitute the initials of a government agency or a labor union for its full name in briefs. However, you may do this in other legal documents. For example:

Watson v. EEOC.

The proper form of the case may be lengthy, such as *Harold P. Pugh, Plaintiff-Appellee, v. Georgia Power Company, a Georgia Corporation, Defendant-Appellant, and Mark Citrin, Defendant-Appellee,* but it can be shortened to *Pugh v. Georgia Power Co.* Sometimes the term *et al.* may appear at the end of the citation. It is a Latin term which means "and others." So instead of typing the entire list of defendants or appellants, you may cite the first surname and then type *et al.* For example:

Pugh v. Georgia Power Co., et al.

When a case is in the lower courts (not appellate courts), the first name is the name of the plaintiff, and the second is the name of the defendant. When the court reaches the appellate division, as in the example, the plaintiff becomes the appellant and the defendant becomes the appellee. In other words, what has happened is the defendant lost the case in the lower courts and appealed the case to the higher court and thus became the initiator of the suit, or appellee. Thus, the plaintiff became the appellant. However, the plaintiff could have lost the suit and appealed it to the higher courts, thus becoming the appellee and the defendant became the appellant. In the appeals court, the first name of the case can be compared to the plaintiff in a lower court.

¶1602.2.2 The Reports and Reporters To cite cases found in reports, identify the case as follows: (1) volume number, (2) official abbreviation of the reporter title, and (3) page number at which the opinion begins. For example:

13 Ga. 234 (1942)

¶1602.2.3 Parallel Citations Both the official and unofficial reports should be cited if available. Cite the official report first. For example:

13 Ga. 234, 23 S.E. 897 (1973).

This case can be found in the *Georgia Reports* and the *Southeastern Reporter.*

The *National Reporter System* is recognized as the unofficial cite. This system of reports publishes the opinions of the federal courts and the courts of every state, those of several states being published in the same bound volume. (See Appendix J for list of reporters in the system.) These reports are unofficial reports of the courts usually published before the official reports. Some states use the *National Reporter System* as the official report. West Publishing Company publishes these reports. The Lawyer's Cooperative Publishing Company also publishes the decisions of the United States Supreme Court, called *Supreme Court Reports,* Lawyer's Edition, which is cited as *L.Ed.* The *National Reporter System* publishes *Advance Sheets,* which are opinions recently passed that have not been published in the bound volumes. These are published in weekly pamphlets. Official reports in some states have advance sheets. This allows attorneys to keep up to date of the court's opinions. The page numbers in the advance sheets are the page numbers that will appear in the bound volumes when they are published.

An additional page number occasionally follows the first page reference, as 13 Ga. 234, 237. The first number is the page where the case begins; the second page number is where that particular part of the case is referenced. Use the designation 2d when you are citing a case out of the second series of that volume. For example:

23 Ga. 289, 23 S.E.2d 811 (1964)

is not the same as

23 Ga. 289, 23 S.E. 811 (1964)

¶1602.2.4 Date The date is usually shown at the end of the citation although some attorneys put the date between the title of the case and the volume reference. Some attorneys do not show the date of the decision of the reference unless it is relevant to the argument. For example:

23 La. 239, 34 S.E. 99 (1973)

or

Modden v. Laxton, (U.S.D.C., D.IOWA, Cent. DIV., 1973) 299 F.2d 899

or

Modden v. Laxton, (U.S.D.C., D.IOWA, Cent. DIV) 299 F.2d 899(1973).

¶1602.2.5 Jurisdiction and Court Show the jurisdiction in parentheses preceding the date where the name of the reporter such as the *Southeastern Reporter,* does not indicate the jurisdiction. For example:

Jennings v. Reagan, (La. 1947) 133 S.E.2d 123, 125.

Show the name of the court deciding the case if it is not the highest court in the state. For example:

Ween v. Colleen Ferrington, (Ga. App. 1982) 204 S.E.2d 422.

¶1602.2.6 Circuit Courts The citations for the federal courts must include the circuit in parentheses. For example:

Nestles Candy Company v. Mary Graves, (D.C. Cir. 1959) 33 F.2d 500.

¶1602.2.7 District Courts Cases decided in the federal district court should show the district, but not the division in parentheses. For example:

Sooner Oil Company v. Ky, Ry (W.D.Ky. 1955) 12 F.2d 635.

¶1602.2.8 Unpublished Cases When the case has not been published in the official reports, but will be later, cite the name of the official report, preceded and followed by blanks. For example:

__Ga. __, 23 S.E.2d 38.

If the case has not been reported, cite by name, court, date, and the docket number, if known.

Bullard v. Bullard, Fulton County Superior Court, August 16, 1982, Civil Action File No. 23445-82.

Always use proper abbreviations for the courts, especially for the lower state courts, whose names vary. Use the abbreviation listed in *A Uniform System of Citations.*

¶1602.3 Secondary Sources

Secondary sources include legal encyclopedias, periodical articles, and books and treatises on law.

¶1602.3.1 Legal Encyclopedias The parts of citations to major legal encyclopedias include: (1) the volume number of the encyclopedia, in Arabic numerals; (2) the official abbreviation for the publication, as *Am.Jur.* for *American Jurisprudence,* or *C.J.S.* for *Corp Juris Secundum,* which are the two major legal encyclopedias; (3) the title of the article cited; (4) page and section numbers; and (5) the date of the edition.

77 Am.Jr., Automobiles § 23 (1985).

¶1602.3.2 Periodicals The citation to articles published in legal periodicals includes: (1) last name of the author, without first name or initial; (2) title of the article; (3) volume number of the periodical, or year if the volume number is unknown; (4) name of the publication, usually abbreviated; and (5) number of the page on which the article begins; and (6) year of publication, in parentheses, unless it has previously been cited.

Hudspeth, *Negligence of Landlords,* 83 Emory L. Rev. 33 (1983).

¶1602.3.3 Law Review Articles To cite law reviews, type the volume and page number and the year. You may underscore or italicize the title of the review. Use quotation marks for the title of the article. Always abbreviate *Law* (L.), *Review* (Rev.) and *Journal* (J.). For example:

23 Harvard L.J. 234 (1933).

There are various ways of citing law reviews. Always check *A Uniform System of Citation* first. The article title may be Roman, and enclosed in quotation marks, and the periodical title may be italicized.

If a law review article is written anonymously by a student, omit the author's name and in place of the name of the article, use "Note," or "Comment," or some other title. For example:

Note, "*Kramer v. Kramer:* Child Custody," 33 *Yale* 343 (1979).

¶1602.3.4 Books and Treatises The citations to books and treatises is different from the way books and treatises are referenced in nonlegal documents, books, etc. The segments of these citations are as follows: (1) volume number, if applicable, in Arabic numerals; (2) the last name of the author or, if needed, only the first initial and the last name; (3) the title of the book, unabbreviated; (4) section or page number if necessary; and (5) usually the edition and date of publication. A long subtitle is usually not necessary because it makes the citation too lengthy. The book title is usually underlined (but not the spaces between the words of the name), or it may be italicized.

¶1602.3.5 Special Case Series There are various law report series, such as *American Law Reports* and *Law Reports Annotated.* Only certain cases are published in these books. The *Law Reports Annotated* are cited by the publication date (year), the letter of the volume (A, B, C, or D), and page. For example:

Rubenstein v. Pacific Bell, 34 F.2d 88, 1924C L.R.A. 22 (8th Cir. 1920).

An example of the *American Law Reports,* second series is:

63 ALR2d 88-92.

In parallel citations, these series follow the National Report citation. It is more common to cite these series in briefs for state courts than in federal courts. For example:

Pittman v. Sheidern, 23 La. 88, 24 S.E.2d 88, 24 ALR2d 34.

¶1602.4 Helpful Hints for Preparing Citations

Variations in the use of citations are common and result from the attorneys' preferences and the differences of court rules. Differences also come from the context of the citation. For example, those citations that are in the body of a text, especially in appeal briefs, tend to use fewer abbreviations and more spacing than citations used as footnotes. Following are rules governing variations.

1. The names of the parties to the case are always italicized except when used in a table of authorities. If you don't have the capability to italicize on your typewriter or word processor, you may underscore. It is best to underscore the *v.* as well. For example:

Gray v. Hewitt, 12 Ga. 23, 23 S.E.2d 88.

2. Title of articles in legal encyclopedia and legal periodicals or title of periodicals may or may not be italicized. Always check with the preference of your attorneys.

3. Consult your attorneys or the court rule book on whether to italicize bibliographical references, such as *ibid. (ibidem*—the same reference), *infra* (below), *supra* (above), etc. Sometimes the phrases that show the history of the case such as *certiorari granted, rev'd, aff'd, aff'g* are italicized or underlined.

4. Always check to see the accepted abbreviations in *A Uniform System of Citations,* or *Black's Law Dictionary,* or the *Blue Book.* The first word or the party name is never abbreviated.

5. Use *Co., Inc., Corp., RR., Ry., Ltd., Assn.* and *Comm.* for company names.

6. Add an *s* before the period to pluralize abbreviations. For example: *arts.* for *articles.*

7. Use *pp* for *pages.*

8. Use § for sections.

9. To save space, check to see if you can eliminate the periods from citations, such as SE2d.

10. Government agencies are typed without periods and spaces except in briefs where the full name is used. For example:

EEOC, NLRB, FTC

11. Omit the period from contractions such as *aff'd, rev'd.*

12. Spell out all names, titles, agencies, etc., in briefs.

13. When a previously cited case is referred to in the text of the brief by a segment of the title used as an adjective, underscore or italicize it. For example:

The *Kramer* case is a well-known landmark case
involving domestic relations.

However, when the reference is repeated in the same portion of the brief, do not italicize it.

14. Do not underscore words and expressions between citations of the same case relating to its history, such as *reversed* or *rev'd,* etc. For example:

In re Howard, (1985) 33 App. Div 23 Ky. Supp. 888,
aff'd on other grounds, 88 Ky. 22, 23 S.W.2d 88.

15. In briefs, the appearance of documents is important, so use spaces in the abbreviations such as 33 S. W. 2d 88. However, in footnotes, it is better to eliminate the spaces between the abbreviations such as 33 S.W.2d 88.

16. Always space between the initials of a personal name such as C. A. Brown.

17. Subdivisions of sections of statutes and constitutions are always indicated in closed-up parentheses such as "§33(b)."

18. Only italicize or underline *case* or *cases* when it is a part of the name of the case.

19. Indent the citation below the quotation if it is not a part of the quotation. For example:

"...will be arraigned on Tuesday, as the rules of the court have indicated."

Griffin Construction Co. v. Samuel (1982), 125 La. 23, 7 So.2d 88.

When it runs over one line, the following lines are indented as well.

20. Periods are not needed in citations unless they appear in the text of a document run in with other sentences. For example:

23 Mich. L. Rev. 2333 (1927)

or

Judge Holmes quoted 23 Mich. L. Rev. (1927).

24. Consult the court rules books or office form files to see what the rules are for the use of commas between the parts of the citation.

25. It is required in some instances that the title of legal encylopedias, legal periodicals and books be typed or printed in all-capital letters. For example:

3 CAL. 24, 3 LA 322 (1936).

26. It is common to capitalize the names of constitutions. For example:

U.S. CONST. amend. X.

27. Citations should appear as if they were a new sentence in the text of a brief or memorandum, preceded and ended by a period. Citations may also be preceded by commas, semicolons, or colons in running text, or they may be separated from the text in a footnote.

28. Do not enclose citations in parentheses. If it is necessary to do so and the citation includes a parenthetical phrase, then you must use brackets to indicate the parentheses within parentheses.

29. A run-in series of citations to different cases is called *string citations;* these are separated by a semicolon or, in the alternative, you may put the different citations on separate lines.

The most important thing to remember when typing citations is to make sure that you are consistent.

¶1603 Finding the Law

Finding the law is a matter of "hunt and search." Researching each book is different, but you can usually start with the table of contents in the front or the index in the back of the book, looking under the subject indicated by different words. For example, if you are looking up law involving an automobile accident, you may look under: automobile, negligence, transportation, accidents, etc. If you cannot find the information you need under one subject, try and think of other possible key words. Keep trying until you find what you are looking for.

Look in the contents of the book to see how it is organized. After you search the particular book, check the pocket parts, which are softbound pamphlets that update the book (placed in the back of the book by sliding the pocket part into a slot). Check the supplements (usually softbound books or pamphlets kept at the end of the set of books). The pocket parts and supplements note amended, repealed, or new laws on the subject.

Annotations to statutes show the court's interpretation of that particular law and are listed immediately following the statute. The annotations give citations to various cases involving that particular law. If there is no annotation you will have to look in the other books to find judicial interpretations of the cases.

¶1604 A General Introduction to the Law Library

This chapter is intended to help you find your own way in the law library, without the assistance of the librarian. The chapter is organized according to the type of books you will use most frequently. It begins with the "ready reference" books you will use often, and takes you through the federal laws, state laws, and other groups of books you might use in assisting your attorneys in the law library. Although the state books vary from state to state, in some ways they are very similar. This chapter will also identify the books by color as much as possible because when you are not familiar with the law library, it is easy to become overwhelmed; the books tend to all look alike.

The books in the law library may be divided into two basic categories:

1. primary sources;
2. secondary sources.

The primary sources are the books that hold the most weight with the court. They are the books that your attorneys will consult first and cite first as authority. They include:

1. Constitutions (both U.S. and state), codes (U.S. and state), statutes (federal and state laws), and ordinances (local laws); and regulations.

The secondary sources are books that set out the writer's interpretation of the law. Secondary sources include:

1. Legal encyclopedias.
2. Treatises—prepared by legal scholars and practice experts covering specific areas of the law.
3. Legal texts—books that usually discuss a single topic, such as bankruptcy, contracts, torts, trusts, evidence, civil and criminal law and practice.
4. Law review articles—written in law school law reviews.
5. Restatements—practical examples that explain particular fields of law.
6. Essays—Publications discussing particular areas of law.
7. Digests—detailed indices by subject on points of law covered by reported cases.
8. Citators—used to track a particular case and determine if it is still valid.
9. Case law from other jurisdictions—when your attorneys cannot find case law (precedent) to support their theory in their own state, they will consult the case law of other states to find cases. American Law Reports (A.L.R. and A.L.R. 2nd through 4th) are good quick sources to get that information.

¶1605 Ready Reference Books

1. *Black's Law Dictionary* is the legal dictionary published by West Publishing Company that gives definitions of legal words and usually cites cases that support those definitions.
2. *Martindale-Hubbell Law Directory* is a set of books that list names, addresses, specialties, and ratings of U.S. and some foreign attorneys. Law firms are listed by the state, city, in alphabetical order. The individual partners in the firm are listed first then the associates are listed next. The individual attorneys are listed in the front of the books by name. Not all practicing attorneys are listed and since it is divided by state, you must know the state to locate an individual. *Martindale-Hubbell* also contains a digest of state and foreign statutory laws with citations to the various state and foreign codes and statutes as well as brief summaries of some of them. Some Uniform Laws are in this last volume.

3. *A Uniform System of Citations*, published by *Harvard Law Review*, sets forth specific explanations of the various accepted ways of citing or listing the law (see ¶1601).
4. *Legal Secretary's Encyclopedic Dictionary*, published by Prentice-Hall, Inc., is a good reference tool for legal secretaries.
5. *The National Reporter Blue Book* and state blue books cross-reference official cites (primary) to unofficial cites (secondary). For example, if you have an official cite in the *Georgia Reports*, you can find the unofficial cite in the regional reporter. Most states have this book, which is updated regularly. There is also a set of books for all the national reporters.
6. *American Bar Directory* is a green book listing the names of attorneys in the United States.
7. *American Lawyer's Guide to Leading Law Firms* published by the American Law Publishing Corporation is a red book that lists the major law firms in the U.S. However, this book has been discontinued. You may find older copies still in your library.
8. *The Bar Register*, published by the Bar Register Company, Inc., Summit, New Jersey, is a green book of selected law firms.
9. The *State Bar Directory* is a directory of the law firms and attorneys in one particular state. These directories are usually published by state bars and are different in each state.
10. *Legal Research in a Nutshell* is published by West Publishing Company. This is a small guide to legal research.
11. *How to Find the Law* published by West is a good general guide to research and writing.
12. *Law Dictionary for Nonlawyers* published by West is a handy dictionary for legal secretaries and paralegals.
13. *Webster's Collegiate Dictionary*.
14. *Court Rules* are state, county, and federal court rules to be consulted as to appropriate court procedures and deadlines for filing and serving court papers or pleadings.
15. *The Lawyer's List* published by The Law List Publishing Co., Inc., Danbury, Connecticut, lists counsel of general corporations and trial practice.
16. *Lawyer's Register By Specialties and Fields and Directory of Corporate Counsel*, published by the Lawyer's Register Publishing Company, Folon, Ohio.

You might also be sent to the library to locate horn books, which are the popular law school books on specific subjects.

¶1606 Guide to Statutes and Codes

Each state has a set of state *codes* or *statutes* annotated which are reprints of laws enacted by the state legislature. These annotated code books usually have a reprint of the state constitution.

The United States Code Annotated contains the Constitution of the United States and the laws enacted by the Congress of the United States. There are two annotated versions of the U.S. Code: U.S. Annotated, published by West, (cited U.S.C.A.) and U.S. Code Service (cited U.S.C.S.), published by Lawyer's Cooperative.

If your attorneys are looking for laws in another state, you can usually find them at the state law library, bar association or large county law libraries and law school libraries. (*Note:* Most court rules require citation to the code or statute rather than the annotated section.) The section number is the same. For example, 26 U.S.C.A. would be cited as 26 U.S.C., etc.)

¶1607 The Reporter System

The *National Reporter System* is the "unofficial" reports of the court's opinions; the "official" citation is the publication of the state reporter system. *For example:* Georgia Reports (cited Ga.). The National Reporter System which is published by West Publishing Company contains the opinions of the federal courts and the courts of every state, with several states published in one single bound volume. (See Appendix J for the names of the reporters, how they are cited, and the courts listed for each.) The series also includes a second series of books (for example, 82 South Eastern 2d. 43). The reporters contain a table of all cases reported, followed by a separate table for each state. In the back of the reporter there is a digest of the cases reported in that volume, arranged according to subject. The name and location of the attorneys are given preceding the opinion.

The *National Reporter System* is updated weekly with pamphlets known as *Advance Sheets.* Advance sheets are also provided for some of the official state reports. These advance sheets keep your attorneys informed of the law immediately. Many attorneys review these sheets as they come in. The page numbers used in the advance sheets are the page numbers that will appear when it is published.

The *Key Number System* is a method of referencing to the *American Digest System,* a guide to other cases dealing with the same matter. They refer to the headnotes used in the reporters. For example, the headnote is "Criminal Law 1024(1)" and this same subject matter can be found in other reporters under the same key number.

There are seven regional reporters that cover the following states:

1. *Pacific:* Washington, Oregon, California, Idaho, Nevada, Montana, Wyoming, Utah, Arizona, New Mexico, Colorado, Kansas, Oklahoma, Alaska, Hawaii.
2. *North West:* North Dakota, South Dakota, Nebraska, Minnesota, Iowa, Wisconsin, Michigan.
3. *South West:* Texas, Missouri, Arkansas, Kentucky, Tennessee.
4. *North East:* Illinois, Indiana, Massachusetts, New York, Ohio.
5. *Atlantic:* Maine, Vermont, New Hampshire, Connecticut, Rhode Island, Pennsylvania, New Jersey, Delaware, Maryland, District of Columbia.
6. *South East:* West Virginia, Virginia, North Carolina, South Carolina, Georgia.
7. *South:* Louisiana, Mississippi, Alabama, Florida.

The *National Reporter System* also includes the *Supreme Court Reporter;* the *Federal Reporter,* which publishes decisions of the twelve United States Circuit Courts of Appeal (F. and F.2d); the *Federal Supplement,* which contains reported decisions of the United States District Courts (F. Supp.); *Federal Rules Decisions,* which contains decisions dealing with the federal rules (F.R.D.), the *New York Supplement,* and the *California Reporter.*

The states are not grouped according to geographical location. The publisher has attempted to group the states together with similar economic interests. The *North Eastern Reporter* includes the states with predominantly industrial interests; the *Pacific Reporter* covers the mining and grazing areas. Since this was done seventy years ago, it no longer holds true that the economic interests are the same.

The U.S. Supreme Court cases are reported officially in the *United States Reports* (U.S.), in the West system and in the *Supreme Court Reporter* (S.Ct.). The decisions of the United States Supreme Court are also published by the Lawyer's Cooperative Publishing Company. It is called *Supreme Court Reports, Lawyer's Edition* and is cited as L.Ed.

Local and trial court decisions are not published in the reporters. For example: a dissolution of marriage of a local couple will not be found in the reporter unless it went up to the appellate court level. However, many United States District court cases are reported (see Appendix J.)

¶1608 The Digest System

The American Digest System, published by West Publishing Company, is a master index to all cases in the *National Reporter System* listed by subject matter. This system is tied into the key number system. The digest contains abstracts of the cases in the *National Reporter System.*

There is a *Decennial Digest,* cumulated every ten years, superceding the *General Digest* for that period. At the beginning of each ten-year period, a new *General Digest Series* begins. Each volume of the *General* references all the cases on every topic published during the period covered by that particular volume. For example, each volume of the *General Digest Series* contains the topic *automobile.* The *General Digest* may contain forty to fifty volumes at the end of the ten-year period, which must be searched to find all the cases on this topic or whatever topic you are researching during the period since the last decennial period. The regional digests published by West are:

1. *Atlantic Digest;*
2. *North Western Digest;*
3. *Pacific Digest;*
4. *South Eastern Digest;*
5. *Southern Digest.*

There are also state digests for all states and the District of Columbia. There is one digest for North Dakota and South Dakota, the *Dakota Digest;* one for Virginia and West Virginia. There are also special digests:

1. *United States Supreme Court Digest;*
2. *Federal Digest;*
3. *Modern Federal Practice Digest;*
4. West's *Federal Practice Digest;*
5. West's *Federal Practice Digest, Second,* which contains digests of Courts of Appeals, U.S. Court of Claims, U.S. District Courts, and old Customs Court cases;
6. U.S. Court of Claims Digest;
7. Military Justice Digest;
8. Bankruptcy Reporter Digest.

The index to a digest system is contained in volumes entitled *Descriptive Word Index,* wherein the descriptive words are listed alphabetically in boldface type. The lighter type indicates the different situations involving the fact item and refers to places in the digest where cases in point may be found. The Key Number System is used here.

The digest of cases is grouped according to different points of law. Each main topic is preceded by an analysis. A table of cases, by plaintiff and defendant, is contained in each digest, with citations to the *National Reporter Systems* and to official state reporters where they have been published.

To use the digest system you first need to find the key number. To locate the key number, you can look in the *Descriptive Word Index,* look at the analysis that precedes each topic, or if you already have a case name in point, you can obtain the key numbers from the headnotes in the reporters, which correspond to the key numbers in the digests.

¶1609 Legal Encyclopedias

Encyclopedias state principles of law supported by footnote references to relevant cases in the United States. They are listed by topic alphabetically. There are two popular encyclopedias used in the U.S.: *Corpus Juris Secundum* (C.J.S.) and *American Jurisprudence Second* (Am.Jur.2d).

¶1609.1 Corpus Juris Secundum System

The *Corpus Juris Secundum System* consists of *Corpus Juris Secundum* and *Corpus Juris.* These books are divided into 430 titles. The *Secundum* contains cases cited since the *Corpus Juris* was published. However, the *Secundum* will reference the reader to earlier cases in *Corpus Juris.*

In addition to topics, these books contain judicial definitions, phrases, and maxims, also alphabetically arranged. The first and last words in that volume are shown on the back. Volume 72 of *Corpus Juris* contains a complete descriptive word index to all volumes in *Corpus Juris.* In *Secundum,* each volume has an index to the topics contained in that volume.

You may research these two encyclopedias by the following three methods:

1. *General Index*—Look in the index in the back of the volume to find the topic that you are researching. It will give the section where the topic is discussed.
2. *Words and Phrases*—Think of all the words and phrases that may describe your topic in the alphabetical list throughout the set. They will cross-reference other words and phrases.
3. *The Analysis*—At the beginning of each title is an analysis which gives the contents of the title. The topics are printed in

boldface capitals and are numbered with Roman numerals. Each topic has a subanalysis.

¶1609.2 American Jurisprudence

There are two sets of *American Jurisprudence:* Am.Jur and Am.Jur.2d. These are published by the Lawyer's Cooperative Publishing Company. They are cross-referenced to the *American Law Reports* (see ¶1607.3). These books are very similar to *Corpus Juris* and *Corpus Juris Secundum.*

¶1610 American Law Reports

American Law Reports Annotated (A.L.R.) initially were only brief statements listing other cases dealing with a particular point involved in the reported case. As the series grew, annotations were added and became more detailed and complex, making it more valuable. West's book *How to Find the Law* describes *American Law Reports 3d* as a compilation of annotations from all United States jurisdictions and where relevant cites cases outside the U.S., each a complete and detailed treatise on a practical point of current law preceded by a report in full of a modern case from a state or federal Appellate Court involving the problem annotated.

An annotation references and discusses all cases involving this particular point of law. The discussion contains an interpretation of all the rules regarding the subject of the annotation, their application to the specific fact situation, and defines relevant words and phrases.

A.L.R. digests are a set of books containing all of the digest paragraphs or headnotes which are classified by subject. The digests are referenced in the main set of A.L.R.

¶1611 Restatements

The *Restatements* explain the law in particular areas. They cover various fields of law, including agency, conflict of laws, contracts, judgments, property, restitution, security, torts and trusts. The American Law Institute is responsible for the *Restatements.* The Institute appoints committee to study and draft restatements covering specific law topics, which restate the common law. Legal scholars are appointed to be reporters for each of the restatements prepared. Although the *Restatements* are not adopted in whole by the highest appellate courts in the states, they are given a lot of weight and are referred to and sometimes approved on a section-by-section basis in the opinions of the court.

¶1612 Treatises

Treatises are prepared by legal scholars and practice experts and expound the theory of law in particular areas. They cite key cases that note the state of the law on a given point in various jurisdictions. Some of the treatises are supplemented by pocket parts and supplements. Others are contained in looseleaf binders, supplemented by new and revised pages from time to time. File these supplements as soon as they are received.

¶1613 Shepherd Citations

Shepherd Citations cites cases and statutes for federal, state, local government municipalities, administrative agencies decisions and reports, as well as legal citations of materials from legal publications such as law reviews and various other legal articles. It is a citator that refers you to cases that are similar or updates the status of particular cases, e.g., cases reversed. It is used to verify legal authorities. Before your attorneys can cite a case, they must look up the case in this citator to make sure the case is still valid.

Shepherd's is published annually and updated quarterly. In the interim sheets similar to advance sheets are published. They are later incorporated into book form.

This citator gives the history of the case and shows what happened to the case on appeal with the following abbreviations:

c = affirmed
cc = connected case
D = dismissed
M = modified
r = reversed
S = superseded

The treatment of the case refers to the decisions reached by the judiciary and is shown as follows:

c = criticized
d = distinguished
e = explained
f = followed
h = harmonized
j = dissenting opinion
L = limited

O = overruled
P = paralleled
q = questioned
v = vacated

¶1614 Comparison of Lexis and Westlaw*

Lexis and Westlaw both offer the capability of performing computerized legal research, but their coverage, format, options and pricing are different. Comparing the two is difficult, especially since each has areas in which one is superior to the other and neither has all the answers or capabilities. It would be ideal to subscribe to both systems and enjoy the best of both worlds. Since this is generally not feasible especially for the smaller firm, it is necessary to choose between Lexis and Westlaw. To determine which service will best meet your special needs and requirements you must understand what each system offers, how it works, the equipment needed, the limitations, and the cost.

The information available through Lexis and Westlaw is stored in groups of libraries and files or databases. These groups are arranged by topics, courts, government agencies and specialized collections. In general the same courts and government agencies are covered by both vendors, but their coverage is different and their collections differ significantly. Lexis and Westlaw can provide a detailed list of the contents of their systems and the dates of coverage. A chart comparing the major files is included at the end of this article in item 18.

The following is a list summarizing some of the characteristics of Lexis and Westlaw as of May 1985. Please note that any comparison of the two vendors is quickly obsolete as both vendors are changing and adding enhancements at a rapid rate.

1. Format

- Lexis is full text.
- Westlaw is full text except for the older cases in a few databases.
- The display and format you prefer will probably depend upon which system you have become accustomed to using. My observation of the two follows:

  Lexis display is good. The online directions and explanations are simple and concise. It is easy to change the format of the display and to edit searches with the Lexis dedicated equipment and the Lexis

*Reprinted with permission of Mary Anne C. Fry, Director of Information Services, King & Spalding, Atlanta, GA, May 1985.

P.C. software. Lexis cannot be accessed with standard P.C. communications software. Lexis menu display is confusing and it is not always clear which code should be entered to select the library and file. To view the Lexis menu online will cost connect time. Lexis offers different options on display format: cite—displays a list of cites; full—displays in full text format; Kwik displays part of the text surrounding the search terms; and Vari-kwik displays selective amounts of text surrounding the search term. The search term is highlighted.

Westlaw's format is different depending upon the type of software used. With standard P.C. communications software, Westlaw's is in "character mode" and the cursor keys cannot be used to edit the search. In character mode editing is accomplished by answering a series of prompts. With the Westlaw P.C. software and the WALT terminals the format is in "block mode" and the cursor keys can be used for editing. Westlaw's menu is excellent for detail and explanations. The codes to be entered to select databases are very clear, but because of the detail it is time consuming to find the desired code. It often requires viewing several screens of menus. This can be frustrating if speed is important, but there is no charge for viewing Westlaw's menu. The online charges begin when the search is executed. When you go back to the menu the online charges will stop. Westlaw offers different options of display: cite, full text, and selected portions such as head notes or summary only. One can view the selected search terms by choosing "term mode" and carriage returning. This will display similar to "Kwik" format. With either type of software it is easy to change the display options.

2. Dates of Coverage

- See the vendors for a detailed list. The dates vary for each court, agency and specialized service. Both Lexis and Westlaw provide printed brochures of their entire contents and dates of coverage.

3. Unpublished Opinions

- Lexis includes unpublished opinions.
- Westlaw captures opinions mainly published by West Publishing Co. It generally does not include unpublished opinions.

4. Key Numbers, Headnotes, Summaries

- Lexis retrieves the opinions from the courts and does not edit them. They do not include headnotes and summaries or the key numbers.
- Westlaw indexes and edits all opinions. Key numbers, headnotes and summaries are exclusive to Westlaw. Westlaw's digests are not on their system, but because of the key numbers and headnotes it can be used like a digest.

5. Shepard's

- Shepard's McGraw-Hill provides both Lexis and Westlaw with a database, but their coverage is significantly different.
- On both Lexis and Westlaw you can go directly from a case you are viewing and Shepardize it without retyping the cite.
- On both systems, Shepard's does not go as far back as the hard copy volumes.
- Neither vendor has yet developed a method of "batch" Shepardizing a list of cites. Each case must be Shepardized individually.

6. Checking Cites

- Lexis uses Auto-Cite which is published by Lawyers Co-Op. According to Lawyers Co-Op it has complete coverage of all the courts back to the 1800s. This will verify whether a cite is correct, and includes whether it was overruled, reversed or cert denied. It also includes ALR ANN.
- Westlaw has Insta-Cite which is published by West Publishing Co. It is a new Service and does not have as complete a coverage as Auto-Cite. It will accept Westlaw cites and the official cites for searches. It includes the parallel cite, the prior and subsequent case history.
- On both systems the cite verification services will provide similar results as Shephardizing and is more current than the hard copy Shepard's.

7. Searching

- Searching by key numbers, headnotes and summaries are possible only on Westlaw.
- Both vendors allow combined file searches in the Federal courts and State courts, but there are more combinations possible on Lexis. On both systems it is more expensive to perform searches in combined files.
- Both vendors use similar search language and Boolean Logic, which is a method of expanding or narrowing a search.
- Both vendors offer the ability to restrict searches with segments or proximity connectors such as: (a) restrict a search by judge, opinion, court, date and title; (b) do proximity searches i.e., a search term within so many words of another search term.
- Westlaw has a "locate" feature. A word can be located within a case after the case has been retrieved. This is not possible on Lexis.
- Lexis has a modify feature which allows you to expand or narrow your existing search request by adding connectors and words at subsequent "levels." Lexis will store the results of the different levels of modification and you can view or retrieve cases from any level.

- Westlaw does not have a modification feature, but you can get similar results from editing a search. However, Westlaw does not store the different levels of editing.
- Westlaw offers grammatical connectors such as: "within the same sentence" and "within the same paragraph." Lexis does not offer grammatical connectors and while the proximity searches have similar results, the number of words selected between terms make a difference, and it is difficult to guess the best number to select.
- Neither vendor has the ability to do "set searches." This could indicate how many times each search term appeared in the search results. It might also indicate the total titles satisfying each search term.

8. Saving a Search

- With both vendors a search can be saved after changing libraries and files or databases.
- Lexis can save the last search results after sign off until 2:00 A.M. the next day. This is per individual i.d. and at no additional charge.
- Westlaw does not save search results after sign off, but does save the search query per i.d. and until the next search is executed by that i.d. There is no additional charge for the save.
- Lexis' new service called Eclipse will allow a search to be automatically run periodically to monitor and update the results. There is an additional charge for this service. Multiple monitors can be assigned to a single i.d.
- Westlaw does not have a monitoring service.

9. Comparative Searches

- During the past 5 years both vendors have made significant changes to create uniformity, but there remain differences which do affect search results and while the same search can now be entered in both systems, it does not guarantee the same results.
- An article by Kelly Warnken entitled "All Systems Are Not Created Equal" explains the results of a comparative search study in a file with identical coverage for both vendors. The article was published in the *ABA Journal,* March 1984, vol. 70, page 87. It explains the study with the following: "in an experiment being conducted by the John Marshall Law School Library in Chicago, experienced computer searchers performed more than 100 searches through U.S. Court cases included in Westlaw and Lexis databases. In fewer than 10 searches did both systems retrieve the same cases." Warnken attributes the different search results to typographical errors. Other contributing factors are difference in indexing and the fact

that both systems do not use the same "common" words. Furthermore, Westlaw counts the "common" words when determining word proximity and Lexis ignores them. The unpublished opinions would also affect the results.

10. Equipment

Both Lexis and Westlaw are constantly adding to the list of compatible equipment and options for accessing their services. The following is the current status:

Terminals:

- Lexis rents their custom terminal (UBIQ).
- Westlaw will sell or rent their custom terminal (WALT).
- Both Lexis and Westlaw support a wide variety of personal computers used with special communications software and 1200 baud modems. Westlaw currently supports more types of personal computers than Lexis.
- Lexis requires the use of special software written specifically for accessing Lexis via a personal computer. It can only be used on those personal computers supported by Lexis.
- Westlaw has special communications software for the personal computers supported by them, but it can easily be accessed with any standard communications software such as Crosstalk.

Printers

- Lexis rents their custom printers that are:

  a. a desk top model, which is buffered to print as you continue your search. It prints on connect time, uses standard print paper, and will highlight the selected word by "bolding" it.

  b. a high speed off-line printer that prints without incurring a connect time charge (cost is 2 cents per line). This printer does not begin printing immediately after execution of the print command. There is a delay of from 5 to 30 minutes. Lexis also offers the service of requesting that the material is printed in Dayton Ohio and mailed at a cost of 2 cents per line and $1.45 for postage and handling.

- Westlaw will either rent or sell:

  a. a desk top printer which is buffered to print as you continue your search. It can hold 3 screens in its buffer, bolds the selected word and uses thermal paper.

  b. a stand alone off-line printer, which can be used with their WALT terminal or with selected personal computers and internal automated systems. Westlaw also offers "Westprint" where the material is printed in St. Paul, Minn., by West Publishing Co. and mailed to you at a cost of 2 cents per line and $15 for postage and handling.

- Personal Computers: With both services any printer that is compatible with the personal computer and software is acceptable. It should print at least 120 characters per second.

11. Vendor Support

- Both Lexis and Westlaw have good vendor support with local representatives available in most major cities.
  They each have an 800 number for customer services where they have specialists for technical support and staff attorneys for assistance in formatting legal research.

12. Training

- Both Lexis and Westlaw have formalized training programs on site and at the firm. They both encourage review and advanced training sessions. The cost will depend upon the individual subscriber agreements.

13. Online Help

- Lexis has a help feature which will offer a selection of concise tutorials. There is also assistance in determining the correct segment to use. Lexis will automatically correct minor errors such as typing "L" for "1." All of this help is charged connect time and is provided without abandoning the search.
- Westlaw has online tutorials which offer detailed lessons in using the system. There is no charge for using these, but you must abandon your search. Westlaw also has a choice of "prompts" which offer online help during the entire search. This, however, will cost a little extra in connect time.
- Both vendors offer practice databases.

14. Cost

- The pricing structure is the most significant difference between Lexis and Westlaw. Which system is the least expensive will depend upon how you use the system, what searches you perform and whether you edit the search.
- Both vendors charge monthly library subscription fees and connect time charges. If you rent the equipment the rental will also be a monthly fee.
- Lexis charges per search with the cost varying per library and file. Lexis also charges for installations and moves of rented equipment.

- Westlaw does not have a search charge, but their connect time charge is significantly higher than Lexis. Westlaw does not charge for equipment installation or moves.

15. News Services

- Lexis provides Nexis which is an online, full text news service.

  Nexis can be subscribed to as part of Lexis or separately. The vendors can provide a brochure indicating the newsletters, magazines, journals and newspapers covered.

  Lexis also offers Info-Bank which is full text articles from *The New York Times,* and abstracts from other major journals and newspapers.

  Dialog can be accessed through Lexis with a separate subscription, but the quality is very poor.

- Westlaw does not offer a news service, but you can access Dialog through Westlaw with a separate subscription. The quality is good. Dialog has over 200 databases. Two of the databases it provides have magazines and legal journals. The articles are generally abstracts.

  MCI Mail is also included as part of the Westlaw subscription. The only charges are usage. MCI Mail includes Dow Jones News.

16. Law Reviews

- Both Lexis and Westlaw offer articles in full text from selected law reviews. Lexis has the entire article from 12 major law schools. Westlaw has selected articles from 200 law schools. Westlaw provides the information necessary to order a back issue from one of the law reviews if the article is not online.

17. Specialty Databases

The following specialty databases are available only through Lexis:

- NAARS—Includes the complete financial portion of annual reports of public companies, accounting procedures, financial data and accounting standards.
- EXCHANGE—Is a collection of company and industry reports and analyses from investment banking, brokerage and research firms. It includes SEC 10-Q, 10-K and 8-K filings. Transcripts of company presentations and reports providing information on countries are also included.
- LEXPAT—Contains full text of utility patents.
- MEDIS—Full text library of medical literature.

18. Comparison of Major Files

This is a generalized overview and does not indicate all the materials that are available. Dates of coverage are not indicated.

FILES	LEXIS	WESTLAW
FEDERAL COURTS	YES	YES
FEDERAL TAX MATERIALS	YES	YES
includes CB, PRR, GCM		
TAX NOTES & TAX MEMOS		
FEDERAL SECURITIES DEC. & REGS.	YES	YES
includes SEC NO ACT LETTERS	YES	YES
FEDERAL TRADE REGS	YES	YES
FEDERAL PATENT CASES	YES	YES
full text of U.S. patents	YES	NO
FEDERAL COMMUNICATIONS DEC.	YES	YES
FEDERAL LABOR DEC.	YES	YES
FEDERAL BANKRUPTCY DEC.	YES	YES
FEDERAL ENERGY DEC.	YES	YES
FEDERAL PUBLIC CONTRACTS	YES	YES
ADMIRALTY	YES	YES
PRESIDENTIAL DOCUMENTS	YES	YES
GOVERNMENT DOCUMENTS	YES	YES
U.S. CODE	YES	YES
CODE OF FEDERAL REGULATIONS	YES	YES
FEDERAL REGISTER	YES	YES
CONGRESSIONAL RECORD	NO	NO
FEDERAL COURT RULES	YES	YES
FEDERAL RULES OF CIV. PROC.	YES	NO
FEDERAL RULES OF EVIDENCE	YES	NO
RULES OF U.S. CT OF CLAIMS	YES	NO
STATE COURTS DEC.	YES	YES
STATE CODES	N.Y., OH.	NO
STATE ATTY GENERAL DEC.	34 ST.	12 ST.
INTERNATIONAL LAW	YES	YES
selected UK & French		
DELAWARE CORP. LAW	YES	YES
SHEPARD'S CITATIONS	YES	YES
VERIFICATION OF CITES	YES	YES
ABA FILES	YES	YES
MILITARY LAW	YES	YES
FORENSIC SERVICES	YES	YES

¶1700 Understanding Real Estate Transactions

To assist in handling real estate transactions, you must have a basic understanding of real estate so that you can be confident in preparing these legal documents and instruments.

This chapter will give you some essential definitions relating to real estate and help you to properly prepare most real estate documents.

¶1701 Key Essentials about Real Estate

¶1701.1 What Real Estate Is

Real estate includes land and its permanent attachments such as grass, shrubs or trees, buildings, fences, certain fixtures, and other improvements.

¶1701.2 What Is the Difference between Fixtures and Improvements?

Generally, fixtures are permanently attached or affixed to real estate. Sometimes, what is and is not a fixture is subject to dispute. For example, a built-in stove may be a fixture if it is permanently attached to the wall and cupboards, whereas a free-standing stove that can be moved about may not be a fixture.

Fixtures include improvements such as landscaping, gutters, curbs, sidewalks, street lights, sewer systems, swimming pools, fences, and other items designed to improve and develop real estate.

¶1701.3 What Is Personal Property?

Personal property, also known as chattel property, is defined as all property which is not real estate and which is movable. Examples of personal property include automobiles, boats, jewelry, furniture, appliances, and clothing.

¶1702 Getting Familiar with Typical Methods of Ownership

By getting familiar with the typical methods of ownership, you will have a better understanding of real estate transactions. State law controls types of ownership.

¶1702.1 Fee Simple or Fee Simple Absolute

Fee simple, also known as fee simple absolute or an estate in fee, is the highest type of interest a person can have in land. It is potentially of indefinite duration, and is freely transferable and inheritable. Corporations, partnerships, individuals, trusts, or estates may own property in fee simple.

A fee simple owner may have accepted title subject to certain limitations on ownership. The most common is a life estate, which grants an owner (Ms. A) a fee simple interest during the owner's lifetime only; the owner may enjoy the benefits of fee simple ownership throughout her life. However, upon her death, fee simple title passes to the individual(s) designated by the person who conveyed the property to Ms. A.

When we speak of Ms. A as being the owner of a parcel of land, it is generally understood that she is the fee owner, i.e., she owns the land in fee, or in fee simple, or in fee absolute. Hers is an absolute ownership, and as long as she obeys the law, she may do as she chooses with her land. She may dispose of it during her lifetime, or devise it by her last will and testament effective upon her death. She may also do nothing with it and have it automatically pass on to her lawful heirs.

¶1702.2 Joint Tenancy

A joint tenancy estate is regarded as a single estate held by two or more persons as though they collectively constituted but one person, a fictitious entity. In some states, this estate is known as a joint tenancy with right of survivorship. The main characteristic of a joint tenancy is the right of survivorship. When a joint tenant dies, his or her interest in the land is terminated, and the estate continues to be held by the survivor or survivors. When there is only one survivor, the estate is held by that person in his or her right only; no other person has any interest in the real estate. Upon the death of the last survivor, titles vest in his or her heirs or devisees. (Compare ¶1702.5, Tenancy by the Entireties.)

In some states the deed is required to include the words "right of survivorship," except in the case of a deed to a husband and wife which creates an estate by the entireties.

¶1702.3 Tenants in Common

A tenancy in common is characterized by only one unity, that of possession. The cotenants own undivided interests, but unlike joint tenancy, these interests need not be equal in quantity or duration, and may arise from different conveyances and at different times. There is no right of survivorship; each tenant owns an interest which on her death vests in her heirs or devisees.

¶1702.4 Community Property

Several states have enacted legislation creating community property. This is defined as property acquired by husband and wife or either, during marriage, when not acquired as the separate property of either. Each owns one-half of community property. Typically, property that is exempt from community property includes property acquired through gift or inheritance. A marital relationship is essential to this type of co-ownership.

Some states without community property laws have adopted the concept of equitable division, which enables a court to divide property based upon certain factors, e.g., length of marriage, financial and nonfinancial contributions to the marriage.

¶1702.5 Tenancy by the Entireties

Tenancy by the entireties is a tenancy owned by a husband and wife. Neither party may convey his or her share of the property individually, and neither share may be attached by a creditor of only one of them. In some states, a conveyance to a husband and wife is presumed to be a tenancy by the entireties unless otherwise specified (compare Section 1702.2, Joint Tenancy).

¶1703 Understanding Title Procedures

¶1703.1 Evidence of Title

When property is conveyed, the owner must provide evidence of good title to the buyer. The form of title evidence may be in the form of an abstract, a Torrens certificate, a title policy, or a title opinion.

¶1703.2 Abstract of Title

An abstract of title is a record of all officially recorded transactions made concerning a certain piece of land since the real estate was first conveyed and recorded upon, to and including the current transaction.

Abstracts are usually done by title companies, although attorneys may do them. In some states title companies are allowed to examine and assist in searching records, to insure the title to the property. In such case, the title company often acts as an escrow or closing agent.

¶1703.3 Torrens Certificate

Although this system is no longer used in most states, it is important to know in case it is used in your state. It is a system of registering the land with the requisite public office. This registration is begun by the landowner who obtains a complete abstract of title to the land. The landowner then files in the proper public office an application for the registration of title. After proper consideration by the court, the court orders the registrar of titles to register the title. The registrar prepares a certificate showing the title as found by the court and issues a duplicate certificate to the owner. The owner must surrender this duplicate upon any change in ownership or encumbrances on the property. A Torrens certificate is considered to be conclusive evidence of the present ownership. The deed remains in the registrar's office.

¶1703.4 Title Examinations

Prior to a real estate conveyance, the attorney must determine if title is clear so that the seller can properly convey title to the buyer. Clear and marketable title means that the property is free from any legal defect and can be readily transferred in the marketplace. In other words, no other party can claim to have a legal interest in the property and the buyer will own the property free and clear. A defect is referred to as a *cloud on the title.*

In many instances, the buyer will obtain title insurance. There are two types of title insurance: owner's policy, which insures the owner's title to the property; and mortgagee policy, which insures the lender's interest in the property. The title insurance commitment may or may not be issued. If the title insurance commitment is issued before the closing, it outlines the clouds on the title and what problems need to be corrected before the issuance of the title policy.

¶1703.5 Defects in Title

The title opinion will reveal any defects in title (cloud in the title). A quiet title action may be necessary to clear the defect in the title and get good and marketable title. The attorney may apply for title insurance, or in the alternative, the attorney may make an examination and issue a opinion of title. The title opinion or title insurance advises the client as to the condition of the title. If there is a problem with the title, the title opinion issued prior to closing describes what action is required to correct the problem. The most typical defects in title are encumbrances, easements, encroachments, and tax sales.

¶1703.6 Encumbrances

An encumbrance is a recorded document, and includes mortgages, judgments and liens. For example, there may be an encumbrance on the property, such as a mortgage or deed of trust recorded to secure a loan obtained on the property. Another example may be a tax lien resulting from unpaid taxes on the property.

¶1703.6.1 Materialman's or Mechanic's Liens Under State Statutes A materialman or mechanic's lien is a lien filed appropriately by a person who has done work on or delivered materials to the property. Such liens are governed by statutes in most states. For example, if a cement dealer delivered and installed cement materials on a certain piece of property and he was not paid, he has a right to a lien for his labor and the amount of his materials from the owner of the property if he follows the procedure set forth in the statute. He can foreclose. If the owner does not pay this lien, he cannot sell the property without paying off the lien or it will remain as a charge on the property against the new owner.

¶1703.6.2 Judgments Judgments also must be paid before the property can be conveyed. Judgments are usually the result of litigation. The most common form of judgment is a money judgment that awards a certain sum of money due the plaintiff by the defendant.

¶1703.6.3 Tax Liens A tax lien is used by local, state, and federal governments to collect delinquent income taxes, sales taxes, federal unemployment taxes, etc. Tax liens are a charge on the property. Therefore, the seller is obligated to pay these liens before the property can be conveyed legally, or the charge will remain on the property and against the new owner. You can convey land with a lien by quitclaim deed, etc., but the seller must satisfy the lien(s) before the property is marketable.

¶1703.6.4 Easements An easement is a right granted by a property owner to use certain portions of the property, such as a utility company. Another example might be when a property owner allows a person to pass through his property, such as a driveway.

¶1703.6.5 Encroachments An encroachment will also cloud a title. An encroachment is described as a projection of a building or other structure (e.g., fence) on one parcel of land onto, or into the airspace of, an adjoining parcel of land.

An encroachment by a building or other structure that rests in part upon the adjoining land may constitute a *trespass,* whereas an encroachment in the airspace above the land of an adjoining owner may constitute a *nuisance,* for which damages may be recovered in a legal action or removal of the encroachment may be enforced by an equitable action. Many states provide that a suit for a trespass must be initiated within a certain number of years or it is barred.

¶1703.6.6 Restrictive Covenants Restrictive covenants are certain restrictions placed upon property by the owner as to the use of the property. These are primarily used by developers of subdivisions. This is used to maintain the value of the property. A covenant is a promise or agreement to do or not to do certain things which affect the appearance or use of the property.

¶1704 Common Documents of Conveyance

Transfer is an act of the parties, or of the law, by which title to property is conveyed from one person or legal entity to another person or legal entity. The term includes voluntary transfers, i.e., by act of the parties, and involuntary transfers, i.e., by act of the law. A deed is the primary means for conveying title voluntarily, although an involuntary transfer, such as an execution sale or a foreclosure sale can involve the execution of a deed. In the latter, the deed is executed by the appropriate officer of the court (such as a sheriff) instead of by the record title owner.

A deed is described briefly as a written instrument, executed and delivered, by which the title to real property is transferred from one person, called the grantor, to another person, called the grantee.

¶1704.1 What Are the Different Kinds of Deeds?

¶1704.1.1 Warranty Deed A warranty deed transfers title to the grantee and covenants and warrants that the grantor is the owner of whatever title is being transferred and that he has the legal right to transfer his title to the property and will defend that title if it is later questioned. If anyone later makes a claim against the property, the grantee can sue the grantor for breach of warranty.

There are general and limited (or special) warranty deeds. The general warranty is against all claimants. The limited warranty is against special claimants. Your attorneys will tell you which form to use in a particular case.

¶1704.1.2 Quitclaim Deed A quitclaim deed does not warrant the title of the grantor to the property against claims by any adverse parties, but simply conveys to the grantee any interest the grantor has or may have in the property. It is often used to release the interests of a mortgagee, or of a spouse in a dissolution of marriage where one party may quitclaim his or her interest in the property to give the other party full title. The grantor gives up any right he or she may have to the property.

A gift of property is often made by a quitclaim deed.

¶1704.1.3 Probate Deed A probate or fiduciary deed merely transfers property to a previous owner by a deceased or incapacitated person. A trust deed conveys property held by a trust.

¶1704.1.4 Grant or Limited Warranty Deed A grant or limited warranty deed warrants that the grantor has not previously conveyed the property to another and that the grantor has not made any liens or other encumbrances in or on the property.

¶1704.2 Who Are the Parties to a Deed?

The seller is the grantor, the one who conveys his or her interest in the property. The purchaser or recipient of the land is the grantee and is one to whom the property is conveyed. The purchaser may be the true grantee, but she also may have acquired the land for the grantee, as an agent for the purchaser. Usually only the grantor signs the deed.

The grantor or grantee is not necessarily a person. It may be a partnership or corporation. The person must not be a minor nor mentally incompetent; a guardian may sign on behalf of these individuals. This should be cited in the first part of the deed. Many states require the spouse to join in the deed; if so, the marital status of the grantor must be noted (e.g., single, widow, widower, or divorced).

In some states a deed may not name a partnership but include the individual partners' names. You would type it: Pete Barwick and Janet Hall, doing business as "Success Strategies."

In some states foreign corporations must have authority to transact business in that state. This is usually done through the Corporation Department of the Secretary of State. Check with your attorneys.

¶1704.3 Basic Elements of a Deed

1. Name of grantor;

2. Name of grantee;
3. Words of conveyance, i.e., I give, I hereby grant, sell or transfer (may include habendum clause);
4. Description of the property being conveyed;
5. Habendum clause—nature or extent of the grant—as forever, for lifetime;
6. Signature of grantor;
7. Date of execution;
8. Notary clause.

¶1704.4 Handling Revenue Stamps and State Taxes

Revenue stamps or documentary transfer stamps may be required in your state as a transfer tax. They are paid when the property is conveyed and are affixed to the deed and cancelled. In most states now a state tax is imposed as a source of revenue. Check your state laws to see if revenue stamps are still needed. If so, you may have them affixed to the deed at the registry of deeds when the deed is recorded or they may be bought by either the buyer or the seller and affixed to the deed. Only minimum stamps are required in most areas if the transfer is a gift.

¶1704.5 Recording Deeds Properly

The purpose of a recording system is to protect future bona fide purchasers for value, lenders, and others by giving constructive notice of instruments of record. Recording is said to be constructive notice of the legal owner of the property. The legal owner is called the record title holder.

Deeds do not have to be recorded to be valid between the parties to the deed and persons with actual notice of the deed. However, recording gives notice to all other persons. A deed that is not recorded is as good as one that is recorded. However, if the deed is not recorded when the seller signs the deed, a subsequent good faith buyer who has no actual knowledge of the unrecorded deed may get good title by his or her later deed that is recorded after the date of the originally unrecorded deed. The subsequent buyer without notice is known as a bona fide purchaser.

To record a deed, first find out where it is to be recorded. Ask your attorney. Type "Please record and return to" and your firm's name and address on the front cover of the printed deed or on the legal back in which the deed is bound. If the deed is not to be delivered to the local recorder's office, send a transmittal letter with the deed after calling the proper public officer, usually the county recorder, and determining the fee for recording. Some offices require that you send the letter by registered mail, return receipt requested. Be sure to describe the parties to the deed in the letter and enclose a check. Place a note in your tickler file to follow up on the deed. If it is not returned within ten days or two weeks, follow up with the designated official.

When the deed is returned, send it to the client with a cover letter, unless the attorney has been instructed to keep the deed in the files. You may want to make a photocopy of the deed showing the official recording office stamp before you mail the original to the client.

¶1705 Land: Descriptions, Surveys, and Subdivisions

The most important thing about preparing legal descriptions is accuracy. The best way to ensure this is to proofread the description with someone else in the office. It's difficult to proofread the description by yourself.

Use the legal description that appears in the deed to the present grantor if it is accurate—subject to changes given by your attorneys when only part of the property is being deeded.

¶1705.1 Understanding How Real Property Is Identified

A legal description of real property may be given by: a description of its location in a government survey (in use in about thirty states at the present time); by metes and bounds; or by reference to a plat recorded in the county recorder's office in the county where the real property is located. The following sections describe each method of legally identifying real property.

Understanding how property is identified will help you to be more accurate in copying legal descriptions. Legal descriptions must be accurate.

Property is identified according to sections and townships or by metes and bounds. Lot and block identification is used in towns and subdivisions. Never identify property by street and number only. It may be included in the legal description but is never used alone as identification.

¶1705.1.1 Government Surveys Property location in your area is described by government survey. It is divided by survey into rectangular tracts. The base lines run east and west, and the prime or principal meridians run north and south. The prime meridians are numbered, i.e., the Fourth Prime Meridian, or they are named. The rectangular tracts are then divided into six-mile squares called townships. The townships are divided in 36 sections, each one mile square, or 640 acres. The sections are numbered from 1 to 36, beginning with the section in the northeast corner of the township, proceeding west to boundary of the township; the next row is numbered from west to east. The sections are then divided into half and quarter sections, and the quarters into quarter-quarter sections, designated by their direction from the center as northwest, southwest, northeast, and southeast.

¶1705.1.2 Description by Metes and Bounds Metes and bounds descriptions detail the lines that constitute the boundaries of the property. Metes are lineal measures and bounds are artificial and natural boundaries. Natural boundaries, such as a large rock or river, often mark the corners and angles. These marks are called monuments. A description by courses and distances constitutes part of a metes and bounds description. A course is the direction from the starting point of a metes and bounds description; distance is the length of the line. A sample of a metes and bounds description is shown in Figure 1705.1.2-1.

All that tract or parcel of land lying and being in Land Lot 107 of the 18th District of Cobb County, Georgia and being more particularly described as follows:

Beginning at a point marked by a nail on the southerly line of the right-of-way of 13th Street (43 ft. right-of-way) three hundred sixty-seven and no tenths (367.0) feet westerly, along the southerly line of the right-of-way of 13th Street, from the point of intersection of the southerly line of the right-of-way of 13th Street with the westerly line of the right-of-way of Crescent Avenue, with the Point of Beginning thus established; running thence in a westerly direction along the southerly line of the right-of-way of 13th Street a distance of 177.67 feet to a point located at the southeast corner of the intersection of 13th Street and Columbia Avenue (a fifty foot right of-way); thence southerly along the eastern right-of-way line of Columbia Avenue a distance of 50 feet to an iron pin; thence east along a line parallel to the south line of 13th Street a distance of 60 feet to a point which point marks the point of beginning, said property being shown on a plat prepared by Southern Engineering dated December 18, 1984, and prepared for Ralph Newberry, which plat is incorporated herein by reference.

Figure 1705.1.2-1 Metes and Bounds Legal Description.

¶1705.1.3 References to Plats and Maps Plats are maps or plans showing the division of larger tracts of land (which larger tracts were described by metes and bounds or the rectangular survey system into numbered lots, showing streets, blocks, alleys, easements, etc.) The plat results from a survey of the tract that is platted. The plat drawing is filed in the county where the platted tract is located. Many plats are required to be recorded, especially those of subdivisions. See sample plat in Figure 1705.1.3-1.

¶1706 Acquisition and Transfer of Real Property

¶1706.1 Seller's Listing with an Agent or Broker

The first step a seller usually takes is to obtain the services of a real estate agent or broker and to sign a listing agreement for a specified period of time. The broker normally charges a fee or a commission if the property is sold during that period. That fee is usually a percentage of the selling price of the property. Ordinarily, the broker has a printed form which the seller signs. However, in some instances your attorneys may prepare a listing agreement. Usually, they will dictate it or will refer you to a form to be modified as they instruct.

¶1706.2 The Purchase and Sale Agreement

When a prospective buyer is interested in purchasing the property, he or she makes an offer to the seller or the seller's real estate agent if there is one. If the property is listed with a broker, the prospective purchaser will convey his or her offer to the broker and the broker in turn will present the offer to the seller. If the seller accepts the offer, a certain sum of money is put down which is referred to as earnest money. The agreement is then put in writing in a purchase agreement, also referred to as a purchase offer, earnest money contract, or a memorandum sale agreement. The document may be prepared by the attorney, the real estate broker, or by the parties themselves. A commercially printed form may be used in routine transactions. A more detailed agreement may be drafted by your attorneys in large commercial transactions.

¶1706.2.1 General Information Included in a Purchase and Sale Agreement The purchase agreement, which is a contract, generally includes the following information:

1. Complete names and marital status of the seller(s);
2. Complete names of the buyer(s);
3. Addresses of the buyer and seller(s);
4. Legal description of the property;
5. Property address (location);

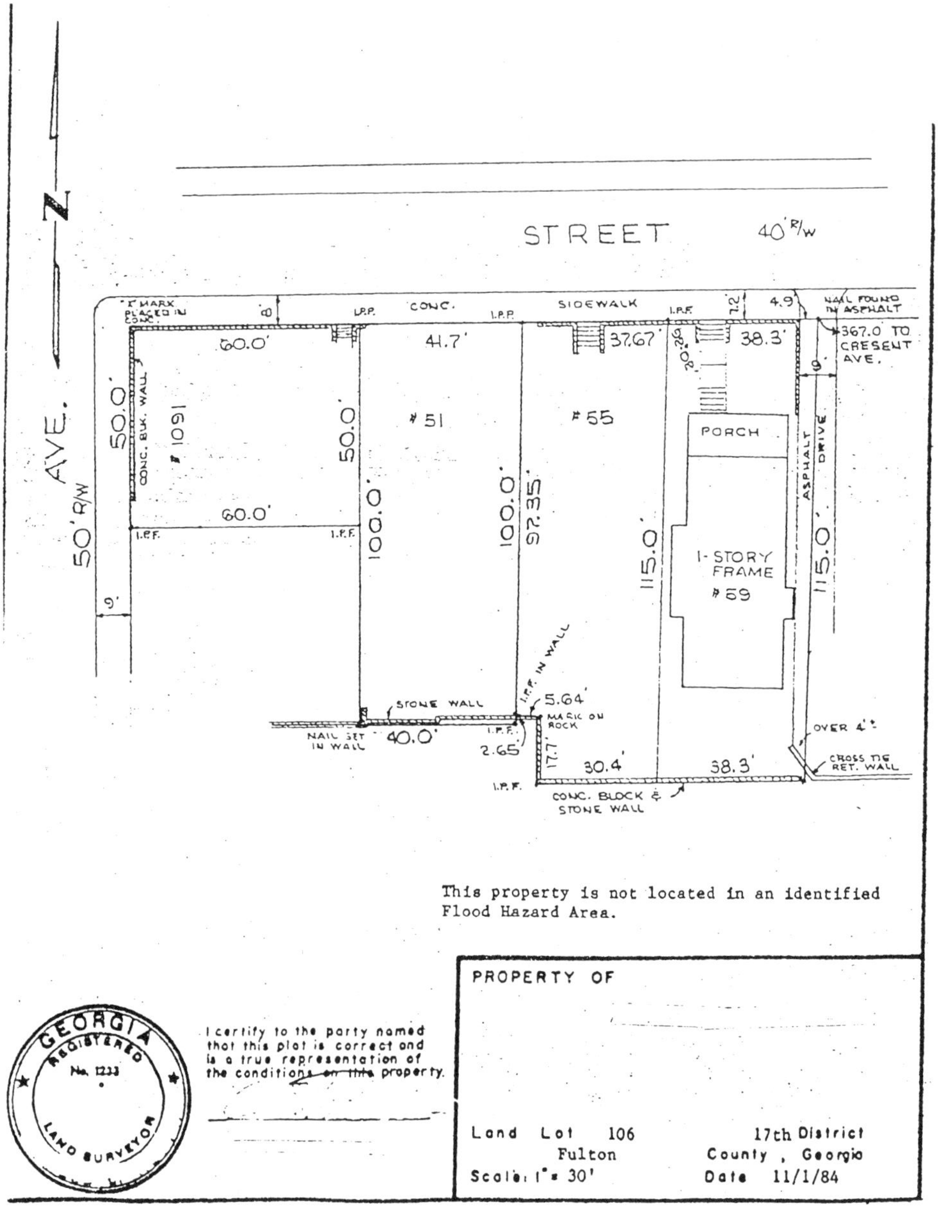

Figure 1705.1.3-1. Sample Plat.

6. Personal property to be conveyed in the transaction (appliances, drapes, window treatments, etc.);
7. Sale price of the property;
8. Financing arrangements;
9. Date of the closing;
10. Other terms and conditions of the sale.

¶1706.3 How Property Is Financed

¶1706.3.1 Conventional Financing Financing that is arranged through a bank, savings and loan association, or mortgage company is referred to as commercial or conventional financing. The interest rates are sometimes negotiable depending upon the credit rating of the purchaser and his relationship with the bank.

¶1706.3.2 FHA and VA Loans Federal Housing Administration (FHA) and the Veterans Administration (VA) financing is available to qualified persons through these government agencies. Many of these loans require a low down payment or, in some instances, none at all. The VA loans are only available to veterans and surviving spouses of servicemen who died while they were on active duty.

FHA and VA loans are made by and processed through private lending institutions, but are guaranteed by the VA or FHA. Those departments of the U.S. Government insure the local lender against financial loss in the event the buyer defaults on the loan. The Federal National Mortgage Association (FNMA), also known as "Fannie Mae," has a similar guarantee to local lenders on qualified loans.

¶1706.3.3 Loan Assumptions Many times a seller is willing to let the prospective purchaser pay him or her the amount of his or her equity in the property plus any additional negotiable amount to take over or assume the balance of the loan. It may be negotiable since banks often condition approval of an assumption upon payment of additional money or an increase in interest. Assumption of a mortgage will not relieve the original owner mortgagor from making payments if the buyer defaults unless the mortgagee (lender) consents in writing or the original mortgage provides otherwise. Check with your attorneys as to the assumption terms and conditions.

¶1706.3.4 Types of Financing Documents Types of financing documents include:

1. Installment real estate purchase contract, either with or without an escrow, sometimes called agreements for deed which is

usually treated as a mortgage in states which use it (Florida, for example).

2. Purchase money mortgage held personally by seller, executed at the time he signs a deed of the real property to the buyer.
3. Deed of trust.
4. Mortgage to lender.

¶1706.3.5 Loan Applications The buyer must submit an application for the loan processed through a lending institution. The buyer must submit a past credit history and current financial situation so that the lending institution can determine if he or she qualifies for the loan.

¶1707 Preparing Real Estate Documents

¶1707.1 Mortgages

¶1707.1.1 Defining Mortgages A mortgage is a form of security agreement in most states. The security is the real property that is described in the mortgage. A mortgage is intended to secure the performance of some act by the mortgagor, such as the payment of money, by the grantor or some other person, and is to become void if the act is performed according to the terms prescribed in the document.

¶1707.1.2 Types of Mortgages Other terms used for mortgages are: conventional mortgage, trust deed, deed of trust, deed to secure debt, trust indenture, or trust mortgage. An agreement for deed is treated as a mortgage in some jurisdictions.

¶1707.1.3 Who Are the Parties to a Mortgage? In a conventional or commercial mortgage, the mortgagor (grantor) is the debtor or borrower and the mortgagee (grantee) is the lender. The mortgagor usually owns the property that is being mortgaged and gives a mortgage to the mortgagee, usually for a loan or the major portion of the purchase price. The mortgagor is sometimes referred to as the "party of the first part" and the mortgagee is referred to as the "party of the second part" in the mortgage document.

¶1707.2 Leases

Leases may be oral or written. In most states, a lease must be in writing if it is for a year or more, if either party wants to enforce it. A lease is not considered an estate in land. It is merely a right to possess the land during the "term" of the lease.

¶1707.2.1 What Are the Various Types of Leases? A lease is the designation given to the contract by which the possession and profits of land are exchanged for rent. It conveys a right to possession of an interest in the land to the lessee, who receives possession of the property, for a period of time, which may be for the life of a party, for years, for months, or at will depending on the terms of the written lease. The word term designates the time and period of the enjoyment of possession. Rent is the return or compensation paid to the owner (lessor) for the use of property. Standard forms of leases are in common use, both as to residential and commercial properties; their formal preparation, however, should be entrusted to an attorney.

¶1707.2.2 Types of Tenancy are listed in the following:

Tenancy at sufferance Tenancy at sufferance is one in which a lessee goes into possession lawfully, but whose right to remain in possession has expired, such as a tenant holding over after the expiration of a lease, or a tenant at will whose right to possession has expired by virtue of the death of the landlord.

Tenancy at will Tenancy at will is created by agreement of the parties, but has no fixed term, and is terminable at the will of either party. Modern landlord and tenant statutes in the various states create certain notice requirements for evicting a residential tenant even if he or she is in possession as a tenant at will.

Periodic tenancy A periodic tenancy is created by the parties agreeing to possession and payment of rent for successive periods of the same length, unless sooner terminated by notice. Examples are tenancies from year-to-year and tenancies from month-to-month.

¶1707.2.3 Who Are the Parties to a Lease? The person who lets real property is known as the "landlord" or "lessor," and the person who receives possession of the property is designated the "tenant" or "lessee."

¶1708 Checklist for Residential Closings

The following is a handy checklist for residential closings. You may modify it according to the laws of your state and preferences of your attorneys.

Preliminary

- Open file.
- Order title examination and tax search.
- Attorney must review results and notify seller of any title defects and the conditions upon which to satisfy same.

- If contract has any contingencies (i.e., contract will close upon satisfaction of certain events):
  1. Set up tickler date for deadline for satisfying the contingencies.
  2. Advise attorney of contingencies.
- If loan is to be assumed, send letter to lender requesting an assumption package. (Assumption package includes conditions for assuming loan and documents to be signed in connection with the assumption.)
- If current loan is to be paid off, send letter to lender requesting payoff; include approximate date for payoff.
- Sales closing statement.
- Owner's affidavit.
- Warranty deed, quitclaim deed, or limited warranty deed.
- If purchase money mortgage, prepare note and mortgage instruments.
- Other documents may include:
  1. Assumption documents, if current loan is to be assumed.
  2. Other documents necessary to cure any title defects.
- Order hazard insurance policy and termite letter.

Preparation of Loan Closing Documents (Third Party Lender)

- Loan Closing Statement, which is ordinarily combined with sales closing statement.
- Owner's Affidavit, which may be same as the document used in sales closing.
- Borrower's Affidavit.
- Note.
- Mortgage Instrument.
- Other documents that may be required by the Lender include:
  1. Name Affidavit, if borrower has used variations of name on legal documents.
  2. Affidavit that borrower intends to reside in the home.

Post Closing

- Prepare checks to parties, lenders, and others (e.g., tax authorities, judgment creditors).
- Send documents for recording. This includes warranty deed and mortgage instrument.
- Check for proper signatures, witnessing, and notary.
- Determine recording costs and taxes that may be charged for deed.

- Prepare cover letter to clerk's office; note names and property in the caption.
- Set up tickler date for return of documents (often six weeks).
- When documents have been returned, order check down of title.
- If owner's or mortgagee's title insurance has been purchased, arrange for issuance of policies.

¶1800 The Litigation Secretary's Guide to Efficiency

If you are not a litigation secretary, most likely you will still have to handle some litigation matters, unless you are in a large firm with a separate litigation department. This chapter will give you some shortcuts to becoming more efficient in handling lawsuits and help you to become more familiar with the litigation procedures (also known as *civil procedure*).

¶1801 Job Duties

- Greet and receive clients.
- Handle telephone calls for the attorneys.
- Prepare client files and other files for the firm.
- Organize and maintain files.
- Prepare court documents (see ¶2100).
- Assist the attorneys in obtaining documents.
- Act as a notary, if required.
- Calendar due dates and maintain a tickler system (see ¶1500).
- Maintain, update, and index form files.
- Arrange for depositions, if requested.
- Obtain needed information for the attorneys.
- Prepare the following documents:

( ) attorney-client contract
( ) medical and hospital authorization (when required)
( ) interrogatories
( ) requests for admissions
( ) requests for production
( ) legal memoranda
( ) office memoranda
( ) court and appellate briefs
( ) motions
( ) subpoenas

( ) stipulations
( ) notices
( ) pretrial statements and/or settlement conference memoranda
( ) exhibits
( ) correspondence
( ) case summaries
( ) settlement brochures, if applicable
( ) requests for charge/jury instructions
( ) assist in preparation of trial book
( ) prepare affidavits
( ) powers of attorney
( ) court orders
( ) objections to discovery
( ) deposition digests
( ) demurrers
( ) complaints
( ) answers
( ) demand for bill of particulars
( ) findings of fact and conclusions of law

- Assist attorneys preparing for trial.
- Arrange for witnesses to appear at trial.
- Assist the attorneys in preparing trial book.
- Maintain firm files.
- Handle attorneys' calendar.

¶1802 Becoming Familiar with Civil Procedures

In 1934 Congress was authorized by the U.S. Supreme Court to adopt a set of court rules known as the *Federal Rules of Civil Procedure* to simplify federal court legal procedures and make them uniform from state to state. These rules were adopted by the U.S. Supreme Court in 1937, and the rules set forth the various steps in a civil proceedings in the federal district courts, including the rules for preparing court documents. They are amended from time to time. An up-to-date version of the rules should be on hand at all times.

Most of the states' highest courts have also adopted rules of civil procedure to govern the procedures in the various state trial courts.

Uniform rules for appellate court procedure have also been adopted and apply when an appeal is brought from a lower court in the federal or state system. If the lower court is a federal court, the *Federal Rules of Appellate Procedure* apply. If the lower court is a state court, that state's rules of appellate procedure apply.

There are four basic phases of civil procedure:

1. pleadings;
2. discovery;
3. trial and judgment (by judge or jury);
4. execution or settlement.

An appeal from an order or final judgment of the trial court is governed by the rules of appellate procedure.

¶1802.1 Pleadings

Pleadings consist of the written claims and defenses that are filed during the beginning of a lawsuit. The various pleadings are prepared and filed in the office of the clerk of the court which has jurisdiction to initiate the lawsuit and narrow the issues.

During this period, several pleadings are prepared: Complaint, Summons, Objections, Answer and Reply (replication). A Cross-complaint or Cross-claim, a Counter-complaint or Counter-claim, or a Third Party Complaint, Answer and Reply may also be prepared and filed by the defending parties.

The Summons that accompanies the Complaint and Objections to any of the pleadings may have to be prepared by the attorney for the moving party.

Complaint The Complaint is the first step in the initiation of a civil lawsuit. The plaintiff's attorney files a Complaint, also known as a Petition, a Declaration, or a Statement of Claim setting forth the plaintiff's causes of action against the defendant. It states (alleges) the specific acts and omissions the defendant did, plus the kind and amount of damages the plaintiff incurred as a result of defendant's alleged action or nonaction.

Summons The Summons is prepared at the same time as the Complaint and accompanies and is served on the named defendant(s) with the Complaint. It is a notice to the defendant(s) that a lawsuit has been filed.

Appearance The defendant(s) must make an appearance in person or by the defendant(s)' attorney by following the prescribed steps within the specific time limit stated in the Summons.

Objections The defendant may object to the complaint by means of a Demurrer, a motion to strike, a motion to quash, or a motion to make the Complaint more definite and certain. The purpose of these documents is to attempt to invalidate the complaint on the grounds that it is not legally valid. Many courts require that these response documents be supported by a Brief, a legal memorandum, or a memorandum of points and authorities. Some of these objections "toll" (momentarily suspend) the time for filing an answer; some do not. Check the appropriate rules of civil procedure.

Answer The Answer is the defendant's prescribed legal response to the plaintiff's Complaint if there is a valid objection as described in paragraph 4 above. In the Answer, the defendant either admits or denies the allegations made in the Complaint (provisions which set forth what happened between the plaintiff and defendant). Also, the defendant may include a Counter-claim against the plaintiff in the Answer, or the defendant may file a Cross-claim against another defendant named in the action, or the defendant may file a Third Party Complaint against a person who is not a party to the lawsuit but is involved in the facts and circumstances alleged in the complaint. Check your court rules of civil procedure if you are involved in litigation for a defendant and your attorneys want you to prepare such supplemental pleadings.

Cross-complaint or Cross-claim The defendant may make a Cross-claim or Cross-complaint against another defendant. This is usually filed with the Answer but may be a separate document. The Cross-defendant is then required to file an Answer. Many times the Cross-complaint or Cross-claim is against the plaintiff.

Third Party Complaint The defendant must prepare and serve the Third Party Complaint the same as an original lawsuit, but the number of the case in which he is the defendant is used in the caption of the Third Party Complaint.

¶1802.2 Discovery

The purposes of discovery are:

1. To narrow the legal and factual issues, thus saving the client both time and legal fees at trial;
2. To obtain basic and factual information for purposes of preparing the case for trial;
3. To ascertain the opposing party's contentions;
4. To ascertain the identity of the opposition's witnesses, including expert witnesses;
5. To ascertain, locate, and preserve demonstrative evidence and testimony;
6. To determine or prove the amount and description of damages, i.e., injury, whether to person, property, or rights;

7. To impeach the witness should his or her answers be inconsistent with his later testimony at trial;
8. To eliminate the element of "surprise," particularly with respect to evidence or witnesses at trial;
9. To hasten settlement;
10. To support a motion for summary judgment or similar dispositive motion or to lay the groundwork for obtaining other pretrial orders.

Many times during discovery, the lawsuit is terminated and the case never goes to trial. At certain points and under certain circumstances a voluntary dismissal may be filed by the plaintiff. Check your court rules of civil procedure for the time and effect of filing such a motion.

In addition to pleadings, you should be familiar with and know how to prepare:

1. Interrogatories;
2. Requests for Admissions;
3. Requests for Production of Documents;
4. Objections to Discovery;
5. Subpoenas;
6. Subpoenas Duces Tecum;
7. Motions;
8. Motion for Summary Judgment and Notices of Hearings or Other Action.

Interrogatories Interrogatories, simply stated, are questions to the opposite party. They may be questions to the plaintiff from the defendant and vice versa. Interrogatories are written and the answers must be given in writing, signed and sworn to under oath.

Written questions may also be read to a witness for oral answer in a deposition under the court rule entitled *Depositions Upon Written Questions.*

A Deposition differs from Interrogatories and Deposition Upon Written Questions in that oral questions (not necessarily planned specifically) are asked the witness who is being deposed. All attorneys are present and usually a court reporter who records the oral questions of the attorneys and answers of the person who is being deposed. The reporter produces a transcript for either or both of the parties involved in the lawsuit. (See Figure 1802.2-1 for a sample set of Interrogatories.) Compare a transcript of a deposition which you will find in a client case file for a case where depositions were taken.

IN THE STATE COURT OF DEKALB COUNTY
STATE OF GEORGIA

THOMSON CEMENT COMPANY,	)	
	)	
Plaintiff,	)	
	)	
vs.	)	CIVIL ACTION
	)	
MOPGARD PROPERTIES, INC.,	)	FILE NO. D-2730L
EDWARD K. IOWI, GARY NELL,	)	
AND DONALD MILLER,	)	
	)	
Defendants.	)	

TO: MOPGARD PROPERTIES, INC.,
and their attorney of record:

S. Samuel Shuping, Jr.
Birnbreit & Kress
230 Walnut Street, N.E.
Atlanta, Georgia 30308

PLAINTIFF'S FIRST SET OF CONTINUING
INTERROGATORIES PROPOUNDED TO DEFENDANT
MOPGARD PROPERTIES, INC.

COMES NOW PLAINTIFF THOMSON CEMENT COMPANY herein and pursuant to Georgia Civil Practice Act Sec. 33 serves upon Defendants Mopgard Properties, Inc., the following Interrogatories and requires said Defendant to answer them as provided by law and requests that said answers be served upon the undersigned attorney within the time required by law. If the whole of a question is not known, so state and answer the part known.

These Interrogatories are intended to, and shall, embrace and include in addition to Defendant and its employees, any agents, servants, representatives or private investigators or others who are in a position or who have obtained information for or on behalf of Defendant.

These Interrogatories shall be deemed continuing so as to require supplemental answers if Defendant or its attorneys obtain further

Figure 1802.2-1. Sample Interrogatories.

information between the time the answers are served and the time of the trial. Any supplemental answers are to be filed and served upon counsel for Plaintiff within thirty (30) days of receipt of such additional information.

INTERROGATORIES

1.

State:

(a) The name of the officer or agent answering these Interrogatories.

(b) The title and duties of such person; and

(c) How long said person has been employed and his or her present position.

2.

List the present employees, agents, servants or representative of Defendant who are familiar with any aspect of this case, their title and address, and the particular aspect of which they would have knowledge.

Specify in detail (including, but not limited to, names, dates, places, documents, and manner and substance of all communications, written and oral) all facts upon which you rely to support the basis of your First Defense contained in your Answer.

SANDERS, LEVIN & ASHTON
By ____________________
Hal J. Riverview

1300 South Avenue
Atlanta, Georgia 30081
658-9087

Figure 1802.2-1. (continued)

Request for Admissions The purpose of Requests for Admissions is to get the opposite party to admit to certain statements, opinions, facts, or the application of law to fact, including the genuineness of any documents described in the request. (See Figure 1802.2-2 for a sample set of Request for Admissions.) Check your court rules of civil procedure for time and manner of responding to a Request for Admission. If a fact is admitted under this procedure, your attorney need not otherwise prove it at the trial.

Request for Production According to the *Federal Rules of Civil Procedure,* any party may serve on any other party a request to produce

IN THE UNITED STATES DISTRICT COURT
FOR THE NORTHERN DISTRICT OF GEORGIA
ATLANTA DIVISION

BROWN & JONES COMPANY,	)	
a Limited Partnership by and	)	
through Alan Crew, Jr.,	)	
a General Partner,	)	
Plaintiff	)	CIVIL ACTION
vs.	)	
	)	FILE NO. C85-1675A
	)	
PAUL THUN, Defendant.	)	
	)	

PLAINTIFF'S CONTINUING REQUEST FOR ADMISSIONS
OF MATTERS AND GENUINENESS OF DOCUMENTS TO DEFENDANT

Plaintiff requests Defendant to make the following admissions for the purpose of this action only, pursuant to Rule 36 of the Federal Rules of Civil Procedure and subject to all pertinent objections to admissibility which may be interposed at the trial.

The previous Request for Admissions numbered "1" through "64" was filed on October 31, 1985, and is incorporated herein for purposes of reference. These continuing Request For Admissions shall continue as follows:

65. Said outstanding principal balance (mentioned in Request No. B-11) has not been paid by MTA.

66. Said outstanding principal balance (mentioned in Request No. B-10) has not been made by Defendant Paul Thun, as a guarantor of said "Note," or in any other capacity.

67. Said outstanding principal balance (mentioned in Request No. B-10) has not been paid by Fred Sibley, Jr., as a guarantor of said "Note," or in any other capacity.

68. Said outstanding principal balance (mentioned in Request No. B-10) has not been paid by either Maker or Fred Sibley, Jr., or Defendant Paul Thun, as principals or guarantors of said "Note."

SANDERS, LEVIN & ASHTON
By ______________________
Hal J. Riverview

1300 South Avenue
Atlanta, Georgia 30081
658-9087

Figure 1802.2-2. Sample Request for Admissions.

specific items of evidence for inspection, copying and/or testing. It also allows any party to permit any other party to enter upon designated land or other property of the responding party to inspect, measure, survey, photograph and/or test or sample the property or any designated objects on the property. During this phase of discovery, most of the documents involved in the lawsuit are produced at a specific time for the other party to examine, and in some cases photocopy or duplicate. This is generally arranged at a specific time and place, usually the office of the attorney producing the documents, and in many cases, at another place. In many states state court rules of civil procedure have similar production rules. (See Figure 1802.2-3 for Sample Request for Production.)

IN THE UNITED STATES DISTRICT COURT
FOR THE NORTHERN DISTRICT OF GEORGIA
ATLANTA DIVISION

BROWN & JONES COMPANY, a Limited Partnership by and through Alan Crew, Jr., a General Partner,	)	
Plaintiff,	)	CIVIL ACTION
vs.	)	FILE NO. C85-1675A
PAUL THUN,	)	
Defendant.	)	

PLAINTIFF'S REQUEST FOR PRODUCTION OF DOCUMENTS

TO: The above-named Defendant and his counsel of record, Richard Stone of Stone & Reinhart

A.

You are hereby requested, pursuant to Rule 34 of the Federal Rules of Civil Procedure to produce and permit the Defendant or persons acting in his behalf, to inspect and copy the documents designated hereinafter. The production, inspection, copying, and all acts necessarily related thereto shall take place at the offices of Plaintiff's counsel of record,

Figure 1802.2-3. Sample Request for Production.

Sanders, Levin & Ashton, 1300 South Avenue, Atlanta, Georgia 30081, commencing at 10:00 A.M., December 1, 1985, and continuing from day to day thereafter until said inspection, copying and related acts are completed by Plaintiff.

B.

These requests are continuing and if, at a time after said Defendant has produced the requested documents or otherwise responded hereto, further documents (called for in these requests but not previously produced) come into your possession and control, then you are requested to further respond and to produce said documents at the named location within thirty (30) days from receipt by you of such documents, and in all events prior to the time of pre-trial conference, or, if none, trial.

C.

When used hereinafter the term "the Note" shall refer to that certain Promissory Note dated April 9, 1985, being the subject matter of this lawsuit between Plaintiff and Defendant and also being described in Exhibit "A" of the Complaint filed by Plaintiff in this action.

You are requested, to bring with you, for examination by counsel for the Plaintiff in the above-styled case, at the place and on the date referred to in Paragraph "A" herein, the following designated books, papers, documents and records which are in your possession or control:

1. All correspondence, communications, memoranda, documents, and other tangible evidence relating in any way to the Defendant's contention that Plaintiff has failed to state a claim against Defendant as set out in Defendant's Answer to Plaintiff's Complaint in this action.

2. All correspondence, communications, memoranda, documents as alleged in Paragraph 5 of Defendant's Answer to Plaintiff's Complaint in this action and other tangible evidence relating in any way to Defendant's contention that the Note in question is not in default as set out in Paragraph 6 of Defendant's Answer to Plaintiff's Complaint in this action.

3. All correspondence, communications, memoranda, and documents between Paul Sibley, Jr., and yourself relating in any way to said Note.

4. All other correspondence, communications, memoranda and documents mentioned, referring to, or concerning said Note.

SANDERS, LEVIN & ASHTON
By ______________________
Hal J. Riverview

1300 South Avenue
Atlanta, Georgia 30081
658-9087

Figure 1802.2-3. (continued)

Objections to Discovery The *Federal Rules of Civil Procedure* provide that party served with the Interrogatories and/or Requests for Admission or Production may object to discovery on specified grounds. The form of objection is usually a Motion for a Protective Order.

Subpoena A Subpoena is used to summon witnesses to give testimony in court or at a deposition. It tells the person served to appear at a specified time and place, which may be at a particular office or place where his deposition will be taken or in court at the trial of the case.

Deposition Subpoena This is necessary to require a person who is not a party to the lawsuit to appear for oral questioning before trial. To take the deposition of a party, a notice of deposition sent by mail to the party's attorney in the case is sufficient service. If your attorney wants to make sure that an opposing party will be available at all times during the trial to be called as an "adverse witness," your attorney may also want you to prepare and serve a Subpoena or a Subpoena Duces Tecum on the opposing party or one of its employees who has custody of certain records.

Subpoena Duces Tecum A Subpoena to appear as previously described with an additional demand that the person subpoenaed bring with him certain documents, photographs, or other items related to the suit to the deposition or to court. For example, a bank officer may be required to bring certain bank account records to a deposition or trial.

Motion Motions may be filed during this phase or at other phases according to the *Federal Rules of Civil Procedure* and most state and local rules of civil procedure. Such motions may be Motion to Compel Discovery (i.e., require the other party to respond to the discovery request), Motion for Protective Order (i.e., to protect the party from embarrassment, oppression, or undue burden or expense), Motion to Dismiss, Motion for Judgment on the Pleadings, Motion to Strike, Motion for a More Definite Statement, or a Motion for Summary Judgment.

Summary Judgment The *Federal Rules of Civil Procedure* provide that the plaintiff may move for Summary Judgment at any time after the expiration of 20 days from the commencement of the lawsuit or after service of a Motion for Summary Judgment by the adverse party. However, a defending party may move for summary judgment at any time. Many state court rules of civil procedure have a similar provision. (See Fig. 1802.2-4 for a sample Motion for Summary Judgment.)

Form
Motion for Summary Judgment

IN THE UNITED STATES DISTRICT COURT
FOR THE ____(1)____ DISTRICT OF ____(2)____

____(3)____ DIVISION

____(4)____,	)	
	)	
	)	
Plaintiff,	)	CIVIL ACTION
	)	
	)	
v.	)	FILE NO. __(6)__
	)	
____(5)____	)	
	)	
	)	
	)	
Defendant.	)	

PLAINTIFF'S MOTION FOR SUMMARY JUDGMENT

COMES NOW the Plaintiff ____(7)____ and moves this Honorable Court as follows:

1.

That it enter, pursuant to Rule 56 of the Federal Rules of Civil Procedure (28 U.S.C.A. §156) a summary judgment in Plaintiff's favor for the relief demanded in its Complaint on the ground that there is no genuine issue as to any material fact and that Plaintiff is entitled to a judgment as a matter of law.

2.

If summary judgment is not rendered in Plaintiff's favor upon the whole case or for all the relief asked and a trial is necessary, that the Court, at the hearing on the motion, by examining the pleadings and evidence before it and by interrogating counsel, ascertain what material facts are actually and in good faith controverted, and there upon make an order specifying the facts that appear without substantial controversy and directing such further proceedings in the action as are just.

Figure 1802.2-4. Sample Motion for Summary Judgment.

Motion for Summary Judgment (Cont'd)

This motion is based upon:

(a) The pleadings, (8) (interrogatories, requests for admissions, etc.) on file with this Honorable Court in this action;

(b) The deposition of ______ (9) ______ on file with this Court; and

(c) The supporting affidavits of ______ (10) ______ attached hereto and incorporated herein by reference.

Respectfully submitted,

____

((11))

Attorney for Plaintiff

(Name, Address and
Telephone Number of Attorney or
Firm)

CERTIFICATE OF SERVICE

This is to certify that I have this day served a copy of the within and foregoing Plaintiff's Motion for Summary Judgment upon counsel for Defendant(s) ______ (12) ______.

____

______ (13) ______

____

____

by depositing a copy in the United States mail in a properly addressed envelope with sufficient postage affixed thereto.

This ______ day of ______, 19______.

____

((14))

Attorney for Plaintiff

Figure 1802.2-4. (continued)

¶1802.3 Trial and Judgment

If the case is not settled between the parties, and if there are no grounds for dismissal or default, the case must go to trial for a decision on the merits.

During this phase of the lawsuit, there are several ways in which you could be helpful to your attorney. First, make certain that the trial date is calendared for the date of the trial, and also prior to the trial in enough time to give your attorney the time needed to prepare for trial. (See ¶1806.)

Your attorneys may ask you to prepare questions for *voir dire*. *Voir dire* is a preliminary examination of a prospective juror conducted prior to the actual trial. It enables the legal counsel to determine the potential juror's qualification to serve as a juror.

An additional document you may be asked to prepare is Requests for Charge, also known as Jury Charges or Jury Instructions. These are instructions to the jury given by the judge after the closing argument. The judge's charge to the jury consists of:

1. The judge's review of the evidence;
2. An explanation of the burden of proof, i.e., which side has the burden of proving the allegations at issue;
3. A statement of the applicable law;
4. Instructions for applying the law to the facts of the case.

Some states have standard jury instructions that may be requested by number in addition to particular jury instructions.

Another important document that you may be required to prepare is a Case Summary. A Case Summary is similar to a trial preparation report wherein all the pertinent information is assembled and condensed in a readable form for the attorneys to use in their preparation for trial or for settlement negotiation. (See Figure 1802.2-5 for sample Case Summary.) The File and Case Evaluation sheet may be used for purposes of settlement negotiations or in preparation for trial. It is a composite summary of the relevant facts and issues in the case.

Prior to trial your attorneys may ask you to assist them in preparing the trial book. (See ¶1806.)

When there is no jury, the judge hears the case, applies the law, and issues a *judgment* in favor of the plaintiff or defendant based on the facts and merits of the case. When a case is heard before a jury, the jury decides in favor of one of the parties on the basis of the facts presented applying the law given them in the judge's charges, and determines the amount of damages. The judgment in civil cases is based on the

James Walter Goodman—Case Summary

Born: 1918, Savannah, Georgia

Died: October 6, 1976

Dependants: Wife: Susan Anne Goodman
Route #2
Atlanta, Georgia 30318
Married: March 14, 1956

Previous Marriage: Carolyn Sneed
Divorced, 1948, Marietta, Georgia

Military History: U.S. Navy, Chief

Medical History: Dr. William J. Jones was his physician for about 16 years. Dr. G. Braun was his physician the past five years. His general health from 1952 to 1975 was good.

3/2/55: Automobile accident which injured his left shoulder.

4/5/72: Complete physical by Dr. G. Braun. Health–Good

8/9/72: Admitted to the hospital with the flu. In January 1974 his first symptoms appeared. Suffered weakness, shortness of breath. He was admitted to South Cobb Hospital one month later for treatment of pneumonia. He was x-rayed on 10/11/72. X-ray report showed pleural calcification and mild chronic lung changes. There was no mention of interstitial fibrons, but mesothelioma was not ruled out.

Exploratory surgery revealed a bronchogenic carcinoma of the left lower lobe and a pulmonary resection (left lower lobectomy) was done. Postoperative radiation to the chest wall and lower esophagus was begun as the tumor was in close contact with these areas.

Final Diagnosis:

Asbestosis in the left pleural space. Dr. McLaughlin's progress notes show a history of fiberglass exposure, no mention of asbestos.

Workmen's Compensation: Previous case settled for $21,000. Lew Insulations. Paid by Zep Insurance Company.

Social Security: No information regarding social security benefits.

Life Insurance: $75,000 paid by Smith Mutual Life Insurance Company.

Medical Expenses:

Medicine and drugs	$ 2,245.45
Medical Supplies	1,195.21
Misc. Doctors	23,000.00
	$26,440.66

Defenses: Assumption of risk–Claimant smoked two packs of cigarettes a day from 1964 until his death.

Employment History:

Annual Salary	Date	Employer
$ 6,400.00	1952-1964	North Insulation Company
8,940.00	1965-1969	United Brothers, Inc.
11,871.00	1970-1975	Lew Insulations

Lost Wages: Total Earnings 1964-1975–$171,915.00

Figure 1802.2-5. Sample Case Summary.

Products Used:	Toyla Block Pipe Covering, Two shot cement and asbestos cloth.
Possible Witnesses:	1. Paul Warren–Foreman, North Insulation Company 9 Outer Road, Norwalk, CN 06854 2. Robert C. Butler–Coworker, North Insulation Company 890 Ridgewood Road, Atlanta, GA 30318 3. Roy Newell–Supervisor, United Brothers, Inc. 4618 Newman Road, Covington, GA 30209
Expert Witnesses:	1. Dr. William La Lane, Charleston, SC 2. Dr. Wilfred Spaeth, Marietta, GA 3. Dr. Fernando Whitney, Riverdale, GA 4. Dr. Robert McLaughlin, Atlanta, GA 5. Dr. G. Braun, Atlanta, GA

Figure 1802.2-5. (continued)

preponderance of evidence. The party in whose favor the judgment or verdict is awarded is the prevailing party.

¶1802.4 Conclusion of Litigation

Upon *judgment,* the losing party may appeal the case to a higher court according to certain time limits and procedures, set by the appellate court rules of the appellate court having jurisdiction of the appeal.

If the judgment is not appealed or if the judgment is affirmed or no stay pending appeal is granted, the judgment may be voluntarily satisfied in these three ways: (1) the losing party may pay the prevailing party monetary damages and court costs; (2) the loser may perform a specified action requested by the prevailing party and ordered in the judgment; or (3) stop a certain action to which the prevailing party objected as ordered in the judgment.

If the judgment is not voluntarily satisfied by the losing party, the prevailing party may obtain a *writ of execution* or a *contempt order* depending on whether the judgment is for money damages or requires a specific action or omission by the loser.

A *writ of garnishment* may be obtained by following the applicable statute and court rules if the judgment is for money damages.

Your attorney may ask you to set a post-judgment deposition hearing at which the loser will have to testify as to his present financial condition. Consult state court rules of civil procedure on availability of this procedure in your state.

¶1803 Checklist for Preparing Pleadings Properly

- Proper court designation.
- Correct spelling of individual parties' names of corporations, limited or general partnership, etc.

- Properly completed summons.
- Proper legal backs.
- Correct amount of filing fees.
- Use of mandatory standard (printed) forms.
- Proper use of numbers, e.g., Arabic (1, 2, 3) or Roman numerals (I, II, III).
- Sufficient number of copies.
- Exhibits attached and properly marked.
- Verification made, if applicable.
- Proper size paper.
- Proper signatures, i.e., attorney and client, if necessary.
- Proper spacing.
- Copies of pleadings conformed. (To conform a signature in a complaint or other pleading insert /s/ together with the person's name either typed or handwritten.)

For example:

/s/ Patricia Graves

- Errors, omissions, and deletions conformed on copies of pleadings.
- A new subject should begin on a new page—not on the last line of the page.

¶1804 Solid Techniques for Preparing Pleadings Properly

1. Obtain a copy of all applicable court rules. Court rules vary from state to state, from county to county, so be sure that you obtain a copy of state and local court rules for your county court system. Also, obtain a copy of the federal and local federal district court rules, if the pleadings are to be filed in the federal district court.

2. Obtain all preprinted court forms. Printed forms are available in some jurisdictions. Check to make sure there isn't a form already available.

3. Check to be sure that the applicable statute of limitations on the plaintiff's claim will not pass and that the time set for filing any other court paper you are preparing will not pass before you can file it. The statute of limitations is the time within which a plaintiff party must file his complaint or within which a counter-claim must be filed by a defendant. Check with your attorneys to be sure that you prepare the pleadings on time.

Failing to file court papers other than the complaint or counter-claim may cause a default or other penalty by the court but it will not keep the plaintiff from filing a new action if the statute of limitations has not run out on the claim.

4. Check with the court to find out how many copies you need. Most pleadings require an original and two (2) copies and sometimes more. You will need: (1) the original to be filed with the court; (2) a copy to be delivered to the attorney for the opposing party(s); and (3) your office file copy. You will need a copy to serve upon each defendant if there is more than one, prior to his retaining counsel. Thereafter, you will need a copy for each party in the case or their attorney if they are represented by an attorney.

5. Check with the court to make sure you use the right size of paper. Many courts, including the federal courts now require letter-size paper, and few attorneys are still using the numbered paper. However, some courts still require legal size court papers and pleadings.

6. Use the proper type style. Most court pleadings should be typed in pica type, which is ten characters to the linear inch and six lines to the vertical inch. Most electric typewriters and word processors are in pica type.

7. Check to make sure your margins are correct. The top margin of the pleading should be at least 1½ inches deep so that it can be fastened in the file. The left hand margin should be set at either 10 or 12 spaces. Many attorneys use a 12 space indentation (tab) as well, but 5 is sufficient.

8. If you use ruled paper, stay inside the ruled margins and line up your typewriter with the numbers. Never go beyond the rule margins or beyond the last number on the paper. Prior to the use of word processors, a Z-rule was made if there were only one or two lines left on the paper. More and more offices are using three or more asterisks or diagonals at each margin of the blank numbered line.

9. Make your page numbers consistent. Page numbers should appear one space before the center of the paper and be preceded and followed by a hyphen. For example:

-2-

The first page is usually not numbered.

10. Check your court rules for the numbering of paragraphs. Some courts require Arabic numbers, (1,2,3) Roman numerals (I,II,III) or spelled-out ordinal numbers, such as First, Second, Third.

11. Indent land descriptions five spaces to the right of the left margin; use single spacing. The right margin may or may not be indented five spaces.

12. Indent quoted material five spaces from the left margin of the body of the text. For example:

The following statement was made by Joseph Moore when he first met Jennifer Long:

> I am glad to see that you came. We were wondering where you were. Did you bring the tapes?

The quoted material should *not* have quotation marks.

13. Capitalize introductory words. Many introductory words and phrases are capitalized such as: COMES NOW (first paragraph of a complaint), WHEREFORE (last paragraph of a document), IT IS HEREBY ORDERED, ADJUDGED AND DECREED (used in court orders), IT IS HEREBY STIPULATED (beginning of a stipulation).

14. Identify the law firm and its relation to the parties. The rules for the location of the name, address, telephone number, and the name of the party the attorney represents vary from court to court. Some courts require it to be at the upper left-hand margin and others prefer it below the signature line. If in doubt, check pleadings that your attorneys have previously filed.

15. Prepare the caption properly. The format of the caption of a case also varies from court to court, but should always include:

1. the name of the court showing its venue and jurisdiction;
2. the title of the action (names of the parties involved);
3. a place for the case number which will be assigned by the clerk of the court;
4. the nature of the document stated in the title of the document.

16. Prepare the verification properly. A verification is a statement that the party involved has read the document and knows or believes that the facts stated within the document are true. Some courts require a verified answer if the complaint is verified. Some law firms verify all court documents. Check with your local court rules. (See Figure 1804-1.)

17. Put on the proper legal backs. Legal backs are usually colored, some are yellow, some are blue. In some areas they are called "blue backs." A legal back encases the document. Some modern court rules do not require or forbid the use of legal backs. The following instruction applies if backs are to be used.

The upper margin of the legal back is folded over the top of the document and stapled two or three times.The endorsement is typed or printed on one of the folded sides, and usually includes: (1) the name, address and telephone number of the law firm and the attorney handling the case; (2) the party that the firm represents, e.g., "Attor-

VERIFICATION

STATE OF GEORGIA,
COUNTY OF ________

Personally before the undersigned Notary Public of the State of ____________, an officer authorized by law to administer oaths therein, came and appeared ____________ who, after being duly sworn, deposes and says that he/she is Plaintiff/Defendant, and that the facts set forth in the foregoing pleading are true to the best of his or her knowledge and belief.

____

Sworn to and subscribed before me

this_____day of __________, 19

____

Notary Public

(Affix Seal)

Figure 1804-1. Verification.

neys for the plaintiff"; (3) the full name of the court; (4) the complete title and number of the case (assigned by the court), including the names of the parties to the case; (5) the title of the document encased in the legal back; (6) the name, address and telephone number of the opposing attorney(s) on whom the document will be served, if applicable; and (7) the date of the document.

¶1805 Basic Elements of Civil Actions

¶1805.1 What Are Causes of Actions and Counts?

For purposes of this discussion a *cause of action* is defined as a "declaration of facts sufficient to justify a filing."

The cause of action may arise out of a civil wrong committed by one party upon another, e.g., tort, breach of contract, libel, slander, defamation, trespass, fraud, etc., or breach of a statutory duty. It is described in a complaint by statements, i.e., allegations, which set forth the facts sufficient to show that a wrong was committed or is being committed by one party against another. The statement may also describe a failure to perform; or an anticipatory breach of duty. Essentially, there are three elements of a cause of action: (1) the plaintiff's right; (2) the defendant's duty; and (3) a breach of that duty.

Counts may be either alternate theories of recovery or wholly separate causes of action, e.g., negligence, fraud, intentional tort, etc. Several counts may appear in one complaint. If so, each count would be numbered (usually by Roman numeral) and set forth separately and consecutively in the complaint.

The following sample complaint illustrates how causes of actions and counts are specifically set forth. (See Figure 1805.1-1).

IN THE UNITED STATES DISTRICT COURT
FOR THE NORTHERN DISTRICT OF GEORGIA
ATLANTA DIVISION

WILLIAM LANE and	§	
KARON LANE	§	
Plaintiff(s),	§	
	§	Civil Action
	§	
v.	§	
	§	File No.__________
CHARLES WOOD and	§	
HALDEN, INC.	§	
Defendant(s).	§	
	§	

COMPLAINT
COUNT I

Come now WILLIAM LANE and KARON LANE, Plaintiffs in the above-styled action and state their Complaint as follows:

1.

The Defendant HALDEN, INC., is a Delaware Corporation qualified to do business in the State of Georgia and is subject to the jurisdiction of this court. Its agent for service is Laddin Corporations System, 1200 Fulton Building, Atlanta, Georgia 30303.

Figure 1805.1-1. Complaint.

2.

The Defendant CHARLES WOOD, is a resident of 1234 Oleander Drive, Decatur, DeKalb County, Georgia, and is subject to the jurisdiction of this court.

3.

That on the 17th day of November, 1979, at approximately 2:50 p.m., Plaintiff, WILLIAM LANE, was driving an automobile owned by him on Corner Street in Atlanta, Georgia.

4.

On November 17, 1979, at approximately 2:50 p.m. the Defendant, CHARLES WOOD, was the operator of a 1979 Chevrolet, 1979 License No. XYZ 1968, owned by the Defendant, HALDEN, INC., which automobile was being driven in a negligent fashion so as to cause Defendant's automobile to collide into the back side of the automobile of Plaintiff, WILLIAM LANE.

5.

At said time and place the Defendant, CHARLES WOOD, was the agent of HALDEN, INC., and at the time the said Defendant CHARLES WOOD ran into and hit your Plaintiff's automobile with said automobile, he was acting within the scope and in the employment of HALDEN, INC.

6.

Plaintiff's leg had been previously injured and operated on approximately nine times and was almost completely healed and Plaintiff had gained almost total use of his leg. As a result of said injury, the metal shank in Plaintiff's leg which gives support and alignment to the fibula between the knee and the ankle shifted position resulting in the breakage of the screws used to hold such shank, causing further injury to Plaintiff's leg. Plaintiff has and continues to suffer from infection of his knee and the resultant drainage thereof. Furthermore, as a result of the injury hereinabove described, the bones have further separated to the extent that Plaintiff has lost extensive use of his leg and may have to undergo amputation.

7.

As a direct and proximate cause of the negligence of Defendants, and the collision thereby, Plaintiff, WILLIAM LANE, was injured and has suffered great pain of body and mind to his damage in the sum of ONE HUNDRED THOUSAND DOLLARS ($100,000.00).

8.

As a direct and proximate result of Defendant's negligence, Plaintiff, WILLIAM LANE, incurred substantial damage to his automobile, in the

Figure 1805.1-1. (continued)

amount of EIGHT HUNDRED AND NO/100 DOLLARS ($800.00) plus towing charges of THIRTY-FIVE AND NO/100 DOLLARS ($35.00) totaling EIGHT HUNDRED THIRTY-FIVE AND NO/100 DOLLARS ($835.00) and was deprived of the use of his vehicle.

9.

Further as a result of Defendants' negligent conduct, Plaintiff, WILLIAM LANE has lost his job and has suffered lost wages in the approximate amount of TWENTY-EIGHT THOUSAND NO/100 DOLLARS ($28,000.00), and has incurred medical and pharmaceutical bills and supplies for his care in the approximate amount of FIVE THOUSAND AND NO/100 DOLLARS ($5,000.00). Plaintiff will, as a result of the aforesaid negligence of the Defendants, incur extensive additional medical and hospital expenses.

WHEREFORE, Plaintiff, WILLIAM LANE, demands:

1. That service be perfected upon Defendants;
2. That Plaintiff be awarded damages against Defendants and each of them in the sum of ONE HUNDRED THOUSAND DOLLARS ($100,000.00) for past and future pain and suffering of body and mind;
3. That Plaintiff have and recover the sum of TWENTY-EIGHT THOUSAND EIGHT HUNDRED THIRTY-FIVE DOLLARS ($28,835.00) for special damages plus all costs of this action; and
4. That Plaintiff have such other and further relief as this Court may deem just and proper.

COUNT II

1.

Plaintiffs reallege and incorporate by reference in this Count, the allegations of Count I, Paragraphs 1 through 5 above.

2.

As a result of Defendants' negligent conduct, Plaintiff, KARON LANE has suffered loss of consortium of her husband, WILLIAM LANE in the amount of TEN THOUSAND DOLLARS ($10,000.00).

WHEREFORE, Plaintiff KARON LANE demands:

1. That service by perfected upon Defendants;
2. That Plaintiff be awarded damages against Defendants and each of them in the sum of TEN THOUSAND DOLLARS ($10,000.00) for loss of consortium of her husband, WILLIAM LANE; and

Figure 1805.1-1. (continued)

3. That Plaintiff have such other and further relief as this court may deem just and proper.

JONES, BROWN & SMITH

____

JOHN I. JONES
Attorney for Plaintiffs

1234 Tailman
Atlanta, Georgia, 30303
(404) 223-4567

Figure 1805.1-1. (*continued*)

¶1805.2 Parties, Capacity, and Status

Real Party in Interest. Rule 17 of the Federal Rules of Civil Procedure provides that every action shall be prosecuted in the name of the *real party in interest,* i.e., the person who is entitled to judgment recovery under the cause of action.

An executor, administrator, guardian, bailee, trustee of an express trust, a party with whom or in whose name a contract has been made for the benefit of another, or a party authorized by statute may sue in his own name without joining with him the party for whose benefit the action is brought.

When a statute of the United States so provides, an action for use or benefit of another shall be brought in the name of the United States.

No action should be dismissed on the ground that it is not prosecuted in the name of the real party in interest, but it saves time to name that party originally in the complaint. A reasonable time will be allowed after objection by the opponent for ratification of commencement of the action by, or joinder or substitution of, the real party in interest. Such ratification, joinder, or substitution has the same effect as if the action had been commenced in the name of the real party in interest, but time has been lost due to the objection.

Capacity to Sue Under the *Federal Court Rules,* "the capacity of an individual, other than one acting in a representative capacity, to sue or be sued shall be determined by the law of his domicile." *Domicile* is the place where a person has their true fixed and permanent home and principal establishment, and to which whenever they are absent, they have an intention of returning.

"The capacity of a corporation to sue or be sued shall be determined by the laws under which it was organized." That means the state in which its articles of incorporation or charter was filed.

"In all other cases capacity to sue or be sued shall be determined by the law of the state in which the district court is held" with some exceptions. The exceptions are "a partnership or other unincorporated association which has no such capacity by the law of such state, may sue or be sued in its common name for or against a substantive right existing under the Constitution or laws of the United States" and "the capacity of a receiver appointed by a court of the United States to sue or be sued in a court of the United States is governed by Title 28, U.S.C. §§754 and 959(a)."

Infants or Incompetent Persons Whenever an infant or incompetent person, i.e., a person who is incapable of acting on his or her own behalf, has a representative, e.g., general guardian, committee, conservator, of similar fiduciary, the representative may sue or defend on behalf of the infant or incompetent person.

If an infant or incompetent person does not have a duly appointed representative, he may sue by his *next friend* or by a *guardian ad litem.* The next friend is usually a relative (natural guardian) or the court appointed guardian of the infant or incompetent's estate. By filing the lawsuit, the next friend voluntarily takes responsibility for the property of the proceedings and court costs. A guardian ad litem is a person appointed by a court for the purpose of that case only. A guardian ad litem does not have the control or management of the person or property of the infant or person of unsound mind but is responsible for complying with any order of the court in that case.

The court may appoint a guardian ad litem for an infant or incompetent person who is not otherwise represented in an action. The court may make any order necessary for the protection of the infant or incompetent person.

¶1805.3 The Importance of Statutes of Limitations

A statute of limitations provides a period of time within which a lawsuit must be commenced, or the claimant will be forever barred from the right to bring the action. A statute of limitations may be as short as one year or as long as twenty years, or even more. One of the purposes of statutes of limitations is to prevent the recovery of "stale" claims. It is more difficult to locate evidence and available witnesses for old claims so, statute of limitations or not, it is advisable to file clients' claims as early as possible in most cases.

A statute of limitations begins to run against the claim once the cause of action accrues. For example, in a contract action, the cause of action accrues on the day the defendant breaches the contract. In a personal injury action, the cause of action accrues on the day of the accident. In an action based on account stated, i.e., a suit based on an account between the parties that has been assented to as correct, either expressly or by implication of law from the failure to object, the cause of action accrues on the date of the last entry in the account.

It is important to realize that failure of a plaintiff to bring suit within the specified period is an affirmative defense to the action, that means that it must be pleaded (stated) in the defendant's answers or response, or the right to claim that defense is waived.

Many laymen know about statutes of limitations but they do not know that they have to appear in court or appear by their attorney and raise that defense. As a result, a default or final judgment may be taken against a defendant in an action on a "stale" claim.

¶1806 How You Can Help Your Attorneys Prepare the Trial Book

The most valuable tool your attorneys can have at trial is the trial book, properly referred to the client's case file. The next alternative is a perfectly organized and complete client file, organized by subject matter and in chronological order for their use in trial preparation.

You can easily assist your attorneys in preparing and systematically organizing the trial book to meet their particular needs. Here are concrete suggestions on what to include in the trial book and how to organize it meticulously to help your attorneys win their cases.

Be sure to allow yourself plenty of time to prepare the trial book so that your attorneys can use it well in advance to prepare for trial. Work closely with them to make the trial book flexible so that you can add to, eliminate, or consolidate items in the book *as your attorneys so instruct.* An 8½ × 11 looseleaf binder will allow you to do this.

Other supplies you will need are folders for organizing the materials used in the preparation of the book, e.g., correspondence, memoranda, exhibits, notes, etc., and colored tabs for subject dividers.

Use the following list of suggested items to reference or include in the trial book:

¶1806.1 Checklist—Contents of the Trial Book

1. Witness statement summary or digest
2. Issues
3. Case Summaries
4. Case Evaluations
5. List of Prospective Jurors
6. List of Witnesses
7. Direct Examination
8. Opening Statement
9. Cross-Examinaation
10. Answers to Interrogatories
11. Evidence
12. Trial Motions
13. Jury Instructions
14. Deposition Digests
15. Exhibits
16. Trial Outline
17. Final Argument
18. Notes

After you complete the organization of the client file and the trial book, prepare a master index and a cross-index by names, topics, issues of law, etc.

¶1806.2 Dos and Don'ts in Handling Exhibits for Trial

1. *Don't* mark or mutilate original documents or other physical exhibits.
2. *Do* be sure of the location of all documents or physical exhibits.
3. *Do* work with copies of important documents.
4. *Don't* file original documents with depositions.
5. *Do* prepare a stipulation for the substitution of copies.
6. *Do* safeguard important documents in a safe.
7. *Do* obtain original documents from the client, not copies.
8. *Do* insist that the opponent produce *original* documents not copies for your copying in discovery.
9. *Do* indicate the source of each document. A simple way is to write the source on a slip of paper or Post-it™ Note and attach it to the document. Do not staple it. The source is the person who will testify as to the authenticity of each document at trial if the document is not to be accepted in evidence by agreement with the opponent's attorney at the trial. (Your attorneys will usually find out at the pretrial conference whether or not the other attorney agrees.)

¶1807 How to Avoid Common Errors in Filing Appeals

Because the secretary's assistance in filing civil appeals is ancillary to the attorney's role, it is imperative that you follow the procedural rules meticulously. Whether the appeal is filed in a state appellate court or a federal appellate court, make certain that you understand clearly the procedural rules and that you follow them to the letter unless your attorneys obtain an extension or other relaxation of the rules by the appellate court.

Since the procedural rules vary in the state appellate courts, it is difficult to discuss the specific state procedural rules. However, many state appellate procedural rules are patterned after the Federal Rules of Appellate Procedure. Moreover, if you can understand the federal procedures, you should have no difficulty understanding and applying the procedural rules of the appropriate state appellate court. The discussion in this section is based primarily on the Federal Rules of Appellate Procedure.

Use the following checklist as a guide to avoid errors in filing an appeal in any federal circuit court of appeals.

¶1807.1 Checklist for Filing Federal Court Appeals

Filing

- ☐ File notice of appeal within 30 days.
- ☐ File bond with notice of appeal.
- ☐ See that the record is transmitted by the clerk within 40 days after filing notice of appeal.
- ☐ Pay docket fee at time and place provided in the federal appellate rules.
- ☐ Expect notice from the appellate court clerk that the appeal has been filed, docketed and appellate case number assigned.
- ☐ All papers, except briefs and appendices, filed by mail must be *received* by the appellate court clerk within the time fixed for filing.
- ☐ Briefs and appendices are deemed filed on the day of mailing by the most expeditious form of delivery by mail, excluding special delivery.
- ☐ In motions requesting relief which may be granted by a *single* judge, the judge may allow the motion to be filed with him, dated the same day, and transmitted to the clerk for filing.

Service of Required Papers

- ☐ All papers filed by a party, except for those required to be filed by the clerk, must be served by that party upon all parties to the appeal or their respective counsel.
- ☐ Service of all papers upon all parties may be personal or by mail. *Personal service* on an attorney of record in the case may be accomplished by serving a copy to a clerk, secretary, or other responsible person at the office of that attorney.
- ☐ Proof of service or an acknowledgment of service by the person served must accompany all papers presented to the appellate court for filing. The certificate of service dated and signed by the attorney which appears on the paper is proof of service.

Computation of Time

- ☐ Do not include day of the act, event, or default from which the designated period of time begins to run.
- ☐ Include the last day of the period unless it is a Saturday Sunday, or legal holiday.
- ☐ If the last day is a Saturday, Sunday, or legal holiday, extend the period of time until the end of the next day which is not a Saturday, Sunday, or legal holiday.
- ☐ If the period of time is less than seven days, exclude intermediate Saturdays, Sundays, and legal holidays.
- ☐ Legal holidays presently include:

  New Year's Day
  Martin Luther King's Birthday
  Washington's Birthday
  Memorial Day
  Independence Day
  Veteran's Day
  Thanksgiving Day
  Christmas Day
  Labor Day

Extension of Time

- ☐ Unless it is specifically authorized by law, an extension of time for filing appellate papers may be requested by written motion directed to the appellate court, except for the filing of:
  1. Notice of appeal;
  2. Petition for allowance;
  3. Petition for permission to appeal;
  4. Petition to enjoin;
  5. Petition to set aside;
  6. Petition to modify or otherwise review; or
  7. Notice of appeal from an order of an administrative agency, board, commission or officer of the United States.

Additional Time After Service By Mail

- ☐ Add three days to the prescribed period of time after service of a paper upon a party by mail when the party is required or permitted to do an act within the period prescribed in the notice.

Content of Motions

- ☐ An application for an order or other relief must be made by filing a written motion with proof of service on all other parties, unless otherwise stated in the federal appellate rules.
- ☐ All required papers, briefs, and/or affidavits must be served and filed with the motion.
- ☐ Response in opposition to a civil motion other than one for a procedural order must be filed within seven days after service of the motion.

¶1808 The Dos and Don'ts of Preparing Appellate Briefs

1. *Do* refer to parties by using the actual names of the parties, or descriptive terms such as "the employees," "the injured person," "the taxpaper," etc.
2. *Do* use the form of citations required by the applicable appellate court rules of procedures. (See also ¶1601.)
3. *Do* make references in the briefs to parts of the record reproduced in the appendix filed with the appellant's brief by denoting the pages of the appendix (not the pages in the original record) at which those parts appear.
4. *Do* reproduce the relevant lengthy parts thereof in the brief, in an addendum at the end, or in pamphlet form (if appellate court rules allow).
5. *Do,* if the appellate rules require that the appellate briefs be printed instead of typed, use at least 11 point type on opaque, unglazed paper and bind briefs and appendices in volumes with pages 6⅛ × 9¼ inches and type matter 4⅙ × 7⅙ inches. (An experienced legal printer in your area usually knows this, but check it out in advance to avoid misunderstanding or delay.
6. *Do* bind pages produced by any other process in volumes with pages 8½ × 11 inches and type not in excess of 6½ × 9½ inches, using double spacing. Consecutive sheets must be attached at the *left margin.*

7. *Do,* where backs are used for appellate briefs, use *blue* covers for the appellant's brief; *red* for the *appellee; green* for *intervenor* or *amicus curiae;* and *grey* for *reply briefs.* Use a *white* cover for the appendix.
8. *Do* serve and file the appellant's brief within the number of days provided in the applicable appellate court rule (See Service of Required Papers and Computation of Time in ¶1808.1
9. *Do,* if your attorney represents the appellee, file the appellee's answer brief within a specified number of days after service on him or her of the appellant's brief.
10. *Do,* if your attorney represents the appellant, file the reply brief within a specified number of days after service on him or her of the answer brief of the appellee.
11. *Do* file the number of copies of each brief with the clerk of the appellate court, check the appellate court rules of the court to which the appeal has been taken to determine the number.
12. *Do* serve a copy on counsel for each party to the appeal or more copies if the applicable appellate rule requires that more than one copy be served on him.
13. *Don't* serve carbon copies of briefs and appendices.
14. *Don't* fail to file the appellant's brief, or the appellee may move for a dismissal of the appeal.
15. Don't prepare any appellate brief in excess of the number of pages limited in the applicable appellate court rules, exclusive of the pages containing the table of contents, tables of citations and any addendum containing statutes, rules, regulations, etc.
16. *Don't* file an *amicus curiae* brief unless it is accompanied by a written consent of all parties, or by leave of court granted on motion or at the request of the court except in briefs presented by the United States, or any officer or agency thereof, or by a State, Territory, or Commonwealth.

¶1809 What Should the Front Cover of the Brief and Appendix Contain?

The front cover of the briefs and of appendices, separately printed, should contain the following:

1. The name of the court and the appellate number of the case as well as the style and number of the lower court case from which the appeal is taken.

2. The title of the case designating the parties as appellant or appellee.
3. The nature of the proceeding in the court, e.g., Appeal, Petition for Review.
4. The title of the document, e.g., Brief for Appellant, Answer Brief for Appellee, Reply Brief or Appendix.
5. The names, addresses, and telephone numbers of counsel representing the party on whose behalf the document is filed.

¶1810 What about Petitions for Rehearing, Motions, and Other Papers?

Appellate court rules may require that petitions for rehearing be produced in the same manner as briefs and appendices. Other motions and other papers may be typewritten or otherwise printed double spaced on opaque, unglazed paper 8½ × 11 inches, or on similar paper if standard legal size, depending upon the appellate court rules in the particular appellate court. Consecutive sheets must be attached at the left margin if the 8½ × 11 inch sheets are used. Legible carbon copies or photocopies maybe used for filing and service.

Motions or other papers must use a caption that sets forth (1) the name of the court, (2) the title of the case, (3) the file number, and (4) a brief descriptive title indicating the purpose of the paper. The motion must be signed by the attorney for the party making the motion. The motion must also contain a certificate of service which must be signed by the attorney.

¶1900 The Role of the Legal Secretary in Corporate Law

In this chapter we may refer to the corporate legal secretary. The term corporate legal secretary is to be distinguished from the term corporation secretary or secretary of the corporation. The latter two terms are used to describe the officer of a corporation called "secretary." (See ¶1902.2.) Your attorney may be appointed secretary of a corporation which he or she also represents as an attorney. In such case, you will no doubt be involved in his or her corporate recordkeeping and duties, as well as business law problems of the corporation.

One area of law that most legal secretaries have to work in is business law. Business law includes the formation and organization of corporations, partnerships, and sole proprietorships as well as business contract drafting and business legal problems.

The purpose of this chapter is to assist the legal secretary in understanding and working with his or her attorneys in the corporate formation and record maintenance phase of business law. Because so much of this work is ministerial or procedural, a career oriented corporate legal secretary can assume a lot of responsibility in helping his or her attorney who is the "secretary of the corporation."

The corporation legal secretary may have a variety of tasks that are described in this chapter. All of these tasks must be done efficiently, thoroughly and in an extremely organized manner. Most of the work can be done in a systematic way. Therefore, you should keep a looseleaf notebook of checklists and forms to be used in this area. Whenever you get a new form or accomplish a new task, document it in your notebook. Write down each step and keep a copy of sample forms that you use. You will probably handle the preparation of the papers necessary for formation of corporations and for the maintenance of proper corporation action records as described in this chapter.

¶1901 What Is the Difference between Corporations, Partnerships, and Sole Proprietorships?

The main difference between corporations, general partnerships (distinguished from limited partnerships), and sole proprietorships is that, generally speaking, a corporation shields its stockholders, officers, and directors from any personal liability. A corporation is a separate and distinct legal entity. If there are any lawsuits and judgments against a corporation, the litigant cannot reach the personal assets of the members of the corporation, unless they allege and prove that the corporation is a shell or alter ego of the members of any one of them. But that is another legal matter. We will assume for the purposes of this chapter that the corporation is or is to be a bona fide registered corporation.

¶1902 What Is a Corporation and What Kind of Corporations Are There?

Basically, a corporation is an institution or entity that is separate and apart from the persons who compose it. A corporation has the power to own property, to contract, to sue and be sued, and to do such other acts as are necessary to carry on the business. The corporation is the owner of the assets of the business and is liable for its obligations. Although the shareholders own the corporation as such (ownership is evidenced by their shares of stock), they do not have title to the assets of the corporation and are not individually liable for its obligations. The existence of the corporation is not affected by the death or bankruptcy of a shareholder or by the transfer of its shares. It has a continuous existence during the period for which it is chartered, which may be indefinite, or until it surrenders or forfeits its charter. The corporation has a centralized management, but the shareholders elect the board of directors (may be one director) that manages it and controls its affairs. The board of directors appoints officers who have power to act for the corporation and to hire employees.

¶1902.1 Shareholders

The shareholders own shares in the corporation. The ownership of the share(s) is delivered to its owner in the proof of a certificate issued by the corporation, called a stock certificate. The certificate shows the registered name of the corporation, the nature of the share, the number of shares, and the shareholder's name. The certificate is dated and signed by the authorized officer of the corporation, usually the president and secretary. The initial operating capital for the corporation is provided by the sale of the stock to the shareholders.

A stock subscription agreement may be executed prior to the formation of the corporation where more than one shareholder is involved. The subscription agreement evidences the future shareholders intent to purchase stock in the corporation.

The shareholders elect the directors of the corporation (board of directors). Many states allow a board to consist of only one director.

¶1902.2 Officers

The officers of the corporation are appointed by the board of directors and follow the desires of the board of directors. The officers implement the policies set by the board of directors. The officers may hire employees or independent contractors to work for the corporation where authorized by the board of directors, expressly or by reason of the general authority given them as operations officers.

¶1902.3 Board of Directors

The governing body of the corporation is known as the board of directors which is composed of the persons elected by the shareholders to run the corporation from day to day. They are usually elected or re-elected at the annual stockholders (shareholders) meeting.

¶1902.4 Types of Corporations

A corporation may be called a *domestic* and/or *foreign* corporation. A domestic corporation has been formed under the law of the state where it operates its business, whereas a domestic corporation is called a foreign corporation in states or countries where it does business other than in the one in which it is formed. For example, a corporation formed in California and doing business there is a domestic corporation, but if that same corporation does business in Arizona, it is considered a foreign corporation in Arizona. That corporation is still considered a domestic corporation in California. In suing that corporation your attorneys would use the corporate name and allege in the complaint that it is a California corporation, regardless of where the action arose. Your attorneys would also allege that it was doing business in the state where the action accrued.

There are three classes of corporations:

1. profit
2. nonprofit and
3. governmental corporations.

A corporation that is formed for profit is a corporation operated for the purpose of making a profit which may be distributed in dividends to the stockholders.

Incorporated churches, lodges, fraternities, schools (not incorporated for the profit of stockholders), etc., are examples of nonprofit corporations.

Governmental corporations are corporations organized for governmental purposes. Incorporated municipalities, such as the Tennessee Valley Authority and the Reconstruction Finance Corporations, are examples of governmental corporations.

Business corporations include:

1. banks and insurance companies
2. public utility corporations,
3. private corporations.

Private corporations consist of three classes of corporations:

1. publicly owned corporations,
2. closely held corporations,
3. professional corporations or associations.

Publicly owned corporations sell its shares to the general public through the major stock exchanges. A closely held corporation generally has a small group of stockholders, sometimes consisting of people in one family, some of whom may be officers or directors of the corporation. Sometimes a closely held corporation can just be one person. The professional corporation or association is usually a group of doctors, lawyers, dentists, certified public accountants, or the like, who practice their profession as a corporation and obtain the benefits of incorporation. Many law firms are now incorporated; an individual attorney may be incorporated as a professional corporation. The professional corporation itself may also be a partner in a law partnership.

¶1903 Step-by-Step Procedure for Incorporation

Step 1. Organize incorporators. Incorporators are those persons who group together for the purpose of incorporating. They put up the capital for the corporation. In many instances, the legal secretary may be named as an incorporator, or *dummy* incorporator. A dummy incorporator is not one of the principals who will own the corporation, but one who merely acts for them until the organization meeting. Of course, the legal secretary will not put up the capital for the corporation.

Step 2. Reserve corporate name. After the incorporators decide on a name, your attorney will direct you to write a standard form letter to the Secretary of State to reserve the name. The Secretary of State will reserve the name, if it doesn't resemble any existing corporation's name. The name must include words that indicate that it is a corporation, such as *Incorporated, Inc., Corporation.* Most states will not permit the use of the words *bank* or *trust* in the name of the corporation unless it is a bank or trust.

If your attorney prefers and the Secretary of State allows it, you can temporarily reserve a name by phone with a follow-up letter. (See Fig. 1903-1.) Some states require a small fee to reserve the name.

To the Secretary of State
of the State of________:

Pursuant to the provisions of subparagraph ______ of section ______ of the ______ Business Corporation Act, the undersigned hereby applies for reservation of the following corporate name for a period of ______ days: ______.

Dated ______, 19_____

_____Applicant
By_____
Its_____

State of ______
Office of the Secretary of State
Certificate of Reservation of Corporate Name
of
____

The undersigned, as Secretary of State of the State of ______, hereby certifies that the corporate name of ______ has been reserved in this office for the exclusive use of ______ for a period of ______ days after the date hereof, pursuant to the provisions of subparagraph ______ of section ______ of the ______Business Corporation Act.

Dated ______, 19_____.[3]

______, Secretary of State

Figure 1903-1. Reservation of Corporate Name Application.

Step 3. Prepare articles of incorporation. The articles, which are often referred to as charters, certificate of incorporation, or articles of association, give the name, purpose, and other information about the corporation. Before you prepare the articles, you must get the following information from your attorney (See also Steps 5 through 13 and ¶1902.3 and ¶1904.6):

1. State of incorporation.
2. The corporate name selected (or second or third choices if the name has not yet been reserved per Step 2).
3. The nature of the business of the corporation, also known as the purpose.
4. Names and addresses of:
   a. Incorporators; and
   b. Initial Directors.
5. The kind of shares to be authorized:
   a. common, preferred, classes, etc.

For closely held corporations they are usually common, but you must know whether the common shares are:

   b. "par" or "no par." If par, you must know the par value, as "$1 par," "$10 par," etc.
6. The number of shares to be issued and to whom.
   a. Get shareholders' names and addresses and their social security numbers.
   b. Be sure to get the *exact* spelling of the shareholder's name.
   c. If shareholders are to own jointly, and want to use "and" or "or," does your state require the words "with right of survivorship" if they want the survivor of the joint owners to own the stock outright if the other dies first?
   d. If the stock is to be owned in name only for the benefit of another, what title should be included? (i.e., trustee, guardian, etc.)
7. Principal office of the corporation.
8. The name of registered agent for service of process (the one on whom a litigant can serve suit papers).
9. Fiscal year of the corporation.
10. Date for annual stockholders' meeting.
11. Amount of initial capital to be contributed to the corporation if your state requires this information. Some states require a specific amount and others do not.
12. Information relating to the designations, rights, preferences, and all other details relating to the preferred stock, if any. (See No. 5.)

Step 4. Determine the number of copies of the articles of incorporation needed. You will usually need three copies: one for the corporation's principal office, one for your attorney, and one to be placed temporarily in the minute book. When the original is returned by the Secretary of State with its notice of the filing date, you will replace the copy in the minute book with the original attached to the Secretary of State's certificate. If the corporation is to be publicly owned, you will need to file a certified copy with the Securities and Exchange Commission. Public registration is a specialized field; the corporate legal secretary in a firm engaging in general business practice will not usually be concerned with that.

Even where a fairly small corporation is involved, you may want a certified copy to use in getting an exemption from your state securities commission if the stock is to be offered for sale within the state. Check with your attorneys.

Step 5. Find a sample form of articles. Type the articles on plain bond paper, either legal or letter, whichever your firm uses. Some states have preprinted forms. You might prepare the original on minute paper and photocopy the other copies on plain paper. (See Figure 1903-2.)

ARTICLES OF INCORPORATION

OF

LEGAL SUPPORT SERVICES, INC.

The Articles of Incorporation of LEGAL SUPPORT SERVICES, INC. are as follows:

I.

The name of the corporation is LEGAL SUPPORT SERVICES, INC.

II.

The corporation is organized pursuant to the provisions of the Georgia Business Corporation Code.

III.

The corporation shall have perpetual duration.

Figure 1903-2. Articles of Incorporation.

Step 6. If you use printed forms, make sure they are up-to-date. Also, be sure you use the forms with the same date of printing.

Step 7. Use pica type and double space the articles. Most states require this.

Step 8. Center the title in all caps.

Step 9. Initial caps for the following words: Corporation, Certificate of Incorporation, Board of Directors and Bylaws.

Step 10. Indented material, including numbers or lettered items are typed five spaces from the left hand margin.

Step 11. Indent the purpose clause.

Step 12. Type a signature line for each person who will sign the document.

Step 13. Find out if a charter needs seals of the signers. If so, type "L.S." or "SEAL" after each signature line.

Step 14. Prepare an acknowledgment, if necessary. Type the acknowledgment for the state of incorporation. Put the state and county where the charter is signed, not the state of incorporation. (See Figure 1903-3.) If the notary is not in the state of incorporation, a certificate of authentication from the county where the notary is registered may be necessary. The certificate merely identifies and substantiates the authenticity of the signature of the notary and indicates that the notary is registered in that county.

ACKNOWLEDGMENT—President or other officer.

State of ______ } SS
County of______ }

On the ______ day of ________, 19____, before me personally came ______, to me known, who, being by me duly sworn, did depose and say that he resides in ______; that he is the president [or other officer] of ______ Company, the corporation described in and which executed the above instrument; that he knows the seal of said corporation; that the seal affixed to said instrument is such corporate seal; that it was so affixed by order of the board of directors of said corporation, and that he signed his name thereto by like order.

[Seal] ______, Notary Public
County of ______

Figure 1903-3. Acknowledgment.

Step 15. Prepare a cover for each copy except the copy for the minute book. Type the following on the cover.

CERTIFICATE OF INCORPORATION OF (name of corporation)

Step 16. Arrange for execution of the articles. Call the incorporators and let them know when the papers will be ready so that they can arrange to sign them without delay. They should sign each original, duplicate original, and triplicate original. All copies should be conformed. Have each incorporator sign his or her name exactly as it is in the certificate. Notarize all copies.

Step 17. Prepare a transmittal letter to the Secretary of State, together with the filing fees and other fees. The public official will review the charter to see if it is acceptable, and if so, return a copy to your attorney with the appropriate endorsement of approval. Note the date of filing on your copies. This date is the official date not the date of signing.

Step 18. File a copy locally, if required. Be sure to include the local filing fee. Note the date of the local filing on your file copy.

Step 19. Affix the tax receipt in the minute book.

¶1904 Preparing for the First or the Organizational Meeting of Shareholders

The additional steps to organize a corporation are done through an organizational meeting which may not actually be held. This meeting may be called a shareholders', stockholders', an incorporators', or subscribers' meeting, depending upon laws of the state. A subscriber may be a signer of the articles of incorporation and also may have agreed to buy stock in the corporation. Some of the items that may be covered are:

- Election of initial board of directors;
- Adoption of bylaws for the corporation;
- Authorization to issue the capital stock.

The secretary or the paralegal needs to do the following to prepare for the organizational meeting:

1. Order the corporate outfit.
2. Prepare waiver of notice of meeting and have it executed by *all* parties entitled to attend the meeting or use a form of Consent in Lieu of Meeting to be signed by *all* parties entitled to attend.
3. Prepare bylaws.
4. Prepare minutes of first meeting of incorporators.
5. Prepare minutes of the first meeting of directors.
6. Prepare bank account resolution.
7. Prepare stock certificates.

¶1904.1 Obtaining the Corporate Kit

The corporate kit consists of a minute book, stock certificate book, a stock ledger, and a seal, if required. You can find names of businesses that sell corporate kits in the Yellow Pages, bar journal or other publications. Be sure to give them the name of the corporation, the type and amount of capital stock to be issued, and par value (if applicable). See checklist in Step 3.

You may need to furnish the preferred stock clause to the stationer from whom you order the corporate kit. You can send the excerpted clause from the articles.

¶1904.2 Preparing the Waiver of Notice of Organizational Meeting

Unless they waive notice, by law the incorporators, directors, shareholders, or subscribers must be given notice of the organizational meeting. If they waive notice of the organizational meeting, which is customary, you must prepare the waiver and have them sign it. (See Figure 1904.2-1.) You may also have to prepare a waiver of notice for the first meeting of directors. (See also the alternative in the form of Consent in Lieu of Meeting described in ¶1904.)

Waiver for organizational meeting.

[Name of corporation]

Waiver—Organizational Meeting of Stockholders

We, the undersigned, being all the stockholders of the _____ Company of _____, hereby call an organizational meeting of the stockholders of said company to be held in the company's office, _____ Street, _____ [city and state], on the _____ day of _____, 19_____, at _____ o'clock _____.m., for the purpose of _____; and we hereby waive all statutory and bylaw requirements as to notice of time, place and objects of said meeting, and agree to the transaction thereat of any and all business pertaining to the affairs of the company.

[Signatures]

[Place and date]

Figure 1904.2-1. Waiver for Organizational Meeting.

¶1904.3 Preparing the Bylaws

The rules that govern the corporation, its officers, directors, and stockholders are called bylaws. Standard bylaws are usually included in the corporate kit. (See ¶1904.1.) Your attorney may tell you to add some additional clauses or delete some. Provisions that may be included are:

1. Location of stockholders' meeting.
2 Time and date of annual meeting of stockholders.
3. The amount of time when notice of the meeting must be given (normally ten days before the meeting).
4. Requirements for special meetings.
5. Time for notice of special meetings (normally ten days before the meeting).
6. What constitutes a quorum (normally a majority).
7. Place of directors' meeting and place where regular meetings are to be held.
8. Provisions for conducting a directors' meeting and time for notice of directors' meeting (normally three to five days prior to the meeting).
9. Provisions for conducting a special meeting and time for notice (normally three to five days before the meeting).
10. Names of officers who are to sign and countersign checks and stock certificates.
11. Fiscal year end for the company.

¶1904.4 Basic Format for Preparing Corporate Minutes

In addition to the minutes of the first meeting of shareholders, the first meeting of incorporators, and the first meeting of the board of directors, you will have to regularly prepare minutes. The corporation will supply the factual information about their meetings. (See Figure 1904.4-1.) Use the checklist in ¶1904.5 to help you type the minutes:

Minutes of annual meeting.

[Name of corporation]
Minutes of Regular Meeting of Stockholders
Held ______, 19____

The annual meeting of the stockholders of the ______ Company was held at the office of the company, ______ Street, in ______, on the ______ day of ______, 19____, at ______ o'clock, ____.m.

The meeting was called to order by ______, the president of the company, who presided at the meeting in accordance with the provisions of the bylaws of the company, and ______, secretary of the company, being present, acted as secretary of the meeting.

Figure 1904.4-1. Sample Minutes for Annual Meeting.

Upon motion of ______ duly made and seconded, and unanimously carried, the reading of the roll of the stockholders entitled to vote at the meeting was dispensed with.

The following stockholders were present in person:

Name	No. of shares
______________	______________
______________	______________
______________	______________

The following stockholders were present by proxy:

Name	Name of Proxy	No. of Shares
______________	______________	______________
______________	______________	______________
______________	______________	______________

being a majority in interest of all the stockholders of the company.

The proxies presented were ordered to be filed with the secretary of the meeting.

The secretary presented and read a copy of the notice of the meeting, together with proof of the mailing of the same at least ______ days prior to the meeting to each registered stockholder at his address as the same appears on the books of the company.

Upon motion duly made and seconded, _______ and _______ were appointed inspectors of election, and were then duly sworn.

Upon motion duly made and seconded the meeting then proceeded to the election of _______ directors in accordance with the bylaws. The stockholders prepared their ballots and delivered them to said inspectors, who received the same and canvassed the votes cast, and certified in writing that the following persons having received the highest number of votes cast at said election, had been duly elected as directors of the company for the ensuing year: _______, _______, _______. The president thereupon declared said persons duly elected directors of the company to serve for the ensuing year and until their successors are elected and qualify.

On motion duly made and seconded, the minutes of the last meeting of the stockholders of the corporation, held on the _______ day of _______, 19_____, were read, as were also the minutes of the special meeting held on _______, 19_____, and the minutes of the meeting held on _______, 19_____.

Upon motion duly made and seconded, such minutes were duly approved, ratified and confirmed.

The _______annual report of the president and directors of the

Figure 1904.4-1. (continued)

______Company was presented and read, and upon motion of ______, duly seconded, it was

Resolved, that said report be received and ordered to be filed with the secretary in the form as presented to the meeting.

[Insert record of any other business transacted]

The secretary was directed to insert in the minute book a copy of each of the following papers:

1. Notice of the meeting and proof of mailing thereof.
2. Form of proxy.
3. Report of the president and directors.
4. Inspectors' oath and report.

Upon motion duly seconded, the same adjourned.

______, Secretary of the meeting

Figure 1904.4-1. (continued)

¶1904.5 Checklist for Preparing Corporate Minutes

- Margins—Come down 6 or 7 spaces from the top of the page to begin the heading of the minutes. On the second page and subsequent pages, come down 4 spaces from the top. The bottom margin should be about 4 to 6 spaces.
- Headings—The minutes should have a three-lined heading, with double spaces, as follows:

MINUTES OF THE ANNUAL MEETING OF STOCKHOLDERS

JARGO LEASING, INCORPORATED

March 2, 1986

- For special meetings, merely substitute the word "Special" for the word "Annual" in the above heading. Pages after the first page should have the following heading, beginning flush left with the left margin which has been established for typing:

MINUTES OF ANNUAL (or SPECIAL) MEETING OF BOARD OF DIRECTORS—JARGO LEASING, INCORPORATED—
March 2, 1986.

- Spacing—The minutes are normally single-spaced, with double-spacing between paragraphs.
- Capital letters—In typing Chairperson, Secretary, President, etc., in the minutes, use initial capitals, i.e., Chairperson, not chairperson.

- Listing Officers—When typing the officers in a resolution showing their election, the following is a good arrangement:

George Keller	Chairperson of the Board and Treasurer
James L. McNaultry	President
Charles H. Davis	Vice-President
Marune H. Olipher	Vice-President and Assistant Secretary
Anne E. Schuller	Secretary and Assistant Treasurer

- Listing Directors—When typing the directors in a resolution showing their election, the following is a good setup:
  George Keller
  Tom H. Smythe
  Samuel E. Jones
  Deborah G. Goodman
- Designation of Registered Agent—The following wording is preferable when appointing a registered agent for a corporation in the corporate minutes as action that the directors had taken:

Registered Agent. After some discussion, the following resolution was adopted upon motion made by Mr. Jones, seconded by Mr. Smythe.

RESOLVED, that Samuel E. Jones be and hereby is named as registered agent of JARGO LEASING, Incorporated, in the State of California, and that the registered office of the corporation be and hereby is designated as the company's office in Los Angeles, California.

- Draft copies and Signature Page—When sending draft copies of minutes to the client for review, *always* mark "Draft" and the date the draft copy is being sent on the top of the copy going to the client. This indicates that this is not necessarily a final copy, but is a copy that they need to review before it is finalized.
- Signature Page—After the minutes have been approved by the client, the signature page may be sent to the client for the proper signatures. The original signature page is sent with a photocopy of the signature page inserted in the minute book. On this copy, a notation should be made of the date the original signature page was sent and to whom it went. Keep this for your records in case anything should happen to the original and you might have to retype the last page of the minutes. The photocopy also keeps your minute book in complete form for the corporate records

until the original is returned. *When the original comes back, the photocopy should be destroyed.* Most corporations don't want copies of minutes floating around for various reasons.

- A statement that notice was given or refer to a waiver of notice.
- Indicate those present and whether a quorum was present. For the stockholders, show separately the number of shares of stock represented in person or by proxy, the persons holding the proxies and the total number of shares represented.
- Show who presided as Chairperson and who recorded the minutes as secretary.
- Refer to the minutes of the previous meeting, if any, and state that the minutes should be read and approved. It is acceptable on special meetings to have the reading of the minutes deferred until the next meeting.
- At annual meetings, state that the stockholders elected a Board of Directors, preferably to "serve for the ensuing year or until their successors are elected and qualified, each to serve at the pleasure of the stockholders."
- At annual meetings of the Board of Directors, state that the stockholders elected its officers, preferably to "serve for the ensuing year or until their successors are elected and qualified, each to serve at the pleasure of the board."
- If applicable, state that certain resolutions were adopted ratifying, confirming and approving the acts of the officers and directors (at the stockholders' meeting), and the officers (at the Directors' meeting) on behalf of the corporation during the year just ended.

¶1904.6 Checklist for Issuing Stock Certificates

The reference numbers shown hereafter are indicated inside circles on the stock certificates shown in Figure 1904.6-1 and stock certificate stub (Figures 1904.6-2, 1904.6-3 and 1904.6-4.)

1. At the very top of each certificate, below the perforations for separating the certificate from the stock book, notations should be made before the certificate leaves your office as to any restrictions to which the stock certificate is subject. The restrictions may be contained in the bylaws of the corporation, in an agreement between the stockholder and the corporation, or in an agreement between stockholders. The word IMPORTANT should be underlined to make it stand out. (See Step 3 in ¶1903.)

(1) Important: This certificate is issued subject to restrictions on its transfer as provided in the Bylaws of the Corporation.

INCORPORATED UNDER THE LAWS OF GEORGIA

NUMBER (2) 3

SHARES (3) --206--

Legal Support Services, Inc.

Authorized Capital Stock 10,000 Shares

This Certifies that (4) John M. Hubbard, Jr., John M. Hubbard, III and Stockton National Bank, Trustees U/T/A William Edward Hubbard II. Dated 9-15-80, Their Successors in Trust and Assigns--- is the

registered holder of (5) -----------------Two Hundred Six (206)-------------------- Shares

Legal Support Services, Inc. FULLY PAID AND NON-ASSESSABLE

transferable only on the books of the Corporation by the holder hereof in person or by Attorney upon surrender of this Certificate properly endorsed.

In Witness Whereof, the said Corporation has caused this Certificate to be signed by its duly authorized officers and its Corporate Seal to be hereunto affixed this 30th (6) day of September A.D. 19 85

SECRETARY

PRESIDENT

Par Value $1.00 (7)

American Seal & Stamp Co.—Atlanta, Ga.

Figure 1904.6-1. Stock Certificate.

PASTE CANCELLED CERTIFICATE IN THIS SPACE

PASTE REVENUE STAMPS FOR ORIGINAL ISSUE IN THIS SPACE

CERTIFICATE No. (8) -10-

FOR ----------- (9) Two Hundred Six --------------- SHARES

ISSUED TO

(10) John M. Hubbard, Jr., John M. Hubbard II and Stockton National Bank, Trustees U/T/A William Edward Hubbard II Dated 9-15-80, Their Successors in Trust and Assigns

DATED (11) September 30 19 85

TRANSFER FROM ORIGINAL ISSUE BELOW

FROM WHOM TRANSFERRED:

DATED ______ 19___

NO. ORIGINAL CERTIFICATE	NO. ORIGINAL SHARES	NO. OF SHARES TRANSFERRED

RECEIVED CERTIFICATE No. -3- (12)

FOR ----------- (13) Two Hundred Six --------------- SHARES

THIS (14) DAY OF (14) 19___

TRANSFER DETAILS FOR SURRENDERED CERTIFICATES

NEW CERTIFICATES ISSUED TO:	NO. OF SHARES TRANSFERRED	NO. OF NEW CERTIFICATES
Reissue: not a sale. (15) Trust U/T/A William Edward Hubbard II	52	18
f/b/o Hazel Montague Hubbard Trust U/T/A William Edward Hubbard II	52	19
f/b/o Katharine Elizabeth Hubbard Trust U/T/A William Edward Hubbard II	52	20
b/b/o Patricia Marks Hubbard Trust U/T/A William Edward Hubbard II	50	21
f/b/o Laura Lewis Hubbard		

Figure 1904.6-2. Stock Transfer Record.

PASTE CANCELLED CERTIFICATE IN THIS SPACE

PASTE REVENUE STAMPS FOR ORIGINAL ISSUE IN THIS SPACE

CERTIFICATE No. -18- (16)

FOR ----------------------Fifty-Two---------------------- **SHARES**

ISSUED TO

(17) John M. Hubbard, Jr., John M. Hubbard III and Stockton National Bank, Trustees U/T/A William Edward Hubbard II Dated 9-15-80 f/b/o Hazel Montague Hubbard, Their Successors in Trust and Assigns

DATED September 30 **19** 85

TRANSFER FROM ORIGINAL ISSUE BELOW

(18) **FROM WHOM TRANSFERRED:** John M. Hubbard, Jr., John M. Hubbard III and Stockton National Bank, Trustees U/T/A William Edward Hubbard II Dated 9-15-80, Their Successors in Trust and Assigns

DATED September 30 **19** 85

NO. ORIGINAL CERTIFICATE	NO. ORIGINAL SHARES	NO. OF SHARES TRANSFERRED
10	206	(19) 52

RECEIVED CERTIFICATE No. -18-

FOR ----------------------Fifty-Two---------------------- **SHARES**

THIS ________ **DAY OF** ________ **19**____

TRANSFER DETAILS FOR SURRENDERED CERTIFICATES

NEW CERTIFICATES ISSUED TO:	NO. OF SHARES TRANSFERRED	NO. OF NEW CERTIFICATES

Figure 1904.6-3. Stock Transfer Record.

AMOUNT PAID THEREON	DATE OF TRANSFER OF SHARES	TO WHOM SHARES ARE TRANSFERRED	CERTIFICATES SURRENDERED		NUMBER OF SHARES HELD (BALANCE)	VALUE OF STOCK TRANSFER TAX STAMP AFFIXED
			CERTIF. NOS.	NO. SHARES		

Figure 1904.6-4. Stock Transfer Ledger (Share Register).

2. Each stock certificate that is issued should be numbered consecutively after the last number issued. A hyphen should be placed immediately before and immediately after the number of the certificate. There should be no space between the hyphen and the first arabic number; there should be no space after the final number and the hyphen. The purpose of this in all places referred to is to prevent alteration of the stock certificates. The same number that is placed here on the stock certificate should be placed on the stub of the stock certificate in the left-hand column (8).

3. At this place at the top of the stock certificate the number of shares should be typed in, preceded by two hyphens, and followed by two hyphens. If the number is larger than 999, it should be typed with a comma separating the thousands from the hundreds. There is no space before or after the comma. This is the item that is most likely to be altered on a certificate.

4. Be very careful in inserting the name of the stockholder. The sample given is the type information that should be shown if a trust is involved. If it is a custodian account, the proper wording is as follows:

"Mary C. Pugh, Custodian for Harry Pugh, a Minor, under the laws of Georgia."

"Mary C. Pugh, as Custodian for Harry Pugh, under the Georgia Uniform Gifts to Minors Act."

If the certificate is made out to a person other than the one shown on the stock subscription agreement or the one holding original stock, if it is a stock dividend, the stub should always show a clear trail as to what has happened. For example, in the illustration given, the master trust at the Stockton National Bank owned the original stock in Legal Support Services Company, which entitled it to acquire stock in Legal Support Services, Inc. The bank had divided up the master trust into four subparts, however, and wanted the stock issued to the separate subtrusts. We issued the first certificate to the master trust (Certificate No. 10) and then cancelled it and reissued certificates nos. 18, 29, 20, and 21 to the four subtrusts (see the lower part of the right column on the attached stub to the stock certificate). An individual's name should be centered with hyphens before and after.

5. The number of shares for which the certificate is issued should be written out at this place, preceded and followed by hyphens. The rule for writing numbers is that the word *and* is used only in separating cents from dollars. For example, the figure 3,406 is written out "three thousand four hundred six" shares.

6. The date of the certificate is very important. It should normally be the day that the payment for the stock certificate is received by the corporation, unless there is some special reason for using a different date. In this particular example, normally this date should not be earlier than the date the corporate charter is recorded in the Register's office of Fulton County or the Secretary of State's Office in Atlanta, Georgia. The certificate should not be dated without discussing the date to be used with the member responsible to the client.

7. For most clients, you should put a gold seal on the stock certificate, and be sure that the corporate seal is impressed on the certificate at this place. Be certain that the corporate seal is impressed, whether or not you use a gold seal.

8. The certificate number should always be filled in on the stub at the same time the certificate itself is completed.

9. The number of shares should always be filled in at this place, although it is not so important to write out the number on the stock stub. If you are writing it out by hand, merely putting the arabic number here will be sufficient. For example, 206 instead of two hundred six; in other words, use arabic numbers rather than writing out two hundred six.

10. The stub should always show the name on the front of the certificate in exactly the same manner, using the same exact words and initials as on the stock certificate itself.

11. The date of the stock certificate should always be filled in on the stub at this place.

12. If the certificate being issued represents shares that are being transferred, the information should be filled in at this place. If it is an original certificate, the notation "original issue" should be made.

13. The number of shares should always be filled in at this place.

14. The date of the receipt for the stock certificate should not be filled in normally until the person to whom the certificate is issued formally acknowledges receipt. The importance of getting a receipt for every stock certificate cannot be overemphasized. If you mail the certificate from your office direct to an out-of-town stockholder, you should send it registered mail, with return receipt requested. It is important that the return receipt be clearly marked and identified so you can certify that the receipt is the receipt for a particular stock certificate. If the receipt is handled in that manner, the return receipt should be affixed to the stub in the stock book. At the time you mail it, you should keep a record, and if the return receipt does not come back

within five days, it should be followed up with the post office. You should not just automatically file the return receipt. It is always better to get the stockholder to sign the stub of the stock book if this is practical. On occasion, with your attorney's permission, you may photocopy the stub, place it in the stock book temporarily and send the original stub to the stockholder with the stock certificate, asking that he sign it, acknowledging receipt, and return it to you for placing in the stock book.

15. The example shown is a reissue of stock which is not a sale. There is no real change of ownership involved, because the master trust has no property other than what is held for the four subtrusts. Therefore, when the bank wanted it reissued, it did not involve a real transfer of interest. You will notice that on the stub of the old certificate, showing the reissue, it is not necessary that the full and complete name of the person to whom the new certificate is issued be shown. For the full information, the person interested can refer to the stub of the new certificate issued.

16. The second stub that is shown as an example shows a transfer of stock from the stub of one of the recipients of the stock. In this example, certificate No. 18 for 52 shares was issued to a subtrust, out of original certificate No. 10 for 206 shares.

17. The name here is the name of the recipient of certificate No. 18 for 52 shares. The date is the date of the transfer of stock, which is the date of new certificate No. 1.

18. The name shown here is the name on the original certificate from which the transfer is being made, number 10. The date shown here is the date of the original certificate, which in this case happens to be the same as the date on new certificate No. 18. It is ususual for these dates to be the same.

19. At the very bottom of the stub is shown the number of the original certificate from which the transfer is being made (206). The next column shows the number of shares transferred in this particular new certificate being issued. In this case, it is 52 shares. At the time a reissue is being made, whether constituting a sale of a part of an old certificate, or a reissue, or whatever it is, there will be stubs in consecutive order showing in the "no. of shares transferred" column numbers that add up the number of original shares shown in the immediately preceding column, all tied into the original certificate.

The importance of being careful in handling stock certificates cannot be overemphasized. These are valuable documents, and you need to handle them very carefully. Ask if you are not sure. When mailing stock certificates, mail by registered or certified mail to avoid unnecessary work in the future.

¶1905 Other Forms You Should Know About

¶1905.1 Resolution Opening Bank Account

Many banks have their own preprinted resolution forms. Always check with the bank where the corporate account will be. Get the forms and signature cards and fill them in before the organizational meeting. You can gather the information from the various forms that you have already prepared.

¶1905.2 Notice of Stockholders' Meeting

The notice of the annual and special stockholders' meeting must be prepared according to the bylaws of the corporation. The notice must give the date and time of the meeting and where the meeting will be held, and the purpose of the meeting. (See Figure 1905.2-1.) If notice is not or cannot be given in the time required in bylaws, see Section 1905.3.

Notice of annual meeting.

[Place and date]

To the Stockholders of the ______ Company:

Notice is hereby given that the annual meeting of the stockholders of ______ Company, will be held at the office of the company, ______ Street, ______ [city and state], on ______, 19____, at ______ o'clock ____.m. for the election of a board of directors for the ensuing year and for the transaction of such other business as may properly come before the meeting.

Stock transfer books will be closed from the evening of ______, 19____, and reopen on the morning of ______, 19____.

Respectfully,

______, Secretary

Figure 1905.2-1. Notice of Annual Meeting.

¶1905.3 Waiver of Notice of Stockholders' Meeting

Notices are sent to all stockholders who have the right to vote. Stockholders may waive notice. They do that by signing the waiver of notice of stockholders' meeting. (See Figure 1905.3-1.) An alternative is to prepare a Consent in Lieu of Stockholders' Meeting containing statements of action taken and resolutions passed and have it signed by *all* the stockholders entitled to vote at that time.

Waiver of notice of meeting.

A. The undersigned, being all the stockholders of ______ Company, a corporation created and organized under the laws of the State of ______, hereby assent and agree that a meeting of the stockholders of said corporation shall be held at ______ on the ______ day of ______, at ______ o'clock _____ .m., for the purpose of ______ [state purpose], and the transaction of other business. We do hereby waive notice and the publication of notice of such meeting, and agree that any business transacted at such meeting shall be as valid and effective as though held after notice duly given and published.

Dated ______, 19_____.

[Signatures]

Figure 1905.3-1. Waiver of Meeting Notice.

¶1905.4 Proxies and Proxy Statement

Frequently, a stockholder may not be able to attend the meeting. He can give his power to vote to another person by means of a proxy. (See Figure 1905.4-1.) Corporations that are listed on the stock exchange must furnish a written proxy statement to each person whose proxy is being obtained. The proxy statement sets forth the matter the designed person may vote on, whether the person given the proxy can revoke it, and other information relating to the vote. It should be remembered that directors cannot vote by proxy in a directors' meeting.

If you think that there may not be a quorum present, you may want to obtain signed proxies well in advance of the meeting. The number of persons that constitute a quorum, required to obtain the vote of the corporation, is set forth in the bylaws. In most corporations, the majority constitutes a quorum.

¶1905.5 Certificate of Assumed Business (Fictitious) Name

If the corporation is planning to do business under another name other than the corporate name, you must prepare a certificate of fictitious name. (See Figure 1905.5-1.) Most states have a statute requiring the registration of an assumed or fictitious name in the county where the business will be conducted under that name. There are penalties for failure to register, including restrictions on the right to sue another or to

A. The ______ Company

I hereby make, constitute and appoint ______ and ______, or either of them, my proxy, to vote for me at the annual meeting of the stockholders of the ______ Company, to be held at ______ Street, at ______, ______.m., on the ______ day of ______, 19____, or any adjournment thereof, for the election of directors, and for the transaction of such other business as may properly come before said meeting, according to the number of votes I would be entitled to cast if personally present.

Witness my hand [and seal] this ______ day of ______, 19____.

B. The undersigned shareholder of ______ Corporation, a ______ [name of state] corporation, does hereby constitute and appoint ______, ______ and ______, or any one of them, the true and lawful attorneys or attorney of the undersigned, for and in the name, place and stead of the undersigned, to appear and act as the proxies or proxy of the undersigned at the annual meeting of the shareholders of said corporation to be held at the registered office of the corporation on the ______ day of ______, 19____, at the hour of ______, ______.m., and at any adjournment or adjournments of said meeting, and to vote all of the shares of said corporation standing in the name of the undersigned, or which the undersigned may be entitled to vote, in the transaction of such business as may come before said meeting, as fully as the undersigned might or could do if personally present, with full power of substitution and revocation, hereby ratifying and confirming all that said attorneys or any of them, or their substitutes or substitute, shall lawfully do or cause to be done by virtue hereof, hereby revoking any proxy or proxies heretofore given by the undersigned to vote and act at such meeting. A majority of such of my attorneys and proxies, their substitutes or substitute, as shall be present and shall act at said meeting [or if only one be present and act, then that one] shall have and may exercise all of the powers of all of said attorneys and proxies hereunder.

In witness whereof the undersigned has executed this proxy this ______ day of ______, 19____.

In the presence of ______

[Signature]

C. I hereby nominate and appoint ______, if present, and if not present, ______, as my attorney or proxy, in the order herein named, to represent me and cast my vote by proxy at the annual meeting of the stockholders of ______ to be held at the office of the corporation in ______ on the ______ day of ______, 19____, hereby ratifying and confirming all my said attorney may do by virtue hereof.

Figure 1905.4-1. Proxy for Annual Meeting.

This proxy is given voluntarily and without any solicitations by any agent of the corporation. Any proxy heretofore given by me for said meeting is hereby revoked.
Dated this ______ day of ______, 19____.

Figure 1905.4-1. (continued)

State of ______
County of ______
__________, a ______ corporation, being desirous of transacting a portion of its business under an assumed or trade name as permitted by ______ [statutory citation] hereby certifies:

1. The corporate name and location of the principal office of said corporation is: ______.

2. The name, other than its own corporate name, under which such business is carried on is: ______.

3. A brief description of the kind of business transacted and to be transacted under such assumed or trade name is: ______.

IN WITNESS WHEREOF, the undersigned president and secretary of said corporation, have this day executed this certificate ______, 19____.

____
By______, President

Attest: ______, Secretary
Subscribed and sworn to me this ______ day of ______, 19____.
My commission expires ______.

______, Notary Public

Figure 1905.5-1. Certificate of Assumed (Fictitious) Name.

defend a lawsuit filed against the corporation if the action is based on acts done in the business being conducted under the assumed name instead of the real corporate name.

¶1905.6 Application for Employer Identification Number

An application for an employer identification number is made on a federal treasury department form called an SS-4. You must prepare this application so that the corporation will have an identifying number for purposes of paying employee taxes and preparing forms, among other reasons. It is filed with the Internal Revenue Service and you can obtain blank forms from them. (See Figure 1002-1.)

¶1905.7 Other Miscellaneous Forms

Other forms you might have to prepare include applications for state and city sales tax licenses, withholding tax registration, unemployment insurance, and workers' compensation forms, which are usually required if your client has more than one employee. Each state is different and your attorney should check with the local workmen's compensation board or licensing agencies. Also, your client will have to arrange to purchase workmens' compensation insurance. You may not have to prepare these forms since many corporations do it themselves. It depends on the client.

¶1906 What Else You Can Do to Assist Your Attorney in Handling Corporate Business

You can do a number of things to assist your attorney in handling the various client corporations' businesses. If you handle several corporate clients, it is important for you to be as organized as possible to keep matters up to date. You especially want to make sure the minute books are kept up to date. Your attorney never knows when the client will request to see its corporate minute book.

¶1906.1 Checklist of Things You Can Do to Assist Your Attorney in Handling Corporate Business

- Prepare for corporate meetings by preparing the notices of meetings, proxies and waivers of notice.
- Record and prepare the minutes of the meetings.
- Issue stock certificates and make transfer of stock, if requested.
- Take care of corporate papers and other documents. (You should keep stock certificates and the like in the firm safe.)
- Maintain the corporate calendar.
- Assist in arranging for the change of corporate name.
- Maintain the corporate calendar and keep a schedule of meetings.
- Keep the corporate seal and minute book in a safe place.
- Keep a list of stockholders, officers, and directors with their current address and telephone number.
- Keep an annual request for information letter form to be mailed to each corporate client each year if you keep the minutes books in your office.

¶2000 Handling Wills, Probate, and Estate Administration

This chapter will provide you with guidelines for handling Wills, probate, and estate administration. The first step is to learn all you can about Wills, how they are written and what provisions they must contain. You could be instrumental in setting up an organized system of preparing Wills if you have a word processor. Set up all the different provisions of Wills, give them a number, create a form book that your attorneys could use to quickly dictate the numbers of the particular provisions of the Will that they want. More on that later.

Probate is a proceeding brought in the applicable court to prove the validity of a Will and to provide for the administration of the decedent's (deceased's) estate and other related matters.

Some states follow the Uniform Probate Code which permits the use of formal (supervised) or informal (unsupervised) probate proceedings.

The county and state in which the decedent resides at the time of death is the appropriate court for administration of the decedent's estate. In some states there are special probate courts or surrogate's courts which handle estate administration.

Probate proceedings involve the proving of the Will and the carrying out of the provisions of the Will.

The attorney works closely with the executor or executrix of the estate. The executor or executrix is given certain authority according to the Will and the applicable laws.

Your role consists of preparing documents, calendaring deadlines, scheduling appointments, and answering routine informational questions from the clients.

Probate and estate administration is not only a difficult legal process, but also a very personal and emotional experience for the client. This chapter will tell you how you can be a helpful assistant to your attorneys. The death of a loved one is a very traumatic experience for anyone. Presenting a very knowledgeable but humanistic attitude toward the client will ease the client's mind. If you know the various steps in estate administration, you will be able to handle the client with awareness and concern. In doing so, you should always treat the client with kid gloves, that is, show and express understanding of and compassion for the client.

As a practical matter, you will probably see the client more often than your attorneys do during the course of the administration of the estate.

Most of you are aware that the Will is the primary document used in estate planning. It is the controlling document that shows to whom the client wishes to leave the his or her property and guides the attorney in carrying out the client's wishes.

The Will is one of the most important legal documents that you will handle in the law office. Just as any legal document, it must have been prepared accurately and also must have been executed properly to protect the party making the Will. A mistake in that area could be costly to the estate of the deceased. Even a slight error or omission could provoke a lawsuit, resulting in tremendous losses in legal fees and court costs. More importantly, the desires and intentions of the deceased may not be carried out according to the decedent's wishes.

This chapter describes types of Wills and gives very practical tips for typing a Will. Estate planning is another matter. This chapter will give you basic understanding of the nature of probate proceedings, and give you ideas on becoming more helpful to your attorneys in this area. As you work with probate administration, always look for ways to systematize the procedures in the process. Ask yourself frequently: "How could this be done more efficiently? Could I write down these procedures to help me in the future? What can I do to save my attorneys' time?"

¶2001 Before We Begin: Some Basic Terminology

To help you understand the process of Wills, probate, and estate administration set forth in this chapter, you need to become familiar with the basic terminology of this area of the law. If you come across a word that is not defined here, check the Glossary in the Appendix.

Decedent. The deceased person whose estate is being administered pursuant to a Will or the estate succession statutes of the state in which he or she resided when he died.

Probate Property. The property of the decedent owned at the time of death is referred to as *probate* or *nonprobate* property. It is probate property whether it passes under the terms of the decedent's Will or under the state succession laws. It is nonprobate if the decedent owned it jointly, and it passes to the decedent's surviving joint owner by the terms of the joint document or by operation of other state laws.

Probate property includes those items of property owned solely by the decedent or in which the decedent had some interest which survived his or her death. This may be any or all of the following items:

¶2001.1 Checklist of Probate Property

1. Real estate, and form of ownership of each parcel of property.
2. Tax refunds for decedent's last tax year.
3. Stocks, bonds, and other securities.
4. Oil, mineral, gas, and timber rights.
5. Life insurance on decedent's life, which is payable to his or her estate instead of to another named and eligible beneficiary.
6. Life insurance owned by decedent on the life of another.
7. Accounts receivable of any business interests of decedent.
8. Mortgages, promissory notes, or real estate. Installment sales contracts payable to decedent.
9. Cash, certificates of deposits, bank accounts.
10. Interests in unincorporated businesses, proprietorships, and partnerships.
11. Annuities, Investment Retirement Account (IRA), and Keogh plans.
12. Pension, profit sharing, and other employee benefit plans.
13. Assets in certain trusts.
14. Automobiles, motorcycles and other vehicles.
15. Personal jewelry and other valuables.
16. Antiques.
17. Coins, stamps, and other valuable collections.
18. Gifts made by decedent within three years of death in excess of the amount allowed by law.
19. Farm equipment, livestock, and crops.
20. Powers of appointment.
21. Valuable art objects.
22. Household furniture and goods.
23. Death benefits.
24. Uncashed checks in decedent's possession.
25. Payroll checks receivable.
26. Other valuable items not mentioned.

Nonprobate Property. Nonprobate property includes all that property that a decedent owned with others in joint tenancy where there was a right of survivorship as described above, life insurance payable to others, and other property where there was a right of survivorship in another, and property the decedent had been holding in trust for others. Property in trust for another is transferred automatically to the recipient without passing through the decedent's estate. Another example of nonprobate property is the residence or other property owned by husband and wife as tenants by the entireties or a bank account or stock certificate owned jointly with the decedent on which express words "with right of survivorship" appear.

Right of Survivorship. This means that the person owns property with another person equally and that if one of the joint owners dies, the property automatically goes directly to the other joint tenant.

Inter-vivos Trust. Property in an inter-vivos trust, one created during life, remains in trust and is transferred pursuant to the trust terms to the recipient without passing through the decedent's estate.

Codicil. A Codicil to a Will is an amendment, postscript, addition, supplement, or change in the original Will that has been incorporated in the Will by preparing, executing, and witnessing just like the original Will.

Testator. A male person making a Will.

Testatrix. A female person making a Will.

Beneficiaries. Those persons named in a Will to receive property belonging to the decedent's estate or those parties who are heirs-at-law of the decedent's estate by reason of state succession statutes which provide for inheritance priorities if the decedent leaves no valid Will.

Devise. To make gifts of real estate by a Will.

Devisee. The recipient of a gift of real estate made by Will.

Bequeath. To make a gift of personal property or money by a Will.

Bequest. A gift of personal property or money.

Legacy. A gift of money or personal property. It is synonymous with bequest.

Legatee. The recipient of gifts of money or personal property. A legatee receives a bequest.

Executor. A male person named by the testator or testatrix to administer the terms of his or her Will and the distribution of his or her estate.

Executrix. A female person named by the testator or testatrix to administer the terms of his or her Will and the distribution of his or her estate.

Administrator. A male person appointed by the court to administer the estate if a valid Will of the testator or testatrix has not been accepted for probate.

Administratrix. A female person appointed by the court to administer the estate if the testator or testatrix has not named an executor or executrix in his or her Will or dies intestate, i.e., without a Will.

Personal Representative. A person, who may be either male or female, who has been appointed as executor, executrix, administrator, or administratrix of the decedent's estate. The Uniform Probate Code, which has been adopted in many states, uses the designation personal representative.

Probate of Will. A legal proceeding which accepts a Will in probate court records. The court will "admit the Will to probate" and upon further procedures the court will direct that letters testamentary issue to the named executor or lawful substitute.

Letters of Administration. The documentary form of authority given to the administrator or administratrix by petitioning the probate court.

Letters of Administration. The documentary form of authority given to the administrator by petitioning the probate court.

Decedent's Estate. The probatable property left by the deceased.

Testate. If the deceased left a Will, he or she is said to have died testate.

Intestate. If the deceased did not leave a Will, he or she is said to have died intestate.

Joint Testators. A man and his wife who make a joint Will which they both sign. This type of Will is used infrequently in some states. Mutual or reciprocal Wills are more common. In this case husband and wife make and sign separate Wills at the same time.

¶2002 The Six Types of Wills

A Will is a legal document drawn and executed in acceptable legal form, in which a person directs how he or she wants his or her property distributed after his or her death. That property is called the decedent's estate. Formerly, the terminology *Will and Testament* was frequently used to describe a Will. The words are often used interchangeably now.

The form must comply with the laws of the state where it is probated even if it was executed in another state.

There are six different types of Wills as follows:

1. *Formal or Simple Will:* A formal Will, drafted by the attorney and dictated to the secretary and typed, or typed on a commercially printed Will form. (See Figure 2002-1.)
2. *Holographic Will:* A Will written by the testator or testatrix in his or her own handwriting and signed by him or her without legal formality. Approximately one half of the states recognize holographic wills under certain circumstances.
3. *Oral Wills (Nuncupative and Soldier's and Sailor's):* A Nuncupative Will is a spoken Will by a person about to die or in imminent danger of death. In most instances, it must be reduced to writing by the witnesses to whom it was spoken within a limited time. Soldier's and Sailor's Wills are oral Wills made by sailors and soldiers in military service or at sea. There are strict laws that govern these Wills and in states in which the Uniform Probate Code has been adopted, they are not recognized.
4. *Contingent or Conditional Wills:* A contingent or conditional Will is valid only upon the occurrence of a specific event. Very few states recognize these Wills.
5. *Joint Will:* A joint Will, which is sometimes referred to as a reciprocal Will, is often executed by husband and wife. They may execute one Will or separate Wills. This type of Will may cause problems should one or the other want to change or revoke his or her Will before the other dies.
6. *Living Will:* A living Will is valid in some states. It is a Will in which the testator or testatrix states that his or her desire is that his or her life shall not be prolonged under the circumstance set forth in the signed documents. This Will may be used in terminal illness if it states that the testator or testatrix does not wish to be on life-sustaining procedures and that he or she be permitted to die. (See Figure 2002-2.)

¶2003 What Are the Parts of a Will?

The following are the clauses that usually appear in most Wills, depending upon the law of the state and your attorney's preferences. The clauses are not necessarily in the order in which they should appear in the Will.

Last Will and Testament of ______

I, ______, of [residing in] the city [county] of ______, state of ______, do make, publish and declare this my last will and testament, and I do hereby revoke all other and former wills and codicils to wills made by me.

First. I direct my executor hereinafter named to pay all my just debts and obligations, including the expenses of my last illness as soon after my decease as is practicable.

Second. I make the following gifts of specific sums of money or specific personal property:

1. To ______ I give [bequeath] the sum of ______ dollars.
2. To ______ I give [bequeath] my ______ automobile.

[Etc.]

Third. I make the following gifts of specific real property:

1. To ______ I give [devise] my real estate at ______ in the county of ______, state of ______, more particularly described as follows: ______ [legal description].

Fourth. I hereby nominate and appoint ______ of ______ to be executor of this my last will and testament and direct that he [it] be [not] required to furnish a bond as required by law and directed by the court [or: to furnish a bond in the amount of ______ dollars]; and, in event ______ for any reason does not qualify for, or ceases to be, executor of this, my last ______, if he [it] becomes such executor, shall [not] be required to give bond, [etc.].

Fifth. My executor and his successors shall have the following powers and duties: ______.

[Testimonium clause and signature of testator]

[Attestation clause and signatures of witnesses]

—Another form.

I, ______, domiciled and residing in ______, make, publish, and declare this to be my last will and revoke all other wills and codicils.

1. My family consists of the following persons: ______.
2. Reference in this will to the term " ______ " shall mean ______.
3. I direct that my funeral expenses (including the cost of a suitable grave marker), the costs of administering my estate and all legal debts allowable as claims against my estate be paid out of the general funds of my estate before any distribution thereof to any of the beneficiaries mentioned herein.
4. I direct that all taxes imposed by reason of my death upon property passing under or outside this will be paid out of my residuary estate.
5. I give and bequeath my personal effects (specify) to the following persons: ______.

Figure 2002-1. Short Forms of Wills.

6. My residuary estate is all of my property remaining after the dispositions specified in paragraph 5 of this will, whenever obtained, and including property not otherwise effectively disposed of in this will and property as to which I have a power to appoint. I give, devise, and bequeath my residuary estate to ______.

7. I appoint ______ as executor (without bond) of this will.

8. My executor shall have the following powers, in addition to those granted by law: ______.

In witness whereof, I have signed my name this ______ day of ______, 19—.

(Attestation)

Figure 2002-1. *(continued)*

Living Will

Living will made this _____ day of _____, 198_____.

I, ________________________________, being of sound mind, willfully and voluntarily make known my desire that my life shall not be prolonged under the circumstances set forth below and do declare:

1. If at any time I should have a terminal condition as defined in and established in accordance with the procedures set forth in paragraph (10) of Code Section 31-32-2 of the Official Code of Georgia Annotated, I direct that the application of life-sustaining procedures to my body be withheld or withdrawn and that I be permitted to die;

2. In the absence of my ability to give directions regarding the use of such life-sustaining procedures, it is my intention that this living will shall be honored by my family and physician(s) as the final expression of my legal right to refuse medical or surgical treatment and accept the consequences from such refusal;

3. This will shall have no force or effect seven years from the date I signed this document as stated above; however, I understand that, if at the end of said seven years I am incapable of communicating with the attending physician, this will shall remain in effect until such time as I am able to communicate with the physician;

4. I understand that I may revoke this living will at any time;

5. I understand the full import of this living will, and I am at least 18 years of age and am emotionally and mentally competent to make this living will; and

6. If I have been diagnosed as pregnant, this living will shall have no force and effect during the course of my pregnancy.

____

________________________ (City), ________________________(County),

Figure 2002-2. Living Will.

and ______________________________(State of Residence).

I hereby witness this living will and attest that:

(1) The declarant is personally known to me and I believe the declarant to be at least 18 years of age and of sound mind;
(2) I am at least 18 years of age;
(3) To the best of my knowledge, at the time of the execution of this living will, I:
    (A) Am not related to the declarant by blood or marriage;
    (B) Would not be entitled to any portion of the declarant's estate by any will or by operation of law under the rules of descent and distribution of this estate;
    (C) Am not the attending physician of declarant or an employee of the attending physician or an employee of the hospital or skilled nursing facility in which declarant is a patient;
    (D) Am not directly financially responsible for the declarant's medical care; and
    (E) Have no present claim against any portion of the estate of the declarant;
(4) Declarant has signed this document in my presence as above-instructed, on the date above first shown.

Witness ____________

Address ____________

Witness ____________

Address ____________

Additional witness required when living will is signed in a hospital or skilled nursing facility.

I hereby witness this living will and attest that I believe the declarant to be of sound mind and to have made this living will willingly and voluntarily.

Witness: ______________________
Medical director of skilled nursing facility or chief of the hospital medical staff

Figure 2002-2. (continued)

1. Title: This is the name of the will such as "Last Will and Testament of Dustin G. Ketchem" or "Last Will of Dustin G. Ketchem." Or if it is a Codicil, it may be titled "First Codicil to the Last Will and Testament of Dustin G. Ketchem," or "First Codicil to the Last Will of Dustin G. Ketchem."

2. Introductory clause: In this clause, the testator's or testatrix's name and residence are recited and it states that he or she revokes all prior Wills and Codicils. Sometimes this part of the Will recites the testator's capacity to make a Will.

3. Debt Clause: This paragraph directs the executor or executrix to pay all debts and funeral expenses as soon as possible after death occurs.

4. Specific Bequests: These paragraphs specify bequests of the deceased and indicate certain monetary or other assets to be given to specific person(s). For example, the testator or testatrix may want to give a special ring to someone.

5. Distribution Clause: These paragraphs, which are also known as dispositive clauses, set forth the testator's or testatrix's intentions for the distribution of his or her personal and real property. (If these paragraphs exceed 26 letters of the alphabet, number the paragraphs instead of using letters.)

6. Trust Clause: These paragraphs which are also referred to as *dispositive clauses* provide for certain property of the testator or testatrix to be set aside in trust for an individual or individuals or institution for a particular purpose.

7. Guardianship Clause: If the testator or testatrix has minor children, this paragraph names or appoints a competent adult, in many cases a relative, who would assume responsibility for the minor children.

8. Residuary Clause: This paragraph provides for the disposition of all personal and real property not provided for in other parts of the Will. This gift made in this clause has the least priority over the gifts made in other clauses of the Will, but it is absolutely necessary to include it to prevent intestacy as to any of the decedent's estate. If any of the decedent's estate is not disposed of by the Will that portion will pass to the heirs-at-law of the decedent under the state succession laws.

9. Appointment of an Executor: This clause names the executor or executrix to handle the testator's or testatrix's estate after his or her death. The executor or executrix is governed not only by the provisions in the testator's or testatrix's Will, but also by rules of the state probate statute. In many cases, the named executor or executrix is the attorney or a banking institution. Sometimes the testator or testatrix will appoint more than one executor or executrix, or an alternate executor or executrix to serve in the event the first named executor or executrix is unwilling or unable to handle the estate. Or the testator or testatrix may appoint co-executors or co-executrices or one executor and one executrix to serve simultaneously.

10. One-dollar Clause: Here the testator or testatrix gives a nominal amount of money to a person to show that he or she was not overlooked in case this person attempts to contest the will.

11. Precatory Clause: In such a paragraph or clause the testator or testatrix may set forth his or her wishes that the executor or executrix handle parts of his or her estate in a certain manner. Since these are often vague, these clauses often cause lawsuits to be filed to interpret their meaning.

12. Payment of Debts and Taxes: This clause directs the estate's legal representative to pay all debts, expenses and taxes. It should tell whether taxes such as inheritance, estate, etc., should be paid from estate funds or by the beneficiaries of the estate.

13. Powers of Executor or Executrix: A testator or testatrix may set forth what powers the executor or executrix may have to administer the estate without requesting authority from the court to handle most transactions, e.g., sale of estate assets. This clause may state that the executor or executrix may not need to obtain a surety bond. The surety bond is required for the protection of both the heirs and the creditors. This is often a commercial bond issued by an insurance company which ensures that the executor or executrix will properly perform his or her duties. This bond requires a payment of a premium similar to an insurance policy. In some states the court may require that the executor or executrix post bond and override a clause in the Will which allows a waiver of the bond. In some states the law provides for other powers for the executor or executrix even if they are not in the Will.

14. Rule Against Perpetuities: This clause supports the rule against perpetuities, i.e., the principle that no interest in property is good unless it vests within 21 years, plus period of gestation, after the end of some person who was living at the time of creation of the interest in the property.

15. Burial Clause: A testator or testatrix may wish that certain items be adhered to regarding his or her burial, e.g., cremation or a closed casket.

16. Testimonium Clause: This unnumbered concluding clause of the Will is where the date and signature appear, and usually begins with the phrase "IN WITNESS WHEREOF" in all caps.

17. Attestation Clause: This is the final clause which states that the Will was signed by the testator or testatrix in the presence of witnesses.

19. Self-proving Clause: The Uniform Probate Code which has been adopted in many states provides a form for a self-proving clause to be signed by the testator or testatrix and the witnesses in front of a notary public. If that clause is used and properly executed, the Will can be filed after the death of the testator or testatrix without producing the witnesses to the Will.

¶2004 Parties to a Probate Proceeding

The person or corporation who wishes to have the Will probated is the petitioner. Usually this is the person or corporation named in the Will as executor or executrix. Besides the petitioner there are three groups of interested parties who must receive notice of the probate proceeding so that they can protect their interests:

1. Heirs-at-law: These parties are the surviving spouse and the distributees who would have inherited the decedent's property or a portion of his or her property if the decedent had died intestate. This includes heirs-at-law who are also named in the Will as legatees, because they might have less according to the Will than they would have inherited if there had been no Will.

2. Executors or executrices and trustees named in the Will who do not execute the petition.

3. All legatees or devisees who are not distributees. These are those named in the Will who would not have inherited if the decedent had died intestate. They will lose their legacies if the Will is not admitted to probate.

¶2005 Hints for Typing an Attractive Will

The most important thing about typing a Will is that it be accurate. You will find it very rewarding to type an attractive and accurate Will. It is prepared very formally; when finished, it is something to be proud of. The client expects the Will to be attractive and error-proof. Again, it is imperative that you type a Will with absolute accuracy and neatness. With word processing, the typing of the Will can be so much simpler and error-free. If your office does not have a form file or Will clauses stored on the word processor, you can simplify your Will preparation by setting up a system on the word processor so that your attorneys can merely select the provisions that they want in the Will that you can prepare without their dictating the clauses.

1. There should be no erasures to the visible eye.
2. Use the same format on each page.
3. Do not end a page with a paragraph or a sentence.
4. Do not start a paragraph at the top of the page. This is to prevent any additional pages being inserted in the Will.
5. Make at least three copies: an original and two copies. The original can be stored in a safe or a safe deposit box. One conformed copy (a copy of the Will that reflects those items that were handwritten or changed on the original document, such as dates, signatures, and corrections), should be given to the testator or testatrix, and one conformed copy should be kept in the office file. Additional copies can be made if the testator or testatrix requests.
6. Number paragraphs consecutively with the use of one of the following headings: FIRST:, ARTICLE I:, ITEM 1:, or I.
7. The attestation clause should start approximately six lines below the signature of the testator or testatrix. If necessary, it can be single-spaced. At least the first line of the attestation clause should appear on the page containing the testator's or testatrix's signature.
8. All witnesses' signatures must appear on the same page, and their addresses should be included in case they have to be located when the Will is probated. An alternative is to type at least one line of the attestation clause on the signature page, with the rest of the clause on the last page with the witnesses' signatures.
9. Type lines for addresses of the witnesses.
10. Prepare a draft of the Will first so that you can determine the proper spacing for the final copy.
11. Use good quality, letter-sized bond paper, or legal numbered paper, if preferred by your attorneys.
12. Double-space, except for the attestation clause and sometimes the "powers" given to the executor or executrix.
13. Number each page two spaces after the last line in the center of the page; you can use a dash preceding the number if your attorneys prefer that.
14. Number the last page one-half inch from the bottom of the page.
15. Triple-space between the body of the Will and the testimonium clause.
16. Type the attestation clause single-spaced. Indent it three spaces from the regular left margin and indent the first line five spaces.
17. Type the witness line three spaces below the attestation clause, at the left margin, and underscore 25 spaces. Type "residing at" and underscore for another 25 spaces.

18. Triple-space between the witness lines.
19. Double-check the spelling of names.
20. Type the back.
21. After the Will is signed, conform copies to the original by typing /s/ in the place where the name was signed on the copies.
22. Certify the copies, if necessary.
23. If your office is going to keep the original Will, give the testator or testatrix a receipt, signed in the firm's name by you or one of the attorneys. Type:

> The Will of (name of testator or testatrix), dated February 14, 1985, is in our possession for safekeeping.

24. Enclose the original in an envelope, marked "Last Will and Testament of (name of testator or testatrix)."
25. If a bank or an institution is named executor, send a conformed copy to it with a transmittal letter.
26. Take any former copies of the Will and make a notation that they have been superseded and put the date of the new Will. It is preferable not to destroy previous Wills.
27. Put the proper backing on the Will and type the necessary information in the required space.
28. Type the testator's or testatrix's name in all caps; all other names are underscored (preferably with red ink).
29. The words "Last Will and Testament" mentioned in the will are initial caps.
30. Do not type a comma before the conjunction *and* when the following phrases are typed: *make, publish and declare* and *give, devise and bequeath.*

¶2006 Execution of the Will

As previously stated, the execution of a Will is very different from most legal documents and should be handled very carefully. An omission or an error could cause a lawsuit resulting in attorneys' fees and court costs to be taken out of the estate. Moreover, the decedent's wishes may not be carried out.

Since most Wills require two witnesses, you may be asked to be one of the witnesses. The procedure of witnessing a Will is very formal. The testator or testatrix "publishes" the Will in the presence of the witnesses by stating that the document is his or her Will. The testator or testatrix asks the witnesses to witness the signature. Although this is not done in some states, the testator or testatrix may initial each page of the Will, usually on the left margin of the rest of the Will. The attorney generally asks each witness to sign the Will in the presence of each other. No one leaves the room while the execution of the Will is taking place and sealed. There is a space in the Will for the address of each witness in case the witness is called upon to prove the Will after the testator's or testatrix's death. This procedure may vary from state to state, but your attorneys will explain to you how it is done in the state in which they practice.

¶2007 Procedures for Probating an Estate

The *Uniform Probate Code* compiled by the National Conference of Commissioners on Uniform State Laws has been adopted by several states, either in whole or in part, or with modification. The purpose of the *Uniform Probate Code* is to establish uniformity in the probate laws and procedures in the various states.

The *Uniform Probate Code* allows some cases to be handled without an attorney, which can save the family of the testator or testatrix a significant amount of money. The attorney and family have an option of deciding whether to administer the estate under the Code or proceed with formal administration under the Code.

The following general steps are to be taken by your attorney in the process of probating the estate in most states. *Probate* includes all administration and proceedings involved in handling the estate not just the official probate process with the court. The purpose of mentioning them here is to tell you the reasons why certain things are handled in a particular way so that you can become more valuable to your attorneys in doing your part of the job.

Step 1. Locate the Will. If the testator or testatrix died testate (with a Will), the Will must be located before probate can be initiated. The first thing you can do is to look in the testator's or testatrix's file if he or she has been a client of your attorneys. You may have to check in the firm's safe or safe deposit box. Or the family may locate the Will among the testator's or testatrix's personal possessions.

It may be in the testator's or testatrix's safe deposit box. To get it out may require a court order if the decedent's spouse does not have joint access.

If the decedent died without a Will, he or she is said to have died intestate. If so, then the probate of his or her estate will be governed by law of the state of his or her domicile. His or her heirs-at-law will be those relatives designated in the estate succession laws of the state where the decedent was domiciled when he or she died, regardless of where he or she died.

The Will may be proved by having one or more of the witnesses to the Will file an affidavit that they were witnesses to the Will and that the testator or testatrix was of "sound mind" at the time of executing the Will. In some states the witnesses will actually appear in court and swear that they witnessed the execution of the Will.

In states that have adopted the *Uniform Probate Code,* a Will may be self-proved if it contains not only the signatures of the testator or testatrix and witnesses but also the acknowledgment of a notary public attesting to the signatures of the testator or testatrix and witnesses, the soundness of the testator's mind, and his or her declaration that the Will was his or her last Will and Testament. No further proof is needed in these states.

Step 2. Reading of the Will. After the relatives of the decedent contact the firm, an initial interview may be conducted with the members of the family, usually the immediate family. If the executor or executrix named in the Will is not a relative, he or she usually will be invited to the interview. If the executor or executrix is an institution, then a representative of that institution may attend the reading of the Will.

A reading of the Will is not required by law. If it is done, it is done for psychological reasons or because of custom. Your attorneys will know what questions to ask and whether to have a reading. They may ask you to take notes. If you do, be sure to take detailed notes. Make sure you remember the names of the people attending so you can identify them when they speak. You might make a diagram of the table where the people are sitting in your notes so that you can identify them when they speak.

If the Will has been located, it may be read at this time. Your attorneys will answer any questions the family may have. You are not permitted to give legal advice to anyone, regardless of any present or prior contact with the family or other persons present.

You can obtain information about the family and the survivors and their relationship to the decedent from the obituary in the newspaper before the meeting. Do not treat that information as complete or unimpeachable although it often is thorough. If you can obtain any information from the file in your office, this will be helpful to your attorneys and the family.

Step 3. File the Will and petition for probate. To prove the Will, the petition for probate of the Will, along with a copy of the Will, certified to be a true and correct copy, must be filed with the court so that a Decree can be issued by the court admitting the Will to probate and directing that letters testamentary are issued to the executor or executrix. The transfer tax affidavit must also be filed with the court, together with a petition for the probate of the Will and a transfer tax affidavit. At least one of the witnesses to the Will should make a sworn deposition to be filed with the court.

Step 4. The Will is admitted to probate. Next, if there are no contests of the Will, the court will issue a Decree admitting the Will to probate.

Step 5. The executor or executrix files a bond. Unless a bond is waived in the Will, the executor or executrix must file a bond. Letters Testamentary will then be issued to the executor or executrix. If a corporate executor is named, they in most instances do not have to file a bond.

Step 6. Letters Testamentary are issued to the executor. Letters Testamentary are issued to the executor or executrix after the signing of the Decree by the judge. These are prepared by the attorney and given to the executor or executrix, giving them authority to take actions on behalf of the estate. The executor or executrix must have a certificate showing that letters have been issued to transact business for the estate.

Step 7. Establish the executor's or executrix's right to handle the estate. The executor's or executrix's right to act is established by three documents: (1) the Will, (2) the Decree admitting it to probate, and (3) Letters Testamentary, which are granted by the court. He or she will need current certified copies of the Letters Testamentary or Letters of Administration to show his or her authority to deal with others in regard to the estate. For example, to control bank accounts or transfer stock or give deeds or bills of sale of personal property.

Step 8. Give notice to all interested parties. Your attorneys will prepare a notice to all interested parties and heirs. An affidavit of service or a waiver of service must be filed with the court. Any heir-at-law should receive this notice so that it gives them an opportunity to object to the admission of Will to probate.

Step 9. File inventory and necessary preliminary estate or transfer inheritances tax reports or returns. Ask your attorney to show you how to prepare these documents, as they are too complicated to explain here and vary from state to state.

Step 10. Publish notice to debtors and creditors and pay debts when allowed by your probate court rules. The court tries to protect the creditors of the decedent. Usually the family members are able to ascertain what the debts of the decedent are. In many cases, the creditors will notify the court. There are different processes for submitting claims to the estate in each state. The executor or executrix may file an intent to disallow the claim or an objection to claim with the court within the time specified in your probate court rules after the claim is presented to him or her. Most jurisdictions also require publication of notice in the local newspaper in order to give constructive notice of the probate proceedings to creditors and others.

Step 11. File tax returns or preliminary reports as instructed by your attorneys. Estate income tax, decedent's income tax, state transfer inheritance tax, or federal estate tax returns may be due depending on the value of the estate and the state in which it is being administered.

Income taxes for the decedent are paid for the year in which the date of death occurs. Tax is paid up until the date of death. The spouse may still file a joint return if the spouse remains unmarried until the end of the year.

The income of the decedent's estate after the date of death is taxed separately. That income is reported on a fiduciary income tax return. All income derived from the probate assets must be reported on this return.

Step 12. Make an accounting and distribution. The executor or executrix or administrator or administratrix (personal representative) files a final account with the court which sets forth all the transactions that have been handled with the estate's assets. The personal representative also petitions the court for distribution of the remaining assets. After a hearing is conducted, if required by your probate court rules, the court approves the account and orders distribution of the assets. Be sure to obtain a receipt from each devisee or legatee when estate property is deeded or given. The receipt is filed with the court. After approved distribution and payment of debts and taxes is completed, the personal representative is discharged from all his or her responsibilities, and the surety bond is terminated, if there is one.

¶2008 Contesting the Will

Any heir-at-law who either was omitted from the Will or was named to receive what he or she feels to be unfair may contest the Will. A petition to contest the Will must be filed within a certain time period. A contesting of the Will is similar to civil litigation. Notice and service on the parties is required. The petitioner must prove that the testator or testatrix was under undue influence, or prove fraud, or mistake in the making of the Will. If the petitioner receives a favorable ruling, then the Will is said to be invalid and will not be admitted to probate. The laws of intestacy then apply.

Use the following checklist to make sure everything is properly taken care of. If in doubt, ask your attorneys:

¶2009 Probate Checklist

1. Attorney's conference with executor or administrator.
2. Obtain copies of death certificate.
3. File Will.
4. File petition.
5. Hearing date
6. Prepare notices of hearing.
7. Send notices to clerk.
8. Prepare affidavit of mailing.
9. Send affidavit of mailing to the clerk.
10. Obtain bond, if necessary.
11. Prepare affidavit of witnesses, if necessary.
12. Prepare order admitting Will to probate.
13. Prepare order appointing appraiser.
14. Prepare letters.
15. Get letters signed.
16. Obtain certified copies.
17. Make appointment date with treasurer.
18. Prepare list of contents.
19. Notify banks of death.
20. Transfer accounts in joint tenancy.
21. File petition for family allowance.
22. Prepare notice.
23. Prepare order for family allowance.
24. File order for family allowance.
25. Publish notice to creditors.
26. Prepare proof of publication.
27. File proof of publication.
28. Prepare inventory and appraisal.
29. Type inventory.
30. Send inventory to appraiser.
31. Conform copies.

32. File original inventory.
33. Prepare inheritance tax affidavit.
34. Send inheritance tax affidavit to controller.
35. Prepare community property affidavit, if required.
36. File community property affidavit, if required.
37. Prepare federal income tax return.
38. File federal income tax return.
39. Prepare state income tax return.
40. File state income tax return.
41. Prepare petition for sale of real property.
42. File petition for sale of real property.
43. Publish notice re sale of property.
44. Prepare order for sale, if required.
45. Prepare petition for sale of personal property.
46. File petition for sale of personal property.
47. Prepare notice re sale.
48. File notice of sale.
49. Prepare order for sale of personal property.
50. File order for sale of personal property.
51. Prepare schedule of creditors' claims.
52. Prepare petition for distribution and final discharge.
53. File petition for distribution and final discharge.
54. Prepare final accounting.
55. Send notice of accounting.
56. File final accounting.
57. Prepare order for final distribution.
58. File order for final distribution.
59. Prepare distributees' receipts.
60. Prepare petition and order for final discharge.
61. Check to see that all attorneys' fees are paid.
62. Close file.

¶2100 What You Should Know about the Court System, Jurisdiction, and Venue

¶2101 Federal Court System

The federal court system consists of the Supreme Court of the United States, thirteen courts of appeal, the district courts, and various special courts.

¶2101.1 The United States Supreme Court

The Supreme Court consists of a Chief Justice of the United States and eight associate justices, any number of whom shall constitute a quorum. The Supreme Court is the court of record of writs of habeas corpus, writs of mandamus, writs of prohibition, penalty cases, and certain cases specified in the state constitution and has original jurisdiction. The Supreme Court has appellate jurisdiction in all cases in law and equity arising under the Constitution and the laws of the United States, and in treaties made, or which shall be made, under their authority. It also has appellate jurisdiction in all cases affecting ambassadors and other public ministers and consulates; and in controversies in which the United States is a party, between two or more states, citizens of the same state claiming lands under grants of different states, and states or its citizens and foreign states or citizens.[1]

The power of the Supreme Court to review decisions of the state courts is limited to those involving a federal question. The Supreme Court, however, has the power to declare unconstitutional any federal or state statute which is contrary to the United States Constitution.

¶2101.2 The United States Courts of Appeals

The United States is divided into thirteen judicial circuits (twelve judicial circuits plus the District of Columbia judicial circuit), with a court of appeals in every circuit. Each court of appeals consists of the circuit judges of the circuit in regular active service.[2] These courts are courts of record, meaning a complete transcript is made of proceedings.

[1]U.S. Const. art III, §2.

[2]28 U.S.C.A. §43(b).

These courts do not have any original jurisdiction but have appellate jurisdiction over the decisions of the federal district courts.

The Courts of Appeals also have the power to review orders issued by certain federal administrative agencies. For example, these courts may review orders issued by the Federal Trade Commission, the Department of Labor, the Federal Aviation Commission, and other federal administrative agencies. In most cases, as a practical matter, the court of appeals is the court of last resort in the federal court system, but, of course, a case may ultimately be appealed from the court of appeals to the United States Supreme Court.

¶2101.3 The United States District Courts

The United States is divided into judicial districts. Although some larger states are divided into two or more districts, there is at least one judicial district and one district court in each state. The federal district courts are courts of record. These courts are the trial courts in the federal court system and have original jurisdiction, exclusive of the courts of the states, of all criminal offenses against the United States.[3] They have broad jurisdiction over civil actions arising under the United States Constitution and federal laws.

The federal district courts also have original jurisdiction of all civil actions wherein the matter in controversy exceeds the sum or value of $10,000, exclusive of interest and costs, and arises under the Constitution, laws, or treaties of the United States (except that no such sum or value is required in any action brought against the United States, any agency thereof, or any officer or employee thereof in his official capacity).[4]

The federal district courts have exclusive jurisdiction, generally, in admiralty and maritime cases, bankruptcy matters and proceedings, those arising out of patent or copyright laws, actions against consuls or vice consuls, actions wherein the amount in controversy exclusive of interest and costs, exceeds $10,000 between: (1) citizens of different states; (2) citizens of a state and foreign states or citizens or subjects; (3) citizens of different states, with foreign states or citizens or subjects as additional parties ("state" here includes District of Columbia and Commonwealth of Puerto Rico); (4) civil actions arising under the Constitution, laws or treaties of the United States; (5) stockholders' derivative suits; (6) actions against the United States, eminent domain proceedings; (7) actions for partition of lands wherein the United States

[3]28 U.S.C.A. §3231.

[4]28 U.S.C.A. §1331.

is one of the tenants in common or joint tenants; or (8) any civil action whether of a local nature against defendants residing in different districts in the same state or involving property located in different districts.

Twenty-four of the states are divided into two or more districts with a court for each district. For example, in Texas, there is the United States District Court for the Northern District of Texas; the United States District Court for the Southern District of Texas; the United States District Court for the Eastern District of Texas, and the United States District Court for the Western District of Texas.

Many of the district courts are further divided into divisions. For example, in Iowa there is the United States District Court for the Northern District of Iowa, Cedar Rapids Division; and the United States District Court for the Southern District of Iowa, Central Division. In Minnesota, however, there is only one judicial district comprising six divisions, i.e., the First Division, the Second Division, the Third Division, etc.

¶2101.4 Special Federal Courts and Panels

The special federal courts include the United States Court of Claims, the United States Customs Court, the United States Court of Customs and Patent Appeals, and Territorial Courts, and the United States Court of Military Appeals, all of which are courts of record.

The United States Tax Court and the United States Court of Military Appeals are not true courts but are quasi-judicial agencies.

There is also a Judicial Panel on Multidistrict Litigation which handles coordinated or consolidated pretrial proceedings of actions involving similar questions of law and fact, filed simultaneously by different parties against the same defendant(s).[5]

¶2101.5 The United States Court of Claims

The United States Court of Claims, which consists of a chief judge, several associate judges, and senior and trial judges, has jurisdiction to render judgment upon any claim against the United States: (1) founded either upon the Constitution of the United States; (2) founded upon any Act of Congress; (3) founded upon any regulations of an executive department; (4) founded upon any express or implied contract with the United States; or (5) for liquidated or unliquidated damages in case not sounding in tort.[6]

[5]28 U.S.C.A. §1407.

[6]28 U.S.C.A §1491.

The district courts have concurrent jurisdiction with the Court of Claims over general claims in which the United States is a party in controversies which do not exceed $10,000.

¶2101.6 The United States Custom Court

The United States Customs Court, which consists of a senior judge and several judges, has exclusive jurisdiction of civil actions involving violations of customs laws, including: (1) review or protest of decisions of customs officials involving imported merchandise; (2) appraisement, classification, and rates of duties; (3) exclusion from entry or delivery, liquidation or reliquidation, refusal to pay claims or reliquidate an entry, etc.[7]

¶2101.7 The United States Court of Customs and Patent Appeals

The United States Court of Customs and Patent Appeals, which consists of a chief judge and four associate judges, is an appellate court having jurisdiction over appeals from: (1) all final decisions of the United States Customs Court; (2) the Board of Appeals and the Board of Interference Examiners of the Patent and Trademark Office, as to patent applications and interferences; and (3) the Commission of Patents and Trademarks, as to trademark applications and proceedings.[8]

¶2102 State Court Systems

The organization of the various court systems in the United States is not uniform. Most state court systems consist of a supreme court, or court of last resort; an intermediate appellate court, usually called the Court of Appeals; numerous courts of regional jurisdiction, that is trial courts where suits are commenced; and inferior (lower) courts, such as probate and other specialized courts. Some states have more than one intermediate appellate court to relieve the congestion of cases in the state's highest court. In California, for example, there are five appellate districts, each with a District Court of Appeals composed of one or more divisions and three justices.

Usually a case is originally brought and tried in a trial court and may, under proper circumstances, be appealed to higher courts having appellate jurisdiction until it reaches the state's highest appellate court or, in some cases, the United States Supreme Court.

[7]28 U.S.C.A. §1582.

[8]28 U.S.C.A. §1542.

Several states are divided into circuits or districts, with a court for each. Other states have only one original trial court, which is composed of geographical divisions. The captions of any document filed in such courts should reflect the geographic division.

All state courts operate independently. The courts in one state do not have control over, or relation to, the courts of another state.

¶2102.1 State Supreme Court

Most state supreme courts, or courts of last resort (not always called the Supreme Court), have appellate jurisdiction over all controversies arising in the state trial courts unless the state has an intermediate court of appeals. Generally speaking, they have original jurisdiction in writs of mandamus, habeas corpus, prohibition, certiorari, and certain other civil actions as specified in the state's constitution.

There is only one supreme appellate court in each state. In Oklahoma and Texas, the Criminal Courts of Appeals are the courts of last resort in criminal cases.

In 45 states the highest court is designated as the Supreme Court. In the remaining five states, the highest court is designated as follows:

Maine	Supreme Judicial Court
Maryland	Court of Appeals
Massachusetts	Supreme Judicial Court
New York	Court of Appeals
West Virginia	Supreme Court of Appeals

¶2102.2 State Intermediate Court of Appeals

State courts of intermediate review exercise appellate jurisdiction over decisions of the lower courts, i.e., superior, circuit, etc. In some states, such as California, they have original jurisdiction to issue writs of mandamus, habeas corpus, certiorari, and prohibition proceedings. In many states, the decisions of inferior courts are first appealed to an appellate court such as a superior court. In California, for instance, appeals from a municipal court are presented to the Appellate Department of the Superior Court. However, an appeal from the Superior Court would be presented to the state's district courts of appeals. In all states, however, an appeal may be taken to the state's court of last resort.

In a few states, the appellate jurisdiction of the intermediate courts of appeals is restricted. In Illinois, for example, the appellate courts do not have jurisdiction over criminal cases involving felonies. And in Georgia, the court of intermediate review, the Georgia Court of Appeals, does not have jurisdiction over appeals involving the Constitution of Georgia, the Constitution of the United States, divorce cases, and other types of "equity" proceedings.

¶2102.3 State Superior Courts

The superior courts are the highest state courts of original jurisdiction. In some states these courts are called circuit courts, district courts or courts of common pleas. They are frequently referred to as "trial" courts. (In New York, however, the highest state court of original jurisdiction is designated as the "Supreme Court.") They have general jurisdiction over civil, criminal, and equity matters. Their jurisdiction frequently extends to two or three counties. As previously mentioned, in addition to original jurisdiction in the first instances, they often have appellate jurisdiction over cases originated in the lower courts, such as municipal, justice, and small claims courts. In some states, their appellate jurisdiction extends to the probate court.

The superior courts in some states have separate "departments" that have jurisdiction over special matters, such as matters of law or equity. In Georgia, as in many other states, there is a separate state court which is often referred to as the civil court, which has both a civil division (with no equity jurisdiction) and a criminal division. The monetary jurisdiction of the superior court in most states is $5,000 or more.

¶2102.4 State Lower Courts

Lower courts include those whose proceedings are directly subject to review by a higher court, such as municipal courts, justice of the peace courts, small claims courts, city courts, traffic courts, police courts, justice courts, magistrates' courts, recorder's courts, village courts, mayor's courts, town courts, etc.

All of these types of lower courts have limited jurisdiction. In criminal cases, they are generally restricted to misdemeanors, preliminary hearings, or inquiries in felony cases. In civil actions, they typically have jurisdiction over cases involving small amounts of money. For example, the jurisdiction of the municipal court in California is limited to civil actions of $5,000 or less. In Alabama, however, courts with similar monetary jurisdiction are designated as district courts.

Generally speaking, lower courts are not courts of record. In many instances, the judges are frequently not lawyers and are appointed (rather than elected) to office. However, some states require qualifying examinations for these judges. The decisions of these courts are subject to review by the higher courts.

Small claims courts (which are frequently designated as conciliation courts), general sessions, magistrates' courts, city courts, civil courts, etc., generally handle small monetary claims, such as property damage claims, claims for wages, collection of rent, wage claims, claims for breach of contract, claims for delinquent accounts and even small personal injury claims. Usually, only the parties involved are allowed to appear, but in some states attorneys are allowed to participate. Most parties find that the amount of money involved, which can be anywhere from $100 or less to $3,500 does not warrant the expense of legal representation. Moreover, the procedures are kept informal so that most lay persons can understand them. The parties simply tell their stories to the judge who then asks questions as necessary. These courts have subpoena power, but it is seldom used. The exclusionary rules of evidence are rarely employed. The parties may bring witnesses, and if a business entity is involved, an attorney or other agent may appear on its behalf.

The procedures involved in bringing an action in a small claims court are often simple: The plaintiff prepares a sworn complaint, which contains his or her narrative statement of facts, and pays a nominal filing fee. The clerk of the court mails a copy of the complaint to the defendant at his or her last known address, directing the defendant to appear on a date certain to defend the plaintiff's allegations, with no written answer required of the defendant. The judge thereafter hears the matter.

¶2102.5 Special State Courts

Courts of special jurisdiction have original jurisdiction over certain restricted matters. The most common special courts are probate courts, criminal courts, justice of the peace courts, chancery courts, juvenile courts, and various other county courts. Probate courts have jurisdiction over the probate of wills, administration of a decedent's estate, and the guardianship of minors and incompetents. Criminal courts have original jurisdiction over criminal cases. Justice of the peace courts, which are quickly disappearing, are usually found in rural areas.

¶2103 Jurisdiction

Since the law of jurisdiction is extremely complex, the discussion of jurisdiction in this section is intended merely to present an overview of the subject.[9] Jurisdiction is defined as the authority or power of a court

[9]Consult your state code or title 28 of the *United States Code*.

to hear a particular cause of action and to render a lawful and binding judgment against one or more defendants. Jurisdiction may be concurrent, that is, two or more courts may have jurisdiction over a particular cause of action. The attorney should choose the best forum for the client's interests.

A court must have jurisdiction over both the *subject matter* of the litigation and over the *person* of the parties in order to hear a case and render a lawful judgment. Subject matter of the litigation is the type of action, such as divorce, personal injury, property damages, etc. Personal jurisdiction refers to jurisdiction over the individual parties, corporations, fiduciaries, or other litigants.

¶2103.1 Subject Matter Jurisdiction

Subject matter jurisdiction can be limited by:

1. *The nature of the case*—example:

A probate court would not have jurisdiction over a traffic violation.

2. *The amount involved*—example:

A suit for one million dollars could not originally be commenced in the small claims courts.

3. *The remedies that the court can provide*—example:

A traffic court would not have jurisdiction over a case involving the death penalty.

4. *The location (situs) of the property*—example:

A suit for foreclosure of property in Nevada could not be brought in California.

5. *The identity of the litigants*—example:

A suit against an ambassador could not be brought in a small claims court.

¶2103.2 Personal Jurisdiction

Personal jurisdiction is automatically obtained by the court over the plaintiff when he or she commences the civil action, whereas jurisdiction over the defendant is obtained by the court through service of process upon the defendant as provided by law (including constitutional limitations) and the applicable rules of civil procedure. If the service of process upon the defendant is defective, the court will not have jurisdiction over the defendant. The defendant, however, can usually waive defects in personal jurisdiction. (See ¶404.)

¶2103.3 Original Jurisdiction

Original jurisdiction is often called "trial court" jurisdiction. It lies in the court which has the authority to hear a case originally, that is, the court where the suit is first commenced. The case may possibly be appealed to a higher court, removed to another court, or transferred to a different location of the same judicial system.

¶2103.4 Appellate Jurisdiction

A court's appellate jurisdiction, that is, the authority to hear appeals from the inferior (lower) courts, is determined by statutory and/or constitutional provisions. Principally, in both the state and federal court systems, both the intermediate courts of appeal and the highest courts of appeal have appellate jurisdiction. The Supreme Court of the United States has original jurisdiction in some matters and appellate jurisdiction in others. However, as do the highest state court of appeals, it normally hears appeals from the inferior courts.

¶2103.5 Federal Question Jurisdiction

One of the forms of jurisdiction in federal court is known as federal question jurisdiction. The two basic prerequisites are: (1) the aggregate monetary damages alleged by a single plaintiff in the action exceed $10,000; and (2) the case involve a federal question, i.e., arise out of the Constitution, laws or treaties of the United States.[10] Two or more plaintiffs cannot combine their claims against the same defendant which total $10,000.[11] In cases brought under certain specific federal statutes, no monetary minimum is required, e.g., title, etc.

¶2103.6 Diversity Jurisdiction

One important basis of federal jurisdiction is diversity of citizenship where the matter in dispute is greater than $10,000. Diversity of citizenship exists where the controversy is between:

1. Citizens of different states;[12]

[10]E.g., 28 U.S.C.A. §§1331, 1332. (No amount required if action brought against the United States, agency, officer, or employee thereof.)

[11]28 U.S.C.A. §§1333, 1343.

[12]The word "states," as used herein, includes the territories, the District of Columbia, and the Commonwealth of Puerto Rico.

2. Citizens of a state, and foreign states or citizens or subject thereof; or
3. Citizens of different states and in which foreign states or citizens or subjects thereof are additional parties.[13]

A corporation is deemed a citizen of the state of its incorporation and of the state where it has its principal place of business. The tests for determining the principal place of a corporation are (1) the location of the nerve center, i.e., where principal administrative and financial transactions are conducted; (2) the state in which the corporation declares is their principal place of business; and (3) the state where the corporation makes the most frequent contacts.[14]

¶2103.7 "Long Arm" Statutes

Most states have "long arm" statutes which give a court personal jurisdiction over nonresident defendants who commit civil wrongs in a state other than the state in which they reside. For example, a resident of Mississippi is involved in an automobile accident while traveling through North Carolina. By statute, a plaintiff could obtain personal jurisdiction over the Mississippi resident in North Carolina where the accident occurred.[15] The theory is that the nonresident motorist, by operating his vehicle in a foreign state, by implication consented to be sued therein in any litigation resulting from an automobile accident occurring in that state. In addition, the statute is designed for the convenience of the resident plaintiff. Similar "long arm" statutes create personal jurisdiction over nonresident property owners, aircraft operators, vessel owners, etc.

In addition, every state has a "long arm" statute which applies to foreign corporations, i.e., corporations incorporated in and located in another state but which are "doing business" in that state, at least with respect to any disputes arising out of business transacted within the jurisdiction. Many state statutes require that foreign corporations become "qualified," i.e., formally registered with the Secretary of State in the state in which they wish to do business.

Service of process can be accomplished on a nonresident defendant where jurisdiction is properly based on a "long arm" statute. Generally, the plaintiff is required to serve a copy of the complaint on

[13]28 U.S.C.A. §1332.

[14]In questions of diversity jurisdiction involving corporations, the most frequent litigation arises out of the question of where the principal place of business is.

[15]*N.C. Gen. Stat.* §1-75.4.

an official designated in the state, usually the Secretary of State, who then forwards a copy to the nonresident defendant. Since this procedure varies from state to state, be sure to check your state statutes. In the federal courts, the procedure for service of process on a nonresident defendant is governed by the law of the state where the suit is filed.[16]

¶2104 Venue

Venue is the place, i.e., city, country, district, or other geographical division, in which an action is to be heard and tried. Although some requirements of venue and jurisdiction are similar, venue should not be confused with jurisdiction. Venue is the *actual location* of the forum and the territorial limits from which a jury is drawn. Venue is determined by statute and usually lies where the cause of action accrued. Venue is designed for the convenience of the parties and, unlike subject matter jurisdiction, it may be waived.

For example, in a civil action involving real property, the cause of action accrues in the county where the real property is located. However, the jurisdiction, that is, the proper court of forum, may be determined by several factors previously discussed, i.e., the amount in controversy, the citizenship of the defendants, the nature of the case, etc.

Generally speaking, in a tort action, proper venue is in the county where the loss or injury occurred. However, the action may also be tried in the county of the residence of the defendant. In a breach of contract action, the county where the contract was to be performed, or the county of the defendant's residence, is usually the proper venue. Some state statutes further provide that in an action involving a contract, the county where the contract was executed may also be the proper venue. Check your state code for specific requirements of venue in various civil actions since they vary from state to state. For specific venue requirements in the federal court system, see Title 28 of the United States Code, §1391, *et seq.*

¶2104.1 Change of Venue

If venue is improper, the defendant may request a change of venue. Usually the defendant must request a change of venue before or with the responsive pleading, or he waives his right to have the case heard in the proper venue forum. In some state courts, a motion to dismiss may

[16]Rule 4(d)(7) *Federal Rules of Civil Procedure.*

be made where venue is improper. Generally speaking, other grounds for change of venue in the state courts might include:

1. Not possible to provide an impartial trial;
2. Bias or prejudice of the judge or jury, if provided by statute;
3. The convenience of the parties and/or witnesses; or
4. In the interest of justice.

Usually change of venue is accomplished by motion in the state courts. Again, you should consult your state code. Some state codes, e.g., California, require an affidavit or a declaration of merits to be filed with the motion for change of venue. In most states, however, change of venue may be stipulated by the parties.

In the federal courts, the grounds for change of venue are as follows:

1. Subject matter jurisdiction;
2. Personal jurisdiction and service; or
3. For the convenience of the parties and/or witnesses. Such a change can be made *only* to another court where the original action could have been brought.

To change venue or to correct the defect of improper venue in the federal court system, a motion, consent, or stipulation of all parties must be filed, except in proceedings brought by or on behalf of the United States. Venue may be transferred without the consent of the United States where all other parties request a transfer.[17] A motion to dismiss may be filed in the federal court for improper venue.[18]

As previously stated, in cases filed in the federal courts, if there is one basic case with similar questions of law and fact that is simultaneously filed by different parties against the same particular defendant, venue may be limited to one district for pretrial proceedings. This is referred to as "multi-district litigation."[19]

[17] 28 U.S.C.A. §1404. (See also §1406.)

[18] 28 U.S.C.A. §1406(a).

[19] 28 U.S.C.A. §1407. (See also ¶2101.4.)

Appendix A
Code of Ethics*

Code of Ethics*

Members of the National Association of Legal Secretaries (International) are bound by the objectives of this Association and the standards of conduct required of the legal profession.

Every member shall:

Encourage respect for the law and the administration of justice;

Observe rules governing privileged communications and confidential information;

Promote and exemplify high standards of loyalty, cooperation, and courtesy;

Perform all duties of the profession with integrity and competence; and

Pursue a high order of professional attainment.

*Reprinted with permission of the National Association of Legal Secretaries.

Appendix B
Legal and Other Abbreviations

A

abstract	abs
acknowledgment	ack, ackgt
acceptance	acpt
account	acct
ad interim (in the meantime)	ad int
Administrator	Admr
Administratrix	Admx
ad valorem	ad val, a/v
affidavit	afft
American Federation of Labor and Congress of Industrial Organization	AFL-CIO
agency	agcy
agency hearing	ct
agent	agt
agreement	K
also known as	a.k.a. or a/k/a
American Law Reports	A.L.R.
answer	ans
District of Columbia Appeal Cases	App. D.C.
article	art.
as soon as possible	ASAP
assignment	asmt
attorney	atty

B

Bachelor of Arts	A.B. or B.A.
Bachelor of Laws	LL.B.
balance	bal
bank	bk
bankrupt	br

barrels per day	b/p/d/ or b.p.d.
because	b/c
beneficiary	benef
between	b/t
bill of exchange	B/E, b.e., b/e
bill of lading	B/L, b/l
bill of sale	b/s
board	bd
Board of Directors	B of D
bona fide purchaser	bfp
bonds	bds
bond rights	bd rts
buyer's option	b.o.
building	bldg
business	bus

C

caps and small caps	c. and s.c.
cash	c
cost, insurance and freight	c.i.f.
cash on delivery	COD, cod.
care of	c/o
caveat emptor (at buyer's risk; let buyer beware	c.e.
certificate; certification; certified	cert, ct., ctf
certificates of deposit	c.o.d.
Certified Public Accountant	CPA
Code of Federal Regulations (and supplement)	CFR + Supp.
chapter	c.
Chairman of Board	C of B
Chamber of Commerce	C of C
check	ck.
chief justice	C.J.
citation; citizen	cit.
civil; civilian	civ.
(court of) claims reports	C.C/s.R.
Clearing House; Courthouse; Custom House	C.H.
client	cl
Code of Federal Regulations	CFR

Code of Federal Regulation Supplement	CFR Supp.
collateral; collection; collector	coll.
collateral trust (bonds)	clt.
commercial	cml.
community property	com prop or cp
company	Co.
concerning, with respect to	re:
conference with	cw
consideration	con
consolidated; consigned; consignment	cons.
contract	K
convertible debentures	cv. db.
convertible preferred	cv. pf.
company	co. or Co.
copy of letter from	clf
corporation	corp
corpus juris (body of law)	C.J.
correspondence from	lf
correspondence to	lt
court	ct
Court of Claims Reports	C. Cls.
court appearance	cta
credit note	C/N
creditor	cr
cumulative	cum.
cumulative with dividend	cum d., cum div
currency bond	c.b.

D

damages	dams
date	d.
Debtor	dr
debenture rights	db, d.b.
decessit sine prole (died without issue)	d.s.p.
defendant	D or (delta)
deposition	dpn
director	dtr
District	dist
dividend	div.

Doctor of Laws	LL.D.
document	doc.
documents upon acceptance	D/A
documents upon payment	D/P
doing business as	d.b.a. or d/b/a
dollar	dol.
draft, drafting	dft

E

enclosure; enclosures	enc.
end of month	e.o.m.
errors and omissions excepted	E. & O.E., e. & o.e.
estate	est
et alia (and others)	et al.
et cetera (and so forth)	etc., &c.
et sequentia (and the following)	et seq., seq.
et uxor (and wife)	et ux.
examine	rev
exchange	exch., ex.
Executive Committee	E.C.
executor	exr, exor.
executrix	exrx.
exempli gratia (for example)	e.g.

F

fair average quality	f.a.q.
federal	fed
Federal Reporter	Fed.
Federal National Mortgage Association (Fannie Mae)	FNMA
Federal Supplement	F. Supp.
Federal Trade Commission	FTC
foreclosure	forc
following (pages; folios)	ff.
for your information	FYI
foreign exchange	FX
forward	for'd., fwd.
free alongside ship	f.a.s.
free on board	f.o.b.
free of charge	f.o.c.
free on rail; free on road	f.o.r.

free on steamer	f.o.s.
free on truck	f.o.t.
freight, insurance, carriage	f.i.c.
freight release	F/R
fully paid	f. pd.
funding (bonds)	fdg.

G

general counsel	G.C.
gold bonds	gd. bds, g.b.
good till canceled	GTC
government	gov., govt.
guaranteed	gtd.
guarantee/guaranty	gu., guar.

H

House document	H. Doc.
habeas corpus	h.a.
Department of Health, Education and Welfare	HEW
hearing preparation	trp
Honorable	Hon.

I

ibidem (in the same place)	I.b.
id est (that is)	i.e.
Incorporated	Inc.
in fine, final at the end	in f.
in limine (at the outset)	in lim.
in loco (in the place of)	in loc.
in the place cited	loc. cit.
in transitu (on the way)	in trans.
initial	init.
in regard to; pertinent to	in re
Interstate Commerce Commission	ICC
interest; interim	int.
investigation	res
invested; investment; invoice	inv.
Internal Revenue Service	IRS
Internal Revenue Officer	IRO

J	
joint	jt.
joint account	j/a
joint stock	jnt. stk.
judge	J.
judgment	judg
L	
landlord	LL
law agent	l.a.
legal; legislation; legislature	leg.
less than carload lots	L.C.L.
let it stand	stet
letter of credit	L/C, l/c
letter from	lf
letter to	lt
liable	l
lien; loan	ln.
lien holders	lienhs
limited	ltd.
locus sigilli (place of the seal)	S.S.
in the place cited	loc. cit.
M	
majority	maj.
maritime; market	mar.
market value	m.v.
maturity (bonds)	mat.
maximum	max.
mechanics' lien (materialman's lien)	m/m
memorandum	memo
memorandum from	mf
memorandum to	mt
Madame	Mme.
Mesdames	Mmes.
Mistress	Mrs.
Miss or Mistress	Ms.
Messieurs	Messrs.
minimum	min.
miscellaneous	misc

month	mo
months after date	m.d., M/D
motion for summary judgment	msj
mortgage	mtg
municipal	mun.

N

name unknown	n.u.
national	nat.
necessary (necessaries)	neces
negative, negotiate	neg.
negligence (negligent)	negl
nemine contradicente (no one contradicting)	nem. con.
net	n.
night letter	NL
non sequitur (it does not follow)	non seq
nonvoting (stocks)	nv
no place or date	n.p. or d.
not	nt
not elsewhere specified or classified	n.e.s. or n.e.c.
nota bene (note well); take notice	n.b.
Notary Public; no protest	N.P.
not elsewhere specified	n.e.s.
not otherwise provided for	n.o.p.
not otherwise specified	N.O.S., n.o.s.
not specified; not sufficient	n.s., n/s
not sufficient funds	N.S.F.
number, numbers	no., nos.

O

obitt (died)	ob., obit
office; officer	off.
omission excepted	o.e.
on account	o/a
on demand	o/d
opinion	ops

Opinions of the Attorney General	Op. Atty. Gen.
opere citato (in the work cited)	op. cit.
opposing attorney	tratty

P

page, pages	p., pp
paid	pd.
patent	pat.
Patent Office	Pat. Off.
payment	pmt, payt.
per annum (by the year)	p.a., per an.
per procurationem (on behalf of)	per pro., p.p., p.pro.
participating preferred	pt. pf.
percent	pct.
pertaining	pert.
petition	pet.
plaintiff	P or (Pi)
police department	P.D.
political, politics	pol.
postscript	P.S.
power of attorney	P.A.
premium	p.m., prem.
prepaid	ppd.
preparation for	prep
preparation of	dft
presumption	pr
principle; principal	prin
proceedings	proc.
profit and loss	P & L, PL
promissory note	p.n.
pro tempore (for the time)	pro tem.
proximo (in next month)	prox.
public resolution	Pub. Res., Public Res.
purchaser	pur

Q

quod erat demonstrandum (which was to be proved)	Q.E.D., p.e.d.
quod erat faciendum (which was to be done)	Q.E.F., q.e.f.

quod erat inveniendum (which was to be found out)	Q.E.I., q.e.i.
quarter; quarterly	qtr.
query	qy.

R

real estate	RE
receipt	rc., rcpt.
received	rec
receiver	rcr
reference	ref
regarding, regards	re
report	rpt
requisition	req
research	res
research and development	R & D
reviewing, review of	rev
right	rt

S

scilicet (namely)	sc.
second	2nd
security deed	sec d.
section	sec.
seller's option	s.o.
seller's option to double	s.o.d.
Senate Document	S. Doc.
shareholder/stockholder	sh
shipment	ship., shipt.
sine die (without naming a date)	s.d.
sinking fund	s.f.
standard operating procedure	SOP
state	st
statutes	stat.
Statutes at Large	Stat.
stock	stk.
study	rev
Social Security Administration	SSA
Status at Large	Stat
subchapter	subch.
subject to approval	s.a.
syndication	synd.

T

telephone call from	tf
telephone call to	tt
telephone conference with	tcw
tenant	t
thousand	M
total loss	t.l.
travel	tvl
trial preparation	trp
trust	tr
trustee	tee

U

upper case	uc
United States Supreme Court Reports	U.S.
United States Code	U.S.C.
United States Code Supplement	U.S.C. Supp.

V

versus	v. or vs.
verbi gratia (for example)	v.g.
vide infra (see below)	v.i.
videlicet (namely)	viz.
volume	vol.

W

warrant	war., wt., w.
warranty	wy
warranty deed	w.d.
with	w/
Withdrawn	w/d
Without	w/o

Y

year	yr.

Z

zero; zone	Z

Appendix C
Dictionary of Legal Terms*

ABANDONMENT—the surrender, relinquishment, disclaimer, or cession of property or of rights.

ABATEMENT—to do away with; annul; to make less.

ABDUCTION—to carry away wrongfully, as in kidnapping.

ABET—to encourage and support wrongdoing; also to incite, instigate or countenance.

ABEYANCE—an undetermined condition as of an estate awaiting an owner.

ABROGATE—to annul, abolish, or repeal by an act of authority.

ABSCOND—to leave suddenly or secretly; to go away and hide.

ABSTRACT—a summary, a condensed version.

ABSTRACT EXTENSION—the updating of an abstract to a certain date by a re-examination of records.

ABSTRACT OF TITLE—a document containing a brief and orderly statement of the grants, conveyances and encumbrances relating to the title and ownership of real estate.

ABSTRACTOR'S CERTIFICATE—a certificate, signed by the abstractor, which accompanies an abstract certifying its contents.

ACCEPTANCE—an official recognition of authority or of a claim; to agree to the terms of a contract.

ACCESSION—the acquisition of property by reason of its being accessory to property already owned; to come into possession of a right or office.

ACCESSORY—a person who aids another in the commission of a felony, even if not present, either before or after.

ACCOUNT—a record of financial transactions.

ACCOUNTING EQUATION—assets = liabilities + equity.

ACCOUNTING METHOD—the method by which income and expenses are determined (see *cash basis* and *accrual basis).*

ACCOUNTING PERIOD—the period of time which a financial statement covers.

*Written and compiled by Paula F. Turner, manager, Management Advisory Services, Holland Shipes Bennett Thrasher, Atlanta, GA.

Accounts payable—amounts owed by the firm to others on a given date.

Accounts receivable—amounts owed to the firm by others on a given date.

Accretion—a gradual increase in land due to natural causes, as out of the sea or river.

Accroach—to exercise power with proper authority; to usurp.

Accrual basis—a method of accounting in which income and expenses are recognized in the period in which they are earned rather than when they are received or paid.

Accrue—to come as a natural product or result; to estimate income or expenses at the end of an accounting period.

Accusation—a charge of crime or misconduct; an indictment.

Acknowledge—to admit the genuineness of a right, claim, or fact.

Acknowledgment—a statement of acceptance of responsibility; a short declaration at the end of a legal document showing that the paper was properly executed.

Acquiescence—passive consent; to accept by not objecting.

Acquisition—to obtain possession of property.

Acquittal—release or discharge of one accused of a crime.

Action—proceedings at law.

Act of God—an inevitable, natural event.

Actionable—having grounds for prosecution as a trespass or libel.

Actuary—an officer of an insurance agency who calculates and states risks and premiums.

Ademption—disposal by a testator in his lifetime of specific property bequeathed in his will; withdrawal of a legacy.

Adjective law—statutes which designate the proper *what, when,* and *how* to bring a legal issue into judicial consideration and judgment; also known as procedural law.

Administrative—having to do with the management of a business.

Admiralty—the law governing maritime affairs.

Admiralty court—a court having jurisdiction over maritime offenses.

Adverse possession—obtaining possession of property through continued use.

Affidavit—a written statement or declaration sworn to or affirmed under oath.

Agent—a representative of a person or entity (principal) with power to act on the principal's behalf.

AGGRIEVED—subjected to ill, undeserved treatment.

AGRARIAN—pertaining to land, or to a division or distribution of land.

AGREEMENT—a mutual understanding; also the language or terms evidencing the understanding.

ALIBI—a form of defense by which the accused establishes his innocence by pleading having been elsewhere than at the scene of a crime at the time the crime was committed.

ALIAS—an assumed name; otherwise called.

ALIEN—of another country; foreign.

ALIMONY—an allowance paid to a man or woman by order of the court for maintenance after a divorce or legal separation.

ALLEGE—to make a statement of fact, but without proving it.

ALLOCATE—to apportion; to allot.

AMICABLE ACTION—an action entered into which is agreeable to all parties involved.

AMNESTY—an act of pardon from offenses against a government.

AMORTIZE—to provide for the payment of debt by paying in installments.

ANCILLARY—subordinate; auxiliary.

ANNEXED—attached or affixed to a document or building.

ANNOTATED—explained by means of critical notes or remarks.

ANNUITANT—one who is entitled to receive an annuity.

ANNUITY—a series of payments paid periodically.

ANNULMENT—an act of making void and of no effect.

ANONYMOUS—having no name.

ANSWER—a defendant's formal written statement of defense, usually signed by the defendant's attorney.

ANTITRUST LAWS—legislation which forbids the carrying on of business practices that may create a monopoly.

APPELLANT—a person who takes an appeal to a different court.

APPELLATE JURISDICTION—the power to review and correct an action taken by an inferior court.

APPORTIONMENT—division and assignment in proportionate parts.

APPRAISAL—the valuing of property by persons qualified to do so.

APPURTENANCE—something belonging or attached to something else as an accessory, as a building to land.

ARBITRATION—the hearing and settling of a controversy by a person or persons mutually agreed upon by all parties.

ARRAIGNMENT—the act of accusing one before the court.

Arrest—to deprive a person of his or her liberty by means of a legal action; to take into custody.

Arson—the malicious burning of a dwelling or other structure.

Articles—the group of clauses or paragraphs forming a contract.

Assault—an unlawful attempt or threat to do physical harm to another.

Assault and battery—the unlawful touching of a person's body or clothing with the intent of doing physical injury.

Assessment—a tax levied on property to be used for improvements.

Assignment—the transfer of title or interest in property by an instrument of writing.

Assize—a trial or hearing by jury without evidence of witnesses.

Assumpsit—an obligation to perform an oral agreement.

Attachment—a legal seizure of a person's property, real or personal.

Attestation—the act of signing a legal document as a witness to the signature of one or more of the parties.

Averment—a positive statement of the facts in a pleading.

Avoidance—annulment; voiding a contract.

Bail—the security given to the court in exchange for a prisoner's release until a later appearance; to become surety for a defendant's appearance in court.

Bailiff—an officer of the court having custody of prisoners under arraignment.

Bailment—a delivery of personal property for a specific purpose, under the terms of a contract, express or implied, with the contemplated return of the property after the contract is executed.

Bankruptcy—the state of being insolvent.

Bar—lawyers, as a group; the legal profession.

Battery—the unlawful touching of a person or a person's clothing.

Being duly sworn—bound by an oath.

Bench warrant—a warrant issued by a presiding judge or by the court directing an offender to be brought to appear before the court.

Beneficiary—one who receives money or property from an insurance policy or will.

Bequeath—to give or leave personal property by means of a will.

Bequest—the gift of personal property by means of a will.

Bilateral contract—a contract with rights and duties on both sides.

Bilateral mistake—an error made by both parties to a contract.

Bigamy—a criminal offense whereby a person marries while legally married to another.

Bill of attainder—a legislative act which inflicts punishment on a person without benefit of a trial.

Bill of exchange—an unconditional written order, signed by the writer, requiring another person to pay an amount of money, on demand or on a certain date.

Bill of lading—a written document acknowledging the receipt of goods which are to be transported to another place.

Bill of particulars—a written statement of information and details of a plaintiff's demands in an action or of the defendant's counterclaim.

Bill of sale—a document issued to the buyer by the seller as evidence of the transfer of title of certain personal property.

Binder—an agreement to cover a down payment on certain real property; also the down payment itself.

Blacklist—a list of persons who are deemed suspicious.

Blackmail—the use of threats, usually in writing, to injure a person, property or reputation for extortion.

Blue Sky Laws—statutes which protect citizens from fraud in securities transactions.

Bogus—counterfeit; fictitious.

Bond—a written agreement to pay a certain amount of money on or before a certain future date.

Boycott—a conspiracy to prevent the carrying on of business by use of threats, intimidation, coercion, or withdrawal of patronage.

Breach—to break or violate a law, duty or legal obligation.

Bribe—a gift used corruptly to influence a public official.

Brief—a written document that states the facts and points of law which is an attorney's basis for argument before a court.

Budget—a financial plan or projection which estimates the amount of money which may be spent during a certain period.

Bureau—a department or branch of government.

Burglary—the unlawful entry into another's home with the intent to commit a theft.

Bylaws—the rules or laws which govern a corporation.

Capias—a judicial writ issued to an officer of the court, requiring a person to be arrested and held in custody.

Capital—The amount of property (wealth) owned by an individual or business; the wealth available for the production of income; also a city that is the seat of government of a country or state.

Capital punishment—death as a legal punishment for a crime.

Capitol—the building which houses Congress or a state legislature.

Caption—the title or introductory heading on a legal document.

Causa mortis—consideration or a gift which is dependent upon death.

Caveat emptor—"Let the buyer beware."

Caveat venditor—"Let the seller beware."

Censorship—denial of rights of freedom of speech and press.

Certiorari—a writ issued by a superior court to an inferior court requiring it to produce certain records for review by the superior court.

Chancery court—a court having jurisdiction over equity as opposed to a common law court.

Chattel—tangible personal property.

Chattel mortgage—a document evidencing a mortgage on tangible personal property.

Chose—personal property, both tangible and intangible.

Chose in action—a personal right to receive personal property or money not in possession but recoverable by a suit at law.

Circumstantial Evidence—evidence of related facts which proves, by inference, another questionable fact.

Citation—a reference to a statute, case record or other authority supporting a statement; a writ issued by the court commanding a person to perform a certain action.

Civil—pertaining to relations between citizens and the related legal proceedings.

Coroner's inquest—an examination by the coroner and a jury into the circumstances surrounding a death and the causes of death.

Corporation—an entity created by law empowered to act in a certain capacity or to transact business.

Corporeal property—property of a material nature, substantial and permanent.

Corpus juris—the body of law.

Corroborating evidence—additional evidence which strengthens and confirms existing evidence.

Counter claim—a cross-claim made by a defendant in response to a plaintiff's claim.

Court—the place where justice is administered; the judge or judges presiding over legal proceedings.

Covenant—an agreement between two or more parties.

Coverture—the legal state of a married woman.

COVIN—a secret agreement between two or more persons to injure or defraud another.

CRIME—a legal offense against society.

CRIMINAL—one who has been convicted of a crime; having to do with an illegal act.

CROSS-EXAMINATION—an attempt to discredit the testimony of a witness by interrogation by the opposing counsel.

CULPABLE—deserving censure or blame.

CURATOR—a legal guardian of another's property.

CURTESY—the right of a husband to a life estate in his wife's real estate.

CUSTODY—guardianship; the control and care of a person or thing.

DEFENDANT—a person against whom a legal action is brought.

DEL CREDERE AGENT—an agent who guarantees his principal against the default of those with whom contracts are made.

DELINQUENT—neglectful of or failing in duty or obligation; faulty.

DEMURRAGE—compensation for the detention of a vessel (or railroad car) beyond the specified time for loading, unloading or sailing.

DEMURRER—a pleading that admits the facts stated in the pleading to which it replies, but denies that they are sufficient to constitute a good cause of action or defense.

DEPOSITION—the written testimony of a sworn witness, taken upon questioning, not in open court but in the course of a commission issued by a court to take testimony.

DEPUTY—one appointed to act for another; a representative agent.

DESCENDANTS—persons born of a certain family or group; offspring; children.

DICTUM—the opinion of a judge not essential to the decision on the main question.

DISBURSEMENTS—amounts of money paid in exchange for goods or services.

DISCHARGE—legal release from debt or obligation.

DIVORCE—legal dissolution of the marriage ties.

DOCKET—an entry on the records of a court of the principal steps taken in a case; a calendar of cases to be called at any time of the court; a trial calendar.

DOCUMENTARY EVIDENCE—evidences supplied in writing rather than "oral" evidence.

DOMAIN—the ownership of land; publicly owned land is often referred to as public domain.

Domicile—an established place of abode; home.

Donee—one to whom a gift is given.

Donor—one who gives a gift.

Dower—the legal right or interest which a wife acquires in the real estate of her husband, at his death.

Duress—constraint by force or fear.

Earnest money—a refundable deposit of a portion of the purchase price of real estate to bind the sale.

Edict—that which is uttered or proclaimed by authority as a rule of action.

Ejectment—an eviction; an action to recover possession of real estate, with damages, for wrongful withholding; also the writing by which this action is instituted.

Emancipate—to set free; to renounce the right to custody of a child who has reached majority age.

Embezzlement—the act of appropriating property or funds fraudulently for one's own use.

Eminent domain—the inherent sovereign power of the state of controlling private property for public purposes by making compensation.

Encumbrance—any lien or liability attached to real property or an estate.

Enjoin—to prohibit by judicial order or decree.

Entrapment—the causing of one to commit a criminal offense by the trickery or persuasion of police.

Equity—value in excess of a mortgage; a court in which suits based on equitable rights may be brought.

Escheat—forfeiture of property, real or personal, for default; confiscation.

Escrow—a conditional holding of something for another.

Estate—the degree, nature and amount of one's lawful interest in any property.

Estate in fee simple—an estate of inheritance free from condition.

Estoppel—an act or admission that cannot be legally denied; prohibition.

Euthanasia—causing death with the intent of ending pain and suffering.

Eviction—the forcing of a tenant from a landlord's property.

Evidence—that by means of which an act is established; testimony.

Executive—having the function or power of executing or performing.

EXECUTION—the signing and delivering of a written instrument.

EXECUTOR—a person nominated by the will of another to execute a will.

EXECUTORY—that which is to be executed or put into effect, especially becoming operative on a future contingency as an executory contract.

EXECUTRIX—a woman who serves as an executor.

EXHIBIT—to present formally or officially; a document or object used as evidence.

EX OFFICIO—by virtue of or because of office or position.

EXPERT WITNESS—a person selected because of knowledge or skill to examine evidence and express an opinion to the court.

EXTRADITION—the surrender by a government of an accused person to the justice of another government.

EXTORTION—to compel another to pay by threats of injury to the person's body, property, or reputation.

FACSIMILE—an exact copy or reproduction.

FACT—a thing done; a deed; the issues raised by the pleadings and evidence in an action upon which a jury must base its verdict.

FEASANCE—performance of a duty; fulfilling a condition.

FEASIBLE—able to be done; practicable.

FEE—a payment for professional services; an estate of inheritance; ownership.

FELONY—a crime punishable by death or imprisonment.

FICTITIOUS NAMES—imaginary names used in legal documents with the intent of replacing with true names as soon as they are known.

FIDUCIARY—pertaining to a position of trust or confidence; a person who holds a thing or funds in trust for another.

FIXTURE—a thing physically attached to real property such as built in appliances in a house.

FORECLOSURE—the barring by judicial proceedings of the right to redeem mortgaged property.

FOREIGN CORPORATION—a corporation incorporated in a state other than the one in which it is doing business.

FORGERY—the act of defrauding another by copying or altering a written document.

FRANCHISE—a special privilege conferred upon an individual by the government; a right granted which allows one to sell another's product.

FRAUD—deception with the object of gaining by another's loss; a false representation of a fact.

FREIGHT—the money paid to a transporter (trucker, shipper, etc.) for the transporting of goods.

FRESH PURSUIT—the power of a police officer to make an arrest without an arrest warrant when in immediate pursuit of a suspect.

GARNISHEE—to secure by garnishment.

GARNISHMENT—a legal proceeding to compel a third party to pay monies owed to a creditor.

GIFT—a voluntary gratuitous transfer of ownership of property.

GOODWILL—an estimation of the value of a company's reputation and relationship with its customers.

GRAND LARCENY—the appropriation of property above a statutory amount.

GRANTEE—the person to whom real property is conveyed in a deed.

GRANTOR—the person who conveys real property in a deed.

GRATIS—free of charge.

GRATUITOUS—given freely without claim or consideration.

GUARANTOR—one who guarantees or warrants.

GUARDIAN—a person who legally is entrusted with the care of another person, property or both.

HABEAS CORPUS—a writ having the object of bringing a party before a court or judge. (A Latin term for "You have the body.")

HEARSAY EVIDENCE—evidence derived from something the witness has heard others say; any evidence depending upon the veracity and competency of some other person other than the witness.

HEIRS—those who upon the death of another, become legally entitled to receive the deceased person's estate.

HEREDITAMENTS—anything capable of being inherited.

HERITAGE—an estate that passes by descent; that which is inherited as a quality or condition.

HOLDING COMPANY—a corporation which is organized for the purpose of owning the stock of one or more other corporations.

HOLDINGS—a right of possession; that which is held in legal title as land in fee, leased or rented or goods held by someone.

HOLOGRAPHIC WILL—a will written in the handwriting of the maker.

HOMESTEAD—the place of permanent family abode, protected in many states from claims of creditors.

HOMICIDE—the killing of any human being by another.

HUSBAND AND WIFE—the parties in a marriage.

HYPOTHECATE—to give in pledge as security for debt.

HYPOTHESIS—a state of things assumed as a basis of reasoning or investigation; an unsupported theory.

ILLUSORY—misleading; deceptive.

IMMUNITY—freedom or exemption from a penalty or duty.

IMPEACHMENT—a discrediting.

INCENDIARY—pertaining to malicious setting of fire; one who commits arson.

INCHOATE—to begin; begun or entered upon but not complete.

INCHOATE RIGHT OF DOWER—the interest a wife has in her husband's property while he is living, which may be converted to a dower's right upon his death.

INCOME TAX—a tax imposed on income of individuals, corporations, partnerships, estates, and trusts by a federal, state, or local government.

INDEMNITY—the compensation of another for sustained loss, damage or expenses.

INDENTURE—a written agreement between two or more parties, all of whom have rights and duties.

INDICTMENT—the formal charging of criminal actions presented in writing to a grand jury.

INHERITANCE—that which is received from descent, as from predecessors.

INJUNCTION—a writ issued by a court or judge which restrains an individual or other entity from doing a certain act.

INSOLVENCY—the inability to meet the claims of creditors.

INTEREST—payment for the use of money.

INTERLOCUTORY—a finding of a court or judge while a suit is pending, but not final.

INTERROGATORIES—written questions answered in writing and under oath during a trial.

INTESTATE—dying without leaving a valid will.

IRREVOCABLE—unalterable; incapable of being revoked or repealed.

JEOPARDY—exposure to or danger of death, loss or injury.

JOINT—joined together in unity of interest or liability.

JOINT ACCOUNT—an account, as a checking or savings account, in the name of two or more persons.

JOINTLY AND SEVERALLY—an obligation or liability incurred by two or more parties.

JOINT TENANCY—the holding of property by two persons at the same time under the same title.

Judge—an officer of a government invested with authority to decide upon the merits of persons, things, and events; to come to a conclusion regarding a matter.

Judgment—an official decision of a court.

Judicature—the power of administering justice.

Judicial—pertaining to the administration of justice; pertaining to a court; established by formal enactment or positive judgment.

Jurat—one sworn to the faithful performance of a duty, as an alderman; the clause in an official certificate testifying that the deposition has been duly sworn to at a stated time before a competent authority.

Jurisdiction—lawful right to exercise official authority, whether executive, legislative or judicial; the territory within or the matter over which such authority may be lawfully exercised; a court or series of courts.

Jurisprudence—the philosophy of positive law and its administration; the science of law.

Jury—a body of persons (usually twelve) legally qualified and summoned to serve on a judicial tribunal (trial) sworn to try well and truly a cause and give a true verdict according to the evidence.

Justice of the peace—a local official of limited jurisdiction.

Justices—judges, as of the U.S. Supreme Court.

Juvenile—a young person; a youth who has not yet reached the age of majority.

Juvenile court—a court with jurisdiction over juveniles.

Kite—to exchange checks for the purpose of gaining time.

Kleptomaniac—one who has an uncontrollable propensity to steal.

Landlord—a lessor; the owner of real property in a lease.

Landlord and tenant—a relationship between an owner of real property and one given the right to use the property by means of a lease.

Larceny—the illegal taking possession of goods or money belonging to another person with the intent of personal gain.

Last will and testament—a document in which a person, called the testator, describes the manner in which he or she wishes to dispose of his or her property after death.

Lease—a contract between a landlord and a tenant granting permission to the tenant to use and possess real property owned by the landlord for a fixed period of time.

Legacy—a gift of personal property left by a will.

Legal age—the age, set by statute, when a person is no longer considered a juvenile.

Legal tender—the money which Congress has declared must be accepted if offered in payment of private and public debts or in payment of money obligations required by contract.

Libel—false statements, written or printed and published either in letter form or in newspapers or magazines that injure the social or business reputation of another.

Libelant—the party who files a libel suit.

License—permission to engage in an act, as a business license issued by a government granting permission to engage in business.

Licensee—a person on another's premises for a purpose which is personally beneficial only, such as a visitor or passenger in an automobile.

Lien—the right of a person other than the owner to retain possession of goods.

Liquidate—to settle the accounts of a business; to determine the amount of indebtedness or damages.

Litigate—to engage in a lawsuit.

Litigation—the carrying on of a lawsuit.

Lockout—the refusal of an employer to give his employees work in an attempt to avoid a strike.

Majority—legal age as set by law.

Malfeasance—official misconduct; violation of a public trust or duty.

Malice—ill will; a wish to hurt others.

Malice aforethought—evil intent on the part of one who commits a wrong.

Malicious—displaying active ill will.

Malicious mischief—intentional destruction.

Malicious prosecution—a suit which was brought without probable cause to believe the charges sustained.

Manslaughter—the killing of another person unlawfully, but without malice.

Matricide—the killing of one's mother.

Memorandum—the written evidence required for contracts under the Statute of Frauds.

Merger—the absorption of one company by another.

Misdemeanor—a crime against society of a less serious nature than a felony usually punishable by a fine or imprisonment in a local jail, or both.

Mistake—a misunderstanding or a wrong impression as to a material fact connected to a contract.

Misrepresentation—a misstatement of a material fact resulting in inducing another to enter into an agreement to his injury.

Mistrial—the ending of a trial by a judge because of the disqualification of a juror or the inability of the jury to reach a verdict.

Mitigation of damages—the lowering of the amount to be paid to a plaintiff because it is more than he or she is entitled to receive.

Mortgage—a claim on a property given to a person who has loaned money in case the money is not repaid when due; a document giving such a claim.

Mortgagee—a person to whom property is mortgaged.

Mortgagor—a person who mortgages his or her property.

Municipal—having to do with the affairs of a city, town, or other municipality.

Municipality—a city, town or other district having local self-government.

Murder—the unlawful killing of a human being which is planned beforehand.

Mutual mistake—a mistake made by both parties to a contract.

Nasciturus—future issue of a marriage.

Necessaries—those things which a person cannot do without, such as food, clothing or shelter.

Negligence—the injury of another person or damage to another's property as a result of carelessness.

Negotiable—capable of being negotiated or sold.

Negotiable instrument—an instrument, the ownership of which can be transferred, such as a stock certificate or bond.

Next friend—a person acting on behalf of an infant or other incompetent person without having been appointed legal guardian.

Nonage—under age.

Non disclosure—concealing the true nature of the subject matter of a contract by one of the parties.

Nonjuror—one who refuses to take a required oath.

Nonsuit—a judgment given against a person beginning a lawsuit who neglects to prosecute or who fails to show a legal case or sufficient evidence.

Notary public—a person commissioned by the state who certifies the genuineness of documents, administers oaths and takes acknowledgments.

Notice—usually, the filing of a notice of appeal in the Clerk of Court's office.

Novation—an agreement by the parties of a contract to substitute another for one of the parties.

Nuisance—an annoying wrong to another party which is both recurring and consistent.

Nullify—make not binding; render void.

Oath—a solemn promise or statement that something is true.

Obscene—offending modesty or decency; lewd.

Occupancy—the holding of land or buildings by possessing.

Onus—a burden or responsibility.

Opinion—a formal judgment by a judge; the written document expressing that judgment.

Option—right to buy or lease real estate or property at a certain price at a certain time.

Ordinance—a law, rule, or statute established by authority.

Ostensible—apparent; pretended.

Ouster—an illegal forcing of a person out of his property.

Outlaw—a person outside the protection of the law; an habitual criminal.

Overdraft—the drawing from an account of more than one has a right to.

Overt—open; evident; not hidden.

Pact—an agreement; a covenant or treaty.

Par—the value of a bond, a note, or a stock certificate that is printed on it.

Parol—oral

Parole—conditional release from prison or jail before the full term is served.

Parricide—the killing of one's parent.

Partition—to divide into parts; an apportionment or distribution.

Passbook—a book in which a bank keeps track of how much a person deposits or withdraws and how much interest is earned on the account balance.

Patent—an exclusive right granted by the federal government to make, use and sell an invention.

Patricide—the killing of one's father.

Pauper—a person supported by charity.

Pecuniary—having to do with money.

Pecuniary damages—monetary payment for damages.

Penal—having to do with punishment or imprisonment.

Penitentiary—a state or federal prison.

Peonage—the practice of holding persons to work off debts.

Peremptory—leaving no choice.

Perennial—lasting for a long time.

Perjury—making a false statement under oath with knowledge of its falsity.

Petition—a written application for an order of court or for some action by a judge.

Petitioner—the person who files a petition.

Petty cash—a sum of money kept at hand to pay small expenses.

Plaintiff—the person who begins a lawsuit.

Plat—a map describing the ways land is divided into lots or subdivisions.

Pleading—an answer to a charge in a lawsuit.

Plenary—full, complete, attended by all its qualified members.

Power of attorney—a written statement giving one person legal power to act for another.

Precedent—a former case that may serve as an example or reason for another case.

Premise—a statement assumed to be true and used to draw a conclusion; property forming the subject of a document.

Preponderance of evidence—strong evidence.

Prerogative—a right of privilege that no one else has.

Presumption—a thing taken for granted.

Principal—the sum of money on which interest is paid; money or property from which income is received; a person who hires another person to act for him or her; a person who is responsible for another's debt; a person directly responsible for a crime.

Privileges and immunities—special rights or advantages.

Probate—the official proving of a will as genuine; to prove by legal process the genuineness of a will.

Process—a written command or summons to appear in a court of law.

Property—a thing or things owned such as land, buildings, vehicles, furniture, jewelry, etc.

Proprietorship—the owning of property.

Prosecute—to bring a case before a court of law.

Prosecution—the carrying on of a lawsuit; the side that starts a legal action against another.

Prospectus—a printed statement describing or advertising something, often used to sell stock, bonds or other investments.

Prostitution—the practice of indiscriminate, sexual intercourse for gain or hire.

Protest—a statement that denies or objects strongly.

Proxy—an agent or deputy's writing authorizing a proxy to vote for another person.

Public—open to all the people.

Puffing—the expression of an opinion that an article is worth a larger sum of money than it really is.

Punitive—inflicting punishment.

Punitive damages—damages awarded to the plaintiff for the defendant's oppressive acts.

Quash—make void; annul.

Quasi—almost real.

Quitclaim deed—a document stating that someone has given up a claim.

Quorum—the number of members who must be present if the business done at that meeting is to be legal or binding.

Ratification—the confirmation or approval of an act or contract.

Rebuttal—the opposing by providing evidence on the other side of the argument.

Receipt—a written statement that money, a package, a letter, etc. has been received.

Recognizance—a bond binding a person to do some particular act; a sum of money to be forfeited if the act is not performed.

Recoup—to make up for.

Recrimination—to accuse someone in return.

Redemption—the buying back, as in paying off a loan, to regain full rights to property.

Release—surrender of a right or estate to another; the document that states such a surrender.

Remedy—the legal means of enforcing a right or redressing a wrong.

Rent—a regular payment for the use of property.

Residual—the amount that is left over.

Residuary—entitled to the remainder of an estate.

Reversion—return of property to the grantor or his heirs; right to possess certain property under certain conditions.

Revocable—a canceling or withdrawal.

Scilicet—to wit; namely.

Seal—to show ownership or authenticity; a per, circle, mark or impression representing ownership or authenticity.

SENTENCE—a decision by a judge on the punishment of a prisoner.

SHERIFF—The highest law-enforcing officer of a county.

SIGNATORY—a signer of a document.

SLANDER—false statements that are transmitted from one person or another by word of mouth and that result in injuries to the reputation of the slandered person.

SMUGGLING—the secret bringing out or taking into a country goods which are unlawful.

SOLVENT—able to pay all that is owned.

SPECIFIC PERFORMANCE—where defendant must perform agreed terms of contract, usually a service or act.

STATUTE—a law enacted by a legislative body.

STATUTE LAW—written law.

STATUTE OF FRAUDS—the name given to certain state statutes which require certain contracts and causes of action to be in writing.

STATUTE OF LIMITATIONS—statutes which govern how much time is allowed to bring legal action before the courts on a matter.

STATUTORY—of or pertaining to statutes or laws.

STAY OF EXECUTION—a delay in carrying out the order of a court to execute a person.

STIPULATION—a condition in an agreement or bargain.

SUBPOENA—an official written order requiring a person to appear at a certain time and place.

SUBROGATION—the substitution of one person for another as a creditor.

SUCCESSION—the right or process by which one person takes the office, rank, estate or other rights or liabilities of another in accordance with law.

SUE—to start a lawsuit.

SUFFERANCE—permission given only by failure to object or prevent.

SUMMONS—an order to appear in a court of law.

SUMMARY JUDGMENT—a decision by a court of law to award victory to one of the parties in a matter without benefit of a trial.

SURETY—a person who agrees to be responsible for another as a bondsman or cosigner.

SURROGATE—a substitute or deputy; in certain states, a judge having charge of the probate of wills and the administration of estates.

SYNDICATE—an association of people formed to carry out an enterprise or investment; also the formation of such an association.

SYNOPSIS—a brief outline of a subject.

TENANCY—the occupany of real estate under a lease or through payment of rent.

TENANCY BY THE ENTIRETY—the joint ownership of real property by a husband and a wife in which the survivor becomes the sole owner.

TENANCY IN COMMON—the joint ownership of real property by any two or more persons in which a decedent's interest goes to his or her heirs.

TENANT—one who occupies land, buildings or other property owned by another.

TESTACY—a state of circumstances created when one leaves a valid will.

TESTAMENTARY—a declaration contained in a person's will that describes what is to be done after his or her death.

TESTAMENTARY CAPACITY—being of sound mind, disposing memory and proper age to make a valid will.

TESTATOR—a deceased man who died leaving a will.

TESTATRIX—a deceased woman who died leaving a will.

TESTIMONY—a statement, written or oral, which affirms a fact or truth.

TITLE—legal ownership of property.

TITLE SEARCH—an investigation into public records to determine ownership of property and discover any liens or encumbrances attached to property.

TORRENS SYSTEM—a system used by a few states to register title to real property.

TORT—a civil wrong or injury.

TORT-FEASOR—one who commits a tort.

TRADE ACCEPTANCE—a bill of exchange drawn by the seller on the purchaser and bearing the purchaser's signature, specifying the time and place for payment of the amount of a purchase.

TRADE-MARK—an officially registered name, symbol, or other device which identifies a product and which is restricted to the use of the owner or manufacturer.

TRANSCRIPT—a written record of a hearing, deposition or trial.

TREASON—the violation of allegiance toward one's own country.

TREASURE TROVE—any treasure which is found hidden and never claimed by its owner.

TRESPASS—the infringement upon the privacy, time, or attention of another person.

TRESPASSER—one who enters the premises of another without permission.

TRIAL—the examination of evidence and applicable laws by a court, usually with a jury, in order to determine the correctness of certain charges or claims.

TRIBUNAL—a court of justice.

TRUST—the holding of property by legal title by one person (the trustee) for the benefit of another (the beneficiary).

TRUSTEE—a person, or agent, such as a bank, holding legal title to property for the benefit of another.

TURPITUDE—baseness or depravity; also a base act.

ULTRA VIRES—having no power.

UNIFORM COMMERCIAL CODE—a set of laws adopted by most states which governs the handling of commercial transaction.

UNILATERAL—affecting only one side, as in a unilateral contract.

UNILATERAL CONTRACT—a contract which obligates only one of two or more parties.

UNILATERAL MISTAKE—a mistake made by only one of the parties to a contract.

UNLAWFUL DETAINER—the unlawful detention of a person in custody or confinement.

USURIOUS—practicing usury.

USURY—charging more than the current legal rate to be charged to a borrower for the use of money.

VAGRANCY—idle wandering from place to place without any visible means of support or a fixed home.

VALID—legally sound and effective; uncontestable and binding.

VALIDATED—to declare legally valid.

VENDEE—a buyer.

VENDOR—a seller.

VENDUE—a public sale or auction.

VENUE—the place (county and state) in which the events from which an action arose took place.

VERDICT—the decision reached by a jury or judge at the conclusion of a legal proceeding.

VERIFICATION—a confirmation that something has been done; a short oath concluding a pleading which affirms that the pleader is ready to prove his allegations.

VERSUS (VS.) (V)—against.

VOID—entirely null and of no legal effect.

VOIDABLE—capable of being voided.

WAIVER—the international relinquishment of a right, claim or privilege; also the document which evidences such an act.

Ward—a child or incompetent person who is placed under the care or protection of a guardian or court.

Warrant—a judicial writ which authorizes a search, seizure or arrest or the execution of a judgment.

Warranty—the guarantee by a seller of the quality of a product or service which induces a buyer to buy.

Warranty deed—a statement made by the seller of real property that the title is good, giving the buyer the right to bring legal action if good title does not exist.

Watered stock—any stock issued by a corporation which is paid for by cash or assets far below the par or stated value of the stock.

Will—a legal declaration of how a person wishes his or her possessions to be disposed of after his or her death.

Witness—one who is called upon to testify before a court; the attestation to a fact, statement or event.

Writ—a written order, issued by a court or judge, which directs the person to whom it is addressed to perform or cease performing some specified act.

Appendix D
Foreign Expressions*

a fortiori	With stronger reason; more conclusively.
a mensa et thoro	From table and bed (commonly translated as from bed and board, a matrimonial separation).
a prendre	(Fr. to take, to seize.) Rightfully taken from the soil.
a vinculo matrimonii	From the bond of marriage (an absolute divorce).
ab initio	From the beginning.
actiones in personam	Action against the person, founded on a personal liability.
ad curiam	Before the court.
ad faciendum	To do; submit to.
ad hoc	For this special purpose.
ad infinitum	Indefinitely, forever.
ad litem	For the suit; for the litigation.
ad quod dannum	To what damages; what injury.
ad respondenum	To answer.
ad satisfaciendum	To satisfy.
ad testificandum	Subpoena to testify.
ad valorem	According to the valuation.
alias dictus	Otherwise called.
aliunde	From another place; from without (as evidence outside the document).
alumnus	A foster child; also, graduate of school or college.
amicus curiae	A friend of the court, not party to the action.

*Compiled by Paula F. Turner.

animo furandi	The intention to steal.
animo revertendi	An intention of returning.
animo revocandi	An intention to revoke.
animo testandi	An intention to make a will.
animus	Mind, intention.
anno domini	(abbreviation *A.D.)* The Year of our Lord.
ante	Before.
ante litem motam	Before suit brought.
arcuendo	In the course of the argument.
assumpsit	To undertake, to assume; an undertaking or promise.
autrefois acquit	(Fr.) Formerly acquitted.
autrefois convict	(Fr.) Formerly convicted.
bona fide	Good faith.
bon ami	(Fr.) Good friend.
capias	To take, arrest (a writ directing an arrest).
capias ad satisfaciendum	Arrest to satisfy (meaning, arrest the debtor to satisfy a judgment).
causa mortis	On account of death.
caveat	Let him beware; a warning. An explanation to prevent misinterpretation.
caveat emptor	Let the purchaser take care; let the buyer beware.
cepit et asportavit	He took and carried away.
certiorari	A writ issued by a higher court to a lower court to send to it the record in a proceeding.
cestui que use	He who benefits by the use.
cestui que trust	He who benefits by the trust.
cestui que vie	He whose life measures the estate.
civiliter mortuus	Civilly dead.
compos mentis	Of sound mind.
contre bonos mores	Against good morals.
contra pacem	Against the peace.

coram non judice	Acts done by court (or judge) having no jurisdiction.
corpus delicti	The body—i.e., the essence—of the crime.
corpus juris civilis	The body of the civil law.
cujus est solum, ejus est usque ad coelum	Who owns the soil, owns it as far as heaven.
cum testamento annexo	(popularly written *c.t.a.)* With the will annexed.
cy pres	(Fr.) As near as (a rule for construing a will to carry out its intention as nearly as possible).
damnum absque injuria	Damage without injury (damage without legal wrong).
de bonis non	A form of administration of an estate where the first administrator died before completion of the work.
de bono et malo	For good or ill.
de facto	In fact, but without lawful title; actually.
de jure	Of right; by lawful title; within the legal status.
de minimis	Trifling.
de novo	Anew; afresh.
de son tort	(Fr.) Of his own wrong.
distringas	To distrain; levy a distress upon.
donatio mortis causa	A gift by reason of death.
duces tecum	Bring with you; as a subpoena *duces tecum* is a writ in which witness is ordered to appear and bring certain things with him.
dum bene se gesserit	During good weather.
durante minore aetate	During minority.
durante viduitate	During widowhood.

e converso	Conversely; vice versa.
ejusdem generis	Of the same kind or class.
eo instanti	Upon the instant.
et alius	(commonly abbreviated as *et al.)* And another.
et ano	And one another.
et cetera	(commonly abbrevaited as *etc.)* And other things.
ex contractu	From contract; out of contract.
ex delicto	From tort; out of tort.
ex gratia	As a matter of favor.
ex necessitate legis	From legal necessity.
ex officio	By virtue of his office.
ex parte	Of the one part; relating to one party only.
ex post facto	After the act.
fait accompli	A thing accomplished and presumably irreversible.
felonice	Feloniously.
ferae naturae	Of a wild nature.
fieri	To be made up; to become.
fieri facias	Cause to be made; a writ directed to the sheriff to reduce the judgment debtor's property to money in the amount of the judgment.
filius populi	A son of the people.
gravamen	The material part of a grievance, charge; the burden or gist of a charge; the grievance or injury specially complained of.
guardian ad litem	A guardian appointed to represent a minor in a particular legal proceeding.
habeas corpus	A writ directed to a person having custody of another to produce that person in court.

habendum	The clause usually following the granting part of a deed defining the extent of ownership.
habere facias psossessionem	Cause him to have possession; a writ of ejectment.
habere facias seisinam	Cause him to have seizing; writ to give possession.
honorarium	An honorary fee; recompense from gratitude.
hostis humani generis	An enemy of the human race.
idem sonans	Having the same sound, as a name spelled differently but sounding the same.
ignorantia juris neminem excusat	Ignorance of the law excuses no one.
ignorantia juris, quod quisque tenetur soire, neminem excusat	Ignorance of the law, which everyone is bound to know, excuses no one.
illicitum collegium	An unlawful association.
impotentia excusat legem	Impossibility is an excuse in law.
in bonis	In goods; among the possessions.
in custodia legis	In the custody of the law.
indebitatus assumpsit	An action in which plaintiff alleges defendant is indebted to him.
indicia	Distinctive marks; postal marks affixed.
in esse	In being; in existence.
in extremis	In his last moments; at the point of death.
infra	Below.
in fraudem legis	In circumvention of the law.
in futuro	In the future.
in infinitum	Forever.
in loco parentis	In the place of a parent.
in pari delicto	Equally at fault.
in personam	A remedy where the proceedings are against the person.

in praesenti	At present; at once; now.
in re	In the matter.
in rem	Against the thing (an action against the property).
in rerum natura	In nature; in life; in existence.
in specie	In the same form.
in statu quo	In the state in which (things were); in the former condition.
in vacuo	In a vacuum.
in toto	In the whole; completely.
in transitu	In transit; in course of transfer.
inter	Among; between.
inter alia	Among other things.
inter alios	Among other persons.
inter vivos	Between living persons.
intra	Within; inside.
ipse dixit	He himself said (it).
ipso facto	From the fact itself; in itself.
ita est	So it is.
jura personarum	Rights of persons.
jura rerum	Rights of things.
jurat	The oath, or "sworn to before me" part, of an affidavit.
jure divino	By divine right.
jure uxoris	In his wife's right.
jus accrescendi	The right of survivorship.
jus ad rem	A right to a thing.
jus commune	The common law; the common right.
jus habendi	The right to have a thing.
jus proprietatis	Right of property.
laches	(Fr.) Neglect to enforce a right at a proper time.
levari facias	Cause to be levied; a writ of execution.
lex fori	Law of the forum (where the cause is heard; where the case is tried).

lex loci	Law of the place (where the cause of action arose).
lex mercatoria	The law merchant.
lis pendens	Litigation pending; a pending suit.
locus deliciti	The place of the crime or tort.
locus in quo	The place in which.
locus sigilli	(abbreviation *L.S.)* The place of the seal.
mala fides	Bad faith.
mala in se	Acts wrongful in themselves; acts morally wrongful.
mala praxis	Malpractice.
mala prohibita	Acts wrongful because the law prohibits them.
malo animo	With evil intent.
malum in se	Evil in itself.
mandamus	A writ issuing out of a court directing a person to do some act by virtue of his office.
manu forti	With a strong hand; forcible entry.
ne exeat	A writ directing the sheriff to prevent the departure of a person from the jurisdiction.
nihil dicit	He says nothing; judgment against defendant who does not put in a defense to the complaint.
nil debet	He owes nothing.
nisi prius	Court where the trial is held.
nolle prosequi	An agreement to proceed no further with the prosecution.
nolo contendere	Plea entered by accused that he will not contest the indictment.
non compos mentis	Not of sound mind.
non est factum	It is not his deed.

non obstante	Notwithstanding.
non prosecuitur	(abbreviation *non pros.)* He does not prosecute.
non sui juris	Without capacity to manage his own affairs.
nudum pactum	A nude pact; a contract without consideration.
nul tiel record	No such record.
nul tort	No wrong done.
nulla bona	No goods. (Wording of a return to a writ of *fieri facias.)*
nunc pro tunc	Now for then. (A record made now of something previously done, to have effect as of the former date).
obiter dictum	A remark made by the judge in his decision, but not necessary to the determination of the cause.
onus probandi	The burden of proof.
ore tenus	By word of mouth.
oyer and terminer	To hear and determine.
pari delicto	Equal in guilt.
pari passu	By an equal progress; equitably; notably.
particeps criminis	An accomplice in the crime.
pater familias	The father (head) of a family.
peculium	Private property.
pendente lite	Pending the suit; during the litigation.
per	By.
per autre vie	For another's lifetime.
per capita	By heads; as individuals (in a distribution of an estate, descendants share and share alike).
per contra	In opposition.
per curiam	By the court, distinguishes the opinion of the court from that of a single judge.

per proc	Signature by an agent under limited authority.
per quod	By which; whereby.
per stirpes	(As if there had been no Will.) Method of dividing an estate whereby a group takes the share which their deceased ancestor would have taken—their right is by representation and not as individuals (per capita), according to the state laws of inheritance.
post diem	After the day.
pur autre vie	(Fr.) For another's lifetime.
praecipe, pracipe	Command; a written order to the clerk of the court to issue a writ.
prima facie	At first view (evidence sufficient in law to establish the fact).
pro	For.
pro confesso	As confessed.
pro forma	As a matter of form.
pro hac vice	For this occasion.
pro rata	According to the rate, or proportion.
pro tanto	For so much; to that extent.
pro tempore	(abbreviation *pro tem.)* For the time being; temporarily.
prochein amy, prochein ami.	Next friend.
publici juris	Of public right.
quaere	Query; doubtful point of law.
quantum	How much; the amount.
quantum meruit	As much as he has deserved (for services in absence of an agreement as to compensation).
quantum valebant	As much as goods are reasonably worth (in absence of agreement as to value).
quare	Wherefore.

quare clausum fregit	Wherefore he broke the close (a form of trespass on another's land).
quasi	As if; almost; bearing a close resemblance to.
quid pro quo	Something for something; a term denoting mutual consideration between the parties to a contract.
quo warranto	By what authority; a writ by which an inquiry is made into the authority by which an officer acts.
quoad hoc	As to this matter; up to this time.
quod computet	That he account.
res	A thing, meaning property of all kinds.
res adjudicata, res judicata	The matter has been decided by a court of competent jurisdiction.
res gestae	Essential circumstances surrounding the subject; the circumstances, facts and declarations which grow out of the main fact, are contemporaneous with it, and serve to illustrate its character.
res ipsa loquitur	The thing speaks for itself (a phrase used in negligence actions where proof of negligence is found from the accident itself).
res judica	The thing judicially acted upon or decided by a court of competent jurisdiction.
res nova	New matter; a point that has not been decided; a new case.

sans	Without.
scienter	Knowingly; signifying the defendant's guilty knowledge of the cause of the injury complained of and which it was his duty to guard against.
scilicet	(abbreviation *SS.* or *ss.)* To wit, that is to say.
scire facias	Cause him to know; give him notice (a writ used to revive a judgment which has expired).
se defendendo	In self-defense; in defending one's self.
semper	Always.
semper paratus	Always ready.
sequitur	It follows.
sic	Thus in the original; in this manner.
sigillum	A seal.
simplex obligatio	A simple obligation; a single unconditional bond.
sine cura	Without charge or care; charged with no duty.
sine die	Without a specified day for further consideration.
sine qua non	An indispensable thing or condition.
situs	Situation; location.
stare decisis	To abide by decided cases.
sua sponte	On one's own initiative.
sub judice	Under judicial consideration.
sub modo	Under a qualification; in a qualified way.
sui generis	Of its own kind; unique.
sui juris	Of his own right; possessing all the rights of a freeman.
supersedeas	That you supersede (a writ commanding a stay of the proceedings).
supra	Above.

tenere	To have in possession.
terminus a quo	The starting point.
ultra vires	Beyond power.
uxor et vir, ux. et vir	Wife and husband.
venire facias	That you cause to come; a form of summons.
verba fortius accipiuntur contra proferentem	Words are to be taken most strongly against the one using them.
versus	(abbreviation *v.* or *vs.)* Against.
vi et armis	By force and arms.
via facti	In a forcible way.
vice versa	On the contrary; on opposite sides.
virtute officii	By virtue of his office.
via voce	By the living voice; by word of mouth.
voir dire	To speak the truth (also, a preliminary examination to determine the competency of a witness).

Appendix E
Special Forms of Addresses and Salutations

Person	Envelope and Inside Address	Salutation
FEDERAL, STATE AND LOCAL GOVERNMENT OFFICIALS		
President	The President The White House	Dear Mr. President:
Vice President	The Vice President United States Senate	Dear Mr. Vice President:
Chief Justice	The Chief Justice The Supreme Court	Dear Mr. Chief Justice:
Associate Justice	Mr. Justice Doe The Supreme Court	Dear Justice Doe:
Speaker of the House of Representatives	The Honorable Jane A. Doe Speaker of the House of Representatives	Dear Ms. (Mrs.) Speaker:
Cabinet officer	The Honorable John Doe Secretary of State	Dear Mr. Doe:
	or	
	The Honorable Jane Doe Attorney General of the United States	Dear Ms. (Mrs.) Doe:
Under (Assistant) Secretary of a Department	The Honorable John Doe Under Secretary of the Treasury	Dear Mr. Doe:
U.S. Senator	The Honorable Jane Doe United States Senate	Dear Senator Doe:

U.S. Representative	The Honorable John Doe The United States House of Representatives	Dear Mr. Doe:
Federal Judge	The Honorable John Doe United States District Judge	Dear Judge Doe:
Former President	The Honorable John Doe	Dear Mr. Doe:
Governor	The Honorable John Doe Governor of ______	Dear Governor Doe:
Lieutenant Governor	The Honorable Jane Doe Lieutenant Governor of ______	Dear Ms. (Mrs.) Doe:
Judge, state or local	The Honorable Jane Doe	Dear Judge Doe:
State Senator	The Honorable John Doe The State Senate State Capitol	Dear Senator Doe:
State Representative	The Honorable John Doe House of Representatives State Capitol	Dear Mr. Doe:
Mayor	The Honorable Jane Doe Mayor of ______	Dear Mayor Doe:
Commissioner	The Honorable Jane Doe	Dear Ms. (Mrs.) Doe:
District Attorney	The Honorable John Doe District Attorney ______ County	Dear Mr. Doe:
City Attorney	The Honorable Jane Doe City Attorney	Dear Ms. (Mrs.) Doe:
Alderman	Alderman John Doe City Hall	Dear Mr. Doe:

Clerk of Court	Jane C. Doe Clerk of the Superior Court	Dear Ms. (Mrs.) Doe:
Ambassador	The Honorable Jane Doe American Ambassador (Country or City)	Dear Ms. Ambassador:
American Minister	The Honorable John Doe American Minister (Country)	Dear Mr. Minister:
U.S. Delegate to United Nations	The Honorable John Doe Chief of the United States Mission to the United Nations	Dear Mr. Ambassador:
American Consul General, Consul, or Vice Consul	Mr. John C. Doe American Consul General (City and Country)	Dear Mr. Doe:
Foreign Ambassador in United States	His Excellency, John Doe Ambassador of Thailand	Excellency:
Foreign Minister in United States	The Honorable Jane Doe Minister of Germany	Dear Ms. Minister:
President of a Republic	His Excellency, John Doe President of the United States of Brazil	Excellency:
British Minister Prime Minister	The Right Honorable John Doe, M.P. Prime Minister London	Dear Mr. Prime Minister:

OFFICERS OF THE ARMED FORCES

General of the Army	John C. Doe, U.S.A. General of the Army War Department Washington, D.C.	Dear General Doe:

General, Lieutenant, Major General or Brigadier General	General (Lieutenant, Major General, or Brigadier General) John C. Doe	Dear General Doe:
Colonel, Lieutenant Colonel, Major, Captain, etc.	Colonel (Lieutenant Colonel, Major, Captain, etc.) John C. Doe	Dear Colonel Doe:
Army Chaplain	Chaplain John C. Doe Captain, USA	Dear Chaplain:
Admiral	Admiral John C. Doe, U.S.N. Chief of Naval Operations Department of the Navy	Dear Admiral Doe:
Fleet, Rear, Vice Admiral	Fleet (Rear, Vice) Admiral John C. Doe	Dear Admiral Doe:
Commodore Captain, Commander	Commodore (Captain, Commander) John C. Doe	Dear Commodore Doe:
Junior Officers (Lieutenant Commander, Lieutenant, Lieutenant, Junior grade, Ensign	Lieutenant Commander John C. Doe, U.S.N.	Dear Mr. Doe:
Navy Chaplain	Captain John C. Doe, Captain, U.S.N.	Dear Chaplain:

CLERICAL AND RELIGIOUS ORDERS

Pope	His Holiness The Pope or His Holiness Pope ___	Your Holiness: or Most Holy Father:

Apostolic Delegate	His Excellency, The Most Reverend John Doe The Apostolic delegate	Dear [Archbishop]:
Cardinal in the United States	His Eminence, John Cardinal Doe Archbishop of ______	Dear Cardinal Doe:
Archibishop in the United States	The Most Reverend John Doe Archbishop of ______	Dear Archbishop Doe:
Bishop in the United States	The Most Reverend John Doe Bishop of ________	Dear Bishop Doe:
Dean of a Cathedral	The Very Reverend John Doe or Dean John Doe	Very Reverend Sir:
Abbot	The Right Reverend John C. Doe Abbot of ______Abbey	Dear Father Abbot: or Right Reverend and dear Father Doe:
Canon	The Very Reverend Canon John C. Doe Canon of ________	Dear Canon Doe:
Sister Superior	The Reverend Sister Superior (Order, if any)	Dear Sister Superior:
Sister	Sister Jane C. Doe	Dear Sister Jane Doe:
Mother Superior	The Reverend Mother Superior	Dear Reverend Mother:
Rabbi	Rabbi John Doe or Rabbi John Doe, D.D. (if with doctor's degree)	Dear Rabbi Doe: Dear Doctor Doe:
Archbishop (Anglican)	To His Grace The Lord Archbishop of ________________	Dear Archbishop:

Methodist Bishop	The Reverend Bishop Doe Methodist Bishop	Dear Bishop Doe:
Protestant Episcopal Bishop	The Right Reverend John C. Doe Bishop of ________	Dear Bishop Doe:
Archdeacon	The Venerable John R. Blank The Archdeacon of ________	Dear Archdeacon:
Protestant	Reverend John C. Doe	Dear Reverend Doe:
Patriarch (of an Eastern church)	His Beatitude the Patriarch of ________	Most Reverend Lord:
Monsignor Reverend	The Right (or Very) Reverend Msgr. John C. Doe	Dear Right (Very) 'Monsignor Doe:
Brother	Brother John C. Doe	Dear Brother Doe:
Priest	The Reverend Father Doe	Dear Father Doe:

COLLEGE AND UNIVERSITY OFFICIALS

President of a College or University	President Jane C. Doe or Dr. Jane C. Doe President, ________	Dear President Doe: or Dear Dr. Doe:
Dean of a College or University	Dean John Doe or Dr. John Doe	Dear Dean Doe: Dear Dr. Doe:
Administrator of College or University	John C. Doe, Ph.D.	Dear Dr. Doe:
Professor	Professor John C. Doe or John C. Doe, Ph.D.	Dear Professor Doe: or Dear Dr. Doe:

MISCELLANEOUS PROFESSIONALS

Attorney	Ms. Jane C. Doe Attorney at Law	Dear Ms. (Mrs.) Doe

CPA	Mr. John C. Doe Certified Public Accountant	Dear Mr. Doe:
Physician	John Doe, M.D. or Dr. John Doe	Dear Dr. Doe:
Veterinarian	John Doe, D.V.M. or Dr. John Doe	Dear Dr. Doe:
Dentist	John Doe, D.D.S. or Dr. John Doe	Dear Dr. Doe:

Appendix F
Professional Associations and Publications

International Word Processing Association
2360 Maryland Road
Willow Grove, PA 19090

Association of Legal Administrators
1800 Pickwick Avenue
Glenview, IL 60025

The National Association of Secretarial Services
240 Driftwood Road, S.E.
St. Petersburg, FL 33705

National Federation of Paralegal Associations
P.O. Box 14103
Ben Franklin Station
Washington, DC 20044

American Bar Association
750 N. Lakeshore Drive
Chicago, IL 60611

The Institute for Paralegal Training
1926 Arch Street
Philadelphia, PA 19103

Appendix G
Client Disbursement Codes

ADMINISTRATIVE

BN	Binding charges
LD	Long distance telephone charges
MI	Mileage and parking
MS	Messenger service
PC	Photocopies
PO	Postage charges
SO	Secretarial overtime
TG	Telegram/telecopy charges
TX	Telex charges

FEES

AP	Appraisal fee
EW	Expert witness fee
FF	Filing fee
RC	Record fee
RG	Registration fee
SV	Service fee

CORPORATE

CS	Corporate seal
NR	Name reservation
SC	Stock certificate
MB	Minute book

COSTS

CT	Court costs
CR	Court reporter
TN	Transcript costs

REAL ESTATE

TE	Title examination
TI	Title insurance premium

MISCELLANEOUS

BP	Bond premium
CC	Certified copy
EC	Exemplified copy
LA	Legal advertisement
LR	Legal research charges
MI	Micrographics charges
NS	Notary service
PH	Photographs
PN	Printing charges
RP	Cost of report

TRAVEL/BUSINESS

AF	Airfare
BC	Business conference
EN	Entertainment
HO	Hotels and lodging
IN	Incidentals
ML	Meals

Appendix H
Typical Areas of Practice

INSURANCE
- Insurance Litigation
- Worker's Compensation
- Social Security

CRIMINAL LAW
- Criminal—Juvenile
- Criminal—State
- Criminal—Federal

FAMILY LAW
- Custody/Guardianship
- Adoption
- Dissolutions

GOVERNMENT AND REGULATIONS
- Antitrust and Trade Regulations
- Employment Discrimination
- Environmental and Natural Resources
- Immigration, Naturalization, and Customs
- International and Foreign
- Labor Law
- Military Law
- Patent, Trademark, and Copyright
- State Laws and Local Ordinances
- Lobby Activities
- Government Agencies
- Inter-Government Litigation
- Utilities

REAL ESTATE LAW
- Sales and Acquisitions—Commercial
- Sales and Acquisitions—Residential
- Planning and Zoning

Landlord/Tenant
Real Estate Litigation
Foreclosure
Title Investigations

COMMERCIAL LAW
Incorporation
Franchise Law
Banking and Finance
Labor Relations
Securities
Patent/Trademark/Copyright
Arbitration
Partnership
Contract
Commercial Litigation

ESTATES AND TAXATION
Taxation—Personal
Taxation—Corporate
Estates and Trusts
Pension, Profit Sharing, and Employee Benefits
Social Security

PERSONAL INJURY
Tort—Motor Vehicle
Tort—Non Motor Vehicle
Product Liability
Federal Tort Claims

OTHER
Oil and Gas
Sports and Entertainment
Bankruptcy and Debtor Relief
Consumer Law
General Practice

Appendix I
Common Work Codes (Acronyms) for Timekeeping

AF	Affidavit
ANI	Answers to interrogatories
BC	Bankruptcy Court
C	Conference with
CC	Conference with client concerning
CO	Conference with opposing counsel re
CONT	Conference telephone call to
CPWC	Conference with client
CRTA	Court of Appeals
EI	Escrow instructions
FDC	Federal District Court
FTC	Federal Trade Commission
ICW	Interoffice conference with
JT	Execution of Judgment
MTW	Meeting with
OET	Obtain extension of time for response
OJTI	Objections to interrogatories
OPCL	Opposing counsel
PCC	Prepare correspondence to client re
PCO	Prepare correspondence to opposing counsel re
PRV	Preparation, review and examination of
RC	Review correspondence
RSHL	Research at library
SHM	Stockholders meeting
SPCT	Supreme Court
STAG	Settlement agreement
TC	Telephone call concerning
TCC	Telephone conference with client
TRP	Trial preparation

Appendix J
Guide to the National Reporter System

Name of Reporter	Cite	Courts Included
Supreme Court Reporter	S.Ct.	United States Supreme Court
Federal Reporter	F.	United States Circuit Courts of Appeals and the District Courts
Federal Reporter, Second Series	F.2d	United States Courts of Appeals, United States Court of Customs and Patent Appeals, United States Emergency Court of Appeals
Federal Supplement	F.Supp.	United States District Courts, United States Court of Claims
Atlantic Reporter	A.	Connecticut
Atlantic Reporter, Second Series	A.2d	Delaware
		Maine
		Maryland
		New Hampshire
		New Jersey
		Pennsylvania
		Rhode Island
		Vermont
		District of Columbia
New York Supplement	N.Y.Supp.	New York Court of Appeals
		Appellate Division of the Supreme Court

New York Supplement, Second Series	N.Y.S.2d	Miscellaneous Courts
North Eastern Reporter	N.E.	Illinois
North Eastern Reporter, Second Series	N.E.2d	New York Massachusetts Ohio
North Western Reporter	N.W.	Iowa
North Western Reporter, Second Series	N.W.2d	Michigan Minnesota Nebraska North Dakota South Dakota Wisconsin
Pacific Reporter	P.	Alaska
Pacific Reporter, Second Series	P.2d	Arizona California Colorado Hawaii Idaho Kansas Montana Nevada New Mexico Oklahoma Oregon Utah Washington Wyoming
South Eastern Reporter	S.E.	Georgia
South Eastern Reporter, Second Series	S.E.2d	North Carolina South Carolina Virginia West Virginia
Southern Reporter	So.	Alabama
Southern Reporter, Second Series	So.2d	Florida Louisiana Mississippi
South Western Reporter	S.W.	Arkansas
South Western Reporter, Second Series	S.W.2d	Kentucky Missouri Tennessee

Appendix K
Selected Bibliography

Law Office Management

Altman, Mary Ann, and Robert I. Weil. *How to Manage Your Law Office.* Supplemented annually. New York: Matthew Bender & Co., Inc., 1973.

Black's Law Dictionary. 5th ed. St. Paul, MN: West Publishing Co., 1983.

Hildebrandt, Bradford W., *Law Office Management and Administration.* PLI, Course Handbook #A4-3079. New York: Practising Law Institute, 1981.

Hildebrandt, Bradford W., and Jack Kaufman. *The Successful Law Firm.* New York: Law & Business, Inc./Harcourt Brace Jovanovich, 1983.

Hoffman, Paul, ed. *Law Office Economics and Management Manual.* 2 vols. with quarterly journals. Wilmette, IL: Callaghan & Co.

Luvera, Paul N., *The Efficient Law Office.* Woburn, MA: Butterworth's Inc., 1981.

Strong, Kline D., and Arben O. Clark. *Law Office Management.* St. Paul, MN: West Publishing Co., 1974.

A Uniform System of Citations. 13th ed. Cambridge, MA: Columbia Law Review, Harvard Law Review Assoc., University of Pennsylvania Law Review, and Yale Law Journal, 1981.

Legal Assistants

Bruno, Carole A., *Paralegal's Litigation Handbook.* Englewood Cliffs, NJ: Institute for Business Planning, 1980.

Kruzman, Robert G., and Rita K. Gilbert. *Paralegals and Successful Law Practice.* Englewood Cliffs, NJ: Institute for Business Planning, 1981.

Larbalestrier, Deborah E., *Paralegal Training Manual.* Englewood Cliffs, NJ: Prentice-Hall, Inc., 1981.

Parks, Wiliam R., ed. *Manual for Legal Assistants.* St. Paul, MN: West Publishing Co., 1979.

Statsky, William P., *Introduction to Paralegalism.* 2nd ed. St. Paul, MN: West Publishing Co., 1986.

Ulrich, Paul G., and Robert S. Mucklestone. *Working with Legal Assistants: A Team Approach for Lawyers and Legal Assistants.* ECON (jointly with Standing Committee on Legal Assistants), Vol. 1, 1980; Vol. 2, 1981. Chicago: American Bar Association.

Secretaries

Blackburn, Norma Davis. *Legal Secretaryship,* 2nd ed. Englewood Cliffs, NJ: Prentice-Hall, Inc., 1981.

Burton, William C., and Steven E. DeCosta. *Legal Thesaurus.* New York: The Free Press, 1980.

The Career Legal Secretary, prepared by the National Association of Legal Secretaries (International). St. Paul, MN: West Publishing Co., 1981.

Clark, Freda. *Secretary's Desk Book of Shortcuts and Timesavers.* Englewood Cliffs, NJ: Parker Publishing Co., 1978.

DeVries, Mary A., *The Complete Secretary's Handbook.* Englewood Cliffs, NJ: Prentice-Hall, Inc., 1977.

DeVries, Mary A., *Secretary's Standard Reference Manual and Guide.* Parker Publishing Co., 1978.

Janis, J. Harold, and Margaret H. Thompson. *New Standard Reference for Secretaries and Administrative Assistants.* 2nd ed. New York: Macmillan, 1980.

Prentice-Hall Editorial Staff, revised by Mary A. DeVries. *Private Secretary's Encyclopedic Dictionary,* 2nd ed. Englewood Cliffs, NJ: Prentice-Hall, Inc., 1983.

Reilly, Theresa M., *Legal Secretary's Word Finder and Desk Book.* Englewood Cliffs, NJ: Parker Publishing Co., 1974.

Sletwold, Evangeline. *Sletwold's Manual of Documents and Forms for the Legal Secretary.* 2nd ed. Englewood Cliffs, NJ: Prentice-Hall, Inc., 1976.

Webster's Legal Secretaries Handbook, Springfield, MA: G & C Merriam Co., 1981.

INDEX

B

U

V

W